Mediterranean Family Structures

CAMBRIDGE STUDIES IN
SOCIAL ANTHROPOLOGY

13

CAMBRIDGE STUDIES IN SOCIAL ANTHROPOLOGY
EDITED BY JACK GOODY

CAMBRIDGE PAPERS IN SOCIAL ANTHROPOLOGY
EDITED BY JACK GOODY AND EDMUND LEACH

Mediterranean Family Structures

edited by **J. G. PERISTIANY**
Sometime Scientific Director,
Social Sciences Centre Athens,
and
Social Research Centre Cyprus

PUBLISHED IN ASSOCIATION WITH
THE SOCIAL RESEARCH CENTRE, CYPRUS

Cambridge University Press

CAMBRIDGE
LONDON · NEW YORK · MELBOURNE

Published by the Syndics of the Cambridge University Press
The Pitt Building, Trumpington Street, Cambridge CB2 1RP
Bentley House, 200 Euston Road, London NW1 2DB
32 East 57th Street, New York, NY 10022, USA
296 Beaconsfield Parade, Middle Park, Melbourne 3206, Australia

First published 1976

Library of Congress Cataloguing in Publication Data
Main entry under title:
Mediterranean family structures.
  (Cambridge studies in social anthropology; 13)
  Includes index.
  1. Kinship – Mediterranean region – Addresses, essays, lectures.
2. Family – Mediterranean region – Social life and customs.
I. Péristiany, Jean G.
GN588.M4   301.42'1'091822   75–20833

ISBN 0 521 20964 1

Printed in Great Britain by
Cox & Wyman Ltd, London, Fakenham and Reading

GN
588
M4

Contents

v

Note on Arabic words and names

Those terms that have passed into English from Arabic: Quran, Muslim, Druze, etc. – also terms that have passed into French: *duar*, *uted*, *machia*, etc. – have been standardized according to the commonest and most correct usage. The transliteration of words, terms and names of historical characters found in classical Arabic (or modern literary Arabic) have also been standardized according to a simple and fairly exact system, not far from that used by the *Encyclopaedia Islamica*. (The chief feature of the system is the use of ' for *hamza*, ' for the letter '*ain*, dots under certain letters and a ¯ (line over the letter) to elongate vowel sounds; the definite article is always *al-*.)

The problem of transliterating colloquial words and expressions has been 'solved' by leaving these, for the most part, as transliterated by the writers, or rather as written down phonetically by them, according to a French form of transliteration, so as to correspond with the usual French forms of place and personal names of North Africa and the Lebanon. (The chief features of this system are the use of ch for sh, ou for u, dj for j, el for al, and numerous contracted forms; accents have been omitted *except* in the case of place and personal names which are subject to considerable variation.)

Introduction

J. G. Peristiany

Sometime Scientific Director, Social Sciences Centre, Athens and Social Research Centre, Cyprus

Over ten years have passed since the conference that saw the birth of 'Honour and Shame'. An additional five have elapsed since the meeting responsible for 'Mediterranean Countrymen', periods marked by a growing interest in the Mediterranean field and the nascent sentiment, on the part of its students, that both they, among themselves, and the people they study, are linked by a common awareness. The heart-searchings as to the existence of a Mediterranean culture (Braudel 1966, I, p. 14), the queries as to its legitimacy as a field of study, are fast receding. Bold advances often coincide with gordian-knot solutions, actions which cut through rather than resolve problems which stand in the way of their development. This new confidence, this new-found ease of movement in our field, receive their institutional expression in the proliferation of Mediterranean sections within wider departments of anthropology. They are also marked by the appearance of periodicals and of new publications using the Mediterranean as a context within which meaningful comparisons may be made and by the continuity of an enduring series of conferences whose latest results are presented in this volume.

In 1970 many of the contributors to this series of seminars were invited to meet in Nicosia as guests of their convenor, the Social Research Centre of Cyprus. The occasion marked the birth of this new Mediterranean Centre and the welcoming, by the old guard, of colleagues who have gained distinction in the Mediterranean field. The theme itself, 'Mediterranean Family Structures', is one of the main foci of Mediterranean anthropological research. It provides an excellent tool for the investigation of 'traditional' values and institutions and a useful introduction to the study of social change.

This volume brings together twenty studies of the family in the Mediterranean, each originating in the author's research in the field. Our main aim has been to present, both to the specialist of Mediterranean cultures and to the student of social relations, a survey of the family in our area and a point of entry to some present-day theoretical problems confronting students of this institution.

Morocco, Tunisia, the Lebanon, Israel, Turkey, Greece, Albania, Yugoslavia, Italy and Spain are the countries providing the immediate frame of reference for these studies. In reality the scope of this volume is wider than its geographical coverage, as a number of the problems discussed here are representative of considerably larger sections of this area. Thus, spiritual kinship is a phenomenon encountered in both eastern and western Christianity, client–patron and rural–urban relations often using its channels. The problems of large patrilineal descent groups and that of marriage with the father's brother's daughter concern not only the Arab–Berber world but also some Christian Mediterranean communities. Again, the degree of integration of women in the various types of family and the reflexion of this integration in the intensity of their identification with their husband's honour, is a Mediterranean-wide problem.

If the family is at the very core of our interests, its depth and constitution are a prime concern of the contributions to this volume. The nature of social groups, their relevance to the methodology of social research and to our understanding of social change are extensively discussed. Apart from the nuclear family, the extended patrilineal patri- or viri- local households and the patrilineage, we encounter social networks and various types of anti-groups, affinal groups and family associations. A constant preoccupation of the authors is to break loose from rigid structural forms, to discover the underlying social reality and to measure the pressures exercised by the rise of social classes.

Indeed, it appears that socio-economic environmental uniformities are undermining the extended households and that the conjugal family is gradually but surely replacing the large groups. This is a victory for what we may call the feminine conception of the family. In aristocratic or powerful families in Europe, the Middle East and the Maghreb, social prominence is related to the control of wealth and people. Women are significant as the currency of alliances; men are the defenders of property and of honour. Women are mainly interested in their progeny and, in varying degrees in the societies studied in this volume, in their own husbands, while they often remain strangers, sometimes almost hostile strangers, in their husband's extended household or in relation to their husband's parental family. Men are committed to the perpetuation of the group with which they are identified. Their social identity is a reflexion of the position of their agnatic group in the ladder of social esteem. Their view of the family is a formal, a political, view. It is a tool in the struggle for power and of its corollary, prestige. The feminine view is a private view and is determined by more immediate accessible ends.

Not only extended households but polygyny is on the wane and we find women in eastern societies not only wishing to limit the number of their offspring but also assuming a decisive position in the family as buffers between fathers and rebellious sons and as protectors of their own aged parents.

The specific aim of this Introduction is to provide as clear a summary as I can offer of what I consider to be the leading argument of each paper or its main point of articulation with the central themes of this volume. I have inserted, during the course of each presentation, an analytical note, of necessity a personal one, not as a critic but as an 'opener of the way' to further discussion. Needless to add that I, alone, am responsible for any bias of interpretation. This can be easily corrected when the reader turns to the original paper.

Having presented in lapidary form some of the conclusions and some of the main themes that run, like Ariadne's thread, through this volume, I now turn to the discussion of individual contributions.

Writing about a Lebanese Maronite village Professor Emrys Peters draws a broad comparison between its kinship terminology and that of other Arabic-speaking communities, demonstrating, in the process, the lack of correlation between kinship terms and the content of relationships. Indeed, a growing number of anthropologists (e.g. Needham 1971) share the view that sociological conclusions may not be drawn from verbal and structural similarities of kinship terminologies.

Lineage organization, such as that observed amongst the bedouin of Cyrenaica, is absent not only from the Lebanon but from a large section of the Middle East, although in the Lebanon, Shī'ite Muslim aristocrats use the lineage idiom to connect themselves to an early hero of Islam or to the Prophet through the descendants of his daughter Fāṭima. In this case the use of a lineage terminology enables these aristocrats to conceive of themselves as an exclusive, high-ranking, group although both the oecological preconditions of a lineage organization and the lineage structure are absent. The language (the lineage idiom) is the medium used to achieve a certain end (a claim to aristocratic descent), but there is no relation between this language and the reality of the organization it is used to describe or, rather, the language is used correctly to describe a fictitious organization. This might serve as a useful sociological definition of trickery.

Among the Maronite villagers those who bear a common name are referred to as *'a'ila*, a family. This is not a corporate group, property in land is not vested in it, the land itself, when seen from a patrilineal viewpoint, being 'dispersed' through female inheritance. The males themselves do not constitute the core of the methods of social grouping. Indeed Peters claims that affinity is 'the instrument of configuration', that social identification is frequently made by tracing connexions through mothers and through affines and that the social vitality of a man and a family are replenished through marriage and through the attraction of affines to their orbit, this last feature also forming part of South Italian marriage strategies as described by Dr Davis.

A patrilineal society using affinity as a means to social identification, and affinity acting as an instrument of social configuration, is an interesting, and, to the anthropologist, a challenging point of view as we might equally well have expected classification through affines to relate, in a patrilineal society, to the intimate, the private, intra-family area and grouping through agnates to pertain to the external, public, domain.

'Affinity', writes Peters, 'has the power to create groups.' What then, is, an affinal 'group'? This group cannot be defined in terms, *inter alia*, of a strictly defined kinship system, of a system of descent, of jural rights and duties vested in it, of a structured system of relations, of a group name or, even, of a generic name for such 'groups' in Lebanese Maronite speech. 'Affinity', writes Peters, 'is a selector which appoints members, so to speak, in the manner of taking a decision to include them.' But who takes the decisions? The 'group', the 'affinal set', is defined in relation to a 'social situation' so that, presumably, varying situations might determine an equal number of permutations in the composition of 'affinal sets' although, when a set has been situationally determined, all the persons in it are said to be accurately identified. Thus, one may conclude that, in this Maronite village, there are as many 'affinal sets', actual or potential, as there are significant social situations relevant to the formation of such sets. At the same time those pursuing wealth and power weave a network of links which ramify with each succeeding generation cognatically or affinally recruited into the 'affinal set' which, through this will to power, acquires a long lease of life.

I have used intentionally the term 'network' as it has been utilized by anthropologists as a technical term in a polemic context dating from 1954 (Barnes 1954) in a sense apparently not dissimilar to that of Peters's 'affinal sets', the resemblance drawing verbally closer through the introduction, in relation to 'networks', of the term 'sets' (Mayer 1966).

According to Peters, the main distinction between network and affinal set is that a network is frequently defined in relation to a particular person chosen at random whereas the affinal set is defined with reference to a particular situation, the set 'existing', in this sense, independently of an individual random point of reference. Nevertheless inclusion in a set does depend on a choice by individuals, the criteria for the choice being contingent on individual interests and on the evaluation of these interests in relation to a social situation at a particular moment in time.

I suggest that the 'affinal set' may be seen as an intermediate step between a type of network, extreme in terms of non-predictability of composition and non-existence of a common context, and that of a jurally defined corporate group. This network may be the result of a series of unconnected choices, each responsible for a network link, while its actors, beyond proximate links, may be equally unrelated, sharing neither common bonds nor common participation in a single social phenomenon, each link being provided not only with its own actors, but also with its own situational context; like a play lacking in any of the three unities. The claim on behalf of the affinal set is that it refers to 'a discernible group of people', interacting in a socially defined situation.

The network, like *la Ronde*, may be a useful descriptive or even a useful heuristic tool. It is, equally clearly, not connected with morphology either in a geographical sense of discerning what is on the ground, in a sociological sense of a 'socially defined situation' or in the anthropological, of an institutionally defined collectivity. The social sciences study what is. Networks, affinal sets and corporate groups exist in the sense that they are all part of social reality. There is place for all these concepts as long as they do not, mistakenly I believe, attempt to usurp each other's functions, thus confusing social categories, field-work techniques and levels or kinds of understanding.

This theme: the nature and constitution of social groups, their relevance to the methodology of social research and to the understanding of social change is discussed, from the perspective of their own field-work, in Professor Khuri's and Dr Seddon's contributions to this volume.

Professor Khuri is also concerned with the theory of groups and with that of descent groups in the Middle East. He studies two Maronite and four Shī'ite family associations in two suburbs of Beirut. Before their growth into suburbs, these localities included a number of important extended families whose prominence, derived from the control of wealth and people, was culturally expressed in long genealogies and large families, each genealogy being supported and nourished by its own history. Family groups tended to split into smaller segments 'often of the lineage order' whenever these segments were able to use a new leader, a new prominent house, as their new core. Indeed, Professor Khuri uses the classical lineage terminology (primary, secondary, tertiary) to describe these segmentations. Here it is the very fluidity of family groups which allows them to shift descent from one line to the other without losing identity, by claiming, for example, to be the cousins of the family group which they wish to join.

A family association is created by the founders registering the association and seeking to receive into it the largest possible number of those bearing the same family name while validating their claim to common descent by the fabrication of spurious genealogies asserting, in one instance, common descent from Abraham. Expanding prosperity and increasing mobility in the two Beirut suburbs were responsible both for the growth of genealogical ambiguity and for the rise of ambitious leaders, each wishing to lead, in lieu of a lineage, an artificially created 'family association' whose main function was to act, internally, as a welfare and protection group and, externally, as a political entity, a receiver and dispenser of privileges.

This artificial creation which uses the terminology but is only a travesty of lineage Professor Khuri calls an anti-lineage. True lineage loyalties are not eliminated, but only suspended by family associations which cut across them. Because of their ad hoc creation, and of the transience of the bonds they create, they merit, in the opinion of Professor Khuri, the qualification of non-groups or anti-groups, a militant terminology underlying this author's opposition to the tenets of the classical school of anthropology proposing the study of corporate and enduring groups as a fit subject (but not, I believe, the only one) for anthropological study.

Here I would like to introduce a further personal *caveat*. In contemporary sociological studies frequent discussions are held concerning the statistical relation between the ideal and the actual, the inference being sometimes drawn that an ideal which is not actualized in the majority of practices is either not a true, or is a declining, ideal. The ideal/actual relation varies in accordance with moments in the life of a society (Peristiany 1975). Again, to summarize Durkheimian argument: from the observation that most unions are mono-gynous one cannot infer that polygyny is not permitted or that it is not con-sidered as the ideal state (Peristiany 1953, xv).

Professor Rosenfeld investigated the marriage patterns of a Muslim and a Christian village in the lower Galilee of Israel over a period of fifteen years. One of his findings is that endogamous marriages, here marriages contracted within the patrilineage, have doubled in number while marriages with women outside the partilineage, or outside the village, or outside both, have decreased proportionately. His search for a clarification of this phenomenon encompasses macro-sociological and micro-sociological explanations.

Professor Rosenfeld examines some of the demographic, historical, structural and economic conditions for the maintenance of Arab social values and of the Arab marriage system and way of life.

In the modern state of Israel, a state lying at the antipodes of feudalism, overall changes are taking place at a rapid rate. Mechanization has been intro-duced in the village and the majority of able-bodied men work away from their homes. But familiarity has not reduced alienation. Work outside the village, being temporary, is considered as insecure so that the 'migrants' remain, in reality, village dwellers, clinging to their village for safety and social warmth. These insecure 'migrants' are also backward agriculturists tied to an ongoing 'residual social structure'.

This may partly explain the preservation of the social system, and thus the stability (but not the increase), of the rate of endogamous marriages. One of the reasons advanced for this increase is the disappearance of a number of villages. As a consequence marriage alliances with other villages have decreased so that the women of one's own village and even more so those of one's own lineage, within which preferential marriages should be contracted, have become more sought after, marriage with them reflecting exceptional prestige.

Dr Cresswell examines, with reference to a Maronite village situated near one of the centres of bygone Druze power, a well-known phenomenon of Middle Eastern anthropology: that of marriage with the father's brother's daughter. This type of endogamy, common to Arab and Berber, was adopted by the Maronites, together with the Arabic language, about three centuries ago. This institution is now dying out in most contemporary Maronite villages in the mountains of Lebanon. One of the interests of this type of marriage is that it appears to set aside the concept of exogamy and that it challenges the notion of marriage-exchange-alliance attributed, i.e. to cross-cousin marriage.

Dr Cresswell's analysis points to the links between this preferential type of marriage and land tenure economics. In this area the lineage with most sons is enabled to increase the size of its cultivation in each succeeding generation through marriage with a patrilateral parallel-cousin. This is in keeping with those theories of parallel-cousin marriage which relate this phenomenon to the economic and political reinforcement of the lineage through lineage endogamy. It is also possible to ask whether the Quranic law, which attributes to daughters one-half of the sons' share, is actually applied and whether marriage with a maiden who is not the Fa Br Da would not also result in increasing the husband's land through the increment of her share (cf. Murphy 1959 and Bourdieu 1972) unless, of course, and this would be an altogether different and special case, the father's brother had no sons (Bourdieu 1972, p. 99).

This type of preferential marriage raises an interesting question concerning the defence of female virtue and, thus, of family honour. Patrilateral parallel-cousins are members of the same descent group living close to each other. Is the division of village life, into strictly defined male and female spheres, asks Dr Cresswell, a means of ensuring the least possible premarital contact between those who, although they live so close together, are also considered as preferential mates?

I suggest that another, possibly fruitful, question which we might ask is that of the relation between personal feminine honour and group honour as they are affected by a woman's conduct in two distinct social contexts, the one in which a woman shares her husband's lineal allegiances even before marriage (as in the case of marriage with the father's brother's daughter) and that in which the wife comes from a lineage with which her husband's lineage may be engaged in a feud.

Professor Cuisenier's research was carried out in the Djebel Anseriin of northern Tunisia. Here, as in the Arab world in general, residence is virilocal, descent patrilineal and marriage polygynous so that the domestic cycle originates with the husband and follows the process of his simultaneous or successive marriages. The author is concerned with the determinants of the various phases of the domestic cycle in Tunisia, the transmission of rights, roles and property on the death of the head of the family, the operation of fission and fragmentation and with the positive correlation obtaining between increases in wealth and the large size of households. The relation between economic factors and cycle stages is most explicit when the eldest son is in a position to break away and set up his own home. Fragmentation of the household also becomes inevitable when each share is too small for subsistence.

The articulation of marriage strategies with economic and legacy tactics is a necessary prerequisite of the survival of large domestic communities, indeed the system necessitates a large number of wives and children. The succession or co-existence of wives and the point of branching out of sons are finely balanced in relation to the needs of the large household. The phasing out of the large Tunisian households and the rise of monogyny as an ideal coincide.

It is methodologically more advisable, and this is the procedure of Professor Cuisenier, to view these as concomitant variations responding to changes in their bio-social environment rather than to ask which conditions the other. The change may also be seen as part of a Mediterranean, perhaps of a world-wide, phenomenon as households, whether they be composed of polygynous, or monogynous families, are tending to shrink in size.

The family composed of parents and married sons – the *dār* – is the 'basic' social unit in the Sahel district of eastern Tunisia studied by Professor Abu-Zahra. A number of these extended families are linked in a larger patrilineal descent unit called the *'arsh*. It is stated that neither the *dār* nor the *'arsh* form corporate units in the sense of being linked, as units, by economic, legal and political bonds. Their main function is to serve as points of reference in the collective status system of the village, as membership of the village is traced through membership of the descent groups embedded in it. Both *dār* and *'arsh* act as ceremonial units, the joint performance of ceremonies publicizing their claim to common descent, long association with the land and, thus, nobility.

The ideal of solidarity and the ideal of actual co-operation between brothers are sorely tested by fraternal rivalries.

Indeed, I understand from the literature on the Arabs that few relations are more embittered than those between brothers who, through competition, have first become rivals then enemies; deep affection and solidarity turning sour and leading to equally deep hatred when the all-pervasive ideal of unity has been betrayed and shattered by individual or sectional needs. 'Who but your brother could have gouged out your eye?' is a proverbial rhetorical question asked in northern, eastern and southern Mediterranean lands whenever the topic of family friction is discussed. 'Fighting like brothers sharing an inheritance' is, in Cyprus, the paradigm of implacable enmity (Peristiany 1965, pp. 88–9).

Here inter-family quarrels are further fuelled by friction and jealousies between a man's co-wives; between the co-wives and the wives of the other brothers; between the daughter(s)-in-law and the mother(s)-in-law; between paternal half-brothers each defending, and spurred on by, his own mother. The opposite is true of half-brothers sharing a common mother, the mother acting here as a pacifier and as a pole of loyalty.

The violence of the strains on the nuclear and the extended Tunisian village family are expressed by a Tunisian proverb current in the community studied by Professor Abu-Zahra, '[when in need] I went to my father's brother and he blinded me. I went to my mother's brother and he abandoned me.' Thus, here again, expectations based on a deeply-rooted social ideal, an ideal round which a chain of values is co-ordinated, generate, when betrayed, a reaction of the same order as the strength of the ideology forming its inner core. The form of the reaction may have a cultural specificity, but the principle is wide in its application.

Wives, until such time as their sons grow up and the wives are integrated in their husband's family, remain peripheral to it and depend on their own brothers for assistance in times of crisis and for burial when they die. This permits the brother of a marginally-integrated woman to meddle in her affairs. A man wishing to be in full control of his home should be careful to choose a wife whose father and/or brother are not powerful and overbearing enough to interfere in its administration.

Dr Seddon examines aspects of kinship and family structure in an under-developed and indigent province of Morocco where polygyny is declining but where men, in opposition to their wives, do not wish to limit the size of their families because, as we have seen, in the case of northern Tunisia, a large house-hold comprising numerous offspring is the most effective social and economic unit.

Dr Seddon distinguishes between nuclear family household and 'budget unit'. The household is composed of nuclear families, or of individuals, both usually linked by ties of consanguinity or affinity. The 'budget unit', a kind of coenobium, is 'a group of individuals sharing a common fund and exchanging goods between them without reckoning'.

When building his model the author proceeds from the smaller to the larger unit while stressing, at each level, that the links bind individuals rather than groups. On the other hand the government uses, for administrative purposes, a model patterned on the tribe and the segmentary lineage system. These form, for the peoples themselves, a conscious model. We might then conclude that kinship and descent links (between groups) provide the people of northeast Morocco with the conceptual framework which allows them to discover and understand their relations to their social environment.

Why, then, are group links and individual links contrasted? Is the people's conscious model (group links) a falsification of reality (individual links)?

Dr Seddon claims that kinship and descent 'serve to obscure the development of horizontal social differentiation and so prevent the emergence of an un-ambiguous class structure in the countryside'. Kinship provides the conceptual framework of the social structure, kinship and patronage are used as electoral vehicles. The fact that the elected representatives of the people are their kinsmen and their patrons 'prevent(s) full awareness on the part of the masses'.

Dr Seddon's paper forces into the open the opposition between what I believe (contra, e.g. Boissevain 1974) to be a non-politically oriented anthropology, an anthropology so far practised equally by the politically and, or, religiously devout and the, in both senses, agnostic and the new *anthropologie engagée. Engagée*, in what sense? In the sense that it assumes that the 'truth', either the actual truth, referring to the here and now, or the ultimate truth revealing a universal process which will come to pass even if it is not actually observed, is that of the class struggle. This 'reality' in-being or in-becoming would, then, be obscured through the study of a society's framework seen as a whole composed of structured parts whose very form and function are conditioned by the internal social forces of its own social system, the functioning of the parts being, in that structural view, to preserve the nature and the equilibrium of the whole.

The study of the social structure and that of its modes of thought which are its emanation and countenance, and which, therefore, may be said to uphold it, are seen as an enfeoffment: one establishment studying another establishment and, in this way of thinking, lending it the support of its scientific recognition as though – and here is the operational part of the argument – nothing else outside the 'structure' existed.

But if outside the 'traditional' structure a new social phenomenon, such as an ideology, or a new form of economy, or a new type of social organization, is emerging then it will affect the 'traditional' structure rather than operate as though it did not exist. Social institutions, social values and social modes of thought are not effaced overnight; societies are not blackboards. Social scientists study what is. The new and the old are part of this reality. Let us, by all means, study social classes wherever they exist and whenever they are relevant (e.g. in Cyprus the honour – 'prestige hierarchy does not correspond to social classes'. Peristiany 1965, p. 14). Let us, also, study all varieties of 'anti-groups' whenever they are helpful to our understanding. My query is whether we should disregard the study of social structures and of concepts permeating the life of a society since the study of their anatomy may obscure changes in their physiology or, possibly, in the evolution of the social species.

One cannot study the relation between being and becoming by investigating only past forms (which is the essence of the accusation directed against students of social structure), or by neglecting the present for the future. Being and becoming are part of the same reality, being *is* becoming. Their separation into two distinct fields will not only impoverish both but it will distort their perspectives. The perspective of the 'traditional' social scientist – and we are speaking in reality of the social anthropologist – will then be limited by those of the micro-society he is studying and the perspective of the anti-structuralist may cause him to disregard that part of the social phenomenon which he considers as more closely connected with the past than what he believes to be the future. If religion and, now, traditional social representations are the opium of the people, the scientist should study both the opium and the people and their interrelation.

In the eastern Adriatic section of the Mediterranean, the Albanians share, with the Serbs and the Montenegrins, the distinction of an extended patrilineal kin-group organization. The Albanians are amongst the least documented Mediterranean people, a substantial part of our anthropological knowledge dating from the early works of Mary Durham and Margaret Hasluck and from Julian Amery's account of guerrilla warfare (in relation to social organization) during World War II.

Dr Whitaker's study of familial roles in the extended patrilineal kin-group of the Ghegs, the sheep-herding highlanders of northern Albania, is based both on his own field-work and on published sources.

The household (*shpi*) formed, in 1945, the time of the field observations, the basic unit of Gheg society. Several brothers and their descendants lived under the same parental roof, joined in a residential and economic unit resembling the *Zadruga*. Up to sixty or more people shared the same 'building complex'. Within it, two specially appointed officials, a 'master' and a 'mistress' of the household (not the master's wife) decided and administered matters of communal interest, thus severely curtailing the domain of parental authority. The Gheg clan was formed of a number of these extended patrilineal kin-groups.

'A man has blood, and a woman kin' is a Gheg aphorism demarcating, in its terseness, the political roles of man and woman.

Members of the closely-knit patrilineal, patrilocal, clan claim descent from a male ancestor. Ideally (as this custom is gradually falling into desuetude) members of a clan formed an exogamous unit which, over several generations, exchanged brides with another clan; the marriages serving to cement their alliance and to resolve blood feuds. Thus, Gheg marriages, like dynastic ones, had political connotations. When the alliance was broken the bride found herself isolated amongst her husband's kin battling against her father, her brothers and her patrilineage – a tragic theme of Albanian epic poetry. Never integrated into their husband's clan, as only patrilineal links are valued, Gheg women remain through life closely attached to their brothers. In rare instances, when the conflict of allegiances was extreme, women killed their children as a desperate outlet to their predicament.

This dilemma is part of the ambivalence of a woman's life. A man is born into a patriline with which he is identified from birth to death. The name, the wealth and the honour of his family are his own and remain in his keeping throughout his existence. To affirm and to defend them is, for a man, an assertion of his own social identity.

Not only the Albanian but, to broaden the issue, the Mediterranean maiden, should preserve her virginity, not so much in order to honour but so as not to dishonour her father and her brothers, thereby undermining, coincidentally, her own marketability and thus bringing further shame to her parents. Her chastity, within marriage, she should defend in order not to dishonour her own children. To her husband's honour as to his lineage, she may remain a stranger. Here I would like to point out the interest of a study relating the social range of a woman's dishonour (to her children, husband, husband's family, husband's lineage and/or only/or not at all, her family or lineage of origin) to the degree of her integration in her husband's kin-group, according to its extension.

A minor French poet said that woman, in her most exalted moments, is no more than a fiddle to a man's bow. The Albanians stress woman's instrumentality equally bluntly by calling her 'a sack for carrying things'. When, as among the Gheg, this 'sack' is used but is never integrated into her husband's lineage, the wife's affections follow the path of her loyalties so that her brother, who is also her protector, tends to be her most loved kinsman.

The relationship between degree of social integration, affectional orientations and feminine conception of honour would well repay study in the Mediterranean area. To this subject the one proposed earlier could serve as an introduction.

The four studies of the contemporary Turkish family are located respectively in the capital city of Ankara and in the large city of İzmir (ex Smyrna) (studied comparatively by Dr Kongar); in Edremit, an agricultural town and the richest olive-growing centre of Turkey situated between İzmir and the Dardanelles (studied by Professor and Mrs Fallers); in a Turkish provincial town (appearing under the pseudonym of Tütüneli) in the extreme southwest corner of Turkey (where Professor Benedict carried out his field-work); and in the small Black Sea coastal town of Ereğli, studied by Professor Kıray.

These four studies concern the Turkish family in relation to the avenues of social change. Apart from articles on change in a rural context, the main monograph on the social institutions of a Turkish rural community is Professor Stirling's *Turkish Village* (Stirling 1965). Although a monograph can claim to depict only one form of a multiform society and only one moment in the life of this form, it may serve as a background to the present studies and as an indication of the distance covered by social scientists in the last few years.

One of the most acute social problems of Turkey, is the mass movement of population from rural areas to urban centres, as these lack the necessary facilities for absorbing immigrants. The result is the shanty-town, the *gecekondu*, which grows on the periphery of organized city life spreading – and this is a common Mediterranean phenomenon – during electoral periods, the modern interregnums. Between 1927 and 1965 the rate of increase of the urban population of Turkey was double that of the increase of the total population. Forty-six per cent of the total population of the three largest cities of Turkey live in *gecekondu* areas, this being a startling figure not only by Mediterranean but by world standards.

The *gecekondu* have their own stratification: traders and shopkeepers at the top, qualified workers and artisans in the middle and the non-qualified at the lower end. One may hazard the guess that this system is not different from that of the city, only that it starts several rungs lower.

Dr Kongar defines the *gecekondu* family as 'relatives living together under the same roof where food is cooked in common', a household in some respects comparable with Dr Seddon's Morocco 'budget unit' (p. 182). Its average size (5.2 in Ereğli, 5.5 in Ankara, 4.7 in İzmir) may point to the urbanization of the *gecekondu* family, as it is smaller than the average Turkish village family (6.2). In *gecekondu* areas family ties do not draw together several nuclear families into a joint family and their weakness is shown by the relative lack of interaction between *gecekondu* kinsmen living within a short distance of each other. Their bonds have ramified outside the family so that work-mates and friends and, increasingly, voluntary associations and trade unions are taking over some of the mutual-aid functions of the family. Thus, the *gecekondu* residents are being increasingly exposed to the formal and impersonal relations which are associated with urban life.

Professor Benedict queries the assumption that a change from extended to nuclear family structure attends the move from rural to urban setting. The very opposite may be true. The extended family, that is, may have begun to disintegrate in the rural area and it is this early loosening of its bonds that may have facilitated migration to the city. Again, once this move has been made, intensive relations between kinsmen may develop rather than decline.

The extended joint household, often depicted as the traditional Turkish ideal, is, in practice, only encountered in a minority of cases. In Tütüneli itself early fission of the family takes place as the authority of the head of the family wanes after the marriage of his sons and there is no mechanism for replacing him after his death.

Dr Kıray stresses that the father–son relationship was axial in the preservation of family solidarity and her observations concerning the father–son conflict, which comes to a head with the son's marriage, confirm recent studies carried out in the Middle East and in the Maghreb.

The birth of a son assures, to his mother, security, and status recognition in her husband's family. The son grows up to be his mother's ally and the champion of her interests not only against his father but against his own wife. 'If a choice is to be made, "the stranger's daughter" (*el kızı*), or daughter-in-law, does not stand a chance,' a common attitude in the Middle East where the 'stranger wife' (stranger in the sense of not being an agnate, a father's brother's daughter) is known as 'the enemy inside the house'.

If bearing a son is likened to the growing of roots in one's own home, his departure, especially his premature departure after a quarrel with his father, is responsible for a sentiment of intense insecurity. A mother is thus prepared to make any sacrifice in order not to lose him.

With the growing independence and rebelliousness of young men against paternal authority mothers are increasingly assuming the role of 'buffers' interposed between father and son. To me Turkish mothers appear to be waging a losing battle. It is clear from Professor Kıray's conclusions that when respect for the father is lacking, this attitude may also extend to the mother, the son gradually identifying himself with his wife against not one but both parents. This has not yet come about in the Fallers's paradisiacal Aegean town, where the inhabitants see their streets as running with olive oil and honey, but it is an index to a new uniformity.

In Ereğli daughters have come to replace sons in at least one respect. Now that the breaking up of the extended family is undermining the security of the aged, daughters are inviting their parents to live with them. This points to the increasing importance of women in the family, to the replacement of the extended patrilineal family by a nuclear family with affinal accretions and to the loosening in the exclusiveness of agnatic bonds.

Professor and Mrs Fallers contend, *inter alia*, in their discussion of sex roles in Edremit, with a perplexing question. Why are Turkish women, who function in public or academic life, as efficient as their western counterparts while being noted for pugnacious self-assurance free of feminine self-consciousness? It is, explain the Fallers, because professional Turkish women commit only the professional part of themselves to their dealings with the public. Their total personality is not involved, the female section being, so to speak, left behind in the home, which is its proper domain.

Social life is so organized that men and women move at ease in two exclusive circles, tangent rather than overlapping even on domestic occasions. Women organize their own activities, attracting to them their own followers and selecting their own leaders. Freedom of action, lack of male–female competitiveness and an assurance developed away from the critical appraisal of the other sex is the outcome. Does one, also, notice a certain detachment, or rather a lack of attachment? The groom is chosen by the bride's family which expects him to be a good provider, a cheerful member of the household, a kind father and a respected citizen; the bride does not look to him for companionship or comfort. This could have been the description of a Victorian household. Two additional characteristics lend this relationship another dimension.

We have already noticed the separate social lives of husband and wife. We are also told that the brother–sister relationship is not only very affectionate but often very intense, perhaps *the* 'most intense cross-sex relationship they will ever experience', so much so that the brother is jealous 'when an unauthorized male approaches either his wife or his sister'. Also that, when a woman misbehaves, the father will hold his daughter responsible, whereas the brother will seek out the other party.

Now this intense relationship between brother and sister is not superseded by that of husband–wife. This last appears to lack the elements of devotion, integration and 'oneness' – even of 'romantic affection' – qualities which characterize the brother–sister relationship. These deficiencies may detract from the plenitude of the conjugal bond. It thus comes as no surprise to be told that when husband and wife quarrel and separate this is 'a matter of little more than inconvenience and mild regret'.

Would it be legitimate to press the argument concerning this male–female separateness to its extreme conclusion so that marriage may be considered as one moment of tangency, long or short according to circumstance, of two worlds which are so organized in (this part of) Turkey as to meet for only brief encounters without trespassing on each other's domain? Or, again, when is a woman not a 'stranger'? When she is a mother (mother–son being, for her, the most important relationship in the family: Kıray), a sister (brother–sister being the most intense cross-sex relationship: Fallers) or, possibly, a sister-surrogate, a paternal parallel-cousin. The first two a man cannot marry. The third he may but, according to Professor Khuri (Khuri 1970, p. 613) writing of this Arab–Berber 'preferential' type of marriage, this results, for the man, in a kind of emasculation as true potency and masculinity can only be fully demonstrated to a stranger. Here the merging of opposites is always made to lack one element. When carnal union is permitted, the partners remain strangers; when they are not strangers at the outset, sexual commerce is either barred or muted.

Professor Tentori's presentation of the family in the south Italian town of Matera is silhouetted against its historical background: the evolution of the social classes between the nineteenth century and the present, a similar time referent to that of Dr Davis.

Here, and I shall concentrate with the author on the earlier period, social distinctions were extreme. At one end of the scale was the duke and the nobility with the representatives of the highest classes, the *signori*; at the other end were the *cafone*, the country bumpkins. The gentlemen lived in the plains, the yokels, until they moved to Matera only a few years ago, dwelled in caves, each conjugal couple occupying one cave together with its children, the family donkey, the family pig, and the domestic fowls. The plains/caves opposition is a variation on the theoretical antithesis between plains (rich) and highlands (poor) to which may be added the rider: the richer the plain the greater the economic and social distances separating its inhabitants.

The social distance between the two Matera extremes was so radical that different church bells tolled on the death of high and low. Kept separate in death, the idea of competition, of mobility or of intermarriage linking the two extreme classes was inconceivable. At the same time the intertwining of social and economic interests, consolidated by marriage, associated the proximate classes, that is the nobility, the higher grades of the civil service and the large landowners, in the formation of a social category, that of *galantuomini*. Technical and trade specialization also graded and graduated the social classes from middle to lower; craftsmen and peasants remaining distinct and seldom intermarrying to this day.

A few decades ago the distinction between the highest and lowest classes was reflected in family relations and in the rules of inheritance. The ideal of the upper class was to transmit almost intact the parental inheritance to the male first-born, whose duty it became to perpetuate the family and its position in society. Among the daughters of this class only the eldest was, usually, endowed and married. The younger brothers and sisters remained celibate and gravitated round the heir or took holy orders, the celibacy of the higher class generating its own, complex, sexual and social problems.

If favouring of the eldest son was a means to preserving the unity of the agricultural enterprise (which constituted the economic assize of the leading families) restrictions imposed on the marriage of daughters ensured that, through the provision of an adequate dowry, the favoured daughter would strengthen her brother's family through a valuable alliance. Celibacy would then prevent the degradation of her family and the confusion of classes. Today the openings provided by prestigious professions have severed the landed estate–prestige–primogeniture nexus, thus rendering unnecessary the enforced celibacy of younger children.

Amongst 'the subordinate classes' all sons and daughters were endowed on their wedding day. The marriage of children of this class coincided with the stage in the biological and economic cycle of the parental family when the need for the children's contribution to the upkeep of this family was acutely felt. The fission of the family, the departure of the children, that is of working hands, when parental strength began to decline combined with the indebtedness incurred through endowments set the poorer classes on 'a continuous road to impoverishment'.

Dr Davis analyses the changes in the rules for the transmission of property in Pisticci, a mainly agricultural hill-town, population 15,000, situated, like Professor Tentori's Matera, in the ancient Byzantine province of Basilicata, in south Italy. '1814' and '1961' have been chosen as points of reference for this comparison.

In '1814' immovable property was inherited by sons while daughters were endowed with movables. In '1961' most property was transmitted at marriage, both children being given land while the daughters received, preferentially, a town house together with personal effects and a cash dowry. Thus, today, the majority of houses in Pisticci are owned by women.

The provision of women with houses at marriage is not, according to

Dr Davis, common in south Italy and he enquires into the reasons for this practice. And why a *town* house? Could it be 'that the honour of a man requires
that his womenfolk should live under permanent public scrutiny' and thus in
town rather than in the country?

Comparison with other Mediterranean areas may be of interest. In Greece
and Cyprus dowries have been taking increasingly the form of city property.
The reasons given for this preference are simple and revealing. Young people
wish to live in the city. Even when the town flat or house is rented it yields a
higher and more stable income than country property. As marriage presents
or dowries form part of the assessment of a maiden's desirability, the parents
do their utmost to enhance her attractiveness in a competitive market. Honour
already forms part of the argument, but, if it is invoked separately, we may add
that fear that a girl may lose her honour if she long remains unmarried forces the
parents (and the brothers) to part with their most precious belongings in order
to 'establish' her. The form of marriage gifts, dowries and investments cannot
escape the influence of an increasingly urban orientation.

Again, the criteria for ranking people, writes Dr Davis, have become
increasingly market-derived and 'the type of market which has been introduced
into Pisticci has ensured that relations between people who are ranked equal
or nearly equal are competitive rather than solidary'. That the *agon* for honour
takes place between equals or potential equals, is at the basis of the argument
of Honour and Shame.

Dr Davis shows, in this 'model' analysis of social change, how political and
economic innovations, to which the family is particularly sensitive, are related
to the new system of transmission of property. I have highlighted a number of
conclusions, or hypotheses, not necessarily those that the author would have
chosen for this purpose, as they may be used as links with some of the theses
presented in this volume.

The relation between family types, form of morality and inheritance in
Galicia, a province in the extreme northwest of Spain, is the theme of
Professor Lisón-Tolosana.

Spain, like most Mediterranean countries, glories in its local idiosyncracies,
in the sense that every valley, every hill, nook and port is distinguished by its
own traditions – a situation reaching its apogee in the case of Greece with its
galaxy of over one hundred inhabited islands.

In Galicia three types of inheritance are customary. In the highlands the
eldest male child (or, failing him, one of his brothers or, for want of brothers,
one of his sisters) inherits two-thirds of the total estate. In the fishing communities and the valleys near the sea a daughter is appointed as the principal heir
to succeed, on the death of her parents, to the most substantial part of the
estate. Finally, in the southeast reaches of this region, the parental estate is
divided equally among all children.

To these three types of inheritance correspond three family types. When the ideal of male inheritance prevails (first type) it is correlated with patrilineal transmission of rights to males, with male authority and with residence with the husband's father. The very opposite holds true when the ideal heiress (type two) is a woman. The correlation is then with matrilineal transmission of rights to females, with female authority in both the private and, in certain contexts, the public sector and with residence with the wife's mother. The family axis, in the first instance, is father/son. It is mother/daughter in the second. In the third instance, when children of both sexes inherit equally, succession is bilineal as the family is bilateral, residence is determined by the couple's particular circumstances and authority is exercised by the husband.

When the patriarchal, patrilineal and male values are heavily accented, the heir's wife leads, in his own parents' household, a life marginal to their own, the husband acting as mediator and constant go-between his wife and his mother. A father, in this social setting, concluded his nightly invocation for his friends, neighbours and all the dead of the parish by adding this tag to his prayer: 'for the welfare of everyone in this house, except for the daughter-in-law who is an outsider'. We have already noted the non-integration of the wives in societies which exalt all bonds between males and masculine lines of devolution of rights, societies such as that of the Albanian Ghegs where one may marry an actual or a potential enemy and Arab societies unless the wife (in the preferential form of marriage) is the father's brother's daughter and thus a member, by birth, of her husband's lineage. With this exception the wife often remained for most of her life on the periphery of her husband's family. The position of the wife is aggravated in the Spanish example by the husband's almost menial position in his parents' household. The internal strains and conflicts of these families result in 5.4 per cent of the wives (of the 195 cases under study) leaving their homes, while 'a considerable number suffer from nevrosis or "bedevilment"'. In the matriarchal setting the position is reversed. Although here the man's sufferings are not described we may refer to the Mediterranean literature on the uxorilocal husband, a shadowy figure in both his home and in his village of residence.

In both instances the male or female heir presumptive, a role they are free to accept or reject, has to live with the parents and care for them until the legacy becomes effective on their death. Their demise, especially in the case of one surviving parent, soon after the appointment of the heir, is seen in the same moral light, as the winning of a lottery ticket: a stroke of good luck, but not as respectable as wealth paid for with the sweat of one's brow.

The usual panoply of moral and utilitarian syllogism is used in defence of deep-rooted beliefs; but with marked constraint when effective disinheritance is upheld. Could this be due to the realization that local inheritance rules antagonize the more prevalent ideology of equality in which this minority custom is embedded, or should we refer to the Levi-Straussian hypothesis that the institutions of all societies tend towards equality? I can only answer that all human societies are differentiated, that in all societies differences are evaluated so that the very core of the institutional and value system of all known societies – indeed their very conceptual framework – is based on inequality. The polar antithesis of this universal *reality* may be a (universal?) *yearning* for equality so that a constant comparison, a constant dialogue, between the actual and the ideal is taking place. As we know of no egalitarian societies we are also ignorant of the converse form of dialogue.

We have been concerned until now with the consanguineal and affinal ties, which constitute the fabric of kinship relations, from the structured patrilineal groups to the more transient bilateral family. The discussion then moved to affinal groups, situationally defined and to anti-groups whose every link is constituted by a particular interaction, their overall articulation in a network being due neither to the linking of all the network's actors by a common objective nor by their membership of a corporate group. Moving from nuclear families and lineages to affinal groups and networks, the bonds become increasingly tenuous. In the last two instances, more subjectively defined and more dependent for their very existence, in the case of affinal groups, on acts of individual volition and, in the case of networks, on the casting of the net.

From anti-groups we move to pseudo-kinship (Pitt-Rivers 1968).

Professor Pitt-Rivers compares the nature and function of ritual kinship in the Catholic and Orthodox worlds, in Spain, Greece, Cyprus and Serbia. *Compadrazgo*, the hispanic appellation by which this institution is often known in anthropological literature, concerns the bonds linking the baptismal and/or marriage sponsor to the person sponsored and the extension of these bonds to some of their kin.

In Christian doctrine it is the baptismal (not the marriage) godparents who are accorded the greater importance, it is only they who are considered essential to the performance of the mystery with which they are associated. The baptismal godparent is a *pro patres*, an anti-parent, his role during the baptismal rite of passage and during the life of the godchild, being that of a spiritual counterpart of the genitor. The godfather only becomes a mundane substitute father (rather than a spiritual surrogate father) when the genitor disappears prematurely leaving his son unprotected.

The relation between godfather and godchild is even more asymmetrical than that between parent and child: unilateral beneficence on the part of the godfather, respect on the part of the godchild. On the other hand the relations between *compadres*, that is between the sponsor and the parent, are expected to be balanced and symmetrical. The sponsor is always the social superior or, at least, the equal, never the social inferior, of the parent. Indeed, *compadrazgo* linking inferior to superior, peasant to rich citizen, agricultural worker to landowner, may be used to provide non-equals with the possibility of collaborating within a context of equality. *Compadrazgo* is, thus, at the very core of many Mediterranean systems of patronage.

In Spain, France, Italy, Greece, Cyprus and Israel, the basic kinship bonds are those linking members of the nuclear family. In Turkey, the Lebanon, Egypt, the Maghreb and the Arab-inhabited parts of Israel, we find that kinship bonds outside the nuclear family *tend* to provide only the necessary elements for a network of dyadic ties. They either do not contribute permanent bonds linking corporate groups or, when they do, as in the case of lineage societies, they may be seen, in the increasingly individualistic modern social setting, as constituting recessive rather than dominant social characteristics. The nuclear family is flourishing. The Mediterranean extended households and lineage societies appear, increasingly, as relics from an undifferentiated world, a world in which it was possible for small groups to enjoy relative autonomy and a degree of autarky.

Dyadic ties depend, for their implementation, on the sentiment of the actors, that is on voluntary decisions rather than on institutional imperatives. *Compadrazgo* bonds conform to this pattern although we often find that these ties may extend over two generations, as both Catholics and Orthodox recommend that marriage sponsors should baptize the issue of the marriage and that baptismal sponsors should sponsor the marriage of their godchild. We also find in Greece, as we do in Serbia, that sons replace their fathers in the role of godfather.

In the northern section of the Mediterranean, that of rural Serbia, we encounter the *Zadruga*, famous in anthropological and socio-economic literature. The *Zadruga* is an extended patrilineal and patrilocal household, itself a section of a patrilineage and a clan. Here, spiritual kinship, *Kumstvo*, links two collectivities rather than two individuals, by establishing a spiritual bond between two conflicting, indeed sometimes feuding, lineages. This it does through its appeal to spiritual values which transcend sectional interests. At the same time spiritual values are embedded in a social environment. They cannot but be enacted in a society whose channels they use while allowing themselves to be manipulated for the advancement of sectional interests.

In Spain, and this phenomenon may also be observed in many parts of Greece, grandparents become the godparents of their grandchildren. Are not the godparents, asks Pitt-Rivers, the 'anti-parents' par excellence, taking their 'revenge' for the breaking up of their nuclear family by becoming, *in partibus*, the parents of their children's children?

A student of East African age-sets would be well placed to follow this argument. He might add that, by usurping a parental role, grandfathers acting as godparents to their grandchildren trespass on the separation, the non-overlap, of the social roles of proximate generations. At the same time they are provided with a means for acting the role frequently attributed to them by Mediterranean popular wisdom: 'A grandparent, twice a parent.'

Dr Kenna's analysis of family life on a Greek island of the Aegean also points to the importance of ritual kinship both in everyday life and in the critical moments of the godson's existence. Here spiritual and social obligations blend in order to provide a godchild with someone to launch him in life and to protect him thereafter while allowing the engaged couple to make their first socially effective choice of institutional friends.

Two quotations from Professor Kenny's paper on the contemporary Spanish family in Mexico lead to the heart of his subject: 'Mexico actually conquered the Conquistadores through her women and continues to do so' and, in a different vein, a statement by members of the old-established Spanish colony in Mexico: 'Fidel Castro (the son of a Spanish immigrant from Galicia) has turned against his own kind', that is, the Spanish immigrants in Cuba.

Spaniards living abroad conserve a 'vibrant feeling' for what they consider as the parent household in Spain, seeing themselves as its expatriated branches. To maintain their Spanishness two converging avenues are open: marry a Spanish woman and educate the children in Spain.

The Spanish male is also considered as a socially desirable mate, old-world virtues such as dependability and a punctilious sense of honour form part of his reputation, while the Spanish woman is distinguished by her identification with *la madre abnegada*, the self-sacrificing and long-suffering mother. This Mediterranean *virtud* forms part of the standard evaluation of the intrinsic worth, of the true hispanism, of a woman. To live up to it reflects credit on both the husband and the children and thus enhances the social standing and the prospects of the family. Thus the idealizations of the 'home' values come to form clusters of stereotypes, conformity to which is used for ranking purposes.

Professor Kenny's study of the Spanish family in Mexico confirms anthropo-logical observations concerning the adaptation of Mediterranean emigrants both to the old and to the new world. The family is the cradle of ethnicity and, within it, the mother is its high priest. Spanish mother, Spanish children; Mexican mother or, now, Mexican maid, and the Conquistadores are conquered.

The present generation of Mexican Spaniards resist both the dominion of their parents and their ethnic ideology which, if my observations are relevant and they resemble Greeks and Greek Cypriots in England and in the United States, they probably consider as the two sides of the same coin. In their view the ethnic ideology serves as an ideational prop to parental authority, both working in unison to slow their emancipation and to prevent their acceptance on terms of equality by their native co-evals.

In kinship, class and selective migration Professor Friedl investigates migration (1930–65) from a Boeotian village to Athens, a study based on field-work both in Vasilika, the village itself, and amongst its migrants.

Vasilika parents have the same city-oriented occupational aspirations for their sons and for their future sons-in-law. This results in the necessity of acquiring, for the daughters, a dowry in the form of city-based property. As these aspirations are common to this village the question arises as to who chose the 'migration route' in order to satisfy them and why he did so.

Professor Friedl discusses macro-sociological and micro-sociological factors affecting social and territorial mobility and examines, within the village, the economic resources of the household, considered as an important determinant, in relation to other factors such as number of children, education, employment history, kin links in the city and escalation in the size of the dowry.

In the village the parents and their unmarried children, members of the same household, operate as a corporate group from which marriage may be seen as a secession. The frequent refusal of men to marry before their sisters is an assumption, by the unmarried brothers, of the responsibilities they share with their parents for the 'setting up' of their unmarried sisters.

A significant conclusion in relation to our theme is to be found in the author's candid criticism of her own research methods. Professor Friedl assumed, at the beginning of her study, that the individual was the proper unit of study but concluded, at the end of her research, that the village family household, its system of values, its economic position, its kin connections, and its age and sex distribution taken together in the Greek national context, set narrow limits within which individuals could operate and over which they had no control,' so that predictions concerning individual behaviour may be made, within a small range of error, by examining the position of the family in the village, and of both the family and its home village in the national perspective. This conclusion emphasizes the measure of conscious or unconscious control exercised by the Greek family over its members. Indeed, it points to their radical relation as individual decisions are, to a large extent, determined not only by the family's social and economic standing within the community but also by the individual's position in the developmental stage of his parental or, if he is married, of his own conjugal family.

The greater the economic resources of the Vasilika village family household, the more likely were the villagers to migrate. When this came to pass the migrants' village status followed them to the city, the top farmers moving to middle-level city positions and the lower grade farmers becoming semi-skilled construction and factory workers.

This conclusion tallies well with recent studies both in Greece (Lambiri-Dimaki 1974) and France (Bourdieu and Passeron 1964) and with Christopher Jencks' study of inequality (Jencks 1972) in the United States concerning the relation between family and education. Indeed Jencks' conclusion that 'the most important determinant of educational attainment is family background' could have been applied, as it stands, to Professor Friedl's Greek, and my own Cypriot, material.

The problems of Dr du Boulay's study are representative of a wide spectrum of modern Greek life. A village on the island of Euboea, small in size and population, the income limited to the essentials of life, the villagers hard-pressed by the ideal of Greek parenthood compelling them to provide a competitive dowry for the 'establishment' of their daughters and the 'highest' possible education for their sons and now – added burden – increasingly for the daughters also.

Living up to these social imperatives absorbs the largest share of the parental income, so that little remains for prestige spending. The levelling of the means available for the display of wealth and power limits the choice of channels of social mobility and highlights the traditional value system in its role of main avenue of local esteem and status.

Every family – and the family is always of the nuclear, bilateral, type – struggles through each of its members to defend its honour, this being the expression of its moral heritage and of its social achievement. I have, elsewhere (Peristiany 1959(a, b) and 1965, p. 14), described this situation as *agonistic*, in the sense of a contest before a chorus, a commenting and evaluating audience.

In this Euboean village success in the struggle for survival, and honour, form the constituents of reputation, honour (*timé*) being the more purely moral evaluation. One of the rules of the game, according to Dr du Boulay, is that a person may lie in defence of family interests or even mock and denigrate the conduct of other families. Then people laugh, and 'before laughter one is ashamed'. The sociologically-oriented French had already clearly perceived that the meaning of laughter can only be understood in its social context (Bergson, *Le Rire*) and that as a social sanction in a society noted for the punctiliousness of its code of honour *le ridicule déshonore plus que le déshonneur* (La Rochefoucauld, *Maximes*).

To protect itself against mocking, the family conceals the actions of its members behind a shroud of privacy while endeavouring to ferret out the secrets of its rivals so as to expose them to public ridicule and, thus, to shame.

We may tentatively conclude that a close correlation obtains between, on the one hand, the defensive use of deception and the offensive use of ridicule and, on the other, the nuclear family's beleaguered and insecure position in the village reputation hierarchy. Secrecy concerning family conduct and an assault of innuendoes directed at the actions of others constitute the defensive strategy, and form part of the offensive weaponry, in the *agon* of honour.

The stark impression of a society in which every family is a self-contained moral entity defending its honour against all comers, when not actively engaged in replenishing its anti-reputation armoury for future use, may be tempered by a number of factors.

Dr du Boulay indicates that the sharp differentiation between the nuclear family and the outside world 'is modified by a number of relations which fan out of the family into the community, linking the family groups in a number of different ways' (du Boulay 1974, p. 143). Thus the family/others opposition is partly neutralized by the links woven by the family with the world outside it, each individual person and each family being at the centre of a web of relations situated within a wider social structure.

The permutation of these webs of relations spun out of the plurality of bonds moderates the bluntness of rivalries. This also performs, in my view, two additional functions. It heightens the possibility of conflict by widening the choice potential, while it reduces its vigour by providing graded rather than contrasted alternatives. Thus, I believe that in modern society, acute but relatively rare conflict is replaced by frequent, if trivial, friction.

A conflict of values implies the possibility of choice. Each choice may be good of its kind, it may, that is, be consonant with the highest value of the particular scale within which the choice is said to be made. But the choice may confront not the values hierarchically graded within the same scale, when the choice will be evaluated in relation to their gradation, but different scales, all, possibly, containing similar values arranged in different ranking orders.

The actor's first task will then be to determine the primacy of an ideal. Will the actor then choose to be at one with an ideal, that is with the highest value in one of the scales, or will he compromise and by compromising adulterate it? Only saints, heroes and, in their heyday, aristocrats, that is persons contemptuous of the social order, could attempt to be at one with an ideal. When the Misanthrope, in the closing lines of the play, cries out, in despair against the limitations imposed by society on his thirst for the absolute, that he is setting out in search 'of a place where one is free to live as a man of honour', the spectator knows that the quest is doomed, for social life is one of compromise constantly curbing the expression of ideals. To live by them, one must live alone, when there will be no occasion to apply them, hence: Misanthrope.

Thus only persons who place themselves outside the social order may embody and enact an ideal without regard to social contingencies. This, and not only the emulation of the gods, is a *hubris*, of which Antigone's actions are the perfect example (Vernant and Naquet 1972, Vol. II, Lloyd-Jones 1971 and 1975). To act the role of sister to perfection, she must neglect all her other social roles and disregard all other social rules and expectations.

This is a paradigm of a conflict of ideals and, through them, of a conflict of the values and prescriptions of the *démos* and of the divine law which inspires them. Although the gods are superior to humans, and although human is the law of the city, the gods are themselves part of the social order. *They are* order. Thus, whatever the choice, one disobeys the gods, or society, or, as I believe, both. The essence of Greek tragedy is the dilemma. On a less exalted level this is the difficulty of living in a Greek village. Whatever the choice, the malicious can fault it either by falsifying the facts, or by attributing false motives for the choice or, and this is the trend of our discussion, by choosing to evaluate it according to a hierarchy of values other than the one which the actor claims to have used. I believe that just as the constant assertion and the putting to the test of a person's worth is a sign of status insecurity in a society where all may claim to be equal, the lack of a clear gradation between ideals, and thus of a clear hierarchy of prescriptive rules, is a reflexion of this type of egalitarian, unclearly structured and thus 'anarchic' social order.

REFERENCES

Barnes, J. A. 1954. 'Class and committees in a Norwegian island parish' *Human Relations*, 7, pp. 39–58.
Bergson, Henri. *Le Rire*.
Boissevain, J. 1974. *Friend of Friends*. Oxford, Basil Blackwell.
Bourdieu, P. and Passeron, J. C. 1964. *Les Héritiers*. Paris, Les Editions de Minuit.
Bourdieu, P. 1972. *Esquisse d'une théorie de la pratique*. Travaux de Droit, d'Economie, de Sociologie et de Sciences Politiques, No. 92. Collection G. Busino. Geneva, Librarie Droz.
Braudel, F. 1966. *La Mediterranée et le monde Mediterranéen à l'époque de Philippe II*. 2 vols. Paris, Armand Colin.
Davis, J. 1973. *Land and Family in Pisticci*. London School of Economics Monographs in Social Anthropology, No. 48. London, Athlone Press.
Dimaki, Jane Lambiri- 1974. *Pros Mian Hellēnikēn Koinōniologian tés Paideias*. Athens, N. Centre of Social Research.
du Boulay, Juliet. 1974. *Portrait of a Greek Mountain Village*. Oxford Monographs in Social Anthropology. Oxford, Clarendon Press.
Jencks, C. *et al.* 1972. *Inequality, a Reassessment of the Effect of Family and Schooling in America*. Basic Books. 1973, U.S.A., G.B. Allen Lane. (The quotation is from the British edition.)
Khuri, F. I. 1970. 'Parallel cousin marriage reconsidered: a Middle Eastern practice that nullifies the effects of marriage on the intensity of family relations'. *Man*, Vol. 5. No. 4.
La Rochefoucauld, François, duc de. *Maximes*.
Lloyd-Jones, H. 1971. *The Justice of Zeus*. Berkeley and Los Angeles, University of California Press.
1975. 'The morals of the majority'. Review of K. J. Dover's *Greek popular Morality in the Time of Plato and Aristotle*, *T.L.S.* 14 March, p. 273.
Mayer, A. C. 1966. 'The significance of quasi groups in the study of complex societies', in Michael Banton (ed.), *The Social Anthropology of Complex Societies*, A. S.A. Monographs, No. 4. London. Tavistock Publications.
Murphy, R. F. and Kasdan, L. 1959. 'The structure of parallel cousin marriage'. *The American Anthropologist*, Vol. 61, pp. 17–24.
Molière, J-B Poquelin. *Le Misanthrope*.
Needham, R. 1971. *Rethinking Kinship and Marriage*. A.S.A. Monographs, No. 11. London, Tavistock Publications.
Peristiany, J. G. 1953. *Introduction to Sociology and Philosophy, by Emile Durkheim*, transl. by D. F. Pocock. London, Cohen and West.
1959a. *Honour*. The Frazer Lecture, 1959.
1959b. 'On Cypriot Honour'. Seminar paper. The Wenner-Gren Mediterranean Conference. Burg Wartenstein.
(ed.) 1965. *Honour and Shame, the Values of Mediterranean Society*. London, Weidenfeld and Nicolson.
1975. 'The Ideal and the Actual, the Role of Prophets in the Pokot Political System', in

J. Beattie and G. Lienhardt (eds.), *Essays in Social Anthropology*. Oxford, Clarendon Press.

Stirling, P. 1965. *A Turkish Village*. London. Weidenfeld and Nicolson. New York, John Wiley.

Vernant, J. P. and Vidal-Naquet, Pierre. 1972. *Mythe et Tragédie en Grèce Ancienne*. Paris, F. Maspéro.

1 Aspects of affinity in a Lebanese Maronite village[1]

Emrys Lloyd Peters

University of Manchester

Throughout the Middle East the language uniformly used is Arabic, and for this reason the interest kinship holds for the social anthropologist is greatly heightened. The entire range of vocabulary used for kinship purposes is understood throughout the area, as a collection of words, by bedouin shepherd and Lebanese businessman alike. Yet the persons to whom some of these words refer, whether they are real or putative kin, differ conspicuously. Thus, to give an example in advance of its more detailed treatment later, the term *'amm* is always used in a particular Lebanese community, by either spouse, to refer to the father-in-law; among the bedouin of Cyrenaica it is not used for this purpose at all. When the same term is applied to persons of like consanguinity in different communities, the content of the relationship is sometimes profoundly different. Thus, the term *khāl* is used to refer to the mother's brother, both by Cyrenaican bedouin and the people of different religious sects in the Lebanon; but among the former the relationship is conspicuously a joking relationship and among the latter it is not. The range in the forms of social organization from, say, Libya in the west to Iraq in the east, includes many varieties: bedouin communities, landowning peasantries, land labourers hiring their labour in different ways to landowners, big landlords employing tied labourers, agriculturally very rich, poor and marginal areas, villages and towns of different sizes and many different economic pursuits, large urban areas, and so on. If it is granted that kinship relationships and other social relationships are to some extent interdependent, then whatever kinship terms are used in the various countries, a variation in the content of kinship relationships is to be expected. It follows from this that when the language of kinship is the same for several communities, it does not mean that they all share a common kinship system – if, indeed, the concept of system is at all apposite when applied to kinship. The argument of this article is partly intended to show that kinship positions and their accompanying terms alter, as do the content of these relationships. This, then, is the most obvious danger when working in an area where there is general uniformity in language. A more serious difficulty arises out of this. Any of the kinship terms are understood as words by people throughout the area. When one of these terms is used in a very restricted sense in one community, and in another community it not only has this meaning but it is used for another disparate category of kin, the very strong tendency, particularly among writers on Middle Eastern peoples, is to impute a primacy of meaning to the term, treating its other uses as derivations. More than this, some scholars transfer this primacy of meaning to the word when it is applied to other disparate categories of kin. This view is based on the assumption, albeit crudely applied in some instances, that if a single term is applied to more than one category of relatives they must share common elements of behaviour: words used in the context of kinship, that is to say, cannot possess a plurality of meanings. There are no logical, lexical or behavioural grounds for making this assumption. Later, evidence will be adduced to support this statement.

Much of the diversity which characterizes the Middle East is squeezed into the small area of the Lebanon, a country whose total length, from north to south is only about 125 miles, and whose width is, roughly, only 35 miles, giving a total area of a little under 4,000 square miles. Within this area the altitude rises from sea level to around 10,000 feet at the peak of Mount Hermon in the south-east, and higher still in other ranges in the north central part. Between these extremes of altitude there is a vast prolixity of topographic forms, and these, coupled with marked local climatic variations, give a range of crops from the subtropical banana to the temperate wheat, and to the barren areas of the high slopes, usually snow covered for many months of the year. With this topographical diversity and wide range of agricultural produce, goes a mosaic of forms of land holding. The differences between local economics and the variety of managerial arrangements that are to be found make the economic diversity of the Lebanon quite striking. Matching this diversity, the population of some 2,000,000 souls includes an equally astonishing conglomeration of cultural differences. Over fifteen of the world's religious sects are represented in the population: Shī'ite and Sunnī Muslims, Druzes, 'Alawites, several Christian sects, some of them ancient schismatic sects, and a few Protestant sects of more recent arrival. This kind of combination of divers ecological, economic and cultural areas, on a national scale, means that it is quite out of the question to think in terms of *the* Lebanese kinship system. While people speak of areas of the country as the domains of this or that sect – and it is true that sects do tend to concentrate territorially – in any small village, the likelihood is that several of the sects will be found there, Muslims living cheek by jowl with Christians, together with some Druze perhaps, and so on.

The brief introduction of these Lebanese complexities is not intended to set the stage for an elaborate cross-cultural comparison. The co-existence of peoples of profoundly differing cultural values and economic interests, dramatizes issues which, where the economy is fairly uniform and the culture homogeneous, are either absent or their significance is obscured. Some cross-cultural references will be made, but only where they will serve to point certain critical differences.

Although this article does not purport to deal with kinship in its general elephantine sense, a few broad statements about it are necessary. And since the concern, henceforward, will be with the formation of groups by people who recognize genealogical connexions through males and females, especially those linked contemporarily by affinity, these remarks, in the first instance, are about some of the more common features of using kinship or its idiom, to specify the nature of groups.

Certain of the stages of genealogical reckoning occur in all the four Arabic-speaking communities which I have studied.[2] In Figure 1, the lines

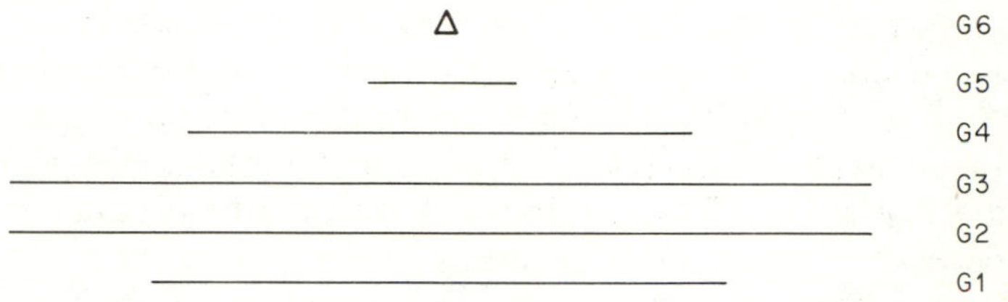

Fig. 1.

represent a hypothetical number of people in each generation (G): G1 are all those unmarried people whose ages stretch from birth to about the early twenties; G2 consists of young adults; G3 is made up of mature adults, and G4 of surviving grandparents. The generations G1, G2 and G3 can be shown as they appear in the diagram for any peoples anywhere, because they represent a statement about the living or the recently dead, and, as such, they are accurate. Diagrams of such kindred will always be similar in shape, and the differences which appear will be differences in the size of the populations contained by the genealogies. What happens to the ascending generations, from G3, if anything, is critical as a statement of the type of group the genealogy is meant to represent. Where descent reckoning is patrilineal, three things are likely to happen at G4: women are excluded altogether (they are sometimes only proffered for the G1, 2 and 3 when requested), the number of males given is reduced compared with G3, and some, at least, of the living are not lineal descendants of the males shown. The number of males given in G5 is greatly reduced to about two to six depending on the size of the population the genealogy has to embrace. At G6, the number of males is further reduced to one. If the genealogy accurately depicted the state of things from the past to the present, then the lines representing the generations G2 to G6 should, of course, be roughly equal in length, since the population in each of these generations should be roughly the same. Obviously, even where genealogical reckoning is of this kind, there might be aged people who remember their grandparents, and this sometimes causes confusion when genealogies are repeated, but the younger people disregard these complications. Reduction of the number of males in the ascending generations is systematic, and it is this which gives the genealogy its characteristic shape. Add to this the fact that the lines of descent are tied together in a knot at the point of a single ancestor, then clearly the shape of the genealogy is a specifically contrived arrangement of people, the single ancestor acting as an emblem conveying to the people themselves the nature of its details. The most evident of these latter details is that people conceptualize themselves as descendants of one person. Why people should wish to conceptualize themselves in this way is made manifest by the form their genealogies take above the point of the single ancestor.

Thus, in a south Lebanese village, the Shī'ite Muslim aristocrats of the early fifties gave a genealogy exactly like that shown in Figure 1, with regard to its shape. Thereafter, save for some idiosyncratic side shoots off the main line, a continuous chain of names connected them either to an early hero of Islam or to the Prophet through the descendants of his daughter Fatima. Sometimes only part of this list of names would be offered, on the understanding that 'it is known' that the line was much longer than this. At other times, usually on request, a complete list of names would be drawn up, totalling some forty-two names in all, in an individual's descent line. The projection of the descent line some thirteen centuries into the past gave the aristocrats the kudos of historical standing; it also gave them contemporary status because it rooted them in early Islam, and this status conferred on them benefits denied to other inhabitants of the village. They were given various dues, received payments for services associated with their status, and they were occupationally privileged. These derived benefits were rewarding enough to relieve almost all of them of the menial tasks of cultivation. Most of them lived a leisured life in comfortable domestic conditions. Until the early fifties the total amount of land they held was considerable, and some of them had sufficient holdings to enjoy prosperity. Their genealogy explained all these facts. Moreover, the single ancestor was the means they had of visualizing themselves as a group of people sharing specific interests, and the line thereafter connected all of them to the status of long ancestry and distinction as Shī'ite Muslims. Visualizing themselves as a group of descendants, they were able to use descent as a means of controlling the movement of property and the negotiation of their marriages, or, at least, to attempt to do so. Through the idiom of descent they were able to conceive of themselves, and to be seen by others, as sufficiently exclusive socially and economically to merit the term 'rank'.[3]

The elaborate genealogy of the bedouin of Cyrenaica, corresponding in shape for the G1 to G6 generations, differs in the kind of elaboration which occurs above the single ancestor at the G6 generation. The entire bedouin population is disposed on pieces of territory of varying sizes. All such local groups possess genealogies of the sort shown in Figure 1, and there are many scores of them. Local groups sharing propinquity demonstrate this genealogically by linking nodal ancestors together as brothers, themselves shown as sons of an ascending nodal ancestor, linked to another as a brother, and so on until the whole population becomes drawn together genealogically at an apical point separated from the living by some eleven generations. A claim to a continuous descent line from this apical point, if it can be successfully upheld, establishes the status of a male as freeborn, and anyone of this status is accredited with rights in land and water somewhere. Successive orders of descendants narrow the area in which an individual has specific rights in land and water. In other words the successive orders on the genealogy rough out blocks of territory in an ordered fashion, and thereby serve as a conceptualization of the territorial dispositions of people in groups. This genealogical apparatus, impressive as a feat of memory, when the names in it are called out in their regular order, is not, in fact, any more of a feat than for someone in England to remember his street, district, town, or parish and county names. The elaboration of a genealogical apparatus of this sort, a lineage system, does not rest on the chance of individuals' powers of recall of names from the distant past. If memory enters into the matter at all, it is highly contemporaneous, for the names of dead ancestors survive in the daily lives of the people, who use them to serve as ready references for a limited and definable number of social relationships. The use of the nodal ancestor in Figure 1 makes clear immediately a number of issues; it defines an exclusive group of males, the political relationships of this group to its neighbouring groups; it states that each male in the group has equal rights with the others to water, to ploughland, to pastures, to protection and succour, and that these rights impose duties, such as protection of fellow members, to pay and receive blood money, and to seek vengeance when any male of the group is slain. Lineality gives this group its constitution, couched in a number of jural rights, duties, and obligations. All jural relationships, how-ever, are not packaged into lineality. The positioning of a man in a particular patriline is a sure indicator of where he has title to water and the amount of his share in a particular well, but it says nothing about the number of animals inherited from his father which drink from it. The inheritance of animals is as jural a relationship as any, but inheritance is on an individual, not a corporate, basis. Marriage, to take another example, is a cluster of jural rights, duties and obligations which lie largely outside the jural relationships of a corporation. In the lives of the bedouin these several clusters of jural relationships, disparate in analysis, are intimately juxtaposed as a motley; other relationships, such as moral, ritual, economic and debt relationships contribute to this variegation. An instance, par excellence, of this is the local residential group, the small camp. In it are bundled the vast complexities of which the list of social relationships given earlier is only a simplification. In it are found men who are virtually all agnates, save for the camps of upstart shaikhs where the agnatic concentration might drop to some 20 per cent of the total male inhabitants. The rights to basic production resources, which give meaning to agnation (and not consanguinity as often implied), draw men together, but this constitution does not state who among them must live together. In an earlier article I was at pains to stress that

affinal and matrilateral connexions – the consequences of the affinity of the
ascending generation – are the selectors which discriminate among agnates to
bring them together as co-residents of small camps. If affinity is of this
importance where lineality is also of such significance, then, in the absence of
the latter, the former's significance is likely to become more critical.[4]

Lineage organization, in any professional sense of the term, is absent from the
Lebanon; and for that matter from most of the Middle East, certainly from its
cities, towns and villages. The examples of the lineality of the aristocrats of a
south Lebanese village and the bedouin of Cyrenaïca have been summarily
explained in this article for two reasons. They will serve as useful cross-
references later in the argument to throw some issues into relief. Also, authors of
Middle East studies, in increasing numbers, insist on accrediting villages, urban
back streets and townships in states with lineage organization.[5] It is quite wrong
to assume because some old codger, an habitué of the local coffee house, has
grandchildren (or even great grandchildren) and remembers his grandparents
(or even great grandparents) who assisted with his rearing, that we are dealing
with lineage relations or a lineage system. Forde, long ago, analysed, with
admirable lucidity, the necessary ecological prerequisites 'for extensive proliferation of unilineal kin and the formation of large and successively segmented
clans'.[6] Yet, where these conditions do not obtain, the full terminology of
lineage analysis, clans, sub-clans, lineage segments is used and these organiza-
tionally disparate situations are analysed as if they are closely akin to those of
the bedouin and south Lebanese aristocrats. For this reason an apology is not
thought necessary for the somewhat instructional tone of the discussion of the
two examples cited.

In a Maronite village of central Lebanon, the main subject of attention here,
two instances of the use of lineality are illuminating. In Figure 2a five generations of males occur in the genealogy.

This number of generations is similar to that required to group the living
aristocrats of the south Lebanese village as descendants of a single ancestor,
and to give the bedouin corporation the focus of a common and putative
ancestral name: and there the similarity ends. The patriline in Figure 2 has
attached to it seven living males only, and a total population of fifteen; the
south Lebanese aristocrats are a total population of about two hundred and
twenty; the bedouin corporation has a total population ranging from about two
hundred to eight hundred people. The patriline in Figure 2 is accurate for all its
generations; the bedouin and the south Lebanese aristocratic genealogies are
inaccurate in the details given for three of the generations, but they are
inaccurate in an ordered manner. The genealogy of the bedouin corporation is
part of a vastly elaborate lineage structure enclosing a total population not far
short of a quarter of a million people. The south Lebanese aristocratic group
is the only large property-owning group in a total population five times its size,
the members of which visualize their identity as cast in the image of a lineage

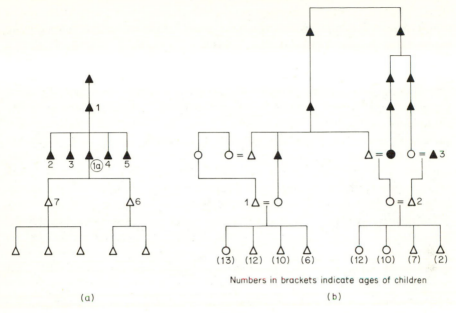

Numbers in brackets indicate ages of children

(a)   (b)

Fig. 2.

framework, but devised by them to catch all those in the population of aristocratic rank. The patriline in Figure 2 is not, by any stretch of the imagination, a lineage group, part of a lineage system, a sub-sib, a minimal lineage segment, or any other kind of group to which the vocabulary of lineage analysis is so irresponsibly and wrongly applied by so many writers on Middle Eastern communities.[7]

The neatness of the patriline in Figure 2 is unusual in the village. It came about in the following manner. The ancestor numbered 1 was an only child. He had five sons – and three daughters for that matter – of whom only 1a had descendants still living in the village; of the others, 2 migrated to the U.S.A., 3 left permanently for South America, 4 lived his life locally as a bachelor, and 5 entered the priesthood. Thus, 6 and 7, two middle-aged brothers, are the fourth generation of males in what is effectively a single patriline. Pride of ancestry and length of continuous descent in one line of males is evident among the people in this small group, and acknowledged by others, although it is not paraded either by them or the others. Moreover, unlike the south Lebanese aristocrats they do not continue their line deep into the past. This small group is a political strong point in the village, and 6 is its *za'īm* (leader). Use of the patriline adds very marginally to the latter's general standing, but it is used only because it does this without introducing complications, and because, for quite fortuitous reasons, it happens to be available. Other men of the village, relatively poor perhaps and of no political standing, can account for as many lineal ancestors – and a greater number of descendants – but they do not make a public show of them, nor do they use them either to differentiate among descendants or as emblems of unity. The distinctiveness of the line in Figure 2 is partly its association with political power, but the *sine qua non* of its use is that it is not encumbered with lateral branches. Were the genealogy more elaborate in the ascending generations, the effect would not be that of a mere encumbrance only, but a history of past embroilments. If it is possible to prune a line of its lateral shoots, as in the present case, the history of past conflicts is confined to a very small nucleus of men in the present. Although patrilineality is atrophied as an agent for differentiation among the living, it is safe for this small group to use it because it does not contribute confusion to present-day issues, while at the same time it provides the group with the distinction of historical association and standing in the village.

The genealogy shown in Figure 2b on p. 33 is of the same number of generations as that in Figure 2a, but patrilineally it is neither as neat nor as singular in its demarcation of people. Only a small portion of its total is shown in Figure 2b, and this because it is rarely used in its complete form; this could probably be elicited, although I had to piece together the portion shown in the diagram. These details were extracted when, conversationally, an explanation was being offered to account for the close friendship of the two unrelated men 1 and 2 in the diagram. The most immediate connexion offered was that their wives are first parallel-cousins. Then it emerged that 2 is related to his wife as a second cousin, their mothers being first parallel-cousins. This additional connexion does not, however, bring 2 any closer to 1. Here it is important to note that the father of 2, shown as 3 in the diagram, was not a native of the village – he had migrated there from a village some distance away. This migrant's first wife died. A stranger at first, his assimilation began when he married the wife shown in the diagram, so that his son (2) if initially not yet an *ibn al-balad* (son of the village), was at least a son of one of its daughters. His father now dead, 2 has no lineal connexions through males, but his mother does connect him to males through males, and it is this kind of connexion, in ideology, which gives a man a secure anchorage among the population in the village, for consan-guineous connectedness is the prime symbol of an *ibn al-balad* status.[8] In short, for genealogical purposes his mother has come to assume, for him, a male role. Substance is added to his status by his marriage to a woman, already in an established position, and both their mothers are closely related as the children of brothers. The latter had several first parallel-cousins, one of whom was the paternal grandfather of 1's wife. The last connexion brings 2, his wife and 1's wife together as genealogically connected, if they wish to use the connexion, and secures an anchorage in the community in terms of sentiments. 'If they wish to use the connexion' is the operative qualification, because, within the span of the generations shown in Figure 2b there are very many more people, but the genealogy is neither conceptualized nor used in its entirety. Pieces are selected as and when required for this or that purpose. Here the attention has been focused on the connexion between two men, 1 and 2. If 2 had not been of stranger paternal origin, it is quite likely that other connexions might have been given. In Figure 2b it can be seen that 1 is linked, through his mother's sister's marriage, to both his wife's father and 2's wife's father, but this is besides the point since the aim was to connect 1 to 2 as an established man of the village, not as a stranger. In other words, the two men are linked together in a chosen manner, not because their genealogical connexions demand it of them but because they choose a selected part of their genealogy to indicate the particularity of their relationship. In a general sense their genealogical relationship would be counted as distant. Certainly, in the context of marriage permissibility second cousinship is thought of as distant, just as if a person wishes to do so for other reasons he will refer to second cousinship as so distant as not to matter. Further, granting that genealogical connexions permitted a wide range of choice of partners, the grounds for the particularization of the relationship between 1 and 2 must lie outside the genealogy. They are conspicuous as friends, as two people joined together in benevolent intimacy.[9] They drive off together to work, some eighteen kilometres distance, and they have a mutual understanding on this. They work in the same place, doing the same job, and they arrange their shift work and time off to coincide as nearly as possible. They live in the same part of the village. They discuss their interest in landed property together. They spend much of their leisure time in each other's company. They are similarly interested in the education of their children, all, except one, attending school. The link between 1 and 2, for all the seeming elaboration of patrilineality, is through women. The full connexion between the two is through five affinal pairings. It is also true that this affinity bonds them only in their generation. For the bond to persist, affinity will have to be renewed in the succeeding generation. Ages are given for the children to show that several possibilities already exist to bring this about. This is suggested as a possibility because this kind of match is consistent with a pattern which commonly recurs in the population. But, it must be emphasized, this does not constitute an approach to a lineage segment nor does it amount to patrilineality: the links are affinal, or through women, or both; and where the ethos emphasizes male descent, reference to women is resolved in affinity at some point.

What is meant by saying that the ethos is patrilineal is that the 'family name' which people bear is passed on through males; women, when they marry, assume the 'family name', and the fiction that those who bear the common family name are related in the distant past is sometimes mentioned. Despite abundant evidence to the contrary, if only in the contemporary disputes over land, the sentiment exists that inheritance is patrilineal – it is sometimes argued that contemporary conditions in which women actually inherit are of recent introduction, although the very people who have pressed this point should know from the passage of property among their own kin that this view is erroneous.

People who bear a common name are spoken of as a 'family' (*'ā' ila*). They are not clans in any sense. They do not have a recognized common ancestor. They are not segmented. Marriage patterns are not woven around them. They do not determine political affiliations. Property, in land or in other forms, is not vested in them, nor controlled by them. They are not used as pressures to seek aid, although they might be used to express a sense of bonhomie when there is nothing else to which appeal can be made. If, however, one of these names is that of an important personage, others of the same name might boast of the fact. With equal ease, a person can abandon the name and choose that of a known ancestor instead. Three men, all originally of one 'family' name have officially altered their surnames, for this, in fact, is what these names are. They are used very much like surnames in Wales: if there are two people named Jones in the same local community they might well take it into their heads to claim that some kind of relationship probably existed in the past.

Nuclei of people formed around men constitute what is usually understood by the term family. The seven living men shown in Figure 2a represent a nucleus of this sort, consisting of a pair of brothers, and their children, who live as close neighbours, and who all share certain property interests. This type of nucleus is called locally a *jib*. There may be several of these with the same surname. Although in the expression of sentiments the *jib* is a male unit, mothers, wives and daughters are included as well as a surviving grandmother. When occasion demands, anyone in the domestic unit, sharing the intimate privacy of common domicile, even if more distantly related than the paradigm suggests, is incorporated into the *jib*. The composition of the *jib* changes with the passage of time, although the term might adhere to a group of people for sometime after the links between its members have become virtually defunct.

Neither the *'ā'ila* nor the *jib* form the foundation on which groups are built, nor are they significant in generating consanguineous relationships. Finally, to dismiss the suggestion, a brief reference to a third concept is necessary. Inheritance, when discussed as a set of rules, is said to be patrilineal. It is expressed as an *'asab* (sinew) relationship, and anyone *'min al-'asab'* (of the sinew) has title to heirship, descending, as one man put it, 'from father to son, for many generations.' There are two objections to this view. First, lineal descent is systematically foreshortened, and factually, deriving necessarily from this, there is no evidence of a group of men holding patrimonial property, save for siblings who have not yet divided their inheritance. Second, women inherit and inevitably disperse property away from the *'asab*. Some women renounce their inheritance in favour of a brother, but this is not the irresponsible act of surrendering, say, a valuable piece of land. It is the use of property for acquiring claims on the recipient, of altering one type of relationship to another of one's choice. Or, a woman might accept a settlement, with or without claims on the receiving heir. Or, ruses might be adopted to disinherit female heirs (an offence in law), but when this is done the manner of doing it secures certain advantages for the daughter. Whatever course is adopted in practice, predictable when the full facts of domestic relationships are available, the critical point is that women, as mothers, wives or daughters are always significant in property relationships. For these two reasons the aggregation of people to form property groups, like the bedouin corporations, is not possible.

Clarification of the issues relating to descent through males, and the gene- alogical status of males as a power for drawing people together into groups, has been necessary to clear the ground of the debris of misunderstandings about kinship in the literature on the Middle East. In the Lebanese Maronite village, groupings based only on males are, at most, highly situational, and the situations to which they refer are few. These groups, moreover, are not defined by imperative rights and duties incumbent on all members. Rather, the senti- ments of possible common origin are used as persuasive pressures to nudge a person to do this or that, like cajoling a reluctant neighbour to come along to a funeral, or – less hopefully – as one of a number of reasons for convincing him to vote for a particular candidate in an election. At the other end of the scale a male group is restricted to brothers, or fortuitously, it is extended to first cousins, when, say, they are bound together by a common interest in undivided property – although this legacy is as likely to be left by a woman as by a man. Accepting, therefore, that patrilineality does not delineate durable groups in the sense of giving them a structure, then the effect of other means for con- figuring relationships is more significant than where such groups are present. Also free of the encumbrance of lineality, and the control it exerts over certain relationships, a much wider field of relationships are penetrated by these means. The main instrument for achieving a configuration is affinity. A foretaste of the sort of thing which commonly occurs in the village was given in the discussion of the partnership illustrated in Figure 2b. The possibility of a match being encouraged between two of the children of the partners was predicted with some confidence, because the partnership is a highly successful one in many respects, and this possible marriage of the future would replicate the kind of connexions in the ascending generations, and it would be consistent with the patterning of marriages among the rest of the village inhabitants. Affinity, it will be argued, is the instrument of configuration, affinal renewal giving it durability beyond the marital history of one pair of spouses.

The manner in which people visualize their connectedness is well illustrated by the following incident. On my first night in the village, a neighbour called to invite me to watch a performance of a card game, played regularly in groups in houses during the winter months, and known as *turnīb*. He introduced himself as my neighbour. There were eight men present at the beginning of the game and two others arrived later. In a manner which was soon to be seen to be characteristic, each person was introduced by his connexion to someone else. The details are significant. In Figure 3 the host (1) began by saying that he was

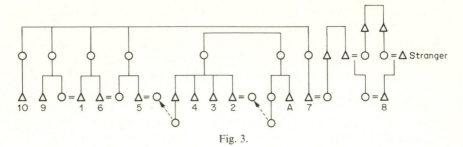

Fig. 3.

my neighbour. Then: 'You know that man of the shop (A) where you bought some things this afternoon. His sister is that man's (2) wife's mother. Next to him are his two brothers (3 and 4). The mother of those three was married to his (5) mother's brother, and he was my (1) mother's brother also. His (5) sister is married to my (1) brother (6).[10] He (7) is my mother's sister's son, and his wife and his (8) wife are related – and he (8) is also related to his own wife.' Later two other men entered together, whereupon the host immediately said, 'His (9) sister is my wife, and their (9 and 10) mothers are sisters.' The host connected all the men present, using only mothers and marriages to do so. In the ascending generation men were used only to link women, who in turn, link 7 and 8 together. Genealogically, it would have been much simpler to represent them as mainly men who had a common grandmother, as shown in Figure 4. It would have

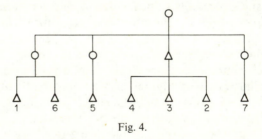

Fig. 4.

been possible to include 8, 9 and 10 much in the way they were introduced to me. This was not the way these men looked at their relationship, although when shown a diagram like Figure 4 they readily agreed that their relationship could be construed in this manner. Later during a discussion of the close friendship in existence between them, one remarked, 'We are a *kutla*.' The latter word is in common use in a political context, when speaking of a bloc of voters, or of a political party as the National Bloc, for example. During the discussion of the word's meaning, the speaker clasped his hands together tightly to indicate a strong bond. When I suggested that it would be appropriate to call them *kutla* Mary (a pseudonym for the common grandmother A in Figure 4), they picked up the phrase with alacrity.

Another manner of casting their relationship would be patrilineally. This

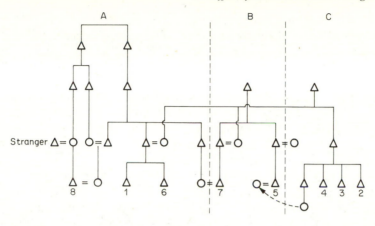

Fig. 5.

would require the use of three patronyms A, B and C in Figure 5, with the explanation that A is linked to B, B to C and A to C through women. Eight of the ten could be accounted for in this way, and the remaining two would require the introduction of an additional patronym for 8 and 9 (they were both of the same *'ā'ila*), since their only connexion to them is through women.

It would be possible to depict all the kinship connecting these ten men on one genealogy, but this would involve a combination of all the links shown in Figures 3, 4 and 5, and many others not shown on any of these. In any event such a depiction would be far removed from the manner in which people conceptualize their kin. Even the representations of links to a common grandmother (Figure 4), and interconnected patrilines (Figure 5), while easily comprehensible to the males they include, these are not the ways in which these men envisage their connexions. When voluntarily giving their relationships the only accurate diagrammatic representation is that shown in Figure 3; and that points to two processes at work: the selection of men by using affinity and the use of women in ascending generations, and the restriction on reckoning links to the grandparent generation, save in special cases such as 8, whose father came to the village as a stranger. Working on these links, the host was able to bring all the men together as relatives of a special sort, and he could have coped in a similar fashion with others of the group, who were absent on this occasion.

The use of lineality, whether through males or females, as shown in Figures 4 and 5, or as used by the Cyrenaican bedouin or the aristocrats of the south Lebanese village, is admirably exclusive in giving general boundaries to groups of kin of either type, and each ascending generation marks a considerable increase in span. But in this Maronite village conditions are so complex and diversified, that, by comparison with the mode of reckoning locally, lineality is much too rough and ready when what is required is precision of reference to individuals. Bilaterality does not solve the difficulty either, for, if this reckoning is systematically traced through a few generations only, large numbers of the population would be linked to any ego. Indeed, I am confident that were I to piece together the multitude parts of kin connexions collected, using all links, it would be possible to include virtually the entire population in one vast web of kinship, largely within the range of the grandparent, only occasionally having recourse to the great grandparent. This is not how the people themselves see it, and unseen connexions, obvious, perhaps, to the anthropologist, are irrelevant. Bilaterality, in other words, is indiscriminate, and cannot, therefore, differentiate into the social groupings evident for all to see.

Reference to a common grandmother and the use of interconnected shallow patrilines are not employed because they are seriously defective in two respects. In the former (Figure 4), three key men are excluded because they are not her descendants and one or two others who should have appeared as descendants are omitted from the diagram because their social relationships with the rest do not merit their inclusion. In the latter (Figure 5), two key men are excluded, and very many other men, not shown on the diagram, should have been included, among whom are some of the direst political opponents of the group, and some from whom they are socially estranged, or both. Their mode of indicating relationships specifies with such discrimination that individuals can be picked out of any kin context, even, when necessary, to the point of specificity of separating brothers. Such precision gives complete exclusiveness. By the same token, bearing in mind that a specific relationship is almost certain to be available, the application of the same method enables contraction or expansion in numbers to suit the circumstances.

Precision in selection does not mean that anyone can be drawn into a group by anyone capriciously. This would be to deny the group stability and rob it of persistence in its social relationships. The fact is that it does persist. I have observational evidence of this for a period of five years for a limited number of these groups, and hearsay evidence, corroborated by genealogical and other data, indicates that they have been in existence for longer. Caprice is removed because a selector is at work: affinity of the present adult generation or the ascending generation. Limits are also set by it, although they are elastic, stretched to include, say, a bachelor brother brought in on one's own affinity, or contracted to exclude him as affinally unconnected, depending on the particulars. This expansion and contraction occurs most markedly at the grandparent generation of full adults, for this is at the periphery of reckoning, and if renewal of affinity has been neglected for that period of time there is serious danger of the link becoming defunct.

Unlike the use of lineality to arrange an entire population into a structure of groups, giving these groups exclusive definition and their members the pre-emptive right of inclusion, affinity is a selector which appoints members, so to speak, in the manner of taking a decision to include them. Affinity is the instrument used to cut through a tangled undergrowth of relatedness, and it carves groups out of what would otherwise be an undifferentiated mass of kin. Without lineality of any sort, whether of a patrilineal, matrilineal, double descent or bilateral kind, affinity has the power to create groups, and it can do so with greater sensitivity.[11] Groups of this kind are not given a designation in the local vocabulary. *Kutla*, the term mentioned earlier, is not used for this purpose. In the context quoted it was inserted conversationally, more as a metaphor than a descriptive term in general use. Nor are they given the name of persons, prominent men among their members. One of them might be referred to as the group of one of its named members, but in another context a different name might be used, depending on the stress of interest the speaker wishes to indicate. The identification of a group is, thus, situationally relative. Nevertheless, they are well known by everyone locally, for although reference to them is situationally determined, the composition of the group is not; so that when reference is made to, say, Robert's group (*jamā'a*, meaning group in a general sense) this identifies all the individuals in it accurately. I propose to adopt the term affinal set to describe it.[12] Reasons for this choice, or, rather, reasons for not employing other terms used in the literature, will be discussed after analysing one affinal set to show its content.

Affinal renewal takes place within a generation, or two generations at most. Unless this is done, affinity loses its impetus to bring people together. Lapsed affinity is the rejection of a link, and, characteristically, it soon becomes 'forgotten', in the sense that it is no longer evoked, and, therefore, no longer serves to steer social relationships. Since affinity is a prime selector in configurating groups of kin, then, when it is allowed to lapse a re-configuration is indicated. This process is demonstrated in Figure 6, which, it must be stressed, is not a unique case, but one which is more manageable than most, and it also contains instances of a variety of forms of affinity to which, subsequently, it will be necessary to refer.

The elucidation of this vast bundle of interest begins with A, a lady in her late seventies. After her marriage, and before any of her three children married, the configuration of her relatives is shown by the shape, X, which, throws a boundary around people of two ascending generations, extending laterally to include her sisters' husbands and their children – her brothers were migrants to U.S.A., and of her husband's siblings three migrated (the daughter of one returning to live in the village), one died a bachelor and the other entered the Church. The only effect of the following generation on the configuration is shown as a trough at its base. I am unsure whether the children of her first maternal cousins were included in her set; they probably were at the time but it is not easy to be precise about events of some fifty years ago. By now, her own children have married and her grandchildren have mostly matured and some of her great grandchildren are in their teens. But the configuration of relatives as she envisaged it as a young mother has become virtually defunct. The only

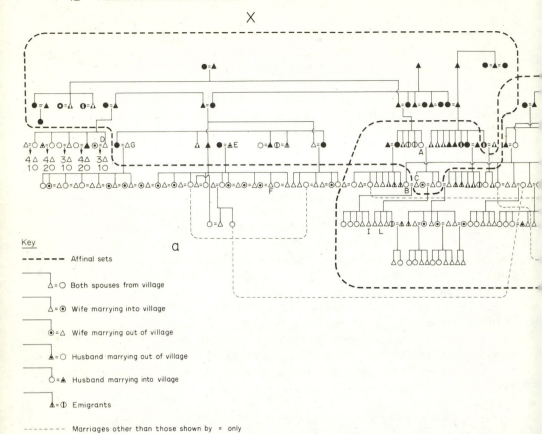

Key

- - - - - Affinal sets

△=○   Both spouses from village

△=⊙   Wife marrying into village

⊙=△   Wife marrying out of village

▲=○   Husband marrying out of village

○=▲   Husband marrying into village

▲=⦻   Emigrants

- - - - - Marriages other than those shown by = only

relatives remaining within the bounds of the configuration of which she is contemporarily a part are her sister's children and the elderly lady, her sister-in-law's daughter. There has, during the lifetime of this one person, been a dramatic change in the configuration of her recognized relatives, placing her in a larger contemporary set,[13] composed mainly of people in succeeding generations; and it is possible that she will live to see a third configuration, at least in its formative process, within the next five years. In other words, she began her post-marital life history in an affinal set anchored to relatives in the past; in her later life history, her view of her relatives first becomes increasingly contemporary, until, at a later stage it becomes projected into the future through her unmarried grandchildren and great grandchildren: a conceptual reversal in the mode of viewing a field of kindred. It is not suggested that this is an inevitable development in a recurring cyclical process. If affinal renewal in succeeding generations had taken place, as occurs in other cases, the conceptualization of her kindred would have had a past anchorage, as well as a future projection. In either event, it is significant in day-to-day behaviour that the ageing members of a kindred

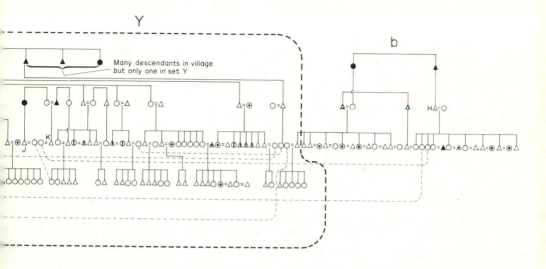

Fig. 6.

conceive of it as configured for them after their children have married,[14] and not by reference to an ancestral link person of the past – only one of the several reasons, incidentally, for the absence of any marked gap between the generations, so evident a feature of some communities.[15]

How dramatic the switch was in configurations, from X to Y, which occurred when C married B, is not brought out in Figure 6, because it would be quite impossible to include all connexions between spouses. Prior to this, A's two mother's sisters and two mother's brothers married men and women of the same patronymic group who were related, and both her maternal grandparents were of this patronymic group, the one into which A and her sister also married. On her father's side, two marriages connected her with this same patronymic group, a woman in her father's generation, and her paternal grandfather. Discounting her two sisters and brother, all of whom emigrated to the Americas, of the fifteen marriages in the two ascending generations ten were to men and women of the same patronymic group, some of them known to be related, but the relationship of others is no longer known. When B married A's son C, except for one man of the latter's patronymic group (but of no known relationship to him), there was a complete absence of any connexions between her set and his – and the marriage of A's sister's daughter to one of B's matrilateral relatives took place later, and they went to live in a nearby hamlet. For three generations, that is to say, two-thirds of the affinal potential was expended in accumulating connexions in one direction; thereafter, in the subsequent affinal set, not one of these connexions has been renewed. What had been a highly and repeatedly successful set of affinal connexions was summarily ended and has by now been discontinued. The configuration of the kindred has shifted remarkably. Why this re-configuration was brought about is a matter to be discussed presently. In the meantime, some explanation of the detachment of parts from A and B's affinal configurations is required.

A small but politically significant *jib*, of which D is the senior living male, is connected to A by double affinity in the ascending generation (D is her mother's sister's brother-in-law's son), a relationship near enough to be evoked if there were any point in doing so. D was a fairly frequent visitor to A's household during the early part of my year's field-work, and of the same political party as C, but his relationship to C, although they are both of the same age generation is too distant to be effective of itself; and their children, although most of them are contemporaries, do not claim any nearer relationship than is implied by a common patronym – perhaps related distantly somehow in the past, but no consanguinity known, as they describe the effect of a common patronym on co-residents in a small community. The children are, however, all well educated, most of them having continued with higher education. Also an age fit between a son of D and a daughter of C added to the favourable combination of factors to predispose a marriage. In these terms, I certainly thought a match was a strong likelihood, and this view was confirmed by D's son, who analytically arrayed the advantages of the match to both sides, for my edification.[16] The opportunity for this match has now passed, and D with his sons are drifting perceptibly away from C and his children. Affinity of two generations ago either had to be renewed now or the attachment would fall into abeyance.

One of A's mother's sister's daughters married a stranger (E). The latter is now C's tenant, renting from him at a highly preferential rate. A dispute blew up over the tenancy, during field-work, and although C felt constrained to concede, the concession was put in terms of *noblesse oblige* – the tenant was aged and not too well off. Kinship was never mentioned, although the tenant is the widower of A's first cousin. More surprising the tenant's son F, a prosperous businessman of some means, is a major political figure locally and of the same party as C. They were closely combined politically from 1969 into 1970, they spent much time together, and were privy to many matters of mutual concern. In all their relationships, and the gossip about them, mention was never made that they were second cousins, and it was not until I put pieces of genealogical information together that the fact of relationship became apparent. Yet the father's (E) tenancy was a privilege granted because of the closeness of consanguinity between him and the present owner's father. Between the sons, that relationship has now been 'forgotten'. Political expediency has already superseded consanguinity.

In 1970, G, like E, a husband of A's first maternal cousin, died. It is customary, during a funeral, that after interment those males who consider themselves to be closely related to the deceased form a line, in order of precedence, outside the church, to receive condolences. Apart from the deceased's sons and his sons-in-law, several affinally related men and two men of his *jib* stood in line as mourners. A's contemporary relatives were unrepresented although sufficient proximity existed between A and the deceased; A's son, drawn neither socially nor politically to the deceased and his children, was able to act as if the relationship was distant. The following generations, released from the need to recognize affinity after it has lapsed for two generations, no longer retain any pretence of relationship.

The entire section of the diagram above 'a' might well have come to be included in C's configuration had there been affinal renewal, but it has now been lopped off. This entire area could still be within C's range of reckoning were it not that the affinity within it has wholly removed its members into other affinal sets. For lapsed affinity is not merely negative: marriages continue to be made and this new affinity is positively diversionary. The marriages shown on the diagram for this section point to the emergence of close affinal links between the children of two sisters, and the other marriages (not shown, because of the diagrammatic complexities they would create) are pushing spouses and their children away from A's descendants into quite different sets.

At the other end, the configuration Y has its perimeter drawn around B's sister's husband, who is certainly included. With equal certainty his brothers and sisters, and their wives and children, are not. The impediment to the extension of the affinity through a sister's husband is not so much a matter of distance, as the fact that the affinity of these siblings has taken them out of B's set into others which are unconnected to it.

Section 'b' has in it a man, H, who, at one time was a powerful political figure in the village, if not the most powerful. Never a wealthy man, he had harvested a store of wealth in relationships by his astute use of affinity. His own marriage gave him a number of valuable affinal connexions (not shown in the diagram) and his first cross-cousin married a stranger (see diagram), an affinal link which he controlled, and they had eight surviving children; this stranger after entering the village emigrated and returned with considerable wealth. One of his (H) daughters married this man's brother's son. One of his other daughters married B's brother at a time when he and his brothers had not moved forward conspicuously in wealth but when they were showing signs of the giant strides they were to make in the future. He had in his possession a most extensive range of other connexions too numerous and too complicated to analyse as a part of this set. Ageing now, and suffering from years of ill health, his problems have multiplied because two of his three sons have married foreigners. At a time in his career when he urgently needed to devolve some of his power, and requiring the tonic of new affinal connexions, he has been denied this support; and his kinship empire is fast collapsing around him.[17]

A foreign wife is a dead-end link. Such links do not lack all utility. It sometimes serves to restrict the affinal range of connexions locally, and men for whom affinity might otherwise be diversionary are available to be caught in a sibling's set. Alternatively, a foreign wife can isolate her husband, or shift him into the social group centred on the foreign wives, of whom there are nine resident in the village. Foreign wives have to make a cultural accommodation as a first step to incorporation, and the fact that they are sufficient in numbers to form a clique among themselves – their husbands join them for recreation, and they attract a few men of clearly defined type to go along with them – gives them a separate identity as a foreign wives group. After a child has been added to the marriage, their general situation shifts significantly; with the birth of a second child, and the increased dependence this implies for a foreign wife on kith, kin, local shop-keepers, on people with whom they can spend some of their leisure time, since they are no longer free to frequent Beirut's cafés and cinemas, accelerates the process of incorporation. But when a foreign wife – or any stranger wife – enters the village, whether she becomes assimilated depends largely on her personality as an individual, and if she fails in this, she remains a terminal point in social relationships, and to this extent disrupts her husband's position as well; by comparison, marriage to a local woman, whatever her personal idiosyncracies, is always a link to other people in the village. There is an increasing possibility that foreign wives will afford international commercial connexions but that has yet to happen. What this form of affinity cannot do, however, is either to increase or diversify the assets in relationships which local connexions con-tribute: and anyone entertaining realistic ideas of acceding to power must perforce secure these, in the first instance at least.[18]

Foreign wives, as partners in an affinal link, are not unlike wives who are introduced into the village from elsewhere in the Lebanon, but with one important difference: Lebanese wives, regardless of their area of origin, are culturally familiar. This means that social assimilation is easy, so that the threat of the partnership becoming a small pool of social stand-offishness to be avoided is removed, and in a general social sense ready acceptability can place the strange wife at the heart of affairs. Like marriage to a foreign woman, marriage to a woman of another village might restrict the range of affinal connexions, and leave their husbands free to move into a sibling set. But at present, these marriages are more likely to produce meaningful affinal links than foreign wives marriages, although much depends, of course, on the proximity of the wife's natal village, her family status and so on.

A similar position obtains when a woman brings a husband from elsewhere to reside in the village. Marriages of this kind invariably indicate dominance for the wife in the partnership. The wife, in this instance, has the significant advantage of support from local relatives. Her husband's entrée into local social life is subject to the openings she provides. It is also likely that the house, or the land on which it is built, or both, is brought into the marriage by dowry, or a patrimonial settlement, or inheritance, or as a combination of any two or all of these means. During the earlier years of the marriage, at least, the power of initiative rests with the wife, and the husband perforce follows her into the social relationships of her choice, however their internal domestic relationships are arranged. Further, since men spend the day-time at work, these husbands (unless they happen to work with men of the village as partners, colleagues or mates) experience more difficulty in assimilating than wives from other villages, who, from the outset, are thrown into social relationships with other women.[19]

Wives from other villages in the Lebanon, or from other countries (mainly European), are married by men reared locally, because the size and demographic structure of the village makes it most difficult to satisfy all marital aspirations. This disability applies to both sexes. Consequently, the number of husbands and wives brought into the village from the outside is no more surprising than the high spinster and bachelor rates.[20] The total population of the village during the winter of 1969–70 was 1,077. I am aware that one has to be bold to offer a precise population figure for any Lebanese village, since it varies conspicuously seasonally – the seasonal variation in this Maronite village is low compared with many others, in particular the Shī'te village in south Lebanon – and it is always difficult to tell which of the people said to be only temporarily resident in various parts of U.S.A., Brazil, Uruguay, West Africa, Kuwait, England, to name only some of the places to which local people emigrate, or in other parts of the Lebanon, are permanent exiles, or which of them are likely to return in the immediate future, twenty years hence, or never to return again. Moreover, it does not include the small percentage of the population, residing on the western periphery of the village, which is essentially part of the metropolitan rim, even though for voting purposes it is part of the village. A discussion of village political affairs would have to take cognizance of this population, just as it would be necessary to discriminate those among the local population whose identity, as far as their passports indicate, are American nationals; but for present purposes, these complications can be safely neglected.

The figure for the total population given here is, then, subject to these qualifications but it is an accurate statement for the time of the census I took. Of this total 50.8 per cent are males and 49.2 per cent are females. Without going into the details of age structure, it is readily appreciable that, despite the near equality in the numerical distribution of the sexes, the total population is so small a universe that finding a suitable spouse is a matter of great difficulty for some at least. This difficulty is magnified when certain norms of behaviour are taken into account. Men do not marry women older than themselves. Cases exist of wives marginally older than their husbands, but the rare case where the gap is conspicuous is an oddity about which to gossip. There are cases, however, where the superior age of a woman has inhibited a younger man from marrying her. A second norm limits the availability of spouses further: first paternal parallel-cousins do not marry. This is not to say that they cannot do so in any circumstances, but there is only one extant case of it in the village. Briefly, prohibited degrees of kinship are negotiable as long as siblings, and ego's direct ascendants and descendants are not implicated. First paternal cousin marriage is possible, but troublesome. There is no civil marriage in the Lebanon. Therefore, for permission to marry within this degree of relationship, among this Maronite Christian sect, recourse to a bishop is a requirement[21] – the closer the degree of consanguinity, the more elevated the Church authority required to deal with it. Permission (akin to the banns in an English church) is necessary for any marriage, and it is given as a document known as a *tahlīl* or dispensation.[22] The *tahlīl* varies in cost from a trifling amount where there is no relationship, to a few pounds if the spouses are second maternal parallel-cousins, the first paternal parallel-cousin marriage *tahlīl* commanding the highest fee of all, fifty pounds or thereabouts. While first paternal cousin marriage is frowned upon, first maternal parallel- and cross-cousin marriages do occur (there are several on Figures 3 and 2b), and second cousin marriages of this sort are quite common. Nevertheless, the practical exclusion of first paternal cousin marriage does reduce the number of possible spouses by about 12 per cent, judging by my data from three other Arab communities and the reports of others working among Arabs.[23]

The effects of these limitations on marriage are not spread uniformly throughout the population. The higher the status of people, the fewer of them there are, and the more difficult it becomes to find a suitable partner. Unlike the Shīʿite village in the south, where marriage for the aristocrats was strictly controlled, there is an absence of rank; but there is clear status differentiation, which, however, between the extremes, is so finely graded that one status shades into another. Moreover, status differences do not inhibit the quite remarkable social ease to be found between any village inhabitants, but without a suggestion of the base familiarity they find offensive in certain western nationals. Coupled with social ease is a marked fluctuation in individual fortunes and taken together they suggest a mitigation of status as an impediment to marriage. Men of relatively humble status do make bids for women of higher status, and, high status women are, therefore, severely restricted in marriage possibilities. An initiative from a woman of high status is, however, a different matter.

The limitations suffered by daughters of high status men are so severe that they have to face the alternatives of marrying down in status, marrying outside the village, or emigrating. Of A's three sisters-in-law (Figure 6) all married below their station, two of them took up permanent residence in U.S.A., and the third went there when her silk interests collapsed. The latter, by dint of hard work, saved enough to return to the village, to restore her fortunes there, opened a small cinema locally, and bought back much of the land she had sold earlier. She lived for forty-eight years after her return, surviving sickness which would have finished off lesser mortals – she recounted with uninhibited mirth how, when in her eighties, the church bell was tolled for her, but without effect! – and lived on into her nineties. Discussing her marriage, she explained that it was an elopement (*khatfa*): 'I helped my sister to go by night. But I went in broad daylight.' I asked her whether the marriages were solemnized. Speaking incomparable, if not impeccable English, she replied: 'Of course, we went to the wishbish'; and it took some minutes of elucidation before it became clear that wishbish was intended as bishop. Her elopement some would ascribe to her being the *grande dame* she was, in every sense of the phrase; but her sister eloped also and, along with another sister, left the village for good. Moreover, her elopement was not mere irresponsibility. 'She married silk', as I was told, and it is true that the husband she chose was prospering in the silk trade at the time of her marriage. It is also true that she was the dominant partner in the marriage, and it is worth noting that she never abandoned her maiden surname. While insisting on her own freedom to choose a spouse, she attempted to arrange a marriage for her daughter, unsuccessfully at first, but after a marriage was negotiated against her will, she gave her daughter careful instruction in the most improbable subterfuge, the marriage was annulled, and she had her way. With her son's arrangements she was successful first time, although in the face of stiff 'family' opposition, and insisted on his marrying her brother's daughter, another lady cast in the *grande dame* mould of her predecessors. The latter's husband left for South America, to return after some twenty years' continuous absence. There has never been any doubt where dominance in this partnership has lain.[24] In the third successive generation a marriage of the same type has occurred and, again, it was an elopement. The wife is the dominant partner and, like her aunt and grand-aunt, she retains her maiden surname, to which her husband, who thinks his children will come to be known by his wife's surname anyway, does not object. Unable to choose a spouse of similar status, these three women chose dominance for themselves in the unions they entered.

The social maturity of women in the village is one of its many striking features, but to examine this would require separate treatment. While admitting the point, it is nevertheless significant that those high status women who have married locally and have resided there, have, in successive generations, perforce married below their station in life and have been, conspicuously, the dominant partners. Men are similarly circumscribed in their choice of spouse, but when they do marry locally the consequences are not at all the same. C married B after he had befriended her brother and engaged in commercial activities. As he was a man of high status in the village, his wife had to manage a household where the onus of entertainment alone (only one of the domestic duties which fall to the lot of a wife in a high status family) is most demanding: I was witness to an invasion of the house – and it is always an open house from the early morning until past midnight – by forty-two adult males, without any warning. A wife, whatever her pre-marital status, matures rapidly in this kind of household; B has long enjoyed a just repute for her managerial skills.

Marriages of the kind C made are not possible for all males of high status. His brother married a woman from elsewhere. Much more critical in relation to the set to which B and C belong is the fate of the children of the succeeding generation. Of the nine children of the two brothers, one of the daughters married by elopement, and eight are as yet unmarried, although six of them are of an age; they have all proceeded to the level of advanced education, and five of them (six, including the married daughter) have received or are still receiving university training either at the American University of Beirut, in England or in U.S.A., three of them proceeding beyond the stage of an initial degree. Educated thus highly, status differentiation has become intensified. They are not, however, the only young people of the village who have gone on to university. There were about a dozen of their male contemporaries receiving university education and about half that number of females. From this, it might be thought that the spread of higher education in the population is increasingly mitigating the obstructions raised by status differentiation; but this is to neglect the different types of education available, from the divers schools for the young to the many kinds and forms of higher education. As things are now, the choice of local spouses for the sons of C, short of close cousins – a practice which this small group explicitly denounces, although adopted by them in the very recent past – is very little. The alternatives are marriage elsewhere in the Lebanon, or outside the country altogether.

Precluded by status from choosing a spouse locally, C's eldest son's (I) marriage, bearing in mind that he is first heir to his father's position, is critical to his affinal set. The diagram (Figure 6) shows that it is made up of three main nuclei: C, his brother and the children of both; C's sister, her children, and their spouses and their children; certain relatives on the wife's (B) side (*jiha*). Considerable local interest is shown in C's son's possible choice of spouse, aware as people are that he is likely to bring a wife into the village from elsewhere. Neither he nor his brother are likely to contribute affinal strength to their set, and their sisters, by the same token, are likely to be affinal terminal points in this respect – although, of course, any of the children may well become lead points in other groups outside the village in future. The eldest son, (I) in short, has become the central character in a Turneresque sort of drama.[25] Bereft of the advantage of direct affinal contributions from his own future marriage, or those of his siblings, he will have to rely heavily on indirect affinal links. Several suitors have come forward for his sister, from within his set and from others outside it.[26] One of these suitors (J) is of particular interest, since, without much hope he tried, failed, and withdrew gracefully. He is now married to B's cross-cousin; but he is also related, as a first maternal parallel-cousin to K, a man of the same surname as C, but who lacks any *'aṣab* relatives in the village, and, consequently, is included with C's set. Further, K and B's brothers are paired as husbands of sisters (*'adīl*). The significance of this will be raised later, and J's wife is, also, his cross-cousin. Multiple tenuous affinal links have given J a foothold at least, in C's set. Direct affinity secures a position for a person; multiple indirect affinal links are less secure, but they contain more options.

The problem facing C's son (I) is made more intractable because he must gain affinal support and the set created in his parental generation is very successful. Unless its affinal connectedness is renewed, it will be threatened in two ways: either it will fall apart or his *jib* will be penetrated in such a way as to make a gap in the set. The latter is a possibility if affinal renewal within the set does not take place soon, for the possibility is real that his father's brother's son (L) will marry D's daughter. Now D has around him only a small nucleus, but he is a man of some substance, as are his sons, in the village. Should this marriage take place the possibility looms that L will leave the set and configure a new one with D and his nucleus. Such dire consequences are avoidable if I is able to encourage successfully a match between a son of his father's sister, and a daughter of his mother's brother.[27] In this event, renewed affinity would lend such strength to the set that, if L does marry D's daughter, her father's nucleus of people will either have to join I's set or remain diminished and relatively isolated.

It seemed to me, considering a variety of factors, that if I can secure the affinal renewal within his set, and if this set were to be connected with that shown in Figure 3 (the diagram does not represent the whole set), and one other, smaller but strong, the total set would be the longest in the village, with the capability of dominating its life in several fields of activities. My data on suitors' hopes admits that this has been a thought in the minds of others besides the anthropologist, with the rider that the conceptualization of the set would not be in their minds. As an indication of the consequences of the enlargement suggested, the men of the set would be able, without any outside assistance, to deal with the entire operations of the building industry, from quarrying for stone and breaking it up either into blocks for stone houses or into small stones for use with cement; and it would include importers of cement and plaster, masons and plasterers to face interiors, plumbers to insert the fittings, a supplier of bathroom and kitchen fittings, another man who could supply tiles (now considered essential for floors, bathroom and kitchen walls), haulage contractors, a furniture maker, a dealer in central heating, and fitters to install them, civil engineering expertise, town planning professionalism, and, finally, an abundance of capital. Impressive as this catalogue is, it does not include all the skills available in the set. It must also be added that the configuration of this set is still only in my mind, that it has not been brought into being – yet; but J's recent marriage delineates the trend and the soundings in the deep waters of marriage are intended to steer the set in this direction. There is, in other words, a discernible pattern which permits prediction of the future course of a configuration, at least within a narrow range of options. Granting this, there must, obviously be a basis to the configuration – it does not exist for its shape, the geometric relationship of its parts; and if it is to be successful as an achievement of the interests of the people in it, then these must be the means whereby members are held bound to it.

Affinity as it is used in this village is an example of sophisticated entrepreneural skill, in the best sense of the term as the action of bringing together two or more disparate skills, relationships, undertakings, and so on in a combination distinctively different and more productive then any of its parts; and not in the common and wrong sense where used perjoratively to mean disreputable dealings. Yet if this is so, then elopement is an uncontrollable, whimsical and hazardous menace, an act of intimidation on the part of a couple to damage the set or configure it according to their individual desire. Reported cases of elopement are numerous; but these numbers belie its relative innocuousness. In the first place elopements are sometimes arranged to obviate the need for dowries: an artful old dodger is reputed to have married off all his daughters by elopement, and his sons in the full pomp of formal marriage, to avoid giving, and to make sure of his sons receiving, dowries. Secondly, a richer man eloping with a poorer maiden is only giving precedence to love, and in doing so, the effect is no worse that the dead-end links referred to earlier, and in some instances, while he might forfeit a dowry, he might gain a number of affines for his set. In point of fact, this form of elopement usually follows a family discussion of the proposal which ends in stalemate, but, when the marriage comes to be accepted soon after it is a *fait accompli*, dowry is given. Thirdly, the couples elope unbeknown to the parents of either the bride or groom or both, aware that they are causing serious consternation or even distress. The three elopements mentioned earlier were of this kind. In all three, women were, in effect, asserting the right to configure their affinal contribution to the set as they wished. Parental choice might have resulted in a marriage contributing more affinal worth, but none of the three elopements damaged the set. Moreover, for all the elopements recorded there is firm evidence that if one or other of the parents publicly opposed to the match does not connive in the elopement, close kin usually work in collusion with the couple. Elopement, seemingly an aberration, is, therefore, planned with the aid of members of affinal sets, and this restricts effects to coincide with their interests. For any individual there are several possible marital choices. Elopement is the assertion by the succeeding generation to configure their affinal relationships as they see things, and not according to the views of mature adults in the ascending generation. Formal marriage is either an acceptance by the ascending generation of the views of the succeeding generation, or a coincidence of views of both generations, or compliance with the views of the ascending generation.[28] Elopement and formal marriage are two ways of making a choice within restricted limits.

After this necessary explanatory diversion, the discussion must now return to the matter of the strength there is in affinity to hold people together. To begin, the reasons for the affinal switch shown in Figure 6 will be examined.

When C (Figure 6) transformed the affinal set he had inherited by marrying B, the people his wife brought into his set had no prior connexions with it. Of the four affinal sets for which detailed data was gathered, only this set transformed the existing sets dramatically. In the others expansion and contraction has been a continuous process, but the switch to a different configuration has not been characteristic of them for the last three generations at least. Why should continuous development characterize one type of affinal set, and switch another? An examination of the circumstances in which the switch took place reveals how certain critical changes affected the sets differentially.

During the war of 1939–45, allied forces entered the Lebanon, and part of the invading and occupying armies was concentrated on the north-eastern perimeter of the village. The presence of these troops set in motion a demand for service labour, and very many of the men of the village, now middle-aged and older, provided it. The army also required supplies, like timber, of which the village had a fair amount on its wooded slopes. Before C married B, he was friendly with her eldest brother and had entered into commercial partnership with him, providing supplies for the army – one had materials and the other negotiated sales. Prior to this, the village economy was based on a rich agriculture, producing a more varied range of crops even than that given in detail for the Shī'ite south Lebanese village.[29] The range in altitude captures the ecological diversity to be expected in an area where the land rises from a coastal plain to 2,500 feet at the centre of the village, and above this on the eastern inland border. Cultivation was intense and rewarding. Rewards depended on labour supply. Those with large amounts of land had to rely on the availability of regular labour. Owners of land were not precluded by rank from contributing their own labour for productive purposes, as were the aristocrats of the southern Lebanese village, but their efforts alone were insufficient. Security of assistance with agricultural tasks was, therefore, a priority. The set to which A belonged fulfilled these needs, catching up, as it did men who had more land than they could work themselves and men whose land was insufficient to occupy them fully and who had, therefore, surplus labour to offer. Labour, during an era when cultivation and harvesting were at the hub of the economy, was an attraction for anyone thinking about the use to which affinity could be put. Connexions which, in present circumstances, defy explanation in terms of status or interest considerations, are intelligible as connexions from the past remaining active in living people who have survived from the era when cultivation was a dominant economic interest. Prior to the 1939–45 war affinal sets were configured on the basis of the interest in land. This was concerned with the creation of a secure labour force, also with a furthering of landowning interests. Men of a set, at this time, were likely to have some of their holdings, at least, lying adjacent, akin to the land-holding arrangements in the south Lebanese village where the patchwork of holdings was given a pattern of ownership by the merging and fragmentation of plots through marriage. (The similarities between the two villages with regard to the variety and kinds of crops grown, the small size of the plots, and their re-ordering with inheritance and marriage settlements on wives (*mahr*) are striking.)[30] Past arrangements within sets are still in evidence contemporarily in disputes over ownership, and in the buying and selling of plots, along affinal lines, previously close connexions, but now virtually defunct.

Since the 1939–45 war economic interests have shifted spectacularly from production to services, the latter of a sophisticated nature for many of the participants. Apart from the list of occupations of men concerned with the building industry detailed earlier, the village has in its population men who are in banking, in hospitals (male nurses and technicians), in medical profes-sionalism, working as sales representatives for international and Lebanese firms, airport workers, airline office workers, in export and import firms, in customs, in Beirut hotels, in coastal garages and tyre depots, in petrol stations, working for oil companies, in the cloth trade, in carpentry, in transport, in the 'taxi' business as independent operators, as mechanics at the airport and else-where, as cooks in various establishments, men who are restaurant owners, shop owners in towns, shop assistants in the capital, in school teaching, in government offices, in the priesthood, university academics, and, for good measure, two research anthropologists.[31] This list is very incomplete, and the occupational categories are given in their crude state – banking, for instance, includes an occupational variety from attendants, to clerks, to managers – and it does not include the women shop assistants, secretaries and so on. Despite its obvious inadequacies, the list is sufficient to demonstrate the great occupational diversity and differentiation which has appeared in the village during the past thirty years, and the overwhelming emphasis on the servicing economy which has developed.

Agricultural activity has declined during the same period. Nowadays, the attention given to the land has become almost recreational for some, and spare time work for others. Most of the households have their kitchen and flower gardens, and many people still tend their olive trees. Many of the manual tasks on the land are done by migratory seasonal Syrian labourers. Cultivation is no longer undertaken to produce surpluses for sale. Proximity to Beirut could make intensive market gardening and flower growing very profitable, but

Beirut also offers considerable occupational opportunities and the chance to make large amounts of money. The village population is educated to take advantage of these opportunities. Land has not, however, become inconsequential. Its value has changed from a productive resource to real estate property. Building land in the village itself has become scarce, with the inevitable rise in price. A substantial amount of land, in one area of what was agricultural land, was bought as a site for a government institution, and those who were heirs to this property benefited substantially from the transactions. Green-belt laws prohibit the use of village land near the coast and the capital for the development of commercial, industrial and housing estates. The existing green-belt laws might be amended in the near future. This would mean riches for many.

The switch of sets in Figure 6, assuming that affinal choices bear some consistency with people's extra-kin interests (and, in the light of the evidence presented, this is a reasonable assumption to make), is intelligible. Obviously a switch of this magnitude is not made simply to acquire more or different relations. It was a function of the slump in agricultural priority in the scale of interests, and the soaring rise in importance of commercial activities. The resultant diversification and proliferation of interests does not, however, impel all sets to switch in similar fashion. Switching, in Figure 6, concentrated in one set expertise in contracting, engineering, planning, finance, politics, administration, and by now, in several professional fields; and, to support the commercial ventures of the people in it, capital in substantial amounts could be made available for the common good by many of its individuals. The affinal set of the agricultural era was in no position to seize the new opportunities that were appearing. It became dismembered and the several parts became incorporated in other sets or formed parts of new ones. Other sets have retained their configuration, renewed affinally since the new economic conditions have come about. The set, part of which is shown in Figure 3 on p. 38 is a case in point. Prosperous nowadays, and likely to prosper more if the government removes the restrictions on village land for development purposes, this set was essentially anchored to agriculture and most of the men were cultivators, working their own land or hiring labour. Lacking any tradition of skills or higher education, they met the changed circumstances by putting their labour into unskilled or semi-skilled work, setting up relatively small-scale enterprises in the building industry, and employing this labour locally and in other countries, Kuwait and Saudi Arabia in particular. The economic changes have not necessitated a change in the composition of this set; affinal renewal has reinforced their mutual interest. People of this group, in the succeeding generation are diversifying their skills, and, in some cases, pushing on to professionalism. Diversification within the set need not make it obsolete. Its effect is not to create unpatterned use of affinity; on the contrary diversity generates more choice, and this, in turn, increases the number of possible permutations in affinal relationships, so that diversity, seemingly destructive of sets, is an agent for cementing their parts firmly together in some cases. Obsolescence caused the switch in the sets shown in Figure 6, but this happened when the specialization of an earlier period so ossified the configuration that it had to be dismantled when faced with profound alterations in the economy after the war. These circumstances are unlikely to be repeated in the near future.

Affinity varies in significance, not only in relation to the types already discussed but, to make explicit what has been shown in the data already, it varies for the individuals in a set over a period of time.[32] At its inception a father-in-law might be the dominant partner in the relationship. Later the reverse might be true. The son-in-law might strike good fortune, and the fortunes of the father-in-law might decline, for a number of contingent reasons. Or the fortunes of both might rise or they might decline. For while the Lebanese economy is a highly diversified service one, its fluctuations can have serious consequences for individuals in the village.[33] The position of an individual in a set during a life history alters several times in many cases, and once or twice in all cases. Hence, the numerically stronger sets are better able to stand economic vicissitudes than the smaller ones. Decline in the financial state of one person is not devastating for the large set. After a few years of marriage, the anticipated benefits of affinity may not be realized. Equally it could, a few years later, yield benefits beyond the initial expectations. So that at any particular time a member of a set might be drawing on its credit and contributing nothing – save that at election time everybody's vote counts. What is most unlikely is that all members of the set suffer decline simultaneously. Rises and declines of individual fortunes do not engender instability unless the set is over specialized in one sector of the economy; then it is likely to collapse and its members disperse. The economic diversity now available adds choice and enables individuals to shift their locus of interests; economic diversity provides a new vigour to affinal sets.

Since there is a plurality of types of affinity, and any affinal link is liable to change both in the sense that the general social standing of any of the people conjoined in a particular link alters, and that the significance of a link in relation to others does not remain constant throughout the life of set, it would appear that affinity, and hence the multiple relationships generated directly through the two spouses and projected indirectly through their children, is in a permanent state of bewildering flux, the only enduring feature being its geometric configuration, which is a design drawn by the anthropologist. Stability in affinity is sustained partly by the patterned relationships to which it gives rise, and it is held fast in a matrix which coagulates around both spouses, together with the couple of dozen categories of people towards whom the spouses, severally, adopt kinship terms or mutate existing ones. Brief reference to these relationships, first as they occur in behaviour, and then as they are represented in kinship terms, is necessary here.

Post-marital residence is overwhelmingly virilocal. Only two pairs of spouses approximate to uxorilocality. These are approximations because one pair lived part of the time uxorilocally and at other times in a dwelling bought by the husband. The other pair began virilocally and remained in this residence for nearly three decades, until, during field-work, and after the husband had returned from a long absence abroad, they lived in a house bought by the wife and built on land that was hers. Some couples at the outset of their married life rent part of a house or a flat, but this is usually a convenience until a new house is built for the husband. The husband is the tenant.[34]

For the vast majority, therefore, marriage sees the departure of a daughter from her natal home to her husband's home, where she might well become not only a wife to one man, but the manageress of a domestic unit which includes her husband's parents and his brothers and, less likely, a spinster sister. Clearly this does not happen to all wives when they marry. If the parents are still enjoying a virile middle age, the young couple might reside in a dwelling alongside the husband's parental home, or in a storey built on to it, or in a lower storey excavated from beneath it. Whatever the detailed composition of the domestic unit happens to be, its managerial authority is the wife, not the husband's mother, or spinster sister. It is the wife who controls the feeding of the family, who deals with the shopkeepers, who is responsible for entertainment, the care of the sick, rearing the children, and keeping the house in good order. Her husband has other forms of authority which do not amount, however, to that of a proprietor. From the moment of marriage both have inalienable rights, as part heirs with the husband's siblings, to the house, details of arrangements made between heirs, for convenience, notwithstanding. Landed property does not differentiate spouses either, for both of them may possess it and both are heirs to each other's property. It is true, since a male inherits double a female's share, that men tend to have more landed property than women, but the unequal distribution of the sexes among heirs prevents the concentration in the hands of males suggested by the plain statement of the law. Also, either sex can make a chance fortune out of land if it is required for building purposes. If both parents are part of the domestic unit, the young wife assumes the role previously held by her mother-in-law, and the husband his father's. With or without parents the control of the domestic unit is essentially a partnership between the spouses, the husband appearing as arbitrator of relationships, publicly if not privately.

The partnership between spouses is more than a domestic-cum-economic arrangement. Marriage is a sacramental union, and since the Maronite Church is under the authority of the Pope, divorce is prohibited. This single fact distinguishes marriage from that practised in the Shīʿite village in south Lebanon, where divorce is permitted, along with plural marriage. In practice, the number of couples (in the three Muslim communities where I have worked) who engage in divorce is low, and the number of men practising polygamy is statistically, if not sociologically, inconsequential. But conceptually marriage is not the same for Maronite Christians and Muslims. Among Muslims marriage is a contract, a witnessed[35] statement of consent by the couple and a declaration of the amount of bride-wealth or marriage settlement, as the case may be. That spouses are not related until they have had children has become an adage in social anthropology. There is a measure of truth in it for Muslims. Among Maronite Christians a man must 'cleave to his wife; and the twain shall become one flesh: so that they are no more twain, but one flesh'.[36] Affinity for them is a kinship relationship in all but the strict consanguineous sense.[37] Whether they like it or not they are joined forever, even beyond the death of one of them in the great majority of cases. Consistent with this view of marriage the spouses speak about each other by terms from the vocabulary of kinship: *bint'amm* for the wife, and *ibn'amm* for the husband. Around the house they address each other by name. Both in the use of kinship terms and in the use of personal names, these Maronite Christians differ noticeably from the southern Shī'ites. Among the latter men and women are referred to as father or mother of so-and-so (their eldest son) in public and in private, unless a man carries the title of *Shaikh*, *Sayyid* or *Ḥājj*,[38] titles which are used publicly but dropped in the privacy of the home. This small difference between the two villages reveals much about the marriage bond. An individual's identity among the Shī'ites is in his son, and his relation to his wife is expressed as a common identity they have in him. An individual, among the Maronites, although he is called father of his eldest son in and about the village, is his wife's kinsman in the home, a notion expressed in a kinship idiom or by the intimate familiarity of a personal name: the primary identification is of spouse to spouse, without the separateness implied in the reference to the son.

Closeness of relationship between the spouses is manifest in the separate forms of behaviour they severally adopt to their spouse's affines. A wife is required to spend much of her time in her sister-in-law's company. It would be difficult for her to avoid doing so in the majority of cases, since they are usually close neighbours or occupants of adjacent storeys in the same house. The term for husband's sister-in-law is *silfa* (from the root *salafa*, to give help by way of a loan). Two women married to two brothers are paired by the use of the term *aslāf*. They move in and out of each other's homes without ceremony, they are to be seen visiting other people together in the afternoon, they sit and gossip together and they freely lend and borrow in a domestic context. Their relationship is so intimate that I first mistook it for one between sisters. They see less of their own brothers and sisters, with whom their relationship is of a more formal visiting pattern, visits usually confined to the late evening, after the day's work is done.

Men married to sisters are paired as *'adā'il* (sing. *'adīl*). The root meaning of the word is equal or corresponding. Explaining its meaning, the relationship was likened, by a man of the village, to panniers on either side of a donkey: the load on one side is counter-balanced by the weight on the other, achieving a nice balance between the two. Sentiments are rarely reproduced exactly in behaviour, and balanced equivalence is little more than a fiction as far as any two men thus paired are concerned. What is true. however, is that a man has the right to interfere in certain of his *'adīl's* affairs. Typically, if the conjugal relationships of a pair of spouses deteriorate, particularly if they reach the impasse of a publicly known crisis, the *'adīl* of the husband intervenes, and does so in favour of the wife: it is wives who pull men into this relationship. Just how an *'adīl* relationship works in practice depends on a number of factors, not least of which is the number of men implicated in it. One man may have five *'adā'il*, his wife being one of six sisters. His relationships are unlikely to be the same with all five, or the same as those of a man with one *'adīl*. Regardless of the peculiarities, whenever there is more than one married sister men will be paired in a relationship which is given a verbal designation, and which carries specific rights and obligations.

Wives married to brothers, and husbands married to sisters, are conjoined in an intimacy of relationships much more profound than a superficial view derived from domestic activities and patterned visiting would suggest. Women and men severally paired in the manner described have a common interest in property because both sexes are heirs, and none of them can be legally disinherited. Consequently, two men married to two sisters are vitally interested in the disposal of their wives' parental wealth, and it often happens that it is these two men who publicly expose the discords among their wives and their siblings. The same remarks apply equally to two women married to two brothers. It follows from this that whenever the relationships of *aslāf* and *'adā'il* appear in families, a minimum of four people have a direct interest in each other's property, two of whom will be heirs and the other two affinally paired spouses of heirs. Save in the rare cases of an only child, a minimum of four interested parties is the simplest reduction of the complexities. The affinally-paired spouses of heirs are themselves heirs to their own parental wealth, and their status as heirs in their natal families adds another dimension to the complexities. Then again, the heirs might number, not two, but five, eight, ten, or more, and the enlargement of the area of involvement widens in relation to the exact number. Many heirs may remain after marriage in the parental set. Whether they remain or leave after the division of inheritance is largely a reflexion of the resolution of the difficulties which arise from it. Pairing of spouses as *aslāf* or *'adā'il* provides the guide to following the pattern of subsequent relationships, especially in relation to participation in affinal sets.

Of the forms of affinity briefly discussed thus far, all of them, except that of the *'adīl* relationship, stem from notions contained in propinquity, actual or assumed. They all presume the departure of a woman from her natal home to establish a new one with her husband, usually in or very near his parental home. This does not mean that there is a complete severance from the wife's parental home or her parents. On the contrary, frequent visiting takes place between a husband and his wife's parents, the husband dropping in on them casually during the day, lunching or taking coffee with them – it would be considered inappropriately dependent, and suggestive of discord in the marriage, if a wife did this – and the wife's parents, particularly her father, drop in equally casually on their son-in-law. Visiting of this kind and visits to a wife's sister's home, or visits by parents and their daughter and her husband to the home of another married daughter, are frequent. They appear conspicuous because such visits entail a switch in habits after marriage, which is immediate and a complete break with the visiting pattern of only a few weeks ago. Much is made in the literature of the mother-in-law relationship. In this village, while it is in evidence of course, the relationship between a man and his father-in-law also presents interesting problems, both of behaviour and of kinship usages.

The most immediate aspect of the relationship between a man and his father-in-law is that suggested by the sentiment that a father gives away his daughter, and the husband, as the receiver, is thereby beholden to him. Stress is placed on this by some fathers-in-law, and evidence of it is to be seen in the demands a father-in-law makes on his son-in-law's hospitality, appearing in the latter's home without warning and expecting to be fed. While purchasing groceries in a local store with his son-in-law, a father-in-law urged me to observe their relationship, how one would insist that he paid, and how the other would protest and insist on paying himself. That, he explained, was their relationship, one of vying against each other to do the most good for the other. The son-in-law whispered to me to watch carefully and I would see how the son-in-law always won the argument!

Some fathers-in-law insist that their sons-in-law are beholden to them, but it is not a norm generally accepted by the people of the village which can be used to bring a recalcitrant son-in-law to heel, much less to quell him. There is no single norm for the relationship, because the prolixity of relationships between them defies standardization. Sometimes they are equal partners, sometimes the father-in-law is pleased and proud that his daughter has done so well in marriage, sometimes the son-in-law's position is so secure that he is not susceptible to threats from his father-in-law, and so on. An instance has been given of a father-in-law cajoling his son-in-law to respond generously to his demands. Other instances could be adduced to show that a son-in-law can do the same; for example, in a political situation a man threatened to send his wife back to her brother, an act of public disgrace, unless the latter complied with his wishes. Other instances could be cited to illustrate many other different elements in the behaviour of this kind of affines, but, whatever the peculiarities of the specific cases and the alterations in them from one situation to another, the fact that marriage is monogamous and permanent is never to be neglected, for it sets the relationship in a mould that gives it a durability lacking where divorce is possible. Today's troubles cannot turn into divorce tomorrow. A single moral norm, unless stated in such vague language that the words mean anything anyone wants them to mean, could not contain the variation in the relationships between father-in-law and son-in-law, their situational shifts, their developmental transformations, nor the relative positional alterations of either or both.

Any attempt, therefore, to reduce this particular affinal relationship – or any other kinship relationship among people of the village – to a single stranded bond, or a skein of easily separable strands is futile. Starting with a term, there are authors who apply this reductionism by relating it to others and ascribing the behaviour between people to the derived meaning they give to it. This is characteristic of writings on the term for father-in-law used in the Lebanon.[39] The term in use in this Maronite village is *'amm*. It is also the word used for father's brother. Among all Muslim Arabs, first paternal parallel-cousin marriage is permitted, among some it is a preferred form (as far as expressed sentiments go, at least), and in a few communities, exceptionally so I am sure, a man has a right to his father's brother's daughter. The relationship, therefore, is an extension of the behaviour of a man to his father's brother.

The fallacy of this view is not difficult to expose. Rates for first paternal cousin marriage do not exceed about 12 per cent of the total marriages in a statistically viable universe. Why, then, should a term and its accompanying behavioural pattern be given to fathers-in-law when only a small minority of marriages are to the first paternal parallel-cousin is left unexplained – the argument for its specific use in the event of first paternal parallel-cousin marriage renders its general use inappropriate anyway. Sometimes the argument is watered down and applied to any patrilineal parallel-cousins as if they are first paternal parallel-cousins. Such confusion is a serious enough error in itself, but numerically the facts do not fit the argument since, save for explicable exceptions,[40] the total for all patrilineal parallel-cousin marriage, in a statistically viable universe, is under half the marriages. Many of these parallel-cousin marriages are also cousin marriages of other sorts; indeed most of them must be, because the parallel form of cousin marriage has persisted for several generations, and this necessarily relates people in a plurality of kinship forms. While the use of *'amm* for father-in-law is present in parts of the Lebanon, it is not common to all Arab communities: among the Cyrenaican bedouin, and throughout Libya, I believe, the term used is *nasīb* whether the father-in-law is otherwise unrelated or a father's brother as well. Collapse of the argument is complete in the face of evidence from this Maronite village: first paternal parallel-cousin marriage is absent, except for one extant case, and there is no genealogical evidence of its occurrence in the ascending generation, but abundant evidence of first and second maternal parallel-cousin marriage, paternal and maternal cross-cousin marriage of the first or second degree, and of other more distant kin marriages.

One author[41] accepts the use of the term *'amm* as father-in-law as incontrovertible evidence of paternal parallel-cousin marriage; and if this form of marriage does not appear in an Arab population – like Maronite Christians – then it must have been practised among them at some remote unspecified date in the past! Another author, opining that the use of *'amm* connecting a father-in-law with paternal parallel-cousin marriage 'seems clearly to be correct', does, however, have the honesty to admit that the usage confounds him.[42] But witless honesty is not the quality required in a guide to lead one through the maze of Arab kinship. A third author,[43] in an article on parallel-cousin marriage (a veritable thesaurus of errors) pursues the argument *reductio ad absurdum.* Father's brother's daughter marriage does not, according to him, 'create affinal but tense relationships associated without marriage', and 'the roles of the consanguine group coincide or take precedence over the roles of in-laws created by marriage. More specifically, the role of the paternal uncle (*'amm*) before marriage coincides with the role of the father-in-law (also called *'amm*) after marriage.' The term *'amm* is in general use for father-in-law, but first paternal parallel-cousin marriage 'constitutes 11 per cent of the marriages contracted between Muslims, and 3 per cent of the marriages between Christians'.[44] Therefore he is wrong on one count in his argument, unless he can explain the affinal use of *'amm* for 89 per cent of the Muslim and 97 per cent of Christian spouses. The argument, without evidence, concerning the coincidence of the roles of father's brother and father-in-law because father's brother's daughter marriage does not create affinity, is based on the view, unrelated to the lives of people, that relationships between closely-related paternal kin (not maternal kin, it must be remarked, however closely related) are harmonious. Marriage within this little charmed circle, therefore, 'contributes to harmonious family relationships'. What it does to disharmonious family relationships is left unsaid. Demolition, brick by brick, of the entire argument would be out of place here; it can wait for another article. In the meantime some of the details relevant to the use of *'amm* in this Maronite Christian village will now be given.

The following are some of the ways in which the term *'amm* is used:
1. It is always used to refer to the father's brother, and as a mode of address.
2. It is always used to refer to the father-in-law and to address him, completely without regard to any consanguineous relationship or lack of it.
3. It is also used to refer to, and to address, the father-in-law's brother.
4. It is similarly used for the mother's brother-in-law.
5. The father's brother uses it to address his brother's son, a reversal of generations in kinship usage common in the Lebanon, and not confined to this relationship only.

6. Selected seniors of the same patronymic group, with whom there is no known consanguinity, but with whom social relationships are intense, are addressed as *'amm*. Such seniors are usually men with few or no actual patrilineal relatives. In one case the only definable relationship was through a mother, and I suspect it was this proximity which was responsible for the selection of one man from very many of the same patronym.

7. It is used to refer to, and to address, a mother's father's brother's son, 'because he is too distant to be called *khāl'* (mother's brother).

In all these instances kinship exists or is presumed to have existed sometime in the past. The term has other uses, some of which are listed below.

8. An unrelated older person is called *'amm*, much as 'sir' was used in this country. A young boy uses the term to a man of proximate generation, but abandons its uses as he reaches manhood; a female retains the use of the term from infancy to womanhood.

9. It is used in banter by young men when one of them wishes to imply that the other is childish, and he himself superior. This is effected by reference to the practice of the father's brother's reversal of the generations when addressing his brother's son as *'amm* (see 5 above).

10. It is also used between peers to suggest that the person singled out ought to know better.

11. It is used to press a point, as when discussing business or in an argument. Here familiarity, real or feigned, is emphasized.

12. It is used to stress a difference in age for pejorative effect.

13. A young woman uses the term to a man if she wishes to quash any ideas he might have of marrying her. This can be insulting, as, for example, when a young girl, after addressing a bachelor about twenty years her senior as *'amm* for many years, entered her twenties and continued using the term: he told her; 'If you call me *'amm*, I will call you *sitt'* (mature lady in this context). To be addressed as *'amm* by marriageable women is, for an unmarried man, condemnation to bachelorhood.

14. When the term *'amm* implies too wide a generation difference or might be thought to be unkind, the diminutive *'ammhu*, literally his *'amm* and sounding like *'ammo*, is substituted. Thus, a nubile girl would address a man of forty, say, in this way, making it clear that girls of her age were not for him, but that there was still hope for him with older women. But it is also used towards a senior, when the term *'amm* would be more appropriate, but would presume a familiarity which the user wished to deny emphatically.

15. As a final example, the statement of a young lady must be included: 'I would not call a man *'amm* if I did not like him.' And that shows the elasticity in the term, as well as choice in its use.

No pretence is made that this is a complete list of all the uses to which *'amm* is put. Nor does it purport to cover its use anywhere other than in this Maronite village, although I am aware that it is used differently in the three other Arab communities with which I am familiar. The question usually raised is: what is the meaning in the word *'amm* common to its various uses? It might be more pertinent to ask whether it possesses any single meaning.

'Amm is put to such situationally disparate uses that there seems slight point in the pursuit of an elusive common meaning, a lowest common denominator to solve all its uses. The common meaning trundled out by anthropologists, and, indeed, by some Middle Eastern peoples themselves, is that it is a term of respect. There is an element of respect, it is true, in behaviour towards some of the persons addressed as *'amm*, like the father's brother, father-in-law, and elders, for example. A man can and does give his father-in-law short shrift, however, when need be; and he can also show disrespect for his father's brother publicly if he considers their relationship warrants it. Respect is also given to persons to whom the word is not implied, like the mother's brother, a learned man, a fair-minded person, and so on. Unqualified, the notion of respect, in discussions of kinship behaviour, is obfuscating.

Seniority is thought by some to be the thread that runs through all its uses. Again, it is admitted that seniority is present in a number of its uses. But seniority and difference of generation are both in the meaning of the term for mother's brother, *khāl*. Why not use this term to do the same work as *'amm*? It would have much to commend it, and for many of the uses to which *'amm* is put it might be more suitable. Yet people of the village would be non-plussed by the suggestion. For although the term *'amm* is malleable, a quality allowing it to take on one shape in this situation and a different one in that, the term *khāl* is not similarly endowed.[45] If the term *'amm*, that is to say, is to be given the prime meaning of father's brother and all this signifies, then its other uses are wrong. The presumption that a common term refers to likeness is quite unfounded. A father's brother and a father-in-law, in relation to ego, are unlike as benefactors, in the respect accorded to them, in the permitted latitude of behaviour towards them, in their residential relationships with him, in their exchange of visits with him, in current financial matters, in the material help he can expect from them or they from him, and so on. In reference to a father-in-law, when a man (or woman) says: 'He is my *'amm*,' what he means is that he is my father-in-law, and not he is like my father's brother. The very suggestion in the latter interpretation would strike people as absurd. A single kinship term has a multiplicity of discrete meanings.

Put in a wider context of kinship terms, the use of *'amm* makes more sense. On marriage, the husband not only addresses his father-in-law as *'amm*, but his mother-in-law, who might have been his actual mother's sister's daughter or some other close relative, ceases to be designated by the consanguineous term, and is called *mar'at 'amm* (father-in-law's wife). Consanguinity yields to affinity.[46] More than this, the children of the father-in-law are called *ibn 'amm* (son of *'amm* and *bint 'amm* (daughter of *'amm*). In other communities where the term *'amm* is applied to the father-in-law, his wife is not called *mar'at 'amm*, nor are the children called son and daughter of the *'amm*, but by a different term (*nasīb*) which, in this village carries no specific kinship designation. Elsewhere the term *'amm* is applied to the father-in-law after marriage, only if he was a father's brother previously, otherwise he is called *ham*; affinity exists, of course, in both cases, but where there is consanguinity it is given precedence by the retention of the term.

Instead of dwelling only on the modes of address used by the spouses to their newly acquired affines, the way the latter address their affines is of equal import. A father-in-law addresses his son-in-law and daughter-in-law as son and daughter respectively. Parents of spouses address each other as brother and sister. To complete this summary of kinship usages, one further fact must be added. The rest of the terms in the vocabulary of kinship which one of the spouses uses, are used reciprocally by the others. The only terms which are not adopted by a son-in-law or daughter-in-law are those for mother and father.[47]

Seen in the light of the whole kinship context, the problem is not one of the use of the same term *'amm* for father's brother, and, after marriage, for a previously unrelated or differently related person, the father-in-law; any more than it is a problem of why the father's brother should be called by the same term as father-in-law. The root meanings of *'amm* refer to what is general, universal, common, prevalent, comprehensive and diffused. Nebulous in its meanings, the term can be applied widely to comprehend disparate categories of people, with a specificity of meaning in one context, a discrete specificity in another, little specificity in a third, and so on. The conjunction of the meanings with which it is endowed is not a likeness in behaviour, rights, duties, obligations and expectations towards all the categories of people to which the term is applied, but the comprehensively diffused common meaning in its root. When used it instantly evokes an image, but so blurred that it cannot be fastened on to any precisely defined behaviour, except contextually.

With the word *'amm* available for the spouses to deal with the intimacies of the elementary families joined by their marriage, the remainder of the kinship problems are resolved by the one spouse adopting the other's kinship usages. The parental use of terms differs in the cognizance taken of the generation disparity. The product of any marriage between two people of the village is to unite the multiple categories of people recognized as relatives by both spouses into a single field of kinship. This is not to say that marriage is a licence to import the entire kinsmen of this field into a particular affinal set. But it does mean that the benefit, bestowed by a marriage on the affinal set the spouses enter, is to create a wide domain in the population to which people of the set have preferential access. Which set the spouses enter depends on the drawing power of the respective affines. Where there is strength of drawing power, one man might capture the immediate affines of all his children. Impressive as the spread of this is in exceptional cases, to be able to draw people in large numbers requires a large number of married children. Not everyone has this numerical advantage. Costs entailed in rearing many children might bite deeply into a person's wealth, and then some or all of the children might withdraw from their parental sets and latch on to those of their spouses. For these and other reasons affinal sets do not inflate rapidly in numbers. Some are no more than small nuclei of people. Given the limited size to which sets can expand, access to the field of kindred which each marriage creates is critically important. This is to be seen spectacularly during the high drama of an election, but it is also in evidence in less stirring times, in small commercial dealings, in property sales, in finding jobs, in funeral arrangements, in staging the high jinks of various village celebrations, and many more informal, voluntary and temporary groupings of people.

People in the village are very aware of what affinity does to relationships and how it can be deployed. An unmarried man arrayed his marriage possibilities for me to see, and gave a sophisticated analysis of each. A married man surveyed his political field and argued cogently for the supreme importance of affinity in building a following. Men make quite explicit the effects of marriage on status. Match-making is talked about frequently and these conversations are sharply analytic. Yet the affinal set is unnamed and unidentified by an exclusive term. It is spoken about as 'our people', 'us', but these idioms are used for other purposes and are relative anyway. The sets unquestionably exist and are clearly drawn in the minds of people. Lacking a name and known only when its composition is known, undefined jurally and not based on a primacy of interest, the affinal set has been shown to possess the authentic characteristics summarized now as follows:

1. It represents, first, a series of negotiated choices by individuals.
2. These choices are arranged to constitute a discernible group of people.
3. The significance of people at the points in this arrangement waxes and wanes situationally, since the asset of a man in, say, a political situation might be crucial, yet inconsequential in a commercial context.
4. The part an individual occupies in the galaxy of points in a set, alters temporally, as individual fortunes rise and decline.
5. The configuration of a set changes with the addition of new affinity and the demise of individuals.
6. Since it is not based on a primacy of interest, the set is differentiated in relation to wealth, occupation, and status.
7. It affords a latitude of choice to the individuals comprising it.
8. Choice is not unrestrained, but available only within the bounds of its morality.

9. Throughout its span, clusters of individuals are subject to legal controls by Church and state: marriage, the first step to affinity, comes under the jurisdiction of the Church, and it has to be registered in an office of the state bureaucracy; inheritance is according to law, ownership of property is registered and holdings cadastrally surveyed. Jural relationships do not, however, wrap people together and bundle them into the same set; they divide as surely as they unite; the wrangling, and sometimes litigation, among heirs is often the reason for this man entering one set and his first cousin entering another.

10. Switching the direction of affinity from one section of the community kills a set and begets a new one.

11. With the power of destruction goes the power of perpetuation, since a switch of affinity is one choice, and affinal renewal the exercise of the choice to retain the set intact into the next generation.

12. Durability, listed last, is not the least of its characteristics. The Church sees to it that the marriage bond is not broken. The affinal knots in the sets remain secure at least until the succeeding generation matures to marriageable age.

An affinal set is not a political group, not a complete power structure, but it makes an admirable starting point for anyone wishing to succeed politically. It is not an occupational group, but divers occupations interlock within it, and it also provides occupational opportunities. It is not a ritual group, not simply because the majority of people attend one of the village's churches,[48] but because the committees which conduct church affairs are not based on it. It is not based on land ownership. It is not a jurally defined group, with exclusive control of specific relationships. But it is to be seen in sharp outline in marriages, funerals and partings, at municipal and national election times, in commercial activities and in the pattern of landholdings. It permeates the fabric of social life. It does not have a single aim, but aims at everything. As a general purpose group, it is elegantly constituted to meet a miscellany of needs.

It is tempting to use the word network to designate this kind of affinal set. A serious objection to the use of network is contained in the statement: 'I define a network as egocentric.'[49] Egocentric patterns end, ultimately, in description. In the affinal set, there is no ego to which others are linked by a single strand or strands. No one in it dominates it at all times, for all purposes, and the strands that connect people are not configured to an ego's connexions with others. All are in it, so to speak, and the patterning of relationships between people is not a function of the configuration but of a particular situation. Conceptually, egocentricity is anathema, as far as the affinal set is concerned, for to alight on an ego – the idiom is deliberate to convey the sense of whimsy in picking on any ego – is to confer a quite unmerited priority. It is like saying that if, in the field, one gets 'the impression of a society inchoate and incoherent, where the haphazard is more conspicuous than the regular, and all is in a state of flux',[50] then grab an ego, chase his links and hope that something will come of it.

A more serious objection to the employment of the term network is that many who favour it regard it as replacing an outmoded functionalism. Boissevain for example, asserts: 'It has become clear to me, as it has to others, that the static, structural-functional model of society does not work at the level at which real people interact'[51] – and do not the Tallensi interact in Fortes's *The Web of Kinship*, or the Nuer in Evans-Pritchard's *Kinship and Marriage*, or the Ndembu in Turner's *Schism and Continuity?* where their behaviour is brilliantly documented? The issue for Boissevain is not a mere matter of anthropological theory, but, first and foremost, a political issue. Structural-functionalism rose simultaneously with the rise of fascism, and, like it, its practitioners 'venerate and thus protect the old order against changes which threaten it' – claptrap, in the exact meaning of the word; anyone in doubt would do well to read Evans-Pritchard's writings on colonialism, as a beginning.[53] Indigent[54] social anthropological-structural-functionalist, colonial-fascist-lackeys-of imperial-governments could hardly have 'bitten the hand that fed them'.[55] It is worth taking a look at his introduction to see who Boissevain thanks.[56]

But leaving Boissevain aside, other scholars in the subject, made aware that structural-functional analyses fail to comprehend adequately all problems, have jumped to the extreme of abandoning this mode of analysis. Mitchell, for example, writes of 'a growing dissatisfaction with structural-functional analyses and the search, consequently, for alternative ways of interpreting social action'.[57] The extent of this 'growing dissatisfaction', is a matter of opinion, just as the growing dissatisfaction with network theory, so-called, may not be as widespread as some of us think; although one of its early converts, and an able practitioner, neatly cuts it down to size in the statement: 'Much anthropological literature has tended to see network analysis as some kind of theoretical breakthrough and not simply for what it is, a technique of data collection and analysis.'[58] Preoccupation with the obliteration of structural analysis appears to have led to a desire to expunge useful concepts employed in such analysis from our vocabulary. Mitchell, quoting Nadel on networks with approval, explains that Nadel says that what happens between one pair of what he calls 'knots' in a network must affect what happens between other adjacent ones, and then comments: 'I personally would modify the "must" to "may" in his statement to avoid the implication of necessary functional integration.'[59] Removal of the imperative drains Nadel's statement of its meaning, as he makes explicit in a comment on Barnes's view of network: 'I visualize a situation in which this interlocking also bears on "what happens" in the relationships, and hence on their effective interdependence. For Barnes, the important thing is the dispersal of the relationships, and the open-ended character of the network; for me, its coherence and closure, that is, its equivalence with a "system".'[60] Lest there should be any doubt about the meaning Nadel attaches to 'interlocking', his brief definition of network will suffice to make his view abundantly clear that he has a functional relationship in mind: 'By "network", on the other hand, I mean the interlocking of relationships whereby the interactions implicit in one determine those occurring in others.'[61] Without this 'implication of inter-dependence', a network of relationships has little in it of interest for him. Rightly, Nadel realizes that once he begins thinking of interdependencies he must, too, think in terms of a structure of some sort.

Opposing structural and network analyses, institutional and interactional, is little more than posturing about positions. Nadel does not deny the validity of network analysis because he employs structural analysis: it is not an either/or choice for him. Why think of interactional behaviour as somehow opposed to institutional behaviour, as if the two are not indissoluably wedded? Why this masochistic desire to amputate that which is serviceable! The desire to do so, in some writers, must surely mean that its origin lies in other than intellectual roots. From the characteristics of affinal sets, listed earlier, the term network as now used is manifestly inappropriate: although as used by Nadel it would have provided a tolerable fit. Set is substituted because the plurality of meanings to the word covers the range of characteristics.

Those who oppose structural-functional analyses have worked, by and large, in industrialized societies, or in countries where modernization, as it is often euphemistically called, is in full swing. At the core of these structural-functional analyses there is always a bundle of jural relationships, the rights people have to this and that, the impelling obligations they have to each other, the claims to which they are entitled. Breach of these jural relationships, if discovered, is punishable. Now in conditions where there is an absence of codified law and officers of the law, the control of jural relationships is literally visible in the camps, hamlets and villages. Where a state bureaucracy exists, the law and its operations is not immediately seen, the nearest police station miles away, and the nearest court even further away. This is not to say, however, that jural relationships do not exist or that they are irrelevant. Jural relationships are in the keeping of different kinds of people in the two instances. In the Lebanese Maronite village, the law is the law of the land not of the village, of the courts not of the moots. In saying this, it is not intended to exclude manipulation, but it is the rules that are manipulated. Manipulation without rules is better described by other words – cheating, threat, deception and a host of other malpractices for which there is a richness of words in our vocabulary. In the affinal sets of this village, durability is given to the relationships they contain largely by the jural nature of the bonds between the people composing them, but this does not mean that choice is eliminated, or that one set of jural relationships determines set membership, or that the jural relationship between two persons coerces both to enter the same set, or that no other kind of relationship exists between people of the same set. Expectancies determine entry into a set, for entry is an act of choice. People are aware that on opting to join a set they are evaluating a number of alternatives in relationships, as became clear in an exchange of views between two brothers. One stated that he was much closer to his set mates than to his father's brother's son. The other told him not to be a fool, that although they both loved their set mates very much, their first cousin was closer 'because we have property together'. The first replied that this was precisely the reason why he always spent his time with his set mates and never wished to see his cousin, to which the second replied that he did not wish to see the cousin either, but that until he got his share of the common property he would not let him out of his sight. Both men were right in the stances they adopted. They were at odds because they were evaluating discrete relationships differently. They both viewed the relationship with their cousin as tiresomely irksome, but the law trapped them in it, and they knew that no amount of manipulation would extract them from it without serious loss. What was not as intelligible to them was that an earlier solution to the property problem between them and their cousin might have put them asunder and into different affinal sets.

Inherited property fetters small numbers of people, no more than the siblings or first cousins of spouses. It never constitutes the base on which large and enduring groups are built. At the beginning of this article the differences between the kinship comprehension of peoples in three Arabic-speaking communities was raised as an issue. Reference was then made to the property relations in these three communities. If heritable landed property is available in all, but the mode of transmitting it is so different that the reckoning of kinship is not merely a matter of degrees of difference but of fundamental disparity, it would appear that the nature of property is different in the three instances.

Property vested in the bedouin corporations in Cyrenaica consists of land and water. Land is abundant measured in acres, but cultivable land in the domain of a particular corporation is always scarce, and in seasons of highly localized rainfall it is very scarce. Division of the land into individually heritable parcels, would, in these conditions, be wholly inappropriate and inexpedient, since then the situation where two or three individuals had a super-abundance of cultivable land and the rest of the people had none, would create annually recurring problems of an intractable kind. One solution is that devised by the bedouin: a relatively large area of ground is owned by a group, the size of which is determined by the carrying capacity of the land. Wherever rain falls, the land is available for all, in equal measures, to plough; the decision concerning the detailed allocation of strips of ploughland is taken summarily by casting lots as soon as the rain falls. Water in wells is of the same nature and its allocation is similarly treated.

In the Lebanese Maronite village the land is (or was) intensively cultivated, the crops grown number over a score, the hillside is deeply serrated, and the land lying between twists and turns this way and that. Elsewhere,[62] I have argued that this topography and type of terrain militates against compact estates and big landlordism. Instead the village land is divided into literally hundreds of plots, some of them little more than twice the area of a house. These plots are individually owned. Among the bedouin land is an estate; in the Maronite village it is a commodity in the Marxian sense.

Landed property is productively different for the two communities; it is used by different assemblages of people and inherited differently. Among the bedouin the utilization of land and water for crops and animals is labour reserved almost exclusively for males, and the women process the products. Consistent with this, men are the owners of land, the productive resource. Conceptually, they are thought of as descendants of a unique ancestor, their badge of identification giving them the status of joint owners. In the Maronite village women participate in production with men, or they did until relatively recently. Here the priority of status accorded to bedouin in relation to land is substituted for a shared status, and unilineality is not used to form groups of either sex.

Among the bedouin a man's status in a corporation is patrilineally defined and is, therefore, prescribed. In the Maronite village a person's entry into an affinal set is prescribed only as a minor; at marriage set membership becomes negotiable. The patrilineality of the bedouin means a cleavage in the comprehension of kinship into the two broad categories: males related to males through males necessitating the inclusion of ancestors to link the living, forming groups in relation to resources; and people related in divers other ways which permit expectations, preferential access to the resources of others and a wide variety of other relationships. Lineality here because it roughs out groups in relation to resources, introduces clarity into claims by restricting the males who share the land and water. The appeal to ancestral connexions does not confuse, but solves the problem of who has rights where. For this reason, the comprehension of this area of kinship is always anchored in the past. In the Maronite village an individual starts life with a comprehension of all forms of kinship – not one area as with the bedouin – projected into the past; but, at marriage it is telescoped down almost to the present, and henceforward it is projected oppositively, into a developing future. Both sexes inherit land, easily divisible, and divided into a mosaic of ownership. Were this 'memory' of past ownership, disputes over particular plots, carried forward into the contemporary scene the entanglements of people would amount to stultification of attempts to settle property issues. Contraction of genealogical 'memory', and its subsequent projection into succeeding generations, cuts off the 'memory' of past property disputes and introduces clarity into claims by reducing the number of claimants, recognizing only a contemporary situation shorn of its historical antecedents.

Comparison with the Shīʿite village of south Lebanon is more difficult. Its total population is almost identical to that of the Maronite village. Agricultural technology is virtually the same. The crops grown are almost identical in kind and variety in both. Topographically the two are comparable. Inheritance rules and practices coincide almost exactly. But in the Shī'ite village rank appears, and in the Maronite village it is absent. The economic surplus in the Shī'ite village, until the mid-fifties, was sufficient to maintain a leisured class freed from work on the land, and a large majority of the population at a high subsistence level. In the Maronite village the economic surplus was always, probably, greater, because it has enjoyed easy access to the market of the metropolis; this is distributed throughout the population in such a manner that everyone enjoys a high subsistence standard, noticeably better housing,[63] with marked differentiation in wealth, but without a leisured class. In the Shī'ite village the leisured class possesses a structured genealogy, and the peasants rarely reckoned more than two ascending generations beyond the older living generation. In the Maronite village, genealogical reckoning is similar to that of Shī'ite peasants. Literacy is high in both villages, but of a more sophisticated kind in the Maronite village than in the Shī'ite village. Consequently the development of professionalism began earlier in the Maronite village and it is, corresponding with difference in literacy, more sophisticated. Migration to the U.S.A., Europe, South America and West Africa has affected both villages, but Maronite migration has been much more rewarding and the prosperity brought to the village has raised the standard of living in general, and, for some, it has meant a transformation in their style of living. Successful migrants from the south were few, and, save for one or two, they did not return; others who went returned little better off. It is not the intention to diminish the differences, but it is surprising that the close degree of comparability in what are generally considered to be fundamentals – land forms, soil and water conditions, range and type of crops, methods of working the land, inheritance – of a situation is coupled with so many differences in the style of social relationships. Between man, his environment and his technological exploitation of it, another factor, culture, interposes.

I am aware that the view is widespread in our subject that an analysis should not be a cultural and material mix. On this view, culture is ultimately reducible to the fundamentals already mentioned. I have never understood why. If one community believes that the approach to God is through a Church hierarchy, and another dispenses with intermediaries, that is as much a fact – a hard fact in the metaphorically odd contemporary idiom – as a statement about water supply, crops or the kind of plough. The effect on social relationships of these two religious belief systems is profound. Maronites belong to a Church organization with its Pope in Rome and his local representative the incumbent of the living which goes with the village church. Whatever support the Church and its large Lebanese priesthood may derive from the local population, there is no section of that population which can live in leisure from religious dues. In the Shī'ite village, there is a local mosque, but no church organization. Claim to descent from the Prophet or one of the early heroes of Islam, if successfully established, enables a man to function as a kind of religious expert. Dues deriving from the functions materially add to a man's wealth. The total number of people benefiting in this way, in the early fifties, was roughly one-fifth of the total population. Since access to this income was based on an historical claim, their genealogy purports to validate it, by depicting a continuous life-line reaching to early Islam. And the genealogy to some five ancestors away from the younger living people neatly catches up all the members of the group, to be conceptualized as a single property interest. Religion and rank go hand in hand.

Allegedly religious notions about modesty in women, in the Shī'ite village, are said to account for certain forms of seclusion among women. Aristocratic women are always veiled in public, and secluded from the public in their households. Peasant women move about the village unveiled but are domestically secluded from the public. The social maturity of women, the general ease in their social relationships with either sex is a marked feature of the life in the Maronite village. Differences of this sort cannot be ascribed to the fundamentals. It is true that since the fifties the practice of seclusion in the Shī'ite village has changed radically, and these changes could be put down, quite plausibly, to changes in production, increased professional opportunities and the like. But this kind of argument does not explain why seclusion was present among Shī'ites and absent among Maronites living in almost identical ecological and technological circumstances; nor does it explain why the same changes lead to certain alterations in female seclusion here and other kinds elsewhere.

Marriage to the father's brother's daughter, while negotiably possible among Maronites, is not a practice; among the people of the Shī'ite village, while it could not be forced, it was a preferred form of marriage. These opposing views are severally embedded in the two belief systems. The significance is obvious: the Shī'ites had roughly 11 per cent more affinal choices than the Maronites, and, since this relationship involved a male transmitting group, then what the Shī'ites can do with affinity is distinctively different. Yet affinal sets, of the kind analysed for the Maronite village, do not appear in the Shī'ite village. Affinity within a restricted range is of great import, but it is not used to serve the multiple purposes of the Maronite sets or to give durability to the relationships of a wide span of people. Conceptually, as was stated at the beginning, marriage is unlike for the two communities. A flood of light is thrown on this by a Shī'ite practice whereby a person wishing to enjoy the freedom of a friend's domestic domain marries the friend's infant or very young daughter – access to houses for unrelated people is usually on a visiting basis or by formally knocking at the door and waiting an invitation to enter, rarely a matter of casually dropping in. A man may make several of these marriages. When the girls grow to puberty, divorce is effected. Affinity, in this instance, is used to make a temporary relationship, severable at any time, and for the purpose of furthering

74 EMRYS LLOYD PETERS

friendship, but without any practical constraints to bind the parties.[64] This, in essence, is the affinity of the Shī'ite village save that in marriage proper a negotiated contract is required. Affinity in the Maronite village, preceded ordinarily by extended courtship, is entered into with deliberation, for it is sure to release immediately an array of immutable relationships, increased by the addition of children to the marriage with the power to strengthen or damage an existing set, or initiate a new one.

No pretence is made that this article is comprehensive. Many of the matters to which affinity intimately contributes have not been discussed. The position of bachelors and spinsters has been omitted. The obvious importance of the affinal set in a man's structure of power has not been taken up. The aim was to deal with aspects of affinity. The choice was decided by the congruence of these aspects with affinity *per se* and not with its relevance to the numerous problems affected by it.

NOTES

1 The data for this article was collected during a year's field-work carried out in 1969–70 and in the summer of 1971. It was made possible by a grant from the Social Science Research Council and paid research leave of absence from the University of Manchester. I wish to record my gratitude for this assistance.

My wife, Stella, as on previous researches in other Middle Eastern countries, took the responsibility for a substantial part of the work; and, thanks to her particular interest in affinity, gave me so many ideas and observed behaviour so carefully, that this article is as much hers as mine.

Laila and Khatir (I omit their surname for obvious reasons, but the people of the village, and they, know to whom I refer) promised much and were always truer than their word.

Dr R. P. Werbner corrected the manuscript and contributed valuably to my thinking in several discussions.

Dr D. Turton was kind enough to let me read his unpublished thesis on the Mursi, a large section of which is an analysis of affinity, with the use of quite superb data. I did not feel free to use it in detail in advance of its publication.

2 The bedouin of Cyrenaica, an olive plantation in Tripolitania (both Sunnī Muslims), a Shī'ite village in south Lebanon, and a Maronite Christian village in central Lebanon.

3 See E. L. Peters, 1963, for a full account of these south Lebanese Muslim genealogies.

4 See E. L. Peters, 1960 and 1965, for a full account of bedouin genealogies and the significance of affinity in influencing the composition of camps.

5 Perhaps the best example of this kind of misconception is A. M. Lutfiyya 1966. Others, randomly selected, are A. Cohen 1965, F. Khuri 1970, R. T. Antoun 1972 and L. E. Sweet 1960.

6 See C. D. Forde 1948.

7 Five of these writers have already been cited; A. H. Fuller 1961, J. R. Williams 1968, and J. Gulick 1955 – an Aunt Sally of a book, easy to hit from any angle – are three more which fall readily into line. There are many more. R. T. Antoun, a meticulous field-worker, who has clearly given much thought to issues of descent and kinship, is nevertheless in error when he criticizes me for giving too much significance to affinal

and matrilateral ties in an article on a south Lebanese village, E. L. Peters 1963 and relegating patrilineality to a manipulative ideology. In the article he cites, he quotes pp. 179, 189, 192–3, where I go to some length to contrast the patrilineage of an aristocracy with the absence of this kind of genealogical arrangement among peasants. He proceeds to state that 'patrilineal descent is the main principle for the recruitment of permanent structural groups' (p. 87). I would not deny that it is one way of recruiting to such groups among the Cyrenaican bedouin and the south Lebanese village aristocrats, but it is not the only means of recruitment, as Antoun should know. Moreover, in the article he cites, I gave a detailed description (pp. 181–9) of the way in which the aristocratic genealogy was constructed, beginning by drawing up 'a list of the mature men who were to be included in the genealogy. They began, that is, with the base of the genealogy, the contemporary group' (p. 181). Thereafter, they arranged the latter into smaller groups, systematically ordering them to converge at a single ancestor. That is not a matter of my opinion; it is a fact. Peasants did not arrange themselves patrilineally in this manner; that is a fact too. I am left quite nonplussed by the insistence of so many writers on the Middle East in giving any kind of reckoning through males such general import, when, at best, its relevance and significance, like any other facts of behaviour, are no more than situational.

8 Note that the connexions required to be accepted as an *ibn al-balad* are not necessarily through males; they can be of any kind. The main determinant is the density of social relationships rather than specific forms of consanguinity, even though connectedness through males is ideologically highly rated.

9 I find it rather sad that one has to define perfectly ordinary words in this way, but they have now come to be used so distortedly that definition, alas, is necessary. The kind of warped meaning to which I refer is given by J. Boissevain 1974, who did a stint of field-work on one Professor Volpe, 'One Sunday morning in March 1963...as we strolled slowly back and forth across the principal square of Leone' before lunch (pp. 1–3). He translates *amicizia* as friendship. But what he describes is cheating, corruption, nepotism and thuggery, '...the chopping motion that means the application of violence' (p. 3). Why use euphemism when we possess a vocabulary which can give precision to descriptions of actions? Worse still, Boissevain attributes the same kind of 'friendship' to us all: 'In fact most of us do the same, although we do not have such extreme educational problems as my friend [*sic*] Volpe...The difference is but one of degree: all of us have problems which we at least attempt to resolve via friends or friends-of-friends...' (p. 3). Boissevain should speak for himself.

10 No. 5 in the diagram (Figure 3) is shown as married to the niece of 2, 3, 4. This marriage was subsequent to the introduction of the discussion, but it is included as evidence of the patterning of marriage referred to later.

11 La Fontaine 1962, has given an admirably clear account of affinity among the Gisu 'who do not have rules of preferential or prescribed marriage' (p. 88). The section in pages 104–19, relating to the changing significance of affinity, limitations on affinal choices, and the uses to which affinity are put, is particularly rewarding. Her later contribution on descent (1973) is also very relevant to several of the issues raised in this article.

12 See A. C. Mayer 1966, for a discussion of groups not unlike those dealt with in this article.

13 I am not yet sure – I hope to continue field-work in the village – whether I have recorded all the people in her set when she was young. It might, therefore, have been larger than shown in Figure 6. I suspect so; those shown are probably only the relatives A has recognized in later life.

14   To avoid confusion in the diagram, I have not included the children of those who have moved out of the sets shown in Figure 6.

15   One of the many pleasant features in the life of this community is the participation of people of two or three different generations in many activities: they join together for fun, at private and public gatherings, and at the annual carnival mature adults mime and mimic along with young people without caring much about dignity of the stuffy sort. Apart for occasions like these, there is a characteristic ease in social relationships even between proximate generations.

16   Perhaps this awareness was his undoing. Women in this village do not take readily to being manipulated, especially in marriage.

17   See N. Yalman 1967, on affinal switching (p. 155), and E. Marx 1967, p. 161.

18   Two alleged multi-millionaires (sterling) live at the antipodal ends of the village and they are connected by affinity – one of them is married to the other's sister. But they are not a part of the local foreign wives group, for, although one of them has dealings with local people, their penetration of local life is fortuitously ephemeral. Their links are international.

19   See La Fontaine 1962, pp. 106–7, for a discussion of the effects of choice on affinity.

20   I do not wish to enlarge on these brief statements about bachelors and spinsters. The problems associated with them are too complex to be discussed here. The somewhat dogmatic statements must, therefore, suffice.

21   An alternative is for the spouses to become Muslims, but this does not occur. The intricacies of inheritance involved in this kind of conversion are enough to act as a bar, and, added to cultural pressures, there is *de facto* exclusion. But there is a case of a man changing his registration to Muslim on marriage to a Muslim woman.

22   This effectively excludes bigamy for Christians, unless it takes place abroad. For Muslims the problem does not arise. Hence there is no word for bigamy.

23   See also E. Marx 1967, pp. 224, 226; F. Khuri 1970, p. 598; R. T. Antoun 1972, p. 125.

24   So little was this lady known by her surname, that when my baggage was delivered to the village on our first day there, it was delivered to another lady of the same surname, who, thinking it was all a gift for her much loved son from his employees, tipped the carrier generously and received it into her house. The hilarity which accompanied the undoing of this comedy of errors set us off to a good start on our field-work.

25   I refer, of course, to Turner's (1957) analysis of the Ndembu character, Sandombu, and the events in his life Turner assembles as one of his dramas. In a structural sense the events surrounding (I) could be made into one of these structural dramas. There, however, the similarity ends. Sandombu, a diseased roadman, was born to lose. But (I), a professional of high promise, holding real power in the balance, endowed with most of life's favours, is being watched anxiously, because, depending on the choice he makes, he might become very powerful or collapse the structure of power built up over several generations.

26   I use the words suitors and proposals here for reasons of brevity. Arranging a marriage is much more a matter of taking soundings in various ways, and it is to these I refer. Once it has been understood that mutual consent has been achieved the presentation of a suit is little more than a formality, but many soundings, in different families, are usually made before this stage is reached.

27   Since writing this article I have received information suggesting that this iron is in the fire already.

28   Most marriages are of the first two sorts. When the third possibility obtains, it results from a parental veto on a particular choice, rather than parental selection of a spouse.

29   See E. L. Peters 1963, pp. 161, 162.

30   Among the Maronite Christians, the marriage settlement is a dowry given to the bride

by her father; in the Shī'te Muslim case it is a settlement on the bride by the groom.

31 There were two others with training in our subject, experienced in giving assistance with research. There were dozens more with unprofessionalized skills in social relationships. It was not without point, when, in reference to one of the latter, I said, banteringly, as a comment to a statement made about him: 'It's alright. I've got a card on him.' Back came the answer like a flash: 'And he has one on you too.' What *is* one to do, these days!

32 The idea that kinship, for any individual, alters during a life history, and is altered relative to the position of others is referred to in E. Marx 1967, pp. 170, 171 and in N. Yalman 1967, p. 185, who also recognizes the stability of the affinal bond as a whole. In this article the alteration in kinship statuses, including the mutation of terms and the adoption of terms with changes in status, has only been touched upon with reference to affinity. It is a fascinating field of enquiry with important consequences.

33 During 1969–70 there were severe troubles between some Lebanese groups and some Palestinian groups. As a result, capital investment dropped, few hotels were full, and the local building industry was badly hit: many young men had to seek employment in Kuwait.

34 When a man builds a house, it is a sure sign he has marriage in mind. As he was completing the shell of a house he was building, one young man told me: 'I have built a house. She must marry me now.' She did not. Undaunted he changed to saying: 'I have a house now. I must find a wife soon.'

35 There must be two male witnesses, or one male and two female witnesses. Witnesses are not a requirement in Shī'ite law, but it is usual to have them.

36 Mark, 10. 7 and 8.

37 Goody in J. Goody and S. J. Tambiah 1973, seizes on the importance of monogamy in relation to affinity, stating: 'so too affinity is in many ways a more important matter when you have only one full spouse, when she is married with property, and when that property is placed in some kind of conjugal fund (p. 47).

38 *Shaikh* refers to a learned man, *Sayyid* to a descendant of the Prophet, and *Hājj* to a Meccan pilgrim.

39 See R. P. Davies 1949, p. 249–50; J. Gulick 1955, pp. 115–17; F. Khuri 1970, p. 607.

40 I have in mind here propertied groups, like the aristocrats of the Shī'ite village in south Lebanon, who, to control their landed property carefully, control their marriages also. The figures for parallel-cousin marriage are consequently high, although many are other sorts of cousins as well, and first parallel-cousin marriages are much less than all parallel-cousin marriages. See E. L. Peters 1963, pp. 177, 178.

41 See R. P. Davies 1949.

42 J. Gulick 1955, pp. 115–17.

43 F. Khuri 1970, p. 607.

44 F. Khuri 1970, p. 598.

45 The term *khāl* is dropped or picked up, in use, at different ages, and in relative changes of statuses, but it is not usually used in contexts where consanguinity does not require it. In these latter circumstances, as for example, towards an older unrelated family friend, the French *tante* is used. More recently the English term 'aunt' has been added to the kinship vocabulary, to express finer nuances of relationships.

46 There was one interesting exception to this. Earlier in the text reference was made to an old lady of ninety who retained her maiden surname. Her brother's daughter, the second *grande dame* to be mentioned, married her son, but she also retained her maiden name for status reasons. As if to give additional point to the retention of the surname the kinship terms they used to address each other continued to be used by them after the marriage.

47   This is stating the matter rather badly. If a fuller analysis of kinship had been intended, it would have been necessary to unravel many more complexities in the kinship uses to which affinity gives rise.
48   There are two Christian Churches in the village: Maronite and Greek Catholic.
49   See B. Kapferer 1969, p. 181 and 1972, p. 167 n.
50   See A. L. Epstein 1969, p. 77.
51   See J. Boissevain 1974, p. 5.
52   These are only a few of the numerous works one could cite which attempt to deal theoretically with the problems of 'real' behaviour – the behaviour Boissevain claims is his concern.
53   See E. E. Evans-Pritchard 1949. He also wrote a number of articles on Italian colonialism in Libya.
54   See J. Boissevain 1974, p. 19.
55   See Ibid.
56   See Ibid, pp. vii and viii of the Preface. He thanks the British Colonial Social Science Research Council, the Canadian Royal Commission for Bilingualism and Biculturalism, The Social Science Research Council of the United States and the Wenner-Gren Foundation for Anthropological Research, among other sources.
57   See J. C. Mitchell 1969, p. 1.
58   See B. Kapferer 1972, p. 167, n.5.
59   See J. C. Mitchell 1969, p. 5, n.1.
60   See S. F. Nadel 1957, p. 17.
61   See Ibid, p. 16.
62   See E. L. Peters 1963, pp. 161–6.
63   This is evident from the large number of well-built, red-tiled houses of the Turkish type built in the past. In the south Lebanese village, there were only a few such houses (so few that they were given names); most houses were built of dried mud and odd stones and the roofs were also made of mud on timber supports.
64   These marriages are, in fact, legal unions, and, therefore, subject to legal constraints; but they are not evoked, to my knowledge.

BIBLIOGRAPHY

Ammar, H. 1954. *Growing up in an Egyptian Village*. London, Routledge & Kegan Paul.
Antoun, R. T. 1972. *Arab Village*. Bloomington, Indiana University Press.
Atiya, A. S. 1968. *A History of Eastern Christianity*. London, Methuen.
Bloch, M. 1973. 'The long and the short term: the economic & political significance.' In *The Character of Kinship*, ed. J. Goody. Cambridge University Press.
Boissevain, J. 1974. *Friends of Friends*. Oxford, Blackwell.
Cohen, A. 1965. *Arab Border-Villages in Israel*. Manchester University Press.
Davies, R. P. 1949. 'Syrian Arabic kinship terms.' *Southwestern Journal of Anthropology*.
Epstein, A. L. 1969. 'The network and urban social organisation.' In *Social Networks in Urban Situations*. ed. J. Mitchell. Manchester University Press.
Evans-Pritchard, E. E. 1949. *The Sanusi of Cyrenaica*. Oxford, Clarendon Press.
    1951. *Kinship and Marriage among the Nuer*. Oxford, Clarendon Press.
Forde, C. D. 1948. 'The integration of anthropological studies.' *J.R.A.I.*, Vol. 78.
Fortes, M. 1949. *The Web of Kinship among the Tallensi*. London, Oxford University Press.
    1969. *Kinship and the Social Order*. London, Routledge and Kegan Paul.
Fuller, A. H. 1961. *Buarij Portrait of a Lebanese Village*. Cambridge, Mass., Harvard University Press.
Goody, J. (ed.) 1973. *The Character of Kinship*. Cambridge University Press.

Goody, J. and Tambiah, S. J. 1973.*Bride Wealth and Dowry*. Cambridge University Press.
Gulick, J. 1955. *Social Structure and Cultural Change in a Lebanese Village*. New York, Wenner-Gren Foundation.
Hourani, A. H. 1946. *Syria and Lebanon*. London, Oxford University Press.
Hughes, T. P. 1935. *A Dictionary of Islam*. London, Allen.
Kapferer, B. 1969. 'Norms and manipulation of relationships in a work context.' In *Social Networks in Urban Situations*, ed. J. C. Mitchell. Manchester University Press.
   1972. *Strategy and Transaction in an African Factory*. Manchester University Press.
Khuri, F. 1970. 'Parallel cousin marriage reconsidered.' *Man*, Vol. 5, No. 4.
La Fontaine, J. 1962. 'Gisu marriage and affinal relations.' In *Marriage in Tribal Society*, ed. M. Fortes. In Social Anthropology No. 3. Cambridge Papers. Cambridge University Press.
   1973. 'Descent in New Guinea.' In *The Character of Kinship*, ed. J. Goody. Cambridge University Press.
Leach, E. R. 1961. *Pul Eliya: A Village in Ceylon*. Cambridge University Press.
Lutfiyya, A. M. 1966. *Baytin, A Jordan Village*. The Hague, Mouton.
Marx, E. 1967. *Bedouin of the Negev*. Manchester University Press.
Mayer, A. C. 1966. 'The significance of quasi-groups in the studies of complex societies.' In *The Social Anthropology of Complex Societies*, ed. M. Banton. London, Tavistock.
Mitchell, J. C. (ed.) 1969. *Social Networks in Urban Situations*. Manchester University Press.
Nadel, S. F. 1957. *The Theory of Social Structure*. London, Cohen and West.
Peters, E. L. 1963. 'Aspects of status and rank amongst Muslims in a Lebanese village.' In *Mediterranean Countrymen*, ed. J. Pitt-Rivers. The Hague, Mouton.
   1965. 'Aspects of the family among the Bedouin of Cyrenaica.' In *Comparative Family Systems*, ed. M. F. Nimkoff. Boston, Houghton Mifflin.
   1972. 'Shifts in power in a Lebanese village.' In *Rural Politics and Social Change in the Middle East*, ed. R. T. Antoun and I. Harik. Bloomington, Indiana University Press.
Pitt-Rivers, J. 1973. 'The Kith and the Kin.' In *The Character of Kinship*, ed. J. Goody. Cambridge University Press.
Seligman, C. G. and B. Z. 1918. *The Kababish. A Sudan Arab Tribe*. Harvard African Studies, Cambridge, Mass.
Sweet, L. E. 1960. *Tell Toqaan, A Syrian Village*. Ann Arbor, University of Michigan.
Turner, V. W. 1957. *Schism and Continuity in an African Society*. Manchester University Press.
Turton, D. 1973. 'The social organisation of the Mursi: A pastoral tribe of the lower Omo Valley, South West Ethiopia.' Unpublished Ph.D. thesis. University of London.
Williams, J. R. 1968. *The Youth of Haoch El Harimi. A Lebanese Village*. Cambridge, Mass, Harvard University Press.
Yalman, N. 1967. *Under the Bo Tree*. Berkeley, University of California Press.

2 A profile of family associations in two suburbs of Beirut

Fuad I. Khuri
The American University of Beirut

This study of family associations raises two issues: one about the general theory of social groups, the other, more specific, about lineage structure in the Middle East. The first issue is whether groups defined by enduring, lasting, relations can, alone, be considered the subject matter of social anthropology.[1] The second is whether lineage membership in the Middle East can be defined strictly by descent lines. The definition of groups in terms of lasting relationships has been strongly opposed by Jeremy Boissevain, who argues that such a definition has made sociologists, social anthropologists, and, to a lesser extent, cultural anthropologists, overlook the importance of what he calls 'non-groups' (cliques, factions, friends, acquaintances) in human societies (1968). Even before Boissevain, others (Barnes 1962; Leach 1961; and Peters 1967) had also challenged the validity of the theory of groups by questioning the primacy of kinship in bringing about corporate actions, particularly in respect to economic and political behaviour. The emphasis social anthropologists place on the element of 'constancy' in groups has, in general, led to the exaggeration of the effect of kinship on politics and economics. This exaggeration is partly due to the fact that the element of constancy is far easier to chart for a group of kinsmen than for an economic or a political group.[2]

In this paper I shall try to show the significance of family associations as non-groups in social action, the roles leaders play in forming groups, and the dynamic character of kinship groups in the suburbs of Chiyah and Ghobeire.

GENERAL DESCRIPTION OF THE SUBURBS

In Southern Beirut, between the pine forest and the Damascus railway line, lie the suburbs of Chiyah (pronounced shiyyāḥ) and Ghobeire (ghbayrī), which are separated roughly by the old Sidon road.[3] The Aley–Damascus highway, which cuts across the Sidon road in the middle of the old section of Chiyah, marks the southern boundaries of the suburbs. However, the land of Chiyah extends further southward to the villages of Borj el-Brajne and Hadath, and the land of Ghobeire westward to the seashore. Official boundaries between them were drawn in 1956 when the suburbs became separate municipalities: Chiyah inhabited mostly by Maronites, Ghobeire by Shī'ites (see Table 1). Between 1925 and 1969 Chiyah grew from a village of 575 households to the two separate suburban municipalities (Chiyah and Ghobeire) composed of more than 5,000

TABLE 1   *Religion vs. district*

| | District | | | |
| | Chiyah | | Ghobeire | |
Religion	No.ᵃ	Per cent	No.ᵃ	Per cent
Shī'ites	337	13.29	1,538	78.43
Sunnīs	223	8.79	379	19.33
Druzes	158	6.23	14	0.71
Total	718	(28.31)	1,931	(98.47)
Maronites	1,164	45.90	11	0.56
Greek Orthodox	232	9.15	7	0.36
Greek Catholic	353	13.92	4	0.20
Other Christians	69	2.72	8	0.41
Total	1,818	(71.69)	30	(1.53)
Grand total	2,536	100.00	1,961	100.00

ᵃ These numbers refer to nuclear families.

households with a population of over 30,000.[4] How did the growth of Chiyah from a single village to two suburban municipalities take place?

Like the local history of other Middle Eastern settlements, that of Chiyah is one of migration. Nobody traces origin to Chiyah proper; everybody says that his ancestors originated elsewhere but settled in Chiyah at some time in the past. All families quote specific dates of settlement in Chiyah, right or wrong. Family origin, on the other hand, is always expressed in terms of ancient Arabic genealogies, never in chronological order. For example, the Ghusn family maintains that it is an offshoot of the *Rabī'a* tribe in Northern Iraq, but settled in Chiyah around the turn of the eighteenth century, after a series of migratory stops in northern Syria, southern Lebanon, and Mount Lebanon. Family origin is so flexible that it should rather be called myth of origin. Family origin may be entirely unfounded historically; sociologically, however, it provides the idiom on the basis of which alliances between groups like family associations are justified.

The people of Chiyah trace the history of their settlement to the end of the eighteenth century, when three Ghusns from the village of Tartij in the district of Kesrouane (Mount Lebanon) are said to have settled in the village. Oral traditions here differ. The Ghusns, who at present own more property than any other family, claim to be the first settlers followed, between 1800 and 1840, by the families of Ni'mah, Na'im, Zakkur, Khalluf, Dahir, and Sim'an. Some of these families, especially the Ni'mahs, the Zakkurs, and the Khallufs, dismiss the Ghusn's claim as an unfounded pretension fabricated deliberately to account for their being the largest landowning family in Chiyah. These families insist that they settled in the village at the same time the Ghusns did, if not earlier, and to justify their insistence, they, like the Ghusns, count descent through five different generations to a sixth ancestor who was, they claim, 'cousin' to the first Ghusn settlers. For lack of documentation, it is difficult to support or deny either the pretensions of the Ghusns or that of other families. As will be shown later, the important point, however, is that these pretensions provide individual members of these families with a wider range for casting alliances, particularly in politics.

Tradition of migration among the peoples of Chiyah and Ghobeire must not be confused with rural-to-urban migration which is a relatively more recent phenomenon. The people of these suburbs make the distinction clear by calling themselves the original inhabitants (*al-sukkān al-'asliyyūn*) in contrast to the newcomers (the rural-to-urban migrants) whom they call 'foreigners' (*al-ghurabā'*). Roughly speaking, the original inhabitants include all the families who were living in Chiyah before 1925, the 'foreigners' those who have been settling there since 1925.

The earliest settlement in Chiyah, according to the old families, dates back to the Shihabi Emirate in Mount Lebanon, between 1788 and 1842. It is said that the Shihabi emirs brought these old families from different parts of Mount Lebanon to Chiyah to work in silk production, at one time the only cash crop in the country. As feudal lords, the emirs used to grant these the right to use land, either on a sharecropping basis or on the basis of a fixed rental payable after harvest. This feudal arrangement between emirs and peasants continued until 1840, the time when the Emirate began to face a series of crises that brought to an end the emirs' supremacy over Mount Lebanon in 1842. When their supremacy over Mount Lebanon, including Chiyah, began to crumble (between 1840–2), the emirs sold their land in Chiyah at a low price to native Maronite peasants or to Shī'ite prospectors. The Maronite peasants were able to buy the emirs' land from the savings they had accumulated from silk production. Among the Maronite families who claim today to have bought land from the emirs are the Ghusns, the Zakkurs, the Na'ims and the Madis. Likewise, Shī'ite families, such as the Kanjs, the Khalils, the Hatums, and the Hajjs and the Farhats, who live today in Ghobeire, also claim that their ancestors bought land from the emirs and settled in Chiyah around 1840. The first three families say that their ancestors came from the neighbouring village of Borj el-Brajne, where other Kanjs, Hatums, and Khalils still live. The last two families, on the other hand, say that their ancestors came from the south of Lebanon.

Eighteen years after the downfall of the Shihabi Emirate, at the onset of the Civil War of 1860, a number of other Maronite families, such as the Malkuns and the 'Iranis, fled the Druze-dominated regions in Mount Lebanon to find refuge in Chiyah. During the Mutasarrifate (the autonomous reign established in Lebanon between 1860 and 1914), Chiyah was estimated to have 575 households of which 400 were Maronites, 160 Shī'ites and 5 Greek Orthodox.[5]

After the first world war, and the beginning of the French Mandate, the organization of Chiyah as a single village with a dominant Maronite majority began to change. One of the most important factors contributing to this change was the construction of a race-course in 1927, in the pine forest nearby, which brought with it the settlement of about 60 new Shī'ite families. These families, particularly the Khansa family which was the largest, were brought from the district of Baalbek (in the Bakaa Valley) to groom horses – an occupation that many of them still carry on to this day. The newcomers chose to settle on the outskirts of Chiyah between the old Shī'ite section and the pine forest, close to both the race-course where they work and to their brethren, the native Shī'ites. The area in which the newcomers from Baalbek settled developed within a decade (1925–35) into a village called Ghobeire, and later (in the early fifties) into a separate suburban municipality.

The founding of Ghobeire as a village came in the mid-thirties as a result of the settlement of the new Shī'ite families and, also, because of the decline of the silk industry. A few years after they settled down on the outskirts of Chiyah, the new Shī'ite families established for themselves a *mukhtarā* (a sort of village headmanship) and a market place (*sāha*), independent of Chiyah. And to reaffirm their independence they called their settlement Ghobeire.[6] Just as the *mukhtarā* gave Ghobeire a semi-autonomous status politically, the *sāha* did so economically. Interaction between Ghobeire and Chiyah was accordingly greatly reduced, more so between the Shī'ites and the Maronites. This reduced interaction became more severe in the mid-thirties after the decline of the silk industry.

Formerly, silk production in the area had tied the Shī'ites and the Maronites together into a single economic enterprise. While both confessional groups raised the silkworm, only the Maronites processed the cocoons. Workers in the silk factory in Chiyah were Maronite peasant girls; the managers and owners were Maronite entrepreneurs. If silk production helped to unite the Shī'ites and the Maronites together into a single economic enterprise, it is no surprise, then, that the decline of this production, in the mid-thirties, helped also to separate them.

From the mid-thirties onwards more rural-to-urban migrants, began to settle in the area at a rate unknown earlier (see Table 2). Muslim migrants, especially the Shī'ites, settled in Ghobeire; Christian migrants, especially the Maronites, settled in Chiyah (see Table 1). This unprecedented influx of rural-to-urban migrants into Chiyah and Ghobeire rapidly turned the two villages into suburbs in the early fifties. Fields (orange and olive orchards) were sold as building plots for the construction of apartment houses (see Table 3);

TABLE 2   *Dates of the settlement of migrants in Chiyah and Ghobeire*

Date of settlement	Chiyah (mostly Maronite)	Ghobeire (mostly Shīʿite)	Total
1900–04	3	8	11
1905–09	4	7	11
1910–14	6	9	15
1915–19	15	12	27
1920–4	21	15	36
1925–9	45	34	79
1930–4	67	32	99
1935–9	101	68	169
1940–4	113	99	212
1945–9	307	281	588
1950–4	290	256	546
1955–9	327	204	531
1960–4	321	174	495
1965–9	203	85	288
Total	1,823	1,284	3,107[a]

[a]In 1970 there were 2,037 migrant nuclear families living in Chiyah compared to 499 native ones, and 1,438 in Ghobeire compared to 523. The difference in the number of migrant families between the total figure mentioned in Table 1 and the figure just mentioned is due to the fact that a number of migrant families did not know when they settled in the suburbs, and were, therefore, excluded, from the table.

new light industries were constructed; new occupations and political groups began to emerge; economic opportunities, educational facilities, and neighbour-hoods all began to take new forms. The two suburbs were indeed undergoing a period of fast organizational change. It was during this period (the early fifties, which I regard to be a turning point for Chiyah and Ghobeire and, perhaps, for

TABLE 3   *Dates of apartment construction in Chiyah and Ghobeire*

Date of apartment construction	Number of individual apartments
1900–09	8
1910–19	46
1920–9	108
1930–9	177
1940–9	322
1950–9	1273
1960–9	2300

all of Lebanon) that family associations began to mushroom in the suburbs, especially among the Shīʿites.

FAMILY ASSOCIATIONS IN THE SUBURBS OF CHIYAH AND GHOBEIRE

Of the twenty-one officially registered family associations in the suburbs of Chiyah and Ghobeire, only four were still operating in 1970, and all of them are

Shī'ite by confession. The rest, two Maronite and fifteen Shī'ite, have ceased
to operate. By operating I mean that they have an elected 'cabinet' composed of
a president, a secretary and a treasurer. The difference in number between the
officially registered associations (21) and the active ones (4) is partly a
bureaucratic problem. To register an association, and therefore make it legal,
three signatures are required, those of the president, secretary and treasurer.
These officials prepare a written statement about the aims of the association,
indicating the date and place of its founding, and submit it to the Ministry of
Social Works. If they receive no reply, negative or positive, from the Ministry
within two months, the association then becomes legal. Seeking legal status for
the association earns the founders, particularly the president, the reputation of
being 'smart' men (wāsiʻal-ḥīlat), who understand bureaucratic formalities.
Legal status gives the founders an unchallengeable claim, not only over the right
to collect membership fees (itself a political act), but also to accept or deny
admission. The only form opposition can take in the face of a licensed association is to refuse to join. Membership in family associations based on
genealogical links is not automatically established the moment an association
is founded. By securing legal recognition the founders simply earn the power to
manoeuvre for membership.

In his work, 'Some structural aspects of the feud among the camel-herding
bedouin of Cyrenaica', Emrys Peters writes: 'The lineage model is not a sociological one, but it is a frame of reference used by a particular people to give them
a commonsense kind of understanding of their social relationships' (1967, p.
261). In relation to family associations in Chiyah and Ghobeire, the 'particular
people' is the founder of the association who uses genealogical links as a frame
of reference to pursue his own individual interest. In this sense, the limits of the
association reflect the founder's interest. The organization of six family associations (two amongst the Maronites of Chiyah and four amongst the Shī'ites of
Ghobeire) illustrates this point clearly.

THE MARONITE FAMILY ASSOCIATIONS

In 1953, Michel, the son of Sij'an Risha Ghusn, founded a family association
that aimed to educate the poor, aid the needy and the sick, establish a club,
and strengthen family bonds (yajmaʻshaml al-ʻāʼila). Michel abandoned his
project only three months after he had begun it. Personal and organizational
factors were responsible for his failure. As Yusuf Ghusn put it, 'Michel belonged
to the Risha branch, the least notable of the family; he was young and ambitious
but did not measure up to the standards of leadership among the Ghusns.' As
a matter of fact, the Ghusns already had two powerful, outspoken leaders when
Michel decided he also wanted to be one. Michel's failure to establish a family
association, however, cannot be explained by lack of personal assets alone –
there are organizational reasons as well.

Those who claim to be Ghusns are known today by four lineage names: Ghusns proper, Rishas, Dahuds and the Khourys. There is agreement that Ghusn, Risha and Eliyya settled in Chiyah together towards the end of the eighteenth century, but disagreement on whether they were brothers or cousins (see the Ghusns' genealogy, Figure 1). Those who say that they were brothers

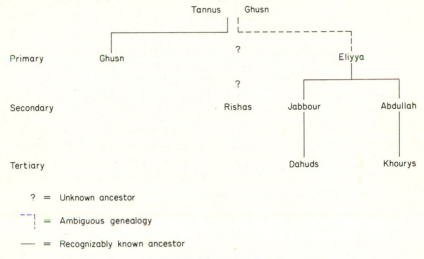

Fig. 1. Ghusn family tree.

insist that the Ghusns proper, the Rishas, some of whom have changed their family name to Ghusn, and the Eliyyas, both those who belong to the line of Dahud lineage or the Khouris (see Figure 1) are descendants of one ancestry and therefore entitled to membership in the association. By contrast, those who say that Ghusn, Risha and Eliyya were cousins insist that there are no valid grounds to include all these lineages in one association. They argue that the word 'cousin' is a loose term, often used as a cultural idiom, either to refer to genealogical links (and here it is pretty loose for it may refer to an actual cousin or anybody sharing common descent) or to common residence in the past.

Coming from the Risha branch, itself an offshoot of the Ghusn family, Michel had no chance of playing the role of an organizer and bringing the Ghusns together into a single family association. The cynics dismiss Michel Risha's attempt to establish a family association as a manoeuvre to ally himself with the powerful and most numerous family in Chiyah – the Ghusns proper.

The other inactive Maronite family association is the 'Iranis', established in 1952 by Alfred al-'Irani from the village of 'Arayya in the Metn district of Mount Lebanon. The 'Iranis, who have been living in Chiyah for about four generations and who count seventeen nuclear families, are, by and large, affiliated to the Katā'ib party, a secular modern party that champions the cause of the Maronites. Because of its relatively small size (seventeen nuclear families), and because its members carry on intensive interaction between themselves, the 'Irani family has no genealogical uncertainties similar to those among the Ghusns. They all trace descent through different ancestors to Yusuf 'Irani whom they regard as the first settler in Chiyah. These two factors, support for the Katā'ib party and an exact genealogy, are responsible for the fact that the 'Iranis of Chiyah are members, not initiators, of, the family association. Faced with a well-defined (at least it is accepted as such) genealogy, Alfred could not claim to re-establish family bonds – they are already well-established. Nor, for that matter, could he claim to unite the family into a single political front – they are already united by the Katā'ib. As will be shown later, genealogical disagreements always reflect political disunity. Alfred 'Irani, as a foreigner not even living in Chiyah, could not possibly hope to use family background to advance his political ambitions. His ambition turned out to be economic. After meeting twice with the 'Iranis of Chiyah, Alfred charted a family tree in which he included the Chiyah branch and sold it to them for fifty Lebanese pounds (about U.S. $17) a piece. Judging from a photograph, I believe the 'Irani tree is too neat to be correct. Today, the 'Irani association established by Alfred in 1952 has ended up in his bank account.

THE SHĪ'ITE FAMILY ASSOCIATIONS

The Khalil family association was first established in Tyre (south Lebanon) in 1921 under the leadership of Kadhim al-Khalil, one of the prominent leaders of the family. He is now (1970) the vice-president of the Free Patriots party (al-Waṭaniyyŭn al-Aḥrār), founded by former President Kamil Chamoun at the termination of his office in 1958. The scope of the association reflects Kadhim's aims at the time. Looking for the widest range of links, real or fictitious, that might tie all the Khalils together, Kadhim traced the origin of the family to none other than Abraham who, in ancient Arabic lore, is called Ibrāhīm al-Khalīl. By doing so, he made it possible for every one bearing the name Khalil, which is very common among the Shī'ites of Lebanon, to join the association. Accordingly, Khalils from the districts of Sidon, Baalbek and Beirut, including Borj el-Brajne and Ghobeire, became eligible to be members, even though no exactly traceable genealogy links them together. By tracing the origin of the family to Abraham, Kadhim earned the maximal range of potential supporters possible on the basis of descent. Genealogical depth (lineally) means wider range of collateral relations; hence, an increase in potential supporters. The reason, therefore, that well-established families have longer genealogies, compared to peasants (Peters 1963), is that such genealogies give them a wider range of support and greater freedom of political action.

It was during the French Mandate in Lebanon, especially between 1925 and 1945, when parliamentary representation was based on large constituencies (all south Lebanon, for example, was one constituency) that such country-wide links as the Khalil association were of the utmost political importance. Later, especially after independence in 1950, when electoral constituencies were greatly reduced in size (Tyre alone became a separate constituency), family associations with national links became politically insignificant. By mobilizing the loyalty of the Khalils in Tyre, Kadhim was able after independence repeatedly to win the Tyre seat in parliament. Unneeded, the Khalil family association with its country-wide links, was forgotten. Instead, local attempts were made to establish micro-associations independent of one another. One such attempt was made in Sidon, another in Ghobeire.

The Ghobeire micro-association which concerns us in this paper appeared first in 1951 under the leadership of Abdul-Karim al-Khalil. He belonged to the Mahdi branch which is at present the most prominent branch of the Khalil family in the suburb. The Mahdi branch traces descent to al-Ḥājj Mahdī al-Khalīl who is said to be one of the descendants of Muḥammad al-Khalīl, the ancient ancestor who migrated from the village of Shur (Tyre district) about five centuries ago and settled in the old Shīʿite community of Borj el-Brajne. In the middle of the nineteenth century, al-Ḥājj Mahdī, with six other Khalils (Yusuf, Qasim, Husain, al-Fàhl, Jabri, Yahya) who claim to be the descendants of Muḥammad al-Khalīl, bought land in what is known today as Ghobeire (then Chiyah) and settled there. These names represent today seven different lineages who, though known locally as the Khalāyilī, (plural of Khalīl), share no exact genealogy. Some say that the seven descendants of Muḥammad were 'cousins' but disagree on the actual linkages between them. Others say that they were 'brothers' but, again, disagree on who was brother to whom. These seven branches, which count about 281 nuclear families, call themselves 'the old settlers' of Ghobeire in contrast to six other Khalil groups who settled in the suburb after 1925 and are known as 'foreigners'. The latter groups, which count about 43 nuclear families, came from different villages of Lebanon, one from the Baalbek area and five from the south.

Under Abdul-Karim's leadership, the association which included the old branches only, was torn by internal dissent: every branch had a candidate for the presidency of the association, a candidate for the local government and an independent spokesman. This lack of unity betrayed the aim for which the association was established – namely, to unite the Khalils into a single political front. Gradually, Abdul-Karim lost interest in the association which continued, for lack of challenge, to have a nominal cabinet until 1969. In 1969, Ali al-Khalil, a medical doctor by profession, and a Mahdi by lineage, tried to revive the association. Once he was nominated president, Ali invited all the Khalils, old settlers and newcomers alike, to join the association but in different capacities: the former as participants in the executive council, the latter as members. What prompted Ali to revive the association was the new political challenge the Khalils had to meet after they lost the municipal election of 1963. The challenge centred around the financing of a sports club established in 1954 under the leadership of Hammoud Khalil for the exclusive use of the seven old branches of the family. This club, though a family enterprise, came to receive continuous subsidy from the municipality at the time the Khalils were in control of it. When the Khalils lost the 1963 elections, they also lost with it the subsidies for the club. Supporting the club financially became, therefore, a symbol of family solidarity, a way of meeting the political challenge.

The club is an independent organization, separate from the association. It has its own fees, its own cabinet, and most of its members are young. Only when the club began to face financial difficulties did the young Khalils, the club members, approach Ali for aid. In order to finance the club and, therefore, meet the political challenge, Ali tried to revive the association founded by Abdul-Karim in 1951. He learned from Abdul-Karim's experience that the failure of the previous association was due to the rivalry for leadership among the seven old branches; hence, his idea of an executive council, composed of seven officials, each representing one branch. The council, as Ali planned it, did not work. Three of the old branches refused to co-operate on the grounds that the council was a trick designed by the Mahdi branch to lay their dominance over the other Khalils. According to Ali, those who refused to co-operate are generally the wealthy who aspire to lead the Khalils. Those who co-operate, on the other hand, are of two kinds: those who are genuinely concerned with the political challenge facing the Khalils of Ghobeire, who generally belong to the old branches of the family, and those who are merely interested in receiving free medical treatment, particularly the newcomers. (This is said in reference to the fact that Ali, medical doctor and head of the associations, does not charge the Khalil patients, especially the poor ones who support him politically.) As of June 1970, the club is threatened by imminent bankruptcy, while Ali is still trying to get the Khalils to finance it. What he is achieving is a leading role in the politics of the suburb. The longer the club issue continues the more influential he becomes: while he is trying to get the Khalils together he is, at the same time, manoeuvring for support.

Another Shi'ite family association operating in Ghobeire is the Hashimite association which has an entirely different organization from that of Khalil. Established in 1950 by Abu-Muhsin al-Musawi, originally from the village of Nabi Shit (district of Baalbek), the Hashimite association includes all the families who live in Ghobeire, and who trace descent to 'Alī Ibn Abī Ṭālib, a prominent Hashimite from Quraysh. These families, locally known as al-asyād (plural of sayyid), claim descent to 'Alī through Zain al-'Ābidin, the son of Ḥusain ('Alī's son), who was the only survivor of the Battle of Karbalā' in Iraq where Ḥusain's troops lost in battle to Yazīd's in A.D. 680. In Ghobeire, the Hashimite association includes the Husainis from Byblos, the Musawis from Nabi Shit, the Murtadas from Baalbek, the al-Amins from the village of Shaqra in the district of Nabatiyya, and the Sharaf al-Dins, the Safyi al-Dins, and the Subhs, from Tyre. All of these families are new settlers in Ghobeire.

Being *asyad*, they have a special religious status in Shī'ite communities: they personify the continuity of the *Imamate*. According to Shī'ites, the Imam is not simply a leader in prayer as he is among the Sunnī Muslims, but an interpreter of the words of God, an objective manifestation of the continuity of the line of 'Alī in whose hands the Caliphate (Islamic government) must rest.

True to its Islamic tradition, the Hashimite association does not 'elect' a cabinet; it designates a secretary. Once a *sayyid* demonstrates his capacity for leadership, he is accepted as the head of the association by sounding out individual opinion, a process referred to as *al-shūra*. To be exact, the association has no head, but a secretary who, with the assistance of any appointed representative from each family, composed the executive board. Like other family associations, the Hashimite's has a written constitution which aims to unite the *asyād* into one bloc, educate the intelligent, and aid the needy and the sick. Since 1950 the association has only accomplished two things: it has given fifty Lebanese pounds to a Murtada *sayyid* who broke his leg by accident and erected an Arch of Triumph for King Husain of Jordan (who is a Hashimite) when he visited Lebanon in 1965. Perhaps the money spent on the Arch was defrayed by the five thousand Lebanese pounds which King Husain had granted in aid to the association.

According to its founder, Abu-Muhsin al-Musawi, the Hashimite association has failed to achieve the primary aim for which it was initially set up – namely, to bring unity to the *asyād* of Ghobeire. Al-Musawi explains this failure by the 'rivalry for leadership among the *asyād*'. The *asyād* of the suburb, who count about 83 households, are as divided as the communities from which they originally came. They share neither the same community background, nor the same political interest, nor even the same genealogy. They are Hashimites by myth, but Musawis, Amins, Murtadas, etc. by genealogy. Theoretically, of course, it is difficult here to separate myth from genealogy; but the fact remains that being a Musawi is one thing, but being a Musawi who belongs originally to the Hashimite house (in the distant past) is something else, at least politically. The former is traceable kinship; the latter, on the other hand, is an inherited religious title. So tense was rivalry for leadership between the *asyād* in the municipal election of 1963 that they were unable to nominate a candidate of their own. Instead, they agreed to support a non-Hashimite. Nevertheless, Abu-Muhsin is still trying to unite the *asyād* families in the Hashimite association. When some of the Hashimites began to suspect his leadership, accusing him of using the association as an instrument to further his personal influence and popularity, Abu-Muhsin resigned his secretarial position, and began to spread the word that Abdul-Ra'uf al-Amine, an employee in the Ministry of Social Works, was qualified for the office. Few people took this gesture seriously, since it is known in the suburb, at least among the *asyād*, that al-Amine is but the shadow of Abu-Muhsin.

The last two Shī'ite associations operating in Ghobeire are those of the

Rmayti and the Baylun families. They are taken together because the founding of the first is related to that of the second. Both families come originally from the village of al-Majdil in the district of Tyre and began to settle in the suburb during the last two decades. In the village of their origin, the Rmaytis, who compose about 80 per cent of the village population, had a traditional monopoly of the leading positions there. The Bayluns, on the other hand, who compose about 20 per cent of the village, were a sort of pressure group supporting from time to time one Rmayti faction against another, depending upon their interests.

In 1955, Muhammad Sa'id Rmayti, an employee in the Ministry of Agriculture in Tyre, came to Ghobeire and invited every adult Rmayti to take part in a general meeting of the family. Though scattered all over the suburb, the Rmaytis, who count about seventeen nuclear families, attended the meeting. At the meeting, Muhammad Sa'id disclosed the founding of a family association and asked those who attended to become members by paying a fee of one Lebanese pound a month. He announced that the money would be spent on the construction of a new mosque in Mjadil. 'It is shameful,' he said, 'that our village, lacking a good mosque, looks like a Christian rather than a Muslim village.' Immediately the question of who should collect the fees became a political issue. Finally, the decision was reached that Ni'mi, Ali, and Mahmud, the better-known among the Rmaytis of the suburb, should be authorized to do so. After two years nobody knew who had paid how much or to whom. All knew, however, that a relatively high minaret had been constructred over the old mosque in Mjadil, under the supervision of Muhammad Sa'id, and that, Muhammad had begun to build a new house for himself. The three better-known Rmaytis from Ghobeire took issue with Sa'id, accusing him of having used the association's money to build a house and threatening to take the case to court. The case was never taken to court; instead, Sa'id returned to them part of the money they had collected and resigned his position in the association. In order to redistribute the money to its donors, Ni'mi, Ali, and Mahmud decided to appoint themselves as the new cabinet of the association, the first as head, the second as secretary, the third as treasurer. Ten years have passed now, but the money has not been redistributed. Moreover, the Rmaytis have not taken a united stand in relation to any issue, even though they retain the cabinet of the association.

Only two months after the Rmaytis formed their association, the Bayluns formed one of their own, under the leadership of Husain Baylun, a shopkeeper. However similar in some ways to other associations (like them, it claims to provide education to the poor, aid to the needy and sick, and to unite the family), the Bayluns' differs in its method of organization. Husain, a semi-literate but shrewd manipulator, never bothered to approach the Bayluns collectively. He neither holds public meetings nor collects membership fees. Yet, he has in his possession a licensed association charter carrying three signatures, his own and two others from the Bayluns. 'To call for a general, collective meeting', he says, 'provokes jealousies.' He adds, 'The Bayluns, after all, are not numerous. I see most of them every day. We talk about the affairs of the association.' It is here, in the lack of meetings and clear membership, that Husain's reputed influence lies. By holding no meetings and enlisting no members, he has made the association entirely his, dependent on his initiative and effort. When Husain's headship of the association was verbally challenged by another Baylun, he responded: 'Let him get another association and become its head.' By holding no public meetings, Husain was able to silence opposition within the family and at the same time, to keep the size of the association secret. The first tactic earned him the title of the unchallenged spokesman of the Bayluns in Ghobeire, descriptively referred to as an 'election key' (*miftāḥ intikhābī*). The second earned him a seat in the municipal cabinet. People are so uninformed about the size of the Baylun family that, of those who claim to know the suburb well, none estimates them to be less than 30 nuclear families while, in fact, they count only eleven. Those who make the estimate try to justify it by saying that the Bayluns have a family association. It appears as if having an association is, by itself, indicative of large family size.

One must not be left with the impression that Husain's unchallenged leadership of the Bayluns rests altogether on tactical skills. He couples his skills with tangible commitments. Every Baylun is entitled to a loan from the association, payable to Husain on credit without interest, provided that the loan does not exceed one hundred Lebanese pounds (U.S. $31). The capital he uses for this purpose amounts to one thousand Lebanese pounds (U.S. $330). It was granted to the association as an 'aid' during the parliamentary elections of 1962 by a prominent politician. To many Bayluns, of whom five are vegetable pedlars, this is a significant commitment which provides them with a workable capital. With one hundred Lebanese pounds as capital, a vegetable pedlar can make a profit of fifteen to twenty-five Lebanese pounds a day thus enabling him to cover his daily expenses and part of his loan.

FAMILY ASSOCIATIONS AND COMMUNITY ORGANIZATION

According to the data from Chiyah and Ghobeire, it is obvious that the number of family associations, active or inactive, founded by Shī'ites exceeds the number founded by Maronites by a ratio of 19:2. The reason for this difference is that while the Maronites of Chiyah have a 'church' the Shī'ites of Ghobeire do not. The Maronite Church (this cannot be said about other churches in Lebanon) provides the people of Chiyah with a common denominator, a meeting ground, a co-ordinator of public services. It provides them with three well-equipped schools, two for boys and one for girls, and a clinic; in addition, on a number of occasions the Church aids the poor, the needy, and the sick. This means that claims by family associations to provide these services have to compete with the Church and its long, well-established experience. The Maronites donate generously to the Church and, in return, they receive anonymous aids and services. The Church does not brag about its services, nor does it try to translate them into political assets, at least not locally. In Chiyah, public services of this sort and politics are separate phenomena – the former are provided by the Church, the latter either by local politicians on a patron–client basis, common among the old families, or by the Kata'ib party, common among the newcomers.[7]

Unlike the Maronites of Chiyah, the Shī'ites of Ghobeire have no such common denominator or co-ordinator of public services as the Church. The *asyād*, who represent the continuity of the line of 'Alī Ibn Tālib and, therefore, are entitled to the Caliphate, are only in principle the co-ordinators of public services and healers of community strife. In practice, however, the *asyād* constitute a faction in Shī'ite communities. Instead of being above conflict, they are part of it (consider the role of the Hashimite association in Ghobeire). It is true, Shī'ites donate (in the form of *zakāt*) to the *asyād*, especially on religious occasions such as *'Āshūrā'*, but these donations are never redistributed in the form of public services. On the contrary, the *asyād* use these donations to enhance their individual properties.

The lack of what I like to call 'consensus organizations' in the Shī'ite suburb of Ghobeire – organizations that are free from factional interests – encourages the formation of family associations in two ways. First, it makes the justifiable and defensible presumption that family associations are founded to aid family members. Second, it gives a political tone to services and projects (personal aid, clubs, credit, etc.) rendered on the basis of family links. The sports club which the Khalils established for the exclusive use of their family is not simply regarded as a family project, but also as a political challenge to other families. Likewise, the credit system of the Baylun's association is certainly understood as uniting them, but the unity is at least partly political. If sponsored by factions and not by consensus organizations, welfare services and projects are automatically translated into political issues. Concerning family associations, the Shī'ites of Ghobeire recognize the political meaning of benevolent objectives so well that they make no distinction between welfare and politics. Because welfare is carried on by the Church, which takes no noticeable part in local politics, this distinction is made clear among the Maronites of Chiyah. This means that the probability of using family associations for political purposes wrapped up in benevolent objectives[8] is greater among Shī'ites who lack consensus organizations than among Maronites who have them.

The presence or absence of consensus organizations, although it explains why family associations occur more frequently among Shī'ites than Maronites, does not explain the sociological conditions that lead to the rise of such associations. To do so, one must examine family organization and proliferation in Chiyah and Ghobeire while these communities were growing into suburbs.

FAMILY ASSOCIATION AND LINEAGE STRUCTURE

Before Chiyah and Ghobeire began to grow into suburbs they had a number of leading family groups (*'ā'ilāt*), each organized around a prominent house (*bait ma'rūf*), an extended family whose pre-eminence in community affairs has been established for at least three generations. The pre-eminence of the *bait ma'rūf*, which is derived from the control of wealth and people, is often expressed in cultural idiom: long genealogies, large families, a history of migration and settlement. A prominent family confers status on all its relations, however inconspicuous they may be. Families without a *bait ma'rūf* are classified accordingly as low-status families. The Khalil family is considered a high-status one because each of its seven branches, mentioned earlier, is headed by a *bait ma'rūf*. Yet Khalils are hardly distinguishable from most Ghobeire people. The *bait ma'rūf* which often leads the family in community affairs, acquires leadership by having socio-economic assets, the control of wealth and people. Whoever acquires these assets earns for himself a leading position in the community.

The fact that leadership rests on socio-economic assets (control of wealth and people) expressed in the cultural idiom (long genealogies, large families, etc.) has an important bearing upon the proliferation of family groups into smaller segments. It means that family groups tend to split into smaller segments (often of the lineage order) whenever these segments are organized around new leadership, new prominent houses. Mobility towards prominent houses carries with it, therefore, a relatively high degree of genealogical segmentation (the splitting off of a line from the main family) which may take place at the primary, secondary or tertiary level upon the lineage concerned.[9] In the Ghusns genealogy (see Figure 1), the Ghusns proper split off at the primary level tracing descent directly to Tannus, the Rishas at the secondary level tracing descent to Tannus through Risha, and the Khourys and the Dahuds at the tertiary level tracing descent to Tannus through Abdullah and Jabbour. The tertiary level at which segments are believed to proliferate in other parts of the Middle East (see Emrys Peters 1967) does not hold true in the suburbs, since within the (Ghusn) genealogy lineages proliferate at three different levels: primary, secondary and tertiary.

Proliferation of lineages is subject to the rise of new leadership, caused either by social mobility or by the dispersal of family groups through migration. This suggests that there is no definite limit at which segments do actually split off genealogically. They may split off at the primary, secondary or tertiary descending generations. It also means that there is no definite limit at which segments of comparable structures but of different sizes can unite. In this sense, family groups which are larger than the nuclear and extended types become historical facts, subject to a great deal of fluctuation. Like empires, family groups expand and shrink depending upon the ambition and power of individual leaders.

What facilitates the expansion and shrinkage of family groups is the fact that links between them are at times recognized to be so fluid that they allow individual segments to shift descent from one line to another without losing identity. Often, if not always, these shifts are marked by change of interest or of political loyalty. By claiming to be 'cousins' to the Ghusns (see above, Figure 1), the Ni'mahs, the Zakkurs, and the Khallufs earn a wider range of manoeuvrability in local politics. If it happens that they ally themselves with the Ghusns, these families would be able to justify their alliance by the 'cousinship' that they claim to share. Shifts of descent and alliances of this sort need not be carried out by family groups as a body, but by individuals, each pursuing his own interests. This is the reason why some Rishas, who allied themselves with the Ghusns, changed their family names to Ghusn when the latter became prominent in the area. While becoming prominent, a man simultaneously enlarges his family.

It is not exactly true to say that large families tend to produce prominent men; on the contrary, prominent men tend to produce large families. If this is so, the definition of a family group, lineage or clan, in terms of a fixed set of generations that reaches to a fixed ancestor, must be qualified. Obviously, this definition tends to reflect the micro-methods the anthropologist uses to record his data rather than the way family groups actually behave. The analysis of relatively small, localized, family groups, the members of which interact very intensively, is apt to yield well-defined lines of descent. Whether descent itself is exact, or is made so as a result of intensive interaction, is very difficult to demonstrate specifically because it requires the charting of descent lines of the same family for a number of generations. Concerning small localized family groups, the definition of lineage by criteria of descent (a fixed set of generations) coincides with the definition of group by sociometric (interaction) criteria (Homans 1951, pp. 82–4). In the suburbs family size determined by genealogical depth is a measure of the prominence of family leaders. Lineages cannot be defined by descent lines alone: exact genealogies, which are considered to be characteristic of lineages, are merely cultural expressions of corporate actions.

This brief account of family organization and proliferation seems necessary for the understanding of family associations in Chiyah and Ghobeire. The founding of family associations depends upon two conditions, competitive leadership and genealogical ambiguity, two phenomena that became more widespread in the suburbs in the early fifties as a result of the economic boom and the social and spatial (migration) mobility accruing therefrom. The way of translating prosperity into status is to challenge the leader of one's own family. This is a challenge that takes various forms: refusing to lend the leader support in times of conflict, criticizing him in public, carrying on social transactions on the basis of strict reciprocity, or trying to become leader. In becoming leader, a man first seeks the support of his kin, which he can accomplish either by gradually eliminating the already established leadership (if the family has any) or by splitting himself from the main family group. When a potential leader splits from the main family, he takes with him his supporters who often happen to be his close relatives; thus, he forms a separate lineage, branch, segment, etc. If continued for two or three generations, political cleavage within the family ends up in genealogical segmentation. Here, again, lack of social interaction, caused by political disagreements, expresses itself culturally in genealogical proliferation. Family groups with many prosperous individuals would be expected therefore to be politically more splintered (in the sense of having multi-leadership) and genealogically more proliferated. This is indeed the case of the Khalils of Ghobeire and the Ghusns of Chiyah.

The stability of resources in Chiyah and Ghobeire before these villages became suburbs, and the limited mobility, social or spatial, that resulted from the stability of resources, contributed to steady family leadership and thus slow proliferation. On the other hand, relative prosperity and high mobility (including migration), which came while Chiyah and Ghobeire were changing into suburbs, gave rise to intense competition for family leadership and, henceforth, increasing genealogical proliferation. Increasing proliferation, caused either by mobility or by migration, creates genealogical ambiguities, not so much regarding the distant origin of the family as the actual linkages that tie the living groups together (the Ghusns are a case in point).

In the face of multi-leadership within the family coupled by genealogical uncertainties, family associations present themselves as logical outlets for whoever seeks to control the family he belongs to. By establishing a formally recognized association, the founder avoids the intricate question of who is related to whom and in what manner. He simply accepts the given – i.e. who-ever carries the family name or shares in its mythical origin becomes eligible for membership regardless of his place of residence, place of birth, or of the exact position he occupies on a genealogical map. In other words, the founder creates an anti-lineage organization whose membership is voluntary. And by creating an anti-lineage organization that rests on the myth of family origin, the founder earns the initiative to act on a broader base than the small, localized segments. The range within which he can manoeuvre for support becomes as wide as he wants it to be. For example, Kadhim al-Khalil, wanting to play a role in national politics, founded an association with country-wide links that could be traced, presumably, to Abraham. By contrast, Ali al-Khalil, who wanted to play an active role in the local politics of Ghobeire, confined membership to those who carried the family name and who lived in the suburb, regardless of whether they were old or new settlers. His interest was regional, unlike Kadhim's which was national. Like Ali al-Khalil, Husain Baylun, whose aim was to be the spokesman of the Bayluns in Ghobeire, founded an association there; but, unlike Ali, he thought that in order to remain the unchallenged leader of the Bayluns he had to avoid recruiting members or holding public meetings. In his view, recruiting members and holding meetings would raise suspicion, invite competition, and expose the weakness of the association – its small size.

THE NON-LASTING CHARACTER OF FAMILY ASSOCIATIONS

Of all the associations, active or inactive, founded in the suburbs since 1950, two, the Bayluns' and the Khalils', seem to be still active, which is in itself a measure of success. The other two operating associations, the Hashimite's and the Rmaytis, though they have a nominal cabinet, have not made any decisions for a long time, which suggests they are no longer active. It is my conviction that I studied the last two associations while they were sinking into oblivion – a common fate of family associations. The question that logically poses itself here is: why do family associations cease to exist almost as soon as they are founded?

Founding an association 'to unite the family' does not, by itself, achieve unity. As indicated earlier, a family association provides the founder with a platform, free from strict lineage ties, to manoeuvre for support. Once an association is founded, it is then the job of the founder to gather support. Likewise, the fact that associations enable founders to ignore the barring effects of strict lineage ties does not eliminate lineage loyalties; it simply suspends them for a while. It is shown in the case of the Hashimite, the Khalil, the Ghusn, and the Rmayti family associations that strong loyalty to individual lineages militates against family unity. Besides, to be a founder is to claim leadership, not to lead. So wary are other potential leaders of the political ambitions of the founder that they tend to oppose him at every public meeting. The timing of such meetings is also significant. General meetings have usually been called for just before local or national elections take place, which leaves members very suspicious of the founder's political intentions. After elections the association is suspended, if not entirely forgotten, until the next elections. Even in the case of the active associations of the Bayluns and the Khalils, the political intentions of the founder are well known – except that Husain, the president of the first association, justifies his political ambitions by the credit system he has made available, and Ali, the president of the second association, by continuous medical aid. Regarding the latter association, the prosperous Khalils, who have no need of free medical treatment, still continue to challenge Ali's leadership.

Sooner or later, I believe, Ali will realize that to head a family association does not alter his popularity negatively or positively. Likewise, Husain's association might very well be forgotten once his credit system becomes unnecessary. Political leadership is based on the continuous provision of services, not on prestige-carrying positions, such as the leadership of a family association. What family associations in fact do is initially to 'feature' (to borrow a word from archaeology) a potential leader. I would like to stress the word 'initially', for here lies the sociological significance of family associations, as well as the reasons for their transient, non-enduring character. As an anti-lineage organization, based on genealogical mythologies that can be stretched lineally, and therefore horizontally, as far as the founder wants them to be, a family association simply lays down the initial foundations, the frame of reference, for political action and for leadership. Whether or not the founder stands up to the test of leadership is largely determined by his personal ability afterwards. In either case, whether the leader succeeds or fails, the association loses the initial function for which it was set up. Accordingly, it may be suspended, forgotten, or it may sink into a social club, as did the Bustani family association soon after it was founded towards the turn of this century.

The sociological significance of family associations lies precisely in the transient, non-lasting, relationships they create as non-groups. They allow for new broad-based leaderships to appear in the face of petty, but lasting, inter-lineage rivalries. Family associations are anti-group organizations where groups (in this case lineages) dwarf individual mobility. The non-lasting relationships that they create act as a lubricant that helps to transfer a man from one status to another, either from an ordinary family member to a spokesman, or from a leader of a branch to a family leader, and then to a national leader. Once the transfer from one status to another is achieved, the association loses its function and is accordingly forgotten: hence, its non-lasting character.

NOTES

1 Eminent social anthropologists, like Firth 1951, p. 17; Evans-Pritchard 1951; Nadel 1951, p. 5; Gluckman 1965, p. 31; Mair 1965, p. 9; and Beattie 1964, p. 13, hold the view that the subject matter of social anthropology is the group defined by enduring, lasting relationships.
2 An example of such exaggeration can be found in Samih Farsoun's paper, 'Family structure and society in modern Lebanon', 1970, pp. 257–307.
3 The data for this paper were collected between January 1967 and December 1969 in the suburbs of Chiyah and Ghobeire. I would like to thank the committee of the Middle East Area Program for granting me the necessary funds to carry out the research, and Ibtissam Sa'id, Abdullah Abu-Habib, Hiyam Shadid, and Leila Jannoun for assisting me in collecting the census data. I would like also to thank Suha Zakhariyya and Michel Kandis for the tabulation of the data.
4 The figure 575 is taken from Ibrahim al-Aswad's book, *Dalīl Lubnān*, p. 592. Ibrahim was the secretary of the tax-collecting office in B'abda town (Mount Lebanon), about ten miles from Chiyah. The other figures, 5,000 households and 30,000 people, are taken from the census carried out during my research project between 1967 and 1969.
5 See Ibrahim al-Aswad's book, *Dalīl Lubnān*, p. 592.
6 The new Shī'ite families say that they were the first to use the word Ghobeire, derived from dust (*ghabra*), in reference to the dust which used to be blown up in the area by the training of horses. Admitting that the word Ghobeire is derived from dust, the old families assert that the dust was caused by the horses of the Shihabi emirs, not by the horses of the race-course, which would, of course, mean that the word Ghobeire was used long before the settlement of the Shī'ites from Baalbec in the area.
7 For the political roles of the old families versus the newcomers, see Khuri 1969.

8   The fact that political ambitions are wrapped up in benevolent objectives explains
    the high frequency with which family solidarity and welfare are included in the
    constitution of family associations, as tabulated in Samir Khalaf's unpublished paper,
    pp. 19 and 20.
9   For the meaning of primary, secondary and tertiary sections, see Peters 1959, pp. 29–53;
    1967, p. 269.

REFERENCES

Aswad, Ibrahim al-. 1910. *Dalīl Lubnān* (in Arabic). Beirut, Catholic Press.
Barnes, J. A. 1962. 'African models in New Guinea Highlands', *Man*, Vol. 62, pp. 5–9.
Beattie, J. 1964. *Other Cultures: Aims, Methods, and Achievements in Social Anthropology.*
    London, Cohen and West.
Boissevain, J. 1968. 'The place of non-groups in the social sciences', *Man*, Vol. 3, pp. 542–56.
Evans-Pritchard, E. E. 1951. *Social Anthropology*. London, Cohen and West.
Firth, R. W. 1951. *Elements of Social Organization*. London.
Farsoun, Samih K. 1970. 'Family structure and society in modern Lebanon', in Louise
    Sweet (ed.), *Peoples and Cultures of the Middle East*, Vol. 2. New York, Natural History
    Press.
Gluckman, Max. 1965. *Politics, Law and Ritual in Tribal Society*. Oxford, Basil Blackwell.
Homans, G. C. 1951. *The Human Group*. London, Routledge and Kegan Paul.
Khalaf, Samir. 1968. 'Family association in Lebanon', unpublished MS., Sociology and
    Anthropology Department, American University of Beirut.
Khuri, Fuad I. 1969. 'The changing class structure in Lebanon', *The Middle East Journal*,
    Winter, pp. 29–44.
    1972. 'Sectarian loyalty among rural migrants in two Lebanese suburbs: A stage between
    family and national allegiance', in R. T. Antoun and I. Harik (eds). *Rural Politics and
    Social Change in the Middle East*. Bloomington, Indiana University Press, pp. 198–209.
Leach, E. R. 1961. *Pul Eliya: A village in Ceylon: A study of land tenure and kinship.*
    Cambridge University Press.
Mair, Lucy. 1965. *An Introduction to Social Anthropology*. Oxford, Clarendon Press.
Nadel, S. F. 1951. *The Foundations of Social Anthropology*. London, Cohen and West.
Peters, E. L. 1963. 'Aspects of rank and status among Muslims in a Lebanese village', in
    Julian Pitt-Rivers (ed.), *Mediterranean Countrymen*. Paris, Mouton.
    1967. 'Some structural aspects of the feud among the camel-herding bedouin of
    Cyrenaica', *Africa*, Vol. 37. pp. 261–82.

3 Lineage endogamy among Maronite mountaineers

Robert Cresswell

One of the more puzzling phenomena which arise in Middle Eastern anthropological research is that of lineage endogamy caused by patrilateral parallel-cousin marriage. This type of union, which occurs preferentially in only 15 of 552 societies recorded in the Human Relations Area Files, somehow does not seem unusual when encountered among the nomadic camel-raising bedouins where it appears to have originated, but does require rather more explanation when found among Christian sedentary agriculturists of the Lebanese mountains. Marrying your father's brother's daughter (FaBrDa) may be an expression of the xenophobic tendencies characteristic of cereal-cultivating areas (Haudricourt 1964), but lineage endogamy contains an inherent obstacle to the acquisition or reinforcement of status in an agricultural society, because theoretically no new land can ever be added to the family's or lineage's possessions through marriage alliances. However, the methods used for colonizing new village territory in the Lebanese mountains would seem to provide a satisfactory explanation for the adoption of this practice and its resultant effects on family structure and relationships.

Probably because the phenomenon is puzzling – one is tempted to add, at least to Western educated scholars – it has not suffered from lack of treatment in anthropological prose, nor is there a dearth of sociological explanation for its existence. The best summary to date of the literature is in Khuri (1970), who points out that the different approaches to this problem have been statistical, functional or cultural. The first approach merely establishes the custom as a significant fact, and the author contributes support to this from his own research. The functional approach explains this type of marriage either as a means of preserving property, or of increasing political power, or of strengthening the segmentary character of the unilineal system of descent among the Arabs. Even if one glosses over the inherent weaknesses of these arguments, Khuri very rightly points out that any marriage system does this, and some much more efficiently than the one under discussion. And, one might add, without summoning up the spectre of circular reasoning intrinsic in the last proposition, for segmentary systems come into being because of unilinear descent groups

101

and preferential or prescribed cousin marriage; therefore the origin of the latter can scarcely be to reinforce the former. Finally, in the cultural approach some authors explain FaBrDa marriage in terms of family honour and modesty. Khuri makes short shrift of these arguments by demonstrating the incompleteness of the ethnographic data on which they are usually based, and makes the point once again that in any case other systems of marriage regulations perform the same task. His own proposition, amply documented, is that this type of marriage is the only one in the Middle East context which not only does not create contradictory roles in the family, but actually intensifies family relationships. Affinal relationships are the same as consanguineal ones.

This is not the place to argue this proposition, which will be done in the context of a work in preparation treating the question. What one can say here is that the author proposes an analysis of the result of this marriage rule and not of its genesis. He does not in any case explain why a goal which is a general trait of all human societies – intensifying human relationships – is sought in only a few societies (approximately one in forty, or 2.5 per cent) through this very particular means, i.e. patrilateral-parallel-cousin marriage. It would seem that the only reasonable explanation is one that would take into account relationships between the fact itself and other aspects of society, particularly the means of production. This paper will try to point out the structural concordance between FaBrDa's marriage and land tenure, at least in one specific locality. One other point should be brought out, although it will scarcely be more than mentioned here, concerning the elementary or complex nature of the phenomenon. Levi-Strauss esteems that only cross-cousin marriage merits the name of elementary structure, parallel-cousin marriage being an epiphenomenon of other more complex social processes. Although it does not create reciprocal links by exchanging women between two or more discrete social groups, and is for this reason reducible *qua* phenomenon to other phenomena, parallel-cousin marriage is elementary insofar as the analytical model one derives from it is non-reducible, and especially insofar as the relationship itself to other social factors is concerned. This then is the whole frame of reference for what follows, which is conceived of as an ethnographical contribution to the problem of whether this trait can be reduced to an elementary social process or whether, as most authors seem to suggest (Barth 1954, Rosenfeld 1957, *et al.*), it is simply the result of other social forces at work. Except peripherally, an anthropological discussion of the problem itself will not be undertaken.

The documents on which this paper is based come from a Christian village in the Chouf in Lebanon, near one of the traditional centres of bygone Druze power. The genealogies were collected orally by the author during a monographical study of the community and present the defects of most peasant genealogies from this region in being shallow and undated. Wives' and sisters' names were elicited, not always successfully, at the time the genealogy was collected, and some additional names and dates were available from the census books kept by the 'mayor'.

The village has been Maronite only for the last hundred years or so. Until the massacres of 1860 the village territory was owned by the Druze, although it seems probable that some of the inhabitants were Christians from north Lebanon, living in the village as sharecroppers. It might be useful to recall that the southward expansion of the Maronites from the seventeenth century onwards took the form in Druze territory of supplying Christian artisans, labourers and sharecroppers for Druze landlords. Following the Egyptian invasion in 1831 the position of the Christian community in general was greatly improved. They gained military power and social status, one of whose aspects was increased economic means enabling them to buy up property from the Druze, impoverished by their struggle against the Egyptian hegemony. Already by 1841 Christians had become restless under Druze nominal power, and Druze resentful of Christian material gains and what they regarded as upstart chaffer. When armed conflict broke out for the third time in 1860, it led to large-scale bloodshed and the intervention of the European powers. In Deir el Qamar, adjoining the village from which the documents discussed in this paper are drawn, 2,600 local Christian villagers were disarmed by the Turkish garrison and slaughtered by the Druze. Subsequently indemnity was offered by the Turkish government to the victims, part of which was paid.

Community history has it that, following the massacres, the ancestors of the present-day lineages chased the Druze out. What is more likely is that part of the village was given to Christian families as indemnity and that the remaining Druze preferred to emigrate. Certain pottery fragments and coins, and a mention of the name of the village in a twelfth-century charter of the Teutonic Order, led one to believe that the site has been occupied for at least 800 years.

The site is some 250 acres of steep mountainside (550 m.) where the only possible cultivation is on terraces. The natural vegetation is an attenuated form of Mediterranean maquis, with possibilities of piñon pine, even cedar, were it not for man and goats. The climate is mild, with hot dry summers, and clement humid winters. The villagers practise two-stage agriculture, cultivating vegetables and a little wheat, often under peach, apple, plum and olive trees. Vines are grown and the grapes used for making jam or distilling araq. One of the original two watermills in the village is still in use, owned by the mayor, with two wheels, one connected to grindstones, adjustable for flour or *burghul*, the other to a blade for chopping olives. The mill also houses the press for extracting oil from the chopped olives. The mill is at the bottom of the slope, and the water it uses comes from two springs at the top. The land around the springs is privately owned, but the water itself is apportioned among the lineages and families according to a schedule which is not always strictly adhered to, and was therefore the cause of a certain amount of friction during the time the field-work was being carried out. Most of the families own a cow and the wealthier ones an ox also. These are used in co-operative work arrangements among nuclear families of a lineage for pulling the scratch plough along the terraces. Only one or two families do not derive their subsistence from their own land or satisfy their cash requirements from the sale of their fruit and sometimes their vegetable produce, and are obliged to work other people's land for shares.

There are approximately 550 people (300 men and 250 women) living permanently in the village. It is not possible to make this figure more accurate because of the difficulty of defining the status of some of the people listed in the census book or on the genealogies, and for various reasons the field-work did not include a house-by-house census. This means that some people that actually live in the village will not be mentioned as inhabitants. For instance, it was only by working with photographs of the different clusters of houses taken from the opposite slope of the wadi that the author discovered the existence of a household consisting of a Muslim man married to a village Maronite daughter. Or again, some persons belonging to prominent lineages are considered as inhabitants, in spite of the fact that they rarely inhabit the village for more than a few weeks during the summer. However, all of the very large colony (at least 200) of immigrants living in Tucoman, Argentina, have been excluded, and the figure of 550 is accurate within 5 per cent of the whole, and within 2 per cent as far as the men are concerned. Births of girls and the existence of women having married out of the lineages are very inaccurately reported. One might add that the age pyramid presents no real anomalies except for the practical dearth of villagers born between 1915 and 1920.

There are ten lineage names in the village. We can call them, in the order of their arrival in the village as tradition has it: Yusuf, Suleiman, Assaad, Hanna, Jeris, Selim, Maroun, Mansour, Boutros, and Elias. The Suleimans are the most numerous, and they share power in village affairs with the Jeris's and the Marouns. In point of fact power and prestige might be said to be diffused generally among the Suleimans, and concentrated among the heads of the families in the case of the Jeris's and the Marouns. The head of the family of the Marouns might be called the head of the village, although the official 'mayor' is the head of the Yusufs, whose lineage is really reduced to a single extended family. The prestige of the Suleimans is further shown by the fact that the mayor signs his name as Suleiman, as does the Hanna family, one of whose members is the village custodian of Church-endowed property, the wāq waqf. This is possible because the mayor married into the Suleiman family, on the one hand, and, on the other, because one of the sons of Suleiman was named Yusuf. The Hannas are also known as Suleimans because one of their ancestresses was the daughter of the original Suleiman. This pre-emption of a prestige-bearing name is possible because of what Peters has so aptly called an 'area of ambiguity' in Arabic genealogies (Peters 1963). However, its use here to attach one extended family, the Yusufs, and one very small lineage, the Hannas, to the most important lineage in the village containing the principal

3. *Lineage endogamy among Maronite mountaineers* 105

property owners, is almost the reverse of what Peters described as obtaining in his Shī'ite south Lebanon village. There, the 'Learned Families', to preserve their power, used the 'area of ambiguity', that took place several generations back, where relationships and names are sufficiently obscure as to render possible the adjunction of new names, to adopt into their lineage any newcomer once he had attained a certain status and power. Here, the outside family itself has taken advantage of the inherent confusion in these genealogies to attach itself to the important village lineage. Arabic speakers' use of teknonymy helps make this possible, in a way, for the Suleimans often call themselves, and are called by others, Abū Yusufs (the father of Yusuf), as do the Yusufs themselves.

In this setting what can be said of lineage endogamy? Table 1 gives for the six

TABLE 1   *Types of marriages in the different lineages of the village*

	Suleiman		Jeris		Maroun		Mansour		Boutros		Assaad		Total	
	No.	%	No.	%	No.	%	No.	%	No.	%	No.	%	No.	%
FaBrDa	6	7	2	4			2	9	2	5	6	14	18	6
FaBrDa including generation differences	16	19	4	9			3	13	8	18			37	13
FaFaBaDaDa FaFaBrSoDa	9	11			2	4							11	4
1st–3rd patrilateral parallel-cousin	28	33	6	11	3	6	3	13	8	18	6	14	54	19
1st–3rd parallel-cousin	30	35	8	17	3	6	3	13	8	18	8	19	60	21
Any 1st–3rd cousin	34	40	8	17	5	10	3	13	9	20	8	19	67	23
Restricted lineage	38	45	9	20	10	21	3	13	9	20	8	19	77	27
Extended lineage	43	51	9	20	10	21	3	13	9	20	8	19	82	28
Village	62	73	28	61	33	69	15	65	26	59	20	46	184	64
Region	73	86	38	83	40	83	21	91	37	84	34	79	243	84
Lebanon	75	88	42	91	47	98	22	96	44	100	41	95	271	94
Other	10	12	4	9	1	2	1	4			2	5	18	6
Total	85		46		48		23		44		43		289	

genealogies comprising more than one or two extended families the numbers and percentages of the different types of marriage practised over approximately the last 65 years. Several comments can be made on the figures of this table. First of all, the overall figure of 13 per cent for FaBrDa marriage in the six genealogies is well within the range of percentages reported from Muslim communities, as is shown in Table 2. Here a digression is necessary to justify assimilating FaFaBrDa and FaBrSoDa marriages to FaBrDa unions in the commentary, these marriages being ordinarily tabulated separately and only

TABLE 2   *Percentages of different types of marriage in Middle East communities*

Marriage with	Suleiman Village	Artas[a]	S. Leb.[b]	Israel[c]	Munsif[d]	Chibayish[e]	Tur'an[f]	Beirut[g]
FaBrDa	7	6	13	15	13	3	38	11, 3[h]
FaFaBrDa	19[i]	13	19			7		13, 6
FaBrSoDa								
FaFaBrDaDa	30	17	26					13, 6
FaFaBrSoDa								
All patri-lateral parallel-cousins	33	19		37				17.5, 6
Lineage	51	28	34		51[j]	28	51	32, 21[h]
Village	73	64	57	60	82	71	82	72, 58
n equals	85	289	264	115	485	84	116	578, 211 3166, 2202

[a] Granqvist, 1931, p. 194.
[b] Peters, 1963, pp. 177–9. The figures are for the Learned Families.
[c] Cohen, 1965, p. 111.
[d] Gulick, 1955, pp. 120–3.
[e] Salim, 1962, p. 49.
[f] Rosenfeld, 1957, p. 36.
[g] Khuri, 1970.
[h] The first figure is for Muslims, the second for Christians.
[i] All higher-order percentages are inclusive of lower order ones.
[j] Within the *hamūla*.

FaBrDa being used in computing percentages. The first and most obvious reason is because the villagers consider them equivalent. Time and again the author was told someone had married his FaBrDa when the genealogy showed it was his FaFaBrDa or his FaBrSoDa. However, objections to transferring this village usage to the analytical plane can be raised, mainly on two counts. For one thing, a first cousin is not a first cousin once removed, and from a purely formal point of view, in any structural model the two terms cannot be co-extensive. As a corollary, the same differential statuses and reciprocal roles do not obtain between the two kin and Ego, although the difference is more one of degree than one of kind. Secondly, the statistics usually quoted in discussions about this problem are based on the exact definition and not the classificatory one.

The latter objection, although perfectly valid, is the more easily disposed of. Many authors give percentages first in terms of true FaBrDa marriage, then of lineage endogamy without specifying the degree of kinship. In this case it is possible for the purposes of comparison to use the figures of 6 per cent and 27 per cent given in the table.

The reply to the first objection can be made in three steps. First of all, it must be emphasized that this type of marriage with a generation difference conforms to the cultural norm in all respects save the strictly formal. The age differences between spouses have the same range and direction as in other marriages, and relationships are the same as in true FaBrDa marriage. Secondly there is no difference between the two types as far as a change or an intensification of relationships within the family is concerned. First cousins and first cousins-once-removed live by the same book of social rules, although the barriers limiting sanctioned behaviour are slightly weaker in the latter case. Finally, and this is connected partly to what has just been said, the sociological results are strictly identical in the two cases. From an economic point of view the same prestations take place, the same religious prohibition applies to both, and the same relationships between the two spouses and their respective in-laws are established. This is not true for marriages between second or third cousins.

Thus, although a dissymmetrical generation relationship between spouses does create structural confusion in the formal model, by introducing a concept of marriage classes through the use of classificatory terminology, into a system using descriptive terminology to designate preferential marriage mates, this difference does not seem pertinent here. The point under discussion is why this type of marriage exists at all in a Christian community of sedentary agriculturists; why a Maronite mountaineer addresses his wife as *bint 'amm*. The hypothesis proposed in this paper is that this type of marriage is linked to problems of land tenure, and that therefore it is legitimate procedure to treat it for its sociological implications and content and not only as a statistical form. This paper is not intended as an exercise in kinship algebra, but as a study of the correlations between two aspects of social reality, and, as Khuri points out, statistics are descriptive and not explanatory.

To recapitulate, as Table 2 shows, statistical FaBrDa's marriage is high for a Christian village and at the lower end of the range of Muslim percentages, which is normal. The same holds true in the village for sociological FaBrDa's marriage comprising a generation dissymmetry, as well as lineage and village endogamy. In this context the 19 per cent of FaBrDa's marriage among the Suleimans stands out, accounting for 43 per cent of this type in the genealogies, as does 33 per cent for all parallel-cousin marriages from first to third cousins and 51 per cent for extended lineage marriages, accounting for respectively 52 per cent and 61 per cent of these types among the genealogies (extended lineage means the two extended families who have attached themselves to the Suleimans are included).

Nineteen per cent for FaBrDa's marriage and 51 per cent for lineage endogamy, then, are high figures, but analysis will show they should probably be higher if effective possibilities are taken into account, for one of the consequences of narrowing the definition of the preferential marriage mate is to restrict the possibilities. One of the difficulties of making this kind of analysis, of course, is the paucity of birth dates in the genealogies. However, it is possible to calculate minimum figures. If one takes the Suleiman genealogy, one finds 19 men and 14 women descended from 5 brothers, and 29 men and 34 women

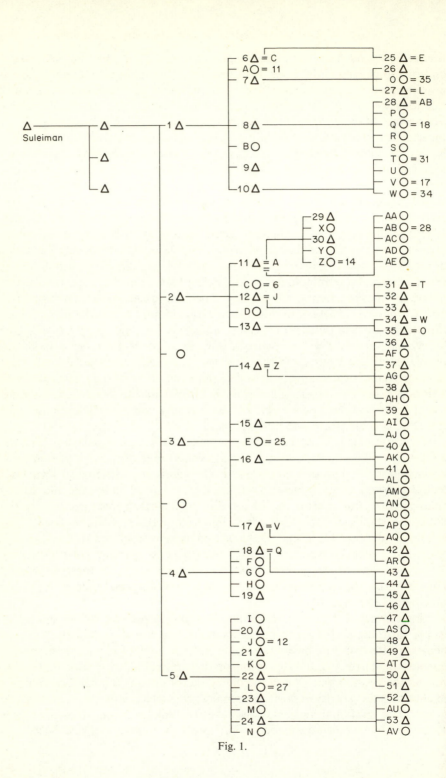

Fig. 1.

descended from these latter (cf. Fig. 1). By postulating that a two-year age difference separates siblings and twenty years a parent and his first child, it can be calculated that 12 second-generation men and 12 second-generation women can marry a patrilateral parallel-cousin, where the man is between 0 and 15 years older than the woman. Six people do, which gives us a percentage of 25 per cent of possible FaBrDa marriages which actually did take place.

One last calculation can be made, but here one must count the number of marriages and not the number of people who marry, so that the figures are not strictly comparable, even if mutually adjusted. It so happens we know that E married 25 on the diagram and that both were born in 1895. It would seem from this, and also by tracing a line through the genealogy to separate those born before 1900 from those born afterwards (31 dates for the three generations) that the natural generation skewing due to age sequences which occurs in any genealogy, cuts this one in half as far as marriage possibilities are concerned. In other words, in the second and third generation fourteen girls could have married a FaBrSo or FaFaBrSo and eight did, which is 57 per cent. This figure is, of course, not accurate, but does give an idea of the real importance of this kind of marriage.

Fifty-seven per cent is an approximation, but it does not seem conjectural to postulate that of every two possibilities of FaBrDa's marriage that arose in the Suleiman lineage since 1860 one actually took place. One should point out here, although it is not really pertinent to the discussion, that if the same relative position of Christian and Muslim populations obtains when one sets up the statistics as a function of what is possible as when one calculates un-adjusted percentages, then the practice of this type of marriage among Muslim villagers must be quite important. Important enough in any case to nullify the argument put forth by some students of kinship that parallel-cousin marriage is a special case, and, because it must be treated relatively with statistics and not absolutely in classes, cannot be considered an elementary structure. In any case 50 per cent conformity to what was, after all, originally an extrinsic cultural norm, although part of the world view intrinsic to the spoken language, and specifically forbidden by the official religion, calls for an explanation.

This latter cannot be only in terms of the phenomenon itself, for then this only shows up as an epiphenomenon on the broader sociological level. A purely structural–functional approach can only bear witness to the existence of this type of marriage, postulate that it serves some purpose, and then point out that in such and such a society it results in the intensification of family relationships, or in keeping property within the lineage, etc. In other words, to analyse the phenomenon in its own terms is to abstract from social relations a fact, which cannot explain itself. On the other hand, to analyse the phenomenon in terms of its structural relationship with other phenomena, which comes partly to analys-ing the relationships between models, is to abstract a function, which admits of an explanation.

To return to the Suleimans, they have practised to a very large extent, up until World War II, let us say, lineage endogamy. They are also the most important lineage in the village. What relationship is there between these two facts? To try to answer this question we shall have to bring into relief the structural implications of FaBrDa marriage. The basic form of cross-cousin marriage requires a model containing four persons in each generation two pairs with a brother and sister in each (cf. Figure 2). At each generation there is

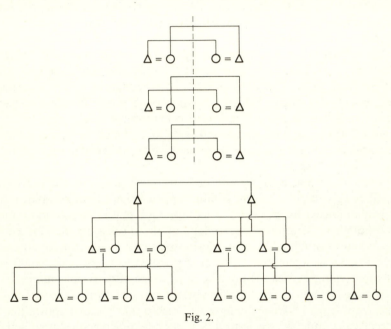

Fig. 2.

either MoBrDa and So, or FaSiDa and So, available. If the society also posses-ses clan (or lineage) exogamy, whether descent is reckoned in matrilines or patrilines, this model still answers all conceivable exigencies. However, in parallel-cousin marriage (whether matri- or patrilateral) the necessity of provid-ing a brother for every male in the position of father in the model means that this latter must provide for the doubling of the number of persons at each succeeding generation, if all exigencies are to be answered. Now, it is interesting to note that this form of marriage seems to have arisen among herders of large animals, in other words among people whose wealth does not derive from the yearly fructifying of a fixed capital, but from the periodic doubling of capital itself. So that the production of wealth parallels in its mode of operation the demographic evolution of the population benefiting from this wealth. This is the contrary of the conditions obtaining in a society of agriculturists, among whom it might almost be said that some form of exogamy has to prevail, if only to make possible the acquisition of new capital. It is not suggested that this parallelism reveals the consciously thought-out origin of this type of marriage, but it seems reasonable to think that it is not entirely fortuitous that the social institution of marriage operates in the same manner as the production of wealth.

This proposed explanation, however, raises another and more serious problem. How is it that this type of marriage was adopted, along with the Arabic language, by Maronite mountaineers, probably during the course of the seventeenth century? Here the answer is suggested by a study carried out in a village in the north of Lebanon, where it was possible to analyse village genealogies and land tenure. Properties had been resurveyed within the ten years preceding the field-work, and a formal written genealogy existed in the village. The cadastral survey shows that today one of the four principal lineages possesses much more than a quarter of the village territory. This was originally divided in three equal parts, and the lineage in question, being one of the four sons of a man to whom was allotted one-third of the territory, should theoretically therefore have only one-half. Although it is not possible to study marriage patterns here, since it is a written genealogy and no women's names occur and few are remembered, this lineage had many more sons than daughters, and land tenure analysis shows that lineage endogamy succeeded in capturing more land for this principal lineage than for others. This, in turn, was made possible because village territory was not completely parcelled out at the beginning, and was therefore valueless as such, for mountain land here has to be built up in terraces for farming, to become capital. In other words, capital was not fixed, so that the lineage with the most sons, and practising lineage endogamy, could, by putting more and more land into cultivation, increase its capital at each succeeding generation in the same way that capital represented by animals increases. The same remark could be made about the traditional system of land tenure in the Syrian plains: *mushā'a*. Here only the community as a whole owned the land, rights to cultivate it being decided periodically by drawing lots, each one of these usually representing one work unit. The lineage with the largest number of constituent families acquires more potential wealth and keeps it in the lineage by practising lineage endogamy.

This theory, conceived to explain the ease with which Arab kinship terminology and marriage customs (a wife is called *bint 'amm*, FaBrDa) were adopted when Arabic replaced Syriac – the kinship terminology of this language apparently indicates MoBrDa marriage, would seem to be confirmed by what has happened in the village that concerns us here. Although lineage endogamy, and concomitant FaBrDa marriage, appear to have almost died out in most modern Maronite villages in the Lebanese mountains, in any case since 1860 when the Turks opened the gates to emigration, in this village we find high percentages for this preferential marriage in the twentieth century. This could arise from a special situation which is limited to this region. The Maronite, in contradistinction to the old Druze, village on the same site is of very recent origin, so that since 1860, when the Maronite villagers were apparently given the site, the same situation obtains as obtained in the early nineteenth century in the north of Lebanon. The unconscious drive to put under cultivation, or to reclaim, as much of the land as possible would have encouraged very highly lineage endogamy. That it succeeds, is shown by the success of the Suleimans. Of course, there is a certain feedback involved. For lineage endogamy to be successful, where wealth is in land and not in animals, families must be large, and where families are large more possibilities for FaBrDa marriage occur. One might add that this trend is also reinforced by prevailing customs of the exchange of gifts at marriage. Although it is extremely difficult to glean from the literature, and from old people's memories, it would seem that the Arab custom of *mahr*, or bride price, did not carry over with the language. And this makes more sense, again where land is concerned and not animals. However, the small terrace, which seems to have been given as dower to the girl when she married, was, and still is, often replaced by a cash sum.

A word remains to be said about the effect of this lineage endogamy on family relationships. It reinforces them, of course, to the extent also that a lineage with endogamous tendencies tends to cluster in one section of the village. In our village there are three quarters, or *ḥāra, al-ḥārat al-sha'wiyya* (farthest point) with about 20 houses contains the lineages of Boutros and Mansour; *ḥārat al-kanīsa* (the church) with 40 houses, those of Maroun, Jeris and Selim; and, finally, *al-ḥarat al-sharqiyya* (eastern) with 60 houses, those of Suleiman, Yusuf and Assaad. The grouping of lineage houses has an effect on an immediate level, that of visiting. Within certain limits lineage members enter all houses as if they were their own, insofar as partaking of meals, for instance, is concerned.

There is one field, that of relationships between the sexes at a same age level, in which family behaviour would seem to be changed by this type of marriage. It would be more appropriate, perhaps, to speak of inter-family attitudes, for the change concerns the relationships between groups of cousins. In societies where all cousin-marriage is forbidden, in other words is considered incestuous, there can be no ambivalence as to sanctioned behaviour between siblings and cousins of the opposite sex. No potential spouse is to be found in this group, so that equivocal behaviour is, and always will be, deviant. If family honour is crystallized in women, only a stranger to the group can sully it without violating the incest taboo. Cross-cousin marriage engenders a certain ambivalence, for some of the group of siblings and cousins now become not only potential, but prescribed spouses. A man can therefore be called on to treat differently two groups of women who stand in the same relationship to him, for towards one of these groups what is today proscribed and incestuous, tomorrow becomes sanctioned behaviour. However, cross-cousin marriage is usually accompanied by exogamy, at least as far as the local group is concerned, whatever the clan or section arrangement may be, so that ambivalent reactions concern an outside group. Now quite a different situation obtains in lineage endogamy with parallel-cousin marriage. The members of the opposite sex, whose relationships with one do not have a clearly-defined nature, since they are subject to an eventual or potential change, dwell within the local group. In a word, the stranger is in our midst. Even if one solves the problem by setting up formal relationships, as is the case between parallel-cousins in Middle East society, indeed between cross-cousins as well, the ambivalence remains.

Thus the lineage, taken as a unit, has to defend its honour, as represented by its women, against the members of the group itself, as well as against outsiders. It can be hypothesized, subject, of course, to verification by subsequent research, that the division of village life into two worlds, male and female, although not nearly so strict in this community as in comparable Muslim communities, derives partly from this necessity. The Arabic maxim, 'I and my brother against our cousins, my cousins and I against the stranger', while expressing the fission by segments which normally occurs within this type of kinship system, also translates an elementary fact of life in its first term.

This short discussion of patrilateral parallel-cousin marriage hardly scratches the surface of the larger problem, that of the origin and the structural ramifications of this type of marriage, although it may possibly add some new data as to the narrower problem of lineage endogamy among Maronite mountaineers. However, the discussion does suggest that analysing the structure of this kinship and marriage system merely in terms of itself, as an autonomous phenomenon, can only lead to treating it as an epiphenomenon when relating it to other aspects of the society in which it is found. In other words, the structure of parallel-cousin marriage can only be fruitfully analysed in correlation with other deep structures, but not by itself, for this latter procedure freezes the phenomenon, which is then related to other social processes as a static fact and not as a process. This necessarily raises insoluble, and, one might add, minor, problems of unidirectional influence. For instance, to set up the Arab kinship terminology as a static phenomenon raises the question of the meaning of *'amm*: has this term primarily a kinship significance with other meanings derivative, or is it used as a kinship term because of its other meanings? To treat *'amm* as a structural, and therefore dynamic, element of the different sociological constellations where it is found: kinship and property, family and polity, prestige and leadership, etc, is to render the problem of its primordial meaning irrelevant, as it should be, for understanding the functioning of the group.

Finally, it would seem a plausible working hypothesis for future research to postulate that this type of marriage can only operate fully under certain specific economic conditions, whether these concern land or herding.

REFERENCES

Ayoub, M. R. 1959. 'Parallel cousin marriage and endogamy', *Southeastern Journal of Anthropology*, Vol. 15, No. 3.

Barth, F. 1954. 'Father's brother's daughter marriage in Kurdistan', *Southwestern Journal of Anthropology*, Vol. 10, No. 2.

Cohen, A. 1965. *Arab border villages in Israel*. Manchester University Press.

Granqvist, H. 1931. *Marriage conditions in a Palestinian village*. Vol. I. Helsingfors.

Gulick, J. 1955. *Social structure and culture change in a Lebanese village*, Viking Fund Publications in Anthropology, No. 21. New York.

Haudricourt, A. G. 1964. 'Nature et culture dans la civilisation de l'igname, l'origine des clones et des clans', *L'Homme*. Vol. IV, No. 1.

Khuri, Fuad. 1970. 'Parallel cousin marriage reconsidered: a Middle Eastern practice that nullifies the effects of marriage on the intensity of family relationships'. *Man*. Vol. 5. No. 4.

Peters, E. L. 1963. 'Aspects of rank and status among Muslims in a Lebanese village', in Pitt-Rivers, J. (ed.), *Mediterranean Countrymen*. Paris, Mouton.

Rosenfeld, H. 1957. 'An analysis of marriage and marriage statistics for a Moslem and Christian Arab village', *International Archives of Ethnography*, Vol. 48.

Salim, S. M. 1962. *Marsh dwellers of the Euphrates delta*. London.

4 Social and economic factors in explanation of the increased rate of patrilineal endogamy in the Arab village in Israel

Henry Rosenfeld

University of Haifa, and the Hebrew University, Jerusalem

THE PROBLEM OF AN INCREASED RATE OF PATRILINEAL ENDOGAMY

In 1954 I investigated the marriage patterns of a Muslim and Christian Arab village in lower Galilee in Israel. I analysed the total number and types of marriages (578 Muslim, 211 Christian) that had taken place over a period of from four to five generations. The subsequent ten years saw great changes in the village: for instance, most of the men worked outside the village and became totally dependent on wages for their livelihood; agriculture had become mechanized and only a handful of men worked their own land; the number of children in school had increased; there was a modern health service; and contact with modern, partly industrialized, cities had been simplified by efficient transport.[1] Consequently, in 1964 and again in 1969 I re-examined the marriage statistics for the same village (248 Muslim and 90 Christian marriages) for the ten-year period 1954–63 and for the six-year period 1964–9 in order to see if and how marriage patterns had changed.[2]

Among other things, I found that the percentage of patrilateral endogamous marriages, those made by men with women of their own patrilineage (*ḥamūla*), had almost doubled among the Muslims and had doubled among the smaller group of Christians, and the number of marriages with women from the village outside the groom's patrilineage, and with women outside the village, had decreased proportionately. We present the figures later on. In this brief paper we attempt to explain this remarkable growth of endogamous, 'traditional' marriage (and the converse decrease in village and outside-the-village marriage) in the face of the pronounced social, economic and political changes that villagers have experienced over the last generation. As a matter of interest, this increased rate of endogamy was mentioned in our earlier article (Rosenfeld 1957, pp. 43–4):

It would be expected, due to modern developments in Palestine and latterly in the State of Israel, that because of greater industrialization and contacts, stranger [outside the village] marriage would increase. It seems, however, that the reverse is true...Clan marriage...

is the gainer, increasing…to 48.1%. Industrialization in Israel…has not encompassed Arab villagers to any great degree, and there is at present little work outside the villages for Arab labourers…Stranger marriage apparently will not increase until the villagers more directly participate in the social and economic changes which occur in the State as a whole. Such a process could well be investigated in another ten or twenty years when the effect of the new State of Israel can be more easily measured (pp. 43–4).

We do not attempt to provide one single answer for the phenomenon of an increased rate of endogamy in the Arab village. The fact of increased endogamy is simple enough, but the historical–social background against which it takes place is complex. Our explanations are both macro- and micro-sociological. In regard to the former, which are defined as factors which have historically determined a life condition, we analyse the socio-economic condition of the Arab villagers in Israel in order to see in what respects the system has changed. In regard to the latter, which are defined as the immediate operative causes that explain a social situation, we analyse those internal village conditions and outside factors that affect the marriage system and marriage patterns.

In a recent discussion of change and barriers to change in the family structure in the Arab village in Israel we have emphasized that with all the changes that the Arab villagers are undergoing (and that some 80–90 per cent of the males in the 15–40 age group seek or find employment outside the village and often in the cities is only one of these changes), work outside the village is rarely permanent. Many Arab workers are unskilled, they lack job security, they change jobs often and basically they are no more than migrant labourers who remain village dwellers. Agriculture in the village is becoming mechanized; nevertheless, it is still backward; there is little irrigation compared to Jewish farming; agriculture is not diversified; crops grown are not industrial ones; and the present technological advances only increase the existing surplus village labour and push it outside the village; there is no local village industry. In brief 'the conditions of insecurity in work outside the village, along with dependence on work outside the village, does not free the Arab worker from ongoing dependence on his underdeveloped village. Outside wage labour is not, as yet, an alternative to the village economy and to the village social structure' (Rosenfeld 1968b, p. 739).

The village social structure is one of patrilineages, extended families, internal factionalism, control over women and restriction on their freedom of movement, bride price and so on; i.e. a social structure in keeping with the agrarian, feudal-type, economy of the past and not with the Israeli economy in which the villagers now earn their living. Thus we could say that an ongoing 'residual' peasant social structure, and the marriage system and endogamous marriage which are its main expressions, continue because the villagers are an insecure proletariat outside the village, and backward agriculturists inside it. This is one of the major reasons that we suggested for the high degree of formal continuity of the extended family. It is in fact the marriage system, i.e. control over women and the decision as to whom they shall or shall not be given in marriage, the careful protection of their honour in order to ensure the smooth functioning of the system, and bride price which is an expression of the social and political status of the families contracting the marriage, that anchors the social structure of the Arab village (Rosenfeld 1968b, p. 740). Because of this marriage possibilities can be little different from what they were in the past. Some men might marry women, including Jewish women, whom they met while working outside the village; others might emigrate from Israel and thus escape the marriage system; some again might refuse to marry village women. However, with so few available alternatives most marriages must follow traditional village patterns. The above is, in part, our macro-sociological thesis: we shall return to it later.

In the study on extended families, however, the main point was, that although radical change had not taken place in the Arab village and therefore there were many signs of continuity of the extended family, the breakdown was nevertheless more rapid, there were fewer instances of its inviolability, sons left their fathers sooner, and more sons left more fathers than ever before; it was in fact simply no longer the same family. Therefore, even though we believe the macro-sociological explanation to be valid for the residual Arab village social structure, it is not as it stands, or by itself, sufficient to explain why over the decade and a half from 1954 to 1969 patrilineage marriage endogamy has unmistakably increased and village and outside marriage decreased. For that some micro-sociological explanations are also required.

First, let us look briefly at some of the figures on types of marriage in Palestine–Israel up to 1954. Of the 578 marriages, which were almost invariably patrilocal or virilocal, made by Muslim men (we shall discuss Christian marriages later) in the village over a period of approximately four generations, 182[3] (31.5 per cent) were marriages with women of their own patrilineage; 234 (40.5 per cent) were marriages with women from other patrilineages within the village; 162 (28 per cent) were marriages with women from other villages.

Now let us look at the figures for the period between January 1954 and December 1969, i.e. during the period of changes for the Arabs within the framework of the state of Israel. Of the 248 marriages made by village men during this period 143 (57.7 per cent) were marriages within the patrilineage; 65 (26.2 per cent) were marriages with women from patrilineages other than their own, and 40 (16.1 per cent) were with women from outside the village.[4] We see, statistically, a great increase in endogamous, patrilineage (patrilateral) marriage and a decrease in marriage with women from other patrilineages in the village and with women from other villages or from outside the village. For convenience the figures are tabulated in Table 1. Although our attention is centred on the more numerous Muslim marriages, we also include the figures for the Christian Arabs who form a little more than a quarter of the village population and some of whom also have homes in cities where they work. Their marriage

TABLE 1

		4–5 genera-tions of marriage up to the end of 1953	Marriages of the 18–39 age group up to the end of 1953	Marriages from 1954 to end of 1969	Marriages from 1954–1963 (June)	Marriages from 1963 (July) – 1969
Total number of marriages made by men	Muslims	578	192	248	120	128
	Christians	211	72	90	56	34
Marriages made with women from the same patrilineage as the man	Muslims	182 (31.5%)	92 (48%)	143 (57.7%)	71 (59.1%)	˙72 (56.3%)
	Christians	45 (21.3%)	25 (34.7%)	45 (50%)	32 (57.1%)	13 (38.2%)
Marriages made with women from the village but not of the same patrilineage as the man	Muslims	234 (40.5%)	58 (30.2%)	65 (26.2%)	29 (24.1%)	36 (28.1%)
	Christians	78 (37%)	21 (29,2%)	14 (15.6%)	9 (16.1%)	5 (14.7%)
Marriages made with women from other villages or from cities	Muslims	162 (28%)	42 (21.8%)	40 (16.1%)	20 (16.8%)	20 (15.6%)
	Christians	88 (41.7%)	26 (36.1%)	31 (34.4%)	15 (26.8%)	16 (47.1%)

ceremonies are held in the village; there are no Christian–Muslim village marriages.

In order to see if there are any tendencies to change during the 1954–69 period analysed, the figures (248 Muslim, 90 Christian marriages) are further broken down so as to cover marriages from 1954 to 1963 and those from 1963 to 1969. We show that the increased rate of Muslim endogamy is stable. Although the number (34) of Christian marriages over the last 6–7 years may not be statistically significant, there is a decrease from the high rate of patrilineal endogamy that appeared between 1954 and 1963. Explanations for these tendencies, Muslim and Christian, appear below in our conclusions.

THE MARRIAGE SYSTEM EXPLAINED

We now turn to the social context of Arab village marriage. This is mainly an historical problem: even if we cannot give the exact reasons for the marriage patterns, the latter are obviously related to social causes past and present. We shall describe these and then try to analyse the marriage system and the marriage patterns that still continue by relating them to social causes.

For a few hundred years, up till the last two or three generations, villagers had been reduced to subsistence level and even below; they lived in conditions of backward technology, subject to feudal overlords, tax farmers, merchants and absentee landlords, within an insecure and hostile environment, threatened by nomadic marauders, and liable to transition from village to semi-nomadic life (Rosenfeld 1964). They sometimes sought support from overlords or patrons (effendis, merchants) outside the village, but because of the subordinate status of the peasants such links were weak or temporary. Within the village itself security was found mainly by associating people into groups. This, then, was and still is the object of the marriage system, even in a modern and non-feudal state like Israel where urban notables and feudal overlords are no longer present.

The marriage patterns of the Arab village must be looked at in terms of a total dynamic system. Endogamous patrilineal marriages are the preferred marriages: males have the right to marry their female paternal cousins. A descent line exists: the social and political potential of the lineage is made concrete when female members are not given to outsiders. However, preferences and rights alone do not explain the dynamics of the system. Small lineages, and hence those which lack the strength necessary to attain security or to enjoy the use of resources and gain the status and recognition from power representatives such as overlords and/or officials, forgo their rights to their females and make alliances by giving their women in marriage to stronger lineages. The strongest lineages gain recognition from the larger power and/or government forces outside the village in the form of titles, e.g. *mukhtār*, *shaikh*, or else receive economic advantages, e.g. salaries, tax dispensations, use of additional land, etc. Other lineages compete with the strongest; they seek to improve their reduced status or disadvantaged economic condition; they attempt to reverse the village status and economic hierarchy by gaining favour from the outside power groups, or by using force against the internal power groups.

Sometimes growth of numbers within any single lineage makes it a contending village political and physical force. In combination with its own patrilineal endogamous marriages, a growing lineage also seeks allies by, among other things, giving and taking women in marriage from other lineages. In order to offset a growing force, the leading and perhaps 'titled' lineage must also seek allies; they do so by taking women from, and by giving women to, other lineages with whom they develop a faction. The security network may be extended by making allies of neighbouring villages through a similar use of women in marriages.

In other words, the preferred patrilineal endogamous marriage can never be a single marriage form. Certainly many marriages are not made for political purposes, e.g. cousins are considered the best marriage partners and hence such marriages take on a momentum of their own; polygyny and remarriage are common and mates may be sought from many different places, etc. However, women are not given freely to those from outside the lineage. When women are not given to yesterday's allies then the latter become today's enemies. New interests appear and new factions are generated and the marriage rates for lineages are not the same. Some lineages, especially large ones, contract 50–80 per cent of their marriages endogamously; others have lower rates. We discuss this point later in another context. Here we state that the prime mechanism for seeking security within the village has been the manipulation of women within the marriage system (Rosenfeld 1968a; 1972).

THE MICRO-SOCIOLOGICAL REASONS FOR AN INCREASED RATE OF (PATRILINEAL) ENDOGAMY

Let us now return to our original question. How did it happen that the rate of endogamous marriages in the village we are discussing has almost doubled over the last decade and a half? This question is posed in terms of the definite social and occupational changes taking place in the Arab village, the termination of agrarian-based feudal-type regimes, and the new security situation; that is, in terms of changes in the social causation that originally promoted the described village marriage patterns. First a series of micro-sociological answers to this question are put forward by analysing the social and cultural processes that occur within the village. These explanations are then functionally interrelated.

1. One obvious possible reason for the increased rate of endogamy can be found in the growth of the Israeli Arab population. The annual rates of natural increase per 1,000 inhabitants for Muslims in Palestine during the Mandate were already high: for 1922–5 they were 23.27; for 1941–4 they were 30.71 (*A Survey of Palestine* Vol. 1, 1945, p. 144): for the year 1966 in Israel the rate was 48.9 (*Statistical Abstract of Israel* 1967, p. 53), apparently one of the highest rates of natural increase in the world. The figures for Christian Arabs, most of whom were and are urban, closely approximate to those for the Jews during the Mandate; 1922–5, 20.16; 1941–4, 18.89; 1966, 26; (for the Jews in 1966, 16.1). To put it simply, as the number of available women within the lineage increases, the number of endogamous marriage opportunities also increase.[5] The Arab population in 1967 was 320,000, approximately twice the number of those who remained in Israel after the 1948–9 war.

2. Closely related to this point is the fact that endogamous marriages are preferred marriages. That is, alongside the rights of males to take their female paternal cousins in marriage, the idea is still strong that cousins are good mates; sometimes desirable mates; are understanding and sympathetic partners; can be relied upon; and have all the prestigious qualities implicit in the lineage itself. Song and story conceptualize cousins as lovers. It is a proper marriage.

3. The potential 'marriage community' has changed. As a result of the Israel–Arab war of 1948–9 at least 650,000 Arabs left the area of what is today the state of Israel; in 1949 the Arab population in Israel was approximately 160,000 (roughly 70 per cent Muslim, 20 per cent Christian, 10 per cent Druze). This drastic population change affected certain areas of the country more than others. The lower Galilee, the area in which our village is located, holds the

majority of Arab villages in the country today, the largest concentration of Arab population and large stretches of land are settled by Arabs only.

This means that more of the local Arab social environment has been retained here than elsewhere and the population changes have been less drastic than in some other areas where they have been total or almost so. Nevertheless, in checking marriages over the last four or five generations for the village in question, we find that seventeen villages within a radius of some fifteen miles, from which the villagers formerly took and gave women in marriage, no longer exist (twelve of these villages were all-Muslim and five were mixed Muslim and Christian; some Christian marriages were with women from the Lebanon; a few Muslim marriages were with women from Jordan and Syria; such marriages were no longer possible after 1949). Marriages with 'stranger' women (from villages other than that of the male) were, up to the end of 1953, the smallest marriage category for the Muslims, but nevertheless they comprised close to one-third of their marriages, 28 per cent; for the Christians of the same village it was the highest category, 41.7 per cent. Of the 248 Muslim marriages from 1954 to 1969 only 16.1 per cent were with 'stranger' women. And of the 90 Christian marriages 34.4 per cent were with such women. Even if there are other factors that could be mentioned in partial explanation for a decrease in 'stranger' marriage (e.g. polygyny is formally forbidden in Israel and fewer women, including 'stranger' women, are required for marriages), the changes for the Muslims are striking. (The changes for the Christians who are not polygynous are less definite and there are indications that, following an immediate decline, the former high rate of outside marriages is today increasing. This point is discussed later on p. 132 in the context of Christian urbanization.)

For our purpose we can state that one of the reasons for increased patri-lineage endogamy is the smaller potential 'marriage community' available as a whole; one's own women become increasingly valuable when the demand for women is still high (e.g. high marriage rates for widows and widowers), and the potential source for women has become limited. It follows that marriage alliances with other villages have been severely reduced.

4. At the time of his marriage a man is still a member of an extended family controlled by his father and his marriage is often determined by his father in consort with the latter's brothers, cousins and uncles; their choice may well fall on an available paternal cousin. A young man does not initiate marriage formalities for a bride; marriages are negotiated between family heads or representatives and not between potential spouses on their own.

Today almost all young men earn wages outside the village and enjoy a certain degree of financial independence. It is, at least in part, through the money they themselves earn that the bride price is paid, some furniture purchased and perhaps a room built. Today, in order to marry, the groom is no longer dependent on the returns from a farmstead controlled by his father; and most men leave the father's extended household soon after marriage and set up a separate one. However, the ability to raise the money for a marriage and to provide some security for the new family remains a problem. Some financial help is required from father, brothers and relatives to meet the combined demands of bride price and housing; for the latter a man requires a plot of land on which to build, or a room that has already been built, and these are his father's property.

The marriage age for men may have risen slightly over the years, but it remains, I believe, relatively early. (In 1965 the median marriage age for Muslim men was 23.8, for Christian men 27.3; for Muslim women 19.9, for Christian women 21.2; however, even the median figures do not fully take into account the high rate of remarriage among Arabs, and therefore we do not have correct figures for first marriages. (See *Statistical Abstract of Israel* 1967, p. 59.) The point we wish to make is that *at the time* of his marriage the groom's independence from an extended family is not complete and he is dependent on the property that is under his father's control. In material terms a first marriage for a young man can be dictated by his father and paternal relatives and, as said earlier, they may choose a lineage female for him. Polygynous marriages, for example,[6] usually take place only after age 30 when the man has greater material freedom and can exercise greater personal choice (*Government of Palestine* 1945, pp. 16–17).

Point 4 is a possible structural explanation for the phenomenon of increased village endogamy at the same time as the family, whatever its semblance of formal structural continuity, has undergone definite changes and is, as was mentioned at the beginning of this paper, 'no longer the same family'. Thus the pressures, or reasons, that dictate whom a man will marry and that operate at one structural point of time in a marriage–family career, i.e. at (first) marriage, are 'no longer' the same pressures or reasons that can keep men, after marriage, within the extended family for any length of time.[7]

5. Restrictions are placed on the freedom of movement of women. Women have almost no opportunity to meet men other than those of their lineage branch; they have even less opportunity to make marriage decisions or reach agreement with men of their own choosing, including male lineage members. Women rarely leave the village and when they do they are escorted. (Female teachers have greater freedom, since they may teach in a village other than their own. But the restrictive atmosphere in all villages places severe limitations on the behaviour of these few women also.) Men (fathers, uncles and sometimes brothers or guardians) decide on the suitability of a candidate for marriage with their daughter, niece, sister or ward; their choice may well rest on a lineage man, and today the latter may be pressured into agreement.

Men receive more education than women (Rosenfeld 1968b, p. 751), and since they work outside the village their experience and knowledge are wider. On the one hand men may have their own ideas about who the correct marriage partner is, e.g. the male may think that his female cousins are not suitable, or he may prefer marriage with a more literate and perhaps urban woman; i.e. although limited, there are other alternatives that he may wish to take advantage of. On the other hand the honour and good name of the family and lineage are maintained by restricting women to the village, and inside it as well, by arranging their marriages when they are still young; and so on. Men place restrictions on women, women are dependent on men, but the marriages of women cannot be delayed for too long. In order to solve the marriage problem of a lineage female, the marriage 'right' of a male to his female cousin may now be forced upon him; in other words, the marriage 'right' and 'preference' is transformed into an obligation. 'As long as men do not grant their women freedom, they must marry them themselves. At the same time, each *ḥamūla* seeks to guarantee a marriage for every *ḥamūla* son or daughter. Pressure is still placed on young men and women to this end.' (Rosenfeld 1964, p. 229.)

6. Arab males do not have a completely free choice of which female they will marry. Just as one male will restrict the freedom of his sisters and daughters, so will others do the same. Men may work outside the village, but they cannot easily meet or talk to Arab women. Thus the marriage system, with some allowance for the educational levels of the spouses, etc., continues to determine the choices available to men; it is a rigid system in the sense that it is the families who make the decision and that spouses do not have a free choice.

It is easier for Arab men to meet Jewish women, and over the last decade or so several hundred marriages have taken place between men from Arab villages and Jewish women living in cities. (No figures have been published and they are difficult to estimate. There are probably less than 1,500 Arab–Jewish couples all told in the country. However three men from our village, two Muslim and one Christian, have married Jewish women.) Mixed Arab–Jewish social groups are rare (if we except certain radical political groups whose very few women members would not in any case have a village background), and they do not usually include women. Thus the prevailing atmosphere is not encouraging, and though marriages between Arab men and Jewish women do occur they are not frequent and do not involve formal negotiations between families over such things as bride price. This means that the women who are available for an Arab villager to marry continue to come mainly from his own village, or perhaps another one, and to be those about whom the respective families must conduct negotiations.

7. As polygyny has been illegal in Israel since 1951 perhaps fewer women are required for Muslim marriages. Because at least some of the women taken as second wives come from villages other than that of the men, the number of 'stranger' women in the 1954–69 enumeration would be expected to decrease and the number of women taken in marriage from the patrilineage and the village would take on increased importance in the rates.

This is probably true, but the effect on the marriage statistics as a whole is not clear. Although it is illegal, 15 men have made polygynous marriages since

1954; 39 men did so during the period up to 1954. (See Rosenfeld 1957, for the reasons for polygyny.) Moreover, since remarriage after the death or divorce of a spouse, especially for men, is common, remarriage for men who now do not make polygynous marriages should be more usual. Young men who are pressured into marriage, usually with cousins, are still promised that they will be given second wives at a later date. The divorce rate is still low in the village (Rosenfeld 1957), but it is probably increasing, perhaps among other reasons, due to the illegality of polygyny and the preference on the part of young men today for divorce instead of polygyny. There were thirteen divorces among the Muslims in the village during the four to five generations up to 1954; and seven from 1954 to 1969. (Polygyny is forbidden among Christians; divorce is difficult and consequently the rate is low.)

8. Although it is difficult to prove that, due to ongoing competition for status and ongoing factionalism in the village, endogamous patrilineage marriages are contracted today in order to build lineage solidarity, it is a fact that the main operative force brought to bear in village politicking remains the lineage. Villagers need not today fear outside forces such as bedouins or hostile villages, that previously required them to defend themselves on the clan level; and the state has made the use of overt clan force within the village almost entirely obsolete. The marriage system and its endogamous patterns develop an ideology over time i.e. they become preferred, desirable, marriages, or, as I have just said, there is a clear political rationale why marriages are not made with other lineages. It is motivations such as these rather than the mechanisms of the 'security system' that cause people to marry as they do. The political–security reasons may be less real today then they were in the past, but since residual patterns, including lineage political factionalism, have not disappeared, there is little reason why the ideological motivations of what is a correct marriage should disappear either. Therefore, we can speak about the political–ideological causation of this marriage system as a living process rather than an exotic 'survival'.

Many villages, including the village whose marriage statistics we discuss, have had local councils for the past few years. That is, the *mukhtārs*, the traditional village heads, are no longer appointed and lineage heads do not provide the traditional councillors. Instead all villagers of voting age vote for a list or for a candidate for membership on a local council. However, voting remains on patrilineage lines; patrilineages may combine around candidates, but the candidates are representatives of lineages or lineage blocs (the latter being sometimes created by consciously directing marriages between different lineages or lineage segments). The point is that lineage members rarely vote for representatives of lineages other than their own. (Sometimes there are problems about women who marry into a lineage and are under pressure from members of their lineage of origin to vote for the latter's candidate: this is another good, but very recent, reason to direct women into patrilineal endogamous marriages.) There are some minor exceptions: there may be a Communist party candidate, a reform candidate, a youth (*shabāb*) candidate; the votes for such candidates may cut across lineages, but they are few in number and extra-lineage parties or associations within the village make little impression on local council voting. In the 1969 local council elections in the village we discuss, only 78 (6 per cent) of the 1,286 votes cast were not votes for a lineage list candidate.[8] The government is not dissatisfied with the continuing *ḥamūla* lists in local council elections, and still manipulates the internal structure as a part of policy. In other words, political solidarity is still stressed at the lineage level; solidarity is served best, although not exclusively, through endogamous marriages (whether or not that is the manifest purpose of the marriage).

9. Until 1966 the Arab population in Israel was under the direct control of a military government. The latter, for what it termed security reasons, but also to protect Jewish labour, restricted and regulated the movement of Arabs in the country. (Rosenfeld 1964, p. 228.) It was not until the latter part of the 1950s that free movement was permitted. We have therefore to consider how far the enforced reduction in possible outside contacts would have encouraged marriage within the lineage and village.

The areas open to entry were circumscribed, and contact with the Jewish population was reduced. The entire Arab population was affected, more particularly so people living in border areas and elements regarded as clearly dangerous by the authorities. In addition the military government was moved by considerations connected directly with the labor market. From 1949 until about 1958 the military government was guided, at least theoretically, by the aim of protecting Jewish labor in those localities and districts that lacked any other authority capable of affording such protection...

In the course of time substantial changes occurred in the restrictive influence of the military government. Civilian bodies enjoyed increased influence in the Arab districts, and the field of activity of the military government was curtailed. There was also deliberate relaxation of restrictions on freedom of movement. More travel permits were issued and the period for which they were valid was extended, while the areas for which a permit was required were reduced. In 1957 the military government lifted the restrictions on access to Afula, Acre, and Nazareth and its environs. In 1959 free movement by day to and from practically all the Jewish centers (except Jerusalem) was permitted. Since April 1962, the regulations have provided for annual permits valid for almost the whole country, with no specification of destination or route. These were the main formal changes, but, as may be imagined, the transition from one stage to the next was not sudden, each change in the regulations being preceded by a more liberal application of the old regulations. It seems that the turning point came in the period 1957–59. Since then military government has not been an important barrier to the entry of Arab manpower into the Jewish sector (Ben-Porath 1966, pp. 51–2).

It is difficult to weigh the effect which such restrictions on movement had on marriage plans and rates. In common with others, many men in our village took a chance and worked in forbidden areas. There were some, mainly but not only Christian Arabs, who had been permanently employed outside before the war, or who had guaranteed employment and/or connexions, and these received work permits in the early 1950s. But in any case, there was countrywide unemployment during the years 1953–7, and work opportunities outside the village only opened up after 1957. For Arabs the restrictions created an atmosphere of repression over an eight- to ten-year period. Theoretically, the situation could have meant a decrease in possible contacts and hence an emphasis on marriage in the lineage or village – another contraction of the already reduced 'potential marriage community'. Although a factor, it was not, as we shall see, a totally definitive one for Muslims who were, in any case, rarely permanent workers in cities; its real importance was in the fewer contacts between male workers and fathers from different villages who might have discussed the marriage possibilities of their daughters and sisters. The Christians (to the extent that they abstained from political activity considered undesirable by the military government) suffered restrictions for a few years at most. The restrictions on movement during the first decade of the state of Israel must therefore be considered as a possible factor for increased internal marriages; it is related to the other reasons mentioned, but its real importance is not easy to assess.

10. In a social environment from which Israeli Arabs feel themselves to be alienated, there may be a psychological or emotional need to seek security and one manifestation of this need could be 'marrying-in'. The state, as I have said, provides the villagers with physical protection and there is no fear of attack from without or within. However, after the establishment of the state of Israel and the 1948–9 war which turned the Arabs into a minority population, it is doubtful whether they have felt themselves, or have been made to feel, unconditionally Israelis. Because of the security restrictions placed on their freedom of movement and of the need for travel permits, amongst other things, they have always felt they were regarded as second-class citizens. Nor have successive wars in 1956 and 1967 improved their sense of security. The point is clear, even though it cannot be expressed in sociological terms, for, of course, Arabs are not aliens; they have roots in the country and plan their future in it; but at the same time there are historical, social, objective, and psychological factors which contribute to their feeling of insecurity and of not belonging. It can, therefore, be said that they continue those marriage links which are the most enduring and they probably set store on them. Conversely, other links are not easily forged. We have already said as much in an earlier analysis of clan (patrilineage) endogamy: .

The direction, because of the effect of the State, could presumably be away from clan marriage, but the increase of both parallel-cousin marriage and clan endogamy, especially for the present 18- to 39-year-old generation, may point up a need for the internal solidarity of the kin in the non-kin oriented State in which, as yet, the former have not become integrated (Rosenfeld 1957, p. 40).

These ten reasons, then, combine to account for the increase in the rate of patrilineal endogamous marriages in the Arab village in Israel. Two of the reasons (Nos. 4 and 6) – that at the time of his marriage a young man is not independent of the demands of his father's extended family and lineage so far as paternal cousin marriage is concerned, nor is he materially independent, e.g. for housing; and that Arab males are not free to make a personal choice among Arab females – if taken alone, would only account for the marriage pattern as an ongoing village phenomenon. The other eight explanations, however, have a much greater effect on the actual increase in the rate of endogamous marriages. These explanations (as numbered in the previous discussion) are:

1. that the number of individuals within patrilineages has increased;
2. that such marriages are preferred and proper;
3. that the potential marriage community has contracted;
5. that the females who are restricted and less advanced cannot have their marriages delayed, and that therefore the 'rights' of the males in the marriage system are transformed into obligations to marry cousins;
7. that the illegality of polygyny and the possibly reduced frequency of outside marriages may give greater statistical weight to lineage and intra-village marriages;
8. that the patrilineage is still a viable political instrument;
9. that the restrictions on movement reduce contacts and hence the potential for outside marriages;
10. that in a social environment which alienates the Arabs, and where they feel alienated, there is a psychological need to 'marry-in'.

THE MACRO-SOCIOLOGICAL REASONS FOR AN INCREASED RATE OF (PATRILINEAL) ENDOGAMY: THE CONDITION OF THE ARAB WORKER IN THE ISRAELI ECONOMY

The micro-sociological analysis explains how and why the ongoing village marriage system operates. On the one hand, the internal system itself potentially 'creates' an increased rate of endogamy, e.g. as in points 1 and 2 above. On the other hand, it is used to solve new social problems as they arise, e.g. as in points 3, 4, 5, 6, 7, and 8; as the two sets of factors combine, the endogamous rate increases. However, in order to understand why this village marriage system continues when, as we saw at the outset, definite social changes have taken place (e.g. the former peasants are now a proletariat, and so on), we must return to our macro-sociological analysis. We must go further into our statement that 'outside wage labour is not, as yet, an alternative ... to the village social structure', and that the endogamous marriage system continues because the labourers are 'an insecure proletariat outside the village and backward agriculturists inside it', and are therefore tied to 'an ongoing "residual" peasant social structure'. This will be discussed later when we clarify the place of the Arab worker in the Israeli economy. We shall lead up to the discussion by first offering a perspective for one of its aspects, that of urbanization.

It would be logical to expect a decrease in endogamy if large numbers of people became urbanized. The decrease need not be immediate; it should appear however in the second generation (that could be tabulated within the marriage rates of their village of origin). That little urbanization of Arab villagers has taken place since the founding of Israel indicates that it is the village social structure which determines marriage patterns.

There is...no evidence of significant rural–urban migration...In 1961 only 25.7 per cent of the non-Jewish population (16.9 per cent of the Muslims and 61.4 per cent of the Christians) lived in towns and urban settlements. Half of the 63,000 Arab town-dwellers lived in the Arab towns of Nazareth and Shfaram (actually a large village without which the urban ratio drops to 22.8 per cent); in Haifa there were less than 10,000 Arabs, in Jaffa about 6,000 and in other mixed towns – Acre, Ramla and Lydda – about 10,000. The 74.3 per cent rural population includes 11 per cent Bedouins.

The per cent of urban population is lower among Israeli Arabs than in the Arab countries (Iraq, 39.2 in 1957; Syria, 38.7 in 1960; Jordan 43.8 in 1961; and Egypt 38.0 in 1960). It is also lower than it was among the Arab population in Palestine toward the end of the mandatory period (36 per cent in 1944). The Arab flight affected cities more than villages and most of the Arab urban centers of the mandatory period ceased to exist as such (Ben-Porath 1966, pp. 8–9).

A process of urbanization, although on a small scale, was taking place during the mandatory period in the second half of the 1930s and the first half of the 1940s. Twenty-four per cent of the Muslim population was urban in 1922, 30 per cent in 1944; 75 per cent of the Christian population was urban in 1922, 80 per cent in 1944 (*A Survey of Palestine* Vol. I, 1946, pp. 157, 159). And as we can see from the above quotation relating to the 1961 census, 16.9 per cent of the Muslim and 61.4 per cent of the Christians were urban – a decrease within Israel.

Urbanization need not be regarded as a process of 'positive' change or even as a necessary one. Life in town may be less rewarding than in a village; villages or suburban areas within reach of city jobs can be more satisfactory places of residence, etc. Although Arab rural–urban migration did take place in Palestine, the rate, at least for the Muslims, was not high. The decline in the migration rate in Israel can be attributed to a number of causes. Firstly, as pointed out in the quotation above, Arab urban centres no longer exist in Israel; the former all-Arab cities of Jaffa, Ramla, Lydda and Acre now contain only a few thousand Arabs. Their inhabitants are almost all Jewish. Among other things, these cities, and such mixed Jewish–Arab cities as Haifa and Jerusalem which formerly had large Arab populations, served as markets and centres where it was possible for urban kin to absorb rural newcomers seeking work and lodging. Secondly, Israel is a small country and transportation is reasonably efficient; a bus ride of an hour, or an hour and a half, will bring most villagers to an urban work place. Thirdly, military–government travel (and hence work) restrictions have only been relaxed over the last ten to fifteen years.

The low rate of urbanization in general, in Palestine and in Israel, is connected with a number of factors. Again, the country was and still is small. Secondly, the greatest rate of urban increase occurred during the full employment of World War II years with its opportunities in the police, public works, army camps etc. at the end of the period of war prosperity many workers returned to their villages. Thirdly, the restrictions placed on women and the strict code of honour operating in the village make it relatively simple to leave women and families in the village while men return home from work a few times in the week or month. Fourthly, part of the family may exploit the economic resources of the village, i.e. land, trees, garden plots, farm animals; these resources may provide either absolutely essential subsistence or a supplement to income. Moreover, villagers who are not totally landless and who hold at least house-plots need not live what might easily become an urban slum existence.

Most important, an explanation of the place of the Arab worker in the general economy helps to clarify urbanization processes. The fact that large-scale urbanization has not taken place may simplify explanations of marriage rates, but it emphasizes the effect rather than the cause. Urbanization is possibly, perhaps even logically, but not inevitably the last stage of a peasant-to-proletariat economic process. However, the key to an understanding of the economic process as it affects the Arabs is not so much non-urbanization, as the condition of the Arab worker in the economy as a whole and the economic condition of the Arab village. Here we can discuss these points only briefly and in relation to Israel. (An extensive and historical analysis is in Carmi and Rosenfeld, MS.) The Arab–Israeli village is agriculturally backward; it has no industry; it does not provide employment except for a few builders, shepherds, some unskilled labourers and miscellaneous personnel. The total income from agriculture of those who were self-employed or wage-earners (probably half of the latter were employed in farming for Jews) was estimated at 25 per cent of the total income of the Arabs in Israel in 1963 (Zahri and Schiezra 1966, p. 15). Another way of showing how totally dependent the Arabs are on wage labour outside the village is by estimating the number of rural Arabs who could be supported by agriculture:

According to the norms of the Ministry of Agriculture in its plans for the Arab village, the present land holdings of the Arab population, with at least double the annual supply of water, would support directly less than 25 per cent of the rural Arab population (Ben-Porath 1966, p. 43).

Today, approximately 10 per cent of the Muslim male population of working age in our village (some 535 men), have full-time jobs in cities, some of them in the all-Arab town of Nazareth. Most of these 50–60 men are restaurant or hotel workers, but at any one time many more Muslim men may be working in the city mainly as skilled workers in the building trades. They move from place to place following the work and building opportunities and their ties with con-tractors. There are also young men, generally in the 15–20 age group, who work in the city in various jobs (restaurants, delivery boys for vegetable and grocery stores, and unskilled labourers in general). Most move from job to job; few are permanently employed, although some of them join the ten per cent with full-time jobs. (Due to the difficulty of distinguishing between temporary and permanent full-time labour, some few of the above have been classified as part of the 10 per cent category.) Because of the nature of their unskilled work, it is difficult to say that more than 5 per cent of the village Muslims are *permanently* employed in the cities.

Most of the Muslim wage-earners work in the wider area of Jewish villages and towns surrounding their village; they work as unskilled and agricultural labourers, and in building and services. Others work for Arab contractors and transport owners from their own village as unskilled labourers in haulage, digging (gathering manure for sale to Jewish settlements by contractors is common in our village), and as skilled workers in the building trades working under local Arab contractors and as work groups. That is, their work does not generally take them very far from the village and they usually return home daily; they are mostly dependent on seasonal work, usually move from job to job and are not fully employed unless there is over-employment in the country.

Many of these men may have begun their work career in cities, but, unable to find full-time or permanent work there, they have sought jobs in the village periphery. In short, very few Muslim men work permanently or for long periods in the city; and in terms of their place in the Israeli economy, there is no prospect of urban work for them. Those Arabs who do work more permanently in the services, transport and the building trades are among the first affected at times of recession. Their wages are not high, though not neces-sarily lower than those of Jews in similar occupations. Lack of job security, the high cost of living and the difficulty of moving (large) families to the city makes such a transition almost out of the reach of Muslim families. The temporary and migratory nature of employment is typical. Lacking permanent work out-side the village, there is thus no process of urbanization that would place people from different villages in proximity to one another and to other town-dwellers so as to make a new generation of (potential) non-patrilineal mates available. It is this state of affairs that has perpetuated the marriage system of the Muslim village Arabs, and it is because of the factors we have analysed that the rate of endogamy has increased from 31 to 57 per cent, that village marriages have fallen from 40 to 20 per cent, and that marriages with 'stranger' women have decreased from 28 to 16 per cent.

The majority of the Arab population (70 per cent) is Muslim. There is little reason to believe that their position in the economy of the country will change or that the percentage of urban Muslims, which is below 20 per cent, will greatly increase in the near future. Although Christian Arabs form only 20 per cent of the Arab population, today probably two-thirds of them are urban. Approximately a quarter of the Christians in the village studied have moved their families to the cities[9] (Haifa and Nazareth) in a process that began some

30 to 35 years ago and still continues. The marriage statistics for the Christians of the village, therefore, although not numerically large, are important because we include those living in the cities. This has been done, perfectly logically, because urbanization is in this case not a single-stage move, but an extended, partial and unfinalized process. With few exceptions, all the approximately 40 Christian families living outside the village still maintain their homes in the village; all have parents, siblings, or cousins there; all visit the village from time to time and hold marriage ceremonies there. Perhaps the most significant thing is that most people over age 40 (and many younger ones too) have built homes, or invested earnings in repairing houses, in the village in preparation for their retirement.

The detailed reasons why most Palestinian and Israeli Christian Arabs were and are urban are beyond the scope of this paper. It is worth pointing out, however, that in 1944 there were three times as many urban Muslims as there were urban Christians: 300,000 as against 100,000 (*A Survey of Palestine* Vol. I, 1945, p. 151). But, as I have said, 75–80 per cent of the Muslims were rural, while only 20–25 per cent of the Christians were so. The fact that Christians become urban today (we are discussing a specific village, but it is possible to generalize) and that few Muslims do, can be explained briefly. The Christians were predominantly urban in the past and there is a possibility that relatively more Christian than Muslim villagers have kin in the city; in our village this is definitely so, there being only two or three Muslim families that have become urban; the so-called urban–rural dichotomy has even less meaning for the Christians; Christians had, and still have, higher educational levels; in the latter respect, Christians enjoyed the support of their churches and missions and especially that of the Greek Catholic diocese, and both the mandatory and the Israeli governments were relatively more careful in their treatment of Christians when implementing policy; Church officials helped many Christian villagers to make the transition to (or, after the 1948 war, back to) the city by helping them find jobs, letting them use church lands for temporary housing, etc.; it seems likely that the Israeli government favoured Christian rather than Muslim Arabs as part of a divide-and-rule policy and it also seems that Christians found it easier to get travel permits for the cities.

Many of the Christians are skilled workers and artisans. Approximately 60 out of some 230 men over age 15 from the village under discussion can be considered as being employed full-time in cities; some of these men have been working and living in Nazareth or Haifa from the time of the mandatory period. In the village also there are few unskilled Christian workers as compared to the high number of Muslim unskilled. Some Christians are permanently-employed municipal employees and, relative to their numbers, more are in the police, more are school teachers (more are secondary school students) and more are self-employed. Almost all those from the village studied who are per-manently- and self-employed in the cities are Christians. We can state that more rural Christian Arabs than rural Muslim Arabs are in a position to compete with urban Christian Arabs for available permanent jobs in the city or to attempt self-employment in the city.

The rate of patrilineal endogamous marriages for the Christians has more than doubled: 45 of the 211 marriages (21.3 per cent) up to 1953; 45 of the 90 marriages (55.6 per cent) from 1954 to 1969. Most of the same (micro-sociological) reasons that we advanced for the increased rate among the Muslim villagers hold good for the Christians as well.[10] There are some differences in weighting, e.g. the restrictions that fall on Christian women are less stringent than those for Muslim women; there is no Christian polygyny; Christian women are better educated (see Rosenfeld 1968b, p. 751) than are Muslim women and there is less of a discrepancy between the levels of Christian men and women both in education and general sophistication, thus reducing gaps between potential marriage partners and making it easier for women to adjust in predominantly Jewish cities.

Of the 90 Christian marriages 36 were made at the time the man was working in the city and usually living in the city, although not necessarily with his parents who might be living in the village; 20 of the latter marriages were made with patrilineage women; some of these women then left the village to join their husbands in the city, the others were already in the city with parents or brothers. In other words, the increased rate of patrilineal endogamy took place during the urbanization process. (The majority of those living in the city are from the large lineage mentioned in note 10.) Of the 16 additional men who married while working and living in the city 3 married women from their own village and 13 married women from outside their own village, in the latter instances often with women whose families had already moved from villages to the city.

When we divide the 90 Christian 1954–69 marriages into two time-periods, those of 1954–63 and those of 1963–9, the number of marriages in each are few, 56 and 34, and each, taken alone, alters the meaning of statistics, and thus any rigid conclusions may be misleading, for example, the transfer of some endogamous marriages from the year 1962 into the latter group could radically change the rates. To join the two, as we have done above, is more satisfactory, given the brief sixteen-year time span. Nevertheless, if we wish to make a prognosis, there may be some significance in the separation: 32 (57 per cent) of the marriages of the earlier group were patrilineally endogamous; only 13 (38 per cent) of the later group were so (10 of the total 34 marriages were made while the man was working and usually living in the city). The rate is still higher than that of the time period up to 1954 (which included four to five generations of marriages), but it shows signs of decrease after the very high increase of 1954–63. Perhaps even more significant is the high increase in the number of marriages, 16 out of 34 (47 per cent), with women from other villages or from the city.

What conclusions then, can we draw from the Christian marriage rates? While urban transition is less of a problem for the Christians, it does not seem that their general place in the Israeli economy will change radically in the near future and therefore, as I have already pointed out, the micro-sociological reasons presented for the increased rates should be valid for them as well as for the Muslims, although not to the same degree, as the decrease from the present high rate seems to indicate. While the 25 per cent who work and live outside the village are not migrant labourers, they are not all completely urbanized. In a formal sense, the village and city are not one single, socio-structural unit, but the Arabs do not themselves feel there is any separation from the economic point of view and very few urban Christians would be able, or would wish, to abandon their village homes and thereby rule out possible return to the village as a dwelling place from which they could go out to work.

The coming generation of Christians should be able to replace those who are at present either municipal and government employees or self-employed, and thus permanently employed in cities. There are, however, few signs that their numbers will increase greatly. It is, of course, a fact that our prognosis is based on examples of careers for only one generation in an Israeli state that has included a decade of military government with restrictions on travel and work.

Many of the Christian children born in the cities will have fewer ties with the village than their parents have had and will receive secondary and higher education in the city. City conditions are less restrictive for young people than are those in the village and natural increase among Christians is in any case only about half that of Muslims and closer to the Jewish rate. This means that the growth of Christian patrilineages is not excessive and the potential for endogamous marriages is not greatly increasing. Most Christian lineages are small and endogamy is therefore technically difficult. (It should also be borne in mind that the high endogamous rates are basically due to the close-knit rural–urban ties within the large lineage mentioned in note 10 and are dependent on their continuity.) These considerations should result in an increase of 'free choices' and of 'non-endogamous' marriages, as the 1963–9 rates perhaps already tend to show. Nevertheless, these possibilities should not be exaggerated. Unless new opportunities arise for permanent urban employment in different branches, including government and municipal employment, the village will remain the basic refuge – a place to live in and from which to seek, and go to, work. Women from lineage and village who are capable of adjusting to both situations will continue to be the best and the 'proper' mates.

Our attention has been concentrated on the 25 per cent of the Christians from the village who have become part-urban, but some of the comments also hold good for the young Muslims who are finishing secondary school, or who are teachers and government employees. Their number is, however, small, and so far, with few exceptions, they all continue to reside in the village. The alternatives to the marriage system (such as flight across the border, emigration, or bachelorhood) which are available to the overwhelming majority of Muslims and Christians are even fewer.

In conclusion, we may say that the Arabs employed in the wider Israeli economy lack job permanence or are migrant labourers, and far too many of them are unskilled. They live in villages with an agriculture and a lack of industry that make them the most backward areas in the Israeli economy. These conditions provide the macro-sociological basis for an ongoing village marriage system. This is why the micro-sociological reasons for an increased rate of endogamy continue to operate. I believe that the definitive link between the macro- and micro-sociological factors is a man's ultimate dependence for his material security on a village house or house plot which may often be the property of his father; this places a powerful limitation on marriage choice or other alternatives. It follows that an absolutely landless proletariat would not be similarly bound to a rigid marriage system.

NOTES

1   The Arab village in question is situated in the lower Galilee of Israel. Its population in 1969 was approximately 3,250 of whom some 75% were Muslims and 25% Christians. Only a few people fled the village during the 1948–9 war. Families are linked together in patrilineal descent and form patrilineages. There are several small patrilineages with less than 20 adults; others number between 30 and 50 adults. Four Muslims and one Christian patrilineages have between 100 and 200 adults. Fifty per cent of the village population are children under age 14. The village is approximately a half-hour's bus ride from the all-Arab town of Nazareth (population 30,000) and the all-Jewish town of Tiberias (population 24,000). The closest large city is Haifa, an hour and a half's bus ride away (population 210,000). The villagers have less than 12,000 dunams (3,000 acres) of un-irrigated land. Most are small owners; some are, agriculturally speaking, landless; a few could be considered middle owners. We say 'owners' and not 'farmers', since probably no more than 20–25% of village income comes from farming. In 1967 the Arab population in Israel was approximately 320,000: 70% Muslim, 20% Christian, 10% Druze. Approximately 25–30% of the Arab population is urban. Approximately 17% of the Muslims and 62% of the Christians are urban. The Jewish population was approximately 2,400,000 (*Statistical Abstract of Israel* 1967). After 1967 the population figures in the Statistical Abstract included the Arab population of east Jerusalem. We use the statistics up to 1967 in order to avoid confusion.

2   The field research on which this paper is based was supported by the Wenner-Gren Foundation for Anthropological Research and the University of Haifa. The paper appeared in Hebrew in *Social Research Review* (University of Haifa), No. 1, January, 1972.

3   In the 1957 paper I explain why I counted 19 marriages of 3 patrilineages, possibly branches of larger lineages, as being village marriages and not endogamous within the respective larger lineages. If they belong within the latter category, then the percentage of patrilineal endogamous marriages rise to 34.7%, that of village marriage decrease proportionately (see Rosenfeld 1957, p. 36). In the 1954–69 statistics they are regarded as branches of larger lineages; since this concerns only 4 marriages, the effect is statistically insignificant (1.7%).

4   Fifty-three Muslim women from the village under discussion married into other villages up to 1954, 20 women did so from 1954 to 1969.

5   Although the rates are unknown it can be assumed that natural increase was not high in the past nor was the number of persons reaching marriageable age. This suggests one clue, among others, to socio-biological origins of preferred and prescribed marriage systems. If it is the purpose of marriage systems to extend relationships and make allies, a system originates when it controls the few men and women available and directs them into correct security-building marriages. By establishing rights and preferences the 'ancient Semitic' or Arab system would operate first to guarantee mates for males from among their female paternal cousins; other systems guarantee other mates.

6   In the past approximately 8% of the men were polygamous, see Rosenfeld 1957, pp. 52–4.

7   See Rosenfeld 1968b for reasons for the more rapid breakdown of the extended family in the Arab village.

8   See Cohen 1965 for differences in voting at local council and national elections.

9   The two main possibilities for urban residence for Arab villagers from the north are in the all-Arab town of Nazareth and the city of Haifa. While there are full-time workers in other cities, e.g. Tel-Aviv, Jaffa and Jerusalem, only four or five from the village we discuss could be considered as having established urban residence. There were approximately 15,000 inhabitants in Nazareth before the 1948–9 war; two-thirds were Christians, one-third Muslims. Today's population of 30,000 is more or less equally divided; many of today's inhabitants are refugees from villages in the northern area. There were approximately 63,000 Arabs (36,000 Muslims, 27,000 Christians) in Haifa before the war; today there are approximately 15,000, two-thirds of whom are Christians.

10   An important fact to take into consideration is that while there are several large Muslim patrilineages in the village we discuss, there is only one large Christian patrilineage. Thirty-nine of the 90 recent Christian marriages were made by men of this large lineage. The other 51 marriages were made by men of 9 other small lineage lines. Most of the patrilineal endogamous marriages, 29 out of the 45 from 1954–69, were made in this large *ḥamūla*; 19 of their 21 marriages from 1954 to 1963 were patrilineally endogamous. Thus, while the large lineage contracted 43% of the Christian marriages, 64% of their marriages were patrilineally endogamous while 36% were so among the small lineages. The smaller lineages, most being composed of few men of marriageable age, make fewer such marriages: it may be difficult to find a female of suitable age from the lineage; a disproportion in the male–female ratio upsets marriage possibilities; if one or two families from a small lineage set up permanent urban residence and/or refuse to give and take women in marriage, the traditional marriage system is distorted for the remaining lineage members, etc. In other words, for many and varied reasons (not the least of which are possible urban transition and lack of concern with village political machinations), small families may have fewer opportunities and incentive for endogamy.

REFERENCES

Anglo-American Committee of Inquiry. 1946. *A Survey of Palestine*, Vol. 1. Palestine, The Government Printer.
Ben-Porath, Yoram. 1966. *The Arab labour force in Israel*. Jerusalem, Maurice Falk Institute for Economic Research in Israel.

Central Bureau of Statistics. 1967. *Statistical abstract of Israel No. 18.* Jerusalem, The Government Press.

Cohen, Abner. 1965. *Arab border-villages in Israel.* Manchester University Press.

Government of Palestine. 1945. *Survey of social and economic conditions in Arab villages, 1944.* Department of Statistics Special Bulletin No. 21 (Appeared serially in the General Monthly Bulletin of Current Statistics, commencing with July 1945 issue.)

Rosenfeld, Henry. 1957. 'An analysis of marriage and marriage statistics for a Moslem and Christian Arab village.' *International Archives of Ethnography,* Vol. 68, pp. 32–62.

1964. 'From peasantry to wage labor and residual peasantry: the transformation of an Arab village.' In *Process and pattern in culture: essays in honour of Julian H. Steward.* Robert A. Manners (ed.). Chicago, Aldine Publishing Company.

1968a. 'The contradictions between property, kinship and power as reflected in the marriage system of an Arab village.' In *Contributions to Mediterranean sociology.* J. G. Peristiany (ed.). Publications of the Social Science Centre Athens, No. 4. Paris, Mouton.

1968b. 'Change, barriers to change, and contradictions in the Arab village family.' *American Anthropologist,* Vol. 70, pp. 732–52.

1972. 'Rural politics and social change in the Middle East: a critique of the literature and an interpretation of the state of affairs.' In *Rural politics and social change in the Middle East.* R. Antoun and I. Harik (eds). Bloomington, Indiana University Press.

Rosenfeld, Henry and Shulamit Carmi. MS. 'The status and condition of the Arab villagers – migrant workers in the social economy of Israel.'

Zarhi, Shaul and Achiezra, A. 1966. *The economic condition of the Arab minority in Israel.* Centre for Arab and Afro-Asian Studies, Givat Haviva, Israel. Arab and Afro-Asian Monograph Series, No. 1.

5 The domestic cycle in the traditional family organization in Tunisia

Jean Cuisenier
Musée des Arts et Traditions Populaires, Paris

Where residence is virilocal, the line of descent patrilineal and marriage polygynous, as in Tunisia and the Arab countries in general, the domestic cycle has as its starting point the husband and his simultaneous or successive marriages. The wives of the head of the family can, it is true, remarry; they will belong successively to as many different domestic communities – each for the duration of one marriage – as they have husbands. The cycle is thus a complex movement, the moments of which correspond to the marriages of the head of the family, the births resulting from them, the marriages of his descendants where these latter remain within the domestic community, and the births of these descendants' children.

But by giving this definition of the cycle are we not evading the problem of choosing the hypotheses for our theory? Where does the cycle start? Does it start when the first couple marries, even where this couple lives with the husband's father and therefore belongs to the domestic community of which that father is head? Or at the father's death, when his possessions and titles to property are divided among his descendants? Or does it start at the moment when the husband leaves his father's domestic community and forms a separate one, whatever moment in the cycle the father himself may have reached? The uncertainty remains when we come to the end of the cycle. Where does it actually end? Is it on the physical death of the head of the family, when he finally goes to join his ancestors in the next world? Is it when his estate is divided among his heirs, if this should take place before his death, and at the precise moment when he relinquishes his functions as head of the family to a brother or a son? Are not some of the transitions imperceptible, and do not certain domestic communities remain as they were for several generations, with the sons succeeding their fathers in the same homes? Are there not to be found, in practice, a thousand different types of case, and a thousand possible patterns? Is it not, therefore, essential to start by choosing our terms and deciding what they are to mean?

I shall therefore use the word *moments* to mean all types of unit of time in the cycle, separated in the time continuum by distinctive barriers; I shall call *phases* the most significant moments in the cycle, characterized by such pertinent events as a marriage of the head of the family, or the departure of one of the children from the domestic community; and I shall term *positions* in the cycle those phases characterized by formal relationships between moments.[2]

The question I propose to deal with is this: what are the phases of the domestic cycle in the traditional family set-up in Tunisia? Are there positional relationships between these phases which mean that the arrangement of the cycle is invariable, even when the other characteristics of the domestic community vary? Do these relationships form a *structure* and are they to be explained as a combination of a few simple principles?

THE PHASES OF THE CYCLE

The phases of the domestic cycle in Tunisia are determined by two different problems. Firstly the problem of the handing down of rights and of the inheritance of rank and individual role. The death of the head of a family means that there is an estate to be settled, and the property is divided up in accordance with the rules deriving from local custom or in accordance with Islamic law. But neither rank nor role can be shared out. Thus, where there are several sons, and above all where the sons are of different mothers, they are naturally left out of the *succession* as regards rank and role unless some special arrangement has been made. Thus, the first phase of the cycle is marked by the way in which the estate and the succession are settled. The subsequent phases are the reflexion of a second problem, which is that of the alliances to be entered into. Each alliance – whether second, third, or *n*th marriage of the head of the family, or first, second or *n*th marriage of his sons – creates a point at which scission may occur. Thus, logically, there are as many conceivable phases as there are possible combinations of alliances. However, social custom has restricted the number of possibilities, and in practice only a few types of cycle are to be found in Tunisia.

HANDING DOWN OF RIGHTS AND HANDING DOWN OF ROLES

The handing down of rights is governed by two norms which are different and frequently conflict: local custom and Islamic law. In actual fact, until recently, except in the big towns, it was generally local custom which was decisive; its basic tendency was to keep the property in the male line by systematically disinheriting the women. Thus, when the head of a family died it was spontaneously decided, by tacit consensus, to follow local custom. Nobody asked *how* the shares were to be distributed, for there were rules laid down once and for all, which were known to everyone. The real question was not which law was to be applied, the Islamic law, which was the learned system imposed by society as a whole, or the local customary law, or *qānūn 'urfiyya*; in practice there was no hesitation and it was always local custom which was chosen. Islamic law was allowed only where there was an appeal against the decision by some lesser heir who had found that that law furthered his cause and who could not be dissuaded from appealing. The real question for those directly concerned is: 'With whom are we to share?' Very often, in the circumstances, this means: 'How can we manage to get out of straightforward application of the provision of Islamic law?' The basic conviction is that land is male property; it belongs to the men who work on it and fight to protect and keep it, and men alone are therefore entitled to pass it on, to receive it and to give it. There are thus two types of disputes. There are those arising between men of the same descent who use different tactics in their handling of customary law but invoke the same rights inherited from the same forebears. And there are others which arise when a claim is made under Islamic law which challenges customary law; here the men are of different descent and invoke different hereditary rights.

Sons and widows

Local custom entitles the sons to equal portions, whoever their mother is. The desire to achieve equality goes so far that the elders who are acting as arbitrators during the discussion frequently go to the point of drawing lots and fractions of lots and do not hesitate to divide and subdivide lands, plantations and flocks or herds into the number of fractions required. On the father's death the sons are thus entitled to claim their share and each to form a new domestic community. One initial source of conflict is that each time the father remarries there is a risk of a scission, and this in fact generally occurs once the sons have reached maturity. First, the sons of the first marriage, then those of the second, and so on, will abandon the domestic community, taking with them their unmarried sisters and their mothers to found new communities of their own. In so doing, the sons and daughters of the first, and even of the second or subsequent marriages, run the risk of being disinherited. Each domestic community thus originates in a situation involving the regular use of a right, or, if we prefer so to call it, a system of chance depending on birth, which is the expression of the debt of the living to the dead. For, essentially, the living are no more than those who hand on what they have received.

I inherited five hectares as all my brothers did. Then I bought nine hectares. That makes fourteen. Of these fourteen I have given two and a half to my eldest son Abdelhafid; he lives separately and he has seven children and his work is not enough to keep them all. I didn't give them to him by deed of *azul*; they are merely for temporary cultivation and use. I have no intention of doing my other sons out of anything; when I die, each will have his due. I am only an intermediary and there's no reason why I should give to one and not to another. God has decided on each one's share in advance and the land merely passes through my hands; I am not the *qasam* who does the sharing out.(1)
[Numbers following quotations refer to the list of informants on p. 155.]

It's different on the father's death. None of the sons has any more right than any other to stick to all the land and refuse to share it with the other heirs. Even if there are only a few of them, when that time comes each wants his share. How could one of them manage to keep it all? It would mean the others didn't need it. If each of us had work which would keep him, we would be quite willing to leave our share to one of our brothers, either permanently out of generosity or solidarity (*karama*), or under a sharecropping agreement, or just for his use, or else we would sell it to him. But this isn't the case; this land is all we have had given us and each should have his share; none of us can allow anything in favour of another. We are all equal: I won't give up my share and I won't prevent the others from getting theirs.(2)

The sharing-out of the different portions is thus the norm on the basis of which one may assert one's rights and the obligation incumbent on the living and owed by them to the dead. In practice, though, the appropriation of property takes place differently. There the rule covering the rights of each, but in practice it is applied in the interests of those who actually hold the land, the agnate descendants, and, among them, primarily the sons of the same father.

We do the sharing out ourselves, it is not the '*udel* who establishes the right of each to inherit, unless there is a dispute and an appeal to the *ḥakim*. So it's a very rough sharing out and we don't take account of all the possible lesser heirs – we only count the main ones who turn up and ask for their share.(3)

Thus, widows have a right to one-eighth if they have surviving children, of one-quarter if they have not. This is the rule which determines the conditions under which there may be an appeal and sets the limits within which the actors in the social drama may make the most of their chances. In actual social practice widows are never alone. They are holders of a right which is basically a right of conveyance and which they themselves are not qualified to exploit; the true contest will be fought out between the father or the brother on the one side and the father, brother or son of the deceased husband on the other.

The complex character of the situations which arise, the keenness of the competition and the degree to which things have recently changed will be clear from the remarks of an old Bejawwi thinking aloud.

And then, in the old days, a widow never took the one-eighth due to her away to her own home. She stayed on in her husband's house, or else she went back to her parents so as to marry again, and if she did that she gave up her share of her first husband's estate...Ah, yes, it would have been a scandalous thing to do.

Before, a father would never have wanted a widowed daughter to keep any part of her dead husband's land if she came back home. Nowadays there are many who would be delighted and would encourage their daughters to do so; if they took back a daughter along with any children she had it would only be because they secretly hoped to get their hands on the legacy. They'd even go so far as to refuse to marry her off again so they could use her land. And yet normally when a widow goes back home it's in order to remarry; once the proper interval (*el 'adda*) is up she usually gets asked for – specially if she's still young and the children are little....

Who takes the children? Normally the husband's family. But it all depends on their situation. If it's a rich family with land, there is no doubt at all that they'll claim the children when they get a bit bigger...Oh yes, they'll prefer the children to get the sort of upbringing which a family provides, and to get them used to the land and the local habits; if they stayed with their grandfather on the mother's side they might get a 'foreign' sort of upbringing...And then there's the land, the family property. This way, no one is outside the family; there's no danger that part of the *melk* may go elsewhere. If it's a poor family and the mother's family is richer, they'll tend to leave the children as long as they can with the other grandfather; it'll mean one less expense, and in the richer family there'll be land and a team of oxen and other farm animals to get used to, and they'll be brought up as *fellahin*. But later on, they'll come back to their real relatives. Before, what wasn't approved of was for a widow who had remarried to take her children along with her to the new husband's home; that sort of thing wasn't liked. It would be a completely strange family and no one would be fond of the children – they might even ill-treat them. There would be no blood-tie and so therefore no affection [*alhanna* = generosity]. The wife's family wouldn't like it either; they'd think it wrong for a strange family to bring up a stranger's children until they were grown up. There had to be an interest somewhere, and here the wife's family was in a worse position than the children's family, because the children were minors and couldn't have their share in their father's estate even through their mother. At worst, the widow could ask for her share and get it, being perfectly aware of the fact that she was sacrificing her children's interests to those of her new husband. She would even be compromising her children's position for later on when they were grown up; they would always be children of a mother who had accepted a legacy from her husband, in other words, who had made her own children do without. That was extremely badly thought of. Meanwhile the wife's family was in the weaker position. Having her children with her, the wife represented too much of a burden. The new husband could persuade her to make things easier by getting her to ask her brothers, for instance, for her share in the estate: she could say it was in order to pay for her children's upbringing. This was indeed a splendid pretext. For the wife's family it was a security to have the little orphaned children; the family could obtain their share in the father's estate and be perfectly sure that later on they would never claim what had been due to their mother.

That was how things used to be. How are they now? It's hard to say. There's no rule, nothing can be made out very precisely [*aqat* = recognize with both the eyes and the mind, and *ahsar* = embrace, circumscribe]. Anything is possible nowadays; families have been known to give over the children to a widow who lives alone, or to her parents, or to her new husband. Worse still, husbands have been seen to repudiate their wives and leave them to keep the children all by themselves so that they may be freer to marry again as there won't be any children to be in the new wife's way at home. It's true that families are readier nowadays to give their own children into other people's keeping, but it's also true that it's now easier for a widow to remarry and keep her children with her. The new husband will want the wife and want her with the children; they will be hers since their family has agreed to give them up. In the old days this was impossible and it was badly thought of for a man to bring up his wife's children; they used to say he was 'growing fruit for someone else to eat', and he would only do so for the children of a dead brother. In that case he would marry their mother so as to bring them up and keep her in the family.

Another thing which has changed is that nowadays one finds more women who give up the idea of remarrying so as to bring up their children. They stay in their husband's family and they work very hard there. Sometimes they work for the other women who still have husbands alive, though they may live independently if the husband already had his own house and wasn't living with his brothers. If the husband has left any land they farm that; if not, they work for the others. Again, they may live on their own but move nearer their own families so as to be under the protection of their relatives. Before, a widow with little children had to remarry; her father or brother wouldn't have her remain a widow, it was too much of a risk. It was dangerous for their honour to have a sister who, being a widow, was no longer 'covered' (*soutra*), and she had to be given a new 'covering' by taking a new husband, or else by coming back home to live. Nowadays, so long as she leaves them alone, they don't care about the rest. The women themselves have changed, too. Before, when a widow had a son it was her duty to remain a 'widow with a son', even against her parents' wish if they wanted to see her remarried. Her conduct had to be a model of all the virtues, and even then her son would be called 'son of a widow' later on. It meant she was prepared to have a hard time and put up with all the offences she would meet with in her husband's family. It was all for her son's sake and it was better to bear it all than to leave him to women who were strangers; it was better for him to be only fatherless than to be motherless as well. At his age it was easier to find a substitute for his father than for his mother; his uncles would be there to see the hereditary rights respected, but no more. So the mother would turn herself into a panther to fight for her son. A son though, not a daughter; no woman was prepared to remain 'a widow for another woman', for later on who would have been able to protect that other woman? It was only for boys that they did such things. Nowadays women like being widows, but only because this way they're more independent. They like being widows because of the very thing people in the old days were so very frightened of; there's no one over them to give them orders (*hakam*). There's no husband – he's dead; no father or brother, since they won't go back home; no brother-in-law (husband's brother), since they can now make themselves independent of these, even if they couldn't while the husband was alive. So they go off and live alone with their children. There are women who refuse to remarry just in order to keep the freedom to do so.(4)

Brothers and sisters

Under customary law a daughter cannot inherit; the land, which is a product of the male line, must remain the property of the male line. It is thus a scandalous thing for a sister to claim her share from her brother on her father's death. The brother cannot refuse it, since the sister's claim is legitimate under Islamic law. But since it is not the sister herself who lays the claim, but the brother-in-law or 'ally' acting through the sister, all possible means of countering the claim are brought into action. Where, on the contrary, the intention is to give over the land inherited to a co-operative production unit, the brother will make no difficulty; the land of his ancestors will be going, not to an 'ally' or a 'stranger', but to a new institution and ceases to be exploitable in accordance with the traditional norms regulating appropriation.

It isn't that we do our sisters out of their rights. God has given them their share and it's unlawful (*haram*) to refuse it to them. It's out of solidarity (*alhanna*) that a girl marries and goes to live with her husband; she will be sheltered from need and will stop being dependent on her family when she becomes dependent on her husband. It's quite right she should give up the idea of doing her brothers out of her share and so making them a bit poorer. If she came to find herself in need, or was ill, or happened to lose her husband, she would turn to her brothers – or rather to what her father had left her. If that happened, a brother could not shirk his duty, which would be to help his sister. It's the same here with the co-operative. A sister leaves her share for her brother to make use of, as the blood-tie between them warrants, and if he is in need he can sell some of it; a 'loyal' (*halal*) sister can't do otherwise than face the hard facts, she can't add still further to her poor brother's troubles. But if, as sometimes happens, the land is just to be given away, there is no reason why the sister, too, should give up her share and get nothing in return; she has given it up only in so far as it could be of use to her brother. Isn't that fair? Anyway in such a case I would rather she took her share, it would rid me of all sorts of things I am bound to because of the blood-ties between us.(5)

When our father measured out each of our shares he had set nothing aside for his widow if she didn't remarry, nor for our sisters either. He divided everything up among the male heirs and everyone – starting with the wife and daughters, who were the first ones to be affected – found this normal. But this doesn't mean they are disinherited; we didn't get the land under a deed of gift, and it wasn't a disguised form of sale either, as happens when some of the possible heirs are to be left out. If my father divided up his property that way, it was because he knew very well that neither his wife – who is our mother – nor our sisters would ask to be heirs. If it so happened that they had some reason to do so, no one could deprive them of their share. If we prevented them from inheriting we would be in the wrong, it would be forbidden by God's law and they would win the case against us if they took it to court. The sharing-out is by tacit agreement and no deed is signed, either in the presence of a notary, or of the 'adûl or the djemaa.

We two brothers shared the estate between the two of us, Salah and myself, but our sisters didn't withdraw their claims. Before the dividing-up was done, Zina kept demanding her share. In reality neither of the girls has any right to the land; the temporary ownership was in our father's name and it was he who received the land from the djemaa. He died not long afterwards, and it was we who cleared the weeds away and did the building. Our sister brought an action (atkhaṣamna) against us and it went on for four years, and finally she lost it; but even so we gave them their shares. Actually Zina brought her case only against Salah. Salah and Zina are one part of the family and Messaûda and I are the other; Messaûda had stayed with me, and I married her in the Djebel Ansariin to her father's brother's son. Zina is married and lives elsewhere; as I said before, it was Salah and his mother's brothers who arranged the marriage. Salah and I shared out the land and the sisters between us and each of us has one sister to look after. In my case there's no difficulty, the sister is one of us, and if we cook one extra egg she has her share of it. In Tunis Salah used to go and see the other sister and she came to see him, and so on. Things were settled that way and we never thought our sister was going to bring a case against us. In fact when she went and lodged a complaint against Salah it was I who appeared against her. The case went on for four years. I wasn't really against my sister and in reality it wasn't she who brought the case; she's a woman and she stays in the home. It was her husband and all the others. I couldn't give my sister anything with her husband attacking me in court. After the case was over and she had lost and it was legally settled that she had no right to inherit anything, I said to her: 'No, Zina, it was we who did the work. You were only little girls and we brought you up and found husbands for you. It was we who cleared away the weeds, but the one who left the eleven hectares was our father when he died, so here's your share.' Zina took her share, but it's my son who farms her land at the present time.

Thus, under the traditional social system, the situation obtaining in the family when rights are to be handed down and roles to be taken over is generally a complex one which leaves room for reference to various different rules, and for playing the alternatives of law and custom, and of solidarity and equity. The initial phase of the cycle is rarely that in which the estate is officially settled on the heirs, since the land is appropriated or held before the property is divided up, and the future fate of the widows and sisters is settled by their marriages. It is not so much the settlements of estates which mark the phases of the cycle as the scissions, for which the dividing-up of the property mostly provides no more than the opportunity.

The ideal type of traditional family structure in Tunisia is the big domestic community. There are few households at the present time which have retained this form of organization, though most of the heads of families, in the Djebel Anseriin at least, spent their childhood in a community of this sort. Many of them look back on the system with nostalgia; others were its victims. All, in any case, take it as their point of reference when assessing current changes. Hence when determining the nature of the phases in the cycle and finding the points where the fission occurs, one must take this same community as the framework within which the whole process is to be studied.

The ideal type of big domestic community and examples of it in practice

1. The ideal type of the big domestic community is where it forms a single household under the authority of the head of the family, *ra'īs al-'ā'ila*, who settles all important matters and manages production as well as consumption.

The descendants of Hadj Mohammed still form a 'tightly-welded group'. We have remained (*mazalna*) [Gesture of clenching the hand, intended to signify that they have remained united]. We are all here; no one has left his parents' home. Who is the head of the family? How is he to be recognized? To start with, the head of the family is responsible for feeding his household; it is he who must give them their daily bread, even if he doesn't actually work to earn it. The head of a family is the landlord; he's probably too old to work, but it's he who feeds his children because the land they live from belongs to him, all his children do is to farm it. He's not just the landlord, he's the one who decides what is to be eaten and how it is to be earned; it's he who leases out the land and decides which land, and how much of it, and at what price. He may not do any farming himself, but it's for him to tell his sons: 'This year we will do this or that.' The children will agree or will end by accepting what he says. It's the same with all the rest as with the bread, or rather the land; he decides how the land is to be used, and what animals are to be used to farm it or are to graze on it. He decides on everything which has to do with the land and with anything which produces food (sheep, cattle, ready money). He hasn't really much to decide when it comes to farming and crops; the land is just farmed as it should be, and that's that – wheat and barley each in its turn, you just have to continue and nothing needs changing. . . . The head of the family also decides on the market transactions – what is to be sold or bought, and where, and at what price and on what terms; that's the head of the family's business. . . . With marriages it's of course the same as for land. Before, the head of the family was supposed to be the oldest, except in unusual cases (if he was out of his mind, for instance), and he was also supposed to be the one nearest the 'trunk' (*eldjedra*). . . . If someone who isn't the eldest in the family is nearer to the origin (*elasel*) it's he who'll be the head.(4)

2. Even where the domestic community involves no more than unification of the work of production, the title is still appropriate. In the local speech the

same word – *ra 'īs al-'ā'ila* – is used also for the head of this type of social structure.

If we count only the three main families living here in Fezzaniin, that makes more than
fifty people. Fifty can't gather round the same fire and the only thing they have in common is the land, and that we farm all together. They consider me to be the *ra 'īs al-'ā'ila*;
I'm the eldest son. My father died when I was seventeen and I had been married since the
age of sixteen; he married me at *bachart* [The verb B-CH-R, meaning to be conscious, to
reach the age of reason where religion is concerned]. I am more or less the head of the family
for all of them; I don't decide on their own affairs – their children or their wives – or
interfere with what they eat or spend, but I'm the one who decides on the big questions.
They come to ask my advice and we make the decision together; they ask me about selling
or buying an animal, or at the beginning of the year when more land is needed and must be
rented or taken on a sharecropping basis, they ask me where it is to be found, whose land
it is to be, and how much of it is to be taken on. Then of course the marriages too. That's
my affair and no one else's. For example, I'm always the one who urges the others to get the
boys married, and where the girls are concerned I'm the one they come to see if they want
to ask for the hand of one of Mohammed's or Ali's girls.(7)

3. On a smaller scale still, the big domestic community may consist of no
more than two households, those of the father and one married son.

My son lives entirely with me. He has his room next to mine and we eat the same food. He
has three children of his own, two boys and a girl. He can't leave me, he's my only son and
my eldest child. Why should he leave me and go and live by himself, when the two of us have
enough land to farm? It would be understandable if he had other brothers; he could take
advantage of the fact that I'm still fit enough to work to go and set up his own home and
get together some property of his own. He's sure of getting everything when I die, since he's
an only son, so he might just as well stay and work with me.(8)

4. In its most limited form, the big domestic community involves no more
than an atmosphere of brotherhood between each separate household, an
absence of any sort of scheming and work done in common. Each of the
married men has one part of his life which is private; this covers feeding,
married life and the way the children are brought up.

How do we all live together? It's simple; with a bit of brotherly feeling, a little mutual
help and above all with a 'touch of the community of Muhammad', a modicum of solidarity, *chara lumat mohammed*, being brothers ourselves, it's possible to live together as we
do. There are no very careful calculations between us, and no stubborn refusals (*elqiṣaṣ*);
there's a lot of giving in to one another. With this attitude and so long as none of us ever has
the intention of harming another or obliging him to do something detestable to him (in
the moral sense) (*lakrah*), everything should go on all right. And that's how it is. Each of us
has his own home, eats what he likes, settles his own affairs in his own way, is free to beat
his wife or children if he wants to, can let them go hungry or let them eat everything up in
one day; let him do as it suits him [*elli isa'du* – what succeeds for him].(9)

Deliberate fission

In the traditional family set-up, the fission was not something improvised;

among the *Bejawwa* it was actually governed by strict rules. There are in fact two distinct types of fission, that resulting from the regular departure of the elder son, who 'sets up' his own home, and that brought about by the father's remarriage, which causes the children of his first wife to leave.

1. Among the *Bejawwa* the home was set up with the father's assistance. However, the operation was not always a straightforward one; sometimes it took the guise of an expulsion of the eldest son for the benefit of his younger brothers.

It's a custom among all of us *Bejawwa*, as soon as a youngster is married he leaves his father and must contrive to set up his own home; but it doesn't happen in the same way now as in my day. I lived alone and so I had to worry about my supplies for the year, but I worked with my father just as though we were living and eating together, though I didn't hope or expect to get anything out of it. It was our land, it wasn't our property. I was the eldest son and I couldn't do otherwise than to farm my father's land for my father; it was our land. It didn't much matter whether I lived with my father or separately, the two things were quite independent and no one linked the two together, and it was the same with all the young people. It was only when you'd finished on the family land that you could go and work elsewhere and help the others, supposing you had enough time left; you got a wage (*udjra*) for that sort of work.(7)

When my mother died, our father made us 'get out' (*kharadjna*) of his house. I was already married, but my brothers were single. He thought that with the house empty of the children he would be able to marry again more easily; a young wife wouldn't want to come and live in a family where there'd be stepsons and their wives and very soon grandchildren too. It's not very pleasant for a young wife to have grandchildren before she's a mother herself! Since then, each of us has been living on his own. When I work for my father, I'm now used to looking on him as a stranger and to thinking of the land I'm working on as someone else's. It's the same on his side, and if I'm going hungry he doesn't give me anything, either from his stores or out of his pocket.(10)

2. The second type of deliberate fission, involving the dispersal of the first wife's children on the father's remarriage, is frequent among all the tribes of the Djebel Anseriin – the *Bejawwa*, the *Riah Daaja*, the *Hamama*, the *Jlass* and the *Drid*.

When the father has had several wives, his eldest children leave him, either because they don't get on with the new wives or else because the father himself has encouraged them to do so, to leave room for the next lot of fledgelings. Some sons have been known to leave their father at the time when their mother left. . . Often no one is left with the father except the children of his last wife, who all keep together with their mother and very often continue to do so after the father's death.

In other words, we older ones who are the first wife's children live separately, away from our younger brothers who are the children of the second wife, and away from one another too; each of us lives on whatever resources he has found to exploit. Meanwhile all the children of the second wife – the present widow – live together on the same resources and eat the same food.(11)

Fragmentation

Where the fission fits into one of the two traditional patterns, it does not affect the big domestic community as an institution. One son 'gets out' and 'sets up his home', or one set of children leaves and the next will be on the way; the big community is merely going through the phases of a strictly regulated cycle. Fragmentation is quite a different thing; it involves a complete break-up of the big community into households independent of one another or hostile to one another, conflicts between half-brothers and breaches between fathers and sons, once the elder brothers have been disinherited in favour of the younger.

In appearance, it is true, it may be a matter of superficialities – quarrels between women, whether mother-in-law and daughter-in-law or first and second wives.

It is easier for the father to keep all his sons under his thumb than for the mother-in-law to keep her daughters-in-law in order, and that's where the frictions occur, as a result of so much going on and on and repeating things. I know some who, when it all starts, forbid their wives to talk about such things and even beat them for it; but little by little they give in and see things as the women do and feel the same way. As for the women among themselves – Heaven preserve me from their quarrels, always about trifles and silly little things. 'I want to eat this or that.' 'I did the sweeping yesterday, it's your turn today.' 'Your son made this mess, it's your job to clean it up,' and so on. It's enough to make life unliveable and everybody finally agrees to separate, more in order to separate the women than to separate from one another.(12)

Nowadays they fly off as soon as their wings are grown. First the eldest, then the next, until the nest is empty. It's the women's fault, they all want the home to themselves, with no one above them; they want to be the one to give orders (*lihum alhukuma*) and it's they who must make the decisions [*ray rayhum* = idea, opinion, decision]. The children go off without anything at all and build their own nests; they all say: 'We are going to set up our nests (*natla' ou bi 'achachna*)'.(13)

But for all their trivial appearance, the clashes between the women are the forerunners of quarrels among the men and prepare the ground for these. The most serious are not those between the male line and the female line but those in which the sons of different mothers find themselves on opposite sides. When the father disinherits his first wife's sons, the breach is complete. It is true that under Islamic law it is illegal to disinherit one's sons, but there is a piece of customary law procedure which makes it easy to get round the law: the sons of the first marriage are made to 'get out', and a part of the land is sold to those of the second. The figure is sometimes only a token one, large enough to make the operation legal in form. There is little defence against such practices, for the first wife's sons can take no legal action against their father; to do so would, moreover, be contrary to the ethos.

Statement by one of the second wife's sons: When my father married again, he had two separate homes; he had divided up the furniture, and his first wife, who was a *Bejawwa*, stayed with her children. My father didn't get on with the sons of this marriage and used to say they didn't want to work on the land; then, one day when he was in a temper, he decided to disinherit them. At the present time we all live together on good terms; we are all brothers born of the same father, and it's all the same today as yesterday. Our father made us a present and we took it; we didn't deprive the others. Our father was the sole owner of his property and he disposed of it as he wished.(14)

Statement by the first wife's son: Our father deprived us of our heritage because we didn't live with him; we lived with our mother and worked for her. He wasn't pleased and wanted us to stay with him so as to work for him. He was put up to it, above all, by his second wife, she wanted everything for her own children. It's true we were the three grown-up and married brothers, but what could we do? We couldn't go and appeal; in any case it was his land and he had done with it as he wished. He sold it, and he sold it to his own children. And then, how could we appeal, anyway?(15)

Hence in the case of the original domestic community, the phases of the cycle correspond to events liable to cause a fission.

There are, to start with, three types of *initial phase*: (1) the phase corresponding to the formation of a new household, which becomes autonomous either because it 'gets out' with the father's assistance, or else because he turns it out on his own remarriage; (2) the phase corresponding, not to the inheriting of the father's estate but to the taking-over of his position in the family. Either the father may come to live with one of his sons after appointing him as the new head of the family – *ra'īs al-'ā'ila* – or else, on the father's death, one of the sons may effectively take over the whole of the estate; (3) the phase corresponding to separation between the brothers, where this is brought about by the father's death and each founds a new domestic community. The initial phase ends either with the arrival of a second wife or else with the departure of the first son.

Next comes a series of phases which vary according to the exact situation with regard to the marriage and the inheriting of the estate. These phases will correspond to the arrival of a second, third, or *n*th wife, and/or the departure of the sons of the first, second, or subsequent marriages. The cycle is completed on the death of the head of the family or – should he do so in his lifetime – when he divides up the land and retires to live with one of his sons, whom he implicitly asks to succeed him. It should be noted that in such a case the son given preferential treatment before the father dies is generally a younger son or a son of the last marriage of all.

The above is a very much simplified description of the cycle followed by the big domestic community. In reality the situations are much more complicated, for two reasons, and we must now go into these in detail. Firstly, the progress of the cycle is bound up with the increase in wealth; secondly, the great variety of situations is due to the social condition of the stockbreeder or *fellah*.

THE INCREASE IN WEALTH AND THE RAPID INCREASE IN THE NUMBER
OF HOUSEHOLDS

The big domestic communities with their cycle in all its many and varied phases
are to be found, in the Djebel Anseriin, only where there is a certain degree
of wealth. The agricultural labourers and the workers employed on the
reafforestation sites – known as the 'tighten-the-belt workers' – live in small
households where there is only one wife, though they may remarry if the first
wife dies or if they have repudiated her for some reason. The big domestic
community makes its appearance only where the means of production – the
livestock or the land – are on a relatively large scale, for these provide the only
real basis for its unity.

What we have in common is the land and the means of working it, so what unites us is just
that – the work. We brothers and heirs are born of the same land and so should agree with
one another and not become divided when they divide up what was to be the link between
us. We are all tied to the land, just as the umbilical cord tied us all to the same mother. The
cord may be cut, but the mother is still common to all. It's the same with the land; each is
master in his own home, but the land belongs to all of us. We work on it, and we share its
fruit (*thamas*). If we say we each own 2.5 hectares, that's only for convenience, and for the
Administrator. When he asks any of us: 'How much do you own?' we answer by dividing
the whole of our land into six parts. But in reality it's only the ground which we divide – we
share the crops.(16)

However, the means of production are both the effects and the causes of a
regular production activity. Thus, the progress of the cycle itself becomes
both the effect and the cause of the expansion of production within the
domestic community; the more men there are to feed and the more women to
marry, the greater will be the amount of labour-power available, but the
greater will be the risk of having to eat into the accumulated reserves in time of
shortage. In the big domestic community the cycle is not a regular process
influenced only by the number of marriages and the number of children and their
sex; in reality the number of marriages and the number of children are partly
determined by the variations in the estate, with an eye to the chances and risks
on the level of production.

EFFECTS AND CONDITIONS OF EXPANSION

There are definite economic reasons for wishing to remain within a big
domestic community, just as there are for 'getting out' of the original community and founding a new one on the same pattern.

As long as one remains inside, it is possible to share a certain number of
production expenses which separate households, each composed of only one
married couple, would not be able to afford. The oxen or mule team, in particular
cannot be maintained unless there is to be regular cultivation of a sufficient

area – a *machia* – amounting, where traditional techniques are in use, to ten hectares. If the fragmentation of the domestic community means that the share given to each brother is below this minimum necessary to maintain a team of draught-animals, the inevitable long-term result will be that each of the newly-formed units will be unable to keep its yoke of oxen and that the whole group will lose its essential character, having lost its hold on an absolutely essential production factor.

It's always the women who split the brothers, and always over trifles. One of them wants to eat one thing and the other doesn't agree and prefers to cook something else, and neither will give in. Or else one of them has pinched the other one's son or daughter. When there's no one left in authority to silence them all, peace is finally restored by giving each one her own home. That's how it starts; the house is divided up, and the kitchen too; but as soon as the kitchen is no longer common to all, each one feels unjustly treated, and somebody will start eating more than he works for. So then the work is divided up, and the land, and the livestock, and it's all over, and each lives separately. And yet you live better all together. The three of us had 22 hectares and a good team of oxen – a household. What can we have now? Not even one ox each. As for sheep or cattle, a flock or herd couldn't live on 9 hectares. Even if you imagine it's going to be more peaceful, you're bound to lose when you all separate.(17)

On the other hand, in cases in which the big domestic community manages to survive, a better organization of the means of production is achieved. With a team of oxen, livestock, and vegetable gardens and orchards, there will be greater productivity, provided there are more than ten hectares per married couple, which is the level at which the traditional techniques become viable.

Three of my sons are married and I have three married daughters too. Ali lives with me; he's the one who farms my land. We live together; he's single at present – he's divorced twice. By his first wife he has a little girl who lives with her mother; she is the daughter of his aunt on his father's side, my sister Nadja bent Salah ben Larbi ben Ali ben Hadj Mohammed Bûtaghane Bejawwi. She was with my son for three years, and then they separated, I don't know why. It was my son who sent her away one day without telling me exactly why; it was in the days before independence when you could marry and divorce as you pleased. Then six years ago he separated from his second wife, Halima bent Belgacem ben Ahmed Bejawwi. It had been a marriage before witnesses, not officially registered, and the separating was done in the same way. As it happens she has married again since. My son has always lived with me; even when he was married we lived in the same house.

My eldest son Rabah hasn't left me either, but he lives with my father's wife and I have given them three hectares to farm. It's Rabah who takes care of all the land belonging to this wife of my father's, M'Barka bent Dahmani Ahûidad Trabelsi. She has no children and she has four hectares which she inherited for herself, and two further hectares she bought from Ali ben Hocine ben Kûider Bejawwi (one of them for fifteen dinars and the other for thirty dinars). That makes nine hectares for them to live on. Actually it's more; Rabah helps his brother on my land too and he takes any extra he needs, either at harvest time or during the year. It's not what you could really call a wage, nor is it *khammeisa*, it's because we all live together and there's no difference – if they haven't enough to eat, I can't have a meal without sharing it. We all take our food supplies out of the same store-houses, and when there's nothing left it's the same for everybody. It's the same with the work; how could

I take on a paid labourer when one of my sons is free? The two brothers share out the work between them, and the livestock belongs to all of us too, except for two cows which belong to my father's wife, and a mare and five ewes which belong to my son Rabah. The rest of the livestock – 14 ewes, 2 teams of oxen, 3 mules, one mare and one donkey – are common property. We also own 50 olive trees in common. Rabah lives with my father's wife because she it was who brought him up; he calls her 'mother' and she treats him as her son. My fourth son, Khalifa, lives with me too. I have married him to a distant cousin of my wife's, the daughter of Mahmoud ben Mohammed ben Ali Bejawwi, who is the son of my wife's uncle (*'amm*). He works on my land and makes one – or rather three – of the family.(18)

From the accounts given by the local people one can see the methods adopted by a father who is doing his utmost to keep the big domestic community together. He seeks, by marriages, legacies, purchases or sharecropping, to get together enough pieces of land to enable the married sons to farm in a profitable way. He makes them all use the same ox-team and lay up their food reserves in a common store, and he chooses their wives, or chooses to have them repudiated, to suit the ups and downs of the situation regarding the succession to the estate.

The tactics are similar where the head of the family is aiming to keep the property together to be farmed in common, notwithstanding the right of the daughters and widows to inherit land: he will make them wait for years and for practical purposes retain the use of the estate.

When my father died, I cleared his land of weeds and planted it, and drew up the contract on behalf of the heirs. My brother had left two wives, and they had one-eighth; he had had a son (who had died single before his father's death), and five daughters, and two of these are now dead. As chief heir (*'aṣaba*) I received a quarter of what was left ($\frac{7}{32}$) and the daughters shared out the rest between them; it must have come to about $2\frac{1}{3}$ hectares each. I got nearly 4 hectares. The widows left the home; one remarried and the other went home to her parents. We had agreed among ourselves that so long as the land had not been finally divided up I was to continue using it. Practically speaking, it was not until after the war that I gave each heir his due: it was when one of my nieces had died and her husband wanted us to give him her share. A bit earlier on the younger of the two widows had been impatient to receive hers too. Even then I kept everybody quiet a bit longer by giving them something or other – part of the crops, and especially small things like oil, fruit and vegetables. But on the whole my nieces didn't give me any trouble, it was almost of my own accord that I gave them back their land, and I believe that if I hadn't wanted to do so, I would be able even today to use at least the shares of those who are still alive. It's their heirs who, having nothing to lose and being more distant relatives, generally decide to assert their rights, even when their share is a very, very small one.(19)

However, the point at which the economic factors governing the formation and progress of the cycle are most visible is the point at which an elder son is in a position to 'get out', to set up his own home. Where the share of each is too small for subsistence to be possible, complete fragmentation will be inevitable.

What use would it be to remain together on just $2\frac{1}{2}$ hectares? If we spread out all the bedding, there wouldn't be room enough for 21 people...No, it wasn't because of a disagreement; on the contrary, as the younger son I found myself in a better position, I was freer to leave than my brother, and that was what I did. I said to myself that if I left my family I would manage to do something or other...No, I don't think that in our case it would have been a good plan to live together: what land was there to farm? If we had all inherited a share in some property we could have stayed together on the same land so as not to split up, especially as we are all children of the same mother and our mother is still alive.(19)

Where, on the contrary, the means of production are sufficient to enable the son to set himself up as an independent unit, everything is done to help him move out. The fission thus becomes a scission, and the new domestic community is set up on the same model as the original one.

I had taken over some land as a sharecropper and I used my father's oxen and other animals, as I could have them as much as I liked and do whatever I wanted with them. In fact my father encouraged me to take on and cultivate as much land as I could. That's the sign of the true farmer; he helped me until I had my own team of oxen, which I needed until I inherited my mother's. We shared the olives roughly half-and-half, and we did the same for the kitchen-garden and orchard (*sania*). We worked there together and shared the fruit and vegetables. So I had to provide nothing for myself beyond the corn, which is the biggest item. The richest fathers naturally give their children land; they give them a *machia* (a plot of land with a yoke of oxen). The children are supposed to be only share-croppers, but not many fathers actually take half their produce, though there are a few exceptions. Others help their sons by giving them a few head of sheep or cattle. My father gave me permission to put whatever animals I had to graze on his land. In return, a father may make use of his son as he likes and use his possessions as though they were his own. It's for that reason that the two are said to belong to the same household.(7)

ECONOMIC PLANNING AND ESTATE ACCOUNTANCY

A minimum amount of land and minimum means of production are not, however, the only prerequisites for the survival of the big domestic community, for the continuation of its cycle in whatever form it may have adopted, and for the units to reproduce themselves on the same model. There must also be economic planning with the aim not merely of preserving the estate in its entirety; unaffected by any deductions for purposes of subsistence, but actually with the aim of increasing it at the same rate as the increase in the number of individual households.

Under the traditional economic set-up, the preservation or replacement of property belonging to the estate was guaranteed by a certain number of *ratios* established by ancient custom; these were the contract of *khammisa*, the contract of *mughārasa* and the stockbreeding contracts. For the head of the family, observance of the norm prescribed by custom was a means of guaranteeing that the system would continue to work satisfactorily and it also provided him with the assurance of being able to tell in advance exactly where any breaking point lay. The use of money, as such, is not inconsistent with these customary-law *ratios*; on the contrary, it is a means of calculating more accurately the quantities to be weighed against one another. But with money, there can be expenditure on new goods, and this seriously upsets the traditional way of equating things. Money is an encouragement to the consumption of 'sumptuary' products such as tea and sugar, appreciated as stimulants, it is true, but also for their 'modernist' significance. When all is said, money payments are less advantageous for the payee than payments in kind. 'You can't find *khammās* these days; all the workers want to be paid so much per day, and in ready cash. For anyone who has the cash it's an advantage, because it comes less expensive in the end than paying them in kind.'(4)

From the point of view of the *fellah*, it is discouraging; as soon as he ventures to work out the cost of his production activity and the returns to be expected in terms of precise figures, he is struck by the low degree of productivity of the hard work he puts in.

It's easy to work out...since everything is done with money. Of my 18 hectares I have ploughed 11; the others have been left fallow, except 2 I have kept to grow a little sorghum. Of those I am sowing, 5 hectares are to be planted with wheat, 4 with barley and 2 with broad beans. That makes 5 quintals of seed for the wheat, 3 for the barley and two double decalitres for the beans. So far, that makes 28,000 to 30,000 francs. For labour I must allow 80 working days at 350 francs per day, which comes to as much as the seed; and I am counting only the autumn ploughing. I haven't included the work of preparing the fields in the spring – that will be entered under last year's expenditure. In any case I shall have to spend the same amount this year. I don't take on any paid labour for the weeding. Traditionally you must reckon as much for harvesting as for sowing – at least you did in the days when you paid in kind. Nowadays everyone wants money and it comes dearer, especially if the harvester is only cutting barley; he doesn't reap any faster than when it's wheat and the crop is worth only half as much. Besides I'd much rather give away half a harvest that's been brought in, than pay out money I don't possess. This year's harvest is going to cost me at least 35,000 francs, plus 5,000 francs for spring ploughing and 10,000 for summer ploughing...Threshing is generally not very expensive and is included under harvesting. You have to allow 120,000 francs for the cost of growing and bringing in 11 hectares of crops. If you lease the same land out to a sharecropper who agrees to give you half the crops, you spend only a quarter of that amount – 12,000 to 15,000 francs. It's better not to start weighing up what you'll be getting out of the land and what you put in; it's a part of God's secrets. You might just as well try to guess in advance what God intends to do as find out what the land is going to give; if you bare your stomach more than decency permits there's always a risk you'll be disappointed.(10)

Thus, most *fellahin* refuse to look too closely into their outlay and their returns; they drive their plough and *tawakul 'ala Allah* – leave the rest to the grace of God! What makes the *fellah* is not so much the size of his lands, the draught animals or the men, as his attitude of mind.

He has no animals or oxen, it's true, but that's not the reason he doesn't farm his land; it's because he has not turned wholeheartedly to his land and nothing else; he'd rather earn his living day by day and tighten his belt (*khaddam ahzam*). If he'd wanted draught animals he'd already have his team; all he had to do was what we have done. With one cow he'd have had a calf. He could have gone short of money that year and looked after the calf, and in two years it would have become an ox. Then he could have waited for a second and he'd have had his team. It would have meant working a bit more – three or four years for someone else – to be able to plough his own land; besides we would easily have lent him our ox-teams for a day. And in four years he'd have had his own team. It's not the land which makes the house, or, nowadays, even the men, though in the old days they used to say: 'A house full of people is more than a house full of goods (*beit erradjal kheir min elmal*). These days it's not all that that makes the farmer's home, it's the courage people have to farm the land, and their faith in the land, and the way they feel towards it. There are farmers' families which don't own a gramme of land of their own and farm other people's, and that is what all our ancestors did, by the way. They lived here and they took other people's land to work on; then they took 10, 20 or 30 hectares and a team of oxen and they all lived together on the same piece of land. When you have the land and you're farmers you have your flock or herd, you raise your animals, and all you need is to be brave and work hard.(21)

It is sufficiently clear from the data provided above that the phases of the cycle and the economic history of the domestic community are one and the same process. I am going to call 'estate planning' the operation which consists, within a given area of calculation, in reconciling legacy tactics and marriage strategy, producing and reproducing draught animals and livestock, taking and giving women in marriage, and keeping one's sons or having them leave. It will be seen that 'estate planning' is the arrangement of the cycle in phases in such a way that within each phase the assets and liabilities balance one another at the very least, and if possible show a profit. The larger the domestic community, the more stable will be the ratios of such figures between one phase and the next. The more children there are, the more likelihood there is that the numbers of each sex will balance. And the more women there are, the greater the chance that relations with 'allies' will equal one another. In the big domestic communities which were typical illustrations of the ideal family set-up, the art of estate planning went even further; allowance was made not only for the way the wives succeeded one another, but also for their co-existence, so as to balance out even more completely the burdens resting on the head of the family. One should hear Sheikh Mahmûd talk of his father, Sheikh Ahmed:

My father married six times. The first wife was Fatima ben Bûmerjil, of Qafaiya. She stayed on with the second wife, an Atar, who died. She also stayed on with the third wife, Embarka Umquauq Jlass. After the third wife he married a fourth one; I can't remember about her very clearly now – she was with him only a very short time and he sent her back home. The fifth wife is a Drid, Halima ben Saâd. The first wife was alive at the same time as the second one and the next ones. The second one died, so she didn't herself live with the third. The third one lived with the fourth, and when the fourth was repudiated she stayed on with the fifth one. The first wife knew the second, third and fourth wives. He married the fifth one only after he had divorced the fourth and the first one was dead. The last wife – my mother Aïcha – had known no one but the fifth one.(22)

Sheikh Mahmûd still cultivates today that same art of arranging for the wives to succeed one another, or to be there at the same time, as it suits him, just as he cultivates the art of making his sons 'get out' by giving them a portion, marrying them off and providing them with the most modern agricultural equipment, with a view to making his land a model of productivity. The ideal is doubtless an out-of-date one, and in any case it is beyond the reach of the majority. It belongs to a culture which daily appears more strange to us, so very strong is the trend in most present-day civilizations to consider the monogamous household as the ideal type of domestic arrangement. The pattern is thus one which no one wants to imitate any longer; it belongs to a culture which is lost, and all there is left for us to do is to try to understand its structure.

LIST OF INFORMANTS

(1) Ramdhan ben Ali ben Brik ben Mohammed Bûtaghan Bejawwi
(2) Abdelhafid ben Mohammed ben Brahim ben Ali Wannas Bejawwi
(3) Ahsen ben Nasr ben Khemi ben Hadj Ali Bûtaghan Bejawwi
(4) Ali ben Brahim ben Hadj Mohammed ben Hadj Rabbah Sidi Rabah Bejawwi
(5) Ahsen ben Mohammed ben Khemis ben Hadj Mohammed ben Ali Bûtaghan Bejawwi
(6) Rabah ben Amor ben Mohammed ben Ali Fraj Bejawwi
(7) Mohammed ben Ahmed ben Shaûsh Mabrûk ben M'Barek Wadjhani Bejawwi
(8) Haj Ramdhan ben Abdallah ben Mohammed Ahlal Riahi Daaji
(9) Hamda ben Belgacem ben Mabrûk ben Hamda Bejawwi
(10) Ali ben Ahsen ben Ahmed ben Haj Abadelawwi Bejawwi
(11) Amor ben Salah ben Athman ben Ali Wannas Bejawwi
(12) Khûmeis ben Amar ben Brik ben Mohammed Bejawwi
(13) Mahmûd ben Sliman ben Amor Mendil Bejawwi
(14) Ahmed ben Abdallah ben Mohammed Ahlal Riahi Daaji
(15) Haj Ramdhan ben Abdallah ben Mohammed Ahlal Riahi Daaji (Cf. 8)
(16) Hamda ben Belgacem ben Mabrûk ben Hamda Bejawwi (Cf. 9)
(17) Mohammed ben Athman ben Ardjab Riahi Arabi
(18) Mohammed ben Abdallah ben Kwider Bejawwi
(19) Ali ben Mabrûk ben M'Barek Wadjhani Bejawwi
(20) Bashir ben Ahmed ben Lakhden Wannas Bejawwi
(21) Mahmûd ben Ahsen ben Haj M'Barek ben Ahlal Riahi Daaji
(22) Haj ben Mahmûd ben Ahmed ben Mohammed Riahi Daaji

NOTES

1 The data collected for purposes of this paper were obtained through enquiries carried out in northern Tunisia, in the Djebel Anseriin, between 1956 and 1967. They were published extensively in J. Cuisenier, *Economie et parenté, leurs affinités de structure dans le domaine turc et dans le domaine arabe*. Paris, The Hague, Mouton, 1975, (*Le Monde d'Outre-Mer, passé et présent*, Etudes LX). See especially pp. 409–67.
2 For an example of the application of these concepts to data concerning France, see J. Cuisenier, 'Age et sexe dans la société provinciale française', *Echange et Communication*, Mélanges en l'honneur de Claude Lévi-Strauss, The Hague, Mouton 1970; J. Cuisenier, 'Société industrielle et famille conjugale', Mélanges en l'honneur de Raymond Aron, Paris, Plon, 1970.

6 Family and kinship in a Tunisian peasant community

N. Abu-Zahra

The University of British Columbia, Vancouver

I went to my father's brother [when I was in need], he blinded
me. I went to my mother's brother, he abandoned me.
            (Jit le-'ammi 'ammani, jit le-khali khallani.)
A Tunisian proverb heard in the village of Sidi Amer.

In this paper I maintain that the extended family – the *dār*[1] – is the model for the
larger patrilineal descent group – the *'arsh*[2] – the latter being composed of a
number of extended families which are genealogically related and which can, in
most cases, trace their descent from the same ancestor. Both of these social
units are based on the principle of patrilineal descent, but the transition from
one unit to another is not clear, and the confusion is echoed in the language
used to refer to them. The *dār* and *'arsh* also have exactly the same social duties,
the only difference being that these obligations are performed more conscien-
tiously by the members of the *dār*. Both are also the social units through which
membership in the community is established. Because of this lack of differentiation between the two units on both the terminological as well as on the social
level, it would be inaccurate to translate *dār* and *'arsh* into the two distinct
anthropological terms of lineage and clan respectively; therefore, throughout
this paper I shall refer to them by their native names. It is also my thesis that
neither of these two descent groups is a corporate unit for economic or legal
purposes, but that they are essentially corporate units for ceremonial purposes
with the main responsibility of supporting their members on occasions for celebrating the life-cycle ceremonies and performing the mourning rites. In the
first section of this paper I give an account of the factors which restrict the social
roles of these units; in the second section I describe how members of the *dār*
co-operate more scrupulously than the members of the *'arsh* on the occasions of
the life-cycle ceremonies.

The information in this paper is based on the anthropological field-work I
carried out from May 1965 to July 1966 in the village of Sidi Amer, in the Sahel
district on the eastern shores of Tunisia.[3] This village was founded more than
three centuries ago by Sidi Amer, a Muslim saint, after whom the village as well

as the religious order of al Ameriya (which he had also established) are named. The Zawiya, where Sidi Amer is buried, is the headquarters of this religious order, and is the most prominent building in the village; it is also the centre of both the ritual and social life of the village. The area surrounding the Zawiya is named after it, and is inhabited by the distinct group of Sidi Amer's descendants, 250 in number, who are referred to as the 'sons' of the Zawiya. Separated from them by the main road which divides the village into two halves are the Ramada people, who take the name of the quarter they inhabit. They are a large group of 2,000 persons who are members of four major 'arshs and a number of unaffiliated families.

Sidi Amer's descendants inherited from their ancestor the land of the village which he owned because he was the first person to settle there. They also benefited from the land and property with which the Zawiya was endowed (hubus),[4] and the 'promised gifts' offered by the Zawiya visitors to Sidi Amer's descendants when their vows were fulfilled. The right to this wealth is derived from their descent from Sidi Amer and this induced them to maintain an interest in their genealogy and made them conscious of their unity: the hubus money, for instance, was distributed amongst them according to their division into five 'arshs. On the other hand the Ramada people came to settle in the village later and worked as labourers on the land owned by Zawiya people, for they did not have the privileges of wealth which goes with descent and a longer period of residence in the community.

Social stratification in the village is mainly based on descent and the claim to a longer period of membership in the community. This emphasis on descent may be attributed to the constant changes in the ownership of olive trees which cannot, therefore, be the basis for social cleavage in the village. The village economy is based on olive-growing supplemented by working in Sousse, the capital of the Sahel, and Monastir, the second city in importance, between which two places the village of Sidi Amer is situated. Every villager owns some olive trees and the number may vary from as little as five to as many as 885, although there are only two men who have the latter quantity. Accumulation of wealth is not possible for, according to the Islamic laws of inheritance, the property of the parents is divided between all the heirs, brothers having two shares each, and sisters only one share each.

The hazards of dry farming also contribute to the variability in ownership of olive trees. In years when there is a poor olive crop or when people need cash, they sell olive trees; similarly, when they have saved some money, they buy olive trees. Ownership of olive trees is also available through special kinds of land tenure, in which the tenant comes to own some of the trees and the land on which they are planted in freehold ownership, as a payment for working on the land. In comparison with ownership of olive trees, descent is more constant. Therefore it is descent and the honour based on a long period of membership of the community, proven by a long genealogy, which are the bases of social cleavage in the village. In the case of the Zawiya people their claim to 'noble' descent is supported by the documented history of the establishment of the Zawiya and by the legal documents concerning the endowment of the *hubus* property to it. Their inheritance of Sidi Amer's land is proven by the inheritance documents which are nearly as old as the establishment of the village. There is also oral as well as written evidence (none of it, however, is historically trustworthy) referring to Sidi Amer as inheriting from his ancestors his *baraka* (divine blessing) and his ritual abilities which he transmitted to his descendants.

The *dār* and the *'arsh* serve the same purpose, i.e. they are the units through which membership of the community can be claimed, and consequently performance of the mourning rites and celebration of the life-cycle ceremonies are the occasions on which membership of the community is ascertained. The main responsibility of the *dār* and the *'arsh* is mutual aid between members, because to have the right to celebrate the life-cycle ceremonies and to perform the funeral rites is the privilege of the members of the community, and above all else is the sign and essential prerequisite by which an individual can claim respectability and prestige. An outsider (*barrānī*) cannot celebrate these ceremonies because nobody will visit him as he has no family or kin who can assist him in the preparation for the celebration or pay return visits to the guests on a similar occasion. Honouring a person by accepting his invitation on one of these ceremonial occasions is the sign that his membership in the community is acknowledged and ascertained. Because the prestige of the host's *dār* is measured by the number of guests assisting on such an occasion, it is no wonder that the basic obligation of the members of the *'arsh* is to assist each other at these ceremonies.

As both *'arsh* and *dār* have the same set of reciprocal rights and obligations, it seems that the only difference between them is that people can, through the *'arsh*, establish a longer period of membership in the community and, thus, prove that they are not outsiders. But if a man is a member of a small *dār* this may be the sign that his family has only recently settled in the village and he is an outsider by origin, which is highly despised. It is for this reason also that the *'arsh* is larger in size than a *dār*, for this is a sign of its depth in time. However, to claim membership of an *'arsh* a man has first to be a member of a *dār*. Thus, in this respect the difference between the functions of an *'arsh* and a *dār* is in the degree of the importance of the function rather than of its nature; yet, because it establishes a longer period of membership in the community, it is more advantageous to belong to an *'arsh*. It is not surprising then that this lack of social differentiation between the two units is reflected in the terminology.

The smallest social unit is the elementary family composed of the husband, wife, and their children and this is called a *dār*. The same word is also used for a larger household composed of the elderly parents, their married sons and the latter's children, when all of them are living in the same house. The same unit is still called a *dār* even when sons have their independent households. People may also refer to any of these units by using the word *familia*, the arabicized form of either the Italian word *famiglia* or the French word *famille* (the Italian language was widely spoken in Tunisia before the advent of the French Protectorate in 1881 and many Italian words have been absorbed into spoken Tunisian Arabic). The *dār* as an extended family composed of the parents and their married sons is thus the basic social unit and is the most important one. Solidarity between members of one *dār* are stronger than those between members of the *'arsh* who are usually members of related *dārs* which claim descent from the same founding ancestor. In legal contexts the *'arsh* may be referred to by the word *fariq*; however, it is not uncommon for both the words *'arsh* and *farīq* to be used to denote a *dār*, nor for the words *dār* and *familia* to be used to refer to the whole *'arsh*. Sometimes, curiously enough, the *dār* is even referred to by the combination of the two words of *'arsh* and *dār*; for instance, one may be told that this is *'arsh dār* el-Hadi, or *'arsh dār* Wunaiyes.

The *dār* is the model for the *'arsh*; the reciprocal duties and obligations between members of both groups are the same but, amongst the members of the *dār*, they are strictly adhered to, as we shall see in the second section of this paper.

One specific connotation of the word *dār* as distinct from the concept of *'arsh* is the warmth and physical nearness the word evokes. The physical proximity of the members of one *dār* is one of its major characteristics compared to the *'arsh* whose members usually live in different towns: members of the same *dār* either live in the same house or in neighbouring houses, while *dārs* of the same *'arsh* may not live near to each other. The value they set on proximity is expressed by the fact that when someone moves it is considered a calamity for him not to be living with his own kin. If a man wants to sell a piece of land for building a house, his brother or his father's brother's son has the first claim to it: if no one in a man's own *dār* wants to buy it, then a member of the *'arsh* has a prior claim to it. Olive groves owned by members of the same *dār* or *'arsh* are situated near to each other: and so are the tombs of members of one *dār* or *'arsh* in the cemetery.

The familiarity between members of one *dār* is extended to members of the same *'arsh* who may call their co-members 'father's brother's son from the same *'arsh*' (*ibn 'amm el-'arsh*). When middle-aged married men and women from the same *'arsh* meet they may kiss each other on the cheek, but this form of greeting is not practised by men and women who belong to different *'arshs*. Members of the same *'arsh* also visit each other more freely than members of different *'arshs*, amongst whom visits are confined to the formal occasions of the life-cycle ceremonies, or visits to console a deceased's family if the latter had previously paid the former a similar visit. In the life-cycle ceremonies members of the same *dār* and *'arsh* celebrate together. All members of the same *'arsh* should also mourn together if any other member dies. 'We rejoice together and mourn together', the villagers say when referring to the unity of their *'arsh*. If a member of a certain *'arsh* slights a member of another by not visiting him on the appropriate occasion, all members of the latter's *'arsh* should boycott the former; this is the worst of all punishments since to be deprived of these visits by the members of a whole *'arsh* is a serious matter.

In both the Zawiya and the Ramada sections of the village neither the *'arsh* nor the *dār* is a corporate unit in the political, legal, or economic sense. Members of both sections of the village are members of the village community and all members of the two groups are referred to by the word *al-Ameri* when they are outside the village. Nor do the Zawiya, nor the Ramada groups, nor the village as a whole, form a final political unit within which it is held appropriate to resort to mediation in cases of conflict. The village community, culturally and morally, is part of the Sahel region and Tunisia as a whole.[5] Order in the village had always been maintained in the past through its shaikh, who was appointed by the government. Today, in addition to the shaikh of the village, there are also the National Guards[6] and the village branch of the Socialist Neo-Destour Party branch, and both of the latter organizations are also responsible for maintaining order. Neither of the two sections of the village, nor any of their sub-groupings, has elder assemblies or chiefs, and no one has formal political authority over anyone else. The only acknowledged authority is that of the head of the family over his wife and children, and his married sons if they are living with him. This is the ideal, but in practice this is not always the case, for there are cases of conflict between father and son. There are also disputes between husband and wife, between members of the same *dār*, between members of different *dārs* from the same *'arsh*, or from different *'arshs*. These conflicts may be about inheritance, divorce, custody of children, drunkenness, or violence.

In a dispute between the members of one *dār* (which is rare), the members of two *dārs* from the same *'arsh*, or between members of *dārs* from different *'arshs*, people take sides in these disputes not only according to their membership of a certain group, but particularly according to their own interests and their relationship with the litigants in the dispute.

All major conflicts are solved in the courts of Sousse and Tunis. Minor conflicts between women such as, for instance, when one woman has given birth to a boy and another woman is jealous because at the same time she has given birth to a girl, or disputes resulting from jealousies between co-wives are all solved by the customary practice of not visiting the guilty party. Order and discipline are maintained by intervention from without the community and are not based on the internal structure of either the *'arsh* or the *dār*.

There are no ritual activities which might unite the members of each *'arsh*, nor are there any political organs such as the council of elders, nor economic activities such as communal ownership of land, which might create a stronger bond between them. Similarly, the elementary families which compose an 'extended' *dār* are economically independent of one another. Each *dār* is composed of the households of the group of brothers and, perhaps, the father's son, who, although they may be still living in the 'divided' house of the founder of the *dār*, have become economically independent and do not share the expenses for the upkeep of the members of their households; the head of each household is responsible for its expenses. Of this arrangement the villagers say that 'they do not share the expenses' (*mush fard maṣruf*), or that 'they do not eat from the same pot' (*mush fard ma 'un*). The wealth of the heads of different *dārs* varies considerably. Also the work in each household is done independently, each housewife being responsible for her own housework. Each of these households would also have its clients who work for it, and its own friends and visitors. Although children of these households can play together and visit each other freely, and even eat if invited, yet women try to restrict their visits to the institutionalized occasions, and they would drop in for a meal only infrequently.

The lack of co-operation between the members of the extended family and the splitting up of the group of brothers is due to psychological as well as social factors. When the sons are first married they stay in their father's house, but soon after his death, or perhaps even during his life-time, the married sons either leave or divide the father's house, and each of them sets up his independent household. In the former case they build their houses next to each other and a whole quarter may be occupied by a group of brothers, father's brothers or perhaps father's brother's sons, and would be named after their *dār*. There are many examples of this in the Ramada quarter.

The reasons why a group of brothers may split up are various; one is the conflict over authority between the father and his sons. If the married sons are working with their father they may aspire to assume responsibility which may be resented by the latter. In one such case the father and his son owned a lorry and carried on together a small business in grain. They did not get on well; finally, the father accused the son of stealing three dinars from him, abused him and struck him in public. As a result of this incident the son left his father's house, joined his wife's family household and was allowed to take part in their business. The father considered it an insult that his son was no longer under his control: he waylaid him in the street and struck him. The son then complained about his father to the police and the father was ordered not to interfere with his son.

In another case, a man struck his father because he disliked his father's sister's son who had been invited to the house by his father. In this case the shaikh of the village and the police had to intervene and punish the son by beating him.

Brothers are also economically independent, each being responsible for his own family. The wealthier brother, be he older or younger, is under no obligation to assist the poorer brother, unless the latter should be completely destitute. There are many examples of this: one brother may be a qualified professional owning a car and a comparatively modern house, and even employing a maid to help his wife with the household chores, while his brother next door may be unqualified and may work as a porter in a school, living very modestly in a small old house without a car or vehicle of any kind, while his wife has no help in the house. In spite of this relative poverty, his wealthy brother would have no obligation to help him, for it is believed that every man should be responsible for his own family. The example is not unusual: there are many similar cases.

The differences in economic standards separating the brothers is manifest in many ways. For instance, the houses of wealthier brothers may be supplied with water and electricity while the houses of poorer brothers lack these facilities; the quantity and quality of their furniture may differ; the women and children of wealthier brothers may be better dressed. The family of a poorer brother will avoid visiting the wealthier brother's family unnecessarily. The wife will refrain from visiting, because her friends and neighbours may think that she is helping her husband's brother's wife with the household chores in return for money or food; she will also resent her children going to play with the children of a wealthier father's brother, as people may think that they are working in their father's brother's house in return for being fed. Similarly, wealthy brothers do not have much in common with their poorer brothers and do not try to associate with them.

In a conflict of interest between brothers, self-interest is most likely to prevail, and this attitude helps to split up a group of brothers, for they will not necessarily and unconditionally support each other but must watch out for their own interests. In one case, a villager quarrelled with another over the inheritance of a share of a house. One litigant was the *ḥaḍra* Muqaddim,[7] a descendant of Sidi Amer who was important in the Zawiya affairs because he was renowned for the efficacy of the charms he wrote. The other litigant was a poor man, although he had influential brothers. Two of his brothers supported him, but a third was neutral. He claimed that he was in mourning for his son, but in fact he was under obligation to the *ḥaḍra* Muqaddim because he used to work with him. When the Muqaddim had more customers than he could attend to, he used to delegate the writing of charms to this man, and they would share the earnings. As a result of this relationship, the man refrained from taking his brother's side in the dispute.

In another case the director of the Agricultural Co-operative asked his brother to make a certain payment to the Co-operative, in accordance with government instructions. In addition, the Co-operative also decided (in accordance with the government's agricultural project for the renewal of the Sahel's olive groves) that a certain number of his olive trees had to be cut down. When the brother heard of this decision he was disappointed since he thought that his brother, according to the principle of patrilineal solidarity, should have exempted him from this payment, and that his olive trees should not have been cut down. His wife and daughters were also upset; they suggested that the father's brother should pay for his mistake and said that they would take their revenge on his daughter who was married to her father's brother's son.

Polygamy is another factor which may create conflict between the group of brothers.[8] Brothers begotten by the same father from different mothers are not as united as brothers from the same mother. It is not unusual for a mother to incite her children against her co-wife and co-wife's children. There was one case in which a son, under his mother's influence, burnt his mother's co-wife with a live coal. As a result of competition between co-wives, sons of co-wives grow up to resent each other and their own wives pick quarrels easily, since the brothers do not try to restrain them. On the other hand, children by the same mother but by different fathers may be more affectionate to each other than to half-brothers by the same father. For instance, a Ramada man married a woman from Monastir and had a daughter by her; she was later divorced and married a Zawiya man by whom she had a son; then she died. The daughter's step-mother treated her badly and her half-brother was similarly treated by his step-mother: this brought the two children together. In spite of the fact that the brother had other half-brothers (by his father) he had hardly any relationship with them except on formal occasions such as the celebration of a marriage taking place within the family, or the two Muslim feasts of 'Īd al-Fiṭr (at the end of the month of Ramadan) and 'Īd al-Aḍhā. He preferred his sister's company to that of his brothers, and they frequently exchanged visits in spite of the fact that they lived in the two separate quarters of the village and women living on one quarter do not exchange visits with people living in the other quarter.

The daily disputes between brothers' wives when they are living together also hastens the splitting up of a group of brothers. Jealousy between the wives when one wife has sons and the other has daughters may cause quarrels. Each wife also likes to have authority in her own household and may resent inter-ference from the other wives in her own affairs, particularly in the disciplining of her children. Similarly there may be disputes between the wives and their mother-in-law over authority in the household. In one case the son's wife refused to continue to live with her mother-in-law on the pretext that the latter beat her grandson for throwing a ball at her and knocking out her front teeth. The wife took advantage of the fact that the mother-in-law was strongly criti-cized by the villagers for beating the child for such a trivial matter (in their eyes), and used this to bring pressure on her husband to leave his father's house. In several other cases it was the mother-in-law who asked her daughters-in-law to leave the house. The general pattern, however, is that daughters-in-law complain about their mothers-in-law and maintain that the latter incite their sons against them. Therefore it is usually the wives who press their husbands to form independent households.

The principle of patrilineal solidarity is also impaired by the practice of adopting one of the wife's brother's offspring if the wife is herself barren.[9] (In a few cases she adopts her sister's offspring.) There are many cases in which the woman said she adopted one of her brother's offspring in preference to her husband's brother's offspring because she was particularly attached to her brother and preferred to have one of his children rather than a child of her husband's brother. A child adopted in this fashion calls its adoptive parents *ummī* and *bābā*, my mother and father, exactly as if they were its natural parents. The adoptive parents are responsible for the child's education. If it is a boy they are responsible for celebrating its circumcision, when the adoptive mother plays the role of the natural mother. If the adopted child is a girl they are responsible for arranging her marriage and buying her trousseau, and at the wedding ceremonies they play the roles which are usually performed by the natural parents. The adopted child usually knows its natural parents and goes to play with its brothers and sisters in their parents' house. The child also bears the name of the natural father, but all its filial duties and social services are devoted to the adoptive parents from whom it inherits property.[10] If it were the custom for barren couples to adopt a child from the husband's family instead of the wife's brother's son, that would tend to strengthen the principle of patrilineal solidarity rather than to weaken it, as tends to happen in the former alternative.

The principle of patrilineal solidarity is also impaired by the ambivalent position of a married sister who belongs to her paternal family and is socially and economically dependent on her brothers, in spite of the fact that by giving birth to sons she perpetuates another *dār* and contributes her work to it. A married woman always bears the name of the *dār* and *'arsh* in which she was born, and when her parents die she inherits a share of their property. This is later transferred to her husband's group through her offspring who inherit her property when she dies.

The social incorporation of a married woman into her husband's *dār* is a very slow process; the gradual incorporation is expressed by various rites of passage which start on the wedding night, and also various ceremonies and gift-exchanges, between the families of the two spouses, take place in the early years of marriage, and on the birth of the first baby, for until then the newly-married woman is still called 'the virgin' (*al-bikr*). The gradual incorporation into the husband's family is only completed when the wife has grown-up sons. Until then her brothers are responsible for her in case of crisis, and for her burial in case of death. In the event of divorce or the death of the husband, the woman's father or brother is responsible for her upkeep in return for her work in his house. Had her incorporation into her husband's family been complete, she would have gone to live and work with one of her husband's brothers, but this is never the case.

A married sister may also receive material support from her wealthier brothers if her husband is in need, and they may find work for him if he is unemployed; in return for these services she has to help her brothers' wives with the household chores. All this would weaken the position of the husband, as he would not have exclusive rights over his wife. If he goes to live in his wife's brothers' house, his authority over his wife diminishes even more and there is the danger that he may himself be incorporated into her family, rather than the other way round.

For all these reasons men who want to have authority in their own house avoid marrying a woman who has a very strong father or brothers. It is not surprising, then, to find that daughters of powerful families are married either to poor men in their own villages or else to outsiders, where the husbands are far away, and their authority in their households is not likely to be impaired by the constant presence of the wife's father or her brothers.

In ceremonial contexts also the mother's brother has an important role to play on behalf of his sister's son; for instance, on the occasion of the latter's circumcision. He has other duties also to perform for his sister's daughter at her wedding ceremonies. The mother's sisters also participate in these ceremonies. Similarly, the sister and her sons have many responsibilities in celebrating the betrothal and wedding of the mother's brother's son.

Although the maternal kin is important, the most significant social group is undoubtedly that of the *dār*: the group of brothers have many important responsibilities towards one another, particularly in connexion with the life-cycle ceremonies. In this respect the *dār* is the model for the *'arsh*.

The solidarity between the brothers begins when they are still in their father's house. The eldest brother is expected to make presents of sweets and money to his younger brothers on such occasions as the two *'īd* ceremonies (see p. 168). On the same occasions he may also be expected to give presents to the brother born immediately after him, who in turn makes presents of sweets to his younger brothers and to his mother.

If the eldest brother is earning money, he is responsible for contributing towards the upkeep of his father's household. He sometimes gives his father the whole of his salary, and in this case the father is expected to build his son a room in his house which the son will occupy when he gets married.

If the father is poor and the eldest son is earning enough money, he may be responsible for the education of the younger brothers. Sometimes the younger, wealthier, brother may contribute to the education of the elder brother's son, but this is an exceptional case which would take place only if the younger has daughters and the elder has sons. In one such case a man contributed to the education of his brother's eldest son because the boy had been betrothed to his own daughter when he was quite small and the girl was newly-born. When the brother's son finished his education and got a job, he married his father's brother's daughter.

The eldest brother is also responsible for buying the trousseau and the wedding outfit for his sisters when they get married.[11] Even when the brothers are married and are living in another town they are still responsible for contributing their share in buying their sisters' trousseau and outfit. Even when the eldest son is married and is no longer expected to give his father the whole of his salary, he still contributes to the household if the father is poor.

In view of these facts it is not surprising, then, that it is the eldest brother who is most respected by his younger brothers and sisters; they address him as 'my master' (*sīdī*). But the eldest brother is the only one to be addressed in this fashion. Exceptionally, where the father is dead and a younger brother is preceded by sisters, he would enjoy the respect usually granted for an eldest brother if he had supported his sisters and bought their trousseau when they got married. Because of his responsibilities towards his younger brothers and sisters the eldest brother ought to have authority over them, and has the right to discipline his younger brothers and sisters, and even to beat them if they do not obey him.

When the brothers are older, co-operation between them is demonstrated in other ways. If a villager is building a house, his brothers and his sons help him and *couscousi* and meat are given to them when the foundations are laid. Similarly, when a woman is roasting wheat and fenugreek for the special food (*'bsīsa*) for the woman in childbirth as well as the guests who go to congratulate her, all the wives of her husband's brothers come to help.[12]

Another expression of the solidarity of the group of brothers is the preference for marriage to the father's brother's daughter, even when the woman has wealthier and more prestigious suitors. In one case, a number of good suitors were refused the hand of a certain girl, and the father insisted that she should marry her father's brother's son. In this case the father was worried about giving his daughter in marriage to an outsider which would have meant her going to live far away from her own family where they were not sure how she would be treated. Moreover, the father was well-off and did not want his daughter to transfer her share of the inheritance to outsiders. Concerning marriage to the father's brother's son, members of the *dār* say: 'May God not lessen the number of our men and women' (*Allah la yeqellina la min erijal wala min en-nsa*). Concerning the prior claim of the father's brother's son to the hand of his father's brother's daughter, they say: 'The father's brother's daughter could always be taken back [by her father's brother's son] even if she is on the camelback[13] [on her wedding night on her way to the bridegroom's house]' (*bint el 'amm mafkuka keif tezal fi jaḥfa*). This implies that the father's brother's son's right is safeguarded if he was away when his father's brother's daughter became engaged to another man.

It is not obligatory, however, for a man to marry his father's brother's daughter to save her from spinsterhood. In one case there were two old maids with a number of younger father's brother's sons. When I suggested to the latter that they ought to marry these older father's brother's daughters, as custom demanded, they answered that they did not want to marry them because the women were old and illiterate, and they wanted modern wives who would be educated, and would wear modern European dress rather than the Tunisian *sefsari* (a white cotton overall which covers the whole body).

Similarly, when a man is uneducated and does not earn enough money, this is good reason for his father's brother's daughter and her parents to refuse to give her to him in marriage. When the presence of such a father's brother's son is pointed out to the mother of an unmarried daughter, she will say: 'How can we give her to a father's brother's son who is both foolish and stupid as an animal?' (*ibn 'amm bhim mahbul ye'tyuha luh*). In one case a woman did not want to marry her father's brother's son because he was not educated or qualified for any profession and was working as a labourer. Her family insisted that she should marry him, since if she were to marry outside the family she would automatically transfer the house she inherited from her father, as she was the only heir, to her husband. Instead the girl eloped with a teacher who was from an inferior *'arsh*. The girl's family sued the man, but the girl declared in court that she preferred the teacher to her uneducated father's brother's son. She married the teacher and although she had a legal right to her father's house, she was not allowed to inherit it.

Co-operation between the brothers has also another aspect: when a man dies leaving unmarried daughters, it is his brothers' responsibility to arrange these daughters' marriages. It is they who are asked for the girls' hands, and the eldest brother is responsible for signing the marriage contract. During the betrothal and wedding ceremonies the father's brother plays all the social roles which are usually the responsibility of the father. If there are no father's brothers, a father's brother's son may play these roles.

Co-operation between the group of brothers is also shown on the following occasions: circumcision, marriage and the mourning rites. On these occasions all the members of the *'arsh* have also to give their support to the family concerned by their attendance, but the members of the *dār* have more specific roles to play: the father's brother has certain responsibilities on the occasion of the circumcision of the brother's son. A wealthy brother may have to contribute to the cost of the circumcision ceremonies of his poor brother's son in order to increase the prestige of his family. On the *maulidiyya* night, the first day of the circumcision celebrations when hymns in praise of the prophet are sung,[14] the father of the circumcised boy is responsible for receiving guests and offering them food; but the father may be replaced by his brother who is also responsible for supervising the collection of money taken up for the father. If the father of the circumcised boy is illiterate, his educated brother attends to the writing down of the names of the donors and the sums of money they paid the father. To explain the absence of the father it is said that his presence is unnecessary since his brother was there. The brother may also volunteer to hire and pay expenses of the band of musicians brought to celebrate the occasion, and later on the brother is paid back out of the money collected for the father. The father of the circumcised boy and his brother are also responsible for paying and tipping the band of musicians when, at the end of the celebrations, they sing the last song for the circumcised and his mother (*ta'lilat al-mṭṭāhir*). For this song they are given three dinars as a tip. On the *maḥḍar* when the women celebrate the circumcision, the father of the circumcised boy may dance with his brothers. On the third day of the celebration when the circumcision takes place, the father's brother is usually one of the two persons who hold the boy's legs apart (the other person being the mother's brother). After the circumcision the father and father's brother may again dance together.

The brothers have other responsibilities during the wedding celebrations. In *khalwat al-'arūs*, when the bridegroom goes to the public bath with the *ḥajjaba* group which includes his unmarried brothers, unmarried father's brothers' sons (and unmarried friends), one of them is always on his right side and is called the *wazīr*. Afterwards the bridegroom goes to the Zawiya to change his clothes and he sits outside the Zawiya surrounded by his *ḥajjāba*, while Sidi Amer's *ḥaḍra* sings religious hymns in praise of the Prophet and Sidi Amer. Later the bridegroom leaves the Zawiya surrounded by the *ḥajjāba*. On the wedding night, the *ḥajjāba* and the maternal kin of the bridegroom accompany him to the bride's house, where the bride's parents are waiting outside the house for the bridegroom to kiss their heads. The *ḥajjāba* should also be present with the bridegroom on the wedding morning when the band of musicians sing for his bride and the women guests. During the wedding ceremonies it is important that the *ḥajjāba* should include some of the bridegroom's mother's brothers' sons, but their presence is less important than that of the father's brothers' sons, whose absence would be noticed and considered odd.

The importance of the group of brothers and sisters is also emphasized on the occasion of funeral rites. The members of the deceased's *'arsh* are also under an obligation to support the deceased's family by consoling them and observing the mourning rites which include postponing for a year any marriage or circumcision celebrations, abstaining from eating fish (which is considered to have the power to avert the evil eye; eating it during the mourning period would expose the bereaved family to ridicule), sweets, pastries, or listening to the wireless. But, in addition to these mourning observances, the immediate members of the family of the deceased have most important roles to perform in these respects.

When a person dies, his mother, sisters, and father's brothers' wives start wailing. They may also be joined by other women, whose presence, however, is less important than the first category of women. The participation of the women of the deceased's family is essential because its prestige will depend on the number of women from the family who are there to wail over him.

When the deceased is being washed before burial, his mother and sisters put the water used for washing him on their faces as a sign of their love and sorrow. No other member of the *dār* is expected to do this. Afterwards the dead man's mother, sisters, father's sisters, mother's sister, father's brothers, and mother's brothers tell him that if he had hurt any of them, or owed any of them money, they forgive him. This they call the *samāḥ*. Thus, the deceased is relieved, in the afterworld, of some of his sins. 'He goes to the next world with less sin' (*yeruḥ lil-akhra mukhafafa min adh-dhnub*), so the villagers say. It is his family's responsibility to render him this last service; other members of his *'arsh* are under no obligation to do so.

In the cemetery before the deceased is buried, his father, brothers, and father's brothers, stand in a line to receive the condolences of the villagers.

As a sign of their mourning the dead man's family do not cook for the first nine days after his death. The villagers send them cooked food, tea and coffee, and as the families of his father's brothers are also considered to be in mourning the villagers send them cooked food also. On the tenth day after death the villagers stop sending food to the deceased's family, and it becomes the responsibility of the deceased's father's sister and his father's brother's wives to send large quantities of food, for there are always other people staying with the deceased's family, or coming from far away places and having to be fed. After the tenth day the dead man's family can cook for themselves.

The father's sisters and fathers' brother's wives of the deceased stay for nine nights in the house to console his family. Friends of the family stay only one or two nights. From time to time, until the fortieth day after death, the former category of women come to stay overnight with the deceased's family, but no one else outside the circle of brothers and sisters is expected to observe this duty.

For forty days after the death, the deceased's mother, sisters, and father's brothers' wives go to the cemetery to receive the condolences of the women of the other faction. These women would not come to the house to console them because of the non-visiting relationship between the women of the two factions of the village. However they may meet in the cemetery.

In view of the above facts it may be concluded that the group of brothers is the most significant social unit, and its importance is mainly manifest in the ceremonial life. In this respect it is the model for the *'arsh* which is mainly important because it supplies its members with the genealogy necessary for establishing long-time membership of the community and hence the claim to 'noble' descent.

NOTES

1   The word *dār* refers to the family as well as the building it occupies.
2   In the Quran, the word *'arsh* refers to the 'Divine Throne of God' (see the following suras in the Quran: IX–130, XXI–22, XXIII–87, 117, XXVII–26, XL–15, LXXXV–15,

XLIII–82). In literary Arabic the word came to denote also the throne of a king; however, in the spoken Arabic in Tunisia, it was not used to refer to the throne of the Bey. The word *'arsh* and the ubiquitous Arabic word for tribe, *qabīla*, are used synonymously in both the spoken and written Tunisian Arabic to denote a tribe (see al-Dayyaf, Ahmed ben Abi, *Ithāf Ahl al-Zamān bi-akhbār Mulūk Tunis wa-'Ahd al-Aman*, seven volumes, Tunis, 1963–6, Vol. III, pp. 50, 83; Vol. IV, p. 93; Vol. V, pp. 124, 161–2, 186; Vol. VI, pp. 30, 39, 68; Vol. VII, p. 60). But in the village of Sidi Amer the word *'arsh* refers to a number of genealogically related extended families who claim descent from the same ancestor. When the villagers are asked whether the word *'arsh* means a *qabīla* they say: 'No the *qabīla* is larger, it branches more.' This particular usage of the word *'arsh* is different from other parts of Tunisia and North Africa where the word means a tribe. An example of this is the usage of the word *'arsh* by al-Dayyaf to refer to the large tribes of Zlass, Frechich or Majeur; and according to Pierre Bourdieu, the Kabyles of Algeria use the word *'arsh* to refer to several villages which compose the tribe. See Pierre Bourdieu, *The Algerians*, translated from the French by Alan C. M. Ross, Boston, Mass., Beacon Press, 1962, p. 3.

3 I would like to acknowledge my thanks to the U.A.R. Ministry of Higher Education for kindly financing my anthropological expedition in Tunisia.

4 In 1957 the Tunisian government promulgated a law by which all *hubus* land was liquidated.

5 Ernest Gellner, 'Saints of the Atlas', in *Mediterranean Countrymen*, J. A. Pitt-Rivers (ed.), The Hague, Mouton, 1967, p. 146.

6 Villages where there are no police stations are supervised by the National Guards who replaced the French *Gendarmerie* after independence. Each Delegation, an administrative section of the Province, has its own National Guards which supervise the villages administered by that Delegation.

7 The *hadra* Muqaddim is the leader of the musical band which gathers every Thursday night in the Zawiya building to sing religious hymns in praise of the Prophet and Sidi Amer.

8 The new Personal Status Code promulgated in 1959 prohibits polygamy.

9 If the adopted child is a baby, the adoptive mother passes it through the top of her garment and receives it from underneath, thus simulating giving birth to it.

10 The customary practice of adoption and the right of the adopted child to inherit is not in accordance with the stipulation of the *Sharī'a* Laws of inheritance. However, the new Personal Status Code which was promulgated on 1 January 1957 legalized the customary practice of adoption and the right of the adopted child to inheritance.

11 It is only well-off families who buy their daughters a wedding outfit; poorer families hire them.

12 In the past the neighbours would also come to help the woman on this occasion, and this was called *et-tu'az*. However, this practice is obsolete now, as people buy many of their needs ready-prepared from Sousse. Now the woman preparing the childbirth food only receives help from her husband's brothers' wives.

13 In the past it was the custom for the bride to go to her groom's house carried on a camel's back, but now she goes in a procession of cars.

14 This celebration is called *maulidiyya* because the anniversary of the prophet when hymns in praise of the Prophet are sung is called *maulid*: from this the word *maulidiyya* is derived which refers to an occasion on which religious hymns in praise of the Prophet are sung.

7 Aspects of kinship and family structure among the Ulad Stut of Zaio rural commune, Nador province, Morocco[1]

David Seddon
University of East Anglia

INTRODUCTION

Even within Morocco the province of Nador is both poor and underdeveloped. Already heavily over-populated, the province as a whole shows an extremely high rate of demographic increase, and the level of unemployment has been rising over the last two decades, despite labour migration to Algeria until 1955, and to western Europe since around 1962. The farming economy, based on wheat and barley, and still the main source of subsistence and livelihood for the mass of the people, is stagnant; there is no industry worth speaking of,[2] and, despite the apparently large proportion of the active population involved in trade and commerce, large-scale entrepreneurs are few, regular employment in this sector is rare, and the income derived from the majority of these 'penny capitalist' commercial enterprises is generally small. (Seddon 1971).

The population of the province is overwhelmingly rural, but the small villages and urban nuclei, founded during the Spanish colonial occupation as military camps and administrative centres, have been growing fast since independence in 1956. This accentuates the pre-existing difference in population density, even in the rural areas, between the hilly regions closest to the provincial capital, Villa Nador, and to the Spanish town of Melilla, in the north, and the more open country to the south.

It is clear that, in Nador, social and economic inequality have a spatial aspect, among others. One source gives the province an average income of $72 a head,[3] with a range of between $100 in the wealthier districts around the urban centres of the north, and $30 in the predominantly rural south, while another puts the average per capita income in the rural areas as low as $18–$20 (Ministère d'Agriculture, n.d., p. 4; Office National d'Irrigation, 1964, p. 37; Seddon 1971). Even within the poorer southern regions of the province, the average standard of living, and cost of living, is higher in the village centres than in the surrounding countryside.

The province is divided into three major administrative units, called circles,

173

each under the authority of a *qāʾid-mumtāz*, and thirteen annexes, each under a *qāʾid*. The boundaries of these annexes coincide largely with the geographical limits of the fifteen tribes of the province, the majority of which (13) are Berber-speaking, and the remainder (2) Arabic-speaking. Nador also comprises twenty-six rural communes, created by royal decree in 1960, ostensibly to provide a basis for the gradual establishment of democratic local government throughout the Moroccan countryside (Seddon 1971b; 1972). (See Table.)

TABLE 1

Circle	Rural commune	Annexe/tribe	Language	Total pop.[a]	Pop. density
Luta	Zaio	Ulad Stut	Arabic	10,500	24
	Ras el Ma	Kebdana	Berber		
	Qaria-t-Arkeman	Kebdana		30.700	50
	Hassi Berkan	Beni bu Yahi	Berber		
	Driush	Beni Ukil	Arabic		
	Tistutin	Beni bu Yahi			
		Benni Ukil		18,800	15
	Driush	Metalsa	Berber	————	
	Ain Zohra	Metalsa		28,100	17
Gelaia	Nador	–	–	18,500	–
	Ferkhana	Mazuja	Berber	28,000	126
	Had Beni Shicar	Beni Shicar	Berber	21,500	127
	Iazanen	Beni bu Gafar	Berber	8,300	131
	Tleta Jbel	Beni Sidel	Berber		
	Tleta Luta	Beni Sidel		22,900	73
	Selwan	Beni bu Ifrur	Berber		
	Beni bu Ifrur	Beni bu Ifrur		25,200	123
Rif	Dar Kebdani	Beni Said	Berber		
	Tazarhin	Beni Said		31,700	78
	Ben Tiyeb	Beni Ulishek	Berber		
	Mehayast	Beni Ulishek		22,100	100
	Kemis Temsaman	Temsaman	Berber		
	Budinar	Temsaman			
	Trugut	Temsaman		36,800	87
	Ijermauas	Beni Tuzin	Berber		
	Midar	Beni Tuzin			
	Tleta Azlef	Beni Tuzin		39,000	64
	Tafersit	Tafersit	Berber	8,200	130

[a] Population figures refer to 1957 and were taken from E. Mennesson, 'Importance social des exploitations minières dans la région de Nador', *Mines et Géologie*, NO. 14, 1961

Zaio is one of the smaller rural communes in the province, both in population and in geographical area; it is also one of the poorest. The commercial, residential, administrative and 'political' centre of the commune is Zaio village, where both the *qāʾid-mumtāz* of the circle of Luta and the *qāʾid* of the annexe of Zaio have their bureaux. Rural commune and annexe alike coincide with the area inhabited by the Arabic-speaking Ulad Stut in such a way that administrative, 'political' and 'socio-cultural' entities appear identical. In this way, despite the development, over the past seventy years, of cleavages which cut across the ties of kinship and family, certain aspects of the 'kinship-dominated', pre-colonial tribal social organization have been maintained in Zaio as throughout the province.[4]

Statistics on the population of Zaio rural commune are rarely precise enough to allow detailed analysis, but the figures that exist, together with genealogical data and life histories collected between 1968 and 1969, are sufficient to delineate certain crucial features of the population geography and demography of the commune. In a short paper such as this I can do no more than indicate briefly, in addition to the numerical data, some of the more important aspects of contemporary kinship and family structures in their economic and political context; providing, as it were, workpoints for a later, more searching analysis.

POPULATION GEOGRAPHY AND DEMOGRAPHY

Sources disagree substantially on the total number of residents in Zaio, and estimates range between 7,527 (Feuille, 1961) and 12,167 (*Qā'id's* Office, 18.6.63), the most recent, and possibly the most reliable, being that given me by the *qā'id-mumtāz* and referring to a census of 24 June 1967, which puts the figure at 11,151.

Population figures for the rural commune as a whole are generally broken down into figures for Zaio village and for the nineteen administrative sub-divisions of the annexe of Zaio, termed *duars*.[5] (See Table 2.)

TABLE 2   *Census of 24 June 1967 (*Moroccans only*)*

Moroccans only	Males	Females	Total	'Families'	Farmers	Employed/other
Zaio village	?	?	1466	333	37	172
duar: A	244	253	497	85	109	27
B	240	247	487	79	38	28
C	349	354	703	98	32	66
D	399	454	853	123	100	31
E	317	297	614	102	57	61
F	268	253	521	84	69	15
G	143	120	263	45	41	3
H	190	206	396	63	40	16
I	61	62	123	22	12	8
J	258	301	559	87	48	35
K	156	136	292	49	27	22
L	380	356	736	129	65	54
M	312	307	619	95	59	30
N	376	403	779	137	84	45
O	128	130	258	46	17	29
P	314	331	645	97	79	16
Q	72	94	166	27	16	11
R	369	374	743	127	85	35
S	221	210	431	63	39	22

It is impossible to provide more than a guess at the rate of population growth within the commune, although the data available suggest a considerable increase over the past fifty years, both as a result of immigration into the area and also from natural increase. The rate of growth is unlikely to be as high as the calculated average growth rates for the province, or even for those of the country as a whole,[6] but most sources suggest that roughly half the population of the commune is under the age of 14. A census carried out in 1968,[7] showed that, in six residential clusters belonging to five *duars*, children under the age of 7 provided between 23 and 32 per cent of the total population, while children under 14 amounted to between 30 and 45 per cent of the total population. Even ten years earlier, according to one source (*Qaid*'s Office, 31.12.59), children under 14 represented approximately 48 per cent of the commune's population. (Detailed examples of population composition in terms of age and sex are given for two residential clusters in Table 3.)

TABLE 3   *Two examples of duar population composition by age and sex, 1969*

	Males	Females	
Duar F (main cluster)			
Age			Total
0–10	26	30	56
11–20	16	6	22
21–30	4	9	13
31–40	7	4	11
41–50	4	4	8
51–60	4	4	8
61–70	1	2	3
70 plus	3	0	3
(Also 4 males under 20 and 2 females under 20)			6
Total			130
Duar D			
0– 9	17	19	36
10–19	14	14	28
20–29	10	17	27
30–39	13	11	24
40–49	6	9	15
50–59	8	3	11
60–69	1	4	5
70 plus	5	0	5
Total			151

The family planning campaign has had little publicity and even less effect, so far. The Spanish doctor in Zaio village has a 'practice' of over 50,000 people,[8] of whom perhaps 10,000 are women of child-bearing age; of these only 40 women (including 12 Ulad Stut from the countryside and 17 from the village itself), have been supplied officially with contraceptives. A few may have bought contraceptives elsewhere in the province and a small number use 'traditional' herbal methods, both for contraception and for abortion.

Although women appear generally to prefer smaller families than their husbands (very few wanting more than six children), they have little control over the matter. The majority of men still emphasize the importance, both social and economic, of having many offspring, and can usually support their outlook with economic arguments of some validity. Furthermore, both men and women point to the very real possibility that one or more pregnancies will produce still-births and that some of the children may die young. The doctor reports that infant mortality is, in fact, still high and that early deaths from typhoid, tuberculosis and diseases associated with malnutrition are relatively common.

Improved medical facilities and better living conditions may reduce mortality rates over the next decade or so. The present age at first marriage (between 14 and 17 for most girls; between 16 and 30 for most men) is fairly low and there are few signs that it will rise to any great extent, for girls at least, in the near future. Fertility levels are high here as elsewhere in Morocco (Coale & Mauldin 1967) and polygamy is becoming increasingly rare. All these data suggest that the rate of population growth from natural increase within the commune is likely to accelerate over the next decade.

The population geography of Zaio is affected to a large extent by immigration and emigration into and out of the rural commune; and also by movements within the commune itself. At the present time, immigration is probably greater than emigration, largely as a result of the development of a major irrigation perimeter in the Sebra plain to the south-west of Zaio village (Seddon 1971; 1973). Perhaps the most significant features of the population geography of Zaio, however, are the gradual rural exodus and the associated growth of Zaio village.

Founded in 1911 by the Spanish as a military camp, Zaio village has grown rapidly since independence to become, in 1970, the largest and most important quasi-urban centre in the south of the province. In 1940 the majority of its 365 inhabitants were Spanish, only 33 being Moroccans; by 1960, of a total population of 662, 485 were Moroccans. My own census records that, in 1969, 2,379 out of a total of 2,414 were Moroccans, the remainder including Jews, Spanish, French and one English anthropologist. The figures available suggest that the village had an average yearly growth rate of about 4 per cent during the twenty years between 1940 and 1960, but a rate of nearly 30 per cent per annum over the last ten years.[9]

FAMILIES AND HOUSEHOLDS

I believe that it is useful initially to distinguish between the conjugal family, as a bio-social unit; the household, as a larger association of individuals living

178   DAVID SEDDON

within one *ḥaush*, or homestead; and the budget unit, as a group of individuals sharing a common 'fund' and exchanging goods between each other without reckoning. In almost all cases the individual members of both households and budget units are linked by ties of kinship and/or affinity, so that all three types of association may be seen as 'kinship associations'.

Average conjugal family size in the rural areas of the commune (that is, excluding Zaio village) is estimated by one source as 6.21,[10] while my own investigations have produced a range of between 4.6 and 6.5 for seven residential clusters belonging to six different *duars*. (See Table 4.) (There are

TABLE 4   *Conjugal family size* (in 7 residential clusters belonging to 6 *duars*)

No. of individuals in family	Number of families						
	Duar A	Duar C	Duar S	Duar L	Duar A	Duar D	Duar O
1	–	–	–	4	–	–	–
2	2	5	5	9	–	4	15
3	3	2	6	6	2	1	11
4	5	3	6	9	4	5	10
5	3	3	1	4	3	3	8
6	8	4	4	5	6	4	11
7	9	6	4	5	1	4	16
8	2	2	9	2	4	2	13
9	2	3	2	4	2	2	9
10	–	–	4	1	2	1	6
11	1	2	3	–	1	–	1
12	–	–	–	–	–	–	1
13	–	–	–	–	–	–	–
14	–	–	–	–	–	–	–
15	–	–	–	–	–	–.	1
Average size	5.8	5.8	6.1	4.6	6.5	5.6	5.8

reasons to believe that all these figures are slightly too low.) Conjugal family size in Zaio village appears, according to the meagre information available, to be smaller than in the countryside, with a calculated average of 4.4,[11] but it is impossible to say whether these suggested differences are in fact significant. There is, however, a number of reasons why both fertility and family size in the village might be below rural levels (Zelinsky 1966, p. 58). Household size, like conjugal family size, varies considerably throughout the commune, but it is quite clear that the average size of households in the countryside is greater than that of those in the village. The average number of individuals in each household in Zaio village appears to be in the region of 5.9 (see Table 8); in the rural areas, basing the more general suggestions on detailed information from two *duars*, the average seems to be closer to between 7 and 8. (See Tables 5, 6 and 7.)

Households vary both in size and in composition. Many factors control these two variables, but the most powerful are (1) the stage in the 'developmental cycle', reached by the family providing the core of the residential group, and (2) the wealth, social status and political standing of the head of the household. This latter factor is likely to be more important in the village than in the countryside, where providing extra accommodation for relatives is less

TABLE 5 *Household size in two* duars *(F and O)*

No. of members in household	Duar F No. of households	Duar O No. of households
1	–	–
2	–	6
3	6	3
4	6	1
5	6	1
6	7	6
7	7	5
8	5	3
9	8	1
10	1	4
11	–	–
12	–	–
13	–	–
14	–	1
15	–	1
16	–	–
17	–	–
18	3	–
19	1	–
20	1	–
21	–	1
22	–	–
23	–	–
24	1	–
25		–
26		–
27		–
28		–
29		1
30		–
unknown		4
Average No. in each household	7.7	7.4

expensive and less unusual. Some indication of the possible variations in household composition in the countryside is given in Tables 7 and 8. I have no detailed data on household composition for Zaio village comparable with that from the *duars*, but the data available suggest broad similarities, with one crucial difference. It is extremely rare in the rural areas to find single individuals living on their own; in Zaio village between 4 per cent and 5 per cent of all households contain single individuals only. (See Table 8.)

TABLE 6 *Household size and composition:* duar F *(cluster i)*

Household	No. of members	Composition
H1	18	Married couple; two married sons, their wives and unmarried children.[a]
H2	5	Married couple; unmarried children.
H3	6	Widow; unmarried children.
H4	7	Married couple; unmarried children.[a]
H5	5	Married couple; unmarried children.
H6	(Empty in 1969)	
H7	(Empty in 1969)	
H8	8	Married couple; married son, his wife and unmarried children.[a]
H9	5	Married couple; unmarried children.
H10	6	Married couple; unmarried children.[a]
H11	3	Married couple; unmarried children.[a]
H12	(Empty in 1969)	
H13	8	Married couple; unmarried children; married son and his wife.
H14	20	Two brothers, their wives and unmarried children; one unmarried brother; one married sister, her husband and unmarried children; old mother.
H15	7	Married couple; unmarried children.
H16	8	Married couple; unmarried children.
H17	9	Married couple; unmarried children.
H18	18	Married couple; three married sons, their wives and unmarried children.[a]
H19	19	Three brothers, their wives and unmarried children; one unmarried brother; old mother.

(Average size of occupied households: 9.5.)

[a] Married couple has married children living elsewhere.

TABLE 7 *Household size and composition:* duar F *(cluster ii)*

Household	No. of members	Composition
H20	5	Married couple; married son and his wife.[a]
H21	9	Married couple; unmarried children.
H22	4	Married couple; unmarried children.
H22a	7	Married couple; unmarried children.
H23	9	Married couple; unmarried children.[a]
H23a	4	Married couple; unmarried children.
H24	3	Married couple; unmarried children.
H24a	3	Man and two wives.[a]
H25	6	Married couple; unmarried children.
H26	7	Married couple; unmarried children.
H27	6	Married couple; unmarried child; two unmarried brothers; old mother.[a]
H28	4	Married couple; unmarried children.
H29	9	Married couple; unmarried children; old mother.
H29a	6	Married couple; unmarried children.[a]
H30	6	Married couple; unmarried children; old mother.
H31	9	Married couple; unmarried children.
H32	5	Married couple; unmarried children.
H33	10	Married couple; unmarried children; old mother.
H34	3	Man and two wives.
H35	4	Married couple; unmarried children.
H36	24	Four brothers, their wives and unmarried children; old mother.
H37	4	Married couple; unmarried children.
H38	9	Married couple; unmarried children.
H39	7	Married couple; unmarried children.
H40	8	Married couple; unmarried children.
H41	9	Married couple; unmarried children.

(Average size of household: 6.9.)

[a] Married man or married couple have married children living elsewhere.

TABLE 8   *Household size in Zaio village, 1969**

No. of individuals in household	No. of households
1	18
2	31
3	36
4	47
5	47
6	57
7	55
8	40
9	33
10	21
11	10
12	5
13	2
14	2
15	1
16	1

Total pop.: 2,414; No. of households: 407; Average no. in household: 5.9; Modal no. in household: 6.
* Information collected by J. D. Seddon and Siyyid Hajjaj Mohamed, May 1969.

TABLE 9   *Household, conjugal family and budget unit:* duar F *(cluster i)*

Household	No. of members	Nuclear/conjugal families	Other individuals	Budget units
H1	18	3	–	3
H2	5	1	–	1
H3	6	1 (no husband)	–	1
H4	7	1	–	1
H5	5	1	–	1
H8	8	2	–	1
H9	5	1	–	1
H10	6	1	–	1
H11	3	1	–	1
H13	8	1	Married son and wife	1
H14	20	3	Unmarried brother and old mother	3
H15	7	1	–	1
H16	8	1	–	1
H17	9	1	–	1
H18	18	4	–	4
H19	19	3	Unmarried brother and old mother	3

There is almost complete congruence, both in the countryside and in the village, between the conjugal family and the budget unit; although even within the budget unit individual members may receive some personal income from their own labour or their own property which they do not share completely with other members. An impression both of the general rule and of the exceptions is given in Table 9.

KINSHIP AND MARRIAGE

The present-day administration makes use of a model of local social organization that is based upon the model utilized by the Spanish during the period of colonial rule between about 1920 and 1956. Both administrative models are founded on the concept of the tribe as a segmentary lineage system (see Evans-Pritchard 1940; Gellner 1969; Peters 1967), and define administrative units in terms of 'kinship', or, more exactly, in terms of 'patrilineal descent'. I have argued elsewhere (Seddon 1973) that the local inhabitants of northeast Morocco themselves made use of a similar model of their tribal social structure in pre-colonial times. Several features of this local 'conscious model' remain operative today, maintained (with what degree of intention it is difficult to say) by the contemporary administrative structure. Thus, the 'tribe of the Ulad Stut' is seen, to some extent both by the local authorities and by the Ulad Stut themselves, as a socio-cultural, administrative and political entity, structured in terms of 'kinship' and 'patrilineal descent', even though these principles do not, in fact, control the nature and direction of social and economic activity within the area. The same applies, perhaps even more strongly, in the case of the *duar*.

Kinship and descent are not the only criteria by which individuals of the Ulad Stut define themselves and in terms of which they act, nor, without a doubt, are they the principles of social organization of greatest concern to the local authorities; but they retain considerable importance as the basis for an essentially 'traditional' view of the structure of rural society in contemporary Morocco. The emphasis on vertical cleavage throughout the social structure given by a model constructed along the lines provided by 'kinship' and 'descent' serves to obscure the development of horizontal social differentiation and to prevent the emergence of an unambiguous class structure in the countryside.

According to the 'segmentary model' based on the principle of descent, the tribe of the Ulad Stut is composed of 19 *duars*, each of which may be seen as a corporate group, the majority of whose members are related by kinship or marriage, or by both kinship and marriage, and each of which may best be regarded as a coherent entity whose members share common interests and cooperate with each other in a variety of ways. Each *duar* is seen to contain a number of constituent sub-segments, or minor 'descent groups', called *uted*; each *uted* being composed of several families. These 'descent groups' differ from those described in the great majority of anthropological monographs in that here, as elsewhere in the so-called 'Arab world', the principle of patrilineal descent is associated with a stated preference for endogamy, rather than with a strict rule of exogamy. In practice, 'descent groups' throughout North Africa and the Near East tend to combine both endogamy and exogamy, the exact balance between the two alternatives at any one time depending upon demographic factors, pressures exerted by the economic and political 'environment', and the complex pattern of relationships produced by a series of strategic decisions, extending often over several generations, concerning marriages made by members of the 'descent group'.

If we look, for example, at the marriages contracted over the past fifty years by men resident in *duar* F in 1968 (see Tables 10 and 11) we discover certain controlling principles. Marriage choices always tend to be made within a

TABLE 10   *Marriages by men of* duar F *(cluster i)*

Household	Husbands *Uted*	No. of wives	Wives in *uted*	in *duar* (*uted*)	in tribe (*duar*)	Other tribes
H1 (A)	I	4	–	IV	S	Beni bu yahi / Ulad shaib
(B)	I	2	–	–	–	Beni bu yahi / Beni bu yahi
(C)	I	1	–	–	S	–
H2	III	2	–	IV	–	Beni snassen
H3[a]	II	1	II	–	–	–
(H4	Gelaia	1	–	–	–	Gelaia)
H5	II	1	–	I	–	–
H8 (A)	II	1	–	–	L	–
(B)	II	1	–	IV	–	–
H9	IV	1	–	–	–	Ait waryaghel
H10	II	2	–	–	–	Kebdana / Djebala
H11	II	2	–	–	R	Beni bu yahi
H13 (A)	III	1	–	–	–	Beni snassen
(B)	III	1	–	–	–	Beni snassen
H14 (A)	III	1	III	–	–	–
(B)	III	1	III	–	–	–
(C)	III	1	III	–	–	–
H15	III	1	III	–	–	–
H16	III	1	III	–	–	–
H17	III	1	III	–	–	–
H18 (A)	III	1	–	–	–	Beni snassen
(B)	III	1	–	–	R	–
(C)	III	1	III	–	–	–
(D)	III	1	–	–	–	Beni snassen
H19 (A)	III	1	III	–	–	–
(B)	III	1	–	–	N	–
(C)	III	1	–	–	–	Jai
Total	26	33	9	4	6	14

[a] Recently deceased.

TABLE 11   *Marriages by men of* duar F *(cluster ii)*

Household	Husbands Uted	No. of wives	Wives in *uted*	in *duar* (*uted*)	in tribe (*duar*)	Other tribes
H20 (A)	IV	1	–	II	–	–
(B)	IV	1	–	–	–	Beni bu yahi
(H21	Duar L	1	–	–	–	Beni snassen)
H22	IV	1	–	– .	–	Beni bu yahi
H22a	IV	1	–	–	–	Beni snassen
H23	IV	1	· IV	–	–	–
H23a	IV	2	–	–	–	{ Beni bu yahi / Metalsa }
(H24	Buzgawi	1	IV	–	–	–
H24a	IV	2	–	III	Q	–
H25	IV	1	–	–	–	Gelaia
H26	IV	1	–	III	–	–
H27	IV	1	IV	–	–	–
(H28	Duar R	1	IV	–	–	–)
(H29	Beni bu yahi	1	IV	–	–	–)
H29a	IV	3	IV	–	–	{ Beni bu yahi / Beni ukil }
H30	IV	1	IV	–	–	–
H31	IV	2	–	–	–	{ Beni ukil / Beni bu yahi }
H32	IV	1	–	—	–	Beni ukil
(H33	Duar A	1	–	–	A	–)
H34	IV	4	IV	–	–	{ Beni bu yahi / Beni snassen / Beni bu yahi }
(H35	?	1	?	?	?	?
H36 (A)	IV	1	–	–	–	Beni snassen
(B)	IV	1	IV	–	–	–
(C)	IV	1	IV	–	–	–
(D)	IV	1	–	II	–	–
(H37	Duar L	1	–	–	L	–)
(H38	Duar L	1	–	–	–	Beni bu yahi)
H39	IV	1	–	–	R	–
H40	IV	1	–	II	–	–
(H41	Beni snassen	1	–	III	–	–
Total	21	29	10	6	4	15

certain circumscribed universe, defined socially, culturally and, except in unusually mobile sectors of society, geographically. In the case considered here (clusters i and ii of *duar* F), all marriages were contracted with women from northern or northeast Morocco; only two women came from further away than 100 kilometres, and both of these were married while the men were away from home in the Spanish military service. *Duar* F is situated in the extreme southwest corner of Zaio rural commune and most of the nearest *duars* are of other tribes: e.g. Beni bu Yahi, Beni Snassen and Beni Ukil. It is interesting and puzzling to note that there appear to be no marriages with women from the nearest Ulad Stut *duar*, *duar* J; at present I can find no convincing explanation for this fact.

Geographical proximity is clearly very important, but is not an absolute control; much less important is the linguistic difference between the Arabic-speaking Ulad Stut and the predominantly Berber-speaking tribes to the west, the southwest and the south. Out of 29 marriages contracted with women from tribes other than the Ulad Stut, only three were with native Arabic speakers (from the Beni Ukil) and, taking all marriages outside the *duar* into consideration, exactly twice as many were with 'Berber' women (26) as with other 'Arabs' (13). The numerical importance of marriage outside the tribe for the Ulad Stut is witnessed by the fact that the proportion found in this *duar* (roughly 42–43 per cent of all marriages), is well below that found in other *duars*, where the figure is generally closer to 48–50 per cent. Possibly associated with this difference between *duar* F and several others investigated is the relatively high proportion of marriages within the *uted* in *duar* F: about 28 per cent on average for the two clusters examined in detail, and as high as about 47 per cent in *uted* III. (See Table 10.)

The analysis of marriage patterns based solely on simple intra- and inter-'descent group' relations is likely to prove seriously misleading. Satisfactory explanations must themselves be complex and should incorporate and account

TABLE 12   *Pattern of marriages of men resident in* duar F *(clusters i and ii)*

Origin of men	Origin of women				
Ulad Stut:					
Duar F	Within *uted*	Within *duar*	Within tribe	Outside	Total
(*Uted* I) 3	0	1	2	4	7
(*Uted* II) 6	1	2	2	3	8
(*Uted* III) 16	8	1	2	6	17
(*Uted* IV) 22	10	6	4	16	36
47	19	10	10	29	68

Ulad Stut: Other *duars*	Wife from *duar* F (*Uted* I II III IV)		From own *duar*	From elsewhere	Total
(A) 1	– – – –		1	–	1
(L) 3	– – – –		1	2	3
(R) 1	– – – 1		–	–	1
5	1		2	2	5

Other tribes:	Wife from *duar* F (*Uted* I II III IV)		Wife from own tribe	Total
Gelaia 1	– – – –		1	1
Buzgawi 1	– – – 1		–	1
Beni bu yahi 1*	– – – 1		–	1
Beni snassen 1	– – 1 –		–	1
4	3		1	4

* Plus 1 probable Beni bu yahi.

for the relationship between individual marriages and shifts in economic and political alignment within the total universe considered in a way that summary numerical data cannot. At the same time, full explanations should account for both 'conservative' and 'innovatory' marriages, and for the relationship between the two types of marriage at any given time. (By using these terms I wish to distinguish between those marriages which perpetuate ties between particular groups and those which seek to establish new ties between groups previously unconnected by marriage.)

The 'present pattern', as summarized in Table 12, should be seen only as a sort of palimpsest: a timeless representation of what was in fact a complex series of interrelated decisions, susceptible, in theory at least, to analysis by more sophisticated mathematical methods (Harvey 1967, pp. 577–96).

ECONOMICS, KINSHIP AND THE FAMILY

The great majority of the active population of Zaio, as of the province as a whole, is involved, to some extent at least, in farming (see Table 2). In only a minority of cases, however, is farming now sufficiently productive to enable families to live entirely off the land, and an increasing number of men seek to supplement, or even to replace, their meagre income from farming by carrying on some form of 'commerce',[12] or by finding paid employment, either in the villages and towns of northeast Morocco or else, since 1962, abroad in western Europe. The majority of active males between the ages of 13 and 60 are involved in at least two 'occupations', and many have a variety of sources of income; but, again, in the majority of cases, these multiple 'occupations' bring in only a small and unreliable income. (Frank 1969, pp. 276–97.) Sources of income may be seen crudely as: sale of farm produce, 'commerce', ownership of rented property, 'regular/professional' employment, 'casual' employment, and 'unemployment benefit'.[13]

Although a distinction is still made between farming (a way of life: self-employment, personal/kinship-type economic relations) and paid employment (work: impersonal/employer–employee-type relations), the two are becoming increasingly indistinguishable. In situations where previously kinsman and/or affines of the same *duar* co-operated in a number of joint enterprises despite differences in wealth and status, a wealthy farmer will now employ agricultural labourers and hired shepherds, and will hire a tractor, or use his own. Poorer peasants in Zaio can rarely afford even the relatively low wages of an immigrant agricultural labourer from the central Rif and will generally work their fields alone or with the help of their own family.

Sharecropping arrangements are increasingly rare and co-operation between members of the *duar* in farming activities is generally limited to the occasional 'lending a hand'. It is usually only the poorer members of the *duar* who do this. The basic 'production unit' is the household, members of which generally work together, even if they are members of different budget units. In some instances they share the cost of seed and the time involved and, after the harvest and sale of the grain, share out the profits and the seed for next year. It is the larger households, with a greater domestic labour force at their disposal, which prove to be the most efficient farming units.

The ownership of land in the rural commune is now predominantly private and individual. Only in the southwestern corner of the commune is the translation of communal '*duar*-owned' land to private individual-owned land incomplete. A smallish number of farmers without land of their own rent from landlords, but the number of landowners benefiting from this source of income is relatively few as the majority of farmers own at least some land, while the landless, or those with too little to farm profitably, tend to seek paid employment rather than to enlarge the area farmed by them. The fragmentation of land-holdings means that farmers who do rent supplementary fields generally do so in *duars* other than their own.

The number of Ulad Stut enjoying what I have termed 'regular/professional' employment is extremely small. The majority of teachers, functionaries in the local administration, gendarmes and 'qualified' individuals living in Zaio are from outside the commune, although perhaps between ten and fifteen Ulad Stut are in this category. Apart from the few individuals who are paid a small emolument for their services at the lowest level of the administrative hierarchy, as *shaikh* or *muqaddim*,[14] men in this category tend to live in Zaio village, and enjoy a relatively high standard of living.

Over the past decade the construction of two major dams across the nearby Moulouya river for the irrigation of three plains in Nador province (Seddon 1971a; 1972) has provided a certain amount of 'casual' employment within the commune itself. With the virtual completion of the irrigation works in 1970 the number of jobs available close to 'home' will shrink rapidly, and unless the development of Zaio village into an important commercial and industrial centre of the Lower Moulouya Irrigation Perimetre takes place as hoped by the national planners,[15] the unemployment problem in the commune, already grave, will increase.

At present the majority of men in 'casual' employment work for periods ranging from a few days to a couple of years away from their homes and from their families. Despite the value of the income derived from such employment, the absence of at least one active male may produce considerable strain and difficulty for the conjugal family left behind and, in the case of a married man, on the close relatives whose assistance and hospitality to the single woman and her children is often expected by the husband if the period of absence is likely to be long. In the countryside the absence of an active male from the household, especially in the case of a small family, may be detrimental to the efficiency of the farming production unit and the majority of men in this situation, where regular well-paid employment is not available, will try and divide their working year between farming and paid employment, remaining at home during the most active periods of ploughing, harvesting and threshing and departing in search of work during the rest of the year.

Although a surprisingly large number of Ulad Stut are employed abroad, both legally and illegally,[16] and some have fairly dependable jobs within the province, the majority of men attempt to create situations of at least some security by combining casual employment with subsistence farming. This results in seasonal unemployment which reaches its height in two 'slack' periods in the farming year: March–April and September–October (see Table 13).

TABLE 13   *Seasonal unemployment in Zaio, 1965*

Men available for the *Promotion Nationale*			
January	200	July	70
February	220	August	200
March	234	September	234
April	234	October	234
May	100	November	220
June	0	December	200

In view of the generally low crop yields within the commune and the low prices for grain on the market compared with those for manufactured and other 'imported' goods in the province as a whole, the continuation of 'subsistence' farming should be seen as a desperate attempt on the part of the majority of the rural population to retain some small measure of security and independence of the fluctuations of the national and international economy, rather than as a continuation of a 'traditional' mode of economic activity. (In fact, the Ulad Stut were primarily pastoralists in pre-colonial times and devoted only a limited amount of labour to agriculture.) The inadequacy of local farming and the lack of jobs available makes the seasonal unemployment a serious phenomenon in the area.

The state provides some assistance for the unemployed, but it is cruelly inadequate. Those capable of manual labour are given 'credit cards' in return for work with the Promotion Nationale,[17] and the old or incapable are given direct handouts. The amount given to the unemployed and the destitute varies but is rarely more than the equivalent of 3.50 dirhams a day at maximum.[18] A man working for the Promotion Nationale will get 8 litres of oil and 45 kg of flour for 12 days' work; there is no guarantee that he will be able to repeat his 12 days work and the exchange of 'credit card' for cash or, more often, for kind is frequently delayed for up to a month or more. For a man with a family to feed the situation may become quite desperate and he may be forced to sell his 'card' to a 'friend' who collects a number of such 'credit cards' and then cashes them (illegally), at the time they become due.

A few rural dwellers carry on some form of commerce in the countryside:

keeping small 'shops', selling wood and charcoal, collecting and selling gravel and stones for building purposes, or selling agricultural produce at the roadside. Smuggling, both between the Spanish town of Melilla to the north of Villa Nador and the Moroccan hinterland, and between Algeria and Morocco, is an activity which involves a surprisingly substantial (but finally incalculable) proportion of the active male population of the commune, but the income derived from this source by each individual is generally small.

A number of rural dwellers carry on commercial activities in the village centres, in the market place and in the shops, both as retailers and as wholesalers. The vast majority of these operate from Zaio village, although a few have stalls in the small village of Selwan in the very north of the rural commune.

In addition to these major sources of income I should mention a number of minor and less generally important sources. A large proportion of the men now over 45 served in the Spanish army and still receive a pension according to their rank. There are also specialists in the 'traditional' arts: midwives, circumcisers, barbers, herbal doctors, 'wise-women' and sorcerers, who receive small 'fees' for the services they render. In the countryside the number of women involved in paid work is very small, and these do it, almost without exception, to supplement a basic livelihood obtained in other ways; a few make mats or clean skins for sale by their sons or husbands in the market, and, at certain times of the year, a number of women and young boys go to pick olives just south of Zaio village.

ZAIO VILLAGE

The great majority of men living in Zaio village have come because they wish to enjoy, together with their close families, the amenities and advantages of life in a quasi-urban environment, and because they can afford to build a house for themselves or else to pay the rent on one to a landlord. The residents of Zaio village have a variety of occupations but, although most of them retain an interest in a piece of land somewhere, very few of them are primarily farmers. The majority are either *commerçants*, (wholesalers and retailers), or have fairly regular and dependable jobs, locally or abroad. The great majority are relatively well-off and the problem of 'urban poverty', although on the increase, is not particularly striking as yet. This is largely because the poor who work in the village come, for the most part, from the surrounding countryside and return home to sleep at night. As Zaio grows, and attracts increasing numbers of poor immigrants in search of work from more distant regions, so the problem of 'urban poverty' will grow; for the seeds are already sown.

The rural exodus is a phenomenon that exists at all levels in Morocco and Zaio provides no exception. Those who can earn good wages locally tend to move to the urban or quasi-urban areas for the sake of the higher standard of living possible there, and often to be closer to their work; those who have found jobs abroad generally begin building on the outskirts of the village after their second or third year in Europe and several have moved their families into these houses, once completed. In Zaio village both the standard of living and the cost of living are higher than in the surrounding countryside. Both are also on the increase.

The village now boasts a 'municipal' swimming pool (completed at the end of 1969), a football ground, a school, a centre for women and girls, a twice-weekly market, a post office and a large number of cafes with TV and ice-cold refrigerated drinks. Electricity was provided by generator until 1961, but now the village is connected to the power station in Uida. Running water is supplied to every residence fresh from the tanks below the spring that rises in the Kebdana hills behind the village; and the existence of bakers, butchers, a tailor and shops selling all necessary household goods and foodstuffs desired by the Ulad Stut housewife make work in the home far lighter and less time-consuming than in the countryside.

Not only the pattern of work but also that of leisure differs in the village from that found in the rural *duars*. In the village there are fewer close kin to prepare meals for when they drop in by chance, and life is altogether more formal, especially for women. Veils, which are rarely seen in the countryside, where almost every individual one meets is likely to be a close relative, are obligatory for women if they leave the house for any reason. In fact, they are rarely allowed out by their husbands and they may remain indoors and isolated, often for days on end, except for their husband and their own children. Only in the much wealthier households, on the whole, will there be several conjugal families living together as part of a larger residential entity.

Children are less necessary as contributors to the budget unit than in the rural areas, where there is always something useful that they can do; partly for this reason, but partly also because they consider themselves slightly more progressive than their relatives living outside the village, and partly because it is so close and convenient, a far higher proportion of residents send their children to school.

Clearly the nature of the 'bread-winner's' activity, and the source and size of his income, have a considerable effect on domestic organization and family life. They also affect relations between the conjugal family and other kinsmen and affines. Men who are adequate wage-earners need not involve themselves in any other enterprise and are not in direct need of co-operation from kinsmen or affines in their work. Few commercial enterprises need a regular labour force of more than two or three, and in cases where a man and his sons, or a man and his brother, cannot cope with all the work it is easy to employ an outsider, who will receive his wage and demand no more. There are exceptions to this general rule, but it is interesting to note that commercial enterprises managed by affines are more common than those run by agnates other than members of a conjugal family or brothers.

The rural exodus does not involve only the regularly employed and the better-off, however; the increasing cost of living, the recurrent years of poor harvests, the low price of grain on the market compared with the high prices of manufactured goods and imported foodstuffs, and the continual influx of Riffians from further west in search of employment at even the lowest wages, are driving many of the poorest of the small peasants and the landless towards the urban areas in desperation and in search of work. Many of the rural unemployed and landless in the province of Nador go to Uida, but some try Nador and, increasingly, even Zaio.

The effect of unemployment on the domestic life of a family is considerable; the man may be obliged to leave his home to seek work and his wife may be forced to turn to others for assistance, if he is unsuccessful. Where the situation is likely to be temporary, kinsmen or friends will help to look after the woman and her children, but if the husband appears likely to remain unemployed for long, most kinsmen will reluctantly withdraw all but the minimum of help, pointing to the drain on their own pockets and the impossibility of a return of the favours given. The woman may then return to her father and her natal family, if members of it are in a position to help; she may become the mistress of a married man and survive on gifts and hand-outs; or she may move to a village or a town to acquire a job, if she is lucky, as a maidservant or factory-worker, a washerwoman or seamstress, if she is less lucky, as a prostitute.

It is extremely rare in the countryside to find single individuals living on their own; usually they are included in a household as a member of one or other of the budget units (see Tables 6 and 7). In Zaio village it is possible to live alone, in a household and budget unit of one. Some of these single individuals are young men, regularly employed as gendarmes or teachers, etc., but the majority are single men and women dependent upon casual and irregular work for a living: washerwomen, waiters, odd-job men, cripples and labourers. They live in tiny rented rooms apart from and unhelped by their kinsfolk. A grubby hostel has recently opened in Zaio village, which provides minimal accommodation for eight to ten single men, and which is run by two women of dubious respectability. Gossip suggests that several of the wealthier landlords are considering several further developments of this sort.

The village is the centre of the rural commune in many ways; it attracts both the wealthy and the poor for economic reasons, and its attraction grows as its size and economic importance grows. It is also, however, the administrative centre, both of an annexe and of a circle. Thirdly, it is where the elected council of the rural commune meets and is thus also the 'political' centre of the commune.

POLITICS, KINSHIP AND THE FAMILY

The rural communes were created by royal decree in 1960 and claimed to represent the basis for democratic local government in the countryside. The purges of 1963 (Waterbury 1970, p. 229), the declaration of a state of emergency and the dissolution of parliament in 1965 (Waterbury 1970, pp. 254–74), and the rigged elections of 1969 and 1970, are simple signs that real popular participation within the framework of a parliamentary democracy is considered to be inimical to the existing political structure.

The control exerted by the local authorities over the elections in the rural communes, and over the deliberations and decisions of the council itself, once 'elected', is considerable throughout Morocco. In Zaio, as far as I could observe, that control is very nearly complete (Seddon 1973). Candidates are carefully selected and support for them is stimulated in a number of ways. They are generally 'friends' or 'clients' of the local administration and members of the local elite, or alternatively, are less well-off individuals, willing to co-operate with the authorities and with the local elite.

The co-operation of the mass of the population in this charade depends on a belief in the existence of a widespread and flexible system of patronage, supported to a large extent by the continuing belief held by the majority in the value and power of kinship relations. The maintenance of a system of patronage (or perhaps one should say of an ideology of patronage) depends on the widespread acceptance of, and confidence in, the power of 'personal' ties (whether of 'friendship' or of 'kinship' in the broadest sense) to overcome the inequalities inherent in the structure of Moroccan rural society.

The old concepts of 'kinship obligations' and 'kinship solidarity' still hold considerable power over the greater, and poorer, part of the rural population, despite the clear, and growing, economic and political inequality throughout the region. It is recognized, however, that 'kinship solidarity' does not necessarily or always have the same meaning as it did previously; it may refer less to corporate action and a common identity than to the willingness of a relatively wealthy and powerful man to assist a kinsman or relative before another man. As long as the gap between the set of beliefs held by the majority of the population and the reality of contemporary rural social structure can be kept below a certain critical level there will be no major upheaval in the countryside. It is therefore in the interest, both of the local elite, and of the administration, to reinforce the belief in the efficacy of a system of patronage.

The horizontal cleavages associated with the developing class structure are masked, or at least softened, by a continual emphasis on the importance of kinship and descent as principles of social action, together with a concomitant stress on the unity, both moral and practical, of the 'descent group' in general and of the *duar* in particular. At the same time, the general belief in the efficacy of utilizing a 'web' of relationships generated by kinship and marriage and supplemented by a network of friends, contacts and patrons, in order to obtain favours and advantages unavailable to less well-placed individuals, is both supported and encouraged by the local elite.

The elections in Zaio in 1969 revealed quite clearly how 'kinship' and 'patronage' are used to divide the population, while at the same time promoting a sense of unity and cohesion. The voting constituencies in the elections had, for the most part, the same membership as the *duars*; only in a couple of cases did two *duars* constitute a single constituency. Thus 'descent group', administrative unit and 'political arena' appeared as different aspects of the same basic social entity. In those *duars* where, despite the activity of the local officials, candidates stood in opposition to those selected by the administration, the unofficial candidate was 'bought off', either by promises of future patronage if he 'saw sense', or by threats of 'blacklisting' and retribution; his support was removed by appeals to the need to maintain the 'unity of the *duar*' and to prevent wrangling between 'brothers', or else by the same methods as those applied to the candidate. The result was the election of a council through whom the administration can exert subtle pressures on the rural population, but who serve themselves and the administration better than they serve the people whose representatives they are supposed to be.

The fact that the 'people's representatives' are still their kinsmen and their patrons helps to conceal the systematic nature of the political and economic inequality that now characterizes the Moroccan countryside, and to prevent full awareness on the part of the masses.

NOTES

1 The field-work upon which this short paper is based was carried out between March 1968 and December 1969 as part of a longer term study directed by Professor Robert T. Holt, of the Center for Comparative Studies in Technological Development and Social Change at the University of Minnesota. The paper itself was written in 1971 and has not been subsequently revised.
2 The only significant 'industrial' development in the province is the mining industry, and that is failing.
3 Which compares poorly with the national average of between $100 and $250.
4 This despite the avowed intention of the Moroccan government immediately after independence to create new administrative and political units which would cut across and invalidate the old tribal divisions.
5 This is the term most widely used, both by the administration and by the locals, but the term *jamā'a* is also used to refer to this same grouping.
6 The rate of population growth for Morocco as a whole is thought to be about 3.2% at the present time, having risen from an average of 2.7% per annum in the period between 1956 and 1960.
7 By myself, with the help of the doctor's assistant, Siyyid Hajjaj Mohamed.
8 It includes all the Ulad Stut and the Kebdana.
9 The sources for this calculation are the Spanish *Annuario Estadistico* for 1944, a report by the *khalīfa* of the circle in 1960, my own census of 1969, and the *Avant Projet* produced by the Office National des Irrigations.
10 Calculated from the census of 24 June 1967.
11 *Ibid.*
12 I use this term very broadly here to include all forms of buying and selling for profit.
13 Described below.

14 The *shaikh*, of whom there are two in Zaio, is an employee of the Ministry of the Interior and acts, together with his inferior, the *muqaddim*, of whom there are seven in Zaio, as an intermediary between the *qā'id* and the rural population. A *shaikh* receives about 100 Dh a month and the *muqaddim* about 50Dh a month ($20 and $10) as payment.

15 Plans for a sugar refinery in Zaio village were reported in the press during 1971.

16 In order to depart officially and legally a man must have a work contract issued by the firm with whom he is to work in Europe. Many leave for Europe as tourists and obtain contracts abroad, or never obtain them and remain in Europe illegally.

17 The state organization which 'employs' the unemployed in small-scale operations throughout the countryside.

18 This amount will buy ½ kg of meat at current prices. Men working for the Promotion Nationale may have families and dependents.

BIBLIOGRAPHY

Coale, A. J. and Mauldin, W. P. 1967. *Report to the Government of Morocco on Family Planning*. Rabat. Unpubl.

Evans-Pritchard, E. E. 1940. *The Nuer*. London, Oxford University Press.

Feuille, P. 1961. *Enquête générale sur les structures agraires dans les zones d'intervention de l'O.N.I.: les structures agraires dans la Basse-Moulouya*. Office National des Irrigations. Roneo.

Frank, A. G. 1969. *Latin America: Underdevelopment or Revolution*. New York, Monthly Review Press.

Gellner, E. A. 1969. *Saints of the Atlas*. London, Weidenfeld and Nicolson.

Gellner, E. and Micaud, C. (eds). 1973. *Arabs and Berbers: from tribe to Nation in North Africa*. London, Duckworth.

Mennesson, E. 1961. 'Importance social des exploitations minières dans la région de Nador.' *Mines et Géologie*, No. 14, pp. 93–106.

Ministère d'Agriculture. n.d. *Situation à la veille du plan quinquennal et programme d'action: Nador*. Roneo.

Office National des Irrigations. 1964. *Avant Projet d'Aménagement et de Mise en Valeur de la Basse Moulouya*. Office National des Irrigations, Mission Régionale de la Basse Moulouya.

Peters, E. L. 1967. 'Some structural aspects of the feud among the camel-herding bedouin of Cyrenaica.' *Africa*, Vol. XXXVII, No. 3.

Seddon, J. D. 1971. 'Social and economic change in Northeast Morocco.' *Current Anthropology*, Vol. 12, No. 2.

1973. 'Local politics and state intervention: northeast Morocco from 1870 to 1970.' In E. Gellner and C. Micaud (eds), *Arabs and Berbers*. London, Duckworth.

Waterbury, J. 1970. *The Commander of the Faithful: the Moroccan Political Elite – a study of segmented politics*. London, Weidenfeld and Nicolson.

Zelinsky, W. 1966. *A Prologue to Population Geography*. New Jersey, Prentice Hall.

8 Familial roles in the extended patrilineal kin-group in northern Albania

Ian Whitaker
Simon Fraser University, British Columbia

The survival of a closely-knit, patrilineal clan system among the sheep-herding highlanders of northern Albania, the Ghegs, until at least the onset of World War II, has been recognized by social anthropologists for some decades.[1] However, attention has to a large extent been focused upon the dynamics of the bloodfeud (Albanian *gjakmarje*), and the consequences of its persistence for political change,[2] whilst there has been little examination of the intra-familial role system. This latter problem will be discussed in the present paper, the data being drawn partly from published sources, and partly from field-work among Albanophone shepherds; the discussion, however, is centred upon the year 1945, after which political changes were set in motion which have had long-term consequences for the traditional structure.

The controlling yardstick by which all behaviour was judged among the Gheg mountaineers was the Code of Lekë Dukagjini, who is said to have drawn up his orally transmitted law (Alb. *kanún*) in the fifteenth century.[3] This governed the relations between the different patrilineal clans, which tended to inhabit clearly demarcated territories – often isolated valleys. It would be periodically brought up to date by inter-clan assemblies (Alb. *kuvënd*),[4] whilst an ultimate court of appeal, and perhaps revision of the law itself, lay in the person of the Hereditary Captain (Alb. *Kapedán*) of Mirditë, itself one of the strongest and most important Gheg confederacies.[5]

Clansmen claimed common descent from a male ancestor who may well have been fictitious. Individual clans might have commonly-recited genealogies stretching back thirteen or fourteen generations.[6] Some had interesting origin-myths which served to provide a validation for the present social order. Thus the three allied clans of Mirditë, Shalë and Shoshi, originally exogamous, claimed descent from a common ancestor who, it is alleged, died a poor man, leaving three sons. The first took the saddle (Alb. *shalë*), the second his sieve (Alb. *shoshi*), whilst the third left empty-handed, saying as he went, 'Good day!' (Alb. *mirë-dita*).[7] The social importance of this myth lay in its providing a rationale for the continuing alliance of the three clans. As Milovan Djilas,

195

discussing the clan myths of the ethnographically similar Montenegrins, wrote:[8] 'Every such fabrication is based on some truth, on facts so reasonable and easily comprehended that even their fabricator comes to believe in them.' It was the common acknowledgement of such myths that served to reinforce the solidarity of the clan.

Ideally the clan was an exogamous unit; frequently two clans exchanged brides over several generations, as was the case with Hoti and Kastrati, and with Vuklë and Selca.[9] In this way an alliance was perpetuated, and since kinship was only calculated patrilineally, [10] continuing intermarriage of this type would not transgress the rules of consanguinity since, as the Ghegs put it, 'A man has blood and a woman kin.'[11] In practice the rule of exogamy had been steadily breaking down and unions within related degrees permitted. Thus marriages between the people of Shalë and Shoshi were rationalized on the ground that the division of the clans occurred a hundred generations ago; in the less warlike Muslim areas a link more distant than seven generations was usually allowed.

This trend away from clan exogamy is documented by the series of Ghegs from whom Carleton Coon obtained anthropometric measurements in 1929–30. He found that of 1,102 persons examined, 1,058 (96 per cent) had parents from the same clan, 11 (1 per cent) were the progeny of inter-clan marriages, whilst the remainder had at least one non-Albanian Gheg (or non-Gheg) parent.[12] The exogamous system was, however, still alleged to be superior, since by bringing in wives from a distance, local rivalry for the same girl would be precluded and the clan would moreover have fewer contacts with her own family which might give rise to tensions.[13] This would only have been the case if the brides were selected from outside groups at random, however, which was not the practice. It is nonetheless true that the greater the distance over which a bride was obtained, the less the chance of frequent contacts between the husband and his in-laws. Such an institutionalized avoidance seems to have been common in northern Albania, and it is perhaps significant that in those few villages of Mirditë where people from several clans lived together, there was a rule of village exogamy, precluding a man from having close affines within easy distance of his home.[14] But whether or not the practice of clan exogamy is disappearing, it was certainly the model marital arrangement, to which the attention of young Ghegs was drawn by both precept and also through fable.

The household (Alb. *shpi*) formed the basic unit of Gheg society. As elsewhere this was based on a marital link, but unlike the common European pattern, the descendants of a couple would live under a man's parental roof, and in this way extended families, often comprising several brothers and their descendants, would form a single residential and economic unit, which in its internal arrangements was similar to the south Slav *zadruga*. The need for mutual defence in this region, which lacked any long-term centralized political control, is often adduced as one of the main factors for the survival of this large familistic unit. The common ownership of the means of production is also an additional causative factor. So basic was the household as a unit that, when, in the famine following the Balkan Wars, the Albanians were the recipients of relief, they expected each family to get equal shares, regardless of the number of inhabitants.[15] The number of people that might live together within the same building complex could include up to 95 persons (in one house visited by Mrs Hasluck in Zdrajshë in 1923),[16] but even in 1944 a local Mati chief had 60 persons living with him.[17]

Such a household would be ruled by an elected master of the household (Alb. *zot i shpis*). He would be chosen from among the older adults, although in some cases he might have been nominated when somewhat younger by his predecessor.[18] Primogeniture was taken into account when making this appointment, but a knowledge of the law, as well as general administrative ability, counted for more. His duties included ascertaining that the fields were tilled and the flocks cared for, allocating different people to different tasks. A semi-permanent division of labour, according to individual skills, would be evolved in the interests of efficiency, and this gave rise to minor technical specialization.[19] The master of the household also had control of the family exchequer. He had the sole right to buy and sell land in the name of the family but he did not receive more than other persons in the event of the family group breaking up and its property being distributed among the members.

The master of the household usually went to market himself to trade on behalf of the group and it was his responsibility to see that all the members of the household were properly dressed and fed, and that the family had proper provisions with which to entertain guests. He paid the taxes and purchased a rifle for every youth in the family who was of an age to fight in the bloodfeud. This rifle was the only significant piece of property owned by the average Gheg male, which he might sell or pledge as he chose. A woman, however, always received a small personal gift of money (Alb. *pekul*) when she left her family to marry, and this remained hers, to be disposed of as she wished, and not to be alienated by the family into which she married.[20]

The master of the household was shown great personal respect, nobody speaking to him first, or in his presence without permission. He had the right to beat culprits within the family, or to starve them into submission. When his physical powers declined he might nominate a deputy, who would represent the family at market and who might gradually assume the full duties of the master.

Analogous to the role of the master of the household was that of the mistress of the household, his feminine counterpart and housekeeper.[21] She was appointed by the master and not elected; she was responsible for the domestic organization of the household, in particular the allocation of tasks to the womenfolk. She never worked in the fields with the other women. She was not necessarily the master's wife – in fact the turnover of holders of this position was much more frequent. She was never under forty years of age when appointed, since younger women were needed for work in the fields, and at about fifty the duties became too onerous and she would be superseded. She had to be impartial, never favouring her own children.

Within his own household the husband had the power to chastise his wife and children, but this authority did not stretch to ordering them to perform any specific tasks; in this respect he was bound, as were they, by the authority of the master and the mistress of the household. We see therefore that the rights of a husband were very severely circumscribed in traditional Gheg society.

The choice of his wife would be dictated as often as not by the shifting pattern of clan alliance, and until in more recent days the practice of clan exogamy broke down, his choice would always have to take account of the state of play in the bloodfeud. Indeed, intermarriage was one of the devices by which the bloodfeud was resolved, generally in addition to a mutually agreed truce (Alb. besë). In this way an unmarried male Gheg might find himself as much the victim of clan politics as the hapless members of royal houses in the Middle Ages. Whilst intermarriage might delay the resumption of the feud, it seldom achieved permanent peace, and hence both parties to the feud would find themselves harbouring womenfolk of their enemies, who were married to clan members. It is this enduring problem of the woman who had married into the enemy camp, and who found her husband and perhaps her sons fighting her own father and brothers, that remains one of the paradoxes of Gheg interpersonal relations. It is one that is overtly discussed only in the epic songs (Alb. këngë trimnijë) which are an important source of information and precept for traditional Gheg values.[22]

It is important to remember that a woman did not lose membership of the clan into which she was born by exogamous marriage. Throughout her life her point of social identification remained her natal kin-group, as represented by her brothers. A woman had the right to protection from her own family throughout her life – her husband only obtained her services at marriage and not her life. Her kinsmen provided her with a standing assurance of vengeance. Miss Durham, whose account of the Ghegs during the heyday of the bloodfeud remains an anthropological document of supreme importance, recorded '... a strong belief that a woman's nearest and dearest is naturally her brother'.[23] In the event of a bloodfeud breaking out between her clan of procreation and that into which she had married, a woman was confronted with an insuperable dilemma. On rare occasions she resolved it by killing her own children; more commonly she abstained from all activity, a course which was strengthened by the rules of the feud which precluded women from taking part other than those who had sworn perpetual virginity (Alb. virgjëreshë).[24] A woman remained, as an Albanian proverb has it, 'a sack for carrying things'. It must, however, be recognized that in the event of a feud breaking out between her clan by birth and that into which she had married, the wife's relationship with her husband, as well as with other males of his clan, was likely to be lacking any emotional warmth.[25]

It is impossible for an outsider to make authoritative judgements about the depth of romantic attachment between marital partners in a culture different from his own, but certainly the Ghegs seem to be highly restrained in the overt expression of sexual emotion. The essential element in marriage was virginity of the bride, and although the epic songs encouraged the young man to find his sexual gratification wherever and as frequently as he will – subject only to the proviso that he does not involve his clan in the feud – this seems seldom to have been the pattern of premarital courtship.

Indeed chastity provides one of the key concepts in the chain of rights which made up the ideal of family honour, on which the bloodfeud rested. Virginity was expected of all women who were unmarried, and at her marriage the proofs of this condition were awaited after the wedding night. In as much as many wives came from a distance, the likelihood of affianced couples having premarital sexual relations was slim, and where this did occur they would connive at the provision of false indications of the bride's unsullied state. For whilst it might be sufficient reason for a marriage to be repudiated by the groom's clan if she were found not to be a virgin, her own clan could take action against the person suspected of causing that condition, as having committed an offence against clan honour.[26]

It is perhaps significant to note that although the levirate was practised until relatively recently, whereby a widow was married *en deuxième noces* to her deceased husband's brother or, failing this, to a male cousin of the same clan,[27] there seemed to be little competitive sexuality between any of the males involved. That this was so strengthens the assumption that romantic feelings between men and women played little part in the expected behaviour patterns of husbands and wives. In brief, I would categorize the marital tie in Gheg society as one based on economic and social factors, involving little power of one partner over the other, few areas of joint decision-making (since both partners were subject to external authority), and containing little emotional dependence.

Among the more significant studies of intra-familial roles, the work of Elizabeth Bott has been widely used by students of the western family, but social anthropologists in general have not availed themselves of her theoretical framework.[28] It will be recalled that Bott distinguishes in husband–wife relations between a joint and a segregated conjugal role-relationship; in the former task-performance is either joint, with overlapping of domestic duties, or complementary, in which task-performance is articulated so that the completion of the work depends on a systematic distribution of labour. In segregated households, on the other hand, there is no overlapping, and task-performance and decision-making are executed by the partners with little reference to each other;

in this latter type of family there is also little common recreation. Bott seeks to show that the adherence of a family to one or the other type depends on whether the marital pair belong to a close-knit or loose-knit social network. The relationship between network and conjugal role-relationships is inverse: that is to say, partners with segregated role patterns tend to belong to close-knit social networks, and those with joint conjugal role-relationships belong to loose-knit social networks. Let us now apply this formulation, which represents some over-simplification of Bott's original hypothesis, to the Gheg ethnographic data.

It would be difficult to imagine a more archetypal example of segregated conjugal roles than the Gheg extended household. Similarly, for men at least, a close-knit social network existed in the everyday restrictions on their behaviour made by membership of the extended household and of the clan, as laid down by the centuries-old traditional canon of Lekë Dukagjini. The dictate of clan honour literally determined life or death. Cases are on record of men who had to remain in the towered fortresses (Alb. *kullë*) for many years while the women did all the agricultural work including the ploughing.[29] A man would derive companionship from other men, and in the evenings the group of people around the fire would be exclusively male, whilst the absorbing topic of conversation would be clan honour in all its ramifications. When ideology and politics intruded it was in terms of clan interests rather than by reference to external principles of morality.[30] Male participation in such discussions was limited by age rather than by reference to genealogical relationships.

As a male my examination of relationships between women was necessarily restricted, but I formed the clear impression that there was much less solidarity between women – who might have come from different clans anyway – and that although there was a clearly defined chain of authority determining task-performance, there was much less consensus between women as to the rightness of any state of affairs, and perhaps very much less concern for the upholding of family honour. Indeed there is some evidence to suggest that where the extended household pattern is breaking down, as it has been universally, the pressure to withdraw from the larger unit has been exerted by the wife on her husband, although the final decision has of necessity to be his. In most instances the woman seems to have gained immediately from the severance of the conjugal from the extended household: she would become mistress in her own house, whereas the husband would still retain obligations in the bloodfeud. Furthermore, in the troubled period of clan rivalry during the second world war, the extended household offered to the man rather more than physical protection, whilst the woman, through her immunity in the bloodfeud, gained less advantage from the collectivity.

This essay has not taken into account the relationships between parents and children, or those between siblings other than their obligations in the bloodfeud: these must await a fuller treatment on another occasion. It may, however, be stated in summary that Bott's hypothesis about the inverse relationship between the intensity of conjugal role patterns and that of the partners' respective networks is confirmed in the case of Gheg males. Womenfolk, on the other hand, seemed to achieve no close relationship with anyone, maintaining residual rights of vengeance by the men of their own clan of procreation, whom they would seldom meet, and not needing to engage intensively in any bloodfeud between clans, by virtue of their exemption through their sex. Close ties between women who have married into the same clan seemed to be uncommon; on the other hand competition for the only post in the household which offered them the chance to exercise authority was perhaps reduced by the more regular rotation of the office than occurred in the case of the master of the household. Equally, however, close ties between a woman and her children were restricted by their membership of different clans, and the practice of clan exogamy precluded any sort of enduring mother–daughter tie. Inter-personal relationships seem, indeed, to have been strictly limited by the provisions of the oral *kanún*, with its constant references to clan honour, and which seems to have inhibited the development of institutionalized relationships with a strong emotional content. Indeed, restraint in intra-familial, as in most social contexts, may be said to have characterized the traditional Gheg role pattern.

NOTES

1 The most significant studies in English are Durham 1909, 1928 and Hasluck 1954.
2 Whitaker 1968.
3 The canon was systematically collated by Father Shtjefen Gjeçov, 1933, 1941. Mrs Hasluck's work depends on this codification in many respects: cf. Kastrati 1955, pp. 124–6.
4 Hasluck 1954, pp. 148–62; Whitaker 1968, pp. 260–1.
5 Clause 1126 of Father Gjeçov's recension reads 'Dera e Gjomarkut âsht themeli i kanûs' (1933, p. 102; 1941, p. 261) – 'The base of the canon is the House of Gjomarkaj'.
6 Durham 1931, p. 155. Baron Nopcsa calculated (1912, p. 248) that the genealogy of the tribe of Berisha stretched back to 1370 and perhaps to 1270.
7 Durham 1928, p. 25.
8 Djilas 1958, p. 5.
9 Durham 1909, pp. 21, 98; 1928, p. 20.
10 Only one case of descent being calculated through women seems to have been recorded among the Ghegs: among the Nikai clan by Miss Durham 1909, pp. 195–6.
11 Hasluck 1954, p. 25.
12 Coon 1950, pp. 11, 28.
13 *Ibid.* p. 22.
14 *Ibid.* p. 28.
15 Durham 1914, p. 101.
16 Hasluck 1954, pp. 29–30.
17 Amery 1948, pp. 104–5. Amery's account of guerrilla warfare in Albania in World War II remains an important contribution to the analysis of social organization at that time.

18   Hasluck 1954, pp. 34–41.
19   Skendi 1956, p. 151.
20   Hasluck 1954, p. 42.
21   *Ibid.* p. 41.
22   Federal Writers' Project 1939, p. 144; Skendi 1954, pp. 85, 87, 195; for a series of love-songs, apparently rather bowdlerized, see Gurakuqi and Fishta 1937, pp. 219–88; Komisjoni Teknik 1939, pp. 207–68.
23   Durham 1928, p. 148.
24   Cozzi 1912, pp. 318–21; Durham 1928, p. 194; Hasluck 1933, p. 192.
25   The problem of the wife living among her own people's enemy has been little discussed. One moving account is Bielenberg 1968.
26   An early example of such a case is in Hecquard 1858, p. 228.
27   The levirate is recorded by many visitors to Albania: Durham 1909, pp. 36, 208; 1928, pp. 74, 202–4; Cabej 1935, p. 223; Swire 1937, p. 89.
28   Bott 1957.
29   For the *kullë* see Rosati 1915, pp. 133–9; Haberlandt 1917, pp. 55–67; Nopcsa 1925, pp. 7–93. Cases of men remaining indoors up to 25 years are on record, and rather more authenticated cases involving twelve years' seclusion – Ippen 1907, p. 17.
30   Cf. Amery's remark (1948, p. 112) of one of the guerrilla leaders: 'The persistance of the bloodfeuds presented Abas Kupi with a serious problem, for every time a clan was won to his cause their blood enemies would side automatically with his rivals.' For an interesting account of the bloodfeud in Mirditë, cf. Frasheri 1930, pp. 123–8.

REFERENCES

Amery, Julian. 1948. *Sons of the Eagle: a study in guerrilla war*. London, Macmillan.
Bielenberg, Christabel. 1968. *The past is myself*. London, Chatto & Windus.
Bott, Elizabeth. 1957. *Family and social network*. London, Tavistock.
Cabej, Eqrem. 1935. 'Sitten und Gebräuche der Albaner' in P. Skok and M. Budamir (eds): *Les Balkans, leur passé et leur present* (*Revue Internationale des Etudes Balkaniques*, Vol. II), pp. 218–34. Belgrade.
Coon, Carleton S. 1950. *The Mountains of Giants: a racial and cultural study of the North Albanian Mountain Ghegs*, Papers of the Peabody Museum of American Archaeology and Ethnology, Vol. 3, No. 3, Cambridge, Mass.
Cozzi, Ernesto. 1912. 'La donna albanese' in *Anthropos*, Vol. 7, pp. 309–35, 617–26. St. Gabriel-Mödling.
Djilas, Milovan. 1958. *Land without justice*. New York, Harcourt, Brace.
Durham, Mary Edith. 1909. *High Albania*. London, E. Arnold.
    1914. *The struggle for Scutari (Turk, Slav and Albanian)*. London, E. Arnold.
    1928. *Some tribal origins laws and customs of the Balkans*. London, Allen & Unwin.
    1931. 'Preservation of pedigrees and commemoration of Ancestors in Montenegro' in *Man*, Vol. 31 (art. 163), pp. 154–5.
Federal Writers' Project of the Works Progress Administration of Massachusetts. 1939. *The Albanian struggle in the Old World and the New*. Boston, The Writer.
Frasheri, Stavre Th. 1930. *Permes Mirdites ne dimer*. Korçe, Peppo-Marko.
Gjeçov, Shtjefen Konst, 1933. *Kanuni i Lekë Dukagjinit*. Shkodër, Françesakne.
Gjeçov, Stefano Cost. 1941. *Codice di Lek Dukagjini ossia diritto consuetudinario delle montagne d'Albania* (Reale Accademia d'Italia – Centro Studi per l'Albania, Vol. 2). Rome.
Gurakuqi, Karl and Fishta, Filip (eds). 1937. *Visaret e kombit*, Vol. 3, *Valle, gjamë,*

vajtime dhe Kange dashunije (Botimiet e Komisjonit të kremtimevet të 25 vjetorit të vetqeverimit 1912–1937, No. 5). Tirana, Nikaj.

Haberlandt, Arthur. 1917. *Kulturwissenschaftliche Beiträge zur Volkskunde von Montenegro, Albanien und Serbien* (Ergänzungs-Band 12 zu Jahrgang 23, *Zeitschrift für österreichische Volkskunde*). Vienna.

Hasluck, Margaret. 1933. 'Bride-price in Albania: a Homeric Parallel'. *Man*, Vol. 33 (art. 203), pp. 191–5.

1954. *The unwritten law in Albania*, J. H. Hutton (ed.), Cambridge University Press.

Hecquard, Hyacinthe. 1858. *Histoire et description de la Haute Albanie ou Ghégarie*. Paris, Bertrand.

Ippen, Theodore A. 1907. *Skutari und die nordalbanische Küstebene* (Zur Kunde der Balkanhalbinsel – Reisen und Beobachten, Vol. 5). Sarajevo.

Kastrati, Qazim. 1955. 'Some sources on the unwritten law in Albania'. *Man*, Vol. 55 (art. 134), pp. 124–7.

Komisjoni Teknik. 1939. *Visaret e kombit*, Vol. 4, *Kangë trimnije* &c. (Ministrija e Arsimit – Komisjoni Teknik, Nr. 13). Tirana, Luarasi.

Nopcsa, Franz Baron. 1912. 'Beiträge zur Vorgeschichte und Ethnologie' in *Wissenschaftliche Mitteilungen aus Bosnien und der Herzegowina*, Vol. 12, pp. 168–253. Vienna.

1925. *Albanien: Bauten, Trachten und Geräte Nordalbaniens*. Berlin, De Gruyter.

Rosati, Umberto. 1915. 'Condizione economico-agrarie dell'Albania,' Part 2 of Umberto Rosati and Gaetano Baudin, *Studi agrologici (Relazione della Commissione per lo Studio dell'Albania Part II)* (Atti della Società Italiana per il Progresso delle Scienze), pp. 127–95, Rome.

Skendi, Stavro. 1954. *Albanian and South Slavic Oral epic poetry* (Memoirs of the American Folklore Society, Vol. 44). Philadelphia.

1956. *Albania*. East-Central Europe under the Communists – Praeger Publications in Russian History and World Communism, Vol. 46. New York.

Swire, J. 1937. *King Zog's Albania*. London, Hale.

Whitaker, Ian. 1968. 'Tribal structure and national politics in Albania, 1910–1950' in I. M. Lewis (ed.), *History and social anthropology* (A.S.A. Monographs, No. 7), pp. 253–93. London, Tavistock.

9 A survey of familial change in two Turkish
gecekondu areas

Emre Kongar
Hacettepe University, Ankara

INTRODUCTION

This paper makes a comparative study of the size, structure, kin relations and
relation to formal organizations of the *gecekondu* family. The intention is to
explore some of the changes that a rural family undergoes when it moves to the
city.[1] The data used have been gathered through two community studies, the
first being the study of the family in İzmir, in which the *gecekondu* family has
been made a separate category,[2] and the second being the study of the Altındağ
gecekondu area in Ankara.[3] In both studies the main technique was survey
research in which structured interviewing was used.

BACKGROUND INFORMATION

THE CONCEPT OF *gecekondu*

One of the most acute social problems in Turkey is the mass migration from
rural areas because cities lack the facilities to absorb the incoming population.
The result of the migration is the formation of *gecekondu* areas where a rural
population wrestles with the problems of adapting itself to urban life.

The *gecekondu* is officially defined as 'the dwelling unit on somebody else's
site which was built without obtaining the approval of the landowner and built
in a way which is not approved by the general legal provisions for buildings and
construction'.[4] It is usually constructed out of second-hand material to a very
low standard;[5] it lacks utilities and, by urban standards, constitutes a health
hazard.[6] *Gecekondu* areas grow very rapidly and the lack, or weak enforcement,
of master plans in metropolitan areas is the major contributory factor to such a
development. At election time the rate of growth of *gecekondus* rises as vote-
seeking politicians pave the way for building new *gecekondus* by legalizing old
ones and by providing utilities for them in order to get the votes of the population arriving from the rural areas.

Gecekondu areas are located around large cities like İstanbul, Ankara and
59.2 per cent of Ankara's population, 45 per cent of İstanbul's population[7]

TABLE 1

Year interval	Annual total population increase (%)	Annual urban population increase (%)
1927–35	1.67	2.50
1935–40	2.06	3.96
1940–45	1.09	1.55
1945–50	2.74	2.57
1950–55	2.97	7.44
1955–60	3.06	6.23
1960–65	2.62	5.99

and 33.4 per cent of İzmir's population[8] live in *gecekondu* areas. These figures seem high when compared to Lima, for instance, where the *barrida* population (which corresponds to the *gecekondu*) was only 20 per cent of the city population in 1964. Again, in Rio de Janeiro the *favela* population was about 16 per cent of the city population in 1964.[9] Though there are other contributory factors, there is no doubt that the main force behind the *gecekondu* phenomenon is the urbanization rate of Turkey. The increase in the urban population (see Table 1) sheds some light on the problem.[10]

As Table 1 shows, urbanization in Turkey gained momentum in the 1950s, and since then the annual urban population increase has been twice that of the increase of total population. This rate of urbanization is very high in comparison to Latin American figures.[11]

The inhabitants of *gecekondu* areas come mostly from rural areas, although some come from small towns and villages. Direct migration from the place of birth to the *gecekondu* area is usual and incomers start by taking up urban-type jobs.[12] With regard to their clothing, diet, and daily habits it seems that they have assimilated some urban patterns.[13] Though Yasa asserts that some rural characteristics, like traditional wedding ceremonies, bride price, etc. still exist among the *gecekondu* population,[14] it is my belief that these characteristics do not exist in the *gecekondu* population itself but can be observed in the relations of *gecekondu* inhabitants with the rural population. In other words, though some of the *gecekondu* population who maintain relations with the rural communities still observe rural traditions, it does not mean that rural traditions (such as bride price, etc.) are followed by the *gecekondu* population as a whole. Furthermore, though some people maintain contact with their rural communities, hardly any of them want to go back. *Gecekondu* areas have their own social stratification. The upper class consists, roughly, of traders, shop-keepers, etc.; the middle class of qualified workers, artisans, etc.; and the lower class of non-qualified workers, porters, janitors, pedlars and the unemployed.

As Turkish cities lack the facilities and other advantages which constitute the 'pull factors' of city life, it seems that the disadvantages of rural life, or 'push factors', are the predominating reasons for migration. Lack of land and mechanization of agriculture are the main impulses behind the 'push factors'. Migration is, therefore, not by free choice. People are in a sense forced to move.

THE GECEKONDU COMMUNITY IN İZMIR

İzmir is the second largest industrial city in Turkey. It has a population of about $1\frac{1}{2}$ million people, 600,000 of whom live within the municipality. The *gecekondu* population of the city consists of about 200,000, most of whom moved into the city more than ten years ago (61 per cent; the comparable figure for İzmir as a whole is 71 per cent). The newcomers to *gecekondu* areas (who moved in 5 years ago or less) form about one-sixth of the population (16 per cent; 12 per cent for İzmir). Ownership of houses is high: 76.5 per cent of the *gecekondu* population are families living in their own houses, whereas in the city of İzmir the figure is only 65.8 per cent.

Income is rather low. The mode of the income distribution among *gecekondu* population is between 250 and 500 TL (9 TL = U.S. $1.00 in 1968) per month per household. The mode for İzmir as a whole is between 500 and 1,000 TL.[15]

THE GECEKONDU COMMUNITY IN ANKARA

The second community to have been studied is the oldest *gecekondu* area in Ankara, the capital of Turkey, in which the service sector is predominant. This is Altındağ *gecekondu* area first settled in the late 1940s. It consists of about 5,000 households with a population about 27,000. A majority of the population (61 per cent) moved to the city more than 10 years ago (the figure for all the Ankara *gecekondu* areas is 53 per cent).[16] The newcomers (those who moved in 5 years ago or less) form about one-fifth of the population (almost the same rate as for all *gecekondu* areas in the city).[17] More than half of the Altındağ population (57.3 per cent) own their own houses (the figure for all *gecekondu* areas in Ankara is 59 per cent).[18] Mod value of income distribution in Altındağ is between 501 and 1,000 TL per month per household. (Yasa and others found an average about 400 TL.)[19]

LIMITATIONS OF THE FINDINGS

As stated before, the data used in this paper have been gathered through two community studies (İzmir and Altındağ) and structured interviewing was used in both cases, therefore any limitations are the result of survey techniques. Secondly, the communities studied are not similar. The Altındağ *gecekondu* area has a population of about 5,000 households. It is the oldest *gecekondu* area and is located in a city in which the service sector is dominant. The İzmir study, on the other hand, covers the whole city which is an industrial one. Therefore, not only do the universes differ, but the characteristics are also dissimilar. One is old-established, the other is more mixed: one is located around a city in which the service sector is dominant, the other is in an industrial city. So these differences must be borne in mind when evaluating comparisons.

A third limitation is the result of treating the *gecekondu* phenomenon as homogeneous and uniform all over Turkey. There is no doubt that it is the outcome of urbanization processes and that, therefore, the population in *gecekondu* areas is in transition, but there the similarities end. In a paper which studies a subject like the family, the differences between the various *gecekondu* areas cannot be taken into account as they should be. To begin with we do not have enough comparative data on the family in the various *gecekondu* areas. Then the characteristics of the different *gecekondu* areas have not been studied according to objective criteria. Moreover, we have no overall vision of the *gecekondu* family.

A fourth limitation is due to the fact that there are not enough studies of the *gecekondu* phenomenon in Turkey itself. The fifth and last limitation is the lack of family studies in Turkey as a whole. Consequently, the findings of this paper must be treated with caution: the writer has used them merely as clues towards further research.

FAMILY SIZE AND STRUCTURE

The average size of the family in various parts of Turkey, according to the various studies, is indicated in Table 2. In this paper 'family' is defined as 'household': i.e. relatives living under the same roof whose food is cooked in common. First of all it should be noted that our findings with regard to the *gecekondu* family size in İzmir are very close to the figure given by the Ministry of Reconstruction and Resettlement. If the small family size is taken as an indicator of urbanization,[20] it could be said that the *gecekondu* family in İzmir and İstanbul is quite urbanized. But in Ankara the case is rather different. An average family size of 5.5 is what Yasa found in all *gecekondu* areas of Ankara. He claims, therefore, that such a high average could be taken as indicating the rural character of the *gecekondu* family.[21] On the other hand, Kıray says that the average size of 5.2 of the family in Ereğli (which is a Black Sea coastal town) approximates to the urban family.[22] This may be due to the context in which the figures are considered. Yasa is studying the *gecekondu* families in Ankara, which is an urban area, while Kıray studies families in Ereğli, which is a semi-urban area. Consequently Yasa thinks 5.5 is more than the city average of 4.63 and Kıray thinks 5.2 is less than the village average of 6.16. I, myself, think Table 2 solves the problem by showing that the average of towns like Ereğli is 5.2 which is very close to what Kıray found in Ereğli. This figure also demonstrates the intermediate character of Turkish towns. Table 2 shows that the average *gecekondu* family size in Ankara is greater than that in İzmir and İstanbul. This may be due to the fact that both İzmir and İstanbul are more

TABLE 2   *The average number of household members*

Turkey[a]	5.7
Cities[a]	4.6
Towns[a]	5.2
Villages[a]	6.2
Central Anatolia (villages)[b]	7.2
Ereğli (villages)[c]	6.3
Sakaltutan[d]	6.0
Elbaşi[d]	5.6
Gecekondus in Ankara[e]	5.5
Hal[f]	5.4
Hasanoğlan[g]	5.4
Ereğli (town)[c]	5.2
Gecekondus in İstanbul[h]	4.7
İzmir City[k]	4.7
Gecekondus in İzmir[l]	4.4
Sindel[m]	4.1
Gecekondus in Altındağ	5.1
Gecekondus in İzmir	4.7

Sources
[a] *Census of Population*, 1965, pp. 672–5, Tables, 53a, 53b, 53c.
[b] Şahinkava, R. *Orta Anadolu Köylerinde Aile Strüktürü* (The Family Structure in the Central Anatolian Villages), Ankara universitesi Ziraat Fakültesi yayınları, 1966, p. 34.
[c] Kıray, p. 201 and p. 115.
[d] Stirling, p. 37.
[e] Yasa, *Ankara'da gecekondu Aileleri*, p. 108.
[f] Erdentuğ, pp. 31–2.
[g] Yasa, *Hasanoğlan*, p. 79, Table 20.
[h] *İstanbul gecekondulari*.
[k] Kongar, p. 68.
[l] *Gecekondus in Izmir*.
[m] Yasa *Sindel*, pp. 34–35.

industrialized than Ankara, which would affect the rate of change in family size and structure. Our Altındağ finding, which is less than the Ankara *gecekondu* average, could be due to the fact that Altındağ is the oldest *gecekondu* area in Ankara. Because the area is older, the population has had more chance to assimilate urban values and way of life which, in turn, affects the family size. It could be said, therefore, that, in terms of size, the *gecekondu* family in Turkey is quite urbanized, and that this urbanization is probably affected by the level of industrialization in the city in which the family lives.

As for the structure of the *gecekondu* family, the comparative percentages are shown in Table 3. Before we evaluate Table 3 it should be remembered that in sociological literature certain structures tend to be associated with certain functions. For instance, extended forms of household are thought of as families of 'great functionality' and nuclear forms of household as families of

TABLE 3 *Percentages of nuclear and proliferated families in various places in Turkey*

Family types	Villages in Central Anatolia[a]	Hasanoğlan[c]	Sakaltutan[b]	Elbaşı[b]	Altındağ gecekondu	Ereğli[d]	İzmir[e] gecekondu	İzmir[f] City	Ankara gecekondu[g]	Sindel[h]
Nuclear	6.8	58.0	55.0	56.0	59.4	61.6	62.5	63.6	72.0	88.5
Proliferated	93.2	41.5	40.0	39.0	26.8	27.2	27.3	27.2	20.0	11.5
Other	0.0	0.5	5.0	5.0	13.5	9.2	10.0	9.2	8.2	0.0

Sources: [a] Şahinkaya, p. 34.
[b] Stirling, p. 38.
[c] Yasa, *Hasanoğlan*, p. 79.
[d] Kiray, p. 114.
[e] Kongar, p. 72.
[f] Kongar, p. 64.
[g] Yasa, *Gecekondu Aileleri*, p. 104.
[h] Yasa, *Sindel*, p. 35.

'little functionality'.[23] But I, myself, do not agree with this and especially not when transitional societies are in question. Even if such an approach were true for 'modern' societies which have completed their industrialization, or for traditional societies which have not yet started their process of change, it is certainly not acceptable for transitional societies in which the rate of change in structure and function is not necessarily the same. The best example of a different rate of change with regard to the structure and functions of the family is given by Yasa. In one Turkish village he found that nuclear family-type household members have extended family-type interactions. For this he invented the term 'narrow family'[24] to describe the nuclear household forms in which the father has the rights and privileges of the family head of extended family-type households. In this paper, however, we follow Levy's classification of ideal family structures without giving them a functional content.[25]

When, with the above considerations in mind, we look at Table 3, we could say that the *gecekondu* family in Turkey has a modern nuclear family structure as far as the composition of the members of the household is concerned. It is interesting to observe, however, that the percentage of nuclear families in the Ankara *gecekondu* area is quite high. This may be due to the fact that Yasa classifies one-member households and households in which there is no married couple as nuclear, whereas I classify them as broken or incomplete.[26] The table also indicates that the Turkish family structure is changing from proliferated to nuclear. If we differentiate between vertical and horizontal proliferations, the transition can be seen more clearly. The percentage and characteristics of the *famille souche* in İzmir and Altındağ are also given in Table 3. It is interesting to observe that the horizontal proliferation of the nuclear family is practically non-existent. It could, therefore, be said that even the proliferated families in the *gecekondu* areas have lost their traditional character and have become transitional.

Table 4 shows us once more that the main characteristic of the Turkish family is patrilineal, Kıray found that the same tendency is to be seen in Ereğli.[27] Patrilineal families form 27.5 per cent of the whole, whereas matrilineal families form only 7.8 per cent. Similar findings were reported by Yasa for the

TABLE 4   *Percentages of family structures in İzmir and Altındağ*

Family types	İzmir City	İzmir *gecekondu*	Altında ğ *gecekondu*
Extended	0.1	0.0	0.4
Famille souche patrilineal	20.3	22.3	20.2
Famille souche matrilineal	6.3	5.0	2.3
Nuclear	63.6	62.5	59.4
Broken and incomplete	9.2	10.0	13.5
Other	0.5	0.0	3.9

gecekondu areas in Ankara. According to his figures, there are five times as many patrilineal as there are matrilineal families.[28] The same tendency is observed by Erdentuğ in two villages in the province of Elaziğ in the eastern part of Turkey.[29] The patrilineal character of the proliferated nuclear families is also reported for the village near Ankara,[30] and can be seen quite clearly in Stirling's study of a Turkish village.[31] But such a patrilineage should be evaluated in the context of dominant family structures. In communities in which the nuclear structure seems dominant, patrilineages would mean sons are taking care of their parents. For instance, in İzmir the head of the household belongs to the younger generation in 65 per cent of the patrilineal *famille souche* structures. One must, therefore, be very careful about patrilineages in Turkey, especially where the family cycle is concerned.

In order to find out how the head of the household sees his authority within the family, I asked questions about attitudes towards children's free choice of a mate and a profession. Tables 5 and 6 show us the results. Unfortunately, our

TABLE 5   *The percentages of heads of households who will let their children decide whom to marry*

İzmir City	İzmir *gecekondu*	Altındağ *gecekondu*	
		For girls	For boys
48.14	45.32	44.5	75.1

TABLE 6   *The percentage of heads of households who will let their children decide their own profession*

İzmir City	İzmir *gecekondu*	Altındağ *gecekondu*	
		For girls	For boys
22.92	17.84	25.2	87.6

data in İzmir would not allow us to differentiate between boys and girls. The results from the tables can be summarized as follows: (1) In İzmir, the heads of households in the *gecekondu* areas are more likely to direct their children on both questions than average household heads in the whole of the city of İzmir. This would suggest that they have not yet completely absorbed urban values. (2) The Altındağ *gecekondu* family seems much more lenient than the İzmir *gecekondus* family when it comes to children's choices. This might be due partly to the fact that the wording of the questions has been changed slightly and partly to the fact that the Altındağ area has a somewhat higher socio-economic status. (3) There is a clear-cut differentiation between boys and girls in favour of the boys; understandably, families are more likely to direct the girls. (4) Most household heads seem authoritarian towards their children's choice of mate and profession. (5) This authoritarian attitude reminds us of the family structure, which Yasa has called 'narrow'. (6) When dominant authoritarian tendencies are seen to go hand-in-hand with the nuclear family structure, it re-enforces our views about the different rates of change between structures and functions.

KIN RELATIONS COMPARED TO RELATIONS WITH NEIGHBOURS AND FORMAL ORGANIZATIONS

Physical proximity to relatives is shown in Table 7 and relationships with them in Table 8. The relatives whose interactions were studied are 'first degree' relatives, i.e. parents, children, siblings, aunts, uncles of both spouses and their children. Interaction between them for the purpose of lending and borrowing goods and money was investigated. Table 7 shows us that more than half of the families have close relatives living in the next neighbourhood or even nearer. On the other hand, Table 8 shows us that the majority of the families tend not to

TABLE 7   *Percentage of families who have close relatives in the next neighbourhood or nearer*

İzmir City	İzmir *gecekondu*	Altındağ *gecekondu*
64.2	68.4	53.8

TABLE 8   *Percentage of families who borrow and lend goods and money with relatives and with neighbours*

	İzmir City			İzmir *gecekondu*			
	Money			Money			
	Borrow	Lend	Goods	Borrow	Lend	Goods	Altındağ *gecekondu*
With relatives	30.0	18.3	11.4	32.5	12.3	12.52	15.1
With neighbours	11.9	8.7	34.3	17.7	10.6	39.1	39.0

combine their resources with those of relatives for the purpose of lending and borrowing goods and money. This picture suggests that the *gecekondu* family is fairly isolated from its relatives. The suggestion is supported by the fact that the majority of the households (67 per cent) in the İzmir *gecekondu* area do not have a reciprocal helping relationship for the purpose of housework with anybody. Such an isolation seems quite significant as the physical conditions (i.e. proximity) for interaction with relatives exist. This certainly suggests that the idea of separate nuclear families under separate roofs functioning as one family under the dominance of the paternal head is not a valid concept in the *gecekondu* areas. It means that neither joint family structure, suggested for rural areas, nor modified extended family structure, suggested for industrial societies,[32] is likely to be found in *gecekondu* areas.

Yasa has also pointed out the weakening of kinship ties. He thinks that because those who find jobs in Ankara through their relatives, kinsmen and acquaintances constitute a low percentage (17 per cent), this is an indication of weakened ties.[33] In our Altındağ survey the figure is only 12 per cent and it is my opinion that it indicates that kinship ties of the *gecekondu* family are already weakened rather than that the passage of time weakens them.

Table 8 also shows us that the lending and borrowing of goods is more frequent among neighbours than it is among relatives. In addition to the figures shown in the table, my additional data on reciprocal help in housework reveals the same tendency. The number of families in İzmir *gecekondus* who have a reciprocal helping relationship with neighbours is greater (17 per cent) than the number of the families who have this relationship with their relatives (14 per cent). Though the difference between the figures is not great enough to allow any meaningful comparative analysis, we can observe a tendency to interact more with the neighbours than the relatives. There is no logical explanation for such a tendency at the moment, except to say that the neighbourhood can be seen as a primary group in *gecekondus* functioning as a substitute for relatives.[34]

The family's interaction with formal organizations in selected areas of life is shown in Table 9. The interactions with formal organizations are important

TABLE 9   *Percentage of families who have interaction with formal organizations in some areas of life*

Areas of interaction	İzmir City	İzmir *gecekondu*	Altındağ *gecekondu*
Visiting with friends at work	40.3	38.7	31.1
Benefits from the visit	48.9	48.5	57.8
Contacts with school and teacher	67.0	62.2	52.5
Benefit from the contacts	90.6	88.6	76.8
Helping children with their courses	63.9	61.35	42.3

as they shed some light on the adaptation processes of the family migrating into the urban environment. As can be seen in Table 9 there is considerable contact between *gecekondu* families and formal organizations, especially over education, and, according to the respondents, such contacts prove useful. Most of the families who have contacted schools or teachers think that this has benefited their children, which suggests that the families believe in co-operating with schools. This gives us one clue about how the *gecekondu* family functions in an urban setting.

A second finding is the intensity of interaction with work life. About one-third of the families are on visiting terms with friends at places of work. This means that one-third of *gecekondu* families support their working members by a primary type relationship. About half of the visiting families think that such visits are a help to working members of the family with regard to their life at work. This could be another clue about the urbanizing tendencies of *gecekondu* families.

CONCLUSION

I have tried in this paper to explore some of the changes that a rural family undergoes when it moves to the city. As stated before, the paper has several limitations. Bearing these in mind, the major point is that it seems as if the *gecekondu* family adapts itself to an urban environment very quickly and ceases to rely on kin. As the Turkish rural family is always thought to rely heavily on its kin, the process of adaptation as well as the independence from the kin means that the *gecekondu* family has undergone a rapid and drastic change. The following factors may account for the change.

1. Most of the families moved to the city because they had no other choice. The majority said they moved because they could not make a living in the village, and could not benefit from their ties at home. Consequently, they came to the city with hopes for the future and a willingness to change and adapt. Hardly any of them want to return to their villages.

2. The move from village to city means moving from *gemeinschaft* to *gesellschaft*. This means, in general, that:

(a) their socio-economic position has changed. Yesterday's farmer has become today's worker, trader or shopkeeper. About a quarter of the heads of Ankara *gecekondu* families have acquired the skills that they need for their new occupation after they moved to the city, e.g. as mechanics, carpenters, tailors, masons, etc.;[35]

(b) the reference group and the social controls to which they are subjected have changed. They have established primary types of relations with friends at work, contacts with schools and teachers and have joined voluntary associations and trade unions. About one-third of the heads of families in the Ankara *gecekondu* area belong to voluntary associations.[36] One-fifth of the family heads in the Altındağ *gecekondu* area belong to trade unions. The population of *gecekondu* is fully aware of formal and impersonal rules and regulations, which have been learned through the difficult experience of building homes. The inhabitants are, therefore, conscious of the change in their milieu.

3. The *gecekondu* dwellers have rising expectations. A majority of them expect better jobs and higher income in the future, and most think that their children will live elsewhere than in the *gecekondu* area. Those who do not own a house expect to own one in the future.

Though convincing up to a point, these factors hardly seem sufficient to explain such rapid and drastic changes. We have, therefore, to look for additional explanations. First of all, it should be noted that to some extent there are substitutes for kin relations in *gecekondu* areas. Formal organizations, friends at work and neighbours are the substitute groups. The *gecekondu* family, by transferring primary relations from relatives to other groups, may easily find substitutes for kin reliance. Secondly, as the migrating families come mainly from the rural areas in which agricultural mechanization, cash-cropping, etc. are already established facts, it may be that the ideal type of kin-relied rural family as the origin of the *gecekondu* family is no more than a myth.[37] It is unfortunate that we do not have enough information about the structure of the rural family in Turkey. Until the appearance of further studies our suggestions must be considered as no more than tentative conclusions. It can tentatively be said that the main reason why the rural family adapts itself so smoothly to urban conditions in *gecekondu* areas is that the process of change has already started in the village.

NOTES

1 The word *gecekondu* literally means a house 'built overnight'. It refers to the shanty-town area in which many migrants to the city live.
2 The study was carried out in 1969. For the methodological approach see K. S. Sirikantan, 'The master sample of the Izmir survey', mimeographed paper, Hacettepe University, Ankara, 1968; and Emre Kongar, *Izmir'de Kentsel Aile* (Urban Family in Izmir), Türk Sosyal Bilimler Derneği, Ankara, 1972, pp. 43–62. I am indebted to the Turkish Social Sciences Association who sponsored the study.
3 The Altındağ study was carried out in 1970, under my supervision, by the Department of Social Work, Hacettepe University.
4 Turhan Yörükan, Ayda Yörükan, *Sehirlesme, Gecekondular ve Konut Politikası*, Urbanization, *gecekondus* and housing policy), Imar ve Iskân Bakanlığı, Mesken Genel Müdürlügü, Ankara, 1966, p. 13.
5 *Ibid.* p. 18.
6 *ibid.* p. 19.
7 *Ibid.* p. 15.
8 *Gecekondus in İzmir*, Ministry of Reconstruction and Resettlement, General Directorate of Housing, Social research Department, Information publication 5, Ankara, 1966.
9 Harley L. Browning, 'Urbanization and modernization in Latin America: the demographic perspective', in *The Urban Explosion in Latin America*, Glenn H. Bayer (ed.), Cornell University Press, New York, 1967, p. 101.
10 Cevat Geray, 'Urbanization in Turkey', *Siyasal Bilgiler Fakültesi Dergisi*, Vol. XXIV, No. 4, p. 159.
11 See Irving Louis Horowitz, 'Electoral politics, urbanization, and social development in Latin America', in Bayer (ed.), *The Urban Explosion in Latin America*, p. 223, table 15.
12 Yörükan, Yörükan: *Şehirleşme, Gecekondular*, p. 21.
13 Ibrahim Yasa, *Ankara'da Gecekondu Aileleri* (*Gecekondu* families in Ankara) SSYB, Sosyal Hizmetler Genel Müdürlüğü Yayınları, No. 46, Ankara, 1966, pp. 160, 173.
14 İbrahim Yasa, 'Ankara Gecekondularında Kentlesme' (Urbanization in Ankara *gecekondus*), mimeographed paper, S.B.F. Iskan ve Sehircilik Enstitüsü XI. Iskan ve

Şehircilik Haftası Konferansları, No. 6, 21 Mayıs, 1970.

15 As all the İzmir figures include *gecekondu* population, the differences between *gecekondu* and İzmir population figures are not as significant as they should be.

16 Yasa, *Ankara'da Gecekondu Aileleri*, p. 74.

17 *Ibıd.* p. *14.*

18 *Ibid.* p. 63.

19 *Ibid.* p. 135.

20 See William J. Goode, 'Industrialization and family change', in Bert F. Hoselitz and Wilbert E. Moore (eds), *Industrialization and Society*, Proceedings of the Chicago Conference on Social Implications of Industrialization and Technical Change, 15–22 September, 1960, Unesco, 1963, pp. 240–1; for some cross-cultural questions, see: Ralph H. Beals, 'Urbanization and acculturation', in S. N. Eisenstadt (ed.), *Comparative Social Problems*, New York, The Free Press, 1966.

21 Yasa, *Ankara'da Gecekondu Aileleri*, p. 104.

22 Mübeccel B. Kıray, *Ereğli, Ağır Sanayiden Önce Bir Sahil Kasabası* (Ereğli: A coastal town before the heavy industry), DPT yayınları, 1964, p. 115.

23 It is possible to see this approach in Eugene Litwak, 'Extended kin relations in an industrial democratic society', in E. Shanas and Gorden F. Streib (eds), *Social Structure and the Family Generational Relations*, New Jersey, Prentice Hall, 1965 and Robert F. Winch, *The Modern Family*, New York, Holt, Rinehart and Winston, 1963, pp. v and 12.

24 İbrahim Yasa, *Sindel Köyü* (Sindel village), Türkiye ve Orta Doğu Amme İdaresi Enstitüsü, Balkanoğlu Matbaacılık Şti, Ankara, 1960; p. 59.

25 In setting forth his ideal types, Levy defines the three categories of societies: (1) societies devoid of modern medical technology (traditional societies); (2) societies with highly developed modern medical technologies as part of generally high levels of 'modernization' (modern societies); (3) societies whose members have imported some modern medical technologies, but who have not yet achieved stable high levels of modernization in general respects (transitional societies). As for the ideal family structures, he distinguishes the lineally-extended family, the nuclear family and the *famille souche*. Ideally, membership of a lineally-extended family unit 'involved representatives of as many generations as possible selected in terms of one sex line, and as many siblings of one sex as possible, plus their spouses and all their non-adult children'. On the other hand 'membership of the nuclear family consists ideally of father, mother, and non-adult children, if there be children'. *Famille souche* is intermediate between these two and corresponds to the transitional society. 'Ideally speaking, the membership of a *famille souche* proliferates vertically along generational lines as does a lineally-extended family, but not horizontally along sibling lines.' According to Levy, the greatest variation between the ideal and actual family structures can be found in transitional societies, with regard to the *famille souche*. See Marion J. Levy jr, 'Aspects of the analysis of family structure', in Ansley J. Coale, *et al.*, *Aspects of the Analysis of Family Structure*, Princeton University Press, 1965, pp. 45–6.

26 For the definition of incomplete and broken families, see: Otto Pollak, 'The Broken Family', in Nathan E. Cohen (ed.), *Social Work and Social Problems*, New York, National Association of Social Workers, 1964, p. 321.

27 Kıray, *Ereğli, Ağır Sanayiden*, p. 114.

28 Yasa, *Ankara'da Gecekondu Aileleri*, p. 105, table 44.

29 Nermin Erdentuğ, *Hal Köyünün Etnolojik Tetkiki* (Ethnological study of Gal village). Ankara Universıtesi Dil ve Tarih Coğrafya Fakültesi Yayınları, No. 109, Ankara, 1956, pp. 31–2, Nermin Erdentuğ, *Sün Köyünün Etnolojik Tetkiki* (Ethnological

218   EMRE KONGAR

study of Sün village), Ankara Universitesi, Dil ve Tarih Coğrafya Fakültesi Yayin-
larından No. 132, Ankara, 1959, p. 20.
30 İbrahim Yasa, *Yirmibeş Yıl Sonra Hasanoğlan Köyü* (Hasanoğlan village, 25 years
later), Siyasal Bilgiler Fakültesi Yayınları, No. 270, Ankara, 1969, p. 79.
31 Paul Stirling, *Turkish Village*, New York, John Wiley. 1965, p. 38, table 2.
32 Litwak says that the 'modified extended' family or the 'coalition of the nuclear
families' who live under separate roofs but exchange significant services with each
other is the ideal type of family structure in industrial democratic societies. See
Litwak, 'Extended Kin relations', p. 291 and pp. 321-3.
33 İbrahim Yasa, 'Types of occupations and economic order in *gecekondu* communities'
in *Regional Planning Local Government and Community Development in Turkey*,
Seminar on Housing and Planning, 14–18 December 1964.
34 For such an approach see William H. Whyte jr, *The Organization Man*, New York,
Doubleday, 1957.
35 Yasa, *Ankara'da Gecekondu Aileleri*, pp. 130–1.
36 *Ibid.* p. 212.
37 See below, Peter Benedict, 'Aspects of the domestic cycle in a Turkish provincial
town', pp. 219–41.

10 Aspects of the domestic cycle in a Turkish provincial town

Peter Benedict
The Ford Foundation, Egypt

INTRODUCTION

Certain assumptions concerning the ideology underlying Turkish family structure are in need of critical examination. The joint extended family-household has long been assumed to be both the ideal and, generally, the actual form of traditional Turkish family structure. Recent studies, however, suggest that the joint extended family as the ideal structure may not be so widespread as previously assumed and that, for particular areas of Turkey, other alternative forms of family structure may be both the ideal and the predominant form.

The composition and functions of the joint extended family in Turkey have been variously described in a number of published studies over the past two decades.[1] Despite a remarkable increase also in a number of general community studies,[2] no other published study to date rivals the single-cover anthropological treatment by Stirling of aspects of social life, such as kinship, marriage, family structure and the domestic cycle, provided in his book *Turkish Village* (1965). Many discussions of ideology and social structure in Turkey, both in and out of the literature, continue to depend heavily upon data and observations derived from his study of two small then-isolated villages in central Anatolia.

Some recent sociological research in Turkey, however, has begun to call into question the validity of the wider application of Stirling's conceptual statements, until now tacitly applied to a number of social contexts. Much of this recent research has added to our growing appreciation of the large enthnographic differences existing in Turkey, differences which tend to limit the usefulness of a single, *Turkish Village*, ethnographic description of rural life. A number of such studies serve a purpose in pointing out that marriage customs differ between regions and ethnic groups, as do matters of kinship terminology, land tenure and inheritance, the morphology of settlements and the exact wording of rain prayers.

Still other studies have attempted to move beyond the simple enumeration of ethnographic differences to examine matters of ideology and their relationship to changing structures and their functions. The rising interest in issues of social change is resulting in a healthy intolerance toward those studies which do not seek to analyse the processes of change in a complex framework of both historical and contemporary factors. Similar to the results of increased enthno-graphic studies, the examination of conceptual issues calls into question accepted generalizations, such as those concerned with the ideology of descent, composition of family and household, and the domestic cycle, postulated in Stirling's useful work.

The purpose of this paper is to examine critically certain assumptions concerning the ideal and actual structure of the joint extended family-household as found in the literature on Turkish traditional society. The discussion begins with a summary description of the household and domestic cycle as it is presented in selected sources in the literature. Secondly, data are used from a study of a southwest Turkish provincial town which suggest a model of the domestic cycle which differs markedly from the 'typical' household career presented in the literature.

A GENERAL VIEW OF THE HOUSEHOLD AND DOMESTIC CYCLE

In his two studied villages, Stirling found the joint household to be a pervasive ideal, an ideal to which all adhere in the organization of their household affairs. The residential domestic group is routinely uniform with few cases of deviations:

The patrilineal joint household is then the ideal at which all are aiming; moreover, most villagers live in such a household for at least one period in their lives, perhaps for two or three different periods.... In a sense the patrilineal joint household is not only the ideal, but also the typical village household(43). Thus the household ideally contains a man, his wife or wives, his married sons with their wives and children, and his unmarried sons and daughters (Stirling 1965, p. 36).

Given this as the ideal, each household experiences a career which has a defined beginning, a trajectory through the fabric of life crises, and a point of termination, or a moment of fission, the latter of which is often described as a kind of social mitosis creating new units in the image of the old. The trajectory is likened to a roman candle which ascends in power and then bursts into small pieces at a roughly predictable point in time. Thus, we read that, whenever possible, 'married life begins under the roof of a senior kinsman of the husband, in most cases that of a father or married brother' (*Ibid*, pp. 40–1). The household grows by the birth of children, the marriage of sons and the birth of grandchildren. There is a strong prescription that sons, married and un-married, do not leave the household of a living father (*Ibid*, p. 36).[3] Then, 'On the death of the head, it [the household] splits into its constituent families, each of which should then repeat the cycle' (*Ibid*, p. 40).

In both villages, however, there are seeming discrepancies between the ideal and the actual composition of households. Stirling observes that extended joint households only amount to 24 per cent in Sakaltutan and 23 per cent in Elbaşı (*Ibid*, p. 38). Such wide discrepancies have been noted elsewhere in the Middle East and justified in various ways. Gulick, for example, does not dwell upon the issue of ideal–actual discrepancies. He suggests that the extended household may be rare in practice, because, as shown through attitudinal studies, Arabs in particular view the extended arrangement as 'temporary' and 'undesirable', held together primarily by economic plight and/or the charisma of tradition-bound elders (Gulick 1967, p. 123).

Elsewhere, Goode found only 18 of 171 households to be extended in form in a Lebanese Druze village (Goode 1963, p. 123). Goode suggests that the commonly held belief that the typical household is an extended one 'may be accepted . . . if we view it as a description, not of reality, but only of *ideals*' (*Ibid*, p. 123). The ethnographic discrepancies, he suggests, result from the gap between a traditional pattern and a secular trend. Stirling's explanation of such discrepancies differs from Gulick's 'no ideal' and Goode's 'ideal, but no longer observed'. For Stirling the problem is a demographic one which accounts for the failure of households to achieve jointness.

Thus Stirling states, 'The reasons why such households [joint extended] are in a minority are far more psychological and ecological than social' (1965, p. 43). Given the best of conditions for the preferred unfolding of the domestic cycle, in a community at any given time only 50 per cent will be joint extended in form. This is a result of fission through the death of household heads, creating small nuclear-like households, and the length of time it takes for a newly-separated household to reach a point where sons marry and grandchildren are born. Thus, about 50 per cent of households will always contain only one married couple (pre-joint or simple in form) while moving toward more than one married couple (joint extended) (*Ibid*, p. 40). It appears, then, that simple households are not explained as a result of an actual structure moving *away* from an ideal, or as Goode suggests, the secular trend versus a traditional pattern (Goode 1963, p. 128), but as a result of structures in the process of moving *toward* a preferred ideal which has been temporarily demographically rent.

Given this prescriptive composition of the household, the most fundamental functional of the household for Stirling is its economic unity or its 'jointness'. The household is a group of people who produce and consume in common. As such, 'It shares all resources belonging to members, it shares out the work according to sex, seniority, and convenience, and it distributes the total income among its members according to need and social position' (Stirling 1965, p. 93). To make this succeed. 'Normally sons and younger brothers hand over to their fathers or elder brothers a large share of their earnings and both sides are apparently content' (*Ibid*, p. 97).

Other authors, discussing the change from extended to residentially-nuclear household arrangements in Turkey, are less convinced of the apparent 'content-ment' found in the extended household. Erdentuğ's work on two eastern

Turkish villages refers frequently to the paucity of joint extended households today in contrast to their dominance in the past (Erdentuğ 1956, p. 31). She suggests that 'nuclear' families are rapidly taking the place of extended families as a result of economic conditions and the desire to lessen internal quarrels (*Ibid*, pp. 32–3). A similar observation is made by her for the Alevi village of Sün (Erdentuğ 1959, p. 19).[4]

Variations on the theme of the joint household are often explained as evasive actions, as responses which serve to resolve conflict between values. For example, in his study of the small town of Erdemli (population 1,711 in 1955), Szyliowicz states that the gap between traditional and new values is being widened by changes in technology (a shift to truck farming and increasing sources of non-agricultural income), military service (which provides new career skills) and shifts in values (new consumption wants and objectives) (Szyliowicz 1966, pp. 87–8).

In Kıray's 1962 study of the town of Ereğli (population 8,815 in 1960), she stresses that the high degree of 'nuclear' households (61.1 per cent of 483 surveyed households) is a result of the changing relationship between father and son (Kıray 1964, p. 115). The most important sources of conflict come from the son's wish to establish a separate household, to obtain financial freedom, and to control his own spare time (*Ibid*, pp. 116–17).

Evidence of the lack of local consensus on the joint household as a predominant feature of social life is found in at least one study which predates Stirling's field-work. Based upon data collected from 1942 to 1946 in the village of Hasanoğlan, Yasa found only about 29 per cent of 267 households surveyed that could be considered joint in structure (Yasa 1957, p. 113). Yasa goes so far as to add that as soon as the married son is able, 'he and his bride will leave the paternal roof at the first opportunity' (*Ibid*, p. 114). In yet another study in 1950 Yasa surveyed the Aegean village of Sindel and found the predominant type of household to consist of a married couple and their unmarried children (Yasa 1960, p. 59). Upon the marriage of a son, the household head attempts to provide a separate room for the newly-married couple if the house is large enough. In this case the new couple is expected to maintain a separate kitchen and separate budget. However, if members of the household are incompatible, or if a separate room cannot be provided, married sons generally move out of their natal house (*Ibid*, p. 62). Yasa believes the increase of new houses in Sindel to be a result of the breakdown 'of extended family units and weekening [*sic*] of kinship ties' (Yasa 1963, p. 12).

Despite their value to a sociological appreciation of family life in Turkey, there are a number of shortcomings in the existing literature on family and household structure.

1. Discussions of ideal residence patterns tend to posit but a single model, that of the joint extended family which purportedly has an extremely wide geographical expression. This traditional pattern, furthermore, serves as a

convenient single backdrop against which structural changes are plotted and their rate measured.

2. The extended household as an actual structure is often depicted to be moving away from the ideal in a set of rather well-defined stages *as a result* of certain disruptive, accelerating, forces of modernization. Some of the literature on Turkey seemingly follows Goode's scheme: 'The stages in the pattern [the secular trend] then move away from the collective operation of the family land, toward rational cooperation among the brothers' conjugal families, and finally to private ownership' (Goode 1963, p. 128).

3. The economic fission of the ideal extended family is often characterized as an irreversible process and as being the catalyst for the complete breakdown of networks of authority, responsibility, aid and social compatibility. From the use of the term 'nuclear' it is often impossible to determine whether economic and residential autonomy alone are implied or whether one is dealing with units which are also socially autonomous.

The material provided in the following section from the town of Tütüneli[5] shows a preferred household domestic cycle which differs markedly from the ideal traditionally depicted. As a frequently occurring form, the Tütüneli example of residentially dispersed 'nuclear-like' families within the town is particularly well adapted to the requirements of a residentially dense town situation. A variety of town-based income opportunities rather than a predominantly agricultural income further support the economic autonomy of dispersed household units consisting of one-couple families. Despite this dispersal and relative economic autonomy, many such households continue to relate to other households of the family in such a way as to perform a number of functions normally associated only with a residentially-nucleated extended family.[6]

THE TOWN AND UNITS OF RESIDENTIAL COMPLEXITY

The extreme southwest corner of Turkey is a rugged mountainous complex bounded by a sinuous coastline. This area, which roughly comprises the administrative province of Muğla, amounts to 1.7 per cent of the total area of Turkey and contains about one per cent of Turkey's population. The highlands consist of a number of closed-in, abbreviated, arid, valleys, each supporting a small town and a number of villages. One such valley in the heart of the highlands at 650 metres in elevation contains the small town of Tütüneli.

Tütüneli is the administrative seat of a county of the same name. The county consists of a combined 1965 rural–urban population of 15,185 individuals, of which 4,616 reside within the municipality of the town and the remainder throughout thirteen villages located in the highlands and the county's small coastal plain. As an administrative centre the small town houses a sizeable number of non-local civil servants who staff the offices of both central and local government facilities. Tütüneli is also a regional economic centre having, in addition to its approximately 275 fixed small-scale retail businesses, a weekly market which convenes on Friday. In its economic role, Tütüneli is primarily a service centre. Scores of craftsmen and shopkeepers work out of workshops and stores located along the two axes of an 'L' which transects the town along its centre.

Similar to many of the other small market towns of this region, Tütüneli displays a rigid bifurcation between public and private space. Nucleated along its commercial 'L'-shaped bazaar street are the various areas devoted to public functions such as commerce, storage, transportation, administration, health, education, religion, and recreation. With the exception of small *mescits*, or places of worship, which are found in residential zones, all of the above functions are restricted solely to the bazaar in the centre of town.

Extending outward from the bazaar area, like bent spokes from a hub, is a seemingly chaotic maze of narrow passageways and lanes. This large area is clearly divided into the four residential districts, or *mahalles*, of the town. Each *mahalle* is further divided into *semts*, or sub-*mahalles*, the minimal neighbourhood unit for townsmen.[7] Located throughout the *mahalles* are the private houses, or *evs*, of townsmen. These houses either singly as fragments of a large family, or in groups as clusters of family houses, constitute the *hane*, or family domestic unit. *Mahalle*, *semt*, and *hane* are the three residential reference points which set the background for an understanding of the domestic cycle in Tütüneli.

The four *mahalles* of the town, containing a total of about 1,150 dwellings, are, at one level, formal administrative units. Each *mahalle* is a political and a tax unit within the schema of local government. Each is required to elect a headman, or *muhtar*, to represent its interests in matters of local government such as for municipal services. In Tütüneli the *mahalle* is also a social unit which, in the past, played a major role in ordering social relations between the four residential quarters. In many ways the *mahalles* in the past served as analogues of four diminutive village communities, exhibiting a partial social and administrative autonomy which is no longer seen today. The inter-*mahalle* differences, however, were never the severe divisive force within community life that they were in large Muslim centres in the Arab world. Contrary to the differences existing between *mahalles* described by Lapidus (1967, p. 86) for cities such as Damascus, the small scale and religious homogeneity of historical Tütüneli did not lend itself to the development of *mahalles* organized around single large lineages, occupational specialization, or sectarian or major social class differences.

A number of examples of *mahalle* solidarity, however, can be indicated for historical Tütüneli. As individual families proliferated, the separate dwellings of married sons tended to be located adjacent to the natal house. It was rare to locate a married son outside of his *mahalle*, thereby resulting in a high degree of residential solidarity for the family within *mahalle* limits. Brides were rarely taken from outside the boy's *mahalle*, contributing to a high degree of *mahalle* endogamy. Exceptions more often occurred in the taking of a bride from one of the villages in a nearby plain. Males seldom entered a *mahalle* other than their own. When they did so without the company of a resident of that *mahalle*, they were usually accosted by the young males of the *mahalle* who were charged with the responsibility of protecting women and girls of their entire *mahalle* as much as the women of their own family (Demircioğlu 1938, p. 9).

Indeed there were few reasons for entering another *mahalle*. A male could frequent his *mahalle's* coffee-house or grocery in the bazaar by passing through a *mahalle* street leading directly to the bazaar area. Within the bazaar, however, workshops were not grouped according to the residential affiliation of their owners. Individual *mahalles* also 'faced out' upon their sector of agricultural land which began immediately at the periphery of their *mahalle*. In this way women could pass directly to their fields, and indeed they seldom had cause to enter another *mahalle*, even to visit other women. Women in the past were prohibited from entering the bazaar area and from attending the weekly market which convened adjacent to the bazaar street. Only within the last fifteen years has this latter restriction been lifted somewhat. The maximal extent of domestic relations, therefore, was limited by *mahalle* boundaries.

Over the past three decades many of these distinctions have all but disappeared. Inter-*mahalle* marriages are now more common than in the past. As a result of such marriages between *mahalles*, a household head may work his wife's fields adjacent to another area of town, and at times may move to the *mahalle* of his wife's family when her inherited land is greater than his own or when his father-in-law is willing to provide a house close to his own. Even when all members of a household have originated from the same *mahalle*, demographic pressures may force the location of segments of the family in different *mahalles*. It is common now for a family to have one or several married sons and daughters residing in another *mahalle*. The ever-diminishing amount of vacant land compels a father to locate his son at marriage wherever space permits. This places an increased burden on patriarchal household heads, who must now not only meet an increased financial burden in purchasing additional urban land for a house site, but who also experience a greatly modified household structure resulting from the compulsory spatial and, often consequential, economic separateness of individual conjugal units.

In many respects the *semt* today continues to be a meaningful residential unit of the town. The origin of individual *semts* is unclear, but many *semts* take their names from a physical feature such as a tall tree, or from the name of a prominent family. Townsmen claim that in the past *semts* corresponded to the territory held by members of individual agnatic lines. Possessing a great deal of vacant space within and at the periphery of the town, the households slowly filled the *semts* through the proliferation of houses of married sons.[8] Later, it is claimed, newcomers to the town purchased land within *semts*, thus incorporating non-kin members in the residential area.

Residents of a *semt* are generally bound together through ties of co-operation and assistance, whether the households are related or unrelated. Often the houses have passageways leading from courtyard to courtyard which allow one to move between houses without entering a public lane or street. The typical *semt* contains several groupings of households which within themselves maintain co-operative ties, economic relations, and close daily social relations. It is from among these co-operating households located in close proximity to one another that people find neighbours or *komşus*. These households join together for such major economic activities as group aid in tobacco fields and the preparation of winter foods, as well as to execute social obligations such as assistance in times of birth, marriage and death. It is important to note that often these bonds between unrelated households of a *semt* take priority over the relations between kinsmen when such kinsmen are geographically scattered throughout different *semts* or *mahalles*.

The physical setting of lanes and courtyards awards the maximum amount of seclusion to women and the round of domestic activities which consumes the household or *hane*. Behind the high walls of whitewashed stone are located the courtyards and private dwellings which are largely isolated from the narrow winding lanes. Within the walls house windows, doors, and veranda face on to a functional courtyard usually containing a water trough, flower and vegetable gardens, several cleared work spaces and, if large enough, the individual houses of married sons. To an extent the disposition of houses, courtyards, and walls is a social map, a document which reflects how rules of residence have affected the proliferation of family segments over time. It is, however, a super-ficial measure insofar as it does not indicate the economic and social networks which in some cases are closely maintained and in other cases have been extensively disrupted.

THE HOUSEHOLD AND DOMESTIC CYCLE: SOME CASES

According to the description provided earlier of the classic form of the joint extended family in Turkey, a household progresses through several well-defined stages. A household grows through the birth of children, who, as they reach maturity, begin to add to the resources of the household through their labour. Upon their marriage, daughters leave the natal household to join the household of their husband, whereas sons are expected to begin their married life within their natal household. Thus, the household membership reduces with the out-marriage of daughters but increases with in-marrying brides. The house-hold eventually increases in membership through the birth of the grandchildren of married sons. At the death of the household head, unless delayed separation of sons takes place, the household divides into the respective units formed by the conjugal families of married sons. In short, there is a continual growth of household membership, of its economic base and of the authority vested in the household head. This growth continues until the death of the household head, the first and final moment of fission.

In Tütüneli the domestic cycle shows a different configuration. In brief, the first phase of the cycle is similar, consisting in the birth and maturation of offspring within their father's dwelling. At times this dwelling is closely grouped with those of agnatic kin to form a household. However, more often it is spatially and economically separate, forming a separate household. During its early career, the household is a remarkably close social unit. Children are expected to remain with their parents until marriage and parents are expected to provide all that is needed for their children until and at the occasion of their marriage. Upon marriage, however, not only daughters but sons as well are expected to leave the natal house and to establish a separate house, ideally through the support of parents and married and unmarried siblings. In cases where the parties are willing and houses are in close proximity to one another, married sons continue to maintain a joint economic relationship with their father. The serial marriage of offspring and their departure represents a period of fission within the natal household. Following this anticipated phase of fission and the resolution of the various marriage debts, the father's household can, and often does, continue separate from those of his married offspring. At the death of the father the estate is apportioned among the survivors and generally consists of agricultural holdings, the father's house, deeds to the houses of the married sons, chattels and cash savings.

Certain features of Tütüneli town life support this two-phased fission within the domestic cycle and the resulting modified arrangements found in joint aspects of household life. The crowded residential conditions of town *mahalles* support the dispersal of married sons to other areas of town, it being increasingly difficult to locate family segments on adjoining plots of communally-owned land. At the same time, the close domestic co-operation found between unrelated households within a given *semt* supports a couple residing separately from the husband's natal household. Further, the economic base of the town supports the continuation of simple households. Rather than having a single agricultural income which would enjoin all members of the family to combine their labour, the range of multiple incomes possible in a town-based economy is conducive to simple households acting as separate economic units. And finally, tobacco, the predominant agricultural activity of the town, is a crop which can be satisfactorily worked by a small family, drawing additional labour for peak work periods from neighbours within the *semt* rather than necessarily from kin.

The narrow street of Nalıncı begins at the end of the bazaar and winds through the residential areas of the *mahalle* of Demirsofu. Along this street live craftsmen, shopkeepers, itinerent marketeers, professional men, agriculturists and civil servants. It is a typical street in this respect, for it displays all levels of income and livelihood endeavours – a diversity which is mirrored throughout the entire *mahalle*. There is great diversity, as well in the composition of the various households found throughout the *mahalle*. In some cases there is an obvious correlation between the term *hane*, or household, and a single unit or house and its members. In other cases, the term *hane* is used by townsmen to describe the economic relationships existing between the separate houses of agnatic kin in close residential proximity, in many cases sharing the same courtyard. Far more often, however, no one word can describe the modified situation which exists when economic relations have been ruptured between the closely-spaced houses of an extended family and the severence of social ties is in various stages of completion.

Table 1 indicates the household types found in a survey of most households of the *mahalle* of Demirsofu. The table attempts to distinguish between households differing in the arrangement of individuals who constitute a *hane*. Within the larger categories of simple (based upon one married couple) and joint (economic unity between more than one married couple), a further consideration of the simple households is made of residential proximity to agnatic kin who also qualify as simple households. The twenty-five simple households considered under IB all began their career as paternal or fraternal joint households and later divided as a result of various forms of incompatibility. They are considered separately from the household forms found under IA which began their career as economically nuclear households, spatially quite separate from their natal agnatic household. The low frequency of joint households is striking, amounting to only 11.4 per cent of the 193 households combined in categories I and II.

Where a joint household exists within a single dwelling there are generally special conditions which prevail. For example, most of the seven paternal joint households under IIA were cases of an only son sharing a large house with his parents. When there are several sons it is mandatory for the father to provide a separate house for each. The father of a Tütüneli bride always demands a separate house as part of the marriage agreement and sometimes demands that the deed be delivered to the new couple, guaranteeing his daughter a house of her own without future conflict over inheritance rights to that house at the death of the family patriarch.

The conflict which is, at times, staved off or, at times, aggravated by the early fission of a household through the marriage of its offspring can best be illustrated through several case studies.

1. Whenever townsmen search for a contemporary example of what families 'used to be like' in Tütüneli they inevitably come around to describing Mehmet Ali and his sons. It is a large family having three sons and two daughters. The married sons and their father share a large courtyard in which

TABLE 1 *Household types by economic structure in the* Mahalle *of Demirsofu,*[a] *1970*

I. *Simple Households* (one married couple)
A. Spatially separate from other married couples of the same family

Married couple[b]	31	
Married couple, children	70	
Married couple, HuMo	2	
Married couple, children, HuMo		
same house	14	
separate adjacent houses	8	22
Married couple, unrelated children, HuMo	3	
Married couple, WiMo	3	
separate adjacent houses	1	
Married couple, children, WiMo		
same house	5	
separate adjacent houses	2	7
Married couple, children, HuFa	2	
Miscellaneous:		
Married couple, children, other kin	3	
Married couple, widowed daughter-in-law	3	
Married couple, children, HuFa 2nd wife	1	
Father with children only	2	146

B. In immediate proximity to other married couples of the same family

Paternal, children (residential courtyard clusters of father and married sons in which each house is economically separate)	14	
Fraternal, children (similar clusters of economically separate married brothers)	4	
Fraternal, children, HuMo (similar to above with HuMo residing with one married son)	7	25
Total I A+B		171

II. *Joint Households* (economic unity between more than one married couple)
A. Within same house

Paternal joint, no grandchildren	1	
Paternal joint, grandchildren	6	
Fraternal joint, no children	1	
Fraternal joint, children, HuMo	1	9

B. Separate adjacent houses

Paternal joint, grandchildren	11	
Fraternal joint, children, HuMo	2	13
Total II A+B		22

III. *Fragmentary*

Widow, alone	15	
Widow, children	16	
Widow, with unrelated child	3	
Bachelor	4	
Widow, widowed Da, grandchildren	3	
Spinster with spinster	1	
Total III		42
Total household I+II+III =		235

[a] Non-Tütüneli born, such as non-local civil servants and in-migrant villagers, were not included in this survey.
[b] Often unmarried children were away at school in another locality.

each has his own house, but the four houses are united into a single household, or *hane*. Co-operation is very good between wives of the brothers and between them and their mother-in-law. All women work together not only in providing for a large domestic setting but also in the tobacco fields of the household head, Mehmet Ali. Mehmet Ali owns all fixed and movable property shared by the household and, in addition, retains the deeds to the sons' houses.

The total income of Mehmet Ali and his sons is merged into one household budget and is administered totally by the former. The family operates a store in the bazaar which sells olive oil, soap and miscellany, and a truck which transports itinerant marketeers between markets. They themselves operate as marketeers buying oil wholesale in Milas and selling it retail in five markets in the province. In addition, the family works and rents out agricultural land and a motorized irrigation network near the town.

Mehmet Ali is a religiously conservative individual, as are his sons. Each of his sons had been apprenticed as a cobbler under the father and other masters at the time when cobbling was a viable trade. When cobbling declined they did not, as did other families, scatter into unrelated occupations but rather worked together in developing other than-new income alternatives, such as motorized irrigation and itinerant marketing. The courtyard of Mehmet Ali is crowded and probably his grandsons will be provided houses upon their marriage in other quarters of the town. This example of a harmonious paternal joint household is rare in Tütüneli, as indicated by the table of household types.

2. Near to Mehmet Ali's household is the courtyard of Hasan, the cobbler. Hasan, close to 65 years in age, lives with his wife and Ali, the younger of his two married sons, in a spacious house at the end of a courtyard. Hasan's other son lives in a house provided by Hasan within the same courtyard. This older son, Celal, has a wife and three young children. Although not more than ten metres separate the houses, there is at the present no economic co-operation between the two, and there exists an extremely strained social relationship between Celal's family and his younger brother and father. The cause of this family rupture reaches back to the time of the marriage of the older son, Celal.

Following the traditional manner, all members of the family helped to defray expenses incurred at the time of Celal's wedding, including the cost of construction of a house. The money needed for the wedding came from Celal's own income as a mason, the father's grocery store where the younger son Ali also worked, the money obtained from the sale of that year's tobacco crop, the sale of a field and borrowed cash. Celal's then unmarried sister also helped by giving the money earned from some day-wage labour during the year.

After Celal's marriage several divisive events occurred. First, the father refused to give Celal the deed to the house until after the marriage of Celal's two siblings. This aggravated Celal's wife and her father. Second, Celal's wife insisted that she would not work the family's tobacco fields with the other women of the family. She demanded, and it was approved, that an adequate section of the family's tobacco fields be set aside for her and Celal (again without deed) with the understanding that after Hasan's death this was to be Celal's share of family land. Third, other members of the family felt expenses were not shared fairly at the time of the marriage of Celal's sister in the year following his own marriage. Celal helped, but it was generally understood that he did not do all he could have done to aid his sister, and again Celal's wife was assumed to have had a part in his reluctance. Hasan was forced to sell some land to help defray the wedding expenses of his daughter, which angered Celal and his brother Ali because the sale of land further reduced the amount which would later be in-herited.[9] Fourth, after a bitter quarrel with his father, Celal gradually began to run his house as a separate *hane*. For some time he had been keeping more and more of his income, and gradually began to insist on more separate meals. Eventually the weakening economic ties with his father's household led to the decrease in the father's authority over Celal's day-to-day affairs. The separation went more smoothly with his father than with his mother who continued to place her impress upon courtyard matters affecting the now largely-autonomous family.

Finally, further friction developed as a result of the marriage of Celal's brother Ali, some three years after Celal's marriage. Celal, surprisingly enough, desired to do more for his younger brother than for his sister; however the brunt of expenses was still borne by Hasan. Ali agreed to live in his father's house after marriage, obviating the need to consider building yet another house. Friction soon developed between the wives of the two brothers. In Tütüneli quarrels between *eltis*, or wives of brothers, are particularly pronounced,[10] and such quarrels are well described in the literature on Turkey. Celal's wife considered the young bride a newcomer in the courtyard and therefore subject to a subordinate role. Also the bride, so Celal's wife insisted, did not show due respect to Celal, the *agabey*, or elder brother. The young bride resided in Hasan's house and soon became the favourite of the mother-in-law. To this situation can be added their quarrels over differences in life styles, the treatment of young children, and numerous daily encounters which further drove a wedge into family relations.

There are in Tütüneli a number of similar cases of families which, beginning as joint households, have within a few years severed their economic and many of their social relations. In many cases continued close residence tends to exacerbate long-standing problems. Some families, however, experience a type of separation at marriage which provides a context in which many functions of the extended family are continued, even though the basic 'eat together' and 'live together' unity is no longer possible. The rule of residence that separates 'house' if not always 'household' does reduce some classic tensions which under-one-roof extended families reputedly experience, e.g. sexual tensions between bride and father-in-law. Where, however, house and household are separated at close quarters, other tensions become paramount, e.g. weakened parental authority.

3. A large number of households along Nalıncı street are simple households containing only one married couple. The actual household composition can be quite varied, as is seen in section I of Table 1 on p. 229. The majority of households, however, consist of a couple and their unmarried children. Haluk is an example of one such household. Haluk's father and mother live at the other end of Tütüneli in a house and courtyard, the latter of which is shared by Haluk's older brother, wife and children.

After the completion of his military service some years ago, Haluk, then aged twenty-two, found he had no vocational training of any use to him. His apprenticeship as a cobbler, which had taken place before he went into service, was now of little use because of a radical decline in the trade caused by factory-made shoes. Haluk began work as an itinerant marketeer, often spending as many as six days a week on the road. When in Tütüneli, through the physical labour and the limited financial help possible from both his father and married brother, Haluk began to build the house which was to be required for his wedding. Because the father's courtyard was too small for yet a third house, his father purchased land elsewhere in town for Haluk's house.

Everyone in the family worked together to meet the anticipated expense of Haluk's wedding – a process which was begun at least two years before the bride was selected. Haluk married a girl who was not from his own *mahalle*, nor from the *mahalle* in which his house, since completed, was located. Because of the distance of the house from his father's courtyard, Haluk's household is almost totally economically separate. In daily decisions, in matters such as household meals, how earnings should be allocated against expenses, the education of their children, and their selection of a circle of acquaintances, Haluk's household is a separate unit. At another level the *semt*, containing neighbouring households unrelated to them, provides a daily orientation within which numerous domestic co-operative affairs are carried out. The *semt* also supplies neighbours who are quick to aid in time of crisis and in daily work-sharing.

Haluk's wife, like most women in Tütüneli, spends at least six months a year in the cultivation of tobacco. In this work she has three spheres of responsibility. Her prime responsibility is to cultivate a small field rented by Haluk.[11] For assistance she draws upon women in her *semt* in what is referred to as *imece* labour.[12] In turn she reciprocates by aiding in the fields of her neighbours. Second in priority, she aids her own mother and unmarried sister in the cultivation of her father's fields. As is customary in the town, she maintains a close relationship with her own natal family. When possible she visits her mother each day for a brief time and at certain peak periods of household and field work she is expected to help as much as possible. In her case, only lastly does she provide assistance to her mother-in-law. This assistance is almost exclusively restricted to the harvest of tobacco, and more particularly to the stringing of the leaves, a process that takes place in the mother-in-law's court-yard during the hot afternoons in August. It is not unusual in Tütüneli to find this order of priority when there is a case of a separate household, such as Haluk's.

Haluk and his wife have never lived under his father's roof nor in his father's courtyard. Haluk is of the opinion that because of this separation he maintains a more harmonious relationship with his parents than does his brother who shares their courtyard. Haluk gives assistance in times of needed co-operation, family crises, and social obligations, but it is understood that it is his brother who is to look after the aged parents. *Semt* neighbours and the close relationship he maintains with his wife's family are two orientations which often take priority over responsibilities toward his own parents and siblings.

These three examples are suggestive of a number of principles and changes which affect all families in Tütüneli. Some major features of ideology can be extrapolated from these examples and others, and their implications explored.

THE HOUSEHOLD AND DOMESTIC CYCLE: SOME GENERALIZATIONS

The Tütüneli household is a very close social and economic unit during its early career. Children are expected to remain in the paternal household until marriage. Compared to what is known of other areas of rural Turkey, the age for marriage is considerably delayed in Tütüneli. Several reasons account for this delay and are related to anticipated household fission.

A boy is not generally considered eligible for marriage in Tütüneli until he has completed his military service at the age of twenty-two, has constructed a house and is relatively well-established in some income-gaining endeavour. There are various explanations given by townsmen for these restrictions which result in a later age for marriage. Townsmen often refer back to the devastating effects of World War I, when only a small number of those males who were conscripted survived to return after the war.[13] They state that in the years since the war the tradition has been for boys not to become engaged, and virtually never to marry, before completing their military service. In his study of wedding customs in Tütüneli in the early 1930s, Demircioğlu also stresses that marriage does not take place until military service has been completed (Demircioğlu 1938, p. 6). Today, prior to his military service, the boy is not generally a major contributor to the household income. For the boy who completes the middle school at the age of fifteen there is generally a hiatus until he is taken for military service five years later. A number, it is true, continue to the lycée, or other upper school, in nearby Muğla. For the majority, however, the intervening period is one of idleness or at best a succession of minor unskilled, day-wage, jobs. Few boys elect to be apprenticed to a craft which might not survive in a rapidly changing economy. Military service is generally followed by a two- or three-year period during which the man begins to earn a livelihood. These earnings are used for expenses already being incurred for his forthcoming wedding and for his anticipated new household. The wedding itself generally takes place when the man is somewhere between 24 and 28 years of age.

The mandatory provision of a separate house for the new couple is an important determining factor for a later marriage age. A major wedding expense for the man's natal household is the provision of a house and this has become a more expensive undertaking than in the past. When described by Demircioğlu (1938, p. 10), building a house within the natal courtyard was still possible. By moving walls and opening other access ways between agnatically related houses, it was possible to construct new houses for sons. However, the increase in the population has since curtailed this proliferation of related households in a nucleated area. It has now become mandatory for the majority to purchase land elsewhere in town in order to build. The cost for the groom's family is about 15,000 TL for both land and house, raising the price of a wedding to over 20,000 TL, a considerable amount in a town where the per capita income does not exceed 4,000 TL per year. (In 1968 9 Turkish Liras = $1.00.) The expense of marrying a daughter is only one-third of that for the son, but it still amounts to the average annual income of a family for two years (see Table 2 for comparison). In this region of Turkey a *başlık*, or bride price, has never been paid to the girl's family. Despite the absence of this custom, families spend a considerable period of time paying off the marriage debts.

In each of the three family cases given, responses to the marriage of offspring differ. Where it was once common to find a family, such as Mehmet Ali's, working as a single unit to meet all requirements, it is now far more common to witness the uncertainties which exist in relationships such as that between Hasan and his sons Celal and Ali. The establishment of the young couple in a house of their own, and the tendency for the house to become a separate household, is increasingly looked upon by townsmen as not only a normal process of household fission, but as a process of anticipatory inheritance.

Before the marriage takes place, the two families involved come to terms over the conditions of marriage. The traditional enquiry concerns the nature of the respective families' reputation, the economic standing of the boy's family, the boy's occupation, the nature of the dowry and other concerns. Townsmen maintain, however, that at this time the bride's father is increasingly demanding certain economic safeguards not made explicit in the past. For example, although the demand for a separate house is a long-standing one, delivery of the deed from a father to his son at the time of marriage is increasingly asked for by the bride's father. Certain marriage agreements go even further in asking the boy's father verbally to commit certain lands to the new couple – lands which will be thus inherited after his death. Celal's wife forced him to obtain such a commitment from his father. In this case it helped to ease mounting tensions between family members. Hasan need not have acted in such an obliging

TABLE 2 *Engagement and wedding expenses (*average cost for 1967–8 weddings*)*

Boy's family		Girl's family	
ENGAGEMENT GIFTS			
1 ring	100 TL[a]	1 ring	150 TL
1 wristwatch	150	1 wristwatch	150
10 gold bracelets	1,500	Clothing (man's shirt, underwear,	
Clothing (woman's dress,		etc.)	150
stockings, shoes, underwear,		Food (sweets)	150
etc.)	365		
Cosmetics	25		
Food (sweets)	10		
Misc.	50		
	2,200		600
WEDDING EXPENSES			
House with plot	15,000	House furnishings	5,000
Furnishings for one bedroom	700	Clothing (man's suit, shoes,	
Three bride dresses (Nikâhlık,		underwear, etc.)	1,000
Kınalık, Gelınlik)	550	Musicians	500
Clothing (woman's scarves,		Food	1,000
coat, underwear, shoes, etc.)	850		
Musicians	500		
Transportation	100		
Liquor	200		
Food	1,000		
	18,900		7,500
Engagement	2,200		600
Wedding	18,900		7,500
Total	21,100 TL		8,100 TL
Or	$2,344		$999

[a] In 1968 9 Turkish Liros (TL) = $1.00.

manner: in another similar reported case a father retaliated against a demanding and intransigent son by unexpectedly selling property and consigning the sale money to another offspring.

Inheritance is bilateral in law and in practice. Although the actual division of land (excluding houses and some chattels) does not take place until the death of the family head, allocation is often clear at an earlier stage. Daughters inherit both from their natal household and through their husband. There are few conditions which can, in fact, disinherit a son or daughter. It should be mentioned, however, that Stirling suggests that, at the time of his study, inheritance by daughters was fairly uncommon. He says that, 'While, therefore, female inheritance in special cases has always occurred, inheritance by daughters when there are living sons is probably fairly new, and increasing' (1965, p. 131). According to the Turkish Civil Code, children each receive an equal share and widows receive one-half the estate in trust, or one-fourth in full possession. In Tütüneli today few cases of dispute enter the courts.

Even if they have physically contributed little to the estate, sons and daughters, equally, demand and receive their share, although not without frequent severe quarrelling outside the court. Again, this contrasts with the findings of Stirling who observed that, 'for a man to leave the ancestral home is to forfeit his immediate rights to a livelihood from the land, and to imperil his hopes of inheritance, since his brothers remaining at home may well take the opportunity to share the land between them and are likely to prove very difficult to dispossess' (1965, pp. 101–2).

Strong bilateral claims on property in Tütüneli are, in large part, due to the nature of the predominant crop, tobacco. Tobacco fields are worked almost solely by women in household or neighbourhood *imece* groups. Men occasionally help in specific tasks such as weeding, but from the planting of the seedling to the stringing of the harvested leaf all activities involve women in small groups. The income from the sale of tobacco is an important economic supplement for the average household. The decision-making involved during this agricultural cycle belongs almost solely to the women of the household, and likewise, in a number of cases observed, the resulting income is largely distributed according to their wishes.

Their engagement in the main agricultural activity of the household gives women a keen interest in the issue of inheritance. As mentioned earlier, Haluk's wife spends about six months a year working in tobacco fields. In addition, she must maintain the household, for which she cultivates small patches of land devoted to subsistence crops such as vegetables, grapes, and some wheat. She receives no share in the sale of her mother's and sister's tobacco, although she provides assistance to them. She does, however, maintain a claim upon property in which she will some day share. The same applies to the assistance she gives to her mother-in-law, although in this case it is Haluk who will inherit the property directly. In other cases there is no assistance, but claims by a married daughter are equally as strong at the time of inheritance. During the period of this study several bitter quarrels were outstanding which were the result of claims to inheritance. It was felt by some that the claims of married daughters residing in other towns were forfeited, as they had not applied their labour to the fields in question for years. Yet these daughters return to Tütüneli after their fathers' death to claim their portion of the land with the intention of selling it to siblings or non-kin. In addition to bilateral inheritance, the land is further fragmented by the high number of land sales to buyers outside the immediate family at moments when cash is needed.

Table 1 and the descriptive material presented here suggest that Tütüneli differs in several respects from traditional accounts of Turkish family life. Not only does the extended kin group in the form of the residentially-nucleated joint extended family seldom occur, but the lack of corporate feeling within kin groups also suggests that it is inappropriate to make a case for lineages in

Tütüneli. A shallow sense of common descent which allows genealogical reckoning up to three ascending generations, and an ability to keep track of the marriages of numerous collaterals, can hardly be conceptualized into a society consisting of brothers and their adult sons united by multifarious concerns, of which the minimal is that of common defence.

In Tütüneli weak corporate kin-group relations are seen in a number of ways. Today, members of a family increasingly tend not to depend economically upon one another after the family begins to disperse through the marriage of offspring. After this fission occurs, the patriarchal family head seldom continues to exercise an unqualified claim on the productive resources of the members of the family. Fraternal joint interests, whether at the level of patriarchal family heads or between married sons, are also increasingly fewer in Tütüneli than they were in the past. The dispersal of the local descent group, the economic autonomy of the proliferating households, and an orientation toward individuals found in one's place of work or the *semt*, mitigate traditional economic functions of the lineage as a corporate group.

In Tütüneli the separate household segments of a family are not dependent solely upon one another in times of crisis leading to moral or physical jeopardy. The male friendships one develops in the bazaar among fellow craftsmen and shopkeepers, the circle of cronies one returns to in coffee-houses and in drinking groups, the political affinity one claims with members of any one of several voluntary associations, and the males who reside in one's *semt* as neighbours, are important ties for a man. These are networks from which needed capital, job information, patronage, advice, and protection can be obtained. For a woman, also, neighbours in her *semt*, her prayer group, or her visiting group, are often more important on a day-to-day basis than her own agnatic kin. In addition, strong bilateral ties allow a man or woman to reach outward through the spouse's network of kin for many of the same things which are so often characterized as corporate group functions.

The applicability of the term lineage has been considered by Stirling in his study of two villages. Stirling describes the weakness of social groups in the villages but continues to reserve the term 'lineage' for them. He observes that the villages consist of shallow patrilineal groups having weakly-defined rights and duties of membership, unequal commitment of members, defence as their main function, and which exhibit a maximal effective genealogical reckoning to three or four generations (Stirling 1965, p. 27). Further, he observes that they are not corporate, not legal or jural in custom or law; they own nothing in common, do not possess common symbols, lack a single head and are neither exogamous nor endogamous (*Ibid*, p. 158). However, despite these qualifications, 'since the non-overlapping groups are defined by descent from a common ancestor through one sex only, it seems pointless to refuse them the name "lineage"' (*Ibid*, p. 158). In short, in this case, the recognition of specific close relations and the obligation to defend one another are the basis of a lineage concept.

Although townsmen in Tütüneli claim that they can, and at times do, call upon kinsmen for defence, the cases are rare where, by degree of relationship, such aid is in fact systematically recruited. When such aid is required, compatibility between individuals often plays as great a role as do kinship ties. Joint action by the family is further hindered by the early separation of sons from their father's household and by the complete fission of the family as a viable unit at the death of the patriarchal family head. Indeed, the family head often begins to lose authority over his sons at the time of their marriage and afterwards it is only with great difficulty that internal conflict, let alone conflict with non-kin, is resolved through concerted action within the family. At the death of the family head fission is generally completed and there is no mechanism for ensuring the succession of a family member to the head of the agnatic line. After the fission it is increasingly difficult for brothers to reach decisions in common. These factors lessen the effectiveness of the extended kinship unit to serve as a defence group. Existing legal institutions in the town and the possibility of recourse to higher judicial authority beyond the town are used when necessary and are often preferred over the recruitment of kinsmen, neighbours, and friends in those cases where social links are too diffuse to allow the supporting of one disputant over the other.

It is, therefore, in the absence of a strong sense of lineage membership – the need to recognize and relate to close relations of a general kind for social, political or economic reasons – that early fission and the domestic cycle described above operate.

The main concern of this paper had been to call into question the broad applicability of certain generalizations on Turkish society which appear in the extant literature. The specific topic has been the limitations of the general model of the joint extended family in purporting to describe Turkish 'traditional society'. Data provided from the provincial Turkish town of Tütüneli show an ideal domestic cycle which differs from the 'classic' form of the joint extended family and which is remarkably adaptable to the conditions of life in a small urban centre. A secondary question has also been raised as to the continued applicability of the notion of 'lineage' to describe weak social groups such as are found in Tütüneli. The pronounced bilateral aspects of social networks found in the face of a lack of local corporate descent groups is considered an important feature in the understanding of household structures.

Studies of rural migrant groups to large urban centres in Turkey have generally assumed such migrants to have come exclusively from residentially joint extended family-households. As a result, the process of social change is often described as a dramatic transition from 'extended' to 'nuclear', and from a family form compatible with village life to one compatible with an urban existence. Recent work by Köngar (see pp. 205–18) discusses the migrant family not as a nuclear family but as a modified extended family, taking into account the continuance of many 'extended-like' family functions in an urban setting. However, few studies have looked closely at changes in family structure which have already occurred at the village and town level for many of those who move to an urban setting.

The data from Tütüneli suggest that it is misleading solely to use residential information to form observations concerning the various functions of households found in the town. A compact arrangement of the houses of married sons within a natal courtyard cannot alone suggest economic or other types of co-operation normally postulated in the model of the extended household. A small sample like Table 1 indicates that of houses so arranged, twenty-five had virtually nothing to do with their close agnatic neighbours and only thirteen exhibited some degree of co-operation. It is also not the case that the 146 spatially separate simple households listed under IA in the same table pursued a strict policy of economic and social isolation from their natal households.

A number of urban surveys have now been completed which are concerned with changing attitudes of recent migrants to Turkish urban centres. In most such surveys the observation is made that a shift from extended to nuclear family structure accompanies the shift in residence from rural to urban settings. Often this observation seems to be based solely upon data concerning household composition. All too infrequently do such surveys attempt to measure the character of the relationship existing between kinsmen residentially separate in their new urban setting. Studies of kinship in western industrial urban settings not only suggest that various kinship ties persist despite (and perhaps because of) the residential separation of families, but also, after a period in which the rural migrant to the city adjusts to his new setting, these ties tend to increase. It seems worth while to pursue two related points in future urban social surveys in Turkey. More concern should be paid to extending the scope of survey questionnaires to include an analysis of the content of continuing relations between kinsmen, relations which are generally described as being normally associated with the extended household in its rural settings. In addition, the investigation of why people move to an urban setting should also include an examination of already existing diversity in rural household structures – which might serve to encourage a rural to urban movement. For many cases in Tütüneli, weakened extended family ties in matters economic and social made it easier for families to migrate to urban centres. As Greenfield (1961, p. 322) has suggested, it might not be industrialization and an urban setting that create a change to nuclear-like families, but rather that the prior existence of such families in a non-industrial rural setting might be the catalyst for economic change.

NOTES

1 Of major interest here are the early work of Yasa, who from 1942 to 1946 resided in the village of Hasanoğlan (1957), and his 1950 study of the village of Sindel (1960); Stirling's 1949–50 study of the villages of Sakaltutan and Elbaşı (1965), Erdentuğ's village studies of Hal (1956) and Sün (1959), and Kıray's town study of Ereğli of 1962 (1964).

2 The reader is referred to the published summaries of research on rural Turkey by J. Kolars, 'Community Studies in Rural Turkey', *Annals*, Association of American Geographers, Vol. 52, No. 4, Dec. 1962, pp. 476–89 and B. Beeley, *Rural Turkey: A Bibliographic Introduction*, Hacettepe University Institute of Population Studies, Ankara, 1969. Beeley's bibliography, although selective, clearly shows the increase in studies by Turkish and foreign researchers.

3 So predominant is this rule of the domestic cycle that Stirling treats cases of the separation of sons as special cases of early separation which are generally balanced in number by cases of delayed separation, namely, fraternal joint-households (Stirling 1965, p. 39).

4 Erdentuğ refers to an interesting departure from the residential pattern. In Hal, she notes that there is a growing tendency for the parents to live with a married daughter (1956, p. 32). In Sün, if a daughter does not have a brother, supposedly upon marriage her husband may move into her father's house. The son-in-law is then eligible, as a true son, for a share of the family inheritance (1959, p. 24).

5 A pseudonym. The field-work on which this paper is based was carried out in 1967–8 and was made possible by the National Institute of Mental Health.

6 Recent work by Farsoun on family structure in Lebanon discussed a similar modification of the extended family. Through continued networks of aid in occupational placement and mobility, and for the pooling of capital, 'the functionally extended family, *unlike the classical residentially extended family, is not residentially nucleated* but nevertheless continues to perform most all of the same functions and with the same basic structure' (1970, pp. 257–8).

7 In large cities the *semt* is a larger unit than the *mahalle*. In Ankara, for example, the *semt* of Altındağ includes the *mahalles* of Atıfbey, Yılmazar, Fatih and Doğanşehir, as well as others.

8 In the Balkans the term *mahala* appears to refer to a territorial unit created by the proliferation of houses on communally-owned ground of a single *zadruga*, or extended household (Sanders 1949, p. 231). This is roughly similar to the notion of *semt* in Tütüneli.

9 In another case, when two married sons refused to aid their father in meeting the wedding expenses of their sister, the father was compelled to sell fields. In addition, the father gave the daughter a sum of money equal to what it would have cost to build a house. The father explained that this was a punishment to the sons who would have that much less to inherit after his death.

10 It is said in Tütüneli that problems between *eltis* form 'the corner of the triangle of *geçimsizlik*', or the inability to live in harmony. The other two corners are *Gelin–Kaynana* (bride–mother-in-law) and *Gelin–Görümce* (bride–husband's sister) problems.

11 Married sons frequently rent fields of their own when convenient or necessary. When bank or co-operative loans are not sufficient, or unavailable, a man will often turn to his wife's parents for aid. For example, as a result of the lack of other alternatives, a young bride worked almost entirely on a section of her own mother's fields. As a case of anticipatory inheritance, her father later decided to give her that part of the

family fields, with the reasoning that it would have been hers through inheritance anyway after his death.

12 *Imece* normally refers to work done for the community by the whole village. In Tütüneli, however, it is used to describe aid between neighbours requiring reciprocity.

13 Relatively little work has been done in historical demography to determine the effects of World War I on the Turkish population. In his study of Hasanoğlan, Yasa indicates that of 263 men between the ages of 18 and 50 recruited in World War I from this small village, 4 'bought out' and only 60 returned (Yasa 1957, p. 124). Yasa also indicates that the average marriage age for men in Hasanoğlan during his study in the 1940s was 22.4, but that nearly 50 per cent of these marriages were prior to the completion of military service. (*Ibid*, p.108.)

BIBLIOGRAPHY

Beeley, B. W. 1969. *Rural Turkey: A Bibliographic Introduction*. Hacettepe University Publications No. 10. Ankara, Hacettepe University.

Demircioğlu, Y. Z. 1938. *Anadoluda Eski Düğün ve Evlenme Adetleri (Old Wedding Customs in Anatolia)*. Istanbul, Burhaneddin Matbaası.

Erdentuğ, N. 1956. *Hal Köyünün Etnolojik Tetkiki (An Ethnological Study of the Village of Hal)*. Ankara University, Faculty of Languages, History and Geography. Publication No. 109. Ankara, Türk Tarih Kurumu Basımevi.

Erdentuğ, N. 1959. *Sün Köyünün Etnolojik Tetkiki (An Ethnological Study of the Village of Sün)*. Ankara University, Faculty of Languages, History and Geography. Publication No. 132. Ankara, Ayyıldız Matbaası.

Farsoun, S. K. 1970. 'Family Structure and Society in Modern Lebanon.' In L. E. Sweet (ed.), *Peoples and Cultures of the Middle East*. Vol. II. New York, Natural History Press.

Goode, W. J. 1963. *World Revolution and Family Patterns*. New York, Free Press.

Greenfield, S. M. 1961. 'Industrialization and the Family in Sociological Theory.' *American Journal of Sociology*, Vol. 67, pp. 312–22.

Gulick, J. 1967. *Tripoli: A Modern Arab City*. Cambridge, Mass., Harvard University Press.

Kıray, M. 1964. *Ereğli: Ağır Sanayiden Önce Bir Sahil Kasabası (Ereğli: A Preindustrial Coastal Town)*. Ankara, State Planning Organization.

Kolars, J. F. 1962. *Community Studies in Rural Turkey*. Annals, Assoc. of American Geographers, Vol. 52, pp. 476–89.

Lapidus, I. M. 1967. *Muslim Cities in the Later Middle Ages*. Cambridge, Mass., Harvard University Press.

Sanders, I. T. 1949. *Balkan Village*. Lexington, University of Kentucky Press.

Stirling, P. 1965. *Turkish Village*. London, Weidenfeld & Nicolson.

Szyliowicz, J. S. 1966. *Political Change in Rural Turkey: Erdemli*. The Hague, Mouton.

Yasa, I. 1957. *Hasanoğlan: Socio-economic Structure of a Turkish Village*. Public Administration Institute for Turkey and the Middle East. Ankara, Yeni Matbaa.

1960. *Sindel Köyünün Toplumsal ve Ekonomik Yapısı (The Social and Economic Structure of the Village of Sindel)*. Public Administration Institute for Turkey and the Middle East. Ankara, Balkanoğlu Matbaacılık Ltd. Şti.

1963. *Sindel (Review of a Village Study)*. Public Administration Institute for Turkey and the Middle East. Ankara, Balkanoğlu Matbaacılık Ltd. Şti.

11 Sex roles in Edremit

Lloyd A. and Margaret C. Fallers
University of Chicago

Lilia gathered somehow...that Continental society was not the go-as-you-please thing she had expected. Indeed, she could not see where Continental society was. Italy is such a delightful place to live if you happen to be a man. There one may enjoy that exquisite luxury of Socialism – that true socialism which is based not on equality of income or character, but on the equality of manners. In the democracy of the *caffe* or the street the great question of our life has been solved, and the brotherhood of man is a reality. But it is accomplished at the expense of the sisterhood of women. Why should you not make friends with your neighbour at the theatre or in the train, when you know and he knows that feminine criticism and feminine insight and feminine prejudice will never come between you! Though you become as David and Jonathan, you need never enter his home, nor he yours.

E. M. Forster, Where Angels Fear to Tread, 1905

To anyone who has worked and travelled a bit around the Mediterranean basin, Forster's lines recall what appears to be a common theme: men are public figures, women private, domestic ones. But this basic pattern varies a good deal, we note, as soon as we think of the particular societies with which we have been concerned as ethnographers. What follows is a preliminary account of sex roles in a Turkish town, with some comparative sallies in various directions.

THE TOWN AS A SETTING

Edremit is a county seat, which is to say it is the headquarters of a second-order political unit, a sub-division of a province. As such, it is the seat of a *kaymakam*, a county governor. It is also a *belidiye*, a municipality with the appropriate corporate rights and responsibilities, and the marketing centre for its 24 attached villages – and for others as well, since it is the largest town between Çanakkale, at the mouth of the Dardanelles, and İzmir. We speak from a coastal perspective, reflecting the standpoint of our informants. Although Edremit's provincial capital, Balıkesir, lies over the mountains to the east, its commercial and cultural life flows north and south. Located on a gulf toward the northern limit of old Greek Ionia, its people have always moved more easily, whether

243

by sea or by land, along the coast toward İzmir or Çanakkale, and beyond toward Istanbul or the cities of the south, than over the mountains into Anatolia. They view their larger homeland as the *Ege bölgesi*, the 'Aegean region', regarding everything to the east as an undifferentiated 'Anatolia', much as Californians speak of the lands beyond the Sierra Nevada as 'the East'.

The coastal strip is narrow, at some spots disappearing entirely, at others widening out as the mountain streams have built up alluvial plains, supporting, and then sometimes choking off such ancient port cities as Ephesus and Miletos. Edremit is not a seaport, though the sea is visible from its hilltops, for the gulf is now too shallow, with the result that the port for the area is Ayvalık, some fifty kilometres away. Edremit is an agricultural town instead, the richest olive-growing centre in Turkey. As a saying favoured by local boosters has it, 'Olive oil flows down one street, honey down another.' The lowest land produces cotton and truck crops, while olives cover the foothills. Further up is government forest, which supports a substantial lumbering industry. Small factories process olives and produce the hemp bags in which they are pressed and the tins in which the oil is marketed. The recent growth of a number of new factories producing tractor trailers, electric welders, retreaded tyres, hay-bailers, and cement mixers, suggests that the town may be breaking through into a new existence as a small industrial centre.

Religion is served by fifteen mosques; education by six primary schools, one middle and one secondary school, as well as boys' and girls' technical schools (the only sexually segregated schools). There are eight banks, three cinemas, a good public library, and a magnificent, well-tended public park-cum-garden which in fine weather attracts thousands of citizens.

TABLE 1   *Occupations and professions (women in brackets)*

Technicians, free professions and related

Architects, engineers and related	11	
Technicians and scientific officials	18	
Agricultural and forestry technicians	8	
Pharmacists and apprentices	9 (1)	
Medical and related	74 (25)	
Teachers	178 (37)	
Law (judges, advocates, prosecutors)	19	
Artists (writers, painters, musicians, entertainers)	64 (13)	
Imams and preachers	35	
Others (all accountants)	7	
Total		423 (76): 8%

Entrepreneurs, managers, office workers

Officials in state service	21	
Wholesale and retail managers and entrepreneurs	50	
Financial (banks and insurance)	9	
Real estate	4	
Extraction, manufacturing, building	46 (2)	
Other entrepreneurs and managers	41	
Book-keepers, cashiers, secretaries	250 (22)	
Total		421 (24): 8%

Occupations and professions – continued

Commercial workers (sellers)

Retail and wholesale merchants and employees	395 (4)	
Itinerant merchants and pedlars	193 (2)	
Others	18	
Total	————	606 (6): 11%

Farmers, lumbermen, fishermen

Farmers, farm managers	391 (10)	
Truck gardeners	214 (29)	
Orchard and vineyard farmers	36 (4)	
Farm and forest machine operators	4	
Herdsmen and shepherds	43	
Fishermen	21	
Farm labourers	328 (25)	
Total	————	1037 (68): 19%

Mining, quarrying

Total		17 0%

Transport and communications

Sea transport	7	
Motor drivers	186 (1)	
Animal transport	140	
Postal workers	28 (5)	
Others	39	
Total	————	400 (6): 7%

Craftsmen and repairers

Casting and forging	8	
Metal manufacturing and repair	308	
Electric goods manufacturing and repair	32	
Textile weavers	30 (4)	
Tailors, shoemakers, quilt and mattress makers	387 (67)	
Wood and cane workers	168 (1)	
Food, drink, tobacco manufacture	157 (1)	
Construction workers	205	
Stone and clay fabricators	27	
Others	77 (2)	
Total	————	1399 (75): 25%

Unskilled workers

Total		459 (2): 8%

Services

Servants, waiters, cooks	356 (47)	
Barbers, bath attendants, coiffeurs, dry cleaners, launderers	200 (18)	
Security services	164 (2)	
Total	————	720 (67): 13%

Not assigned to occupations

Military	6802 (1)	
Other	65 (1)	
	————	6867 (2): 56%
Total		12332 (326)
Less military		5488 (325) 99%
(above percentages based upon this total)		

This, then, is the setting for our discussion of the roles of men and women. In proceeding to the main business, we call attention to the figures for the two sexes in Tables 1 and 2 on occupation and education. Three hundred and twenty-six women are, at any rate from the census-taker's standpoint, scattered throughout the extra-domestic labour force of 5,488. (As noted, this

TABLE 2 *Men's and women's education*

	Men	%	Women	%
Age 6 and over:				
Illiterate	3,470	23	3,554	44
Literate, no graduation	3,218	22	1,424	18
Graduated primary or above	8,108	55	3,054	38
	14,796[a]		8,032	
Age 11 and over:				
Primary graduate	5,762[a]		2,573	
Middle graduate	1,126[a]		274	
Lycée graduate	346[a]		75	
Occupational school graduate	670[a]		104	
Higher	211[a]		31	
	8,115		3,057	

[a] Male population inflated by some 6,000 at local army base.

excludes the local army installation.) Women are present in varying numbers in all major sectors, but the largest groups are women tailors, teachers, nurses, secretaries, farmers and service workers. In terms of level of education, the ratio of women to men decreases as one goes up the ladder. Twice as many women as men are illiterate and women graduates of universities and other institutions of higher education are a small fraction of their male counterparts. There are, however, thirty-one of the latter – an unusual number for a Middle Eastern town of this size.

Note: This paper presents the pooled observations and ideas of its two authors. In the context of this subject, in a society in which men and women lead very separate lives, joint authorship by a man and a woman has obvious advantages. Although we employ the 'we' of collaboration, we worked separately most of the time.

THE WOMEN (M.C.F.)

The world of women – most women – in Edremit is the private world of the house and courtyard. My conclusion, which may seem paradoxical, will be that the women of this secluded world are in many respects more independent than the 'emancipated' women I know in Europe and America. I shall describe four women of Edremit and analyse the meaning, for them, of the cultural emphasis upon separation of the sexes, taking note of some present tendencies toward change.

I first met Emine a few days before the end of Ramadan when I was taken to visit her by a friend who was having a new dress made for the feast (*Şeker Bayram*) at the end of the month. We went in the evening and it was dark in the streets up in the poorer part at the top of the town. The walls of the houses lining the streets are forbiddingly bleak and stark. In Edremit houses are not attractive or welcoming on the street side. As we pushed open the door which led directly from the street into the courtyard of Emine's family's house, it was even darker inside. But when we shouted, a door across the courtyard was opened and I could see a room – a very small room – completely filled with women. It was as if a spotlight had been turned on a cosy scene on the stage of a theatre. We were welcomed, and we crossed the courtyard and entered; space was made to fit us in on the bench which ran around the room.

We stayed about an hour and I gradually made out that in the confusion of the crowded room a master tailor – that was Emine – and five apprentices were making clothes. The others were having fittings, gossiping, or putting in the evening with their small children in a spirit of sociability. All were glad to have a new subject – myself – as the centre of conversation. We talked of clothes (including examining all of mine); of sicknesses in the community and of the differences between Christianity and Islam. The young girls sang pop songs which they had learned from the radio, from records, or from the movies, knowingly discussing every singer's personal life and every word of every song ...all love songs and mostly about frustrated love.

As the evening grew late, the women drifted away home and my friend and I made our way back down across town, avoiding passing close to any of the crowded coffee-houses open on the neighbourhood squares – filled with men. The men would not go home until they knew that the women were at home. No messengers would be sent or special signals given but it would be known in the coffee-houses that the women were going home.

Emine is the oldest of five children. She had her workshop in a room in the family's house. Her mother and younger sisters worked in the house and court-yard most of each day and visited or were visited by women from the neighbourhood.

Emine's father drives a horse cart (what my father's generation called a 'dray') all day. He comes home for dinner after evening prayers in the mosque but leaves again after dinner to go to the coffee-house on the square or to the movies. Besides his business with the horse cart, the family has 50 olive trees, 10 of which Emine's father bought, while her mother inherited 40 from *her* father. During the olive season Emine's father works part of the time in the orchard and when harvest time comes the mother and children help harvest. If they have any spare time during this season, they help Emine's father's brother's family with harvesting or join a crew of neighbourhood women who are hired for wages to work for a rich man who owns thousands of trees. Emine did not pick olives this year because her tailoring business was doing so well. I was impressed, as I watched her work, by her skill, her self-confidence and her ability to handle five apprentices.

While I was in Edremit, Emine became engaged to a policeman. The women and older men of each family arranged the engagement to Mustafa, who lived in the next town and was the son of a second cousin on her mother's side. Emine and he knew each other by sight and agreed to the engagement, although they never talked to each other about it. However, Mustafa's sister, Şeri, was a frequent visitor after the arrangements for the engagement had begun. The two girls had known each other for five years casually and they increasingly visited each other, went to the movies (on women's day) together, and planned the wedding together, along with both mothers. The girls treated each other not as close friends but with correct and careful respect. The engagement gifts were exchanged and the engagement festivities were planned.

I attended the engagement party, a supper for 50 to 60 women. After supper about 100 to 150 women and children gathered in the courtyard of the lumber company which adjoined Emine's house. Music was provided by a three-instrument gypsy band whose one male member played behind a closed door. The women and children sat on the ground and on hired chairs in a large circle. When we had all gathered, Emine came from her house to the centre of the circle and danced the first dance with Mustafa's sister, Şeri. After that most of the younger women and girls in turn took off their coats and scarfs, danced a few turns with Emine, put their coats and scarfs on again and sat down. Certain women were especially encouraged by the crowd to come to dance in the centre of the circle and they danced in marvellously erotic postures. The group clapped and laughed, some raucously, some nervously.

When all had danced, the party was over and Emine and Mustafa were engaged.

After the engagement Mustafa and Emine met occasionally at her house and went for short, formal walks around town, accompanied by his sister, or mother. It used to be the fashion never to meet before marriage, but this was the modern world and Mustafa was a civil servant in a militantly modernist government, so they walked together, chaperoned, about once a month.

Months later – toward the end of our stay in Edremit, after Mustafa and his family had provided a house and furnishings and after Emine and her family had assembled kitchen equipment, linen and clothing – the time of the wedding was fixed. It was the usual three-day celebration. The household goods were on display, relatives gathered and on a Friday night, at Emine's house again, there was dinner for 50 to 60, with the men of both families eating separately in a nearby courtyard. All evening (I was told) the men danced with each other, dances similar to those of the women, and, like theirs, sometimes explicitly erotic. The men drank as much as could be afforded.

We women ate in the lumberyard and again we formed the circle for dancing. This time Emine came out wearing her grandmother's wedding dress. In Edremit, just now, it is the fashion on the first night of the wedding for the bride – in a spirit of recalling old customs – to wear one of these handsome, heavy velveteen dresses, embroidered in gold thread. In the past, 40 or 50 years ago, each bride of any substance had such a wedding dress. This time, too, Emine first danced in the centre of the circle with Şeri, and then with each woman present.

Saturday night followed much the same pattern, except that now Emine wore a long white, western-style wedding dress and veil. Before the opening dance Mustafa's mother arrived, carrying a large decorated bowl of henna which she kept on a chair at the centre of the circle during the whole evening.

Toward the end of the dancing on Saturday evening, a bus drew up in the street outside. The dancing stopped and Emine's father came to the door and tied a ribbon around her. Then, men in the back and women in the front, we all drove to the next town, to Mustafa's house. There Mustafa's older brother cut the red ribbon with which Emine had been bound and Emine kissed the hands of Mustafa's grandfather, his father, his grandmother and his mother and older brother. Then all the women retired to the back of this courtyard for more dancing while the men went to the coffee-house. Later we all piled back into the buses and went home. After most of the guests had left, Emine's friends painted her hands and feet with the henna to make her more beautiful.

On Sunday, the official government ceremony was held in the office of the marriage officer in the town hall, and Emine and Mustafa were married.

Azize is a little, round woman. When she is 'dressed up', she wears a very tight red dress and spike heels, and on the street a black cloth coat and a scarf. She has been married three or four years, but as yet has no children. She and her husband live in the household of her husband's parents, which also includes his unmarried sister when she is on holiday from teacher-training school. Her husband also has three married sisters and they and their families visit the house almost daily. So Azize lives in the midst of her husband's family and is known as the 'bride' (*gelin*). She came as a 'bride' from a nearby town and had almost no contact with her husband before she was married. She spends most of her time in her husband's house, but is occasionally allowed to go for several days at a time to visit her mother and father and sometimes, 'if her father allows it', her mother comes for several days to stay in Edremit with her.

Mornings Azize and her mother-in-law, and sometimes her husband's sisters, prepare food, sew, and do other household chores. In the afternoons – except during the olive season – they dress up and go calling, occasionally going with a group of women to the park or to the movies. Azize seldom leaves the house without her mother-in-law.

During the year we were there, one of the sisters-in-law and her husband had the opportunity to go to Germany to work. They left their daughter in her grandmother's care and the child joined the household. When the three generations went walking in the afternoon, it was possible to see that amusing picture, very characteristic of present-day Edremit, of the older generation in a long black *çarşaf* and black head scarf, the 'bride' in a street-length cloth coat and coloured head scarf and the young girl in a short skirt.

Also during the course of the year Azize's brother became engaged and later married one of Azize's husband's sister's daughters, so the two families had exchanged men and women. At this time, then, Azize came to play one of the important roles of Edremit women, already mentioned in connexion with Emine's marriage: the supervisor of much of her brother's forthcoming wife's activities for months before the wedding, and the first to dance at the wedding festivities.

It was during the arranging of this marriage that I noticed something which was to become quite clear to me during the year – the particularly close feeling between many brothers and sisters. Only when her brother was around did Azize seem happy and relaxed. Since the two families were on quite good terms, the brother was fairly often in the household of his future bride's family. The engaged couple continued to behave very formally toward each other, and the relationship was further strained by Azize's and her brother's obvious attachment to each other. My impression was that frequently brother–sister relationships had an almost romantic quality.

The only serious quarrel I witnessed in this rather large and quite easy-going family was during the preparation for the marriage. Azize was at one point felt to be siding with her brother against her husband's relatives with respect to the amount of money to be spent on the clothes for the bride.

Makbule is an attractive thirty-two. Her father is a well-to-do merchant who is an important public figure in Edremit, a well-educated, well-read, cosmopolitan man with an educated wife. His wife, Makbule's mother, is proud of her ability to read and write Ottoman, as well as modern, Turkish, and of her skill in keeping one of the most attractive houses and gardens in a seaside suburb of Edremit. They have one other child, a son, who was recently graduated in economics from the University of Istanbul.

Makbule was sent to school in Istanbul when she was eight, to an English-speaking lycée, and during her time there she went as an exchange student for one year to America. She speaks fluent and colloquial English.

While she was in her last year of lycée in Istanbul, after her return from abroad, her family arranged her engagement to a man who had recently graduated in law from the Sorbonne. She and he were married the following year.

Makbule's husband is an adventuresome entrepreneur in a country hungry for his kind of talent. He correctly sees opportunities in the business world of Turkey and he is busy, both at his place of business in and around Istanbul, and in Europe. For Makbule, Istanbul was lonely after her son was born and at the time we knew her she was living in Edremit in her parents' house, starting her child in school there. Her husband travelled a lot and was seldom home, but his family lived three or four doors away and the two families were daily involved in social and familial interaction.

These two families are particularly interesting because, as families firmly established in Edremit, not alienated from provincial life, but at the same time fully aware of changing patterns and standards of behaviour in Turkey and the rest of the world, they daily make decisions which are slightly changing their lives. And as they make these decisions, since they are leaders, they are influential in establishing new patterns of life in the town. Makbule's daily activities embody these subtle changes as she works at traditional philanthropic activities, participates in the work of the Parents' Committee of her son's elementary school on the 'new curriculum', helps her mother find a suitable wife for her brother and joins the first class for those learning to drive a car. She nightly reads the Quran with her father (in Turkish) because, he says, her schools didn't teach her about her own religion; she is helping her mother-in-law redesign her house to include the first domestic central heating unit in Edremit. She leads a life independent of her husband, who comes to Edremit when he has time.

Makbule leads a style of life so familiar to me in many ways that I could not help being startled by her independence of her husband, her acceptance of her arranged marriage and her plans for finding a wife for her jazz-playing, skin-diving, Max Weber-reading brother. One day I asked her whether she thought there was any value in our system of knowing a man before marriage. Quite casually she answered, 'There is so much time after marriage to get to know him.' She went on to say that surely, since families have to co-operate, it is most important that many members of the family help make the decision.

Fatma was a village girl who received a lycée education in Edremit and then found a job as a bank clerk. Since the Atatürk reforms, some women have been moving from the private space of the home into the public space of business, schools and government. Fatma has risen in rank and now is assistant manager of the bank, with men as her subordinates as well as her superior. One of the men employees of lesser rank than she is her husband. This does not strike anyone as strange.

Fatma and her husband met in the bank and asked their families' permission to marry, but the marriage, to an observer from outside, seems extremely similar to most other marriages in Edremit. Most of Fatma's life outside the bank is spent with women, most of her husband's life with men. In the bank, both behave as bank officials. In the bank she wears a smock which serves to seclude her female identity as the *çarşaf* or coat does that of women in the street. She meets her male colleagues and customers strictly in her role as bank clerk.

What, then, does sex role mean to women in Edremit? For young girls it means being included in the tasks of the household, learning the wide range of skills necessary to be a working member of a group of women keeping house. And it means being judged by the women on one's ability to preserve food, roll dough, pickle olives, sew, dance, manage small children, and appear respectfully pious.

For growing girls it means learning the modest, discreet behaviour appropriate in public so as not to attract the attention of non-family men, and thus the scolding and abuse of older women.

For girls between seven and twelve it means, nowadays, being in school – co-educational school – and learning ways of behaving in the public world with boys of similar age. I did not spend much time in schools and do not know the subtleties of behaviour in this crucial institution, though on another visit I hope to make extensive observations of young students in school. My impression is, however, that girls and boys in school keep quite apart and have relatively little personal interaction, simply because this is the pattern they know at home, in the town and among the teachers.

For all women, sex role means learning forms of social behaviour to make oneself a welcome member of women's society: some women learn to joke and to be the clowns of social gatherings, others are sympathetic listeners and still others are noisy givers of advice; many sing and dance (often gracelessly), but all learn ways of contributing to the social gatherings of women.

Women of modest means gather in small groups for work and – in the brief moments of the afternoon or evening when they are not busy – for sociability. Most well-to-do women participate in a very formal style of visiting: each member of a social group has a day (*misafir günü*) each month when she is 'at home' to her circle; others bring handwork and spend the afternoon. This formal visiting is found particularly attractive by wives of civil servants and army men who move frequently and for whom it provides a custom through which they can make friends. On certain occasions the women of prominent families meet for philanthropic business. At many levels women gather to play cards.

Many, many occasions in Edremit call for a group of women to have a religious gathering in a home; usually it is a *mevlûd*, a recitation of the poem on the life of Muhammad. Very infrequently do women go to the mosques, even on important religious occasions.

Women's society in Edremit has its specialists. The religious services are conducted by women who have either oral or, sometimes, reading knowledge of some Arabic for Quran reading and who are remarkably skilled in the recitation and leading of the *mevlûd*. Women hairdressers and beauty parlour operators cut hair and give permanents, but their major function is to prepare girls for engagement and wedding parties, making for them elaborate hairdos. (One is reminded of the part formerly played in preparation for marriage by the *hamam* – the Turkish bath – now no longer much used in Edremit.) As the example of Emine indicates, there are women tailors, all of them working in homes, There are women known to be experts in traditional curing, magic and fortune telling, as well as licensed nurses and midwives.

Thus, the women's world has a complex social structure of its own, quite apart from the occupational roles filled by some women in the public sphere. Women organize, conduct and participate in a wide range of work activities, sociability and ceremonies at a distance from the world of men. To it they bring their own leaders, skilled specialists and loyal followers. The separate structure allows freedom of action for women, away from men.

What is marriage when there is so much separation? The husband is very, very often chosen for a woman by her family. She has various ways of affecting the choice and it is unheard of in Edremit for a girl to be forced to marry against her explicit wishes. Basically, however, it is the responsibility of other members of the family to find a husband for her, and since she does not take full responsibility for the choice, she feels less than full responsibility for the outcome. Often she hardly knows her husband before the marriage. She has a sense of fate about it – and resignation.

What are the expectations which Edremit women have of husbands? They want them to be good providers, kind fathers, cheerful members of the household, respected citizens of the town. They do not expect men to be a major source of companionship, comfort or help in the daily work of the house. They appreciate 'worthwhile' men, but are actually slightly contemptuous of all men and feel that they are a burden to be borne. They expect men to be self-indulgent in their free time.

But marriage is more than gaining a husband. It means being required to work and play, from marriage on, with a certain group of women. There is no doubt that a woman contemplating marriage takes great care to evaluate the women she is becoming involved with and that her opinions are respected as judgements are made about the women of the future in-law household.

Marriage is clearly a *rite de passage* – a chance, once in her lifetime, for a girl to be 'queen for three days'. For these three days, the whole world seems to revolve around her. But the emphasis during the entire three days is upon large groups of women coming together in solidarity; the ceremonial emphasis is not on the couple. The decisive ceremonial gesture from the bride's standpoint (apart from the formal requirements of the state), is her first dance each evening with the groom's sister. There is a real sense in which the bride 'marries' the *görumce*, as well as the groom. Usually the present from the 'groom's side' to the bride at the wedding party is presented by the groom's mother. The whole rite can be thought of as a ceremony of women joining other women.

For the bride, of course, it means too that she is now a full adult woman and head of her own household, unless she and her husband join one of the parental households. In any case, such arrangements usually do not long survive the birth of children.

The other key figure in a woman's life is her brother. For most young people in Edremit there is little opportunity to know any person of the other sex except one's brother or sister. I have strong evidence that in Edremit the brother–sister tie is often very intense and very affectionate. Girls are expected to listen to and 'obey' their older brothers and they feel a sense of constraint to be 'respectful' to them, but at the same time they count on them for companionship, advice, help and defence. Cousins are called by the same kinship term as brothers, but since cousin-marriage is fairly common, cousins are potential husbands and are not treated as brothers. Into later life, the men with whom women feel most comfortable and upon whom they can most depend are their brothers.

Public education has now made it possible for a few women in Edremit to work in the public world – the world which traditionally belonged to men. They work in banks, the post office, offices of local and national government and schools; one or two are doctors in private practice. These women act as 'professionals' in these capacities, interacting with the public with the part of their person which is trained and skilled. They do not act as total personalities and certainly not as 'females'. It is this ability to focus on their job skills when at work, to have habits of behaviour which do not necessitate orientation to men as males, which makes me find them different from the women I know in the United States who work in the public world. American women have such a drive to relate themselves to males that whatever they do, whether personal or professional, is very often done for some man, in some way. These Turkish women who work in the public sphere bring with them from the separated world of the women a sense of independence of men which makes them more able to concentrate on the tasks at hand. In the academic, business and professional worlds of Turkey, the women who have stepped through the screen are giving no quarter to the men with whom they are in competition and they seem more free to conquer the problems of the professions than their counterparts in America.

But other pressures are at work: for example, the bureaucracies of the army and the civil service are large, and at the same time more influential, models of behaviour than their numbers would indicate. Since these officials are transferred around the country, and since it is the custom for them to take their nuclear families with them, all towns have such families. Their style of life is widely known and it influences others. It involves much greater mutual dependence of men and women. These families act socially as nuclear families to a much greater degree than do local families.

What imperatives do nuclear families have? I can only speculate: Do both men and women press for a larger role in the choice of their future marriage partner if they are going to live in the nuclear-family manner rather than in social groups based on separation of the sexes? If this is so, young men and women in Edremit will need institutions to bring them together. At the moment this occurs, if at all, in classes in the lycée, that most ambiguous of Edremit's institutions. Since such a fundamental change of social pattern may be implied in its structure and activities, it is easy to see why the town is very uncertain about the lycée – proud of it and at the same time wary of its consequences.

Not only does the emergence of a nuclear-family pattern possibly imply increased emphasis on personal choice of marriage partner, it probably also implies increased dependence of women on men, because in a nuclear family the dominance of men is less easy for women to escape. On the other hand, the pattern of separation may prove more resilient than one might suppose: new, more 'portable' institutions may emerge to facilitate its continuation under conditions of greater mobility.

Other possible influences for change in the role of women in Edremit are the cinema and foreign travel. One cannot live long in Edremit without wondering about the effect of three large cinemas, filled every night of the year with every kind of citizen. Some nights, on the way home from the movies in discussion with friends, one comes to the conclusion that the effect is nil – that what has been seen is relegated to the realm of fantasy; other nights one is convinced that local society will not be able to withstand the impact. Of course, neither of these conclusions is correct; the effect is subtle, tangential and long-term. The same is true of the alternative models for the role of women known to the many Turks who each year go to work in Germany. Every year thousands of Turkish men, and increasingly women as well, go to Germany to work on one-, two-, or three-year contracts. Some of the men bring back German wives.

It is tempting to predict that all these influences will strengthen the nuclear family. It is then an easy step to suggest that under those circumstances women must become more dependent on men. If so, the paradox with which we started is really not a paradox. The separated women of Edremit are now more independent, at least psychologically, than American women, but they may increasingly lose this independence as they gain freedom of movement. Edremit women are now, perhaps, to use an ironical American expression, 'separate but equal' in many senses.

THE MEN (L.A.F.)

The world of men is the public world of the street, the place of business, the mosque and above all the *kahve*, the coffee-house which, despite its name, purveys mainly tea. Women are not excluded from the first three; they pass along the streets to do business in the shops, markets and government offices, but for them this is foreign soil, entered by necessity. They move through it briskly, well-covered and, when possible, in groups. Even many younger, more 'modern', men, who occasionally stroll with their wives on fine summer evenings along the streets and through the park, prefer to do most of the food shopping themselves. A few women attend mosque on special occasions – during the month of Ramadan and on other Muslim holy days – but they are separated on these occasions from the male congregation behind curtains, in a balcony. The coffee-house, however, is inviolate. The one exception I observed resoundingly proves the rule: one poor mad creature who is always pregnant by some 'shameless male', frequents the coffee-houses, and after a few minutes of friendly, incoherent banter, she moves on, after which the patrons devote an additional few minutes to excoriation of the unknown 'filthy atheist' responsible for her condition. The male code is upheld by its very adaptation to her special needs.

Much of the male world has been dealt with in our earlier outline of the occupational structure of the town, which men very largely dominate, despite the inroads made upon it by the few 'new women'. The most economical way of adding what needs to be added is the life-cycle way.

Small boys tend to be rather spoiled and indulged – more so than girls, though toddlers of both sexes are much made-over. Almost all boys now go to school through the six primary grades and at somewhere around the age of six or seven undergo circumcision, *the* rite of passage for the male (marriage, in many ways its female analogue, is a woman's ceremony). We attended, among others, the circumcision of Ismail Aksu, a rather thin, wan little boy, the only son of a moderately prosperous farmer.

It was a two-day affair. On the first morning I met Ismail's paternal grandfather, strolling about the town in the company of a coeval friend (there is a strong age-grading tendency in male sociability), receiving congratulations, while the boy's father slaughtered two sheep for the occasion. The boy's four sisters were taken to the hairdresser's, while their mother and a squad of neighbours and kinswomen prepared food in the courtyard kitchen for the guests, who must have numbered at least 200 of both sexes in the course of the two days. In the late afternoon something like 100 women gathered to dance to the music of a gypsy band hired for the occasion. Ismail's father's brother's wife stained the thumb and two fingers of Ismail's right hand with henna – the occasion is called *kına gecesi*, 'henna evening', as is the evening during the marriage ceremonies when the bride's hands and feet are similarly decorated. He thus spent this evening with the women, who made much of him and pinned money to his clothing. Circumcision, which would come the next day, would formally transfer him to the world of men.

When we arrived on the morning of the second day, the whole second storey of the substantial house was filled with seated men, packed together and spilling down the stairs, and I was asked to join them. They had come for the chanting of the *Mevlid-i Şerif* of Süleyman Celebi, the poem on the life of the Prophet which commonly marks life's most solemn occasions in Turkey. A cantor, hired especially for the occasion from the office of the Mufti, sang the *mevlid*, as well as a number of passages from the Quran, and prayers were offered for the boy and his family, and for the Republic ('make [it] victorious over all its enemies by land, sea and air, O Lord God'). *Lokum* – Turkish Delight – was distributed and rosewater was sprinkled on everyone's hands. Then, following a lavish meal for all, the men went to the mosque for midday prayers, at the conclusion of which several dozen of them returned together in a procession, led by the cantor and the *imam* of that particular mosque congregation. At the door of the Aksu courtyard, hands outstretched with palms upward in the Muslim posture of supplication, the men stood and again prayed for the boy, his family and the Republic. The mosque congregation (*cemaat*) was constituting itself in preparation for receiving little Ismail into the universal (male) Muslim community (*ümmet*).

Meanwhile, Ismail was brought out mounted on a horse and dressed in a suit, white shirt and tie, his head covered with the white pillbox cap bearing the word *maşallah*! (God preserve him!) that is customary for such occasions. His father's brothers paraded him about the town as men pinned money on his clothing. Then he was taken upstairs, dressed in a gown and placed on the lap of a father's brother, who held him for the operation. The boy was terrified, the more so as his playmates had been terrorizing him for weeks about the coming ordeal. But he was now repeatedly urged to be brave and not to cry out. The hired operator slipped into the room and did his work with professional speed and skill, while below in the courtyard, at a signal from the window, another uncle slaughtered a cock and the boy's mother and sisters wept. Ismail was not quite up to the occasion, but his uncle's hand muffled his cries, making it possible for everyone present to congratulate him on his lion-like courage. The small hero was then placed on a bed decorated with paper streamers and cloths in the form of a canopy (recalling the campaign tents of Ottoman sultans) and made to receive a line of well-wishers who presented him with gifts of money. Thus small Ismail became a man.

When a boy leaves primary school, the paths his life may take are several. A few of the brightest, with adequate financial resources, will go on to further schooling, which will make them bureaucrats, free professionals, businessmen or military officers and will often remove them from the local community. The average boy, however, unless he takes up his father's occupation, will now be apprenticed to a master craftsman to learn a trade – though some may now circumvent apprenticeship via the town's technical school. The master–apprentice relationship can be crucial to the formation of a boy's character – almost as much so as his relationship with his father, for the master to a substantial degree takes the place of the father at the very time when the boy is entering adolescence, which Turks call, very expressively, *delikanlık*, the phase of 'crazy blood'. During these years the workplace can be a near-total environment, for craftsmen work incredibly long hours. Several men have told me at length about their craft-masters and how they influenced their moral development – how they strive to emulate a good master, or avoid the example of a bad one, in handling their own apprentices. From the shop of a good master, people say, a young man emerges from the 'crazy blood' stage hardworking, *temiz* and *namuslu*, 'pure' and 'honourable', in both the narrower sexual, and the broader, general moral, sense, including especially business ethics.

Whether boys work with their fathers, attend technical school or serve an apprenticeship, by the age of eighteen or nineteen they have acquired a skill while forming the peer-group ties that knit together the male community. (For those few who go on to higher education, of course, these skills and ties are formed elsewhere.) Then comes military service, usually far from home, providing the youth with some sense of his nation's size and diversity; and then sentimental reunion with friends and brothers, expressed in arm-in-arm strolls along the streets and through the park. But just at this time, after ten to fifteen years of intense involvement in all-male society, marriage looms on two fronts: the young man and his sister must help seek out spouses for each other, along with other members of the family – primarily the nuclear family, since cousins of all sorts are among the likely candidates. The young peoples' contribution to the spouse-hunt can be important, for they know the reputations of their respective peers rather better than do their elders. The latter are sounder on other considerations, such as property.

A good deal has been said above about brothers and sisters from the woman's standpoint. The relationship is certainly a focal one for both parties – perhaps for many the most intense cross-sex relationship they will ever experience. Men are deeply sentimental toward their mothers and affectionately protective toward their daughters, but the sentiment of brothers toward sisters is something else again. Reared in radical separation from other peers of the opposite sex, they have grown up with sisters in the intimacy of the household and they are made to help seek spouses for these sisters at the very time that they themselves are about to marry. For both, marriage means breaking this highly-charged bond. It is revealing that a man experiences the same sentiment, *kıskanç*, for which the only possible English gloss is 'jealousy', when an unauthorized male approaches either his wife or his sister. It is little wonder that marriage partners must be chosen by others and that they take so long 'to get to know each other'.

It is this complex, perhaps, that provides much of the affective underpinning of the honour-and-shame pattern in Aegean Turkey. That part of the male subculture which has to do with women stresses their weakness, dependence and vulnerability. Women, I have heard men say, are ten times as passionate as men. They are like gunpowder, which the presence of a male may ignite. It is difficult to avoid the conclusion that men are protecting their women from impulses which they feel and fear in themselves. A man is dishonoured when the chastity or fidelity of any woman of his family is threatened, but the not infrequent killings of 'enemies of virtue' seem most often to involve offended brothers or husbands. A father's honour, too, is threatened by his daughter's vulnerability, but he, it seems, is more likely than a brother to hold *her* responsible. In the best-known of local myths, Sarıkız, the 'blonde girl', is sent away to the mountains with her flock of geese when her father hears rumours that she has lost her virtue. A brother would have sought out the other party.

As he passes into middle age, a man relaxes – not from work, for as *aile reisi*, 'head of a family', he must provide for it as best he can, including, most importantly, acquiring the means for satisfactory circumcision ceremonies for his sons and weddings for his daughters. But he relaxes from the passions and anxieties of youth. He attends mosque more frequently and once having married, circumcised and educated his children to the best of his ability, he may perform the *haj*, grow a beard and subside into a life of pampered self-satisfaction. His wife and he may get on well and become quite affectionate, though never demonstratively so until one of them dies. (It is almost as indecent for a married couple to embrace in public – for example, at parting or reunion – as for an unmarried couple to do so.) Or they may quarrel and separate, a matter of little more than inconvenience and mild regret. He is more apt to remarry than she, but she, too, may try again before giving men up as a bad job. The marriage bond is not sacred; it is a civil contract. Even the more pious often dispense with any sort of religious ceremony. The man who is friendly with his wife spends more time at home, but even he must join the male moiety in the coffee-houses and cinemas when his wife has guests, and he may not return until they have gone. If he is a craftsman or shopkeeper with a workplace of his own, he has the option of entertaining friends with tea or coffee there.

We have stressed the separateness of the worlds of men and women, but in fact we did not experience the full force of this aspect of life in Edremit. We were visitors from abroad and allowances were made for us – for the fact that we behaved more as a 'couple', in what our friends recognized as Western style. Since we attempted to avoid the more egregious violations of local sex-role behaviour, we were regarded as respectable deviants. The people of Edremit are extremely hospitable and we were entertained as a couple, in a spirit of kindly tolerance, in many homes in which, we suspect, such mixed sociability is normally confined to close kin. Only for such transient isolates as civil servants, teachers and military officers is extra-familial sociability by couples at all common.

A society's capacity to mislead by offering to the observer its more adaptable and inquisitive members was brought home to me by the man with whom I achieved the closest personal friendship, but who was not one of these. He is a craftsman, a man of little formal education, but a true autodidact who reads serious books for pleasure. He is very well-informed about national and world affairs, which we discussed at length and frequently over endless cups of tea, and is deeply and undogmatically concerned about the health of the Turkish polity. His religious views are tolerant and sceptical: a truly enlightened man. But he resisted my repeated invitations to visit our flat and finally, with great embarrassment, he explained why. He would be 'ashamed' (*utanırdım*), he said; he meant that he was afraid that my wife might be present. He knew he shouldn't feel that way (he is a strong believer in Atatürk's modernizing reforms), but that was how it was. He couldn't help it, he said, because he had been brought up that way. A free spirit ideologically, he is a simple traditionalist in domestic manners and quite representative, in this respect, of the men I knew. 'Though you become as David and Jonathan, you need never enter his home, nor he yours.'

We conclude, then, that while Forster's sketch is in some degree pan-Mediterranean, it is only partly so. What we understand him to have meant by his statement about the 'brotherhood of men' prevailing at the expense of the 'sisterhood of women' is not that the men of an Italian town were equal in power and wealth or that their relations were particularly harmonious. What he meant to suggest was that men's monopoly of the town's public space made it possible for them to interact, in whatever manner, unencumbered by the contingencies of their individual ties with women. It must follow from this, he apparently reasoned, that the women were pining away, each in her own home, awaiting the return of their lords and masters. (It is perhaps relevant to recall that Forster's observations are now three-quarters of a century old.) Now this, as we have shown, is not the case in Edremit. If relations among males there are relatively unencumbered by their relations with females, it is also the case that females' relations with each other are similarly, if in lesser degree (since male authority and possession of public space do inhibit women's movements), free of male interference. Our point is not the familiar one that women, submissive in public, manage to influence their fate by domestic scheming, manipulation and hen-pecking. This is true, but probably universal. Our point is rather that in Edremit women have an institutional structure and sense of solidarity of their own, parallel to those of men, which give them a substantial field for self-assertion and a psychological independence of men – an independence underscored by the performance of those women who break into the public sphere.

12   The new role of mothers: changing intra-familial relationships in a small town in Turkey

Mübeccel Kıray
İstanbul Technical University

Submission by women to the authority of all their male relatives, the patrilineal-extended family composition, and the segregation of the male and female worlds, even within the home, are well-known aspects of Turkish family life. A great deal of knowledge exists on male behaviour both within and outside the family circle, but very little is known about women, their role in the life of the household, or how they establish their relationships with other members of the family. It has even been stated that village men consider their wives 'just like animals'. However, many realistic novels introduce women with strong personalities who not only influence the lives of their male relatives, but even reorganize the whole community in which they live.[1] In Middle Eastern societies, at least, women have been called 'carriers of tradition', which would imply that they resist change.[2] Equally important, however, are the laws of the Turkish Republic which, after 1926, defined new and equal rights and status for women. These laws are partly responsible for the obvious change one sees in the lives of women who are no longer segregated, those who do not live in patrilineal-extended families and who do not submit to male authority in many Anatolian cities and settlements.[3]

In order to understand the new status of women and the channels and means through which this has been achieved, there is a clear necessity to examine the new relationships which women are establishing and the mechanism by which the change in such relationships is effected.

It is also necessary to determine what type of interaction is taking place between various members of the family within its original framework and to understand which functions are changing hands because of new relationships and which are not. In addition, it is important to study the aspects of family life which are not affected by new relationships and the position and role of women in this changing structure. In order to obtain a clear picture of the interrelationships between members of families and why and how such relationships evolve, a strictly analytical study of a specific case should be made.

The subject of this paper is such an analysis of changing intra-familial relationships in the small Black Sea coast town of Ereğli.[4]

261

In Ereğli both family structure and intra-familial relationships appear to be changing; however, the family – like society at large – does not necessarily become disorganized as a result of these changes. The aspects of family life which have changed, those which have not and those in the process of change, all present themselves as an organized, interdependent whole. So much is this the case that terms designating different kinds of disorganization, such as anomie or cultural lag, are inadequate in the analysis of this slowly changing whole. It is therefore imperative to see which aspects, relationships and values provide the necessary links in maintaining an interdependent whole in such a changing structure. It is also important to be able to analyse the new family structure as being different from the prior traditional one, and as undergoing a process which makes change comprehensible. The relationships, institutions and values which cause change, but at the same time permit integration between the different factors, need special attention. It is particularly necessary to study the circumstances which bring about change of a type which is relatively slow within the old structure, while keeping the new family structure in a reasonable state of integration and equilibrium. Buffer mechanisms, as these factors are called by us, cause a type of relationship not seen in the previous inter-dependence, but which constitute a new configuration of norms, relationships, institutions and values in a particular society at this peculiar stage of change. In Ereğli such a family analysis was possible to achieve by searching for the emergence of new intra-familial relationships and by looking at the special role played by women in general, and by mothers in particular. It seems that women, and particularly mothers, function as buffers in providing a smooth change in intra-familial relationships, while serving to adjust and integrate the family within a changing society.

The difference in composition of households in Ereğli reflects the definite changes that have taken place in the family structure and in intra-familial relationships. Of all the households studied, only 9 per cent had the characteristic composition and function of the patrilineal joint extended family, where father, mother, married sons, their wives and their children, as well as unmarried sons and daughters, live as a single unit.

However, it can be claimed that another 27.5 per cent of the families, although not all conforming to the classic patrilineal extended family, still presented variations on that theme. It seemed that in all these cases, where the father, mother, or only the father, lived with the son, the father's traditional powers of authority and control were passed on to the son. Interviews clearly indicated the latter's overt acceptance of the role of head of the household. Although the form of such families resembles the traditional patrilineal type, distorted by demographic factors, further observations of power and authority within such families lead one to the conclusion that the functions and interrelations in fact point to the existence of a new order.

Most important of all, perhaps, is the high rate of nuclear families consisting of only one married couple and their unmarried children. More than 60 per cent of the independent units were found to be such nuclear families, which indicates a fundamental change in relationships. It should be noted that 7.8 per cent of these families included the wife's parents, a situation which is highly irregular in terms of traditional patterns. The fact that the married daughter, her husband and their children live with her parents is important, and needs further analysis concerning her relationships and status as a daughter compared to her other relationships. There is yet another family type which can be termed 'distorted', where there is no lineal extended family, but various other relatives, from either the father's or mother's side, live together. The existence of this type also indicates how far the family and relationships between its members have changed.

To understand such diversified family arrangements, the interaction of the members as reflected within these different compositions will be analysed.

FATHER–SON RELATIONSHIPS IN CHANGE

The father–son relationship used to be the most important, since it served to perpetuate the multifunctional structure of the family. This relationship was seen clearly in the patrilineal extended family where married sons lived in the same household as their father under the latter's dominance and authority. Traditionally a family, and particularly a father, strongly desires sons. After childhood, the father takes care to see that his sons find jobs or learn the family trade, that suitable girls be found for them, and that at the end of his active years the welfare of his family can be entrusted to them, thus commencing a new domestic cycle.

Because of change, such relationships have become less rigid. Conflicts have arisen and sons have begun to rebel. In fact, the low ratio of married sons living within their father's households reflects this break from the traditional form.

The major conflicts between father and son correspond to three different periods in the son's life. Firstly, independence is asserted in early youth when the son begins to have his own way in matters of work and entertainment, then later on, in marriage, when the desire for a separate house is felt, and finally with maturity when he goes in search of an independent job. These periods, and the conflicts contained in them, are all related to the perpetuating processes of a traditional society where the configuration is complete. During change, friction and crisis are to be expected, and do to some extent exist; this is where the mother steps in and facilitates the change by playing the very important new role of buffer between father and estranged son.

The first type of conflict between father and son concerns the latter's work and leisure habits after he has joined his father's business. Fathers say that their boys are 'good-for-nothings', that they are lazy and irresponsible and only want to enjoy themselves. However, such statements contain an important contradiction: in general, older men tolerate drinking, smoking or keeping late hours in boys of eighteen and nineteen. They say that boys should do wild or foolish things, and that it is in their blood. As a result, boys are called *delikanlı* (with wild blood) during their early youth. But fathers strongly object to their own sons' leaving the shop during working hours in order to see their friends, go to the beach or the cinema, or if they have too much to do with girls. The boys themselves feel no particular responsibility towards their work so long as they are neither employees nor employers in the business. They therefore try to avoid work as much as possible, which in the end severs their ties with their fathers.

In many cases this conflict does not become serious, and mothers step in to calm the two parties by trying to arbitrate between them. She intercedes on her son's behalf, sometimes even to the extent of sharing his guilt.

The other much-discussed issue concerns the son's marriage and where the new couple will live after they are married. In fact, in the present study the home they chose was discussed almost as much as the selection of the bride herself. Sons and the bride's family usually insist on setting up a new home, and conflict is aggravated when the father and son work together in a family business, as this means that the common income has to be divided. However, in the majority of cases the reason for establishing a new residence, or, even more frequently, that given for the separation of a young couple, is the potential and real conflict between the mother-in-law and the bride. It should be added that this reason is often provided by fathers to enable them to disclaim any responsibility. A father's assertion that he has given his consent over separate houses definitely confers his assumed authority upon him. In this way he solves a most important conflict between the two 'lesser' members of the household, over whom he has absolute authority, through the generous gesture of allowing them to have a separate house, and thus re-establishes the disturbed peace in the family.

However, it must be remembered that mother-in-law–bride conflicts in Anatolian families are legendary. They are the subject of many folk songs, jokes, tales and anecdotes. It is only now that in the eyes of the men of the house this has suddenly become an important enough reason for separation. Obviously something new has developed. In this area one of the most important changes in intra-familial relationships is taking place. While the son's submission to his father is disintegrating, neither party is willing to take the responsibility or blame upon himself, and they conveniently shift it to the shoulders of the women (the mother-in-law and the bride). It is well known that in the past no conflict between women could make the men change the established household pattern, and it is probable that the son's wishes are most significant in these situations. If and when a move is made according to the bride's wishes, she is enabled to express and realize her desire, and the son, understanding her feelings, can somehow manage to make his father receptive to the idea. Here the role assumed and played by the mother is significant. She uses her influence on the father to make him agree to allow separate households, because her desire to please her son comes first. Secondly, she alone is in a position to judge the severity of the dispute, the feasibility of a second household, and to advise both the father and the son to separate. Among all those involved, the father, the son, the daughter-in-law and the mother, it is only the last who directly and intimately interacts with everybody. She agrees to the separation even though she is aware that the bride will not join her household with subservient status, nor will she offer any physical help. Although the mother is usually ambivalent in her feelings on the solution, we find that instead of trying to leave the conflict between the father and son unsolved, she prefers to take it on herself and solve the problem once and for all, although she has no desire to see her son leave or to be deprived of the help of his bride.

The second important source of conflict between father and son concerns the job provided by the father, which opposes the son's desire to be financially independent. Among the tradesmen and artisans of Ereğli, who constitute the great majority of the working population, sons begin their apprenticeship at thirteen or fourteen years of age. From then until the time he actually participates in, or takes over the full management of the business, a boy receives only pocket-money from his father, and the amount increases slowly over the years. It is only after the father dies or becomes incapacitated through old age or illness that the son finally acquires financial control. The tradesmen of Ereğli call this process 'turning over the cash-box' (*kasayı devretme*). Conflict arises when the son wants more money and/or responsibility, and if this remains unsolved, he may even leave the town and settle in another city. Many such sons only return just before the death of their father to await their inheritance.

Mothers like this solution least of all and would do anything to avoid it. They use all their skill in manipulating family relationships to ensure that the father will solve the problem to their satisfaction. For instance, they may find another job for the son, or open a separate shop for him. A third way is to associate the son in the business in such a way as to make him a partially independent partner without actually turning the business over to him. Comparing the two solutions, either the son's leaving town or his being provided with another job, the latter appears to be the most frequently reached. This may show the mother's willingness to make herself appear as a humble loser to convince the father and son that the new job is better. No discussion between father and son can take place without the mother's knowledge; even if she is not present, she will certainly hear about it later from both sides. Without a great deal of aggressiveness, she will put her own ideas forward in an attempt to calm the anger of her husband, and persuade her son to have patience until a solution is reached. Eventually this strategy works.

Fathers do not usually admit that any such conflict exists, and are very reluctant to concede that their rights and duties have changed with the times. It seems that this reluctance is not because fathers consider such conflicts to be ordinary, or even that they have no complaints, but rather because they are resisting the new way of life and are sure that they will succeed in solving the problem according to their own wishes. Usually, however, a father will agree to accept his son's demands, although it is only through the skilful persuasion of his wife that it seems as though he gave his consent by using his own judgement, thus leaving his authority intact. With the help of continuous discussion of the issues with the mother, both parties can usually be led to believe that neither's role has changed and so authority can be formally retained. Thus it is mothers who bring about the gradual changes which guide relationships between fathers and sons to a new configuration with as little crisis as possible; this is a major departure from the disharmony of the past.

Although a new balance in the father–son relationship is being achieved through the mother's mediation, new problems are arising. The traditional father–son relationship provided the family with a built-in security system. Responsibility for the welfare of the family, particularly for aged parents, fell upon the son, who accepted this when the time came to do so. It used to be merely normal for a son to remain with his parents and care for them, but when he leaves the house, takes an independent job, and severs his ties with his father, parents can no longer rely upon him in their old age. This intense insecurity and fear of being left alone in old age, and having to depend on strangers, can be strongly felt in Ereğli. Society has not yet provided any new relationships or institutions to take the place of the old father–son relationship which would obviate this insecurity. The acquisition of a house and investment in real estate, which brings in rent, is one of the buffer mechanisms used in dealing with this general feeling. More directly, however, insecurity changes the role and place of the daughters and gives new roles to the mother in the family, as will be discussed later.

MOTHER–SON RELATIONSHIPS

For a woman the most important relationship in the family is that with her son. As a bride she is an outsider and is always made to feel so. Her status is low, and no matter how good a daughter-in-law she is by any standard, she will only receive final recognition when she has given birth to a son. It is not until then that she gains higher status and feels herself to be accepted by her husband and his family. As a result, all her hopes and fears, and her plans for the future, are concentrated and expressed in the love she shows for the growing boy. This explains the extraordinary spoiling of male children by women compared with their treatment of girls, and the tolerance with which parents accept the behaviour of their sons. A mother can always rely on her son to protect her and defend her interests in intra-family disputes or fights, particularly against the father. The son is second to the father in authority and in influence within the home, and a mother would never consider severing her ties with him or becoming less affectionate towards him. Through her son she can gain status and authority in the household similar to that of her daughter-in-law after the birth of a son. Generally a son takes his mother's side in any conflict between her and his wife, and he is normally expected to do so. If a choice has to be made, 'the stranger's daughter' (*el kızı*), or daughter-in-law, does not stand a chance. The mother's desire for her son's well-being reigns supreme.

Today this mother–son relationship is also undergoing change, as another traditional basic inter-dependence moves towards a new configuration. In many cases, mothers and sons unite in rejecting the father's authority, not only to prevent his arbitrary decisions as in the past, but also to force him to accept new modes of behaviour or new values. This co-operation becomes particularly effective when different behaviour patterns and values pertaining to women are in question. This is especially evident when new and expensive household items, such as radios, refrigerators or electric irons, are desired, when a father refuses to permit his women to go to the cinema or to open-air concerts of Turkish music in the park, or to purchase new styles of clothing, or, more importantly, when he will not accept his wife's open participation in the making of some crucial family decision.

Sons who change their behaviour towards their fathers also begin to change in their actions towards their wives and mothers. Consequently, often a mother can no longer count on supreme power over her daughters-in-law if her son starts to take his wife's side against his mother. This causes some constraint in mother–son relationships, but it is still too early to see whether the mother will ultimately be the gainer or the loser in this matter.

DAUGHTER–PARENT RELATIONSHIPS

The attitude of both mothers and fathers towards their daughters is one of both affection and firmness. The mother–daughter relationship is intimate from the moment the latter leaves school. The female child is constantly with her mother, in doing housework, as a companion on excursions and as a close friend. Fathers are affectionate and may be proud of their daughters, but this relationship is very different from that between mother and daughter, or father and son, being a spontaneous one based partly on affection and partly on indifference until her marriage. Everyone in the house, particularly the father and the sons, has a right to interfere with the daughter's life. Even after her marriage they keep an eye on her to see that she is properly protected and that she suffers no more than the usual pressure from her in-laws. In fact, if a girl is unhappy and her marriage is not successful, she can find refuge with her father or brother. However, prior to marriage, in her own household if a daughter has a problem she only solves it through her mother; her brother may also help, but his attitude would tend to be authoritarian and intolerant. Again, it is the mother who negotiates with both the father and the brother to settle the question in the best interests of her daughter. The mother's role as mediator is becoming particularly important and difficult as the present-day girl's unusual demands increase because she spends more time with her girlfriends, dresses differently, goes to school or works in an office. When a daughter starts to show a preference for a young man, no matter how innocent it may be, the reactions of her father and brothers may be very definitely negative and prohibitive. At this time she looks to her mother to find an accomplice. Although the daughter may show anger, nervousness and grief, her mother tries to do all she can to hide her daughter's behaviour under the cover of their intimacy and friendship. Since nowadays a girl has more chance to speak to young men, mothers may appear to play the role of angry old women towards their husbands and sons as well as towards their daughters. It is only through the mother than any permissiveness is allowed in a girl's behaviour.

Marriage is a girl's sole aim, but not simply because it means the beginning of a new way of life as a young woman. When a girl marries, she is uprooted from her own natural environment and goes to live in a different place among total strangers in close, intimate and, in some cases, basically hostile circumstances. This is a very difficult experience for her. However, girls are brought up to accept the idea that they will have to adapt themselves to their husband's family, who may well be hostile towards them and that they will become second-class members in that strange environment. This is a thoroughly different socialization process to that of boys, who are constantly reminded that they will eventually replace their fathers in the important position of control and decision-making occupied by the latter. Indeed, almost from childhood, sons are given this privileged status. As a result of this, girls are always able to adjust to adverse circumstances more easily than boys.

In Ereğli little pressure is put on girls regarding choice of marriage partners. They are often consulted, and their right to refuse is respected. Today there is no question of marriage between two young people who do not know one another, and conditions are such that they always have a chance to seek out and speak to each other. The type and intensity of their relationship may vary from simply observing each other in the street, in shops, at the cinema or in the park, to actually having a secret affair. In more conservative families, special occasions are arranged when the boy and girl can see each other from a distance. In families where both sexes visit together, the boy and girl are given as much chance as possible to speak to one another and to participate. In all the accepted and unaccepted modes of contact, the mother plays the most important role, and during this time children communicate with their fathers only through their mothers.

Both boys and girls express their wishes through their mother, and, no matter how wild these wishes may be, she will always find a middle course to satisfy both the children and their father. It is for the mother to reconcile her husband to this and to effect a compromise between the values of the older generation of women and the present relationships between the two sexes, thus avoiding open conflict. In this area, as in others, the diminishing authority of the father and the changing roles of the sexes have resulted in new responsibilities and functions for the mother. She is, in the fullest sense of the word, a 'buffer', the most important balancing mechanism, who imposes, yet slows down, the transition of family relationships.

There is another way in which girls are presently experiencing a change in their traditional relationships with their parents and particularly with their mothers. At the time of their marriage, when they move to the house of their husbands' families, daughters have usually had little to do with their new relatives. However, as was mentioned above, 7.8 per cent of the families studied were 'extended', and included members of the bride's family. Of these families, 50 per cent had the bride's mother living with the couple, which reflects a new relationship both for the girls and for the mothers.

Separate houses for newly-married couples often leave young women alone with two or three children and without help. Since they have refused to live with their husband's families, they can hardly ask for help from them, because the traditional pattern is for the bride to help with the work in the mother-in-law's house, and not vice versa. The young couple, therefore, ask for the help of the girl's mother. In more isolated parts of Turkey it would be disgraceful for a girl's mother to live with her son-in-law, but in Ereğli, due to pronounced change, many young couples insist on living in separate houses. As a result, if a girl or her mother need one another's help they live together. This situation causes two different types of adjustment problem, but the question of conflicting values is not prominent.

Mothers residing with their daughters give the latter an opportunity to lighten the burden of household chores and are of particular help in sharing the work of raising a family. In this way the girl's mother, after the boy's mother has ensured that they have a separate house, takes it upon herself to provide more congenial living conditions for the new family. Her relationship with her son-in-law is usually friendly, because she clearly recognizes his superior place as head of the household and as the oldest male. Here again, one can see the altruism of women, which enables change and adjustment without extreme friction.

A more significant aspect of the relationship between the girls' parents and the nuclear family, if they live within the same household, can be seen when the older generation needs the help of the younger. In fact, parents often seem very willing to live with their daughters and sons-in-law, though in the past emphasis was always laid on the loyalty of sons. Father–son relationships, and patriarchal authority, the chief pillars of a traditional society, are changing fast. One of the most important functions of the extended family, that of providing security for the older generation, has not been taken over by any new institution. A daughter's request for her parents to live with her husband and her in a new relationship is becoming more commonplace than for parents to live with their sons. It is interesting to trace the way in which this change is viewed. Now one hears such phrases as 'daughters are loyal', or, 'daughters are more considerate', in contrast to the behaviour of sons. This is because a daughter will welcome her parents to her house when a son will not. Hence, in the absence of other institutions which could provide security to the aged, the daughter not only becomes a renter, but she acquires new functions as a buffer mechanism and as such provides the required balance within the process of change that Ereğli is experiencing.

HUSBAND–WIFE RELATIONSHIPS

The husband–wife relationship is a very varied one in Ereğli. It is still true to say that the wife is completely subservient to her husband, especially when the latter's relatives live under the same roof. It is equally certain that as the years go by the wife's status rises. She gradually becomes the central figure in the family as her children grow up, marry and have children of their own. However, the establishment of nuclear families does bring fundamental changes to these relationships. First of all, the subservience of the wife is reduced. In traditional families husbands never talk to their wives about their work. Husbands and wives live in separate worlds, in the way they express interest in such things as births and deaths, business and politics, relatives and friends, holidays and weddings. Today, however, this segregation is decreasing as husbands and wives share in activities, and men find reliable advisers in their wives in many matters. Very few husbands today refuse their wives' comments or advice on any important matter. Many even stress that they prefer their wives' advice to that of the older members of their families who have been unable to keep up with today's fast changing relationships, institutions and values. Such co-operation between husband and wife directly indicates that the absolute authority of the husband is on the wane.

Today in Ereğli there is certainly more communication between young married couples. The education of children, medical care, entertainment in mixed company, family visits, picnics, travel together, going to the cinema together and, to a lesser degree, the fact that women have begun to work outside their homes, have all contributed to break down the traditional, rigid segregation in husband–wife relationships. The woman's altruism, her endurance in difficulty, her almost natural acceptance of a humble role and her capacity to adjust, make her the most crucial person in bringing freedom and emancipation into her daughter's life. Finally, in nuclear families, the wife's intelligent, silent observations from outside give her the status of being the best adviser to her husband.

All in all, it is the wife's buffer functions that provide an avenue for smooth change in intra-familial relationships, as well as the adjustment and integration of the family to the new and changing demands of society at large.

In Ereğli the family seems to adjust itself to changing social conditions through the changes in the family's internal relationships caused by mothers in particular and women in general. The roles they assume in these new relationships smooth the way for further change and integration. Women fulfil these new roles with the help of two behavioural characteristics learnt from traditional relationships. The first is the skill acquired during her socialization in asserting her influence in an effective, though round-about, way when the supremacy of her male relatives is almost absolute. The second is her ability to adjust to a hostile environment with humility and modesty, but at the same time with definite determination.

Obviously the women and mothers of Ereğli are not like Nora of the Doll's House, but they do play a most important part in changing the most resistant sex roles of a traditional society with the least possible friction.

NOTES

1   See, for example, Yaşar Kemal, *Teneke*, Istanbul, Varlik Yayınları, 1957. Yaşar Kemal: *Mehmet My Hawk*, London, Pantheon Books, 1961 (original title *İnce Memed*, Istanbul, Remzi Kitabevi, 1953). Fakır Baykurt: *Yılanların Öcü*, Ankara, Bilgi Kitabevi, 1959.
2   L. H. Melikian, 'Authoritarianism and its correlates in the Egyptian culture and in the United States', *Journal of Social Issues*, Vol. 15, 1959, p. 3.

  In a recent study, as yet unpublished, Çiğdem Kağıtçıbaşı found that among İzmir secondary school students in their last year, in the face of conflicting role demands caused by a traditional environment and by their education and social class status, the girls were more pessimistic regarding belief in external control and affiliation orientation than were the boys. For an opposite view, see Serim Yurtören, *Fertility and related attitudes among two social classes in Ankara*. Unpublished master's thesis, Cornell University, 1965.
3   See, for example, Nermin Abadan, 'Turkey', in *Women in the Modern World*, Raphael Patai (ed.), Free Press of Glencoe, 1967, pp. 82–106; and 'The Place of Turkish Women in Society', *Siyasal Bilgiler Fakültesi Dergisi*, Vol. xxiii, No. 4, 1969, pp. 131–44, Ankara, Hamide Topçuoğlu, *Kadınların Çalışma Saikleri ve Kadın Kazancının Aile Bütçesindeki Rolü*, Ankara, Kültür Matbaası, 1957.
4   Ereğli is a town on the Black Sea coast whose population was 8,815 when the material was collected in 1962. It is a district seat, as well as a secondary centre in the province's most important coal-mining area, and functions as a coal port. Most important of all, however, it provides an exchange flow for the agricultural surplus from the surrounding rural area and for other multipurpose relationships between the villagers and townspeople. The material reported here was obtained by various techniques, including a survey of household heads with 484 questionnaires on various aspects of the town's life by which information on the composition of households was also gathered.

13   Social classes and family in a southern Italian town: Matera*

Tullio Tentori

Instituto Universario Orientale, Naples

Matera is a city in southern Italy and the capital of the province of the same name. Its population is 39,931 people, according to the 1961 Census.[1] The visitor who goes there is urged to see the half-deserted zone called the 'Sassi', a group of caves dug into the rocks of a canyon called the Gravina. Unfortunately, until a few years ago most of the city's population lived in these caves. In 1950 I had the opportunity to carry out anthropological research there for Unra-Casas, now called Ises, as part of a study group organized by Professor F. Friedman. In that year a programme had been initiated to remove at least one group of people from these impossible dwellings, and a project was planned for the construction of the first of a series of villages outside the city to which the peasants who lived in the 'Sassi' could be transferred. I had occasion to speak to many people about the project, and the local bourgeoisie expressed its opposition to it, stating as a pretext the view that the Materan peasant was not used to living in the countryside and preferred to travel two or three hours every morning to reach his fields (sometimes leaving Matera before dawn) rather than abandon the city. To this justification was added another, often more cautiously expressed, that 'great Matera' could not be destroyed in order to build villages around it for the peasants who lived in the 'Sassi'.

To give an idea of the condition of the 'Sassi', we can describe the area as three contiguous zones, Barisano, Caveoso and Casalnuovo, but the latter is not considered one of the 'Sassi' because it is not composed primarily of caves. Until the 1940s these zones were without a sewage system (sewage was thrown into uncovered ditches which descended to the stream below) and without public fountains (much less water in the houses). Electricity began to be installed around that time.

Each cave was inhabited by one family, composed of a married couple and all their unmarried children. A cave was usually only a single room, sometimes subdivided by partitions half its height in order to separate the large bed where

---

* For further information on Materan culture see T. Tentori, *Il sistema di vita della comunità materana*, pp. 99–185 of T. Tentori, *Scritti antropologici*, Ed. Ricerche. Roma 1971.

the parents and the very young children slept from that of the older daughters and again from that of the older sons. If the family owned an ass (which was a necessity for carrying equipment and other objects to the fields) it stayed in the back of the cave, near the parents' or the boys' bed. Chickens lived under the beds, and the pig, if there was one, went where it liked.

Not only the poor lived in the 'Sassi'; there were also a few, very old, houses belonging to *signori* (members of the upper class). These habitations were situated almost at the height of the plain which gave on to the edge of the canyon. Also almost on the border between the brink of the canyon and the plain is the *piazza*, which contains the cathedral and the palace of one of the most important nobles of the past, Duke Malvezzi.

Until some decades ago the community was clearly divided not only by the distinction between residents of the 'Sassi' and those of the 'Plain', but also by the more substantial class distinction which separated the world of the privileged from a subordinate world. This distinction was favoured by, among other factors, a different system of structuring family relations and also a different way of transmitting inheritance. On the one hand these factors prevented the dispersion of the patrimony of the dominant class (and in particular of the especially privileged within its ranks), while on the other they favoured the continual fragmentation or subdivision of family wealth in the subordinate class.

The idea of the polarization of the society into two parts was so deeply rooted that even the Church expressed it in some of its practices, for example, that of using different kinds of church bells to announce the birth or death of a noble (or at any rate a *signore*) and those of a poor man.

In the community's structure, the two categories of people were united only by ties of dependence and servitude.

THE WORLD OF THE *signori*

The subordinate world classified as *signori* all those who could enjoy life, those with whom no *cafone* (country lout) would permit himself to compete or to whose level he would dare to aspire. The members of the leading class, on the other hand, considered themselves superior to the subordinate world by natural and unquestionable birthright. Their way of eating, dressing, marrying, observing juridical and religious norms, and their life style in general, all distinguished them from those of humble birth.

Not all the *signori* had the same degree of prestige and power. There were some who considered themselves so highly placed that they refused to pass their whole lives in Matera among people who, although of the same rank, seemed to them their inferiors. They therefore passed much of the year in other cities, sent their children to study outside Matera, and avoided marrying Materans. Instead other *signori*, although among the economically fortunate, were held in low esteem by the old families, just as some members of these more ancient houses who had suffered economic decline kept up the appearances of prestige.

Moreover, those privileged by virtue of their birth (those born, that is, within the ranks of the leading classes) did not in reality all enjoy autonomy and independence. Only the head of the family had the despotic power to command and make decisions. The other family members were dependent on his will, which was governed by respect for the behavioural norms which operated to defend the family's prestige.

The life of the real *signore*, the landowner, was characterized by the possibility of enjoying idleness, for he had the various categories of shepherds, servants, etc. doing manual work for him. His *fattore*[2] had the task of organizing this work and keeping him free from worry. Indolence, therefore, had the value of a symbol of social superiority. The idea of work, on the other hand, was associated with the values of inferiority, condemnation, burden. Work, stripped of any rationalizing moral conception, was seen as the 'evil' of the subordinate world, as a weight which could neither give satisfaction nor produce wealth.

The agrarian structure of the economic system was so organized that within the great families it favoured the first-born. The other offspring, in contrast, could only rarely and with difficulty find economic autonomy, which they did through professions which made them self-sufficient (careers like the courts, the army, etc.). They usually remained dependent on their father, however, and, on his death, on the first-born, as a result of the custom of placing power in the latter's hands mainly to avoid dividing the land. Although this practice was officially abolished in the first half of the nineteenth century, it in fact continued in both its original forms and in spurious ones for a long time afterward. During the period when I carried out research, there was still a certain tendency to favour the eldest son, or to place the family's greatest hopes on him or on the son who could be relied on if the eldest failed to perform his duty. But the crisis and transformation of an economic system based on land as the only source of income, and the increased possibility of channelling sons into autonomous professions, was already beginning to diminish the importance of the relation between land and family. The *signore* no longer needed to practise primogeniture to protect both his property (once the only source of subsistence for the family) and his children.[3]

In the period in which our research was done, the younger children could get married without difficulty, but earlier, when the practice of primogeniture was at its height, only one of the sons (obviously the eldest) had the good fortune to be able to marry and therefore receive legitimate satisfaction of his sexual needs. In the old community the limitation regarding the other sons had led to an inordinate importance being placed upon sexual activity, both as a result of its exaltation by the privileged son and as a reaction on the part of his less fortunate brothers. The expression of sexuality was, however, subject to various restrictions, both in conversation and behaviour, between people of opposite sex, of different generations, or occupying different roles within the family and social structures. These restrictions required formal more than real respect. The high number of illegitimate births demonstrates this, as does the tendency of those who could not marry to seek a solution to their sexual problems in extra-marital relations. These were sometimes temporary or occasional and sometimes enduring. Relations with women of the subordinate class who were servants in the homes were temporary. Much seduced by the 'young gentlemen' (and not by them alone) were the shepherds' wives, whose husbands had to be absent from home for long periods (*quindicine* = fifteen days, or sometimes even longer) in order to watch over the herds in the mountains or the country-side. Experiences with these women are a theme which often appears in popular poetry; it is also found in the song 'Maria the shepherdess' (still widely sung at the time we carried out our research), which recounts a piquant and dramatic episode that occurred not many years ago.

Romantic factors were excluded from both temporary relations and the more stable ones. Marriage was an event in which the desires of the contracting parties were not supposed to be taken into account, since it was determined by the interest – regarding both economic factors and prestige – which the two families had in effecting a relationship between them. If personal desires did become involved, they had to be subordinated to family interest and thus withdraw.

Among the children who did not marry there were some (usually one in each family) who were destined for an ecclesiastical career. This occurred independently of their real inclinations, and it naturally led to a lack of enthusiasm and to a reserve in embracing the duties inherent in their status. It also led to the rather frequent phenomenon of the *de facto* existence of the 'priest's family', a usage against which even the ecclesiastical authorities were impotent.

Another manifestation of the separation between official and real status was the double family of some landowners: a 'facade' family which accorded with the man's own status and the social conventions, and another family whose existence was concealed (even if not very much). The father respected his duty regarding both families, at least as far as maintenance was concerned.

A vestige which still remains today of the practice of primogeniture is the tendency to marry off one's children (and above all one's daughters) in their order of birth. When we were carrying out our study we encountered the case of a father who turned down the suitor of one of his daughters because he had an older daughter at home whose hand no one had yet asked in marriage. The suitor would either have to wait until this daughter was married off before himself marrying the younger one, or else change his views and ask instead to marry the older girl.

THE SUBORDINATE WORLD

However lacking it may have been in affective and moral cohesion, the family among the upper classes was structured so as to carefully defend the economic and social interests of the traditionally dominant world in Matera. The opposite can be said regarding family structure and the system of property transmission in the Materan subordinate world.

But let us begin by indicating the characteristics of the subordinate classes. Their primary activities, especially in the last century, were agriculture and herding, cornerstones of the economic system of the old community.

There were various categories of peasants. The most fortunate of them were the *vrazzali*. Their descendants, who grew rich after 1870 with the purchase at low prices of the ecclesiastical wealth which had been confiscated by the state, were, along with the descendants of those unscrupulous *fattori* who had become accustomed to carrying out their own interests more than those of their employers, the owners of the few industrial and commercial enterprises existing in the province – at least according to the gossip of today's impoverished aristocrats. Once, their average wealth could be calculated by the possession of four horses and around ten hectares of land.

The mass of the peasants possessed so little land ('a handkerchief of land', to use an expressive local phrase which is also used in other regions of southern Italy) that they had to take on occasional work as well in order to earn a living. There were also many peasants who did not possess even this 'handkerchief of land'. These people were partly dependent on, if not fixed employees of, a given *signore*, and they were hierarchically organized according to their tasks, which went from *garzone* ('boy', general helper) to *massaro di campo* (field bailiff). Others were occasional day labourers who were hired in the mornings in the city's *piazza*, where they traditionally gathered.

The shepherds were usually salaried employees. A career as a shepherd began at adolescence, with a period of apprenticeship as a *uagnone* (boy) to another shepherd. If the apprentice showed the appropriate aptitude he was promoted to *uagnone jranni* (older boy); then at around 18 to *abbiscitatore* (substitute); and finally to shepherd with the task of caring for a herd. The *casiere* (the man whose job it was to make the cheese) was chosen from among the best shepherds. After being a *casiere* one became a *massaro*, responsible for the entire herd and for all the people listed above and the activities they carried out.

The shepherd lived in the countryside and was sent home for 48 hours every two weeks. Only then did he feel sheets beneath him, for the rest of the time he slept fully dressed in straw huts on makeshift pallets.

ATTITUDE TOWARDS THE FAMILY IN THE SUBORDINATE WORLD

Both the peasant and the shepherd were obliged to stay away from their homes for long periods of time. When they returned, they were too tired in the few hours they passed there to preoccupy themselves with its problems, and sought at the most only the enjoyment, so long deferred and repressed, of matrimonial relations. It was therefore really the woman who kept domestic life going, and she found in this function a compensation for her lack of formal authority in public life and the dissatisfaction of her wretched existence as one of the poor.

Moreover the father, although estranged from family life, made irrational and excessive use of his authority, especially over the children, sometimes brutally employing physical violence to punish even small infractions. This could not favour the formation of close affective ties between himself and his offspring. But the children until they reached marriage – an act which conferred on young people of both sexes the status of mature members of the society and gave autonomy to the males especially – were subject to their father's authority, which was total and despotic. For example, even though when they were grown the sons had to address their fathers with the formal *voi* rather than the familiar *tu*, they could not dispose of their own earnings; could not smoke in the father's presence; and could not return home as late in the evenings as they pleased, etc.

Marriage meant freeing oneself of all these subjections in the correct way, the way established and accepted by the community.

The choice of a marriage partner was not, however, made directly by the parties concerned, and, for reasons of interest, this was true of the dominant classes as well. In the subordinate class interest could not play a role, and what mattered instead were factors of a psycho-cultural nature and those which regarded the organization of time and physical obligations.

In fact the youths, ingenuous and brutalized by work, were used to conceiving of love only as the satisfaction of sexual needs (even though within the legitimate bounds of marriage). They were kept far from girls by a barrier of taboos and social prejudices which tended to separate the young of opposite sex and to consider any encounter between them as bearing the risk of falling into a state of sin. The youths were therefore little adapted to sentimental skirmishes. Nor did they have the opportunity to create love stories with girls of their own age, who were always kept under guard by their parents. There was therefore no resistance to letting others resolve their problem for them.

As for the girls, they evidenced their desire to marry in a thousand ways: the care they took in making a trousseau; the scrupulous respect given to the social norms and conventions prescribed for 'good' girls; the observance of the various superstitions which assured them of getting a husband; recourse to marital predictions, etc. Yet they could not arouse the youths' attentions by taking initiatives which would have destroyed their reputations and compromised forever their possibilities of arriving at their coveted goal, marriage. They could only act in secret, that is, by having recourse to magic and *fatture* to tie the youths they cared for to them.

The person who took the initiative to bring about a marriage in this situation was the youth's mother or one of his female relatives. And she carried out her task with great diligence. The tales and gossip that ran through the neighbourhood, or from one neighbourhood to another, were for this woman a precious source of information which permitted her to make an inventory of all the girls who might constitute good matches for her son or brother or relative. Once she had set eyes on the best suited of these girls she took the youth aside for a talk (the *discorse*), telling him that the moment had come for him to get married: '*tu t'aie nzura*' (you must get married). To which the youth responded, '*Acchiateme la zita*' (find me a bride), and accepted the match proposed for him without discussion.

Just as the youth made no opposition, neither did the chosen girl when she was later informed of the match. She was silent *per rispetto* (out of respect), that is, because of that formal obedience which children were expected to have before their parents. Her parents did not even pose themselves the problem of whether or not their daughter liked the future partner. The partner's name may also have had no meaning, since it might be the case that she had never seen the person concerned. The matter was simply that of accepting one's fate. No element of romantic love played a part in determining or favouring a marriage choice. Love, it was thought and said, comes after marriage.

The period of engagement was absent of emotion and of any kind of amorous interest. It usually lasted for more than a year, and during this lapse of time the two young people never had the possibility of being alone together, or of exchanging intimate confidences. They always met in the presence of another member of the family and took walks accompanied by a relative who might even come between them physically to prevent them from being too close to each other. This supervision, for all its attentiveness, was probably useless: although perhaps in a few cases there may have been a tendency to evade it, the majority of young people had neither the intention nor even the idea of contravening a norm so deeply rooted in custom as this one. Failure to observe it would have compromised the girl's reputation. But in any case the very organization of their lives would have rendered any brief escapade impossible for the fiancés.

In the ritual sphere, the beginning of the engagement was marked by the giving of a ring. But before this official act occurred, the *parlamento* (parley), an agreement between representatives of the two families, took place. It was held in the home of a neutral family, that is, a family not closely related to the family of either future spouse. At the *parlamento* the parents of the young people had to agree on the dowry and, with the help of a literate friend, draw up a list of how much each would give. This document had a function similar to that of the *capitoli* (marriage contracts) among the *signori*, and it was called the *carta della zita* (the bride's paper) or *la carta con la quale si azzetta la dote* (the paper with which dowry is agreed on). It ended with lines referring not to economic considerations but to the integrity of the girl. Its final words, which followed the list of objects the girl was expected to bring to the marriage, were in fact *e la zita come si trova* (and the girl as she is at present, or in other words a 'virgin', the assumption being that she was one at the time the *carta* was drawn up).

Both the peasants and the shepherds were anything but well off. And they committed themselves to giving more than they could really afford, for various reasons: the joy and euphoria induced by the happy event; the desire to avoid making a poor showing; and the insistence of the young people themselves on having as much as they could with which to begin their new household.

The *carta* listed the items to be given by both families. The girl's family was expected to provide her personal linen and dresses, sheets, blankets. mattresses and a linen chest. The material needed for these items was until the beginning of the century, woven on household looms, and all the sewing was done at home.

Some days after the *parlamento* (the agreement about the dowry), the *trasuta* (the 'entrance') took place. The future groom paid a visit to his wife-to-be in her own home bearing the engagement gift, a ring which was called the *spoletta*. The old people today remember that when they were young the ring was a simple gold circle with another tiny, rhombus-shaped cross-piece of gold soldered on to it. The *trasuta* was in the nature of a family party, and biscuits and wine were offered to the guests. Not infrequently it was the first occasion on which the fiancés met, and they raised embarrassed and bashful eyes to scrutinize each other, perhaps more curious than anxious about their fate. After the *trasuta* they might meet on certain occasions, for example to take a *passeggiata* on feast days, naturally not alone but, as we have already explained, in the presence of some person who could effectively watch over them.

On the day before the wedding, both sets of relatives met for another important act, that of verifying whether the goods promised and listed in the *carta* were really available to the spouses. Given the tendency to promise more than could readily be given, quarrels often broke out. When these were serious the engagement was broken. This was not a source of great affective regret for the young people involved (although it may have induced some anxiety about the social repercussions of the rupture) because love was not considered as existing in that period and was not expected to come into being until after the marriage.

MATRIMONIAL CHOICE IN RELATION TO SOCIAL CLASS, NEIGHBOURHOOD, AND PERSONAL QUALITIES

The main groups in the hierarchy of social classes at Matera were the following:

1. Nobles (usually called *galantuomini*).
2. Professionals and functionaries.
3. Large landowners.
4. Intermediate class (of little consistency, its ranks being composed of

teachers and merchants, and further down the scale of *fattori*, guards, ushers, etc.).

5. Craftsmen.
6. Peasant small owners and renters.
7. Salaried workers (mainly employed in agricultural work and herding).

The first three groups formed the leading class, also called, as throughout southern Italy, the class of 'gentlemen' (*galantuomini*). Until the nineteenth century, the word *galantuomini* only referred to professionals and landowners, who often intermarried among themselves. Later, as the result of more frequent marriages between both these groups and the nobles, the term came to include the latter as well.

The last three groups listed formed what we may call the subordinate world.

Rigid traditional norms prohibited marriage between members of the dominant and subordinate worlds. And within each of these large categories there were considerable obstacles to marriage between persons with different degrees of prestige. Among the three upper classes, however, economic interest began to undermine this principle.

In the subordinate world, the tendency to avoid marriages between craftsmen and peasants still existed, although less markedly, when we carried out our research (by which time the shepherds had almost completely disappeared). If a craftsman's daughter marries a peasant she has made a bad marriage because she will have to adapt to the fatigue of country life, to which she was unaccustomed in her father's house, and to living with people who carry home the burden of a strenuous life working a poor and barren land with tools which are still today rudimentary. But, most of all, such a marriage is considered degrading from the point of view of prestige.

A peasant also considers marriage with the daughter of a craftsman (or with any girl not of his own life style) an inconvenient arrangement, because the girl is not as useful as a country girl and does not know how to follow her husband into the countryside and help him if she is needed there. A recent episode shows that the resistance on the part of peasants and craftsmen to falling in love with each other still exists. In 1951, at a dance in one of the caves of the 'Sassi', a craftsman, carried away by the music, accidentally stepped on the foot of a girl of peasant origin. In the Materan symbolic language of love, to step on someone's foot when that person is one's own age and of opposite sex signifies a marriage proposal; it was a way of expressing one's interest and asking about the girl's intentions. Thinking of this, the craftsman concerned thought it gallant to say to the girl he had troubled, 'Well, forgive me, it means I'll marry you.' To which the girl promptly replied, 'It's not possible. I'm a peasant's daughter and you're an *artiere* (craftsman).'

Among the lower classes marital choices did not, however, relate only to an individual's position in the hierarchy and to social and professional interests.

They were also local, for there was a tendency to circumscribe the possibilities of marriage to persons living in the same 'Sassi' or in a similar position within it.

This local endogamy was probably partly a reflexion of social endogamy (since within the inhabited area each of the classes tended to live in a given zone). It also reflected the occupations of different ethnic groups living in different zones of the 'Sassi', and was also partly a result of the fact that it was mainly the women who arranged marriages.

Let us consider this last factor (even though with all the obvious limitations). Women in old Matera, whether they belonged to the upper or the lower classes, went out of their houses as little as possible and only when necessary. Widows remained confined to their homes for many years. In the families of the bourgeoisie the servants, up to not so many years ago, must often have included an old woman and a very young girl. The former took care of matters internal to the household but did not leave it, while the latter, because of her youth, could go out without compromising herself and was therefore used when it was necessary to carry out errands outside; it would have been scandalous for a grown woman to go outside to do them. When I carried out my research in 1951 I frequently saw upper-class men make purchases at the market in the morning before going to work or to their offices, in order to avoid having their wives go out. I remember that the widow of a shepherd told me she had never seen 'upper' Matera.

But if they did not walk in the city (or, more correctly in the 'Sassi'), how could the women gather information to suggest or decide on a *zita* (fiancée) for a relative? It is necessary here to recall the structure of the 'Sassi'. These were subdivided into many neighbourhoods (*vicinati*), sometimes clearly physically demarcated by furrows or folds in the earth. The neighbourhood contained around eight or ten families, and within it the women went out freely, gossiping with each other about all the people known to their little world. Naturally the objects of this gossip could not have lived very far away: one neighbourhood, two, three, four . . . and the limits of the well-known world had been reached. A fiancée was therefore usually chosen from within this area. By remaining within an area which gossip could cover, it was possible to know whether the girl was 'serious', in good health (and how many girls in order not to let their illnesses become public knowledge avoided sending for a doctor?), conscientious in her work, and knew how to take care of all those tasks and use all those small techniques that a good wife should know (in the past, spinning; today, sewing a dress, etc.). In this way the choice remained restricted to the area or the zone.

IMPOVERISHMENT AND THE PRESERVATION OF INHERITANCE AMONG THE LOWER AND THE UPPER CLASS

The aspiration of every young person of either sex was to marry, in order to gain freedom from the father's tutelage and, above all, his oppression.

In the subordinate classes, where there was neither the need – nor the possibility – of dividing family wealth among the heirs, all the children could marry, and, as we have already seen, they received their shares of the dowry on their respective wedding day.

It is necessary to keep in mind in this regard that peasant families were large. Interviewees often told me, 'What entertainment do we poor peasants have besides making love? And if children come, what can we do about it? We don't know any way of preventing them from arriving.' But even though the birth-rate was high, not all the children survived. Infant mortality was frequent and not all children born arrived at marriage. But even those who survived were numerous, considering the expenses their fathers had to face for their marriages. By the time they were ready to marry, their father was usually in his period of full working efficiency, but beginning to feel the exhaustion and the burdens of a life of hardship passed working in an unhealthy and unhygienic environment. And after he had met all the expenses of the marriages involved he would himself be in serious difficulties, often heavily in debt and now at an age in which he could not work as hard as he used to. And at this point he began to feel the lack of support from his children.

In fact, given the system of brutal and authoritarian relationships, his children did not feel affection for him. By tradition, moreover, each of them on marriage began his own independent household. And when the old parents, no longer capable of doing productive work, needed their children's help, the latter could not take them into their homes (or, more commonly, 'caves') since they themselves were in economic difficulties both because of the permanent level of poverty on which they lived and because they had to begin to provide for their own offspring.

So old parents were abandoned, and they had no choice but to knock on the door of the old-age home, one of the few institutions which, for all its faults, was nevertheless active when our research was carried out. Sometimes only neighbours gave the old people help. Where there were adopted children[4] they showed greater humanity towards the old than the legitimate ones, if the cases told to me are true. This different behaviour may be explained by the gratitude which adopted children undoubtedly felt towards those who had taken them in, removed them from orphanages, or rescued them from difficult situations.

In conclusion to what we have described in the foregoing pages, it seems evident that

1. the different utilization of the institution of the dowry was
   (a) for the leading classes, whose income came mainly from the ownership of the land, a way of defending the unity of their agricultural enterprises (which included pasturage and animal raising) and of impeding their fragmentation into smaller unproductive farms; and
   (b) for the subordinate classes, a continuous road to impoverishment;

2. the despotic nature of the authority role of the family head
(a) constituted, for the leading classes, an element of cohesion (even if only on a formal level), because it was united with the family head's real power to control the dependent members of the family;
(b) was, for the subordinate classes where it was united with the real power to control only until the children reached marriage, such a fragile element of cohesion that it encouraged the children to leave their father's home as early as possible and to be indifferent to even the most serious problems of their parents.

The contradictions and frustrations produced in the individual because it was impossible for him to satisfy expectations aroused by his culture (the value placed on sexuality, for example) and because of the authoritarian oppression inherent in the hierarchical family and social structures, find a compromise solution. We might call this solution *the use of a double moral standard*. Lip service is paid to the formal standard and a show is made of respecting it in certain situations. The real standard is that which is put into practice even if it sometimes contrasts with the formal one.

Within the Materan family, family cohesion in the affective sphere is generally exalted by the members of the group. But it seems to be a myth which was either created to defend a cultural stability among some social classes, or else which arose within the framework of the intercultural controversy between the North and South in Italy. The situations in which some degree of family cohesion is visible are those where the formal moral standard demands some defence of the family's prestige (for example, defence of the honour of the women) or those which arise out of gratitude (the case of adopted children, who do more than the legitimate ones to help the parents, perhaps because they see the act of their adoption as not only, or not so much, an act of love as a testimony to their own salvation from a condition of social inferiority).

The lack of family cohesion in the Materan community encourages the formation of other institutions, chief among which are
(a) the neighbourhood (which functions as a source of assistance on occasions when the family cannot or will not do so);
(b) the old-age home (which has the function of providing food and shelter for poor old people who have been abandoned by their children).

In short, the 'violence' perpetrated on individuals (inside the family as well as in the sphere of relations between the social classes) has a detrimental effect. It impedes the development of the community (the impossibility of social integration and the lack of incentive for, and use of, the innovative capacities of individuals) and also prevents the existence of an honest moral standard (the double family, the 'priest's family', the abuse of women of the subordinate class, etc.).

NOTES

1   In 1732 the population amounted to only 2,777 people and by 1769 it had grown to about 13,000 (of whom 200 were priests). Between 1881 and 1891 population growth was stemmed by heavy trans-oceanic migration. In 1901 Matera had 17,000 people, in 1931 somewhat more than 20,000, in 1951 30,390, and in 1961 39,931.

2   *Fattore* (literally, 'the man who does', 'the man who acts') was the name given to the man who administered the landowner's holdings.

3   The essence of the practice of primogeniture among the *signori* consisted in transmitting the family lands intact to only one of the sons (to the first-born, the eldest), and only this son had the possibility, as well as the duty, of assuring the family's continuity through his marriage and procreation. The younger sons did not marry and they therefore did not receive 'dowries', relying instead on the older brother for their needs. Among the women, usually only the eldest married and received a dowry; the others either entered convents or remained spinsters at home (and they were jokingly referred to as 'house nuns').

4   It should be noted that adoption was not a very exceptional occurrence. It could be done by vow in various circumstances; a child could be adopted if children of one's own age were lacking or if one of them died at a young age.

14 An account of changes in the rules for transmission of property in Pisticci 1814-1961

J. Davis
University of Kent at Canterbury

INTRODUCTION

All sorts of things get called social change.

> Liholiho...walked over and ate (with the two dowager queens). The commoners... raised a joyful shout, 'The taboos are at an end and the gods are a lie'. Hewahewa...now took a torch and set fire to one of the temples...the structure of Hawaiian religion at once fell in ruins.

> ...I have described two different patterns of conflict – that between the descent groups and that between the council of chiefs and the sacred king. Is it possible to indicate the types of change wrought in the social and political structure by these conflicts? We cannot indicate specific changes, for these depend too heavily on a particular series of historical events, on factors impinging on the kingdoms from without, on the roles played by key individuals...

> Whereas the traditional native diet consisted of roots, tubers, mealy fruits, vegetable flour, fats, oils and vegetables, the present pattern of expenditure for diet in *evolué* households shows a different tendency.

> Social change occurs when, and only when, new norms develop...Some understanding of the emergence and spread of new norms may be gained from the study of new institutions. Voluntary associations are of particular interest in this respect...Young men's associations in many different parts of Africa have shown a consistent pattern of development...

> The concept of structural differentiation can be employed to analyze what is frequently termed 'the marked break in established patterns of social life' in periods of development. Simply defined 'differentiation' is the evolution from a multi-functional role structure to several more specialised structures.

> In Tocqueville's day we were 24 states and 13 million people.

These quotations, all taken from sociological or anthropological works published between 1958 and 1966 serve to show at least one thing: that the identification of what a social change is, is perhaps a rather more difficult task than we commonly imagine. And the reasons for this, I think, are, first, that we now take it as axiomatic that all societies are continuously changing, and that social processes are never entirely repeated: any set of institutionalized actions can be shown to be different in some degree from the set which preceded or followed it, and because it is *different*, changed. And secondly, that we do, on the whole, try to avoid the sort of description and analysis which is represented by the first quotation on my list – which is, I had better add, rather cruelly selected. For, if we abandon the sharp focus 'on a particular series of historical events . . . on the roles played by key individuals', then we become disoriented: we can focus on roots, tubers and mealy fruits; or look for concrete indicators – such as new institutions – of the more nebulous real social changes; or get caught up in the sort of exasperating metaphysical condition where we have to redefine social change as 'the marked break in established patterns of social life' – and then to redefine *that* as structural differentiation, somehow hoping that no one will notice that in doing so we have traced back to Aristotle.

We are none of us simply content with measuring changes in numbers: the increase in political sub-units or in population does indeed represent a different state of affairs, but we use quantitative changes to illustrate qualitative ones: from 13 million to 200 million is a big increase, but it is not a social change unless 'new norms develop'. And we must be careful, too, before we suggest that big increases cause new norms: this could be to do no more than to substitute the key figure for the key individual. The focus is diffuse and diverse because we are conscious that the description of social changes requires a holistic account: changes in diet are consequent on changes in social and economic structure; the appearance of new institutions does indicate the presence of new norms; and so on. We are aware of the connectedness of social things and cannot allow ourselves a sharp focus.

Broadly speaking, we find two sorts of account of social changes. One is the double equilibrium account: state of affairs x is compared and contrasted with state of affairs y, say a hundred years later. In the best possible case, state of affairs y is known thoroughly, while good records exist for state of affairs x. But even so equilibrium x is an omnium gatherum, with information collected from a period extending sometimes as much as 50 years on either side of the hypothetical year of equilibrium. The gap $x-y$ is then filled in with events, personalities, broad trends of conflict, climacterics of consensus, guess work, and subtle reinterpretations – all of which somehow, ineluctably, produce equilibrium y. The other type of account is the eyewitness account. Here there is hard information: 'The first meeting was convened to consider the case of a driver who jumped off his tractor to help someone without first putting on the brakes . . .' but usually a very short time perspective: the broad changes are lost from sight; and – though not in the book from which that passage is cited – the sociology comes in by tying the events described to big labels – structural differentiation, evolution from a multi-functional role structure, and so on – often with ludicrous results.

THE TRANSMISSION OF PROPERTY IN 1814 AND 1961

The reason for telling you this, when you know it better than I, is that this paper incorporates an attempt to specify its procedures, as well as to provide an account of social changes. It seems to me that it is worth while to be explicit about procedures. While I do not think I have done anything which is unusual in sociological accounts of social change, I have, I hope, been able to discuss criticism of the more telling weaknesses common enough in this sort of account of social change by specifying procedures.

In 1814 the Pisticci land tax register (Cadaster) recorded the distribution of land as in Table 1. The rest of the land (47 per cent) was municipal and state

TABLE 1

	Landowners (%)	Amount of land (%)
Nobility	0.8	34.7
Magnates	6.4	5.4
Artisans	7.7	0.5
Other men	71.6	7.6
Women: spinsters and wives	2.9	0.4
widows	10.0	0.6
Heirs of 80 dead people	?	3.8
	99.4[a]	53.0

[a] Total not 100 due to rounding.

demesne, or belonged to the churches of Pisticci. The capitation fee for winter pasturage on this land was the municipality's chief source of revenue; the land was also subject to common rights to collect wood and wild fruits. House-ownership – and then as now Pisticci had a concentrated settlement pattern – was distributed as in Table 2. This pattern of distribution of taxable rights in

TABLE 2

Owners	Houses (%)
Men	77
Women: married, spinsters	7
widows	13
Heirs of 27 dead people	2
	99

fixed property is the chief evidence for saying that these rights were transmitted in the male line; there is other evidence which suggests that

    (i) all sons received such rights;
    (ii) they received them at the death of their father;
    (iii) daughters got parapherns and a cash dowry if they were rich.

The evidence for these last three points is a number of odd, scattered documents dating from between 1650 and 1800, and some statements in secondary sources. So far as point three is concerned, there is no evidence about Pisticci at all: it is guesswork based on evidence from other towns and supported by the figures from the Cadaster. It is worth making one other remark about the nature of the evidence: the odd documents are precise and explicit about what different people did at different times. From these we extrapolate to a whole population. The figures from the Cadaster are 'real', in the sense that they apply to a population of landowners who pay taxes on the basis of them.[1]

The argumentative procedure is different from the one based on documentary evidence (an extrapolation to the whole population of 1814 of data which relates to a few individuals widely scattered in space and time). We ask of the Cadaster – what system of transmission of property could produce such results? And the answer is got by considering the possible systems of property transmission, and what their consequences might be: one which could produce these results is the right one. Records do not generally provide us with accounts of rules of behaviour and we have to reconstruct as best we can by a variety of methods. I think it is true that in Pisticci in 1814 they transmitted fixed property to sons (and failing them to daughters) at the father's death, while daughters got a marriage endowment in movables. But '1814' is a sociological construct – derived in a variety of ways from a variety of disparate sources. We are no longer dealing with reality, but with a notional state of affairs which is acceptable in terms of our culture. Indeed it is absolutely necessary to perform operations of this sort if we are to avoid the trivialities of dealing with current developments – the horrors of translating 'Osmin has sent his children to school this year' into 'Osmin's multifunctional role structure . . .' etc.

The '1961' equilibrium model is constructed in a slightly different way: again on the basis of the Cadaster, which was up-to-date for that year, but also on the basis of personal observation in the years 1964–6. But since the Cadaster, by 1961, was very large – about 35 volumes of 600 pages each, I had to take a sample. And since I wanted participantly to observe my sample, as well as to collect public record data about it, I chose an area rather than a statistically random sample of individuals. The people who provide the data for '1961' are therefore selected because they had rights to land in an area of manageable size (420 hectares) which I thought – rightly, I think, – was typical of other peasant-farmed areas of Pisticci. But I wanted to relate these figures and notes to the all-Pisticci distribution of land. The latest set of figures of the sort required for this operation were collected in 1946. So, '1961' (transmission of property) is also a construct which is different from other ethnographic presents – of say, pre-colonial African communities – only in that the public records are rather more precise and detailed. It is made up from:

(i) figures for the universe, collected in 1946, with adjustments made for major changes such as agrarian reform;
(ii) figures for the sample area, true of 1961;
(iii) notes taken of observations made in 1964–6.

The evidence is quite unequivocal. The rules for families with land and houses are stated as follows:

Parents ought to give land to their children (sons and daughters) as they marry, and ought to retain only a small portion at death;

Parents ought to give a house to their daughters as they marry; they can give a house to a son if they have no daughters;

Parents should provide daughters with parapherns and a cash sum when they marry.

In the first two cases parents may retain a life interest.

Cadaster figures of land ownership – for the sample area only – show the outcome of these rules:

(i) Women are 53 per cent of the people with taxable rights (52 per cent of the population of Pisticci as a whole are women).

(ii) 39 per cent of the land was acquired by the present owners from their parents at their marriage; 23 per cent was acquired from their parents, or close kin in some cases, by inheritance; (and 21 per cent was bought; 17 per cent is 'other' and 'unknown').

House ownership is rather more problematical It is recorded in a different register (*catasto urbano*) to which I had no access. My estimate is that between 60 and 75 per cent of houses are owned by women; that a further 10 per cent are owned by spouses jointly; and that about 75 per cent are acquired from parents at marriage. This is based on an examination of marriage contracts for 1960–2; enquiries made of occupants of houses; and census data on titles to occupancy (22 per cent of all houses are rented; but not all houses are occupied; moreover houses in the country 'go with the land' and can go to sons. So the situation is very complex).

We can summarize all this by saying that in '1814' Pisticcesi had partible inheritance of all fixed property by sons; and in '1961' they had bilateral transmission of land at children's marriage; and transmission of town-houses to daughters at their marriage. In both cases, daughters' marriages are further endowed. In '1961', nevertheless, some land and some town-houses were inherited.

ELEMENTS OF CONTEXT

That is the social change I wish to give an account of. It is as clear-cut and simple as one could wish, even though the procedures for establishing that it has occurred are less simple than they appear to be at first sight. Part of the reason is exactly that one wants to make the two states of affairs as clear and precise as possible and this requires a variety of sorts of information from a variety of sources. We must now try to say what can legitimately be said by way of 'explanation'. It should be noted that there is no instant we can point to and say –

that is the decision, *that* is the moment. We might then analyse the moment, identify the context of the decision and show how it was brought about by social forces, or whatever: we would produce a sociological interpretation of an historical event. But we have no event; we can assert that lots of people have made choices and decisions – we can see the consequences, but we cannot know anything about them in the way that we can know something about the decisions to draw up the clauses of Magna Carta, for example. We have to look, therefore, for changes in the context in which decisions were made and to assert that these made it possible, or easier, to choose certain courses of action which were formerly closed or difficult. Insofar as such an account is explanatory at all, it asserts connectednesses between things and that changes in one are met with changes in others. It makes no attempt to assert causal primacy of one set of changes over another. It is distinct from 'sociological interpretations of history' because it has no precise time referent, no event.

STRAIGHT EXOGENY

The Napoleonic code was introduced in the Kingdom of the Two Sicilies in 1799 and the Piedmontese civil code was imposed from 1861. Since these enjoin bilateral partible inheritance, there is no need for further explanation: Pisticcesi changed their inheritance system because they were told to. Or so an explanation could go. But we must discard this for various reasons. First, Frederick II of Hohenstaufen's codification of South Italian law, the *Liber Augustalis* of 1231, enjoined inheritance *absque sexus discretione*: Pisticcesi *could* have practised bilateral partible inheritance for nearly 600 years before 1814, but they did not. Item: the purely historical explanation does not account for the new distinction between town and country property, and between daughters and sons. Item: it does not account for the new practice of transmitting property at the marriages of next generation rather than at the deaths of the members of the owning generation. In other words, because we are interested in the choices people make, and can show that they could have made the choice earlier, but did not; and can show that when they do make the choice they tack on other choices, then we are forced to conclude that a purely exogenous explanation of this sort is not sufficient. Certainly, the enforcement of a legal code was important: not the laws themselves, but the controls which secured conformity to them. The growth of government control is, however, a general phenomenon and has other consequences.

CHANGES IN THE DISTRIBUTION OF PROPERTY

For example, throughout the years 1800–1951 a series of laws and administrative regulations ordered the redistribution of demesne land (not only in Pisticci). Roughly speaking, at twenty-year intervals areas of demesne between 750 and

1,500 hectares were redistributed to landless farm labourers: in 1814 there were 11,300 hectares of demesne; by 1950 there was a negligible amount left. Some of the land was usurped, some of it was bought, but most of it went to the landless labourers. This had two consequences for the statistics of distribution of property. First, the proportion of property owners in the town is far higher in 1961 (75 per cent of the active population) than in 1814 (4–6 per cent of the active population). And secondly, because the demesne was doled out in small parcels of about 1.2 hectares, the number of small holdings is much higher – though some of the really big estates of 1814 were broken up and swelled the middle to large holdings of the local *borghesia rurale*. We see the results in Table 3. The figures in Table 3 do not explain anything – indeed, the processes

TABLE 3

Size of property (hectares)	1814			1946		
	Properties		Land[a]	Properties		Land
	N	%	%	N	%	%
	(a)	(b)	(c)	(d)	(e)	(f)
0 – 0.50				1,528	37	1
0.50 – 2	615	91	7.3	1,508	36	8
2 – 5				623	15	9
5 – 10				187	5[b]	5
10 – 100	48	7	9.2	180	5	23
100 – 200	4		5.1	17		11
200 – 500	3	2	8.2	9	1	13
500 – 1,000	3		14.0	4		14
1,000 + +	3		56.2	2		16
	676	100	100	4,058	99	100

[a] Excludes all public property – and the 100% here is therefore about half the 100% of column f.
[b] This category was significantly enlarged in 1951 by some 449 new properties created from land expropriated from the bigger properties. The land expropriated was 9% of all Pisticci land, i.e. 12% of all land held in properties of more than 100 ha.

which gave rise to the changes they represent do themselves require painstaking analysis. In brief summary we can put the figures under the heading 'effects of increasing government intervention' – though this does some violence to the facts. They are important in this argument because they are connected with the growth of population in Pisticci.

GROWTH OF POPULATION

In 1814 the population was between 4,000 and 6,000; in 1861 it was 6,597; in 1961 14,847. The increase, taking 1861 as the base year, is 100–225. The significance of this is that it is unusually high for the region, Basilicata, of which Pisticci is a part. There, the increase is 100–124; in South Italy as a whole the increase is 100–185. Pisticci's population in fact behaves like that of the neighbouring Puglia. Failing better information than we have from historical demographers the assumption must be that rates of natural increment did not show wide variation from one region to another, nor, within regions, from one town to another. Slight variations, undoubtedly; but not enough to account for Pisticci's increase being five times greater than Basilicata's. So we must look to other causes: and of these, the available evidence strongly suggests that the failure of Pisticcesi and Pugliesi to emigrate is the main cause. The estimable I. G. MacDonald (1963) has produced figures for Puglia which show that there is an inverse correlation between emigration rates and a wide distribution of property rights. In other words, where land is widely distributed people emigrate less than where it is narrowly distributed. The redistribution of Pisticci's communal demesne is of patent relevance. To this we should add that demesne lands were distributed with a tenure in emphyteusis which, among other clauses, prohibited any conveyance of the rights *inter vivos* for a period of twenty years after the initial grant. Therefore the redistribution not only created a new category of smallholders, but effectively tied its personnel to the soil: it was difficult for a man to sell up and go away. We can thus see a cause–effect relation between the changes in the distribution of land and population growth between 1800 and 1960: because of the redistributions, causes which operated elsewhere did not operate in Pisticci.

INTEGRATION INTO A NATIONAL SOCIETY

This is a very broad class of changes, which includes the closer control of inheritance and the redistributions of demesnes. More particularly I wish to refer here to the diversification of the local economy and to the growth of white-collar jobs as the result of more intensive administration, with consequent opportunities for social mobility.

Diversification of the local economy

In 1814, we may be sure, more than 95 per cent of the active population derived its main income from the land: the pharmacists and the police appear not to have been local men, and hence to have had no land in Pisticci; but the lawyers, doctors and priests were normally landowners. Artisans, then as now, tended to work part-time at their trades, and so did shopkeepers, but both these are categories with very small populations. The 1961 distribution of the working population, by principal source of income is shown in Table 4. There are two important points to make about the figures in Table 4. The first is the familiar one that they refer to principal sources of income: the majority of Pisticcesi have more than one source. They are part-time farmers and part-time lawyers; or they work as clerks and rent their land; or they work their own land and also other people's land for a wage, and so on. Most enterprises are peasant-like: fragmented, under-capitalized, seasonal. If Pisticcesi are not specialists they nonetheless have a diversified economy and the reason for this is partly that land-holdings tend to be too small and too scattered to provide a living; also that the type of non-agricultural enterprises which has been introduced is not sufficiently secure to permit specialization, nor sufficiently demanding of the

TABLE 4

Sector		N	%
Agriculture		3,724	58
Industry:			
Artisans	649		
Builders	1,096		
Other	5		
		1,750	27
Services:			
Commerce	254		
Transport and			
Communication	203		
Banking and Insurance	23		
Public Admin.	283		
Other	207		
		970	15
	Total	6,444	100

Source: ISTAT (1964).

labour force to force it upon them. Secondly, the contrast between the number of people with land rights (nearly 9,000) and the number of people with incomes principally from the land – about 3,700, some of whom are, of course, landless labourers – indicates the extent to which the use of land rights may be symbolic rather than economic. Particularly in the case of the very smallest holdings (1,528 of less than half a hectare), and those which, though bigger, are held under multiple ownership – of, say, more than five persons – we seem to be in the presence of symbolic action, rather than the manipulation of economic resources. Symptomatic of this is the tendency to create joint holdings to cover each of the close kinship relations a man may have; or the practice whereby a grandparent gives some land directly, by-passing the intervening generation, to each of the grandchildren who bears his or her forename. These are cases that are quite common, and in which the transfer of land rights *inter vivos* has important, if not dominant, symbolic meanings. It is obvious, I think, that symbolic meanings are a luxury permitted by the relative unimportance of the economic value of the land in some sections of the population and that this is a consequence of the particular way in which the economy has become differentiated in the last century (i.e. by the creation of undemanding jobs at all levels of the occupational hierarchies) and of the social mobility which has resulted from the creation of new jobs in the middle ranges.

Social mobility

The white-collar jobs are almost all new. In 1814 there were shopkeepers, some local administrators, some professionals, but the careful policing, administration and schooling of the population is a phenomenon mostly of the last 70 years. New welfare measures – health and hygiene, poor relief, labour exchanges, agrarian reform – have all required new personnel. The elementary schools alone have more than 60 established and unestablished teachers now, against about ten in 1920. And so on. In 1961 the census records 401 people as belonging to the category of 'entrepreneurs, professional workers, executive and administrative grades and clerks', but it should be recognized that most of the people employed in the service sector, and even some of the building labourers, have positions of high prestige in Pisticcesi eyes. We may say, therefore, that there are approximately 1,000 occupational positions of high prestige in the town; and we should not forget that some Pisticcesi are employed in white-collar jobs in the provincial capital or in Rome or in Bari. We might guess, without too much danger of wild inaccuracy, that there were at most 100 such positions in 1814 – but probably far less than that.

This increase has had two immediate consequences. First, there is now a white-collar category of some importance, and relatively accessible to the peasantry: education is available to all, and some of it is free, while the white-collar workers are not yet a hereditary group. Secondly, the mobility of these families makes land available, at rent, for sharecropping, or for labouring, to people who otherwise do not have enough. It is rarely sold, for it has symbolic value to non-cultivating owners. Finally, it is worth noting that many of these new recruits to the ranks of the *Schreibmachtig* in '1961' were descendants of people who received land during the redistributions of demesne. This information is incomplete and rather piecemeal, but 15 of the 42 established elementary schoolteachers had ex-demesne land in emphyteusis; 5 or 6 out of 27 shopkeepers on the main street; one out of three Cadaster clerks; 2 out of 5 legal Registry clerks; one out of 4 priests, and 2 out of seven paid political officers. This averages out at about 1 in 3, and is probably an underestimate.

In this section I have discussed the diversification of the local economy, which has provided new sorts of economic opportunity at all levels of activity, and the social mobility which results from the increase in jobs in the middle levels. These changes can be related to changes in social rules rather more closely than the changes discussed in the previous two sections. In particular, for present purposes, I would draw attention to the way in which land is used symbolically – a new phenomenon so far as one can tell, but certainly new in the degree to which it occurs and in the consequent uneconomic fragmentation. This is made possible by the redistribution, and by the type of undemanding diversification of the local economy.

I see the other main consequences for rules of behaviour as belonging to the area of social stratification, which deserves a special section to itself.

CHANGES IN SOCIAL STRATIFICATION

One reason this deserves a special section is that the argument requires a certain amount of uninhibited speculation about '1814'. We can argue backwards from '1961' when talking about social mobility, because we have data, and because we can show that the present state of fragmentation of land is the consequence of processes which we know to have been created during our period. But this is more difficult when discussing changes in the criteria for ranking people.

What I *want* to argue here is – briefly – that in the last century and a half the criteria for ranking people have become increasingly market-derived; and that the type of market which has been introduced into Pisticci has ensured that relations between people who are ranked equal or nearly equal are competitive rather than solidary. This argument is supported by sub-arguments of varying type, plausibility, and empirical basis. Because they are of diverse kinds it may aid assessment if I list them separately.

(a) We would expect a local community which has been increasingly integrated into a national society to adopt – gradually – universalistic market criteria of evaluation of goods, persons and activities. In particular, we would expect power and wealth not only to be correlated (for they are that in all societies) but their use to be liberated from non-legal social controls – for the use of power and wealth to be increasingly independent of other activities. Pisticci in '1961' was – as I have argued elsewhere (for example, in 1969 (a)) – by no means entirely market-integrated, but the cash evaluation of persons and actions was a fairly common phenomenon. This type of argument is standard in sociological accounts of social development: societies with widening horizons tend to adopt criteria of evaluation which are independent of the local culture. Its plausibility is based on the fact that it does enable us to describe and communicate fairly accurately some of the patterns of change commonly met with in developing societies. Its empirical base is that in Pisticci in '1961' market-evaluations were fairly common and that development ('increasing integration with the national society') has occurred since 1814: therefore, I *assume* that market evaluations were less common in '1814'. There is no direct evidence for '1814'.

(b)(i) A similar argument can be applied to marriage: no direct evidence is available for '1814', but we know that homogamy is now sought after, and achieved, in most matchmaking: homogamy being defined as equality of spouses in health, wealth and morality. The argument, then, is that wealth has become an increasingly important consideration in the assessment of homogeneity. It can be re-phrased as: since 1814 marriage has ceased to be a significant channel of social mobility: people now marry equals; social mobility is now achieved by marketing operations (renting, sharecropping land, marketing the produce and converting the proceeds to educational qualifications for a member of the family, or to savings or capital to support a new enterprise). This argument is a special application of (a).

(ii) It is possible, on demographic grounds, that a population of 500 peasant landowners of various ages, with their wives and children, could not have been self-reproducing. If this were the case, some marriages must necessarily have been hypergamous or hypogamous. This is a neat argument; but not enough is known about the demographic characteristics of the population to make it more certain than speculative.

(c) A further consequence for relations within socio-economic categories is that these become more competitive: people are tied to the land; their own resources are limited and inadequate; the population increases: *ergo*, the competition for supplementary resources becomes more acute, and market evaluation of goods and services does not get transposed into market struggles over life-chances, or into class-consciousness; rather, the struggle for resources is conducted with patrons and against rival clients.

SETTLEMENT AND AGRICULTURE

I have argued elsewhere (Davis 1969a, 1969b) that the settlement pattern and the system of transmission of property at marriage are crucially related. It is because the farmers do not live on the land but in a concentrated settlement that they are generally able to retire before they die, at about 60–65 years old, and to endow their children's marriages with fragments of their patrimony. When Pisticci's population consisted mostly of farm labourers, before the redistributions, they lived in a concentrated settlement; when they became part-time farmers with property rights it was therefore possible for them to transfer property at marriage. But why should it be necessary? Why should they choose to do this? We can suggest possible constraints in the lack of capital to build farm houses and, more negatively, in the type of extensive agriculture which did not require people to live on the land. Again, the association of inadequate farm incomes and the need to diversify the household economy by supplementing farm incomes with money from other sources. And I argue that there are positive advantages to be gained in the competition for these resources if the competitors live in town rather than in the country. But once again, the significant root cause, as I see it, is the imbalance in the development of the local economy: a wide distribution of land and a scarcity of capital, and a diversification of the economy which did not create jobs requiring specialization.

CONCLUSIONS

We started out with a straightforward double equilibrium problem: the '1814' partible inheritance by sons at their father's death is replaced by the '1961' distinction between town and country property, with sons excluded from town property and most property transmitted at marriages. What I have tried to do is to show how the institutional framework of Pisticci society changed, permitting people to choose to do things which they had not formerly chosen to do. The emphasis has been on those changes which seem, on the basis of some sort of sociological common sense, to be closely relevant. Very broadly speaking, these are changes in the political and economic (rather than legal or religious or domestic) spheres. This is partly because we have more information about these, but mostly because we all know that the family is a dominant institution in Pisticci as in other Mediterranean peasant communities. For this reason – its place in a 'multi-functional role structure', its lack of specialization – we expect it to be precisely sensitive to political and economic changes. So we look at redistributions, population growth, changes in social stratification and modes of political representation. The redistributions increased the number of small landowners; they caused (by inhibiting emigration) a population growth which was so great that, even with the conversion of pasture to arable, pressure on resources continued to increase. Because there was no capital to invest in agricultural improvement there was no incentive to move on to the land: there were, indeed, positive inducements to stay in town, because access to supplementary resources was easier there. The wider distribution of land was not, therefore, accompanied by any change in the settlement pattern, and I suggest that the absence of farmhouses is one feature which permits farmers to divide their land progressively among their children as they marry. The administrative and legal regulations of redistribution are one manifestation of the trend to closer government control: the tougher enforcement of the laws of inheritance, which enjoin a bilateral partible system (but not division at marriage, nor the town property – country property distinction), is another probable manifestation. The special problems created by these changes – the inadequacy of holdings, the increasing population – were in part met and countered by the diversification of the local economy and the increase in white-collar jobs in the town. But this was a bastard modernization. It did not demand specialization; it did not force changes in the agricultural system; it permitted the economically irrational fragmentation of property rights, and the symbolic use of conveyances.

The '1814' population was relatively small; it consisted mostly of labourers – some journeymen, some permanent ones – foremen, muleteers, *salariati fissi*, but very few owner-cultivators. As the population increased and land was distributed, the nature of the competition between the sellers of labour changed. Whereas formerly – we may guess, with an acceptable degree of plausibility – it was a competition for basic incomes in which a man who failed could clear out, it became a competition for supplementary incomes: the basic income was assured and it was more difficult to clear out. As pressure on resources increased (because the population increased), the need for supplements increased and success in the competition became more important. Moreover, increasing government intervention created the ends of social mobility – white-collar jobs – and the means to be socially mobile: education and the market in land and produce. It is important, but also difficult, to be clear about the nature of this competition. The arena is the market in labour, in land (tenancies, share-cropping, of land made available, among other things, because some families were socially mobile) and in produce (goods are sold and converted into educa-tion, houses, more land, a shop, a workshop, or savings to support a new part-time enterprise). But the market is not one which can be described without reference to social, moral, controls. It is, we may plausibly guess, increasingly subject to national market forces; but even in '1961' we cannot explain varia-tions in prices to individuals, or the choice of labourers, or the differences between the market for grain and olives and the market in, say, oranges and peaches, without reference to the local idioms of moral controls and the characteristics of ranking in terms of honour (Davis 1969(b)).

It is necessary to mention non-economic factors because the varying imperfections of the different markets cannot be discounted: they have to be accounted for in terms of the moral evaluations which operators make of each other. And it is necessary in this argument because I want to suggest that as success or failure in the economic competition becomes more crucial, so the reputation and moral evaluation of families have greater consequences. In other words I want to suggest that, as what I have called bastard modernization supplants bastard feudalism, the consequences of having more or less honour, and of family reputation, become more widespread and take in areas of activity which did not exist in '1814' but which were introduced between then and '1961'.

As the consequences of family reputation extend into new spheres of activity, and as it becomes an important instrument in the political and economic struggle to get access to more varied resources, so too, I think, there are changes in the ways in which new families are created, i.e. in the criteria of mate selection and in the material endowment of the spouses. For example, we can suggest that the contemporary feature of Pisticci marriage strategy, that people try to cast as wide a net of affinal relations as possible, is a fairly recent one: this is because mobility is increasingly achieved in the market – with all its bastard features – rather than by marrying land, and the possibilities of finding oneself allied to an up-and-coming family are thus greater. Another example is the en-dowment of marriages at the time of marriage which assures the basic economic viability of the family: the husband's ability to support his wife, to keep her without exploiting her labour on the land is an important component of their joint honour, which has in turn important consequences for his ability to get access to other supplementary resources which he needs to maintain a growing family. Of course, the endowment of a marriage by both sets of parents does not increase the total endowment of the new family, for, in a family with an equal number of sons and daughters, the admission of daughters' rights to the country patrimony merely halves the size of the marriage portions; and if each child then marries homogamously the endowment is the same as it would have been had sons alone received an endowment – and that would have been in one piece.

Both bilaterality and transmission at marriage seem to be associated with homogamy (wealth) of marriage partners. Bilateral transmission and homo-gamy seem to lead 'naturally' to marriage endowments rather than to inherit-ance: in marriage negotiations the precise quantities and qualities of goods contributed by one set of parents can be matched against the goods contributed by the other. Nor do we, perhaps, see much difficulty in assuming that, if all children have a right to property at the time of their marriage then the outcome of negotiations will tend to ensure equal contributions from each set of parents. Similarly, if children are to be equally endowed at marriage, and property is as widely diffused as it is in Pisticci, it could seem 'natural' to us that a principle of bilaterality is recognized. What I am saying is that there is a complex inter-dependence between these three things, which is difficult to describe and even more difficult to analyse because it seems so 'natural', so 'right' and appro-priate.

It is, I have suggested, associated with the increasing importance of family honour during the nineteenth century, as supplementary resources become more numerous and more necessary; it is also associated with a closer enforcement of the law, which I suggest should be seen in the context of a gen-eral trend towards closer integration into the national society; with a wider distribution of property, and with the increased political and economic import-ance of women's behaviour as a component of family honour. And by this I mean that, ultimately, I am inclined to see the endowment of marriages by brides' parents as a recognition of the importance of women in Pisticci society.

Why should women get houses? This again requires us to refer to the political manipulations necessary to get a living. Because the economy is unbalanced, and because the struggle to improve life chances is conducted not only in market terms but also in terms of honour, and because the honour of a man requires that his womenfolk should live under permanent public scrutiny, we can see that women should live in town and not in the country. So far so good: however, this does not explain why women should get the houses, and I must confess that I am at a loss to see why they should, unless we are prepared to plunge into a series of symbolic analyses in which Country is symbolically associated with uncouth masculinity, agriculture, absence of politics, poverty, immorality and lasciviousness, and Town is associated with the opposites of these notions. I have, in fact, described these associations elsewhere (1969(a)), and there I was able to assert that Town has as one of its component notions the fact that most houses are owned by women. But it would be quite another sort of argument to suggest that, in the nineteenth century, and *because* there was this series of consonant notions associated with Town, people decided to give houses to daughters. The series Town–Country do in fact have the simplicity and 'naturalness' of Left–Right series; but it would be difficult, one might think, to assert that the 'naturalness' has any causative power. It is worth pointing out that Pisticci is uncommon in this respect: none of the neighbouring towns endows women with houses and it is not common elsewhere in South Italy.

I would like to end this paper by making some general points about the study of social change. This account of the changes in rules for the transmission of property tackles an unmistakably anthropological problem. It is typically an anthropological area of interest: land tenure, inheritance, marriage. It is problematic, in that it requires an explanation, or something like one, from us. And it is anthropologically problematic because we are not satisfied with a simple historical explanation ('the law was enforced'), but have to go searching for the changes in connected institutions and activities. This account has tried to show that there are such changes in land distribution, population, ranking and the local economy which are consistent with the changes in property transmission on which the account is focused. At some points I have been able to say that one change was caused by another (redistributions and population growth *causes* increased pressure on resources). At others I have said that some changes permit others (bastard modernization permits diversification without specialization), while so far as bilaterality, homogamy (wealth) and transmission at marriage are concerned, I have simply said that these seem indissolubly interdependent, even though we know that they are not necessarily and universally associated. And I have appealed to general principles (when horizons are broadened, people adopt evaluative criteria which are independent of local cultures), which I take to be based on a sort of basic, pragmatic sociologically common-sensical generalization. This is one dimension of the eclecticism to which we are forced when we try to give a contextual account of social change.

Another dimension is the way in which I derive the accounts of '1814' and '1961'. This is a mixture of historical documents, guesswork, observation and enquiry. Both '1814' and '1961' are amalgams of information gathered from different years and, for '1814', from different communities. This procedure seems to me to be both legitimate (i.e. it is frequently done by anthropologists) and necessary: if we reject the key individuals/roles/legal enactments approach, we do this because we prefer to try to get some notion of changes occurring across a broad front of social institutions; some priority-less account of changes which neither requires us nor permits us to assert that on such and such a day such and such a change was caused by some specific event. But this desire to produce what I have called a contextual account of social change does require us to reconstruct '1814' and '1961'. It also requires us to speculate about possible connexions and possible arguments, and to use our anthropologically-disciplined intelligences to discriminate between the possible and the impossible or, as it may be, the acceptable and the unacceptable.

It is worth making explicit what sort of account of social change this is not. It is not historical. Not only are there no 'causes'; not only are the main foci of attention things which historians do not usually concern themselves with; but there is also no essential time-referent. '1814' and '1961' are artificial. The intervening period is deliberately timeless and it is possible to be rather more precise about the sequence of events than I have been.

The resulting account aspires to be a model in two ways. The first is as a type of account of social change: this is how I think we ought to write about social changes. Others, more fortunate in their data, may be able to be more accurate and less speculative about their two states of equilibrium, and they may be able to assert necessity more often than I have. But we ought, I think, to try to give a contextual account.

The second is as an account of the specific changes in rules for the transmission of property. That is to say, I think it is correct to take as of primary relevance changes in population, in property distribution, in the place of the family within the larger society, and in the place of the local community within the national society.

NOTE

1 It is sometimes said that Cadasters are unreliable guides to 'what really goes on'. It is, of course, true that very often there is a difference between owner and cultivator – and the degree to which the property rights are distinct from cultivation rights in any community is a matter of great interest, worthy of careful study; but it would be wrong to suggest that the Cadasters are therefore in some sense 'unreal': they record liabilities to pay tax, which are real enough. Moreover, people take care to register changes in these liabilities – they manipulate them, give them away, divide them and so on. In an agricultural community with a property suffrage the liability to land tax is a qualification for voting; just as – in more recent times – the absence of liability is a qualification for receiving land, work and subsidies from welfare and development agencies. So, whether or not taxed rights correspond to cultivation rights, what the Cadaster states is the case is real in its consequences, and we need not be afraid to base arguments on it.

REFERENCES

Davis, J. 1969a. 'Town and Country.' *Anthropological Quarterly*, Vol. 42, No. 3, pp. 171–85.
   1969b. 'Honour and Politics in Pisticci'. *Proceedings of the Royal Anthropological Institute*, pp. 69–81.
ISTAT. 1969. *X Censimento generale della popolazione, 1961*, Vol. 3, Fasc. 77. Rome (ISTAT).
Macdonald, J. S. 1963. 'Agricultural organization, migration and labour militancy in rural Italy.' *Economic History Review*, second series, Vol. XVI, pp. 61–75.

15　The ethics of inheritance

Carmelo Lisón-Tolosana

Universidad Complutense, Madrid

The following lines refer to Galicia, a region of 29,434 square km in the extreme northwest of Spain. Culturally the region shows a considerable degree of homogeneity. The people all speak the same dialect, practise identical or similar rites and draw from a common substratum of ideas, beliefs and values. Moreover, they all believe that they are part of a group who differ from the rest of the Spanish. Nonetheless, my aim in this paper is to emphasize certain local differences. My line of argument is, in fact, very simple; I shall underline the relations between ways of inheritance, types of family and forms of morality. I would like to show how certain forms of inheritance correspond to certain forms of family and morals which are not only different but opposed. From another standpoint this paper could well be titled the ecological background of morality. It should be borne in mind, of course, that the consequences of particular types of inheritance and family are very far-reaching, and if one is to understand not only the social structure but also the special history of the region itself, they must be taken into consideration. However, as I have dealt with this elsewhere I shall limit myself now to the analysis of the topic indicated.

Firstly, inheritance. In the mountainous zones of the region the general rule is, with some exceptions, to 'marry at home' the eldest male child whether or not he is the first-born, or, failing him, one of the other male children. A daughter is only 'married at home' when she has no brothers. In this area to 'marry at home' means to inherit two-thirds of the total estate of the parents, while receiving an equal share of the remaining third, which is divided among all the brothers and sisters. Note that the heir becomes immediately the legal owner of the property while the parents keep its usufruct during their lifetime. In return the heir and his wife and children must live in the same house with his parents, looking after them and attending to their every need. He must work his parents' lands under their direction and without remuneration, and must pro-vide at his own expense the funeral obsequies that they request. The surviving parent enjoys the usufruct of the entire estate during the remainder of his or her lifetime. The heir must allow his unmarried, or widowed-and-childless brothers and sisters who have not received their portion of the inheritance to live under the paternal roof with free bed and board. In return for their unpaid work on the family farm these brothers and sisters must be fed and clothed. Likewise, the parents feed and clothe the heir, his wife and children. Failure on the part of the heir to fulfil any one of these conditions may invalidate his position.

Observance of this form of succession becomes less rigid as it comes down to the valleys and plain. Here the heir no longer receives the lion's share. His inheritance may consist of one-third of the total estate as well as a share of the remainder which is divided equally among all the brothers and sisters. Or the parents may bequeath the house they live in as a special legacy to the son they have chosen as their heir, while they divide all the fields equally among all the children, and so on. In other words the special legacy the heir receives apart from his brothers and sisters varies in amount from one place to another and one could generalize the assertion that the further from the mountains the smaller the extra bequest to the son chosen as heir. Notwithstanding the smaller legacy, the rights and duties of the heir remain the same as those described above.

Another pattern of inheritance predominates among the fishing villages and valleys near the sea. Here a daughter, not necessarily the eldest, is the one who inherits. The legacy she receives also varies locally, but she is normally bequeathed the house and the surrounding fields, or the house and a field as well as an equal share of the remainder with her brothers and sisters, etc. The heiress lives with her husband and children in her parents' home; she enjoys the same rights and is under the same obligations towards them and her brothers and sisters as the heir in the former case. Her position in the house is also the same.

In the south of the region lies the province of Orense. Here the division of the inheritance among the children follows a simple line. The entire estate is divided equally among all of them just as, in principle, rights and duties are equally shared by them all. The newly-married couple may live where they choose, and according to the traditional ruling it is of no importance as to who remains in the family house.

Three types of family correspond to these three types of inheritance and I shall underline briefly their chief characteristics. When the heir is a male the transmission of rights is patrilineal, the husband possesses the authority, the inheritance follows a male line and the residence is patrivirilocal. The basic relation of this patrilineage is centred around the dyad father–son. The son lacks authority as long as his parents live, but he is bearing the burden of the farming with his labour. Thus the heir finds himself in an ambiguous position. On the one hand, his obligations as a father and a husband increase but, on the other hand, his role lies in the future, his authority and decisions count for nothing and he has no independent income. Although married and a father he has not yet come of age. The discrepancies between his positions as son, as father and as husband are evident; he is made to be a person both of and under age at the same time. Meanwhile, frequently, his brothers and sisters are urging the father to alter the legacy in their favour. Tensions and frustrations mount and outbursts are often violent.

The subjection of the heir begins before his marriage. Very often the legacy is only made out in his favour on the condition that he accepts as his wife a girl chosen by his parents. His brothers and sisters are not subject to such a condition as they do not have to continue the lineage. Naturally when the parents select their son's bride they are thinking of her dowry, of a financial settlement which will benefit the estate. When the patrivirilocal residence forms part of the legacy the husband brings his bride into his parents' home. Her arrival alters the internal forces and the roles which have hitherto prevailed. For the time being she is bound by heavy obligations: she must work hard in the house, attend and look after the parents-in-law and labour in the fields; her rights are limited to her receiving free food and clothing. In reality she is exchanging her present services for a future position, that of the wife of the heir when, on the death of his parents, he comes into his own.

Such negligible rights and onerous duties, the fulfilment of which is closely superintended by the mother-in-law, provide a breeding-ground for conflicts. The daughter-in-law lacks authority, can take no decisions and has no independent income. Indeed her personal situation can be summed up in two words: submission and toil. Her incorporation into the family circle is slow and difficult, her position is illustrated by the following case: an old man, the head of the lineage, used to pray the Rosary each night surrounded by his offspring. Towards the end he would recite Our Fathers for the neighbours, friends and all the dead of the parish and used to conclude: 'For the welfare of everyone in this house except for the daughter-in-law who is an outsider.'

Two alternatives face the daughter-in-law: either to put up with the difficulties and drudgery, or to abandon the home. In extreme cases, when she reckons her place in the house is really unbearable, she leaves for good. However, by taking such a decision she destroys her husband's legacy and in doing so deprives one of her own children of his eventual inheritance, and as the husband goes with her, the *famille souche* is broken while she and her husband and children find themselves homeless, without money or work. They are forced to begin their lives again from scratch. Such a drastic step indicates an intolerable situation over many years. In only 5.4 per cent of the 194 cases studied has the daughter-in-law left the house for good, but there is a considerable number of married women with patrivirilocal residence who are emotionally disturbed, suffering from neurosis and 'bedevilment'.

The position is completely different when the woman herself is the heiress. In this case the inheritance follows the female line, the transmission of rights is matrilineal, the authority belongs to the wife – not the husband – and the residence is matriuxorilocal. It is the mother who has authority and takes the decisions. She – not her husband – directs the tasks on the farm. She – not the husband – settles matters concerning the parish and the council, she has control of the family finances, she chooses the future husband of the heiress. The basic dyad in the line is mother–daughter although the latter lacks authority and money, while the centre of discord is the daughter's husband who is an outsider. His obligations are unconditional labour for the house and absolute obedience to the mother-in-law who may occasionally ration the nights during which he sleeps with his wife lest there should be too many mouths to feed. Should he turn on his mother-in-law she may chasten him by compelling him to perform distinctly feminine tasks, an affront to his masculine dignity, such as churning the butter, washing the clothes, or scrubbing the floors. Besides, it lies within the mother's power to throw him out and, if she has another daughter, to 'marry her at home' instead and bring in another son-in-law. Such a threat always rings in the ears of a stubborn or insubordinate son-in-law. Moreover, should he leave the house on his mother-in-law's orders or because he decides to after reviewing his situation, he is by no means certain that his wife will accompany him.

A few examples will indicate the atmosphere in this type of family. A woman had a sheep for sale; some buyers from outside the village heard of it and spoke to the husband who asked them 500 pts for it. 'We'll give you 400', they replied. 'Oh no, go and talk to the wife.' Off they went and managed to buy it from her for only 350 pts. In the tavern the husband repeated the ensuing dialogue: 'I asked her, "Did you sell that sheep?" "Oh yes." "And for how much?" "For 350 pts." "Well, well, they'd have given me 400 pts." If it had been me who'd sold that sheep at such a price she'd have skinned me alive, but as it was her she can just go and chase herself.' Mother and daughter will cook up special sweets and dainties for themselves without sharing them with the husbands. The patron saint of the district is a female, her advocation is Our Lady of Easy Childbirth and Milk. In the same district they tend to visit a male witch rather than a female one, a significant inversion of the predominance of the woman in the manipulation of the mystic–magic world. To meet a woman on leaving the house first thing in the morning is considered bad luck anywhere else in the region, but not here, of course, and so on.

The third type of family is that where the inheritance of both parents is divided equally among all the children, the succession is bilateral, husbands hold authority *de jure* and the choice of residence is not determined by defined, traditional patterns but by a multiplicity of circumstances, chiefly by economic factors, work or space. Since this type of family is only too well-known I will not describe it here.

If such marked divergences are upheld in something so important as inheritance and the family, it is only to be expected that each of the forms described here will be supported by *ad hoc* rationalizations. It is to this I shall refer now, beginning with a lengthy quotation, which clearly expresses local reflexions upon the equity of bequeathing the bulk of the inheritance to one child alone.

In some cases, [says the informant], the son named as heir may win his inheritance within four hours, because there has been more than one case of the testator dying four hours after making his will. It's something immoral that, at no cost to himself, he earned it in four hours flat, just because the parent died without the son having to spend anything on medicines, nor losing any sleep sitting up with him, nor sacrificing himself at all. But then you'll get another case where the father has chosen the son who is to inherit. To start with, perhaps, this father is a skinflint, or else his wife is, or maybe both of them are. Then they're never satisfied with the treatment they get, or with the profits made on the farm. Then maybe there's another son outside the house [i.e. who has been passed over] who is working on the father [to alter the will in his favour]. There are all sorts of things. Later, perhaps, the father or the mother falls ill and spends five or six years in bed and the son and his wife have to nurse him and sit up all night with him; then, indeed, the inheritance is well earned. If he's a dutiful son he is letting himself in for a load of trouble when he accepts the legacy. I agree with what they say today: 'I am not going to suffer my father,' or, 'I'm not putting up with my mother.' Because, of course, if they live with their son they must live with his wife, an outsider, who has nothing to do with the family, there-fore they've no feelings for her, she's a nobody. Or else she doesn't get on with her mother-in-law, or her sisters-in-law, or her father-in-law. So then the husband finds himself constantly having to act as a mediator between his wife and his mother, which is no mean task. For this reason many people are opposed to these forms of bequest. Yet, on the other hand we get the case of the parents who find themselves abandoned by all their children, for we've recent cases and not far from here, who grieve night and day. They reared three, four or five children and now find themselves alone. They cook and eat their solitary meals when once they were surrounded by children and grandchildren, a flock of a family all under one roof. And today, to see an old couple of seventy-five or eighty years living alone in a house, it's not much of a life, they cannot look after them-selves properly. There they are on their own, like a pair of saints on a side-altar. I think it is better that this sytem of leaving most of the estate to one child should die out, but we old people have to accept a new system, we must find another way in which the children will help and care for us. But at present we are not used to the idea that an old man should enter a home for old people; we would say that either he or his children were mad. However, it will reach the point when nobody will be thought mad for doing this, only the old people will search for shelter in the place where they'll be looked after best.

So this form of inheritance raises the question of morals. Should one or should one not follow the traditional norm? Which son or daughter should be pre-ferred? Does one deal fairly with the sons and daughters passed over? Tradi-tion provides some answers but have not the circumstances changed? Under these new conditions will not the parents resent the disappearance of the famil-ism inherent in the *famille souche*? Is there not even now an ever-increasing demand that they make adaptations which are at first painful?

Theoretical and practical answers differ, my concern here is to underline their rationalization. The following is the opinion of a peasant who is an expert in these matters and, as such, has ample and direct experience:

When something is general, one knows that when one does the same as everybody else does, it is because it is most beneficial. Whether by a law or custom when something is generally done it is because it is advantageous, it has something to it. In cities there are more welfare centres than there are in villages, you will find old peoples' homes, asylums, etc. Here there is nothing of the kind and although a father may die in such a way that he requires no attention from anyone, he may also linger on for a year and then for another and another, and he will need someone to wash him and make his bed and you can't expect that from any welfare centre here. So a father who has the means says: 'I'll appoint one of my children to look after me and to inherit from me.' Should he die after only a couple of days' illness, the heir can consider himself lucky. However, he may survive a year or two in which case the inheritance is well-deserved. For this reason I am one of those who believes I've no obligation to wander round from house to house eating here today and there tomorrow. I've got my house here, and I reckon that it's here where I should sleep, here where I should eat and here where I should take my ease. If the sun gets too hot I shall sit in the shade and if it rains I've got a shelter.

The argument is straightforward. There is a traditional norm; it is not without purpose and it should be observed. Decisions taken in accordance with custom are moral. Furthermore, the reason for the custom seems obvious: the exchange of an inheritance for a secure old age.

A father of sixty-eight years reasoned thus: 'I have three sons in South America, another one lives with me. When I go about choosing an heir I can hardly choose my sons who are in America. I must appoint this one [who was present] as he is bearing the burden of the farm. Moreover, should I fall ill and need anything, it is he who will have to help and care for me. My wife is ill now and I can only work a little. I can only take the cows to pasture up in the mountains during the morning and in the meadow in the afternoon. It is my son who works, who earns and supports my sick wife and me. It is only natural that he should inherit.' The son added: 'Nor would it be fair to share out later the improvements I have made to the farm by my own efforts and labour.' Only one of the four sons works on the family land and the father keeps the profits, only one of them looks after the parents when they are infirm, therefore it is only just that he should be rewarded with the inheritance. Nonetheless in this case the cultural norm holds sway. It has not occurred to the father to follow the same reasoning concerning various daughters he has living at home, working for him and looking after him when he is ill. It is normal to think according to the local cultural category. Once more this is the final reason for morality.

Nor should it be forgotten that charity begins at home and that the lands to be divided are few and, therefore, not enough for all the children. 'If I were to divide everything equally among my children and keep something back for myself, my children wouldn't farm it for me, so I would have to find someone to farm it or else sell it in order to live. However by leaving the bulk to one child I have someone who is under an obligation to look after me. It is the only way. My other children, as they know already, must look elsewhere for their living.'

Increasing emigration to other parts of Spain, or to Europe, has provided a new reason of a moral nature for continuing this form of bequest. 'Today one must bestow and bequeath almost everything to one heir only, because it is he who is in an inferior condition compared to his brothers who already have their way of life. We consider the heir to be at a disadvantage,' therefore he must be compensated. After all, who wants to live in the country? Here they are driven to make a special bequest so as 'not to destroy the house, but the house destroys one which is worse'. In these villages the obligations imposed on the heir are not offset by the reward of the inheritance. This form of inheritance has begun to chip away the heart of the most powerful tradition. The parameter of morality begins to be the actual individual chosen to inherit, appraising his rights and duties, his views about the lack of equity between him and his brothers who live better than he does without family responsibilities; thus the house and the parents begin to move into a second plane.

Yet, to continue the former point, the number of hectares and their fertility is decisive.

The homestead [the house and the fields immediately surrounding it] amounts to nothing among nine children, so if a bequest is made, one will be left the homestead and the rest know already that they must make their own way. As a recompense they will receive outlying fields. Besides it is also very unjust that a married couple [the son and his wife] spend ten or fifteen years with me and thereafter are no better off than the rest. For during these fifteen years they will have received no reward, nor will they have made any money, but have been no better than a servant who gets no pay except his keep. This is a sorry state of affairs. The father must support the son, as though he had been a small boy, and he should support his wife and children, so it would be very, very unjust if a man spent ten or fifteen years with his father and in the end found himself without anything or was even thrown out of the house.

In other words, the working of this system demands personal sacrifices and bestows rewards. It is immoral to expect the former of a son without conceding him the latter.

Approval of the special bequest generally coincides with areas where it is still the tradition. But where the rule is an equal division of the estate, the system of bequeathing the bulk to one child is condemned. People questioned in the province of Orense told me: 'We don't do as they do in the province of Lugo, where they leave the whole lot to one child while the rest are cast off like foundlings.' Sarcasm is evident in this phrase. An old man remarked: 'If I were in charge of affairs, that law of special bequest would disappear. They are all equally one's children, they all came out of the same place, so why leave everything to one and nothing to another? The one who gets left nothing has to go and work for someone else. If a father intends to leave everything to one child he should avoid having more than one.' In one village in this province they told me: 'Here there is someone from the province of Coruña [where it is the custom to favour one child with the inheritance] who hardly received anything because they left it all to his eldest brother, and the funny thing is [note the surprise of the speaker] that the brothers and sisters did not fall out; for if they leave nothing to a child here, that's the end, he will never speak to his family again. He says now that his children will get equal treatment; he has married here.' This case is corroborated by another speaker: 'My sister in the province of Coruña knew of another of these cases and she said to the father who had made out the legacy: "Have you no heart? Are they not all equally your children? And what does your son the priest say?" "Look," he replied, "It's the custom, so what am I going to do about it?" She said: "Don't tell me you've got any heart or soul; you ask any priest and if your son doesn't tell you the same as me he doesn't know his religion, he's not studied the same books as other priests." My sister got quite red in the face in her agitation.'

The above quotations reveal climates of conscience which are diametrically opposed. The moral principle they invoke to sanction the practice of equal treatment is the equality of all the children. To them this is obvious, natural and even physiological. If this argument does not suffice, one should appeal to the clergy, the repository of Christian morality. There remains a third level to corroborate the necessity for equal division: this is to avoid family tensions between parents and children, between brothers and sisters. To pick out one as heir is to antagonize the rest. The reply of the father who has done so is clinching: he obeys the custom, the cultural norm he has internalized, just as the woman is familiar with the contrary cultural norm and, feeling and thinking according to hers, she rejects the alien one. The surprise felt at contrary cultural imperatives is evident. They cannot understand each other because in this sense they belong to two opposing cultural worlds; they speak a different language.

Now if the parents do not purchase the sacrifices and attention of their children how can they be assured of the care they will require in their old age? The system of values provides the answer. In Galicia the most despicable persons are those who alter the stones which mark the divisions between the plots in the fields or those who bear false witness. Innumerable and harsh terms exist to censure such people. However, in the district of Ribadavia, province of Orense, they do not make special bequests and the hierarchy of censure is reversed. The worst person of all who is 'a renegade, a scoundrel, a son of a . . . , a wretch, is the child who ill-treats, or neglects, or does not feed his aged parents properly. This is worse than altering a boundary stone, worse than being a false witness, in one sense he is as bad as a criminal.' In this scale of values to behave badly towards one's parents is the 'lowest of the low'. The morality of the equal division of the patrimony is a special case; it is included in the code of general values. This is to be expected when no institution exists which requires *ad hoc* bases of morality.

The internalization of these opposing cultural norms is revealed on another deeper plane, indirectly and unconsciously, as the following stories would seem to indicate:

This happened to a cousin of mine. When his father died he left no will [he didn't name an heir] so everything was divided among his son and two daughters. This included the house in which my cousin received the kitchen and his sisters another room in which they had to cook. It is just a year since one of them died. One of the sisters heard a noise among the pans and noticed a light. The next night it was the other sister who saw the light while the first sister could not see anything. This light was their father's soul. On the third night the father approached the son, who felt someone knocking on his bed and asked who was there. 'Don't move the bedclothes son, it's a cold night. I want you to have a Mass said for me in the hermitage chapel. Unless it is said for me I'll never get to heaven.' 'I'm not going to,' answered the son. He was not prepared to go because his father had not named him as heir. So one of the daughters went to the hermitage and the father never turned up again. The son used to weep bitterly when relating this.

Up there in the mountains, when laying out the body of a wicked woman they wrapped her in a habit. Because of this she could not go to heaven and she could not go to hell but wandered abroad. She had left all her capital to one son and nothing to the other and I believe that this was the reason she wandered abroad. The son who had got the capital had wrapped her in this habit on her death and thereafter he heard everynight: 'Ay! Ay!' He went to confession and the priest advised him to wear medals which had been blessed. He then went to the place from which the ghastly cries came and asked what she wanted. 'Bring here a long scythe and thank the one who put medals on you [to protect him against her] otherwise you'd be coming with me.' He then had to hack the habit off her, or rather act as if he did, for it would be her spirit or her ghost. He cut it off and she disappeared with a bang.

This next story has been written down. An old widowed sailor with few fields named his daughter as heiress. The son was forced to leave the paternal roof and go and earn his bread in the wide world. Meanwhile the daughter administered the house and land bequeathed by the father, and her husband went to sea in the boat which belonged to the old sailor. The father began to feel remorse at the thought of his son wandering about the world like a beggar. He told his daughter who hastened to reassure him. Time passed, the old man died and his soul began to beat on the roof at night. One night his voice was heard: 'Daughter, daughter! Help your old father who is wandering about the world in torment because of the wrong I did! Help me, daughter, help me and give to your brother what is his.' The daughter finally decided to do so and the soul of the father never appeared again.

The first tale is gathered from a village which lies in one of the most traditional nuclei of patrilineal inheritance. In this case the application of the norm was not difficult for the father as he only had one male child. Notwithstanding he died without naming him as heir. For no apparent reason the father has not behaved as he ought, he does not care whether the family name continues. So his soul wanders about in torment. He needs help and seeks it first from one daughter and then from the other. But he has to go to the son and, as he knows the son is angry with him, he begins his appeal: 'Don't move the bedclothes, son, it's a cold night.' Nonetheless, the son has a strong moral reason for denying the paternal request abruptly. He does not mind if his father cannot go to heaven; after all it is his fault for not having done as he should. It is his sister, who has benefited by his father's omission, who goes to the hermitage. Later, however, when some time has passed, the son who, backed by the cultural moral, had felt resolute enough to refuse to listen to his father's petition, recalls and relates the incident and his rejection from another standpoint, the 'natural' and moral perspective of Orense. He feels himself to be the son of one who, after all, was his father. Placed in this situation, he suffers remorse at his refusal and every time he tells the story he 'weeps bitterly'.

The second tale shows the reverse. In the province of Orense it is not customary to appoint an heir; the division of the estate into equal parts is the rule. In spite of this 'up there in the mountains' live odd people, including 'wicked' people, who do not know what they should do. From the start the woman is judged and represented as a 'wicked woman' who was queer enough to leave all her capital to one son. As a result she had the deserts of such people and she was condemned to wander abroad in torment. The son with the capital – not the other – goes to summon her, and he is ready to do whatever she asks. At the meeting, the mother's ghost is outraged when she is unable to take her son with her, one assumes to a hot place, and she disappears with a bang. The son had accepted something he never should have, hence the danger he incurred. The ethics of inheritance are crystallized in collective representations of mysterious and supernatural sanctions; these provoke dreams and visions and determine their content.

The third story, similar to the first tale, on account of its ambivalent structure, is in one sense even more expressive. On the sea coast, matrilineal inheritance is the norm and yet the old sailor who has acted in accordance with it feels ill at ease. Are not all one's children equal, as they reiterate in the province of Orense? Then why this cultural favouritism? Culture violates 'nature' and is thus a source of remorse. However, the problem cannot rest there because an equal division of goods and lands does not make sense if, as a result, none of the children can exist on the output of their portion. The conditioning of the environment operates rigorously; cultural precepts are but its translation and expression on another plane.

There are two basic options with which to tackle the problem: unilineal inheritance (patrilineal and matrilineal) or cognatic inheritance. These are the answers provided by the local culture. Each of them is normal, indeed correct, in the respective areas in which they are practised. Moreover they are reinforced by moral bases which are rationalized, internalized and unconscious. 'Nature', according to the popular concept in Orense, would seem to support cognatic inheritance. Such a system requires no other moral basis; all the children are equal. The culture which ordains unilineal inheritance has predominated more widely, and for longer, in the region, but its moral base is weaker, it is 'unnatural', hence the indecision and remorse expressed in folklore and found of course in real life. In the final analysis the dilemma presents two poles. One must either be motivated by ecological factors or by those held to be 'natural'. However, every solution offered for the dilemma – like every cultural solution – solves some problems but occasions others.

In theory, unilineal inheritance according to the basic norms is straight-forward. At the root of the matter, implicit beneath the whims, interests and prizes of the parents and the ambition of the children, is the recognition that in the last resort all the children are interchangeable, that all the remaining brothers and sisters are of the same blood. From another angle we find that acculturation does not always go deep; and that although, on account of the cultural norms, resentment is usually at work unconsciously and is expressed in folklore, it also breaks out from time to time and can be seen directly.

On the other hand, the combination of the cultural norm 'unnatural' with a certain degree of arbitrary subjectivity shown by the father – according to the children passed over – is producing an attitude which bodes ill for the continuation of the unilineal system of inheritance. If we add to this the positive appeal of the city as opposed to the negative appeal of the country, and increasing possibilities of life beyond the confines of the fields, the system of favouring one child with the bulk of the inheritance as described here, will disappear as a cultural system. The heir will be the son or more likely the daughter who wants to stay at home, a filial not a paternal decision, on conditions imposed by the child not the parent, so that the system will have been turned upside down and the favoured ones will be the parents who have a child who is willing to take care of them.

Lastly, these three varieties of inheritance give rise to three sub-types of family as I have shown. And it should be noted that in spite of their fundamental differences, the three are considered to be normal, and indeed morally right, in the areas where they are found, while in the areas where they are unknown a description of them provokes laughter, indignation or sometimes a desire to imitate.

16 Ritual kinship in the Mediterranean: Spain and the Balkans[1]

Julian Pitt-Rivers
London School of Economics

Julian Pitt-Rivers
London School of Economics

THE NATURE OF THE INSTITUTION

There is a large measure of homogeneity throughout the Catholic world in that institution of religious sponsorship that is commonly referred to in anthropological literature as *compadrazgo*.[2] The pretext for establishing ties through sponsorship may vary in accordance with local custom; the duties of the sponsor, both towards those he sponsors and their parents or kin, may vary also but, stretched as it may be in one direction or another to cover the exigencies of each society, the *compadrazgo* is always recognizably the same institution and its rules, despite the variations in detail from place to place, carry the same general sense. Only when it departs from its religious pretext, centred on the rite of baptism, do we find it changing its nature and, put to other uses, merging into the structure of political patronage which in colloquial Spanish has been called *compadrazgo* by analogy, or into the simple sponsorship of lay events. These fictive forms employ the idiom of *compadrazgo*, but their sense is not the same and we can no longer recognize in them the same institution; but this is hardly surprising for institutions, once placed in a changed context of ideas, commonly change their function and implications even though they may not change their form. In order, then, to examine an institution in its entirety, in all its transformations and despite its variants, we must decide which of its characteristics are essential and which are contingent: where to draw the line between the 'genuine' and the 'spurious' examples of it.

We take as essential to *compadrazgo* its connexion with baptism (which indeed provided, historically, the pretext for its inauguration), and suggest that its fundamental sense derives from the recognition that a parent cannot stand as sponsor to his own child, that is to say, putting it in theological terms, that spiritual and physical parenthood are antithetical to one another.[3] However, once the *compadrazgo* severs its roots in the font and the *compadres* are no longer related as physical parent and sponsor of the same child, the *compadrazgo* becomes something different which may be regarded as spurious from the viewpoint of the original institution, though of course it is spurious in no other sense, nor is it for that reason any less interesting than the 'genuine' form, nor any less important. But the two must be distinguished before we can attempt to explain the relation between them. Any general statement must delimit the field of data to which it applies and this is not a task that can be entrusted to the customs of ordinary speech which, in this case, happily class under the same rubric political skulduggery and the spiritual salvation of infants. For ordinary speech lives on analogies and abstracts a given sense from a word in order to extend it to cover phenomena which are quite different in every other sense. Already at the start spiritual kinship owed its vocabulary to physical kinship, though its nature is opposed precisely to this, and in the same way the fictive forms of *compadrazgo* borrow the vocabulary of the literal forms without admitting any adherence to the norms of ritual alliance. Thus the relationship between 'political *compadres*' is essentially venal and calculated where genuine *compadrazgo* prohibits venality and calculation, while a man's fictive *comadre*, far from being sexually excluded by the incest prohibition deriving from spiritual affinity, becomes in many instances simply his illicit sexual partner. Not only in the Spanish fictive form, *comadre de carnaval*,[4] but in the colloquial usage of many cities of Latin America,[5] the *comadre* is opposed to the wife, not by the absence of sexual relations but by their illegitimacy. Hence, if the passage from physical to spiritual kinship implies a reversal of the sense of the terms, so does the further passage from ritual kinship proper to sexual, social or political alliance. From godsib to gossip is but one letter's distance graphically, but in significance the two concepts are so different that the former is not commonly recognized as the etymological origin of the latter. If, as I have written,[6] ritual kinship is what physical kinship aspires to be but, on account of its social consequences, is always prevented from becoming, so political *compadrazgo* is what ritual kinship becomes once its spiritual roots have been forgotten. It tends always, however, to move in that direction, to 'go political', for the viability of exploiting sacred ties for political advantage is so patent.

Compadrazgo's roots are embedded in Christian doctrine which validates the prohibition of sponsoring one's own child by reference to the notion of original sin transmitted in the act of physical generation and washed away by the spiritual regeneration conveyed in the rite of baptism, but the opposition nevertheless recalls the functions of blood-brotherhood and ritualized friendship in non-Christian societies which commonly prohibit the choice of ritual kinsmen from among the members of ego's lineage. It is not my intention here, however, to pursue either the doctrinal aspect of *compadrazgo* or the parallels to be found in other cultures.[7] In *compadrazgo* only the physical parents are formally excluded from the role of godparents and close kin are, on the contrary, frequently recommended for it by the edict of custom.

Sponsors are first of all required at baptism when the child is received into the Christian community and given its Christian name by the godparent who takes it from the priest at the font before returning it to its parents. Prior to baptism it was regarded as a 'Moor', an animal or at any rate scarcely human. At confirmation, according to Catholic doctrine, a child also requires a sponsor, though custom often omits to attach any social importance to the godparent on this occasion or to recognize any relationship of *compadrazgo* between this sponsor and the parents. On the other hand, much importance is frequently accorded to the sponsors of a marriage, though this has never been a function recognized by Catholic doctrine, which only required witnesses with whom no spiritual affinity was ever created. Other occasions concerning the child's well-being are also in the eyes of custom pretexts for establishing relations of *compadrazgo*; curing ceremonies or the sponsorship of a festival in honour of the Infant Jesus are commonly found among these in Latin America. In all cases, however, the baptismal godparents are accorded prime importance. The godparent commonly pays for the ceremony and the baptismal godparents are expected, in addition to their supposed responsibility for the child's religious education (which in fact is not often taken seriously), to make gifts to the god-child on certain occasions specified by custom which mark its progress towards adulthood: a religious medallion to protect it from the evil eye, for example, or the first pair of shoes or long trousers, or the first long dress. Help in the education of the child is often hoped for from the godparent, but there are no further demands on him once it has attained the age of marriage. Sponsorship, then, governs the passage of the individual from the family of origin to the family of orientation, a cycle initiated and terminated by the birth of children who bring a new nuclear family into existence and by doing so destroy the unity of the old one. Baptism gives social significance to the physical fact of birth and ushers the newborn member of the physical family into the community. At each stage in the child's advance towards maturity this function is echoed, for a change in the structure of the family is implied. The reiteration of the notion of sponsorship on the occasion of confirmation, its popular extension into the sponsorship of marriage, its evocation whenever rites of passage are to be performed and even the role of the godparent in a child's funerary rites – he often must pay for the coffin – rub in the essential point: godparents take the place of parents in sponsoring their charges at the crucial points where the individual destiny of the child, rather than the preservation of the familial unit into which he was born, is at issue. This is most clearly seen in the custom of those parts of Andalusia where the parents of a child enter the church neither on the occasion of its baptism nor of its marriage.

In accordance with the theory of the rites of passage a person must be separated from the unit in which he has a status before re-entering it in a changed status. During this transition he is commonly in the care of someone whose relationship to him is opposed to his ties with the members of the unit in which his status is to change. Thus, in patrilineal societies it is frequently the mother's brother who plays such a role in the rites of initiation. His concern for his sister's son is purely for the boy as a person, not as a member of a lineage to which he himself is only allied by marriage. The godparent may be said, then, to be the guardian of the child as an individual person rather than as an offspring and therefore to be a kind of 'anti-parent' bearing no legal or social responsibility for him, but only the religious duty of ensuring the salvation of his *individual* soul and if, as it is said to be the purpose of the institution and as occasionally occurs, the godparent replaces the parent in raising the orphaned child, it is only because the godchild's parents' nuclear family had vanished before he was old enough to depart from it by founding one of his own. The godparent replaces the parent only in providing care in order to bring him to maturity, he does not replace him socially as he would were he to adopt the child and give it his surname. The godparent, as guardian of his destiny, looks into the future to the day when his charge will become an adult, the parents, who bear responsibility for him in the present, attach him to the past and to the social structure in which his place is granted to him by virtue of his membership of the unit they have allied themselves to create. Hence the notion that *compadrazgo* is 'fictive' kinship, that the godparent is a 'fictive' parent (though the clerical label *propatres* has been thought to mean this), is in fact totally misleading, for it ignores the opposition between physical and ritual (or spiritual) kinship which is the basis of that institution morphologically and historically, and the key to the understanding of the rules that govern it. The godparent is not a surrogate for the parent, but only a substitute for him in the roles from which the parent is excluded on account of his physical and social paternity and where he must be replaced by his contrary. And on the material plane the parent is only replaced by the godparent partially and exceptionally when his premature disappearance threatens the child's chances of attaining the age at which he no longer requires a guardian: i.e. full adulthood, the point at which the role of godparent is effaced anyway. This anti-parental role is, therefore, for the anthropologist as opposed to the theologian, a function of the process of transition from one generation to the next which involves the destruction of the parental family and its replacement by the filial one, an aspect of the developmental cycle of the domestic group. In the rural society of southwestern Europe with which we are first of all concerned, the domestic group is no more than the nuclear family and the developmental cycle is uncomplicated by the requirements of the larger kinship unit. This interpretation may raise misgivings in a reader well acquainted with the literature of *compadrazgo*, because the people themselves so often liken godparent to parent – especially in Italy, where the godfather and godmother are said to be a second father and mother.[8] Such statements (which are no different from those often recorded regarding bloodbrotherhood) refer only to the sentiments which are thought proper in such a relationship, not to the rights and duties involved which are totally different. The constant stressing of the analogy between ritual and literal kinship in the face of the patent differences is in itself an indication of value regarding the nature of the institution of *compadrazgo*: taken in conjunction with the prohibitions attaching to that institution, it should be interpreted as a technique of exorcism, of eliminating from the consciousness of the participants the conflict of aims inherent in the opposition between literal and ritual parent whose function is precisely to assure the continuity of the individual personality through changed statuses, that is to say, the transition from one generation to the next.

The opposition between the person as an individual and as a member of a social unit – in this case, a nuclear family – is perfectly illustrated, in the naming system of modern times, by the fact that he receives his Christian name from his godparents and his surname from his father (or in the Spanish naming system, his surnames from his father and from his mother's father). The person as a Christian soul is opposed to the person as a social cypher, an element in the system of descent. As an individual he is differentiated by his Christian name from other individuals and especially from his siblings within the family from whom he is not otherwise differentiated; as a member of that family he is identified with its other members by their common surname. In keeping with this distinction, those who depart from the world into the seclusion of a monastic order leave their surname behind in the world. The king calls people by their surname but God knows us only by our Christian names.

The naming system of modern western Europe marks the opposition with greatest clarity perhaps, but those that preceded it were no less significant in this regard. Over-generalizing grossly, one can say that the Christian name defined the man as an individual and to this was appended a descriptive name based either upon his descent, birth-place, profession or personal characteristics. These were the sources of the modern surname. This name, whatever it referred to, tended in any case to be inherited by his children, for a child is first of all identified by reference to the family into which it is born before it has acquired any distinct identity of its own. Regardless, however, of whether the descriptive appellation by which he was finally known related to his personal characteristics or to those of a forebear, the child as an individual soul, named by a godparent after a saint under whose protection his destiny was placed, was distinguished from the man as he is seen by society which named him by his *social* characteristics.

It is unfortunate that there is as yet no anthropological account of the history of the naming systems of Europe, but it is significant in the context of this essay that the naming systems of eastern Europe differ from those of the West. In particular, the retention of the father's Christian name in patronymic form in addition to the surname has implications in the realm of sponsorship, for it means that the name given by godparents to the father is retained by the child as a teknonym and passes from defining the father as himself to defining the child by his place in society. It is the destiny of every individual as such to start his life with his future ahead, undetermined as to his social value, and to end it with his past behind him, institutionalized and converted into an ancestor. His individual name becomes a category name for his descendants if he is retained as the point of reference by which they are labelled, whether as their father or as the eponymous founder of the group. In eastern Europe both the immediate forebear and the eponym are retained. The system of the Arabs appears at first sight to present an anomaly, for a man may be called 'Abu' (father of) followed by the name of his son, that is to say, the son's first name provides the teknonym for the father rather than the reverse, but this is no more than an inversion of their formal naming system, used to stress affective and informal relations and its significance resides in this. The misunderstanding between Evans-Pritchard and his informants, recounted in the introduction to *The Nuer*, illustrates that, despite the difficulty of translating the nomenclature from the British to the Nuer system, both cultures recognized the distinction between individual name and collective name. The opposition between spiritual and social parenthood (represented as physical parenthood), which is given a theological explanation, in the context of Christian doctrine, is, at a higher level of abstraction, simply a manifestation of the universal structural opposition between the personal and the collective destiny of a man.

I have already mentioned certain duties of the godparent towards his charge. An attitude of beneficence is expected of him which concords well with the absence of responsibility for him in the world. The godchild owes his godparent nothing in return for his gifts which are 'free gifts' – as one might expect from the bestower of spiritual grace; *padres de gracia* is one of the terms for godparents in Spanish – and they may be interpreted as manifestations of that grace which is the essence of the relationship. To undertake in any sense the guardianship of a child not one's own already implies a gratuitous goodness which looks to a reward in Heaven rather than in the here and now, and in any case the inequality of age between the participants rules out an immediate return of the godparent's favours. But when the godchild attains the age when he *might* reciprocate, the relationship lapses. He has nowhere a specific duty to care for his godparent in old age, nor to return any service for what he has received. He owes only great respect and, in certain places, the formal duty of a congratulatory visit on his godparent's feast day. The relationship is one that excludes all salacious reference and sexual union is unthinkable. Indeed, in the view of the Church, it was until recently an even more grievous sin than incest with a physical parent.

In contrast to this unilateral beneficence, the relationship between the sponsor and the parent (the *compadres*) is essentially mutual and balanced. The sponsor is always, if not the social equal, then the social superior – never the inferior, save in certain exceptional cases – yet the reciprocity is ideally complete and no detail of conduct distinguishes the spiritual from the social parent; each must call the other *compadre* and speak in the respectful third person. The equality of mutual esteem pervades, in theory at least, the relationship between the two, even when they are related as employer and employee; indeed moral equality is opposed to, and combined with, social inequality and it is this that gives the institution its particular tenor and function in this context. The reciprocity is not, then, a matter of material calculation, but of the heart, a question of mutual trust: each must be at the other's service, ready to help whenever needed in whatever way required. You can refuse your *compadre* nothing, it is said. Such an open-ended reciprocity lends itself to exploitation, especially when the participants are not in fact equal, as the examples of its use between the owner and his peons on the *haciendas* of Latin America show. But, according to the theory of *compadrazgo*, each is committed irremediably to the other by their common concern for the child.

The complementary nature of their roles in relation to the child reposes on the Christian notion of dualism: man is both a physical and a spiritual being, therefore he requires parents of each kind. But the relationship resulting between the two kinds of parents is equivocal and this sets it aside from the normal run and gives it a sanctity which is illustrated in the combination of intimacy with extreme respect. Sex and rivalry, the prime preoccupations of ordinary life, are taboo in this relationship wherever it is taken seriously: not only are sexual relations between *compadre* and *comadre* incestuous, but sexual joking between *compadres* is excluded. To quarrel with a *compadre* is to desecrate one's self. The tie is, thus, the opposite of a juridical relationship whether contractual or statutory; it is a matter of sentiment, not of rights.

It is usual for the parents of the child to invite the person of their choice to be the sponsor, though in some places he may offer his services and even demand the role. But in either case mutual consent is essential. Moreover, one cannot envisage entering into such a relationship without an act of will on both sides, for the necessary sentiment and respect can scarcely be commanded.

The act of individual will is an essential constituent of all forms of ritual kinship, which is differentiated from literal kinship by this fact. Literal kinship is established in accordance with the kinship system without regard for the consent of the participants, and the rights and duties attaching to it are specified by custom, not dependent upon the kinsman's wishes. *Compadrazgo* is thus a relationship between two individuals and, even in those parts of Mexico where it is customarily extended to include the parents of the participants, it can be avoided if they do not choose to exchange the ritual embrace which initiates it. This voluntary aspect of the *compadrazgo* displays its association with the notion of grace which is always connected with free will and the state of the heart. Whether grace is bestowed by the Deity or by humans it is always an emanation of the will, not the fulfilment of a statutory or contractual obligation. In this way *compadrazgo* resembles friendship, and it has rightly been described as 'ritualized friendship'. It differs from ordinary friendship only in that by being ritualized it is rendered irrevocable. Yet its sacred character does not always suffice to save it from the paradox of friendship: that while friends express the state of their heart in acts of favour and esteem without any thought of a return – for friendship is false if entered into out of calculation – nevertheless, the failure to make a return implies the absence of reciprocity in sentiment and this puts an end to the friendship. Since *compadrazgo* cannot be ended, great care is commonly taken to test the character and sentiments of the person envisaged as *compadre*, for if he proves false there is no recourse to sanctions. Hence, also, the fear of destroying the spiritual and sentimental purity of the relationship sometimes looms so large that one must expressly avoid asking favours of one's *compadre* and should even choose him from among those who live at a distance in order to escape the temptation of sullying the relationship with day-to-day concerns of utility. This point of view is commonly expressed in Italy. In other places, however, the potential material advantages are frankly exploited. It becomes sometimes the guarantee of fair dealing, and those engaged in commerce may choose their *compadres* at strategic points in the locality. Or, where the relationship is entered into by persons of different status, it may be used to guarantee the fidelity of the patron's clients; the social inferior may equally choose a *compadre* who is able to help the whole family. Honour, public support and service is traded against protection, influence and beneficence. It is to be noted that, precisely because the relationship between *compadres* is conceptually one of equality, it is effective in circumstances of factual inequality: it provides the possibility of intimacy and trust between persons whose difference of class would otherwise make this difficult. Hence, in Andalusia, for example, it became the nerve of the structure of patronage in the nineteenth century. Thus, according to social circumstances, from one society to another, and from one period to another, the *compadrazgo* varies in the use to which it is put. The relative stress laid on its spiritual nature or political potential is manifested in the rules of choice. When it is suggested that the powerful man able to afford protection should be chosen as *compadre*, or when men boast of the number of their godchildren, we are on the road to a political transformation of the institution which will take us into realms where spiritual affinity is forgotten.

However, prescriptions regarding the choice of a sponsor are sometimes much more specific than the mere recommendation to choose someone near or distant, equal or superior, with whom one might hope to cement a relationship of mutual trust and goodwill; they frequently recommend a specific kinsman.

These rules vary from place to place. In Spain they range from those areas of Andalusia where the landowner or employer is expected to 'baptize' his dependant's children, to others where *compadres* are normally kinsmen. The importance attached to the institution varies also. The urban classes give it less heed than the rurals; the upper classes give it little and do not use the terms of address; and in the Levante of Spain no one gives it any importance at all.

Throughout most of rural Spain, however, the rules conform to certain general provisions:

1. Each child must have a godfather and a godmother who must be married or at least engaged to be married.
2. Each child must have different godparents from its siblings. (This rule is not always followed.)
3. Godparents must be chosen from among the closest kin outside the nuclear family: preferably the parents and siblings of the child's parents.

Additional rules which are not necessarily logically consistent with one another are found in great variety:

(a) The godparents of the marriage must 'baptize' the first child. Alternatively, or in addition, the godparents of baptism of a man must be chosen as the godparents of his marriage.
(b) The godparents of the marriage must be the husband's *elder* brother.
(c) The choice of godparents must come alternately from the husband's family and the wife's. And this rule is sometimes combined with another rule regarding the choice of Christian name: that the name is chosen from one side of the family and given to the child at baptism by godparents chosen from the other side. Thus, in the township that I studied twenty years ago[9] the rule was that the first son was given the Christian name of his father's father by his mother's parents, the second son that of his mother's father by his father's parents – and the same rule applied in the naming and sponsorship of girls: the first daughter was named after father's mother, the second daughter after mother's mother, the godparents being chosen from the close kin of the opposite side to the name: uncles or married siblings of the parents.

Sometimes the grandparents (contravening rule 2 above) served a second time.

The importance accorded to grandparents is perhaps the commonest feature of the system of *compadrazgo* in Spain. Are not grandparents the 'anti-parents', par excellence? Their nuclear family was broken up by the marriages of their children, but they take their revenge, as it were, in the guise of godparents to their grandchildren whose personal destinies will, under their patronage, eventually mature to break up the family which broke up theirs, and prolong their line of descent, over-reaching the time-span of the nuclear family, into the future. No longer head of a nuclear family once their children have grown up and married, they become founders of the lineage which descends from them. The principle of the alternation of generations, so evident in those kinship terminologies which possess only a single reciprocal for the grandparent–grandchild relationship comes to light in the rules of sponsorship: I am to my grandparents what I could not be to my parents, and to my grandchildren what I could not be to my children.

In an earlier analysis of the *compadrazgo* of Andalusia I laid stress on the practical function of these rules of preference in the appointment of godparents: affines become ritual kinsmen and the rules of respect and sacralized amity provide a tie of a different sort – and a direct tie – between those who are previously linked only by the fact that they are spouse's kin and kin's spouse. Moreover, the rule that the godparents should be married entails that, except in the case of the grandparents, one is a lineal kinsman and the other an affine of the child's parents. The superimposition of ritual kinship on a relationship of physical kinship may change little in the conduct of those who are accustomed from birth to speak in the second person, as indeed they continue to do (except sometimes in Latin America where brothers, or even father and son, may call each other *compadre* and speak in the third person), but the tie of *compadrazgo* between affines brings a new basis to their relationship which overlays the potential hostility between families who are otherwise linked only by marriage. Thus wives become *comadre* of their mother- and sister-in-law; those who are kin-in-law become kin-in-God, and owe each other a respect which their simple alliance through marriage does not demand. This was the practical function – the mitigation of tensions between affines – which first struck me. But to give this as the explanation of the institution rather than of the prevalence of such recommendations regarding the nomination of sponsors is to indulge in the most uncompromising functionalism. The superimposition of spiritual kinship on the relationship of kinship by descent or alliance implies that the personal destiny of the child is opposed only to his membership of a nuclear family out-side which he must fend for himself, aided or not by kinsmen whose solidarity with him cannot be taken for granted. The ambiguity of extra-familial kin ties is consecrated by the usage of the word *primo*, first cousin, to mean a person who can be fooled. Much as one would like to trust one's cousins for reasons of sentiment and allegiance to a common familial past, the pressures of the social structure, far from prescribing solidarity, promote through the division of in-heritance the conflicts of interest that only the sacred bond of *campadrazgo* can palliate.

Kinship outside the nuclear family does not provide the basis of any group solidarity, but only a network of dyadic ties deriving from the sentiment of common origin and common attachments. In order to have any value it requires to be sanctioned by personal sentiment and this is validated in the *compadrazgo*, for in fact those who do not like each other waive the rule. The recommendations to invite one or other person to be sponsor are always subject to the state of heart of the persons concerned.

THE CASE OF KUMSTVO

The Greek Church attaches quite as much importance to sponsorship as Rome, in fact more today, since the incest prohibition between co-parents is still in force. In Greece, and in the Greek communities of the United States and elsewhere, the institution is respected and the popular belief persists that a person should not marry his spiritual sibling (i.e. the physical child of his godparent). The retention of such archaic forms can, in the first place, be attributed to the historical fact that the Eastern Churches were not affected by the restrictions to the extension of spiritual affinity imposed by the Council of Trent which abolished them in the West. In brief, the Greek Church accords much the same sense to sponsorship as the Catholic Church has done down to modern times, and the Greek world provides similar preferential rules for the choice of godparents: the same recommendation that the marriage sponsor should 'baptize' the children of the marriage (not just the first child),[10] and that the baptismal sponsor should be sponsor at the marriage of his godchild. Indeed, the latter rule is incorporated in the blessing at baptism. 'May you live to marry him,'[11] i.e. complete your charge by bringing him to full adulthood.

It appears, then, that the explanation I have given of the fundamental sense of the institution will hold as well in the Greek as in the Roman Church, despite the dogmatic differences and certain differences in family structure between the two areas. A greater importance is attached to extra-familial kinship as a rule, but the Greek kindred is bilateral even if the stress on patrilinearity is sometimes more marked than in the western Mediterranean. Moreover, the same naming system is found, by which children are named alternately after the patrilateral and matrilateral grandparents.

However, when we turn to the material from rural Serbia, presented by Hammel,[12] everything changes: the institution of *kumstvo* appears quite anomalous. The ritual requirements of the Church are accepted regretfully, it seems, and the social ties established through sponsorship are of quite another order. It is true that baptism is still preponderant as the pretext for inaugurating the ties of *kumstvo*, and sponsorship at marriage is no less important. The first hair-cutting of the child (incorporated in the baptism in the Greek as in the Roman Church) furnishes here a supplementary occasion to establish *kumstvo*. The attitude of respect shown to the godfather is even more marked. The degrees of spiritual affinity prohibiting marriage are more extensive and one encounters the same belief that one must avoid financial entanglements with *compadres*.

On the other hand, *kumstvo* cannot be established with any member of the *zadruga* (extended family household), the lineal kin or even the clan, nor with any matrilateral or affinal kinsman. It is inherited from one generation to the next, being treated like a good in itself. It can supposedly even be bought or acquired in exchange for something else. It is vested in the *zadruga* of the baptizer, and, if it falls into abeyance through the absence of a suitable replacement in the next generation, it is the privilege of that *zadruga* to name the successor, for, as it is said, it 'belongs to them'. When this right is not or cannot be exercised, or is relinquished by the *zadruga* whose sponsorship may have brought ill-fortune, and the parents are left without any indicated *kum*, the choice reverts to the domain of destiny, and the child is placed at the crossroads where the first stranger to find him is invited to be his godfather, even though he may be a Muslim or a gypsy. When a *zadruga* divides, the *kumstvo* is among the goods divided. The institution has great political importance for, apart from the sacred trust established between lineages, it may also be used to compensate a homicide or to end a feud: *kumstvo* is 'given', that is to say, the role of godfather is given, to him who would otherwise be an implacable enemy. It is also given to the person to whom one owes one's life, promised in exchange for a favour, transmitted with the sale of a property, or offered to a powerful family by newcomers in the region.

The explanation of the nature of *compadrazgo* which I have given above seems to apply poorly to rural Serbian *kumstvo* in view of these facts and, since it is still the same institution from the religious standpoint, a further explanation is required of these anomalous features.

1. It does not, save in the first instance, depend upon the personal ties of the parents and the reciprocal sentiments of the *compadres*, but on the inherited right to the role.
2. It no longer fulfils the function of mitigating the tensions between affines, nor of balancing matri- and patrilateral ties, nor of ensuring the passage of the nuclear family from one generation to the next, though it is still in evidence on the occasions of the rites of passage in the godchild's career.
3. The terminology does not distinguish between godfather-godson and co-parent, but the same term is extended to all members of the *zadruge* involved. (On the other hand the southern Serbs distinguish terminologic-ally between the physical and the spiritual co-parent, thereby mitigating the ideal reciprocity of the relationship.)

It is no longer a relationship limited to the individual destiny of the child. Indeed it is not, in operation, a relationship between individuals as such, but between *zadruge*, as Hammel shows. Is it, he asks, to be regarded as an extension to their family of a tie created between individuals, or, on the contrary, a tie between individuals by virtue of the tie between the household to which they belong? The latter is certainly the case in Serbia, for the relationship between family groups is maintained through the choice of sponsors from among their number as long as there is a child to be baptized and a baptizer, and it lapses only in default of one of these.

Even when a fresh invitation to be *kum* is issued it is clearly conceived in terms of its collective aspect. One might, however, argue that when the choice is remitted to the hand of destiny by placing the child at the cross-roads, it is a negation of the collective usage of *kumstvo* and a return to a purely individual treatment of the institution. In the same vein Montesquieu's parents' choice of a beggar to be their son's godfather represents the negation of the political value of the ties of *compadrazgo* to another member of the nobility. In each case the godparent is chosen not on account of who he is, but on account of what he is not. The significance of the choice is purely negative; anyone will do, so let God decide. This appeal to the Divinity for grace through a person unknown (the stranger) or without social significance (the beggar, who was perhaps also unknown) amounts to a rejection of the political aspect of the institution and a reaffirmation of its spiritual origin. But this appeal remains in both cases the exception. The essentially collective nature of normal Serbian *kumstvo* is seen all the more clearly if it is compared with the forms of *compadrazgo* found in Latin America, which extend the term *compadre* to the ascendants, and even in rarer examples to the whole family group, for there it is always initiated by the free choice of *compadres* and there is no notion of an obligation to reproduce the tie between the same families. This is, indeed, a case of the extension of an individual tie to a whole family, but in *kumstvo* the collective aspect is primary.

For this reason Hammel decides to explain *kumstvo* by analogy with kinship. In brief, he maintains that *kumstvo* forms a system of generalized exchange in which unilateral sponsorship can be likened to unilateral alliance. Thus the *zadruga* undertaking the duties of godparenthood (i.e. owning the *kumstvo*) is always superior in prestige to that of the godchildren, who gain prestige through the alliance in the same way as, in the hypergamic system of marriage in India, those families who give their daughters in marriage to a higher caste gain prestige through doing so. Hammel does not observe that this is always the case in the rest of the Christian world, where there is *no* notion of a collective relationship and, therefore, no possibility of a system of generalized exchange – one can hardly speak of a system of generalized exchange between nuclear families when they are those of children and their parents – and where the dogmatic reason for the superiority of the spiritual parent over the physical parent is not given. This appears to me to weaken the argument. It does not in any case invalidate his contention that the counter prestation of *kumstvo* is accrued prestige, but demonstrates only that this need not entail a system of exchange.

Viewing *kumstvo* in this way, Hammel sees it as providing the 'alternative social structure' which gives the book its title. I shall not linger over what is implied by the notion of *alternative* social structures with regard to the definition of social structure. Can a society have more than one, and, if so, in what way are they alternative? One cannot suppose that a choice is offered to those who are dissatisfied with the ties of cognatic kinship to replace them by ties of alliance or ritual kinship. In fact, I believe Hammel means no more than that people are linked by 'blood', by marriage, or by *kumstvo* (as I would put it: by grace) and that these different kinds of tie are exclusive of each other. In accordance with an ancient, and to my mind regrettable, tradition he calls each set of relations a social structure. Hammel quotes a grey-bearded informant who explained to him 'we have a clanship, we have alliance, and we have *kumstvo*' and no one would deny the necessity to distinguish clearly between them; but by viewing each as a structure in itself rather than as part of a total structure, as alternatives rather than as elements in articulation, Hammel places *kumstvo* in parallel with kinship, neglecting the conceptual opposition between the two. This makes it more difficult to see clearly the nature of Serbian *kumstvo*, which appears to me to be a very good example of the exploitation for political ends (collective this time not individual) of an institution which still retains its roots in the font and whose social function depends upon this. It remains to be explained why it is so different from the *compadrazgo* of the Hispanic world.

Let me return to my original thesis regarding *compadrazgo* and reduce it to its bare essentials. Every generation sees the destruction and creation of families, and the passage of individuals from puerile to adult and from junior to senior status. This process determines that while individuals remain the same person, the units in which they are combined are replaced as they grow up, found families, grow old and disappear into the ranks of the ancestors. The rites of passage place the seal of recognition upon these changes. The affines of one generation become the cognates of the next, the people to whom I am related through my wife will be related to my son through his mother. Throughout all these changes in time the person remains the same individual and as such he is distinguishable from the person *qua* member of a collectivity; in addition to his activities as a member of a group he has other relations to which these collective allegiances are irrelevant. Moreover, in addition to his kinship with co-members of the same group he has other kinds of kin relations (giving rise to no solidary group) which are unique to him and his full siblings. All kin relations outside the nuclear family are of this type in the bilateral systems, but not all in societies which have corporate lineages. Regardless of differences of structure, we can distinguish between ties established between persons in terms of the social units to which they belong (structurally determined ties) and those which are conducted on the basis of mutual attachments or antipathies as persons. That these attachments or antipathies should have a structural setting does not mean that they are structurally determined and does not prevent them from being personal in the sense that they entail no necessary consequence in the field of relations between groups. The extension of the basic collectivity, therefore, determines the field within which relations are structurally defined. The ambilateral nuclear family of the Mediterranean knows no extension; it *is* the basic collectivity. The lineage system of the rural Serbs extends the basic collectivity to the level of the clan.

Now it can be observed that certain types of affective relationship are restricted to those persons who are not assimilated by the social structure. These are undertaken on the basis of a concern in the person as an individual not as a group member. The mother's brother in many patrilineal societies (or the father in matrilineal) is able to have such an attachment to his sister's son (or son) because they belong to different basic collectivities. In lineal societies certain duties concerning the personal welfare of individuals are entrusted to the non-lineal kin, and this is particularly the case in mortuary services where the disposal of the corpse, the physical person, the individual man, is undertaken by those who are opposed to the lineal kin whose concern is with the dead man's spirit and his subsequent significance as an ancestor. In other societies these duties attach to affines of whom the same can be said. In others again it is the pseudo-kinsman, especially the blood-brother, as among the Azande, to whom such a duty falls, for he is by definition the man with whom such personal ties have been formed. For this reason he can normally only be chosen from among those who are not lineal kinsmen.[13]

The society of southern Europe might appear anomalous in enjoining the choice of a close kinsman to be a pseudo-kinsman until it is recognized that, given the kinship structure, he belongs to precisely the category of kin which is opposed to the members of the structurally significant unit, the nuclear family. As has been noted, brothers and sisters are eligible only if married and therefore no longer members of it. In Serbia, where the basic social unit is an extended patrilineal and patrilocal household belonging to a patrilineage and a clan possessing a common name, a common patron saint and feast-day (*slava*), we would expect to find that the role of the baptizer should be filled from beyond the category of patrilineal kin. The matrilateral kin might seem indicated. But the matrilateral kinsmen are not without structural significance either, as Hammel points out (p. 16). It is the mother's brother who plays a vital part in the division of the *zadruga*; unlike the mother's brother in many patrilineal societies, he is thus intimately concerned in the structural realignments of the lineage. Moreover, women have a right to inherit property even though they usually pass up their share if they have brothers; the in-marrying son-in-law is a common feature and Hammel finds 'some recognition of bilaterality in all the words which designate household groups' (p. 28).

The personal destiny of the child is entrusted, thus, to a non-kinsman, since the relationship with kinsmen, lineal, matrilateral and affinal (matrilateral in the next generation) is structurally significant. The 'anti-parent' is not just anti-parent in the English sense of the word but 'anti-*parent*' in the French sense, i.e. anti-kinsman. Yet the personal destiny of the godchild hardly appears to be the major conscious concern of the *kum*. If, as Hammel and I are agreed, *kumstvo* is effectively a relationship between collectivities rather than individuals, this is only to be expected. Nevertheless, that it may be put to political use in this way does not eliminate the ritual significance of the institution any more than does the choice of a powerful patron as *padrino* in Andalusia. The godfather, however he may have been chosen, still officiates at the rites of passage of his godchild. It is still a *ritual* relation between individuals even if it is a *political* relation between *zadruga*. It is initiated as such and it is still regarded as sacred. This is apparent in a number of ways: in the avoidance of mundane entanglements with *kum* (p. 90), in the power of the *kum*'s curse

(p. 42), and in the role of the stranger chosen by hazard at the crossroads as the *padrino* who is intended to bring good fortune to his charge. The good fortune of the collectivity is first of all ensured by the survival of the individuals who compose it. Moreover, *kumstvo* is still said to be a 'relationship contracted out of love and friendship' (p. 9). But in Serbian rural society love and friendship are none the less submitted to the pressures of group solidarity. How can sacred trust be respected among warring lineages if it is not itself vested in a collective relationship? Yet it cannot be concluded from this that the institution is *by its nature* collective, but rather that it is put to use by the collectivities of which the social structure is composed, just as in Andalusia it is put to the shifts of the systems of patronage. In both cases its political utility depends upon the fact that the assumptions upon which it is founded controvert those of the social structure. In Andalusia the ideal equality of the institution is opposed to the inequality implicit in patronage; in Serbia the spiritual tie between individuals is opposed to the collective solidarity of the lineage. It provides not an alternative social structure, but an alternative *to* social structure.

It must be noted that the bond between godparent and godchild is absolutely irrevocable while there exists the possibility of renouncing the *kumstvo*, in the collective sense, that is, the right to become godparent. Indeed, the relationship comes to an end automatically if the family produces no sons, for on the marriage of the daughter her husband's, not her, baptismal godparent (or his replacement) will be godparent of the marriage. The collective nature of the bond of *kumstvo* is superimposed upon its individual nature by virtue of the prolongation effected by the rules of nomination to godparenthood. These rules are all found elsewhere and it is only when they are applied within the social structure of tribal Serbia that they produce the institution described by Hammel. The rule that the baptismal sponsor should be sponsor at marriage, deriving from the notion that to complete his duties he should bring his godchild to the foundation of a new nuclear family, has already been mentioned with regard to Greece, as has the converse rule that the sponsor at marriage should baptize the first child or the children. Both these rules are found in Spain also. If both rules are followed and if one adds to them a further rule also encountered in Greece: that sons replace their fathers in the role of godfather,[14] then all the necessary elements are present in order to ensure that the *kumstvo* remains vested in a patriline. Add to that the rule that all the children of a marriage have the same godparent and *kumstvo* becomes a collective relationship between lineages.

Its acquisition of a political function follows inevitably from the nature of the relations between lineages, but this by no means curtails its sacred character. On the contrary it is essential to it, for thanks to this it is able to contravene the rules of rivalry between lineages and prevent or put an end to feuds. When, by the logic of the social structure, men should fight and annihilate each other's group, *kumstvo* can be invoked to lay that logic in abeyance. Its sacredness serves not to mitigate the tensions between different nuclear families within the kin, as in Andalusia, but between different lineages within the community. Social utility it has, deriving from its sacred nature as in certain forms of *compadrazgo* in the West, but whereas in Andalusia it is used to promote the material interests of a nuclear family by linking it to a powerful patron – and this use is also found in non-tribal Serbia – in the cases examined by Hammel for tribal Serbia it ensures political peace between lineages. In the society of classes and nuclear families it creates ties between classes or between close kin. In that of social equality and the lineage system it creates ties between lineages. But in both cases it is able to perform its function because it derives from premises other than those of the social structure, going beyond them to the dualistic nature of man and invoking the sacred, which is always exonerated from the logic of everyday life.

The institutions of complex societies must contend with many different social contexts and insofar as this contributes to their significance we must expect them to change from one place to another. I have attempted here to show how the *kumstvo*, so well described by Hammel, which appears to be very different from the *compadrazgo* of the rest of the world, is none the less essentially the same institution and that these differences are to be attributed much more to the social structure in which it is incorporated than to a fundamental difference in its nature.

NOTES

1   With reference to E. A. Hammel: *Alternative Social Structures and Ritual Relations*, Englewood Cliffs, New Jersey, 1968.
2   This is no doubt on account of its importance in Hispanic society and the volume of anthropological literature devoted to Latin America. I use the term, as others have done before me, to include the whole network of ties initiated by the sponsoring of a child at baptism, or at a subsequent religious ritual such as confirmation or marriage. Strictly speaking, of course, the relation between the sponsor and the sponsored should be referred to as *padrinazgo* and *compadrazgo* should refer only to the relationship between the spiritual and the physical parent of the same child. However, it is evident that they are interdependent and form a single system of relationships to be classed as ritual kinship, which may on occasions include the physical children of the *compadres*. To refer to this institution as spiritual affinity would imply that we were concerned only with the theological concept, whereas it is its social aspect that is the subject of this article.
3   The commonly repeated explanation of their differentiation, that the early Christians found it advisable to provide the neophite with a replacement for the parent in case the latter should fall victim to the persecution, is hardly supported by the fact that infant baptism was not yet customary when the persecution ended. Saint Augustine still assumed that it was normal for a parent to sponsor his own child at baptism. The prohibition to do so was only established much later and in the course of the development of the concept of spiritual affinity, not for any practical consideration. Explanations on the basis of commonsense are to be mistrusted as much in history as in anthropology.

4   The *comadre de carnaval* was the girl with whom a fictive *compadrazgo* was formed for the duration of carnival. This relationship, established for a period of authorized licence, often developed after the fiesta was over into serious courtship and marriage.

5   Examples of the colloquial usage of *comadre* to mean 'paramour' may be cited from popular songs:

From Lima:

'Compadre que a la comadre
No se le mueve las caderas
No es compadre de veras.'

From: Belén, Catamarca, Argentine (from field-notes of Dr. Esther Hesmitte)
'La cabeza me duele y los ojos me arden
De tanto menear la tipa
De mi comadre.'

6   Article on 'Pseudo-kinship' in *Encyclopedia of Social Sciences*, New York, Crowell Collier & Macmillan, 1968.

7   I have examined the theoretical problems raised by these in 'The kith and the kin' in J. Goody (ed.), *The Nature of Kinship*, Cambridge University Press, 1973.

8   Gallatin Anderson, 'Il Comparragio: the Italian Godparenthood Complex', in *Southwestern Journal of Anthropology*, Vol. 13, 1. 1957, pp. 32–53.

9   For a more detailed account of the rules there see 'Ritual Kinship and the Family in Andalusia', in *Bulletin of the New York Academy of Sciences*, Series II, Vol. 20, March 1958.

10 In Cyprus the marriage sponsors, who are numerous, 'baptize' the children of the marriage in order of their importance as *Koumbaroi* of the marriage. After this they are called by the name *Koumbaros myrodykes* (the sponsor of the myrrh). J. G. Peristiany in Peristiany (ed.), *Contributions to Mediterranean Sociology*, Mouton, 1968, p. 90.

11 Philip P. Argenti and H. J. Rose, *The Folklore of Chios*, Cambridge University Press, 1949.

12 I am grateful to Professor Hammel for his careful reading of this essay, which has enabled me to correct certain errors of interpretation of the Serbian ethnography. None the less, a fundamental difference in our interpretations remains, deriving from our different theoretical positions, as will be apparent to the reader.

13 This is so in Serbia where, Hammel tells us, the tie was instituted in connexion with the danger of death and celebrated, literally, in the cemetery. He does not mention the blood-brother in connexion with mortuary ceremonies. With regard to the point made here see my essay 'The kith and the kin', in J. Goody (ed.), *The Nature of Kinship*, Cambridge University Press, 1973.

14 Irwin T. Sanders, *Rainbow in the Rock: the People of Rural Greece*, Cambridge, Mass., Harvard University Press, 1960, p. 170.

17 Observations on contemporary Spanish families in Mexico: immigrants and refugees

Michael Kenny
The Catholic University of America, Washington, D.C.

It is not uncommon for villagers in Spain to include, in their view of community, many of those who actually live outside the physical boundaries of the village.[1] A family in Spain may have good practical reasons for doing so, especially if the remittances that help to support them come from wages earned by a relative working in Mexico City or, now, in Hamburg or Sydney.

I contend that, rather than simply duplicate abroad the home model of the family, the Spanish migrant positively exaggerates both family and ethnic models especially where there is a strong institutional structure to support the idealized types. My aim here is to support that contention by at least a brief analysis of family values among Spaniards in Mexico today.

Clusters of villages, particularly in the northern provinces of Spain, have been sending their sons by a process of chain-migration to specific urban centres in the New World since the 1830s. The two sub-systems – one in the Old World, one in the New – are linked by an alternating flow of migrants and material resources which bring in their train suppositions important for the analysis of both social control and change. I prefer to think of this movement as a form of transcontinental 'transhumance', for by this term I would stress the importance of the reciprocal rather than the unidirectional flow.

Until recent years the return flow was a privilege enjoyed largely by the group in Mexico that I refer to by the term 'the Old Colony',[2] for there was no political restriction on their movement. These were joined, in the years immediately following the outbreak of the Spanish Civil War in 1936, by several thousands who had fled from Spain; this group I refer to by the term 'the Refugees'[3] which is the name accorded to them by the Mexicans and used also by the Old Colony. For obvious reasons, the relationships that the Refugees were able to keep up with the Spanish homeland were much more severely limited, certainly until 1966 when General Franco declared an amnesty.

Each group – the Old Colony and the Refugees – set up its own institutional structure of formal voluntary associations. Old Colony associations were noted more for their eleemosynary nature; Refugee associations, more for their political or professional character. But only an ideological difference divided

335

the two separate hospitals or the two sets of regional associations, e.g. the Catalans, Asturians, Galicians.

Elsewhere I have shown that the associations especially the regional ones, supply a familiar Spanish environment for the immigrant, a kind of ecological hearth-rug which assuages the loneliness of expatriation.[4] They are, too, centres in which the Spanish family model most consciously survives.

It would be trite to call these centres a home from home, but in effect they serve that purpose. In this regard I find Le Play's classic concept of the stem-family still surprisingly apt. I believe that Spaniards abroad conserve a vibrant feeling for the parent household (the stem) in Spain and see themselves as branches breaking off by their need to migrate. Nostalgia, positively institutionalized in these centres, helps to idealize this model however much grim reality may negate it. Romanticized from abroad, the stem-family appears to them as a haven of safety, a cultural womb to which all may joyfully return, especially those who fail in the business of migration. The actual homecoming may be a shock for all concerned. After a particularly disillusioning trip back home, I heard a Spanish migrant in Mexico City say, in all seriousness, 'Home is a nice place to visit but I wouldn't want to live there.' Even despite the shock of reality, or when migrants cannot return home and their memories grow dim, they seek to duplicate the home model abroad, and their associations encourage this extension.

Given this structural similarity in the associations and the marginal position of both Spanish groups in Mexican society, I feel justified in my arbitrarily homogeneous treatment here of family values.

It is unnecessary for me here to describe this model as it applies in Spain for there are ample accounts of family life there.[5] I know of no study of Spanish family life in Mexico, although studies of Mexican family life are not lacking and one at least of these includes a small percentage of Spaniards in the sample.[6] From this sociological study, carried out in the late 1950s, there emerges a rather cold statistical picture of the average middle-class family, but since half of the total sample resides in Mexico City and Veracruz it will help to illustrate my point, for I restricted my attention to these cities.

The average age of the father is nearly forty-seven years, some six years older than his wife. The couple are Catholic and marry under both the civil and religious rites. The father may own his own business, or be a simple employee, or belong to one of the liberal professions; he earns, on average, $144 a month. With their three or four children they live in their own mortgaged house or flat (value about $6,000) consisting of two bedrooms, sitting and dining room, kitchen, bathroom, patio, and maid's room. They have a small car, radio, refrigerator, and other electric-domestic appliances, but they spend nearly 70 per cent of their income on basic necessities, including over 12 per cent on medical attention. The study brings out the strong provincialism of the families who prefer to marry someone from the same city. A final point is made that only a small percentage (some 6 per cent) marry foreigners.

In its bare state this statistical picture of the Mexican middle-class family generally accords with my own findings on the Spanish expatriates, except that I have recorded a smaller average number of children for the Spaniards and, of course, their medical needs are covered by their Spanish association membership fee. The study tells us nothing, however, about changes in organization and values of the immigrant family.

The conscious Spanish family model has a matrifocal base. It is clear that the Spanish woman is in great demand in Mexico and she generally enjoys a more comfortable and a higher social position than she did in Spain. One rarely, if ever, finds a Spanish woman earning her living in menial tasks such as domestic service. Indeed, emigration may project her from domestic service in Spain to the status of employer of maids in Mexico. This premium on women from the 'peninsula' would seem to be not only a contemporary truth. 'The conquerors shaded the land with churches but neither sowed enough wheat nor brought enough women.' Cortes, well aware that the Spanish woman was the strongest link for binding the conquistador to his new domain, continually attempted to increase the number of immigrant females.[7] A perceptive member of the Colony (described as a man of the extreme centre, politically) summed up the situation for me in these terms: 'The history of the Conquest should be re-written; Mexico actually conquered the Conquistadores through her women, and continues to do so.'

Among Spaniards residing in Mexico City and Veracruz in 1887, over 86 per cent in the capital were men (73 per cent in Veracruz); second, nearly 83 per cent of the Spaniards in Mexico City (nearly 57 per cent in Veracruz) were in the age brackets 11–20 and 21–40, whilst over 77 per cent in the capital (72 per cent in Veracruz) remained unmarried. A survey of statistics on Spanish immigrants into Mexico from 1887 to 1958 shows that until 1933 the ratio of men to women was 3:1; moreover, during this period the women returned to Spain at a significantly higher proportionate rate than the men. From 1933 on, this trend was reversed to the extent that during the years 1933–8 and 1948–53 more Spanish women than men immigrated into Mexico; yet their rate of return to Spain continued to be proportionately higher than that of the men.

A combination of these macro-statistics with my own findings at the micro-level gives us an emergent pattern. The majority of the Colony's male members arrived as bachelors in their early teens. It took them, in most cases, more than twenty years 'hard labour' to make good before they thought of marriage. In the earlier years they had little option but to marry Mexicans or to enter into an illicit union with them; after 1933, they had a greater choice of Spanish women. Eventually, in spite of their initial protestations to the contrary, the endogamous preference repeatedly emerged in my conversation with them. I even found a number of cases of marriage linking the two groups of Old Colony and Refugees, a unique form of the highly infrequent contact between these groups.

For their part, the Refugees came in an organized group, many already with their wives and children; others succeeded in bringing over their families after a few years. A study by Mauricio Fresco reports more than 4,000 women and 8,000 children among their group, a rather high estimate in my opinion.[8] The Refugee men who were bachelors often spent lengthy years, too, carving a niche in the economic structure before they took the step of marriage, quite often with well-to-do Mexican women.

I feel bound to mention the disruption to family life that migration, voluntary or forced, often supposes.[9] There are many cases of Spaniards in Mexico who emigrated at a more mature age (when the Colony was well established), leaving their wives in Spain with the promise of bringing them over when conditions were favourable. Exile, of course, divided some Refugee families too and, in not a few cases, this physical separation was exacerbated by an ideological discord. In Galicia, the northwestern province of Spain noted for its cohort migration, these abandoned wives are described as 'the widows of the living'. The longer the absence from his legitimate spouse in Spain, the more likely that the immigrant will enter into an illicit relationship, consensual union, or even bigamy, abroad.[10] Hence, programmes for reuniting families are a common feature of official governmental and Church immigration policies today. With considerable pleasure Don Alberto, an old informant of mine, from Veracruz, told me, 'There are plenty of those who marry, or rather shack up with, a Mexican – perhaps Indian – woman without ever the family back home hearing of it.' Given the intense and very pointed communication between immigrants and their natal villages, I found this hard to accept, but it *is* possible in isolated rural areas of Mexico.[11] Alberto referred to those who had 'married' their dark-complexioned Mexican cooks or maids and fathered one illegitimate child after another. There was the well-known case of the Spanish millionaire who, after thirty years in Mexico, returned to his village with this type of numerous progeny. The cultural shock expressed in no uncertain terms by his co-villagers was so bitter an experience for him that he returned to Mexico and never re-visited Spain. I can also record cases of bigamy by Refugees who had left their wives in Spain. This is a forceful step in the assimilation process and one from which the immigrant can rarely retreat, for it also effectively cuts him off from any family participation in his own immigrant associations.

Such behaviour might be tolerated for the Spanish male, never for the Spanish woman. The care with which a daughter's future is planned is quite remarkable. The ideal is to send her back to Spain, if not for basic education under the care of the stem-family, then at least to a finishing school or similar environment in which it is hoped she will acquire a Spanish husband. This may well account for much of the high rate of return revealed in the statistics. If she stays in Mexico the parents will ensure that she marries well. Her dowry may be no more than her European heritage.

In order to compute an endogamous pattern demographically for Mexico City and Veracruz one would need to use concepts such as Dahlberg's 'isolate' (the group of intermarrying people) which, in Levi-Strauss's view, throws open to anthropological investigation the marriage system of a complex society.[12] I can at least confirm the trend from my own findings. Mauricio Fresco, a Mexican ex-diplomat and an accepted authority on Spanish immigration, apparently offended many Mexican Hispanists by declaring that the Italians make better immigrants than the Spaniards. 'They (the Italians) almost always marry Mexicans and never boast about their ancestors as do the Spaniards.' He went on to say that Mexico itself must share the blame for the segregation of Spaniards because restrictive laws and conditions make even the naturalized foreigner only a third-class Mexican.[13]

This endogamous preference among the Spaniards, plus their legal and effective segregation from certain Mexican institutional structures, does not prevent Mexican women from being absorbed into the Spanish immigrant social system. The Spanish male is a desirable mate for the socially-conscious Mexican Hispanist. Industriousness, stability in the home, and ethnic heritage, are three of his main qualifications. He is often not as well-educated or as well-bred as his Mexican wife, a fact I have observed rather more in the Colony than among the Refugees. For the potential Mexican wife, money cannot be the sole criterion in her choice of a husband, since she might have plenty of rich Mexican suitors. 'I never speak English when my husband is around', confided the American-educated Mexican wife to me at a Colony fiesta, 'because he gets annoyed, you know, not understanding any other language than Spanish. Oh! he's the master of the house alright. I have to do literally everything for him – so Spanish, you know, but a fine dependable man.' And she sighed.

A contrasting case is described in a novel about the exiles: Elias Carrasco from Madrid who married a Mexican girl in 1945 has 'educated and polished her', but keeps her in ignorance about his most intimate thoughts and his past in Spain. A disillusioned man, he finally leaves Mexico City and takes his wife and two children to begin a new life in the provinces, a logical step for those who felt too keenly the pressures of their own ethnic or ideological group.[14]

Both these cases depict the Spanish husband as a dependable family man, in direct contrast to the usual prototype of the irresponsible and often absent father in the lower-class Mexican home.

There is a striking similarity between the ideal types in the U.S.A South and those of Spaniards in Mexico. 'The ultimate symbol of quality folk is gentle (Southern) womanhood protected and defended by honorable (Southern) manhood . . . Expectations are high for both; purity, gentility, and unimpeachable behavior for the woman; honor, masterful direction of others, and a willingness to die in defense of principles for the man.'[15] I summed up these values several years earlier in my concepts of Immaculate Motherhood and Honourable Manhood in Spain. The point I wish to make here is that both Spaniards in general and Mexicans of the middle and upper classes hold these values in common. Even if Spaniards did not adhere to these values in such a homogeneous form in Spain, it is likely that they conformed to a model often thrust upon them or at least expected of them abroad by older residents and Mexican society at large. Values such as these become frozen into fabricated stereotypes which are then used as criteria for ranking whole families in a vertical scale.

We are told that three of the basic themes in Mexican and Puerto Rican family values ensure that the father is considered the dominant and superior figure in the household; that there is an emphasis on child training to teach obedience and submission to the father; and that the mother is held in such affectionate esteem by the child that this love may interfere in the husband–wife relationship when the child grows up.[16] *Mutatis mutandis*, one could claim that these themes were equally relevant for the Spanish family. To these I would add the forceful concept of *la madre abnegada* – the self-sacrificing and long-suffering mother – which women perpetuate and men take advantage of. Yet this outward cry of submission to male dominance is more apparent than real. In the majority of Spanish households, even in Mexico, it is the woman who is the prime minister of the home and it is she who usually manages the finances (though the higher the social scale the less this is true). In her person resides the store of social credit for the family, a credit form of reputation which the husband continually seeks to augment in the outside world. In an alien land noted for *machismo* – the aggressive masculinity of its men – the pollution potential of the Spanish woman is accentuated.[17]

Changes in the role and dependency of relationship between husband and wife are affected by many variables and would require a study in itself. I can do no more here than point out that in those cases where the family model and ideal values are adhered to most consciously, division of labour and definition of roles between the sexes is most pronounced and more constant. This is particularly true when the backgrounds of husband and wife are quite different, as in the cases of the Spanish–Mexican marriages I referred to earlier. It also appears true of marriages in which the husband is considerably older than the wife. I believe the change is more apparent among Refugee couples whose backgrounds were similar and who were often thrown into a relationship of increased social inter-dependence during the first critical years of settling in Mexico. The example of the Refugee woman forced to support her ailing husband is a case in point. In Elizabeth Bott's terms, the joint conjugal role relationship is less common among members of the Old Colony than among the Refugees, who carry out many more activities together with a minimum of task differentiation and separation of interests.[18] Their social networks are more dispersed, their interests more diverse. I would qualify this to some extent in the case of the more dedicated regionalist (such as the Valencian) or the hard-core political Refugee. These networks – simple extensions of the family in some situations, manipulable personal communities in others – are themselves gradually Mexicanized by the children as they grow up and by the changes in values that long residence and assimilation bring.

For, if the children of the Spanish immigrant grow up in Mexico, their assimilation is considerably hastened. If the parents' social horizon was limited the chances were that the boy would be a replicate product of the *comanditario* system like his father, unless he rebelled.[19] The richer his father the more likely that the boy would be spoilt and would not conform. 'It takes three generations to make a gentleman,' runs the English saying, but it takes only two in Mexico where social class is closely pegged to and defined by economic class. The Spanish saying is therefore more apt: *Padre bodeguero, hijo caballero, nieto pordiosero* ('Father a grocer, the son a gentleman, the grandson a beggar'). I have often heard veteran members of the Colony bemoaning the fact that their sons have turned out to be wasters or have grown away from them; that they have had to bring over from their natal villages a poor but distant kinsman, train him to be a right-hand man, and turn him into a son-in-law to take over the business. Wolf has noted a similar phenomenon among Spaniards in Puerto Rico.[20] In Mexico after 1936, a young Refugee, already in Mexico but no ostensible friend of the Colony, could be tempted to fulfil this role.

The son need not, of course, be a waster to alienate himself from the family enterprise; his choice of another occupation, especially if it is a professional career, will effectively do this for him. Incidentally, this very choice may create an irrevocable educational and cultural gap between him and his uncultivated parents. Many 'Colony' children were sent to Spain or to the U.S.A. to be educated; and this is true even for children of Refugees, especially since the amnesty granted to the exiles by Franco. This is nothing new. As far back as 1921, the Mexican press was complaining that 95 per cent of the Spaniards who are 'well-off' send their children to schools abroad rather than in Mexico.[21]

The statutes of most Colony associations do not give the *criollo* (i.e. the Mexican-born) son the same rights as his father, so that he could have no voice in the administration or direction of these centres. Thus the *criollo* in Mexico City who had a Spanish wife was particularly annoyed, since his wife *could* enjoy these rights but he did not. 'If I'm fit to run the family business I should also be allowed to run an association if I want to,' was a familiar complaint. Other *criollos* I know who are intense Hispanophiles seek solace in the direction of Mexican organizations promoting *Hispanidad* (the sense of an Iberian heritage) such as the Fraternidad Iberoamericana or the Instituto Cultural Hispano–Mexicano. Colony parents, in moments of refreshing candour, admit to a fear of their children becoming too Mexican. They cite with some trepidation the *criollo* Fathers of Independence in Mexico (e.g. Padre Hidalgo), and cases such as Cuban Premier Fidel Castro (the son of a Spanish immigrant from

Galicia) who has turned against the Spaniards there, i.e. against 'his own kind'.

It is not difficult to see why the children, especially the sons, become so quickly Mexicanized and even reject their cultural heritage. The tale of the absent father in Mexico is a classic one. The immigrant, particularly the Colony member devoted so exclusively to making his way to riches, had little contact with his offspring. He was already at work in his store, printer's shop, bakery, or textile business before the children were up in the morning, and he returned home at night when they were already abed. Having shut the shop for the day he entered into his own little Spanish world. What little leisure time he allowed himself was usually spent playing dominoes with Spanish regional friends in the association's recreation rooms. The children were, therefore, more often than not reared by the Mexican maid. If the wife were Mexican the children fell even more into her orbit, however Spanish the husband himself remained. It is not altogether surprising that some of the children become more Mexican than the Mexicans. Nor are they subjected to the same legal restrictions as their immigrant parents. Anyone born and naturalized in Mexico may become President of the Republic of Mexico or hold a high administrative post without discrimination.[22] The Minister of Education in 1961 – Jaime Torres Bodet – was the son of a Catalan; and Uruchurtu, the Mayor of Mexico City in 1961, was the son of a Spanish Basque who, according to my informants, was not kindly disposed towards the Spaniards.

The case of the Refugee children is more complex. Some, like the Niños de Morelia, knew the anguish of flight alone; they suffered the hunger, hardship and insecurity without any firm guide. This group of nearly 400 children between the ages of four and fourteen were evacuated from Barcelona to Morelia in Mexico during the early part of the Spanish Civil War in 1937. According to Foulkes, they have totally and successfully integrated as Mexicans. She states that their experience exerted no ill-effects on them; nor did the ideologies under which they were trained remain with them for, she claims, they are now apolitical and 'a-religious'.[23] A group of them told me proudly – with perhaps a touch of bitterness – that they were 'Mexicans born in Spain'. Others learnt of the Spanish Civil War from its most intimate first-hand participants – their parents. The endless and deliberately repeated post-mortem of battles lost by the parents, was like a masochistic exploration of a familiar wound, nightly over the dinner table. The plans, the erratic enthusiasm, the vain hopes and gruelling nostalgia of their fathers, became, for the children, a learning experience by which they too 'fought' and participated in their parents' patriotism. I was assured by two respected intellectual sons of Refugees that even those who were born in Mexico, criollos in fact, are riddled with a guilt complex or angered at the parents for constantly reliving a past in which they had no part. Whilst they were in camps in France waiting to come to Mexico they 'fought' in their own way, they said, by scholarly achievements and by publicly manifesting their ethnicity – their Spanishness. Later, in Mexico, they founded militant movements such as the 'Movimiento 59' which flowered briefly but soon languished.

Among the second-generation Refugees I noted a determination to carve a niche or career *for themselves* rather than depend on their fathers (as the sons in the Colony might do). They claimed that those of their fathers, who left Spain with little education or talent were quickly corrupted by a bourgeois and material life in Mexico; whereas others, more educated and gifted, were able to achieve the sort of success they never would or could have done in Spain. As to their own future, these young men and women saw it in terms of a need to decide once and for all whether or not to return to Spain. Two particular informants of mine, both in their early thirties, yet already fearing the mental pause of middle age to come, felt that the decision had to be made before they reached the age of forty. They themselves were prepared to make the sacrifice, although both were successful innovators in the literary and artistic fields in Mexico and worked closely and easily with Mexican colleagues.

'Adapt or die' is the unvoiced cry guiding the fortunes of every immigrant. And adapt they do, for the percentage of failures who are repatriated to Spain is remarkably small. Yet to adapt oneself is not the same as being assimilated. Of course it involves deep and sometimes rapid changes. When the Mexican and Spaniard lose their awareness of each other's distinct cultural origin, then, and only then, can we say that the process of assimilation is complete.[24] No one can say exactly when or how this occurs. But the danger in studies of minorities lies in seeing only the negative aspects of the assimilation process. One cannot see the assimilated trees for the non-assimilated wood, so to speak. One's contacts and informants always seem to be those who have preserved their cultural identity; the assimilated have disappeared into the new cultural scene. I believe, therefore, that all studies of immigrants should eventually be complemented by studies of the second and third generations, and also by studies of the views of the receiving society about immigrants in its midst.

Assimilation is too often depicted as an all or nothing, irreversible, process. A study in depth of family relations among immigrants would not only indicate the fortunes of the family as a *group* in both the behavioural and structural assimilation processes, but also reveal the differential assimilation of children. In cases, for instance, where one son is sent back to Spain to be educated but another receives his education in Mexico, we might be able to plot not only differential assimilation but also differences in 'isolate' inter-marriage patterns and, possibly, the disruption and disunity in family organization and values. Moreover, I believe that the parent–child relationship is not always the most significant one. In the cases of young immigrants consigned to the care of kinsmen or co-villagers under the *comanditario* system, in the case of the Niños de Morelia, and, indeed, in the case of an unknown number of other Refugee children, the important relationship is not that of parent–child but that of guardian–ward. This may be a more lasting and profound relationship than the tenuous bond between a child and his parents whom he may see again only after many years' absence, at their death-bed after an emergency trip 'home' for that purpose.

Although I cannot substantiate this by sufficient statistical evidence, it is my firm impression from my own samples that Spanish immigrants in Mexico have fewer children than they normally would in Spain.[25] I cannot explain this simply by saying that the Colony type is obsessed by work and marries late or that the Refugee type who worked equally hard did not want to establish roots in Mexico; yet there is more than a grain of truth in these statements. Nor could I substantiate this from Spanish females; there is a male bias in my informants that I could not counter. But I do know that the wealthy immigrant who has no children at all makes his natal village his heir and immortalizes himself by dedicating monuments of charity to the village in his name. His reluctance to involve himself totally in the national culture of Mexico can only be explained by his clinging to a different set of cultural values. In the case of the fathers, they preserve an authentic tradition through their ethnicity; in the case of the children ethnicity has ceased to be the main criterion which regulates the pattern of daily life.

NOTES

1 This is probably true of many Mediterranean societies. I am indebted to Dr Robert Cresswell for pointing out that, in the Lebanon, population figures given by villagers are often misleading because of this fact.

2 In practice it is not possible to give a reliable statistic for this Old Colony group, although for 1950 there were an estimated 37,540 Spaniards in all Mexico. Between 15,000–20,000 refugees are known to have been brought to Mexico between 1939 and 1949.

3 Writers on migration might prefer the term émigrés who are supposed to regard their exile as temporary, whereas refugees are supposed to have the intention of settling permanently in the new country. The move from a status of émigré to that of refugee is, in effect, a conceptual statement of assimilation.

4 Michael Kenny, 'Twentieth-Century Spanish Associations in Mexico City', in *Socio-Economic Change in Latin America*, Alberto Martinez Piedra (ed.), Catholic University of America Press, 1970.

5 For Spain see appropriate sections in my *A Spanish Tapestry*, London, 1961; also in Carmelo Lisón-Tolosana, *Belmonte de los Caballeros*, Oxford University Press, London, 1966; and in Julian Pitt-Rivers, *The People of the Sierra*, London, 1954. Oscar Lewis's *Five Families* (1959) and *The Children of Sanchez* (1961), deal exclusively with Mexicans. So do such articles as Norman D. Humphrey, 'Family Patterns in a Mexican Middletown', in *Social Service Review*, 26 (June 1952). See also Claudio Esteva Fabregat, 'Familia y matrimonia en Mexico: el patron cultural', in *Revista de Indias*, pp. 115–18 (Jan.–Dec. 1969); the author is Spanish-born but his detailed treatment is entirely concerned with the Mexican not the Spanish model. No one has really grappled with the problem of distinguishing between the two models and I do not pretend to do so here in such an overview.

6   In J. Gomez Robleda and Ada D'Aloja, *La Familia y La Casa*, Cuadernos de Sociologia, Mexico D.F., U.N.A.M. (n.d., but completed in the late 1950s), the authors include some 40 cases (out of a sample of 689) in which one of the spouses was Spanish. Their work is regarded as a contribution to the few studies of the growing middle classes in Mexico.

7   See Carlos Girón Cerna, 'El Indigenismo y El Indio,' *América Indigenista* (Mexico), Vol. I, 1, 1941. And Nancy O'Sullivan-Beare, *Las Mujeres de los Conquistadores*, Madrid, Compañia Bib. S. A., n.d.

8   See his *La Emigración Republicana Española*, Mexico D.F., Editores Asociados, 1950, p. 53.

9   Compare a similar phenomenon in the Greek islands where there is an excess of females left on the islands because of the exodus of males. Many of these can never marry and, according to Kasperson, are responsible for an additional element in the traditional Greek melancholia (p. 21). See Roger Kasperson, *The Dodecanese: Diversity and Unity in Island Politics*, Illinois, 1966.

10 So, too, might the wife back home, of course; but it is more difficult for her to do this positively. Professor Tentori has mentioned to me the seduction of shepherds' wives in Italy, whose husbands – transhumant migrants of a sort – were away for long periods. No doubt parallel cases could be found in Spain.

11 In this, they seem to be following a pattern set by earlier conquistadores in Puerto Rico, who kept their wives in the cities and concubines in the countryside. See Mayone Stycos, *Fertility in Puerto Rico*, New York, 1955, p. 108, citing J. Rosario's *A Study of Illegitimacy and Dependent Children in Puerto Rico*, 1936, pp. 8–10.

12 See Claude Levi-Strauss, 'Social Structure', in *Anthropology Today*, University of Chicago Press, 1953, p. 535.

13 Personal interview, Mexico City, 1 December 1961.

14 Carmen Mieza, *La Imposible Canción*, Barcelona, Plaza y Janes S.A., 1962.

15 See Marion Pearsall writing on the southern regions of the U.S.A. in *Anthropological Quarterly*, April 1966.

16 See e.g. R. Fernandez Marina *et al.* 'Three basic themes in Mexican and Puerto Rican Family values', *Journal of Social Psychology*, XLVIII, Nov. 1958, pp. 167–81, where changes are noted in the Puerto Rican pattern because of the intrusion of North American values.

17 By the Spanish male, in particular. One might argue that the ideal type of behaviour for a Spanish woman is so frozen into a stereotype imposed by the Spanish male and expected by the Mexican, that she may have to 'mexicanize' herself in order to be able to behave like urban Spanish women in Spain today.

18 Elizabeth Bott, 'Urban Families: Conjugal Roles and Social Networks', *Human Relations*, VIII, 4, 1956, p. 346.

19 The *comanditario* system was one whereby young recruits for Spanish business enterprises in the New World were brought over from the same region, often the same village, as that of the business proprietors.

20 Eric Wolf, 'Kinship, friendship and patron–client relations', in ed. Michael Banton, *The Social Anthropology of Complex Societies*, A.S.A. Publications, London, Tavistock, 1966, pp. 6–7.

21 See the article by Benito Garcia Prieto in *El Dia Español*, 21 December 1921.

22 Unlike the Poles in Britain, some of whose sons have been rejected as volunteers in the British armed forces on the grounds that they might present security risks. See report 'Interpretations of Integration', *News Letter*, Nov./Dec. 1966, published by the Institute of Race Relations, London.

23 *Los 'Niños de Morelia' y la escuela 'Espana – Mexico'*, Vera Foulkes, Mexico D.F., U.N.A.M., 1953, p. 60.

24 Emilio Willems has a stimulating discussion 'On the Concept of Assimilation' in a letter to the Editor of the *American Anthropologist*, 57, 1955, pp. 625–6.

25 This seems to be in general agreement with the finding of G. C. Myers and Earl. M. Morris (see their 'Migration and Fertility in Puerto Rico', *Population Studies*, 20 (1966–7)), where they state that migration tends to depress fertility throughout the childbearing period.

18   The idiom of family

Margaret E. Kenna
University College, Swansea

In this paper about family life on the Aegean island of Nisos I hope to show how the idiom of family, used in relationships of wedding sponsorship and god-parenthood (*koumbaria*), reconciles the ideal of family independence and self-sufficiency with the need for co-operative ties outside the family.

One of the main bases for trust and co-operation between island families is established through interaction in the religious rituals of marriage and baptism. Relationships between resident island families, Nisiot families now living in Athens, and non-Nisiots, are also created through *koumbaria*.

THE ISLAND OF NISOS

Nisos is a small island about twenty hours' boat journey from Piraeus. It has a population of 394 individuals, 183 males and 211 females. The main bases of economic life are subsistence farming and shepherding. The sale of sheep and goats in the spring to visiting meat-merchants is a major link with other islands and the mainland. Subsistence farming rarely provides enough grain for flour and olives for oil to last from one harvest to the next. Island men spend three months in Athens as seasonal summer migrants working as builders' labourers to earn cash for buying essential supplies and also for capital, consumer and 'luxury' goods to maintain and raise status. This temporary migration, as well as permanent migration, is a long-established pattern of island life. There is a settled émigré Nisiot community in Athens which provides a 'home' for seasonal migrants and for would-be permanent migrants.

There are many different sorts of ties between the island and émigré communities and some of these are not immediately relevant to the theme of this paper. Besides ties of kinship there are also contractual ties such as those between émigré landowners and their island half-shares tenants, and between pasture-owners and shepherds who rent grazing for their flocks. Many émigrés return to the island for summer holidays and to see to the upkeep of their island property. At this time many weddings and baptisms are held, and émigrés are asked to be wedding sponsors and godparents. They also offer themselves as *koumbari* for there are many advantages in being *koumbaros* to an islander just as there are for the islander who acquires an Athenian *koumbaros*. I shall discuss the balance of rights and duties at a later point.

THE FAMILY HOUSEHOLDS

The pattern of household organization on Nisos is based on the nuclear family. The island population numbers 394 individuals living in 125 households. Ninety-one of these are nuclear family households at different stages in the domestic cycle: from households of newly-married couples and couples with young children, to elderly couples whose children are married and living either on Nisos or in Athens. The remaining 34 households are mostly those of single individuals: bachelors, spinsters, widowers and widows.

Daughters and sons move out of their parents' household immediately on marriage. No unmarried person lives with a married sibling or other relative. No sick elderly relatives are brought into the household but are cared for in their own homes. There are thus no joint or extended family households. This is not just a grouping of the population into separate buildings: household units are discrete entities.

THE IDEAL OF INDEPENDENCE

A household is set up when a newly-married couple move into a house which is part of the bride's dowry and it continues until both partners are dead. The islanders insist that the life and fortunes of each family household are united and cannot include those of other families, however closely related. Each nuclear family regards itself as a unit with its own specific interests. Co-operation with other individuals and families may help to achieve these aims, but helpfulness and altruism never dominate self-interest. As other families are thought to hold similar aims of self-advancement they are seen as possible threats because it is felt that it is impossible for everyone to be successful. For one family to succeed means that others must fail. One family's success in a large harvest, a child's success in an examination, acceptance by an influential person of a request to stand as *koumbaros*, necessarily reflects on other families not so successful. Thus members of a family can only be really sure of each other for they have the same common goal. They conceal from others any piece of information, trivial, or important, in case capital can be made out of it.

To retain his self-respect a man must regard himself as subordinate to no one. His position among his peers, his own self-respect, and the respect accorded to him by others, is partly determined by his own actions but depends also on the behaviour and reputation of other family members, particularly the female members. He must make sure that no breath of gossip or scandal touches them, and they in turn can exert pressure on him by public sullenness, tears or disobedience which show up his lack of control.

THE FACTS OF INVOLVEMENT

The new household which is created at marriage is an independent unit and yet at the same time meshed into the existing network of each partner. It is possible for a couple to raise their status in economic terms and in terms of public opinion as to their honour. However, the reputation and status of their respective natal families will always provide a basis for comparison of the new household's success, and also a means of justifying adverse evaluations and interpretations. The choice of spouse is affected by the factors of health, family reputation, age, and wealth, which depend on the situation of the individual's natal family. Sickly offspring damage a family's reputation, a poor family cannot afford to dower a daughter until she is older than the expected age for marriage, a family scandal will discourage reputable suitors or prospective brides, despite their suitability in terms of age and wealth.

A couple set up house with the bride's dowry (a house given to her by her parents, its furniture and fittings, and possibly a few grain terraces and olive trees) but the groom will not get the land which is his share of his natal family's estate until his parents die. A newly-married man must therefore create a network of contacts for employment on the island as a labourer, working for men who have land through inheritance or purchase, and contacts for work in Athens as a builder's labourer during the lull in farmwork after harvest in June until there are island jobs again in October. He becomes involved in relationships of dependence and situations of obligation, putting himself in the position where others can make claims on him in order that he can later make claims on them. For example, a farm labourer tries to make an employer beholden to him by offering his labour at a time, such as harvest, when labourers are greatly in demand. The employer is then obliged to employ this man when jobs are few. The relationship builds up so that although the workman is paid, his labour is given 'as a favour' because he arranges working days to suit his employer's plans. It is thus impossible to establish and maintain a household without getting involved in social relationships based on interdependence. At his father's death a man inherits the fields which are his natal family estate; the quantity and quality of his inheritance depend on his parents' efforts. Just so, the transfer of house and dowry lands to a daughter is an indication of the ability of her parents to build, buy or otherwise acquire such property.

The aim of each nuclear family household is to become independent and economically self-sufficient; in order to achieve this end the household head becomes involved in relationships of dependence and in situations of obligation and debt.

INDEPENDENCE AND INTERDEPENDENCE

The husband and father represents his family to other island families and to the outside world. His relationship with his parents and his married siblings is one of equality between independent households. Although a father can exert moral pressure on a married son, he cannot expect him to work without reciprocation or payment. A married son will help his father with farmwork but not, as when he was unmarried, as an unpaid subordinate. He fulfils obligations to his natal family by placing their claims for labour high on his list.

By sharing in his wife's kinship relationships a man adds affinal relationships to his already existing kinship ties; criteria of self-interest determine which ties are maintained and strengthened. Ties are likely to be stressed if distant relatives or affines are neighbours or have neighbouring fields. Kinsmen outside the nuclear family are involved in each other's reputation. They stress a relationship, even if distant, if it brings reflected glory and shun those whose dishonour may attach to them. A man's co-operation with his married brothers and sisters, with his wife's parents and her married siblings can also be described in terms of a relationship of mutual advantage between independent household heads. The moral content of the relationship is expressed in the fact that each party to it acknowledges obligation to the other and recognizes claims to reciprocal services. Each has the right to ask for help and co-operation and the obligation to give it on the understanding of long-term reciprocity.

TIES BETWEEN HOUSEHOLDS

There are networks of different and overlapping ties between family households. Different types of ties include: kinship, affinal, and *koumbaros* relationships, contractual ties between employers and workmen, ties of neighbourhood between households in certain areas of the village, or between those whose landholdings are near each other.

Each kind of tie involves certain rights, obligations and expectations. As the link between any two households is likely to be made up of several sorts of tie, the way in which the associated rights and duties are expressed directly and indirectly in the total relationship of household to household is variable and capable of manipulation because there is no way of deciding exactly how that particular combination should be expressed. Judgements of relative value, choices and decisions, are all made in the light of certain commonly held principles such as honour and family independence which are ideally absolute but are evaluated in practice according to variable factors such as stage in the domestic cycle.

These networks of multiplex ties and their practical expression in mutual interaction are nonetheless ties between family households striving for economic self-sufficiency and social independence.

THE IMPORTANCE OF *Koumbaria*

In a situation where co-operation and trust are thought to be possible only between members of the same nuclear family household, and where ties outside the family are essential to maintain it, trusting and co-operative relationships outside the family are only possible if they are phrased in the idiom of family and backed by moral sanctions which are strong and, in many cases, stronger than those of kinship. These aspects are implicit in the religious ceremonies which create *koumbaros* relationships between the main participants.

The man who performs the central act in the wedding service and sponsors the marriage by garlanding the groom and bride becomes the couple's *koumbaros* and they become *koumbaros* and *koumbara* to him; a woman who garlands a couple becomes their *koumbara*.

THE WEDDING SPONSOR

Choosing a wedding sponsor is one of the first acts of independent choice which denote that an individual has attained full adult status. The choice takes into account qualities of sociability and good humour, for the most public aspect of the sponsor's activities is his acting as master of ceremonies at the wedding celebrations. The choice must also take into account reputation and respectability, for the future position of the newly-founded household is assessed by others and forecast by the *koumbaros* in terms of his position. The couple have yet to establish themselves as an honourable and respected household with a sound economic basis which will later provide dowries for daughters and land for sons. The *koumbaros* by accepting and performing his sponsoring role makes a public statement that the couple will in his opinion achieve such a position. He aligns and involves himself with them, they in choosing him affirm his position and involve themselves in his reputation. The choice is also affected by the sponsor's economic and political position, that is, his resources of land, money, personal influence, and network of influential kinsmen and friends. The *koumbaros* is expected to help establish the couple in the first months of marriage. He helps in practical ways and by using his influence with administrative officials, important islanders and members of the émigré community. He has an obligation to offer to the groom any work he wants done on his own lands and to hire the bride for olive-picking and harvesting. The couple in their turn must try to meet any requests for help and assistance, ideally putting their *koumbaros* before anyone else, but actually putting his claims equal with those of their closest relatives. If the *koumbaros* is himself the groom's employer his standing as *koumbaros* increases his control over fixing the days and the type of work.

It is the duty of the *koumbaros* to help a newly-married couple on the way to becoming an autonomous household. Parents and parents-in-law have other children and other commitments, so although they are involved in the success of the marriage because this reflects on them, they must also remain a separate and independent household closely involved only with those members who remain. They cannot be fair to unmarried children if they are helping to build up the newly-created households of married children. It is thus the *koumbaros'* role to ensure that the newly-married couple have an advisor and helper, ideally throughout their married life but usually only during the period when they are trying to get established. The couple need a kindly and established *koumbaros* to help them acquire their own network. When they do the *koumbaros* has fulfilled his duty to help smooth the first months of marriage. If he has proved reliable and helpful the relationship may well be made lasting by the groom's asking him to stand as godparent to the first child.

In practice, the extent to which the possibilities of the relationship are realized, varies considerably. The islanders emphasized that a wedding *koumbaros* was chosen mainly for his social skills, the good humour and sociability essential for the successful organization and liveliness of the wedding festivities. A young farmer who had been a wedding sponsor on seven occasions, said: 'To be a *koumbaros* is fun – and there's no expense involved', and then went on to compare wedding sponsorship with the serious nature, and expense, of god-parenthood.

GODPARENTHOOD

A relationship of *koumbaria* also exists between a married couple and the person who acts as godparent to their child. Usually in Greece the parents and godparents call each other by the same terms of address and reference as are used in wedding sponsorship. On Nisos the child's physical and spiritual parents address each other as *synteknos* (m.) and *synteknissa* (f.) which literally means 'together-child' and can be translated as 'joint creator of the child' or 'co-parent'.[1]

The islanders explain this by saying that the child's physical parent 'makes the child for his own pleasure' – *yia to gousto tou* – whereas the godparent makes it possible for the child to be a *Christianos*. The word *Christianos* not only has the meaning of 'member of the Greek Orthodox Church' but also means 'a human being', as opposed to an animal, 'a civilized person' in contrast to 'a savage', and in particular, 'a Greek citizen and member of the Nisiot community'. The tie between the child and the godparent and between the parents and their *synteknos* is based on the importance of being a *Christianos*. Without a godparent the child cannot be named and without a name he or she cannot become a member of Nisiot society nor inherit the property which goes with the name and marks full adult status. The parents recognize the extent of their obligation to their *synteknos* for his vital role in establishing their child in the community by giving him preferential help, putting his requests before those of any other potential employer, and he in turn helps them both in practical ways and by using his influence on their behalf.

The godparent provides a complete set of clothes for the child to wear after baptism by total immersion, a gold cross to be worn on festival days, and gifts of money for parents, grandparents, other close relatives, the priest, and guests at the christening party. The behaviour of the parents to their *synteknos* on the day of the baptism is predominantly one of formalized respect with self-conscious use and acceptance of *koumbaros* as a term of address and reference. This is particularly so if the godparent is a member of the émigré community. If he is a villager, especially one with whom there is already an established tie of neighbourhood or kinship or *koumbaria*, behaviour shows the friendly but still respectful intimacy which later characterizes all effective *koumbaros* relationships.

The godparent continues to give the child clothes and presents over the years, to follow growth and development, and to use his influence and contacts to smooth difficulties and arrange favours in any circumstances in which the child's welfare is directly or indirectly involved. The help and favours given to the godchild's parents are an extension of the godparent's duty to make sure that the child is materially and spiritually provided for. The godchild must answer any request for help and ensure that the godparent is well looked after in old age, particularly if there are no children or close kin on the island. Often the godparent is asked to perform the engagement ceremony for the godchild, blessing the rings in front of an ikon and asking the two young people if they are entering voluntarily into the betrothal.

LATER CONTACT WITH THE *synteknos*

The relationship between the family of the godparent and that of the godchild is considered to be one of spiritual kinship. Intermarriage between families so related is forbidden by canon law, to the degree of third cousin, just as marriage is prohibited with any consanguine to this degree. Local custom says in addition that a godparent should only stand sponsor to children of one sex in case any of the godchildren wish to marry each other, as this is also forbidden by canon law. The islanders say 'they cannot marry because the oil came from the same house', referring to the oil provided by the godparent, which is blessed and used in the baptism. The godchildren of any one person are said to be related to each other by their bond of spiritual filiation to the godparent. They are called *stavradelphia*, 'siblings of the cross'. I found no evidence that the reciprocal rights and duties between godparent, godchild and godchild's parents extended to the godchildren of a common godparent, but it seems likely that ties of spiritual kinship between co-godchildren might serve as grounds for seeking assistance and favours. There is one small piece of evidence for this: all the godchildren have a photograph taken with their common godparent.

Although a godparent should only baptize children of one sex, it is not expected that boys should have godfathers and girls should have godmothers. A man or woman can baptize either a boy or a girl but must thereafter only stand godparent to children of that sex.

The child calls the godparent *nonnos* (m.) or *nonna* (f.). The godparent refers to the godchild as *vaptistikos* or *vaptisteros* (m.) or *vaptistika* or *vaptistera* (f.) meaning 'the boy (or girl) I baptized'.

The other children in the family call their sibling's godparent *nonnos* or *nonna*, 'as a sign of respect', although they are quite clear that the relationship with this *synteknos* of their parents is unlike that with their own godparents. When they are older they address the sibling's godparent as 'uncle/aunt' or 'grandfather/grandmother' depending on the age difference and generation gap. A person's older siblings may call his godparent *theios* 'uncle', while his younger siblings will call him *pappous* 'grandad'. In general, any individual of a junior generation, no matter what chronological age, uses kinship terms in addressing members of the senior generation when there is a distant unexplicit kinship tie or a link of some other kind between the families. The change in the term of address for a sibling's godparent (from *nonnos* to *theios*) indicates a lessening of involvement and identification with the natal family. The sibling's godparent no longer belongs to a special category of persons with a particular type of relationship to all the godchild's family, but now belongs, as far as the siblings are concerned, to the wider category of respected members of the senior generation. The siblings cease to be involved in the *koumbaros* relationships of other members of their natal family, and begin to establish their own *koumbaros* relationships, retaining only the tie with their own godparent.

THE IMPLICATIONS OF CHOICE OF GODPARENT

Because of the importance of the mutual claims and obligations of those involved in the godparental relationship, parents take care to ask at least one influential islander to be godparent to one of their children. Such men as the village president, council members, the schoolmaster, and the post-office clerk have as many as six godchildren and have acted as wedding sponsors on many occasions, besides having ties to families for whom their wives, and in some cases, unmarried children, have acted as sponsors and godparents. Important members of the migrant community in Athens are asked to become wedding and baptismal *koumbari* on their summer visits to the island. Such a *koumbaros* may be influential in helping the new husband find work, or in later years in finding the godchild a job in the city, or in using contacts to manipulate a situation to the godchild's or his parents' advantage. The Athenian *koumbaros* relies on the support of his island *koumbari* for himself or for his own patrons, in the political context of island, city, or national affairs.

Several island families chose a childless or unmarried godparent for one of their children. This child, usually one born after the first son and the first daughter, would be expected to inherit the godparent's property in return for care in illness and old age and for performing funeral and memorial ceremonies. Some of these families said that they had been approached by the prospective godparent who asked to stand as godparent under these terms. There is a clear balance made in the arrangement between the godchild's duty to care for the physical and spiritual welfare of the godparent, and the right to inheritance after the godparent's death.[2] The godparent fulfils the required duties over the godchild, makes the godchild his heir, and in turn can be sure that he will be cared for in old age and that the funeral service and cycle of memorial ceremonies necessary to ensure that his soul gets to God will be carried out. The care-inheritance aspect of these godparent–godchild relationships is made more explicit in instances in which island godchildren were legally adopted by childless godparents in Athens. I knew of three families from which a child had been adopted by city godparents. In each case there was already a kinship link between the godparents or spouse, and the godchild's family, and the child was one of the youngest in a large family.

Islanders and migrants are aware that calculations of advantage and future gains for each party to the relationship are involved in the choice of godparent. Each party feels that the balance of rights and duties is fairly favourable to himself. An influential islander or member of the migrant community may feel that he will have little opportunity to exert claims for help or labour on his godchild's father, and will himself be involved in gift-giving and have pressure put on him to get favours for the family. On the other hand, a farmer, particularly a skilled workman, may feel that his child's godparent will make unavoidable claims on his time and skills. Often each party is suspicious of the other's intentions. Before making a direct request, the parents, or the prospective godparent, sound out the possibilities of acceptance or refusal of godparenthood. Parents often start a rumour of their intentions which they know will reach the proposed godparent whose reaction will be relayed back to them. They can then ask directly or choose an alternative. A prospective godparent also uses the same tactics.

In several cases, parents chose as godparents individuals who had no established ties in the island community. Examples of such individuals are: policemen stationed on Nisos; fishermen from the large refrigerated boats which fished in the area, and who occasionally came up to the village to sell part of their catch and to buy provisions and cigarettes; meat-merchants who visited the island before Easter to select sheep and goats to transport for slaughter for Easter feasting; and a taxi-driver on a large neighbouring island who took an expectant mother to hospital after meeting the caique which brought her over from Nisos.

There are clear advantages in most of these relationships with 'strangers' as far as an islander is concerned: bureaucratic matters can be arranged, preferential sales or purchases made, and other favours performed for him. For the 'stranger', the non-islander, becoming a godparent on the island involves the duty of carrying out such favours, but also establishes a role for him within the island community and provides a set of rights and duties without which small comforts, favours, and a guarded acceptance of him by the islanders would be unobtainable. The *koumbaros* relationship gives the 'stranger' a basis and a reference point for himself and others during the times he stays on the island. The fisherman and the meat-merchant godparents have rights to hospitality rather than seeking paid board and lodging. They are included in the men's news and gossip-groups, and this gives them the advantage of knowing island conditions better or more easily than other strangers can. A policeman-*koumbaros* is not expected to be a house-guest because his term of duty may last several years, but he is given, or found, a house for a favourable rent through his island *koumbaros'* good offices, given presents of fruit, vegetables, and other produce which would be difficult to find for sale, and shares of illegally dynamited fish, or partridges shot out of season, to ensure his complicity. The policeman expects in return to get a wider knowledge of island affairs through access to freer and franker sources of information – his island *koumbaros* and family – than he would from acquaintances and coffee-house gossip.

Thus while islanders try to choose influential godparents for their children, there is also competition to be chosen as a godparent. Both sides want to establish a relationship of mutual obligation, from which each expects to get the things he wants. The balance includes: for the godparent, preferential help on the land, political support, care in old age, and the assurance of properly performed funeral and memorial ceremonies, and on the other hand, for the child's parent, preferential wage labouring jobs, influential contacts, and the possible inheritance of property for the child.

The man of mature years who has never acted as a wedding sponsor or godparent is free from the claims for services and favours based on the relationship, but he is also without the opportunity to exert reciprocal claims. Not to be a *koumbaros* implies that a man has nothing to offer, as a wedding sponsor, or as a godparent, and this 'nothing' is an evaluation not merely of his economic position and lack of influential contacts, but also an assessment of his lack of honour, which tends to be correlated with economic status. To choose such a man as *koumbaros* reflects badly on the couple making the choice, and, by implication, reduces their reputation for honour, and their own evaluation of it, to the level of the *koumbaros*.

There are families with little land and few resources who are highly respected and sought after as *koumbari*, but generally, low economic status is given a low moral evaluation, and families in this category seek *koumbari* from those of similar status who consequently do not possess a wide range of ties among islanders and migrants. Similarly, one index of the prestige of islanders with a regular income and/or large land-holdings, is the number of *koumbaros* relationships in which they are involved. For example: the *proedros* had seven ties as godparent with island families, and had been a wedding sponsor many times; one of the councillors, of the *proedros'* party, had five godchildren and 'more wedding *koumbari* than I can remember' (he mentioned more than ten names); another councillor had six *koumbari* ties; a councillor of the opposing faction had five *koumbari* ties with island families; the post-office clerk had been a wedding sponsor nine times, a godparent three times, and was in a *koumbaros* relationship with six other families through the godparental ties of his wife and eldest daughter.

It is rare for *koumbaros* relationships to be reciprocal. In the instances where there is 'doubling up' so that a wedding sponsor later becomes a godparent, or a godparent's child stands as wedding sponsor to the godchild, it is nearly always the already sponsoring family, that performs the sponsorship, and the other family which asks to be sponsored again. There are very few instances of, for example, a godparent from one family, a wedding sponsor from the other, over two or three generations. There are, in fact, so few of these instances that it is difficult to generalize about the reasons for their being exceptions which might prove the rule of the unilateral nature of the sponsoring relationship.

'DOUBLING' AND CONTINUED ASSOCIATION

Often those chosen as *koumbari* are members of a family with which a previous *koumbaros* tie existed. A man asks the child of his godparent to act as his wedding sponsor, and may himself be asked to become godfather to the child of a couple to whom his parent acted as wedding sponsor. A *koumbaros* tie can also be 'doubled' when a wedding sponsor later becomes godparent to the first child of the marriage.

In his analysis of ritual relations in the Balkans, Hammel (1968) discusses similar data on doubling and agnatic succession to sponsorship roles. Sponsoring relationships, he says, have a 'collective character' and 'are best viewed as being contracted between groups rather than between individuals, or at least between individuals by virtue of their group membership' (p. 89). (The 'group' here is the *zadruga*, the partilocal joint or extended family.)

Similar institutions in other parts of Europe 'are more easily described as a system of individual dyadic contracts in which group members *may* become involved by extension' (p. 45).

There is no evidence that on Nisos *koumbaros* relationships are systematically continued between families, nor that *koumbaria* is regarded as an inherited or heritable relationship. *Koumbaros* relationships also exist with families with whom there is a kinship or affinal tie. A man acts as wedding sponsor for his siblings, his parallel- or cross-cousins, and for unmarried siblings of affines; he may stand as godparent to siblings', cousins' and affines' children. It seems that the establishment of a *koumbaros* relationship between members of families already linked by actual or spiritual kinship ties emphasizes that the mutual rights and obligations involved are mandatory only for the nuclear families concerned in that particular relationship. The more flexible, optional ties between families linked by kinship, affinal, or previous *koumbaros* ties can only be set into the context of firmly binding rights and obligations by creating a *koumbaros* tie between the members of newly-formed nuclear families, and thus reconstituting the basis of the relationship. Each nuclear family must establish its own ties in its own right.

Although Hammel says 'the ties of ritual, consanguineal and affinal kinship are generally mutually exclusive' and shows how and why the three sets of ties are usually separate in the Balkans, he also quotes a Greek informant as saying 'why go out and make a new relative when he is already a relative?'[3] As I have tried to show, these ties are not mutually exclusive on Nisos and the possible reasons are the size of the island population, the extent of contact with non-residents, and the autonomy of each nuclear family. The interests of siblings diverge from each other and from the natal family once they set up separate households on marriage, and the creation of *koumbaros* ties counter-balances this division into separate nuclear families by binding the sponsoring and the sponsored families with links of spiritual kinship. Pre-existing ties from the natal family are re-phrased and re-established in the context of the existing and operative nuclear families.

FUNERAL AND MEMORIAL SERVICES

One of the most important aspects of kin and *koumbaros* relationships is the duty to perform the funeral service, *kydheia*, and the required number of memorial services, *mnemosyna*, for the souls of the dead, and finally, to exhume and reinter the bones when the corpse has rotted.

The obligation usually obtains between children and parents and is seen as a reciprocation by the children for their parents' care for them in youth, particularly for their provision of lands for sons and dowry for daughters. The connexion between these ritual duties towards others and the inheritance of property is most explicit in the cases of those who are unmarried or childless, or with no descendants or collateral relatives on the island or in Greece. Such a person approaches an islander who has the reputation of an honest and fairly devout man and broaches the topic of his own advancing age and preparations for death and the after-life. If the younger man has small children and is likely to have others the old man offers to stand as godparent to one of the yet unborn children. The two men will then be *koumbari* and the rights and duties they have towards each other, one for care in life and after death, the other to inheritance for his children, are set in a religious context with the strongest of sanctions on observance. If it is not possible to establish a *koumbaros* relationship, there is not the same degree of confidence that promises on each side will be fulfilled.

But once the old man gets his will drawn up and the younger man and his wife show by their care and attention that they will look after him, the contract becomes a moral one.

Relationships with *koumbari* show the same recognition of moral rights and duties combined with calculation of self interest as is exhibited in kinship relations. The relationship is however different from kinship in that most *koumbari* are chosen: both sides enter the relationship voluntarily. The moral component is thus more explicit and hence more manipulatable than in ordinary kinship ties.

A Nisiot household usually has a number of *koumbaros* links. One tie is with the wedding sponsor, there are ties with children's godparents, with the spouses' own godparents if they are still alive, and also with families to whom husband, wife or their children have acted as wedding sponsor or godparent. Different aspects of each tie may be stressed according to need and some ties remain almost inoperative until circumstances encourage their renewal, as when parents decide to send an intelligent child to High School in Athens where an émigré godparent can provide a home during term-time.

The rights and duties in *koumbaros* relationships are economic in that they are concerned with jobs and with skilled and unskilled labour. They are politically important because they involve decisions about the allocation of these jobs, and competition to control decision making and access to officials and administrators in the government bureaucracy.

Koumbaros relationships regulate the pressures of supply and demand for labour, needs which alter with the yearly cycle and with each year's specific problems. *Koumbaros* relationships are the major context for patron–client ties within and outside Nisos as a physically bounded community and as a community of residents and migrants. Nisiots, like Sarakatsani,[4] use *koumbaros* links to create personal ties with individuals in official positions, so that they can use these individuals and their networks of relationships.

Many *koumbaros* ties are with members of the émigré community, some of whom have official positions, and jobs in business and trade, and who have ties with others in similar positions. Some ties are with non-Nisiots affines of émigré families. There are ties within the island with members of various government organizations, the post-office clerk, the police, the schoolteacher, and through them with senior officials in the hierarchy.

These ties are not like those of the Sarakatsani, 'across the frontiers of community'[5] (ibid) and with those outside the 'field of values', but they *are* formed to provide ways of manipulating the impersonal mechanisms of bureaucracy and the labour market to the advantage of the family. *Koumbaros* relationships are explicitly and implicitly similar to relationships between members of the same family household. The idiom of family is used in behaviour, expectations and evaluations of actions between *koumbari*.

A couple's wedding sponsor, older than them but younger than their parents, someone who is likely to have young children but none on the brink of marriage so that he can help the couple without conflicting claims from his own children, acts as a stand-in parent or older brother. I do not want to over-emphasize the family aspect of wedding sponsorship for I think that the island-ers view the role as a first stage or trial run for godparenthood. While it is true that the couple trust their sponsor because he is their *koumbaros* it is also true that they chose him because they thought him trustworthy. A sponsor who 'proves' himself nearly always becomes a *synteknos*; this suggests that sponsor-ship in itself is not thought a particularly binding relationship. The couple wish to continue the relationship with one who shows himself reliable and trustworthy, so they ask him to become their *synteknos*.

OTHER FAMILY AND KINSHIP IDIOMS

This paper would not be complete without some reference to the use in daily life of family and kinship terminology between unrelated individuals. Kinship terms such as *theios* or *barba*, 'uncle'; *theia*, 'aunt'; *pappous*, 'grandfather'; are systematically extended to particular unrelated individuals with whom the speaker comes into frequent contact, as in the example of other children in a family and their sibling's godparent. Children very often use kinship terms to address unrelated adults: 'uncle' and 'aunt' for adults of the parents' generation, 'grandfather' and 'grandmother' for those even older. Kinship terms are also extended to individuals whom the speaker usually addresses in another mode. A young adult who usually calls an older man and his wife who are non-kin, *Kyrios* Iannis and *Kyria* Margarita (Mr and Mrs), may on a particular occasion call them *theios* Iannis and *theia* Margarita and the use of these terms creates an atmosphere of affectionate respect, implying intimacy. The couple can ignore the implication of the kinship terms, or they may respond in a friendly way. If so, the younger person can make a request – the loan of a grinding stone, a pur-chase on credit, a message to a shepherd grazing his flocks near the couple's fields – without feeling that there is too much obligation on one side and condescension on the other.

I am not suggesting that kinship terms are used in a conscious strategy to influence non-relatives to behave like kin. I do think that when an individual wants a request to be granted as a favour in a reciprocal setting the model which springs to mind is one based on mutual aid between close kin. It is important for individual self-esteem for the request to be granted as a reciprocal favour and not as a patronizing gesture over a wide status gap. No man wants to imply that there is such inequality of status that there is nothing he can do to return a favour, or to feel that he is in someone's debt in a short-term exchange of aid.

Kinship terms are also used in situations where there is no thought of a reciprocal relationship but rather as an indication that respect is recognized or required. Kinship terms for members of the older generation are used to address unrelated individuals older than the speaker to imply a kindly interest tinged with respect. 'Take this seat, grandfather' says a young man about to leave a crowded café to an elderly widower standing at the door looking round for somewhere to sit. Kinship terms used to individuals younger than the speaker imply that some degree of co-operation, obedience, and attention is demanded. An old man who wants cigarettes bought for him calls *Ela pedhi mou* ('Come here my child'), to a boy playing in the street outside his house; an old woman grasps the arm of a younger women or a girl to help herself up the church steps saying *To cheiri kori mou* ('Your arm, my daughter').

As well as being used as a sign of intimacy and affection, kinship terms can also be used to convey lack of respect. A young man who calls an older man *barba*, 'uncle', can imply that the older man is a doddering old fool, or that there is no need to call him *kyrios* as he commands no respect because he lacks status. A telling point in discussion is clinched by calling the listener 'my child', thus asserting the speaker's superiority.

A man who needs help in a practical task such as holding a struggling donkey to treat a sore may call out to a passer-by for help, *Re koumbare ela 'dho* ('Hey *koumbaros*, come over here'). The speaker is opening himself up to the passer-by, acknowledging his need for help, asking for the sort of favour appropriate in a *koumbaros* relationship. By giving the passer-by an admission of inability to manage on his own, the speaker puts him in a position both of superiority and obligation: to repay by acting like a *koumbaros*.

I am aware that there are indications in behaviour as well as in terminology that a situation is seen by one actor as best managed in a kinship idiom. By acting like a kinsman towards non-kin an individual can indicate and imply a moral dimension in the situation. Behaviour of this sort is recognized by other actors and responded to either positively or negatively. As an observer from another culture I was unable to recognize instances of this sort of behaviour unless there was a clue of terminology. All I can do here is to comment that the idioms of kinship and family are used in behaviour alone as well as in behaviour and terminology. Family and *koumbaros* relationships have strong moral components and sanctions: individuals try to impose a moral dimension on a particular situation by referring explicitly or implicitly to the model of these relationships by using kinship or *koumbaria* terms of address and by adopting behaviour appropriate to such relationships.

CONCLUSION

Koumbaria uses the idiom of family behaviour to resolve the conflict between the ideal of family independence and the necessity for ties outside the family to maintain it. The idioms of family and *koumbaria* are also used in non-kin encounters to indicate the moral dimensions of the situation.

NOTES

1   Middle-aged and elderly islanders used the term *synteknos* in conversation, but younger people used it as an obsolete technical term to make precise distinctions between sponsors and godparents in discussions with me on *koumbaros* relationships.
2   Compare with Hammel's assertion, 'I find no evidence that property can be inherited by ritual kin in the absence of consanguineal heirs'. E. A. Hammel, *Alternative Social Structures and Ritual Relations in the Balkans*, Englewood Cliffs, New Jersey, Prentice Hall, 1968, p. 91.
3   Hammel, *Alternative Social Structures*, p. 85, n.
4   J. K. Campbell, *Honour Family and Patronage*, Oxford, Clarendon Press, 1964, p. 218.
5   Campbell, *Ibid*, p. 218.

19   Kinship, class and selective migration[1]

Ernestine Friedl
Duke University, North Carolina

In spite of a growing literature on migration, reports on case studies which trace specific individual migrants over a span of time are still relatively rare.[2] The advantage of such studies, as this paper hopes to illustrate, is that they permit observation and analysis of the specifically local, social, and cultural conditions under which the selection of migrants occurs, the social and cultural conditions which affect the outcome of the migration at the point of destination, and the effect on both sets of circumstances of the changing economic, social, and political conditions of the national system which provides the environment within which the migration takes place. One can also investigate the relationship of the objective conditions and the migrants' perception of them to their stated motives for migration, and to the outcome of the move. The data, then, permit the delineation of a process rather than a statement of correlations.[3]

The study presented here describes a case of voluntary rural–urban migration in a developing country. The rural area is the village of Vasilika in the Greek province of Boeotia, the city is Athens, and the data are concerned with migration from the village to Athens between 1930 and 1965.

Research began with a field study of Vasilika in 1955–6, with a second brief field session in 1959. At that time there was clear evidence that migrants from the village had not severed ties with members of the community, and that they were exerting influence on the culture of the village (Friedl 1959; 1962; 1964).

In 1956 the village had a population of 216, divided among 48 households. By 1965, 22 household heads had relatives living in Athens who had grown up in the village, 3 had such relatives both in Athens and in the provincial towns, and 5 had them in provincial towns only, leaving 18 household heads with no village kin who had migrated to larger centres. In this study I disregard those who went to and stayed in provincial towns. A total of 53 migrants (35 men and 18 women) went to Athens to settle or to study and were there in 1965. These 53 individuals are the subject of this paper.

I knew at the start that the migrants had not left the village in family or other groups, and that they were not settled in any single region of Athens. It was also obvious that, in the course of the 35 years, some villagers had stayed in the village and had no intention of migrating. Two problems therefore presented themselves. (1) How had the selection of migrants occurred? (2) What, if any, consequences for their urban histories had the process of selection imposed?

In this situation it seemed best to use the individual as the unit of study. This research strategy assumes that individual actors allocate their time and energy with reference to a set of goals, that they have an awareness of the restrictions of their environmental setting which make some behaviour intended to accomplish the ends rewarding and some not, and that allocations will be continued or changed depending on the actual outcome of earlier behaviour. In other words, individuals keep on making decisions, and one important part of the process is the conscious weighing of alternative choices.[4] By comparing the statements of individuals as to how they arrive at decisions with the objective environmental constraints and opportunities within which they operate, it should be possible eventually to predict which sets of conditions will result in which kind of decisions.

During the summers of 1964 and 1965 I interviewed, in their own urban homes, all but 5 of the migrants. Information about these 5 was obtained from their rural and urban relatives. No formal questionnaire was used but similar information was elicited from each person. My husband and I participated in a variety of social events in 6 of the migrants' Athenian households. We also met some of the migrants back in the village when both they and we returned for ceremonial occasions. At these times we started and participated in discussions on the subject of *astifilia*, 'love of the city', as the Greeks call the process of urbanization. Since 6 of the migrants left Vasilika in the 1930s, 10 shortly after World War II, and the remaining 37 between 1951 and 1965, there was an opportunity to talk with, and to observe, migrants of different ages and with different degrees of urban experience.

The earlier study of Vasilika had established that a prominent village norm was the value attached to striving for the improvement of the conditions of life for one's children. Villagers also believed that it was the function of the members of the elementary (nuclear) family, acting together, consciously to manipulate its resources toward that goal (Friedl 1962, p. 18; also 1964). The major criterion for improvement was movement upward in a rank order of occupations. The ranking was based on a combination of the level of education required for the occupation, the opportunities for security and advancement it afforded, and the consumption standards that the income from it could support. At any level an occupation accrued greater prestige if it permitted life in Athens rather than in villages or provincial towns. (Cf. Safilios-Rothschild 1967a, p. 375.)

A rank order of occupations which the villagers considered realistically possible for their migrating sons and their prospective sons-in-law was roughly as follows:

A. Those requiring post-gymnasium education:
   liberal professions (law, medicine, engineering, university professorship);
   upper-level civil service or equivalent post in private enterprise;
   commissioned posts in armed services or police;
   gymnasium professorship.
B. Those requiring at least gymnasium, and often additional training as well:
   middle-level civil service or equivalent post;
   non-commissioned posts in the armed services or the police;
   elementary-school teaching;
   priesthood.
B'. Those in which a respectable income and independence compensate for
   lower educational qualifications:
   ownership or management post in retail store or other commercial enter-
      prise;
   commercial brokerage.
C. Those in which educational qualifications may vary, but tend to be lower
      than for those in A and B, and in which income is lower:
   low-level civil service;
   office work;
   proprietorship of small store;
   artisan ownership of a shop;
   clerkship in a store.
D. Those in which academic education is not required:
   skilled construction or factory work;
   unskilled factory work or farm labour.

Running parallel with the values attached to this series of occupations was the value placed upon farming as a way of life. The position of the farmer with between 40 and 100 stremmata (4 stremmata = 1 acre) would be rated as equivalent to the B and B' occupations in the foregoing list. Ownership of a farm of fewer than 40 stremmata meant that wage labour or other sources of income were also required, and therefore ranked at or below the D level.

Aspirations for daughters centred on marriage to men in the rank order listed. The specific means for achieving such marriages was for fathers and brothers to acquire dower properties in Athens or in a town in the form of a house or apartment. To put it another way, the first aim of village men was to acquire an education or skill, the first aim of village girls was to acquire real property. Girls might, as a secondary means of improving their economic and prestige status, try for an education either for teaching or white-collar jobs, or for some skill such as dressmaking. In such cases, the girls might save before marriage to supplement their fathers' and brothers' efforts to buy a lot or a house, and, after marriage, they might supplement their husbands' income by working.

It is clear, then, that except for the possibility of retaining or accumulating substantial amounts of land in the region, the Vasilikans assumed that a better life would require migration to towns and occupations other than agriculture.

This set of values existed between 1956 and 1965 at a time when a considerable number of villagers had migrated or were leaving the village and achieving their goals. The Vasilikans' aspirations were congruent with, and reinforced by, observed events. The recollections of those who left Vasilika before 1956 suggest that in the 1920s and 30s the values of the villagers were similar; what was lacking was the practical opportunity for any significant number of villagers to achieve them. If, as the evidence indicates, there were no serious differences of opinion about the importance of, or the means toward, upward mobility for children, the question of why and how some villagers but not others chose the migration route becomes more urgent.

When, then, were the restrictions or constraints on the one hand, and the opportunities on the other, which were balanced by the villagers in the effort to make a decision, and how did these coincide with objective reality?

Three different sets of economic, political, and social conditions in the village, in Athens, and in the Greek nation as a whole, correspond with three major waves of migration from the village:

Phase I, 1931–6.   Pre-World War II;
Phase II, 1945–50.   Post-World War II and the Greek Civil War;
Phase III, 1951–65.   Recovery and development.

Within the village the significant differences among the households lay in their economic resources. The differences in Vasilika in this respect were sufficient to affect the rates of migration among the various groups and the subsequent placement of the migrants. The village households, as of 1956, can be grouped into four categories, A, B, C, and D, in the descending order of economic resources, occupation, and style of life.

Category A: eighteen households
    Own 40–150 stremmata of land;
    Frequently supplement income by running a store, keeping bees, etc;
    Household members normally do neither wage labour, nor (except by
        arrangement with siblings or brothers-in-law) any sharecropping;
    Annual cash income estimated at $600–$1,500.
Category B: nine households
    Own 15–40 stremmata of land;
    Supplement income by sharecropping and wage labour;
    Annual cash income estimated at $300–$800.
Category C: sixteen households
    Own 15 or fewer stremmata of land;

Supplement income by sharecropping and wage labour;

Annual cash income estimated at \$200–\$600.

Category D: five households

These were shepherds; their annual cash income is not estimated.

These D households will not be referred to again, save in so far as their members served as an available labour force within the village itself, since they did not participate in the migration to Athens until after 1965.

PHASE I, 1931–6

In the first phase the total migration from Vasilika which ended in settlement in Athens consisted of five young men and one woman. I shall call these six 'pioneers', and shall use the term 'first-migrant' for any subsequent migrator who is not linked by close kinship with a previously-established resident of Athens. All the pioneers came from Category A. This fact is typical of the whole migration picture: it began with the top economic stratum, and this stratum continued to be heavily represented.[5]

Preparation for migration was believed to require education or training beyond the six-year village school. The families' decision in the 1920s to give the five boys mentioned a secondary education was based on the family's evaluation in each instance of its economic and human resources. The labour of the young men was viewed as surplus, and the resources sufficient to maintain them during their schooling. Each of the boys had one or more brothers old enough to supply the labour for the farm under 1920 conditions, and to help in the accumulation of dowries at the moderate level then required for their sisters. (Significantly, no A category household with only one son sent him to be educated.) The choice of the particular son to be educated was not based on age ranking within the family. The boy to be sent had to be at the proper age for the educational opportunity then opening up, and had to have shown some academic talent.

The prospective equal division of the land among the children, by inheritance or dowry (the total number of living children in each of the pioneer's families ranged from four to seven), would have drastically reduced the resources of each of the children as compared with what the parents had had. The joint support of one child's education therefore increased the land share available to each of the others because the education was construed as constituting his share of the inheritance.

Information about secondary school educational opportunity and encouragement to take advantage of it came from the local school teacher. There was a Middle School (three years beyond the six-year village school) in a larger village five miles away. This made it unnecessary for the families to face the constraints which the absence of relatives at a distant educational centre would have imposed. Transportation costs were nil; the boys walked back and forth each week-end, at which time they were also furnished with sufficient bread and cheese to last out the school week. The outlay in cash or kind was for lodging, books, and school supplies, which these families could afford.

Finally the prospects for earning a living at a liberal profession or of obtaining a civil service post in Athens were predicted as favourable. In 1922 some one-and-a-half million refugees came from Asia Minor into Greece through the exchange of populations; about 150,000 settled in Athens (Pentzopoulos 1962, p. 97). This population increased the labour force in a period of low industrialization and immediately after the disruption of the Greek economy by the first world war and its aftermath, so that the market for common labour from rural areas was not propitious. But the settlement of the refugees increased the need for administrative government personnel.

After completing the Middle School in 1926, four of the boys went on to gymnasia in provincial towns twelve or fifteen miles away, for what at that time was a three-year course. Although the greater distance added to the expense of transportation, and made lodging more expensive, the gymnasium diploma was an eligibility requirement for certain civil service exams and the university. The fifth boy did not complete gymnasium, but went to a police school in Athens instead. By 1936, he was earning an urban living and he is the man who brought his Vasilika bride, our sixth pioneer, to Athens at that time. She was a sister of one of the other pioneers.

The others finished gymnasium, one going to Athens for the purpose, where he boarded with his sister (the young woman mentioned above) and her husband and earned his way during the day while attending night school.

The decision of the four gymnasium graduates to proceed further with their education (for three this meant a transfer to Athens) was the next important step, for it would have been possible to acquire a low-salaried post with only the gymnasium diploma. Their actions were influenced by the great competition for posts requiring only a gymnasium education, and what seemed like a greater chance of success if they joined the fewer eligibles with university or other higher level training (cf. for a later period, Argyriades 1968).

The police officer's training and support were provided by the government (his opportunity had come through the patronage of a member of parliament from the rural area); the night-school gymnasium graduate earned something for himself, and the other three were supported in Athens by remittances from their brothers back in the village.

ATHENIAN CAREERS: EMPLOYMENT, MARRIAGE AND HOUSING

The period between the completion of their training and the outbreak of World War II was spent in searching for positions, with intermittent success, and with occasional periods back in the village. The men balanced the relative lack of opportunity in the cities against the constraints imposed by the contemplated loss of their own and their families' *filótimo* (honour) had they returned to take up farming after their lengthy and expensive educations. Furthermore, agricultural methods and yields were improving in the village, so that there was not even a specious justification for their return (Naval Intelligence Division 1944, Vol. ii, pp. 55, 64). By the mid-1940s all had, through civil service examinations, achieved permanent, salaried posts in Athens on a level with other men of their training. All had developed networks of friends in Athens, through whom they had learned of available vacancies. Their careers therefore exhibit a pattern of assistance both from the rural family and from individually-acquired urban friendship ties.

Notably absent as a social mechanism for support in urban adjustment was membership in an association of compatriots. The pioneers themselves initially formed a miniature group, living near one another in rented quarters, but the marriage of three of them was followed by settlement in different parts of the city.

Once established in their posts, these five men lived lives characteristic of middle-class salaried Athenians. Two, while in their early 30s, married, without arrangement, rural school teachers who came to teach in Athens and supplemented their husbands' meagre initial incomes. The policeman, as we have seen, brought, by an arranged marriage, a farm woman from Vasilika itself to become his wife; the income from her dower share of land, worked by her brothers, eked out his salary. Incidentally, since the state and not his family had supported him through the last part of his training, he was still regarded as entitled to some land as part of his inheritance, and continued to enjoy the usufruct of this holding.

The two remaining men, like many other Athenians, married late, one aged 40 and the other 50. The first found a rural wife by arrangement, the second married an urban friend. These two, as well as the earlier-marrying pair, followed the current Athenian and village pattern of having no more than two children each.

The five have all been promoted in their organizations and, in 1965, three were retired or close to it, looking forward to the pensions that had bulked so large among their goals. Each owned either a house or an apartment in a good residential section of the city near its centre, and not in the newly-developing outskirts. These had been acquired either with the assistance of the wife's dowry, or through a generous loan programme for civil servants, or by a combination of the two. Their children, all girls, have had, or were expected to acquire, a gymnasium diploma; one girl has had education beyond the gymnasium.

The description which the pioneers give of their early experiences make clear the severe emotional stress they were under and the real physical hardships which their early poverty engendered. These hardships and the fear that they might not successfully uphold the honour of their families were counter-balanced by the emotional support the family gave them and the feeling of the migrants that they were important participants in a family enterprise.

The description of the careers of the pioneers was given in some detail because their histories illustrate principles of choice and limiting conditions which are significant for all subsequent migrants from Vasilika. The careers of these pioneers also had some specific consequences. Their example served the younger generation of villagers as successful models for migration. More importantly, all but one of the six pioneers were the first links in a chain forged by the migration of their nieces and nephews. The pioneers' presence in Athens and their acceptance of an obligation to help their brothers' and sisters' children to leave the village accounted for 34 per cent of all the subsequent migrants from Vasilika. The pioneers provided an urban opportunity of significant proportions by their acceptance of a supportive role. In a sense, they were thereby repaying their village families for the assistance they had received.

PHASE II, 1945–50

There was no new migration from Vasilika during the immediate pre-World War II period or during the war and the German occupation, which ended in 1945. Ten migrants, five men and five women, left the village to settle in Athens during the second phase, 1945–50, despite the guerrilla warfare in the countryside and the unsettled conditions in Athens during the Greek Civil War of 1947–9. These ten were distributed as in Table 1. The considerations

TABLE 1

Village economic category		Kin-linked			First-migrant		
		Men	Women	Total	Men	Women	Total
A		3	1	4	0	0	0
B						1	1
C		1	2	3	1	1	2
	Total	4	3	7	1	2	3

which led to the decision to move in the case of two men of the A category households were similar to those of the male pioneers. They had one new advantage, however. Both men, or boys as they were when they left the village, had relatives in Athens. One had a brother who was a pioneer, and the second had a godfather in the city. The third man was the first only child to migrate. The presence of an uncle pioneer in Athens, and of a relatively young father who could handle the labour on the farm influenced his decision to leave.

The woman in the A category represents the first example of what we have earlier called a secondary avenue of improvement for women, education beyond elementary school. By virtue of being the niece of two pioneers, she had ample supervision in the city, and her household had the resources to see her through gymnasium education in Athens. After finishing, she went back to the village for several years, but eventually returned to Athens and obtained, by examination, the civil service post she was still occupying in 1965.

The B category first-migrant woman exemplifies what became the most frequent basis for the movement of women from the village: marriage to an Athenian. Her husband was an artisan from a neighbouring village who had set up shop in Athens before World War II and returned to Athens in the late 40s, soon after which event they were married. With the aid of her dowry, they eventually built a house in an outlying section of the city. This phase also marks the first movement of C category migrants out of the village. Here the considerations were different from those we have already discussed. The families did *not* have the economic resources to support the children in town. What then led them to disregard this limitation and how did they overcome it? In the case of one young man, it was a combination of his kin link with one of the pioneers, and a situation in which, with few land resources, only one sister, and a talent for studies, his prospects in Athens were better than those in the village. He also worked during the day for a time and went to school at night.

The other male C migrant had neither resources nor kin links. He did have two other brothers who could stay on the farm, and his association with the village was less strong because his father was not native to Vasilika but had married into it (cf. Friedl 1962, p. 65). His was the only case in which a man apparently went to try his luck at getting a job in the city without kin links and without the thought of continuing his education.

The three girls in the C category are three sisters, one of whom went to Athens first and so became the first-migrant through whose auspices the other two sisters later went. Here, the girls were older than their one brother; the father's chances for providing dowries for them with his minuscule land resources and low-paid railroad job were not good. The presence of a woman acquaintance of the parents in the Piraeus seems to have been the decisive element that enabled the eldest daughter to try for a gymnasium education. She chose lodgings at the terminus of a railroad line where she could receive food sent from home. She left the gymnasium to take a factory job, and soon married her landlord's son, an office worker. She facilitated the migration of her sisters, one of whom worked in a factory; the other learned dressmaking.

If for this purpose we include mention of a C migrant who went to a provincial town but did not reach Athens, it may be noted that every C household in which there were children between the ages of about twelve and twenty sent such children out of the village.

For all the C cases, the lack of land for supporting the children in the city or town was weighed against the equal lack of opportunity for work in the village. Between 1945 and 1950, the farm labour requirements of the region could be satisfied by the children of farm families with reasonable amounts of land. In Athens and the towns, the turbulent conditions provided interstices into which people might fit themselves.

The five migrants from A category households or from a C household with A connexions had educational and employment histories which paralleled those of the male pioneers. The unsettled political conditions lengthened the time required for their education; they went back to the village for varying periods, and the civil servants spent some time serving in provincial towns before they were rewarded with posts in Athens.

One of these five men was still unmarried in 1965; two were over thirty when they married, and the other two were in their late 20s. Two of the marriages were arranged, and involved wives brought from a village. For all four married men, housing was provided through their wives' dowries. The girl in this group married in her mid-twenties, and chose her own husband; it was her husband who had access to housing.

The career of the single B migrant, a woman, has already been discussed. Four C category migrants exemplify patterns some of which are repeated for later migrants from this group. Except for one of the girls who married in her early 30s, the rest, both men and women, married in their early 20s. The three women chose their own husbands, one, as we have seen, moving into his household; the other two eventually accumulated enough funds with the help of their fathers' dowry contribution to build houses in outlying sections of Athens.

After their marriages, two of this group of migrants left Greece to find work. The man has settled in Canada; the woman and her husband are temporarily working in Switzerland.

PHASE III, 1951–65

Phase III was marked, on the national scene, first, by the completion of the recovery from World War II, the German occupation, and the Greek Civil War; and then by steady economic growth and development. During this period, 37 villagers, 25 men and twelve women, established themselves in Athens. The largest number absolutely, nineteen, came from A category households, representing 50 per cent of the young people in those households eligible to migrate. From the B category, seven migrated out of eleven eligibles, or 63 per cent; from the C category, eleven out of 34 eligibles, or 33 per cent.

The term 'eligible' in this context refers to those boys and girls who could be expected to consider migration, if the patterns characteristic of Phases I and II were to be further exemplified. All movement out of the village between 1931 and 1950 had been undertaken by unmarried boys who had recently completed the village school, by girls in late adolescence if they left before marriage, or by girls who left in order to get married. Therefore, 'eligible' refers to all boys of twelve years and over and all girls of sixteen or over. Up to about sixteen it is still possible for girls to undertake further education or training.

The 37 migrants were distributed as in Table 2. Many of the conditions under which this large group arrived at decisions to migrate and to stay in Athens

TABLE 2

Village economic category	Kin-linked			First-migrant		
	Men	Women	Total	Men	Women	Total
A	7	7	14	3	2	5
B	3	1	4	3	0	3
C	3	1	4	6	1	7
Total	13	9	22	12	3	15

were similar to those already discussed. In this section, it suffices (1) to summarize, for both the rural region and Athens, any differences from the situation encountered by earlier migrants, and (2) to try to explain the continuing pattern of variation in migrants' careers attributable to their original membership in rural households of different economic resources.

Several new circumstances were the same for all economic groups. First, there was the constantly increasing availability of kin in Athens. Even the first-migrants of the early 1950s were, by the 1960s, capable of providing supervision, information, and contacts for their younger relatives. A second common condition was the expansion of employment opportunities at all levels in Athens, and in the 1960s in western Europe, with no accompanying increase in the size of the Greek adult working population. A third consisted of the technical improvements in agriculture introduced through new government farm policies. Finally, the previous migrations and the continuing pattern of movement out of the village began to have feedback effects in the Boeotian plain. One of these was intangible; as we have seen, the earlier, successful, migrants provided models for the later Vasilikans to emulate. The tangible feedback was the demographic change which resulted in a different man–land ratio.

A CATEGORY MIGRANTS

Decisions to migrate

The limiting need to retain at least one son to work the land had been diminished (1) by improved agricultural technology resulting from the increased availability of government credit for machinery and fertilizers which both lessened the need for manpower and increased the yield to the point where letting out some land for sharecropping was economically practicable, and (2) by the availability of C and D group labour for peak work-periods, and for share-cropping, for those households with larger land holdings than the home-staying members could farm. As a consequence, four households were willing to permit all their sons to migrate during this period, in contrast with one in Phase II and none in Phase I.

Another new consideration was the increase in marriages of girls in A category households to townsmen. The normal expectation that a wife's dower land would match the prospective inheritance of a farmer was severely diminished, because only poorer girls were now constrained to stay on farms, and they had small dowries. This consideration was particularly important in households with several sons who had to share the patrimony.

The expansion of the Greek military establishment, concomitant with Greece's status as a NATO ally, created more opportunities for commissions, so that two of these households encouraged sons to take up military careers.

For the migration of women, the new element for these households was the increase in the dowries required by educated urban grooms in white-collar occupations (B or B' level). By the early 1960s, a girl's dowry might be about four to five times the annual cash income of an A category household. The established practice of gradually accumulating resources for a daughter's dowry either facilitated the payment of an initial instalment on an urban house, or contributed to its gradual construction. For the six women who went to Athens as brides from this economic group during this Phase, those with urban kin had the advantage of relatives who could act as marriage brokers (these were all arranged marriages) and could be trusted to recommend honourable grooms.

Another new situation for women during this period was represented by two cases in which the girls had married men in provincial towns, and whose husbands were successful enough to move them and their children to Athens.

If 50 per cent of the eligible young people in A ranked households did migrate, what about the situation of the other 50 per cent? About three-quarters of these were young men who were staying in the village to run what were sufficiently substantial farms to make it worth while to take the chance of receiving only a small dowry. Several of these men enjoyed farming and were glad to be able to stay in the village. One woman in A category married one of these men, her fellow villager, thus joining two substantial families.

The other quarter of those who stayed in the village were virtually all as yet unmarried women who had either not gone for further education at all or who had begun gymnasium in provincial towns. The presence of half of these women in Vasilika in 1965 was a function of their ages. They were then 25 to 32 years old, within the normal range for still unmarried girls in this group. At the time when they would have been the right age to enter gymnasium they had no relatives in Athens or in provincial towns. For the few who had kin links at the appropriate age, various idiosyncratic family situations prevented their additional schooling.

Education and employment history

Because this phase covers a span of fourteen years and some of the movement out of the village occurred in the last years of the period, many of the men and the husbands of the women were still in the process of building careers. Some few were still university or gymnasium students. Among the remainder, almost all the men had education or training beyond the gymnasium. One man had an A level, the others B or B′ level jobs. The husbands of the women migrants were at the same occupational level, except that no woman's husband was in an A level occupation. (Warriage and housing for *all* migrants in Phase III will be discussed below.)

B CATEGORY MIGRANTS

Decisions to migrate

The increase in the proportion of B young men and women who left the village is attributable to the increased agricultural yields which provided for these households just the additional margin needed to facilitate the temporary support of children in Athens during their education and training. Several of the first-migrant men from this group used the military and police training route to urban support. Those few eligibles who had not left were again either unmarried women or men staying on the farm.

Education and employment history

Since almost all of this group left the village in the 1960s, half of the men were still students or in training. The others were in B or B′ occupations as was the husband of the one young woman who migrated as a bride.

C CATEGORY MIGRANTS

Decisions to migrate

The proportion of C migrants in this phase, one out of three eligibles, is conspicuously low and requires some explanation. The increased opportunities available in the village for agricultural wage labour or sharecropping arrangements, already discussed in connexion with the A category migrants, approximated those available at unskilled or semi-skilled labour in Athens. Only such low-level jobs were open to those without education or training beyond the village school. A C category boy who aspired to an Athenian career above this level had therefore (1) to deprive his family of his help or wages during his educational years, and (2) to draw from the family's meagre resources at least the small amounts needed to sustain him in the early years of this period. For those who tried the educational route (and some did), the precariousness of the balance was so delicate that any failure in school, even a temporary one, easily tipped it in favour of giving up, as unrealistic, the higher aspirations which they had nourished.[6]

The women of the C group did not migrate because they could take advantage of the shortage of prospective brides available to the A and B farmers. They married up into wealthier rural households for which, in former years, their dowries would have been deemed quite insufficient.

In a sense, therefore, what is surprising is that eleven people from this economic group did reach Athens. Once again kin links tipped the balance for some of the men, and for one woman for whom an Athenian marriage was arranged.

For the first-migrants, earlier successes in provincial towns with a subsequent move to Athens accounts for a few, and the military training route for some others. One new pattern emerged here for male first-migrants: they married Athenian girls they had met during their compulsory army service and their wives' Athenian parents became their link to jobs and housing.

Education and employment history

In 1965 one-third of these men had completed gymnasium or were in the process of getting career military training for non-commissioned posts. The rest were

TABLE 3   Phases I, II and III.
Summary of employment history of all migrants and husbands of women migrants

Occupation levels	A category migrants			B category migrants			C category migrants			Total
	Men	Hsbnds of women	Total	Men	Hsbnds of Women	Total	Men	Hsbnds of women	Total	
A	7	0	7	0	0	0	1	0	1	8
B and B′	7	9	16	2	0	2	2	0	2	20
C	1	1	2	1	1	2	3	2	5	9
D	0	0	0	0	1	1	4	3	7	8
Student levels										
Post-gym	2	0	2	1	0	1	0	0	0	3
Gym or equiv.	1	0	1	2	0	2	1	0	1	4
Total	18	10	28	6	2	8	11	5	16	52[a]

[a] These 52, with one unmarried girl who was a low-level civil servant during the day and studied at night, make up the 53 migrants. Two women represented in the table above by their husbands were still working, one in a B level job and the other in a D.

mostly in C and D level jobs, as were the husbands of the women migrants. One of the women, with her husband, was temporarily working in Germany.

PHASES II AND III (*All migrants*)

MARRIAGE, HOUSEHOLD AND HOUSING

Among all the Phase II and III migrants who were no longer students in 1965, more than half were still unmarried; 8 out of 11 A category men, 1 out of 6 B, and 4 out of 11 C. They ranged in age from 26 to the early 40s and most were in their middle 30s.

Setting up a household and starting a family is a serious matter, and more serious still where property or a higher standard of living is involved. The men were waiting for advancement in their posts to the point where they could either command a larger dowry from a village girl, or could find educated working urban women so that their double income could be sufficient to set up a household. Actually two of the three A category men who did marry chose to exemplify the Greek proverb, 'A shoe from your home town even if it is patched', and acquiesced in the efforts of their Vasilika relatives to find them wives from neighbouring villages. The third had a marriage arranged with a rural bride from a different part of Greece. One C category man also married a rural girl. In each case, the girl brought with her a dowry sufficient to supply the couple with housing.

Throughout the migration period, a higher proportion of C category men married in their 20s. Several of them were able to do so because Athenian girls found them attractive; the girls' families acquiesced, and the boy was assigned the urban version of the role of in-marrying son-in-law. At least at the start, the parents offered the young couple housing, and in some cases offered their sons-in-law employment and training. This 'good marriage' syndrome was the means by which a few of the C category migrants, in time, developed exceptional careers.

The migrant women from A category households married later than those from other economic groups. A higher proportion of C women not only married earlier but also came to Athens alone and later arranged their own marriages.

But about a quarter of all the married women married men in Athens whose parents had been the migrants. In every case, the groom brought his bride into his parents' household in the standard virilocal pattern of the villages. Here, the girls' dowries provided for some furniture and housing improvements. This situation engendered a number of three-generational extended households, as did the in-marrying son-in-law arrangement referred to above.

Housing has been mentioned often in passing; it is time to consider it in more detail. The city of Athens has grown in an ever-widening semi-circle from the Acropolis, and its houses have started creeping up the sides of mountains surrounding the Athenian basin. As more houses appear further away from the city, land values for the nearer zones go up. These zones which started without paved roads, sewers, or piped water, are then gradually improved by the enlargement of the single-room houses, or their demolition and replacement by apartment houses, a favoured form of investment. Public utilities, then, also improve (Ekistics 1965, p. 73).

The migrants from Vasilika, both married and unmarried, were located in more than a dozen different districts in the Athens–Piraeus area. Kin-linkage again played an important part; those with relatives in Athens tended to rent rooms and later to acquire houses or apartments near their relatives, with the result that there are three regions of the city where more than two kin-linked households from Vasilika are concentrated. For the rest, information on land values, construction costs, and the like, came only from friends and colleagues.

The majority of the A category married migrants were settled in 1965 in old or new standard middle-class housing in the belts not far from the centre of Athens or Piraeus, and hence equipped with electricity, running water, baths, and water-closets, while almost all the C migrants were in more distant belts where, except for electricity, none of the amenities just mentioned was available. The B migrants occupied a middle position. Nevertheless, all houses were owned rather than rented. In many cases, houses had been occupied as soon as walls and roof were completed; their owners were carefully limiting all other expenditures in order to be able to complete the house and add to its amenities, and additional dowry instalments were also being used for that purpose. Because real estate taxes in Greece are negligible for low-salaried people unless the house is used to produce income, costs of upkeep are limited to charges for garbage collection, water, and the like.

For none of the migrants in outlying sections, despite the absence of piped water and water-closets, did such housing mean insanitary, crowded slum conditions. The number of persons using each house was small, since no migrant in this kind of housing had more than two children. Indeed, only four of all the married migrants were the parents of as many as three (cf. Safilios-Rothschild 1967b). Houses are usually widely spaced. Back-yard latrines are ample for the small number of users. The Athenian climate makes it possible to heat houses with space electric or kerosene heaters during the four coldest months, and this also keeps down the cost of housing. Cooking is done with bottled gas, and electric refrigerators are not uncommon. The women maintain the standards of orderliness and the touches of elegance they were accustomed to in the village.

DISCUSSION

KIN AND CLASS: EDUCATION AND EMPLOYMENT

There are several conclusions to be drawn from the histories just discussed. First, the decisions are made on the basis of the economic resources of the nuclear family household of the migrant and are subsequently backed by these and by the families' strong emotional support. In the village, the parents and their unmarried children who constitute one household operate as a corporate group; any siblings in either generation who have already married are normally not part of that corporate group. The frequent reluctance of men to marry before their sisters have been dowered is a reflexion of their prospective separation from the responsibilities of their parental households once they themselves have married. Exceptions to this pattern occur if several brothers remain in their parents' household after marriage, or if their father dies while some of the children are still young. Brothers may then continue to act jointly, at least with respect to the fortunes of their unmarried siblings.

From the standpoint of a prospective migrant and his parents, the parents' siblings and the married children of the nuclear family who are no longer members of the corporate household constitute the most important potential source of aid and assistance. These take the form of giving information, using contacts, and providing moral supervision of the young. Housing may be provided, but if it is for a longer period it may have to be paid for. Assistance by these non-members of the corporate group is very rarely given in straight cash payments; this remains the prerogative of the corporate household.

The brothers and sisters of a migrant or of his parents are not the only source of aid; they are part of a pool which includes godparents, more distant kinsmen, friends, and political patrons. But siblings in both generations, if available, are the most likely first choice, and their presence or absence may be crucial at the point at which decisions to move to the city are made, and for the first placement in school and in jobs. Once a man or woman has lived in Athens, friends become important sources of information, particularly about jobs and about potential grooms for a man's sisters.

A second conclusion to be drawn from the data is that the class position of the villagers as defined by the relative quantity of land their households owned, for the most part determines the class and status level of the occupations they or their husbands will occupy in Athens. The move to the city meant, for the A category farmers, a shift from the class and status of small-holder to that of middle-level management and white-collar positions in government or private bureaucracies; the shift for most C category migrants was from sharecropping and wage labour to low-level bureaucratic posts and skilled or semi-skilled construction and factory labour. The B category migrants moved between the lower levels of the A and the upper of the C. This generalization for the B category migrants holds for the entire subsequent discussion and they will not henceforth be mentioned separately.

This second conclusion is directly related to the first because it was the process of kin-linkage that affected the life chances of each group of migrants. Because the A category households could afford to send sons earlier and could keep them studying longer, these men attained higher level posts. A generation later, when their nieces and nephews were ready to think of leaving the village, the pioneers were sufficiently well placed to have information about superior schooling and housing, and eventually to have access through contacts to better jobs. At the same time, the village households could support their children at higher standards and for longer periods. This chain continued for these A families; about 60 per cent of the migrants from this group are kin-linked.

Among C category families first-migrants did not start leaving the village until at least a decade after the A migrants had; they had fewer resources to start with, and less chance for advanced education. Therefore the probability that there would be C-migrant relatives in Athens was lower; in addition, the level at which those who were there could give assistance was lower. Only about 43 per cent of the C category migrants were kin-linked.

A third conclusion is that the military and para-military police force constituted a substitute for the family and its kin, particularly for B and C migrants. Room, board, supervision and training were given at government expense; jobs were available if a young man could successfully complete training. This fact enabled some C migrants to transcend D level occupations.

From the subjective standpoint of the migrants and their village kin, the urban occupations achieved by all the migrants involved upward mobility. The prestige of the jobs, and the security they afforded at the employment levels existing in Greece in the mid-60s, were considered better than those offered by the positions they could have achieved in the village.

KIN AND CLASS: MARRIAGE AND HOUSING

The conclusion that the class level in the village had determining consequences for urban careers can be drawn also for the marriage and housing histories of the migrants. The higher the economic levels, the greater was the probability that men and women would marry late. This is partly a result of the longer period of education required for the superior positions toward which men of this class aspired; it is also due to the willingness of both men and women to postpone marriage until enough economic resources could be accumulated to form the basis of a standard of living which this group considered appropriate for its status.

Another class-linked phenomenon, as we have seen, was the location of the housing occupied by married migrants, with a larger proportion of those in the higher economic groups living near the centre of the city.

Household composition

A statistical survey of household composition among all the married migrants shows that nineteen live in new, exclusively nuclear family households, while only nine live in households which include a parent or parents of either spouse. This 68 per cent to 32 per cent contrast must not be interpreted as a change in values with respect to household composition as a result of urbanization. To do so would obscure the fact that a three-generation household is impossible in the absence from the urban centre of members of the ascendant generation. From this point of view, the data would tend to support, if anything, the hypothesis that no change in values had occurred. No married Vasilika migrant, male or female, lived in a separate exclusively nuclear family household if the parents of their spouses were already resident in Athens.[7] Actually, the matter is best understood not in terms of values, but rather as a system in which household membership is generated by decisions as to how to allocate resources. Whenever a parental household is already established, at any economic level, the incorporation of the young couple obviates the necessity of providing new housing for them immediately, and resources are released for other purposes. This phenomenon is not, then, class differentiated.

Choice of husbands without kin assistance

Also undifferentiated with respect to class is another phenomenon. All the women who came to Athens unmarried, whether for education or for work, found husbands for themselves. Again, the unavailability in Athens of kin normally responsible for arranging marriages, parents and elder brothers, seems to have been the crucial factor. Athenian uncles and aunts served to help the girls win approval for their choices from their parents; if no older Athenian kin were available they used their own powers of persuasion. Parental approval remained of some significance because the willingness of the older generation to contribute a part of the dowry was still helpful.

MIGRATION OPPORTUNITIES: PERCEPTION AND REALITY

The implication of the foregoing description and analysis has been that the migrants' and their families' perception of their own situation corresponded with realistic opportunities. I believe that this is indeed the case. Although such a conclusion may appear to impute an excessive degree of *savoir faire* to rural Greeks, the data support the interpretation. Nor should we be surprised. As small-holding farmers with some commercial crops, in a country whose economic and political situation for the first half of this century has been notably unstable, their survival depended on adjusting crop production, marketing patterns, saving systems, and their own labour to the changing conditions. Gathering information about the larger world was vital to their survival, and its collection from teachers, merchants, relatives in other villages, soldiers, and passing government officials was a well-developed art.

There is also, of course, an element of self-fulfilling prophecy in the situation. For example, once the villagers are convinced that a humanistic education is the qualification required for jobs, they send their children for such an education, thereby disqualifying them for jobs which require other kinds of training. His academic qualifications then impel the young migrant to search hard for a position commensurate with his training.

In any case, the initiatives for rural–urban migration and the outcome of the effort were dependent on the changing conditions of Greek culture and society between the 1920s and 1965.

NATIONAL ENVIRONMENT

In the standard evolutionary discussions of adaptation among primitives the ecology of the situation, the interaction between the culture of the population, especially its technical and organizational aspects, and the physical environment, are considered relevant frameworks for the analysis of change. In the study of the adjustments of rural migrants to urban settings, the relevant environment is constituted not only by the physical characteristics of the city, or its climate and ecology, in the sociological sense of the word, but also by the codes of law, the method of their enforcement, and by the occupational, educational, administrative and fiscal structure of the city and the nation (Leeds 1968). The urban and national structures are not extrinsic (Southall 1961, pp. 5, 14–16), that is, possibly ancillary or non-essential, but primary and relevant aspects of an environment within which migrants function (Leeds 1969).

Not only the migrants from Vasilika, but those coming from all regions of Greece were faced with similar national conditions. There is some evidence that migrants from other regions achieved similar goals and followed similar paths. This parallelism is the more striking because the region around Vasilika is one with low migration rates, and with better educational facilities than most of the rest of Greece (Baxevanis 1965, p. 89). Yet a study of 400 randomly selected migrants to Athens and a control-group of non-migrants in Athens done by T. Gioka for the Athenian Social Sciences Centre showed that migrants had higher occupational levels than non-migrants, that they arrived in Athens often with the aid of kin links, and that they began by living with relatives, but soon left these earlier migrants to disperse themselves throughout the city (Gioka, personal communication).

A comparative study of migrants to Athens and to Yannina from Epirus in northern Greece, and from the island of Paros, shows similar results (Moustaka 1964). Both rural areas are poorer agricultural regions than the Boeotian plain, and their educational facilities are less adequate. Consequently the level of income and education with which these migrants start is lower than that of Vasilika's migrants; their range of urban occupations begins at a lower level, and a higher percentage of them become artisans and factory workers. Nevertheless, the reasons that these migrants give for their move, the ways in which they find employment, their low levels of unemployment, and their satisfaction with their migration all parallel the situation which I described for Vasilika's migrants (Moustaka 1964, pp. 47–50).

What were some of the national conditions which constituted an environment for migration? There is space here for a brief summary of some I believe to be most significant.

1. A short period of political stability and with economic development as a national goal.

2. A rural economy which permitted the support of sons during their urban education and the accumulation of dowries for daughters. The situation was the result of national government policies of extending credit for machinery and fertilizers, and subsidies for certain cash crops. National cotton production, important for Boeotia, was 99,000 tons in 1953, 184,000 in 1960, and 205,000 in 1965. National tobacco production, also an important Boeotian crop, had similar spectacular increases (Candilis 1968, p. 182). As we have seen, the labour force needed in the countryside decreased with improved methods, but the opportunities for landless families improved as the landed children migrated. Although the cost of labour increased, the profits of the farmers also rose.

3. An Athenian economy which could provide jobs for the migrants (cf. Hammel 1968, pp. 5–6). The population of Athens has increased from 4,000 in 1833 to over 2,000,000 in 1965. The latter figure represents a quarter of the Greek population. Since 1928, after the influx of the Asia Minor refugees, except for the decade between 1940 and 1950, the annual growth rate of Athens had been about three per cent. The annual growth rate of the national economy as measured by the gross national product between 1955 and 1965 was six or seven per cent. Athens had a concentration of the industry, although largely small-scale, that had contributed a gradually increasing share of the gross national product, and the index of industrial production showed a steady increase from 1947 to 1965 (Candilis 1968, pp. 185, 186). The size of the labour force in Athens had been reduced by the demand for labour in western Europe and the emigration of Greeks during the period under discussion to Switzerland and Germany, with some continuing emigration to Canada, Australia, and the United States. At a rough estimate about three per cent of the Athenian labour force emigrated in 1962 and 1965 (*Statistical Yearbook of Greece 1967*, pp. 43, 128). Even with an unemployment percentage of 8.6 in Greater Athens for 1961, Gioka's and Moustaka's researches suggest that it was not migrants who were unemployed.

Opportunities in the civil service, public utilities, banks, the armed forces, and in construction expanded in the post-World War II years for political as well as economic reasons. Moreover, government policies did not then encourage the development of provincial industries which might have given some of Vasilika's population the alternative of becoming rural commuters.

4. Fiscal policies which maintained the value of the drachma and controlled

inflationary pressures. From 1956 to 1963 the average annual increase in the level of prices was less than two per cent, and it went only slightly higher in the next three years (Candilis 1968, pp. 92, 93).

5. Policies which permitted an expansion of housing. Regulations designed to prevent construction in areas not yet supplied with piped water and the like were not strictly enforced. Statistics covering the decade between 1951 and 1961 indicate that, for the country as a whole, the number of houses had increased more rapidly than the population, and that the occupancy ratio (persons per dwelling) had decreased inside and outside Athens. There was also a 25 per cent decrease in the number of persons per room in the Athenian area during the decade, with a 1961 average of 1.49 persons per room, and the trend continued (Ekistics 1965, pp. 65, 66).

A Doxiades Institute study for 1962 shows that almost nineteen per cent of the new dwellings built that year were privately-built single-room houses, situated in marginal areas of Athens, without paved roads, water conduits, or sewerage (Ekistics 1965, p. 67). Since neither the nation nor the municipalities depend to any great extent on real estate taxes from non-income-producing property, independent householders are not burdened with a heavy tax load.

6. The system of cheap bus transportation, in which lines are extended as the residential areas expand, places even the most outlying houses no more than a half to three-quarters of an hour's ride from the centre of the city.

CONCLUSIONS

The most significant single conclusion to be drawn from this presentation is that the most important variable with respect to migration and its outcome was the level of the village family household's economic resources; the greater the resources the more likely were the villagers to migrate.

At the beginning of this paper it was asserted that the individual was the proper unit of study, and that it might be possible to predict the specific decisions that ne would make under certain sets of conditions. Our conclusions indicate that the village family household, its system of values, its economic position, its kin connexions, and its age and sex distribution taken together in the Greek national context, set narrow limits within which individuals could operate and over which they had no control (cf. Hammel 1969). If hindsight had been foresight, the probability that a particular person would migrate and the probable development of his career could have been predicted within a small range of error.

What about the individual not as a unit of study, but as a human being capable of influencing his own fate? First, there were a very small number of cases not classifiable by the criteria used in this study – what some migration studies call 'epiphenomena', a love affair, a strongly idiosyncratic personality, an illness – which had effects outside of the expected limits. Second, the constraints under which the migrants operated provided some range of opportunities; the point at which a particular individual fitted into that range seems to have been a result of his particular, personal talents. Space limitations, and an effort to retain some degree of anonymity for informants have prevented a detailed description of the vicissitudes through which many of the migrants went. Those with the intelligence, diligence, vitality, and with skill in knowing how to manipulate contacts to their own advantage, arrived at better situations than those less well-endowed.[8]

One general outcome of all these processes, then, was an adaptation to the urban environment without personal or social disorganization. A second general outcome was that although all the migrants improved their economic and social position by absolute standards – they did not substantially change their relative position in the class and status structure of the village or the nation.

NOTES

1   Research on which this paper (completed in 1970) is based was made possible by a grant from the National Science Foundation, which is gratefully acknowledged.

    Several earlier versions of this paper have had the benefit of criticism from the participants in the City University of New York Seminar on the Mediterranean: Bette Denitch, Edward Hansen, Mervyn Meggitt, Joyce Riegelhaupt, Lucy Saunders, Muriel Schein, Jane Schneider, Peter Schneider, Sydel Silverman and Ronald Waterbury. Gideon Sjoberg, Eric Wolf, and my husband, Harry L. Levy, were kind enough to make comments. My thanks are due to all of them.

2   Oscar Lewis carried out such studies but did not present the results in a systematic way. Cronin 1970 and Metge 1964 include data on both the rural area from which migrants come and the urban areas to which they go but do not trace specific individual careers.

3   Among the many studies of migration, attention is drawn particularly to those of Tilly and Brown 1967 for general discussion and bibliography as well as for data on Wilmington, Delaware; and to Taylor 1969 for a discussion about West Durham in Britain. They raise questions similar to those raised in this study.

    The entire volume in which the Taylor paper appears is germane as is also Spencer and Kasdan 1970.

4   The use of this approach has been influenced by Barth 1967, and Boissevain 1968.

5   Occurring within the years of Phase I, but not involving migration to Athens, were the cases of three villagers, two from A category families and one from B. The first two began but did not complete Middle School Studies. The third went on to training in agricultural extension work, and is a geoponist in the Peloponnese. These, as well as the other non-Athenian migrations, five cases in all, are disregarded in the rest of the paper.

6   The same precarious balance was characteristic of the A category migrants in the 1920s, when the entire higher educational enterprise was new for the villagers, and it had similar results. See note 5.

7   One widowed mother lived with the brother of the husband of one of the migrants.

8   For a fuller description of similar manoeuvres see Denitch 1970 on Serbia.

REFERENCES

Argyriades, Dimitri. 1968. 'The ecology of Greek administration: some factors affecting the development of the Greek Civil Service', in J. G. Peristiany (ed.), *Contributions to Mediterranean sociology*. Paris, Mouton, pp. 339–48.

Barth, Frederik. 1967. 'On the study of social change.' *American Anthropologist*, Vol. 69, p. 661–9.

Baxevanis, John. 1965. 'Population, internal migration and urbanization in Greece.' *Balkan Studies*, Vol. 6, pp. 83–98.

Boissevain, Jeremy. 1968. 'The place of non-groups in the social sciences.' *Man*, Vol. 3, pp. 542–56.

Candilis, W. O. 1968. *The economy of Greece, 1944–1966*. Praeger Special Studies in International Economics and Development. New York, Frederick A. Praeger.

Cronin, Constance. 1970. *Sting of Change. Sicilians in Sicily and Australia*. University of Chicago Press.

Denitch, Bette S. 1970. 'Migration and network manipulation in Yugoslavia', in Robert F. Spencer (ed.), *Migration and Anthropology*, Proceedings of the 19th Annual Meeting of the American Ethnological Society. Seattle, University of Washington Press, pp. 133–45.

Ekistics. 1965. 'Reviews on the problems and science of human settlements.' Vol. 20, No. 117, August. Athens Center of Ekistics.

Friedl, Ernestine. 1959. 'The role of kinship in the transmission of national culture to rural villages in mainland Greece.' *American Anthropologist*, Vol. 61, pp. 30–8.

    1962. *Vasilika, a village in modern Greece*. New York, Holt Rinehart & Winston.

    1964. 'Lagging emulation in post-peasant society.' *American Anthropologist*, Vol. 66, pp. 569–86.

Hammel, E. A. 1968. 'Economic change, social mobility, and kinship in Serbia.' Mimeograph. Paper read at American Anthropological Association Meetings, Seattle, 21 November.

    1969. 'The pink yo-yo: occupational mobility in Belgrade, ca. 1915–1965.' Berkeley, California.

Leeds, Anthony. 1968. 'The anthropology of cities: some methodological issues', in *Urban anthropology; Research perspectives and strategies*. E. M. Eddy (ed.), Southern Anthropological Society Proceedings, No. 2. Athens. University of Georgia, pp. 31–47.

Leeds, A., and Leeds, E. 1969. 'Brazil and the myth of urban rurality: urban experience, work, and values in "squatments" of Rio de Janeiro and Lima', in *city and country in the third world*. A. J. Feld (ed.), Cambridge (Mass.), Schenkman.

Metge, Joan. 1964. *A new Maori migration: rural and urban relations in Northern New Zealand*. London School of Economics Monographs on Social Anthropology, No. 27. London, Athlone Press.

Moustaka, Calliope. 1964. *The internal migrant. A comparative study in urbanization*. Athens, Social Sciences Centre.

Naval Intelligence Division (British). 1944. *Greece; a geographical handbook*. 3 vols. London.

Pentzopoulos, Dimitri. 1962. *The Balkan exchange of minorities and its impact upon Greece*. Paris, Mouton.

Safilios-Rothschild, Constantina. 1967a. 'Class position and success stereotypes in Greek and American cultures.' *Social Forces*, Vol. 45, pp. 374–83.

    1967b. 'Some aspects of fertility in urban Greece.' *Proceedings of the World Population Conference*, 1965. Vol. II. New York, United Nations, pp. 228–31.

Spencer, Robert F. (ed.). 1970. *Migration and anthropology*. Proceedings of the 19th Annual Meeting of the American Ethnological Society. Seattle. University of Washington Press.

Statistical Year Book of Greece. 1967. Athens.

Taylor, R. C. 1969. 'Migration and motivation: a study of determinants and types', in J. A. Jackson (ed.), *Migration*. Cambridge University Press, pp. 99–133.

Tilly, Charles and Brown, C. Harold. 1967. 'On uprooting, kinship, and the auspices of migration.' *International Journal of Comparative Sociology*, Vol. 8, pp. 139–64.

20 Lies, mockery and family integrity

Juliet du Boulay

St Antony's College, Oxford

The village in Greece in which I carried out my field-work had, when I first went there in 1966, thirty-three houses and a population of 144. It lies in a mountainous area of the island of Euboea at a height of approximately 700 metres, facing northeast across the sea, and, in common with very many villages of that time, existed on subsistence farming eked out by cash cropping the resin in the forests. I am giving the village itself the pseudonym of Ambéli, and the market town with which it had the closest connexions that of Kateríni.

For nine years, from 1957 to 1967, a road linked Ambéli with Kateríni, but in the winter of 1966 a gale tore down the bridge which spanned the ravine separating the village from the main road, and since then, although there have been numerous plans for one, no road has actually materialized. Even before that, however, there was no regular bus service or transport of any sort to the village, because the road was too steep to allow it, and it is this lack of communication with the outside world that is given by the villagers as the chief reason for the high rate of emigration from the village. This has reached the proportions at which, with all the young men working abroad and all the girls having married into lower villages, all the remaining families, except for the very old, are working towards eventual removal from the village. It is now[1] the sheer lack of *kósmos*, people, in the village which, as well as the lack of a road and other attendant amenities, turn the villagers' thoughts to dreams of more prosperous and populous communities.

The village has a large territory of 12,500 *strémmata* (one *strémma* = 0.2471 acres), consisting mainly of forest and some arable land, which it bought from the Turks in 1853; but because of the poor communications, this land has only theoretical value since the timber in it remains largely unexploited. The villagers' cash income is derived largely from the resin trade, and each villager works approximately two days a week in the forest during the resin season. The rest of the time is spent in the fields cultivating wheat, vetch, lentils, beans, chickpeas and so on, for subsistence. Any surplus from these items is used in sale or exchange. Income in the village varies from 20,000 drs to 40,000 drs per annum (1 drachma = approximately $1\frac{1}{3}$p).

The social situation in Ambéli may be described simply as one in which competition between the different groups, developing frequently into hostility, is a typical and basic relationship. In this, Ambéli shares a similar situation to that described by other writers on Greek society, where the overriding concentration of every individual's loyalty on his family brings it about that each family finds itself inevitably in a certain state of opposition to the others. The degree of this opposition varies with a number of factors relating to kinship and friendship, but in even the closest relationship between two houses the seeds of hostility are always latent.

Competition between the different houses may be defined briefly as being over wealth and reputation. These two factors are frequently synonymous, and are united in the concept of *prokopí*, or progress, an idea which is applied universally in Ambéli to indicate the saving up of enough cash to build a house in Kateríni or elsewhere, and to move out of the village. There is, however, a sense in which reputation, seen more fundamentally as honour (*timí*), is a quality which is independent of wealth and seen in terms of purely moral qualities.

The nature of the struggle for reputation is determined chiefly by the factors already mentioned. Emigration on the part of the men and marriage into the lower villages on the part of the women has reduced the working force of the village to such an extent that no family can cultivate its property fully. In addition to this, even the forest land cannot be exploited for timber because of the lack of adequate transport. This means that the cash incomes of the villagers are severely limited and that there is a comparative equality of wealth. The fact that all families now try to send their children to the gymnasium for further education, and to save up as much cash as they can to provide good dowries for their daughters, means that even those families who earn more than the others do not spend this money on prestige objects, or on a different way of life within the village from that of their fellow villagers. It is thus true to say that, on the whole, the terms in which prestige is defined are, from the point of view of the village, self-defeating: the only prestigious individual is one who has left the village, and so by the time he has gained this prestige in village eyes he has left the sphere in which this type of evaluation operates.

Within the terms of village life, therefore, there is a very limited possibility of acquiring prestige through a place in a fixed hierarchy of wealth and power. The result is that, instead, people jockey for position in a relative hierarchy which is evaluated in accordance with conformity or non-conformity to the value system. In this value system the absolute demands of *timí*, in the sense in which this is connected with the qualities of honour and shame, as well as the more relative standards of the honourable man which are concerned with wealth, hard work, progress and so on, are all relevant.

Social life in Ambéli may therefore be described, in one of its aspects, as a type of see-saw, continually in motion, with the various groups and individuals permanently engaged in attempting to discredit one another, so as to rise, if only temporarily, in the social scale. In this situation, lies and mockery play an important part.

It is however very important to stress that this is one aspect only, and not the most crucial one, of village life. This chapter is concerned with the topics of lies and mockery, and how these can prevail over a large area of village relationships; but it is also concerned with the relation of this behaviour to something even more central to the society, and this is family integrity.

I deal with family integrity primarily in terms of how the individual manages to sustain a particular view of himself and his family not only as honourable but as qualitatively more honourable than most of the families with which he is surrounded. But it is important to remember that this sense of honour lies in certain basic realities which are fundamental to the villager's life. By means of the house, an entity which is thought of as more or less synonymous with the family, the villager is provided with his basic relationships to Christ, the Mother of God, and the Saints; to his immediate social world in the form of his nuclear or extended family; to the dead; to strangers; and to nature. Thus he experiences within the house the fullness of his religious beliefs and of his social dedication; and in its context life and death attain a value and a significance which far outweigh the acrimony and unrest of the wider social scene. The villager's view of himself, therefore, must not be seen as the manipulation of certain concepts, but as the experience of certain realities. There is all the difference between the two.

The lying and mockery which are one of the characteristics of life in Ambéli are related to two principal features in its social structure. These are the exclusive nature of the elementary family, and the nature of the moral code which, at its most severe, is beyond the capacity of most individuals to live up to all the time. These two facts are interrelated as follows:

The family, since it is the only group within which unconditional obligations are recognized, provides the villager with the only context in which he can live and act according to the most positive values of his society. Within the house, therefore, mutual trust, support, love and inter-dependence characterize his relationships. However, because society is fragmented into a number of groups all with the same exclusive loyalties, the solidarity of the family involves its members in behaviour to the outside community which is the reverse of the behaviour which is the norm within it. Kinship ties to some extent mediate between the family and the community, but even these are flexible and need to be reinforced by other criteria. At the limits of blood relationship the situation is reached in which the dominant relationship between the families is one of competition and hostility.

The main area for competition lies in the sphere of reputation, and it thus becomes everybody's business to find out what everybody else is doing in the hope that they can find something to criticize. This hope is in fact often fulfilled.

There are two reasons for this. Firstly, a rigid value system which covers in principle all human conduct is, when applied in particular to different shades of human situation, unable to save itself from paradox. At what point, for instance, should loyalty to the family and therefore total defence of its interests be subordinated to the demands of neighbourliness? Where exactly should self-esteem draw back from a quarrel which may be read either as a proper defence of individual and family rights, or as laughable bickering over a trifle? Secondly, there is the fact that the existence of sheer self-will, even in a society as rigidly structured by role as this one is, is bound to generate a conflict between the individual and the severity of the morality to which he is meant to conform.

Criticism is aided not only by the fact that people do wrong, but also by the fact that the value system has two aspects, either of which may be referred to at will to justify the self or condemn the other. There is the system of values which is concerned specifically with honour and shame; and is projected into the principal roles within the house and acted out within the community largely in terms of *tá symphéronda* (self-interest). However, there also exists a strong awareness of an ideal set of values, typified in the life of Christ, according to which not only does a man not murder or steal in order to further the good of his family, but he does not lie, cheat, gossip, or infringe the rights of others either. It is with reference to this standard – unattainable in social terms and yet recognized by all to be the norm of the perfect life – that many accusations are framed. Eavesdropping, gossiping about neighbours, inventing scurrilous explanations of events, lying to destroy another's reputation – all common occurrences in village life and all accepted among friends as being a perfectly legitimate way to keep in the endless business of defending personal secrets while finding out about those of others – are sharply condemned by those who happen to suffer from these things at the time.'*Étsi kánei ó kósmos?*' they ask, indignantly – 'Is this the way people behave?' – referring unconsciously to the standard of the perfect life, while of course it is exactly the way they themselves will behave five minutes later if the situation arises.

Balancing the two factors in society which make it inevitable for its members to go against its value system, are two other factors which resolve the conflict at a point long before it becomes a threat to the system itself.

One is the fact that the very severity of the moral code provides the means whereby people may adapt its rules for their own ends, for it is precisely in the proliferation of definite standards of conduct for varying theoretical situations, and in the ideal rigidity of their application, that the actual flexibility of the system lies. The same ambiguity which is found in the conflicting pull of loyalties in a given situation and which makes it often impossible for one individual to do right by all parties, also gives the individual a chance of self-justification by appeal to a loyalty to other values held in the same scheme. In this way the system can in many cases be accommodated to the individual when the individual finds that he is unable to keep to the highest requirements of the system.

The second way in which this pressure on the individual to conform is minimized, lies in the institution of the lie. Here the individual does not appeal to alternative standards within the value system to justify his action, he simply denies the action altogether.

So far, therefore, we have a situation in which the love and trust found within the house is related to the hostility which is found, predominantly, outside it. This hostility expresses itself largely in criticism of others which, because of the nature of the value system and the villagers' conception of an ideal world, finds ample scope. It is noticeable, however, that the high standards which they apply to others they by no means apply always to themselves, and in the following section I shall try to explain how it is that the villagers are able, without any sense of paradox, to act according to one standard while criticizing their enemies according to another. This explanation lies, I think, in the nature of self-interest and in the two ways in which the individual (or the family) is aware of his own honour.

Because of the categorical nature of the loyalty which the individual owes to his family, self-interest, or, more literally, the good of the group, which is what is meant by *symphéronda*, is inevitably concentrated on the house. Since in the house the social values are harmonious with those of the sacred world which the house images, the defence of the family and the battle for *symphéronda* are seen not only as a necessity but also as a moral good. Self-interest thus becomes a value in itself, and it is this value, rather than any notion of a disinterested ethical obligation to another, which in one way or another is the deciding factor in most of the situations making up village life.

The point regarding honour[2] is closely related to this, for the overwhelming reality to the villager of his house and family, and the values which are found within it, provides him with a deep sense of his own integrity in defiance often of circumstances and of what the community may be saying about him.

It may appear at first sight as if this statement runs counter to the accepted view that honour in Mediterranean societies lies crucially in public reputation rather than in private virtue: that if a person is denied a reputation for honour by the community then he has literally no honour. The contradiction, however, between these two statements is only superficial.

Firstly, honour as such is in this society rarely lost. It is competed for, but it is competed for in a relative sense – X has less honour than me, therefore I have more honour than him. It is rare that honour as such, as a basic moral quality, is irredeemably lost. What is lost are various of the aspects of reputation whose loss is usually temporary and may be made good by any one of a number of means. The result of this situation is that while a family may realize that it has lost ground with the community over its management of a certain event and may suffer deeply because of it, this loss does not normally affect its sense of the continuing reality of its own honour. Secondly, every family is supported in its own evaluation of itself – or at least in a favourable evaluation of itself – by a number of relatives and possibly friends, and these people also form a part of public opinion. And thirdly, because honour is a quality which materializes essentially with relation to the family, each family gives to its own members an experience of love, trust, mutual responsibility and communion with the sacred world in which all believe, which they do not find anywhere else. The villager *experiences* the honour of his own family, while he only *knows about* the honour of others; what he experiences of others is, except in the case of close blood relations, in terms of the more generalized aspects of *filótimo*. Since this not only is an aspect of honour rather than its totality, but is also not by any means characteristic of the relationships between the different houses, he is reinforced in his basic assumption that his own honour is greater than that possessed by the majority of the community. It is on this assumption amongst others on which his suspicion of the apparently innocent acts of others is founded, and it is this which provides the virtually unshakeable foundation on which his activities within the community are based. Except in the case of extreme catastrophe, each family remains throughout all vicissitudes convinced of its own essential virtue, and of the community's unfounded envy which prevents it from recognizing that virtue.

A reputation for honour is therefore, to the villager concerned, an external recognition of his own inner state. It is a recognition which is vital, but it is nevertheless one which he is, in his own opinion, unquestionably due. This fact is central to an understanding of the complex of gossip, mockery and lies that form so large a part of village life.

In a society where there is, so to speak, a divine sanction for the pursuit of family interest, it is plain that the result would be pure anarchy were it not for certain sanctions which act as a check on unlimited self-seeking. Chief of these sanctions is the mockery – *yéloia* – of the community.

This is a phenomenon which arises naturally out of the competitive nature of society and the desire of all the different families to catch each other out in wrong-doing.

On discovery of some offence, the discoverer immediately relates it to his or her friends and relations, and in no time at all the story is all round the village and everyone is, as they say, 'laughing' (*yelane*). The more serious or ludicrous the offence is, the more people mock the principals of it. The more they laugh, the more the victims of the laughter are humiliated, because the chief ingredient of laughter is lack of respect, and it is this above all that is the enemy of reputation and self-esteem.

The relation of mockery to the value system and to the roles related to it is through the quality of shame – *ntropi*. The function of shame in enforcing a pattern of honourable behaviour is best illustrated by the almost invariable explanation given when a person refrains from doing something he in fact wants to do – 'He is ashamed'. And the parallel statement, 'Before laughter one is ashamed', indicates exactly what it is that one is ashamed of. It is not, that is to say, the wish to avoid an abstract and private shame that is indicated by the words, 'He is ashamed', but the wish to avoid a public shame in the form of the adverse opinion and mocking comments of others.

Mockery, therefore, may be said to work through shame to preserve honour. This is done by reconciling what the individual wants (according to his self-will) with what he should want (according to his role) and by identifying the interest of the house with his correct behaviour to others. In causing the individual to lose standing in the community and thereby making him ashamed of his action, mockery brings about this identification between otherwise antipathetic interests.

As well as being motivated by competition, mockery has the additional merit of being fun. It is often said as an explanation for the extent of malicious comment in the village, 'People like to laugh', and this must be taken literally not just to indicate that people like to increase their reputation by destroying that of others, but also that people like to amuse themselves, and that witty comment is one way of doing this. It is this that gives to mockery an ambivalent aspect in the social structure, for although mockery to a large extent works as an agent of social control, in that people fear it and therefore try to avoid it, it can itself become an agent of disruption when it takes the form of spreading lies about others 'in order to laugh'. For although the community is highly skilled in ferreting out the truth of events, and in disentangling different versions of an event from all the various strands of self-interest and differing loyalties that accompany them, it also 'likes to laugh' and is quite capable, depending on the circumstance, of suspending its disbelief in the cause of its own entertainment.

It is as a preventive mechanism that mockery is plainly the most effective agent for social control. Children are told: 'Don't do such and such, people will laugh', and one frequently hears people rejecting a possible course of action because, as they say, 'they laugh'. People are scrupulous about observing the niceties of relationships with those with whom they wish to keep on good terms – for instance sending round a plate of food in return for a gift previously offered – in case, as it was said to me, they laugh and say, 'Look at her, she doesn't know anything'. People will try to avoid quarrels, women and girls will be meticulous in their public deportment, private eccentricities will be sternly suppressed for fear of the community's mockery.

Mockery is incurred also not only by gross deviations of behaviour, but by anything that is out of the normal. People always go to church in their best clothes, feel compelled to have at least one new dress a year, conceal evidence of poverty such as selling any of their rugs or dowry articles for fear lest people should laugh at them. It is in these cases that mockery is seen to cause not only emulation in a positive sense of the highest ideals of society, but also a rigorous standardization of behaviour over the minutest details. An example of this is seen in the behaviour of a woman who married into Ambéli from another village and has a beautiful voice, although she will never sing except at special festivities, because she says, 'People will mock me and say, "Listen to the woman from Ayia Ioanni singing "'' – a comment which achieves the double aim of poking fun at her both for singing and for being a stranger from a poor village. Another example of the way in which simple events are used as ammunition for mockery is seen in the self-reproach of a woman who on her way to a nearby village failed to notice that an embroidered blanket had fallen off her mule. Turning back to find it she said, 'I hope no one else finds it because they will laugh and say that we couldn't even get to Palaiohori without losing a blanket.'

In addition to its preventive aspect, mockery also has corrective and punitive aspects. As a corrective measure mockery is effective whenever a person is involved in a course of action from which he or she may draw back without losing face – as for instance in the case where a woman in mourning for her first cousin wore a dark yellow headscarf because it was more becoming to her, but changed it to the correct dark brown after she heard that people were mocking her. In many cases, however, such as for instance during a quarrel or an engagement, values such as self-esteem, self-interest, and so on, can all create a situation in which, in spite of the mockery of the community, it becomes impossible for the principals to withdraw. Here there is a conflict between the interests held in the particular situation with relation to the other party, and those with relation to the community as a whole, which mockery is unable to resolve. It is in such cases, as well as in cases of an action discovered by the community which cannot be undone, that mockery becomes purely punitive.

As has been argued above, there are two main escape mechanisms held in the logic of the value system which allow a certain latitude for individual preference, while not challenging the supremacy of the values themselves. The chief sanction, also implicit in the value system, is mockery, while secondary sanctions, exercised by the individual or the group on behalf of their own interests are withdrawal of support, quarrelling, or taking offence. It is impossible to assess in precise terms the degree to which the sanctions control deviations and that to which the escape mechanisms allow individuals to deviate with relative impunity from the highest values of society. However, in principle it is plain that, since the value system of the village continues to survive, there is a far greater standard of adherence to these values than there is lapse from them. One of the great contributors to this survival of the value system is that it is the very fact of an observed lapse from the system that causes an immediate reaction in terms of a flood of gossip, and reaffirmation in the highest terms of those values which have been defied.

Closely related to this search for laughter and the search to avoid being laughed at, is the double phenomenon of curiosity and secrecy in which all members of the community are trained from youth up.

Since everyone automatically suspects everyone else of concealing faults or of trying to deceive them in some way, it is the business of every family to find out as much as they can about others by whatever means are available. Eavesdropping, questioning, checking the answers given by some with those given by others, angling for information in various kinds of unobtrusive ways, are all common means in this unceasing battle for knowledge. When there was doubt in the village as to whether an engagement had been finally agreed upon or not, one woman told me to say, '*Mé geiá*' ('with health' – the customary greeting on such an occasion) to the family concerned, in order to see the reaction. Unwisely I did this, and the news was all round the village in a few hours, together with the woman's cautious answer, 'We haven't arranged anything yet.'

Information, however, is sought not just about the truth of events, but also about the truthfulness of people regarding those events. A man from Katerini who brought some suitcases up for me one day was seen in Ambéli by a villager, who later said to me: 'I asked Thanassi what he had been doing – I knew of course – and he said, "I've been taking the stranger up to Ambéli."' A woman one evening asked me where I was going, and I answered, 'To Anna.' 'To eat?' 'Yes.' Later I found out that she had already known that I was going to have supper there, and that her question was designed to find out whether I was going to lie rather than what I was going to do.

The various kinds of motivation that can prompt questions of this sort are well illustrated by the question invariably asked of everyone who has seen a village girl's fiancé – 'Is he good?' These are: (a) that they are curious about the man, (b) that they are curious to know how one will react, (c) that they want to hear that he is not good so that they will have something to talk about, and (d) that they want to catch you out and get you to say that he is not good so that they can then go to the person concerned and make trouble.

In such a community, discretion in general obviously becomes a paramount virtue, and discretion as regards the family vital, and for this reason children are trained in a secrecy which is all the more essential because it is continually being tested by the outside world, who see in a child's possible unwariness a good source of information as to what is going on in the fastnesses of other houses. One evening I was in a house and the paraffin ran out, and the eldest boy, a child of eight, was sent to the café to get some more. As he was going he was told, 'If anyone asks you where you're going, say you're going to feed the animals. Say nothing else, see?' And when he returned he was asked: 'Who was in the café?' He told her. 'Did anyone ask you what company you had tonight?' 'No.' And a similar example occurred when two other women and I were sitting telling fortunes from cards, and the son of the house, aged ten, returning after a visit to another house, was asked, 'Did they say, "What is your mother doing?"' 'Yes', he answered, adding ironically, 'And I said, "She's sitting playing cards."'

It is not just from a hostile community that secrets are kept, but also in certain cases from close kinsmen who are not in the same house, simply because it is recognized that complete security does not exist outside the family. However, the fact that relationships consist in telling people things about oneself as well as about others means that all but the most vital secrets eventually get confided to a relative, and it is this fact that causes a break-up of an otherwise intransigent situation in which curiosity and secrecy meet head on. For because of the exclusive and limited nature of the individual's categorical obligations, those kinsmen in whom confidences have been reposed owe undivided loyalty not to the family from whom they have received the confidence, but to their own nuclear group. Thus the lines of communication are kept open, and the sanction of mockery given the means by which to take effect.

Confiding in friends is an even more dangerous process than confiding in relatives, because the extreme flexibility of this type of relationship makes it likely that the friendship will sooner or later suffer a setback or come to an end, and when this happens the secrets entrusted to either party when the relationship was good are all revealed, with a good deal of exaggeration and accusation, to an interested community. And even during the course of friendship the relationship may in general be unstable enough to provide no real security, while deep enough in moments to encourage the giving of confidence. One example of this occurs in the betrayal by one woman to another of a friend with whom she had a working relationship on account of their sons both sharing the same boarding house in Kateríni. This woman had become pregnant but did not want anyone to know because she was preparing to have an abortion. However, she unwisely told this friend of hers who, within a few hours, was saying to another: 'Maria has eaten something. Something has happened to her. She's eaten too many beans.' And, on receiving no response to this, insisted with meaning, 'Something has happened to her, *I* think.' When I remonstrated with her over this blatant piece of mischief making, she said, 'Maria is stupid. If she didn't want people to know, she shouldn't have told anyone.' This, of course, is the literal truth.

Secrets, however, must be kept not only by words, but also by actions, for the public nature of village life makes it such that the villagers read the lives of others from the signs and indications much as a hunter tracks an animal by its prints. Rice being bought at a shop indicates meat for a meal and, therefore, probably a visitor for lunch; a strange animal tied up outside means perhaps a prospective bridegroom for the daughter of the house; a girl away with her goats for longer than the customary time means perhaps an illicit rendezvous in the forest. This means that excessive care must be taken not to give the wrong indications even when the action behind these indications may be perfectly innocent. It means also that if a secret is to be protected, false trails must be laid to deceive the curiosity of the community even before it has been aroused. A case in point is that of the priest who was acting as match-maker for a particular family. The prospective bridegroom was a mason from a nearby village, and, so as to give the village nothing to speculate about, the two went to the café and there began to talk about prices and materials for reconditioning the church. After a while the priest got up saying, 'Come to my house and we'll discuss the matter further' and, relating this to me much later, said, 'So we deceived the community and they realized nothing.' It is relevant here also to mention that in Greek the word for 'to deceive' is the same as that meaning 'to laugh' (*yeló*), and may be interpreted freely as 'to have the laugh of' – an interesting indication which makes the connexion between lies, deceit, mockery and laughter still more apparent.

It is plainly only a short step from concealing secrets and causing people to make false assumptions about one's actions, to actually telling lies, and the often heard phrase, 'You can't live without lies', accurately sums up the situation in Ambéli.[3] Since, as has been explained, it is impossible for the villager always to conform to the value system, it becomes in many cases necessary not for him not to break it, but rather to break it and not be found out. The curiosity of the community is, in fact, such that any violation of the code will inevitably be found out unless the cover-up is foolproof, and even then lies about matters important enough to be of interest to the total community are, in the last instance, usually revealed. However, even in these cases the steadfast continuance of the individual of his protestations of innocence, and the fact of his support by his kin, will enable him to cast a smoke screen over the proceedings and to preserve to some extent at any rate his *egoismós*, if not his reputation.

Lies are therefore used to conceal offences against the value system; they are used in the service of curiosity to trick an informant into giving some information which the questioner needs; they are told in order to destroy people's reputations, to make trouble, in order to avoid giving offence, and are even used purely for fun as a sort of esoteric entertainment of which an example follows later. However, it must be said also that in spite of the prevalence of lies in this society, and in spite of the concept of the truth which accommodates such lying into the demands of the value system, lying is itself subject also to a form of social control. Since within this system of honour and shame there exists also an ideal code of behaviour with reference to which lying, cheating, gossiping, and so on, are all considered bad, these things are, within the framework of the values in which they occur, self-limiting. The inveterate gossip is disapproved of, the incorrigible liar is no longer believed, the cheat is made to feel ashamed. These are all, therefore, mechanisms which carry their own sanctions and which, therefore, when they are in danger of causing a greater disruption than society can bear, simply collapse under their own weight. Not only is the lie by no means a totally effective way of sheltering the liar from the community's mockery, but also the community, although it likes to laugh, has a good deal of common sense and tends to know roughly the likelihoods of each situation, even though the standards according to which each person judges that situation will vary in accordance with his particular alignment at the time. So neither the defensive nor the slanderous lie have got unlimited power, and, in the case of the latter, the network of kinsmen and supporters around any particular victim of slander helps to produce a situation in which an equilibrium between the victim and the community is kept.

I have divided lies up into eight types, under two main headings – those concerned with defence and those concerned with attack. To take those concerned with defence first:

1. Chief of these is the lie to conceal some failure of oneself or of one's family to live up to the highest requirements of the social code. These failures can be intentional, committed out of personal desire and impatience with the restrictions of the value system, and consist of such things as casting beans or playing cards in order to tell fortunes, gossiping about another or betraying a confidence, breaking mourning customs, and, in the case of a woman, having a love affair, and so on. On one occasion a woman boasted to me of how she had, by urging on her horse, left behind a party of people on their way to the market town, and had been the first to greet a new baby. The first person to do this is normally taken as godparent, and this woman was duly accepted. However the woman's brother-in-law's sister had been in the party, an unmarried girl, and the woman herself had been put in charge of her by the girl's mother. In leaving the party, therefore, she had committed a double sin, (*a*) in breaking the *parea* or company, a thing never normally done, and (*b*) in failing to chaperone this girl adequately. A quarrel of gigantic dimensions blew up afterwards, and the next I heard of this story was the woman indignantly informing me that she hadn't been able to remain behind with the party because she had a high-spirited mare and had not been able to hold it. This story she put out to the community also, and was supported in it by her close relatives.

2. Lies to conceal unintentional failures – such as a poverty which involves the need to sell a commodity not normally sold, the fact of a man having been rejected by some woman he has made advances to, the fact that a proposed marriage has not succeeded because the son or daughter in question has been turned down – are all common also, and are intimately associated with the notion of family honour. The question of marriage is particularly tricky, especially as regards girls, as the failure of a proposed marriage which a certain family has tried to arrange impugns both the honour and beauty of the girl and the economic stability of the house, since the points on which an engagement stands

or falls are the beauty and reputation of the bride and the size of the dowry. In the event, therefore, of a girl being turned down, the effort is always to make it known that in fact the girl has turned the man down – he was balding, he had sunken eyes, the bride would have had too much work to do, and so on. If, however, the community cannot be prevented from finding out that in fact it was the man who had turned the girl down, then it is said that someone in the community slandered her unjustly.

3. This brings us to a third category of lies, those attacking others by false imputation. The power of this particular sort of lie is considerable, particularly with respect to questions such as marriages, simply because a girl's honour is not something she possesses by virtue of being honourable, so much as something she is given by the community by virtue of the fact that she is seen to be honourable. The community, then, is always at liberty to say, as two women did of an apparently virtuous girl who had just got engaged, 'She pretends to be good.' And indeed in a community where the expression, 'How do you know what goes on in someone else's mind?' (*pou xereis ton allone?*) or 'How do *I* know what *she* is?' (*ti xero ego ti inai afti?*) are frequently heard, it is easily seen that this distrust of the motives and actions of another is a genuine pheno-menon which is related to the fact that the honour of another is not as apparent to the individual as his own honour, and that therefore anything *might* in fact be true of that other, even though nothing is obvious.

This basic agnosticism, then, about the characters of others, the necessity for a girl's behaviour to have been more than impeccable if she is not to have even one slanderer, and the general desire of the community in any event to mock, causes a situation in which, so they say, not one engagement can take place without someone slandering the particular girl involved. I was told: 'If they can't say that the girl has been with a man, if she stays inside all the time, they will say that she is lazy, or that she is ill. If she goes out and talks to people in the road they will say that she is loose and that she talks to all and sundry. Something can be found, even if the girl is an angel. Why? People want to laugh. They break the engagement and they sit back and say, "Now what is she going to do?"'

This type of lie, that slanders another, automatically breeds a further one which links up with the fourth type:

4. This is the lie to avoid trouble or quarrels. The essence of gossip is that it is behind the back of the one gossiped about. Face to face that gossip becomes an insult, and a quarrel is then inevitable. The form that such gossip takes is often, for example, for two women A and B to criticize a third, C. Later, on reflexion A, for instance, realizes either that the other will probably betray them, or that she has in her hands a good means of stirring up trouble, and for either reason or from a mixture of both, will go to C and tell her all that has been said, imputing it all to B. The excuse given for this sort of report is a spurious loyalty of the order, 'You ought to know that. . . .' In any event, C will then go to

B and confront her with it, on which B, if she does not want a quarrel, will either deny having said anything, or else say that A said it.

This situation has a number of permutations, but this is the basic pattern. The value of the lie here is that if everyone lies enough about what has been said, or who has said what, no one will have to apologize and the subject of the gossip will be deprived of the necessity to have a quarrel with either. She will in her own mind come to some conclusion as to what she thinks the truth of the situation is, but the denial of all parties to have said what has been said will calm down the situation until time has passed and the whole thing been forgotten. Everyone's face will have been saved, and 'words', the real consolidator of quarrels, will not have been said.

This type of lie, to avoid trouble, often occurs also when an individual finds himself in a situation of conflicting obligations – for instance the obligation to help a neighbour while preserving some commodity for the use of the family. In a situation such as this, therefore, it avoids insult to the neighbour and preserves the owner's honour, as well as serving the family's interest, to say that there is none left, rather than that there is some but that she will not give it. The same situation also occurs in reconciling *filótimo* with self-interest, as I saw on going with a certain woman to another village, when just as we were leaving, another woman asked us if we would wait while she went and fetched something she wanted us to take with us. 'We'll be going next week', said my companion, and the other woman was satisfied. Later I asked her, 'Are you going next week?' 'No.' 'Then why say so?' 'It was a lie. You can't tell the truth all the time.' 'What will you say to her next week?' 'I'll say that I changed my mind.' 'Did she know when you said that you were going next week that you were lying?' 'No.'

5. Self-interest takes a more illicit turn when it comes to a question of lying for material gain. Cheating on a deal, pretending 'cunning', is one of the virtues of a clever man and a good provider, on the grounds that everyone cheats everyone else, the clever man cheats the stupid, and that's the way the world goes round. However, to cheat out of the context of a financial deal, simply to acquire something without paying for it, earns universal condemnation. Giving false witness at a trial, however, comes under a different sort of judgement. By the time a quarrel over boundaries has reached the court, the actual rights and wrongs of the case (if they were ever accurately known) have usually become deeply confused, and the case is much more concerned with vindicating the honour of the rival parties than with the actual piece of land over which the whole thing started. Giving false witness, therefore, in so far as a man is laying claim to land that is not his own, is simply part of the general struggle for prestige, and as such is, of course, never admitted by either party, and continually indulged in. There is, however, a sin involved, not because the false witness is attempting to take a man's rightful property from him, but because he has to lay his hands on the Bible and take an oath which he has no intention of keeping.

6. There are also lies for sheer concealment, with no particular motive except for a love of secrecy and a fear of the unknown power of the community. The need for the lie here, as in other cases, is generated not so much by the love of lying, as by the need for secrecy in the face of the ruthless curiosity of others. If no one asked what people were doing, there would be no need to lie. But since everyone always asks, for instance, children, what their mothers are doing, from childhood up people learn to counter with a convincing lie. This confuses the enquirer at the same time as avoiding the insult – 'I won't tell you.'

7. This lie to conceal is allied with the lie which is told purely out of mischief, to confuse the authorities (as in the case of the man who, when asked information about a certain piece of land that had been sold to someone he did not even know well, said, 5,000 drs, while the answer the next man gave to the same question was 15,000 drs), or to have private fun at the expense of others. I was an on-looker at an extraordinary joke where one woman, Maria, pretended to steal another woman's flowers, and where both of them elaborated on this action over a period of days to see if a mutual aunt living next door would come and betray her. 'If she doesn't come,' said the second woman, Vassilo, 'I'll say, "I wonder who can possibly have taken my flowers. I had two pots here before, and now there is only one."' I asked what was the proper course of action for this woman to take, and was told, 'Not to speak at all, if she is good.' Of course she did come running round straight away, and the apparent victim of the theft pretended to be very angry and went round to everyone saying how awful it was that Maria had come and taken her flowers without asking her. . . . Maria's scornful comment on the whole thing afterwards was, 'Thus we make fools of them all.'

There was, however, an additional motive for this joke, and that was as a way of resolving a situation in which two people wanted the flowers but in which only one could have them. Maria was Vassilo's second cousin, whereas the other woman, the one who figures in the betrayal, was Vassilo's husband's sister. It was therefore in favour of the latter that Vassilo's obligation lay. Since she did not want to give the flowers to her, but preferred to give them to Maria, they concocted between them this way round the situation as a result of which, as Maria said, 'I kept the flowers and Antigone didn't take offence with Vassilo.'

8. Finally, there is a very large category of lies which are undertaken out of absolute necessity – those told in defence of a friend or a kinsman. Here the obligation, though not categorical, is strict, particularly if good relations need to be maintained. The community will try to find out certain things from you, and there are two courses open in such a case – to betray, or to lie. Only one example need be cited here, and this concerns my going down to Katerini to tape-record some women singing some church music. These women were at the time in the second year of the five-year period of prescribed mourning for their mother, and for thirteen years previously custom had prohibited them from any secular singing as, after a five-year period of mourning for their father's death,

their mother had been taken seriously ill and had remained so for the eight years until her death. By this time it was natural that they should have got impatient with some of the customs of formal sorrow, and since they were both good singers they both sang me, in a low voice so that no outsiders should hear, a number of demotic songs of various traditions. On my return to Ambéli I went to supper with a family, who asked me where I had been. I answered that I had been to Kateríni to tape-record Anna and Maria singing the *Parákleisis*. Immediately they asked, 'Did they sing you any songs?' 'Of course not,' I had to reply, 'they are in mourning.'

Lies, therefore, as part of the network of friendship and obligation, are far-reaching and extend into the field of official relations and patronage with the understanding that a friend supports one's interests, right or wrong. Non-support in many cases can equal in the other's mind non-fulfilment of an obligation, but at the very least it is important for a friend or relation to conceal if necessary the actions of those he is friendly with, and to back them up in any lies they may be telling about any situation. A friend who fails to do these minimal things is no friend.

Some structural implications of the lie as it occurs in Ambéli may therefore be enumerated as follows:

1. The lie reconciles the need of the individual to break the code on occasions, with the need for subscription to the moral code which is vital if the code is to survive. In this case, actual violation of the code does not question or invalidate it, because verbal subscription to it reaffirms its centrality to village life.

2. Where the lie conceals some unavoidable failure of the family to live up to the requirements of honour it acts simply as a mediator between the situation of the individual and the code of the community.

3. Where it occurs as a denial, overt or implicit, of intent to offend, it acts as a mechanism to break a deadlock without violence, and by minimizing the totality of the confrontation it allows both parties to escape from the situation without either quarrelling or compromising their honour.

4. The lie as a mechanism for sheer concealment for the sake of concealment, or in the case of non-betrayal of a friend, serves a vital function in reconciling the need for individual families of the community to lead a private life with the sanctions (curiosity leading to mockery) which must operate if the moral code is to have force.

It would obviously be unrealistic to argue that the lie has a solely constructive function in Ambéli, for, as many of the examples quoted above show, it is responsible for a large measure of disruption, quarrelling and unhappiness. However it is true to say that even in the case of the most vicious form of lying, that of slander, it is possible that the need of the individual to put himself or herself above the reach of even the most malicious enemy is a factor which helps to maintain behaviour at something approximating to the high standards that society ideally demands. And it is also incontestable that, given the other components of the structure of society, the lie plays a vital part in mediating relations between the individual and the community, and that in doing so it helps to promote the continued validity of the moral code of honour and shame which would otherwise either break under its own inherent contradictions or be broken by the villagers' inability to conform to it.

A final section on the understanding of truth in this society is relevant here, for it may seem from the foregoing list of lies as if the factual truth in each situation is of little importance. It is not, however, that the facts in each case are unimportant to either party – to the victim or the victor – but that the use made of the facts, and the degree of importance attached to them, varies according to the situation of either.

The reason for this may be analysed as follows. Because the reputation for which everyone strives is something which is given by the community, this reputation, and, in the last extreme, honour itself, in a very literal sense only has reality if the rest of the community grants it that reality. At the same time, however, the individual has in all but the most extreme cases a positive experience of his own honour which provides him with a continual sense of being in the right, even where in specific instances he may realize that he has done wrong. The combination of these two aspects of honour brings it about that it is more important to be thought to be in the right than it is actually to be in the right, and that deceit comes to be regarded as an indispensable element in social relations.

It is not, however, that the villager is the victim of a sort of self-hypnosis or that he lives in a world of almost total self-delusion as to the practical significance of his own actions, for, except in the case of real confusion over, for instance, the correct drawing of a boundary line, he knows perfectly well where his actions have accorded with the social code and where they have not, where he has told a lie and where the truth, and what implications may be drawn from either. But because the truth of the honour of his family is to the villager a reality much more important than the factual truth of what has actually happened, the lesser truth of the pragmatic event is manipulated to clear the way for the greater truth of family honour to appear.

Thus it appears that the villager lives according to two standards of truth which mirror the two ways in which he experiences honour. Because of the greater reality to himself of his own honour as he experiences it within his family, the truth for himself is that he is always essentially in the right, and his business is to convince others of this. The empirical facts of his own behaviour are in such cases subordinate to the greater reality of his own honour, and may be concealed or manipulated at will. However because in the realm of logic and the material world it is the factual event which justifies a good reputation, and because the honour of others has less reality to the villager than their lack of it, he is relentless in his evaluation of the actions of others according to the factual truth of what actually happened.

Deceit, therefore, and the avoidance of public mockery, appear as phenomena intimately connected with the structure of the value system and as part of the legitimate means by which the honour of a family is preserved and the prosperity of the house maintained. This is well illustrated by the words of a woman who, explaining how deceit can save a house from catastrophe, ended emphatically, 'God wants people to cover things up' – '*O Theós thélei sképasma*'.

NOTES

1   This paper was delivered in 1971, and refers to conditions prevailing at that time.
2   It is relevant to point out here that the adjective *tímios* (fem. *tímia*), honourable, is heard in the village very much more often than the noun *timí*, honour, except where this is used specifically to denote feminine honour or chastity. This is similar to the circumstance described by Campbell for the Sarakatsani: 'Although the Sarakatsani use the adjective *filótimos* to describe a person who "loves honour", they do not use the substantive *tó filótimo* "a sense" of this honour, which is a concept of popular thought extremely common in many parts of Greece. It is clear, however, that *egoismós* is a close analogue.' J. K. Campbell, *Honour, Family and Patronage*, 1964, p. 307. A possible explanation for this infrequent use of the noun *timí* is that it is not usually the totality of honour which is in question, but one or more of the attributes of honour: while someone may well not behave in an honourable way over a particular matter, it is only in rare circumstances that a man or a woman is thought to lose their honour completely.

It must also be noted that although *filótimos* is with the Sarakatsani used synonymously with *tímios*, this is not the case in Ambéli. To say in Ambéli that someone is *tímios* is to credit them essentially with the virtues which are necessary for the protection of the house and family – those of responsibility and maturity, and especially the inward-looking virtues of dignity, sobriety, chastity and so on. To say someone is *filótimos* is to say that they have a proper sense of obligation to the community, that they understand the duties of neighbourhood, relationship, and the need to help others in a crisis. The virtues of *timí* are shown largely in relation to the house and family, those of *filótimo* in relation to the wider community. The difference between *filótimo* and *timí* in Ambéli is well illustrated by the fact that the girl who was notorious in the village for having lovers was nevertheless universally known as *filótimi* because she was generous, open hearted, hard working, and rarely quarrelled with anyone.
3   The lie, *pséma*, is to be understood here as a literal untruth told with a deliberate intent to deceive. It has not, however, the overtones of moral failure which the same word causes in English.

Index

The authors of items listed in the bibliographies are not included in the index unless extensively discussed in the text.

References to broad geographical areas are given at the foot of the page throughout the index: these should be used in conjunction with the individual headings.